What's New in This Edition

This edition has been updated to include coverage of all the exciting changes that have occurred in microcomputers since the previous printing. The most notable event was the release of Windows 95 by Microsoft. This new operating system is a quantum leap from its predecessor. It includes a new user interface as well as a new tasking architecture. To exploit this new operating system, Borland has released the latest version of its C++ compiler. But, even without the enhancements for Windows 95, Borland C++ 5 offers many new features to simplify the development process. The new features covered in this book include the following:

Namespaces—These are used to separate libraries in your program and enable you to reuse code without concern for naming conflicts.

Runtime type information (RTTI)—This is used to add a little safety to C++ programming by giving you a way to retrieve information about an object at runtime.

Templates and the Standard Template Library—This idea is just now becoming widely used; it provides an easy way to add general functionality to your program.

Windows 95 common dialog boxes—This chapter covers the new format of the standard dialog boxes in Windows 95. It also offers a comparison to the Windows 3.*x* boxes, in case you are programming for the previous operating system.

Windows 95 common controls—Some of the things added by Windows 95 are new kinds of controls—ones that programmers had to code for on their own. The coverage shows how to easily include tool tips, progress meters, up/down controls, and tabbed controls in your programs.

Integrated Resource Editor—As well as covering new features of the Borland development environment throughout the book, a chapter is dedicated to coverage of the new resource editor.

Teach Yourself
Borland® C++ 5
in 21 Days,
Third Edition

Teach Yourself
Borland ®C++ 5
in 21 Days, Third Edition

Craig Arnush

SAMS
PUBLISHING

201 West 103rd Street
Indianapolis, Indiana 46290

This book is dedicated to Mary Q. Smith (If That's Her Real Name) for all that she is and all that she is becoming.

Copyright © 1996 by Sams Publishing

THIRD EDITION

International Standard Book Number: 0-672-30756-1

Library of Congress Catalog Card Number: 95-068852

99 98 97 96   4 3 2 1

Interpretation of the printing code: the rightmost double-digit number is the year of the book's printing; the rightmost single-digit, the number of the book's printing. For example, a printing code of 95-1 shows that the first printing of the book occurred in 1995.

Composed in AGaramond and MCPdigital by Macmillan Computer Publishing

Printed in the United States of America

Trademarks

Publisher	*Richard K. Swadley*
Acquisitions Manager	*Greg Wiegand*
Development Manager	*Dean Miller*
Managing Editor	*Cindy Morrow*
Marketing Manager	*Gregg Bushyeager*

Acquisitions Editor
Grace Buechlein

Development Editor
Anthony Amico

Production Editor
David Bradford

Technical Reviewers
Ellie M. Peters, Larry Richardson

Editorial Coordinator
Bill Whitmer

Technical Edit Coordinator
Lynette Quinn

Formatter
Frank Sinclair

Editorial Assistants
Sharon Cox, Andi Richter, Rhonda Tinch-Mize

Cover Designer
Tim Amrhein

Book Designer
Gary Adair

Production Team Supervisor
Brad Chinn

Production
Steve Adams, Michael Brumitt, Charlotte Clapp, Jeanne Clark, Mike Dietsch, Sherri Fugit, Jason Hand, Sonja Hart, Mike Henry, Steph Mineart, Casey Price, Brian-Kent Proffitt, Laura Robbins, Bobbi Satterfield, Lauta Smith, SA Springer, Susan Van Ness, Todd Wente

Indexer
Cheryl Dietsch

Overview

Contents

Acknowledgments

I would like to thank, as always, Grace Buechlein at Sams Publishing for having the patience to deal with the likes of me. Also, thanks to all those at Sams who participated in putting this book together and eventually into your hands. This especially includes Phil Paxton, who taught me how to play that damnably addicting game of cribbage just when I needed it most; made it hard to write about it when I spent all my time playing it.

Thanks also goes out to Ellie M. Peters, who helped me immensely as the moving target slowly got large enough to fall over and crush us all.

Thanks go out to Ian Spencer, whose OLE chapter is still being borrowed, and thanks to James Thayer for his work on the common controls.

Last but by *absolutely no means* least, super-special thanks with sugar on top go out to all the people who took the time to contact me and let me know where I'd screwed up in earlier incarnations of this book. I wish I had room to list them all, but I'll have to settle for Keith Thompson, who was going to be listed earlier but got lost along the way.

About the Author

Photograph courtesy of MQS.

Craig Arnush is an independent software consultant in San Diego and is an expert on C++ and Windows. He volunteers his time answering technical questions on the Borland CompuServe forums as a member of Team Borland. Craig can be reached via his CompuServe account at 71333,3052 or via the Internet at craiga@netcom.com. His Web page is located at http://ourworld.compuserve.com/homepages/craiga/.

Introduction

This book has three major goals: teaching you to program in C++, teaching you to create Windows applications using Borland C++, and teaching you the new features of Borland C++ 5. No prior programming experience is required. However, knowing how to program in other languages, such as BASIC or Pascal, certainly helps. This book is not for the faint-hearted, because becoming familiar with the new features of a new compiler is hard enough, but also learning to program in C++ and learning to write Windows applications in C++ are two nontrivial tasks!

The book contains 21 chapters, one for each study day. The material in some of the chapters tends to be fast-paced in order to meet the goals of the book. Each chapter contains a Q&A section, a quiz section, and an exercise section. In the back of the book you'll find the answers to the quizzes and to many of the exercises. You will also find four extra-credit bonus chapters, containing topics that just didn't fit into the rest of the book.

Day 1 gives you a brief tour of the Borland C++ IDE, the Windows environment that you use to develop C++ programs. The chapter also presents your first C++ program to demonstrate the basic components of a non-Windows C++ program.

Day 2 looks at C++ program components in more detail. The chapter discusses the preprocessor as well as naming and declaring variables, constants, and functions.

Day 3 covers C++ decision-making constructs and loops. The constructs include the various kinds of if statements as well as the switch statement, and while loops including the for, while, and do-while loops. The chapter demonstrates how to use the for loop as an open loop. In addition, the chapter discusses skipping loop iterations, exiting loops, and nesting loops.

Day 4 covers user-defined types and pointers. The chapter discusses enumerated data types, structures, unions, reference variables, and pointers. The text demonstrates how to declare and use pointers with simple variables, arrays, structures, and dynamic memory.

Day 5 examines functions and how they're constructed. The chapter discusses the differences between preprocessor macros, regular functions, and inline functions.

Day 6 presents arrays in C++. The chapter covers both single-dimensional and multidimensional arrays, discussing how to declare and initialize them. In addition, the chapter discusses sorting and searching single-dimensional arrays.

Day 7 focuses on C-style strings and the STRING.H library, which is inherited from C. The chapter covers topics like assigning, concatenating, comparing, converting, and reversing strings. In addition, the chapter discusses searching for characters and substrings in strings before moving on to formatted stream input and output, as well the famous printf function. The latter function supports versatile formatted output.

Day 8 introduces you to the world of object-oriented programming (OOP). The chapter covers the basics of OOP and presents C++ classes. The text discusses the basic components of a C++ class and the rules related to using these components.

Day 9 introduces namespaces, which are used for separation of libraries in source code, and runtime type information, which is used to add a little safety to C++ programming. The very powerful templates are then introduced, followed by the Standard Template Library that makes such good use of them.

Day 10 discusses the basic stream file I/O, which is supported by the C++ stream library. The chapter covers common stream functions, sequential text stream I/O, sequential binary stream I/O, and random-access stream I/O.

Day 11 covers the string class, an alternative to strings, and the functions in STRING.H that work with them. This class conforms to the preliminary strings class from the ANSI C++ committee and is defined in the Standard Template Library.

Day 12 presents very simple OWL-based Windows applications. Object Windows Library version 5, or OWL5, is included with Borland C++ 5. It is a C++ library for use in Windows programming, and using it shortens the time and effort needed to develop a Windows program.

Day 13 focuses on drawing text in a window. The chapter presents both nonscrolling and scrolling windows, and it illustrates how to draw text (as graphics) in these windows.

Day 14 presents the OWL classes, which model static-text controls, edit controls, and pushbutton controls. The chapter also presents a nontrivial, command-oriented calculator as an example that uses these controls.

Day 15 focuses on creating and using dialog boxes. The chapter shows you how to use resource files to define modal and modeless dialog boxes. In addition, the chapter discusses data transfer between a dialog box and its parent window.

Day 16 presents the OWL classes that model the check-box control, the radio-button control, and the group control.

Day 17 covers the OWL class that models list-box controls. The chapter discusses both single-selection and multiple-selection list boxes. The programs in the chapter illustrate both kinds of list boxes.

Day 18 presents the OWL classes, which model the scroll-bar control and the combo-box control. The chapter also discusses how to create history boxes using combo boxes. In addition, the chapter presents a version of the calculator program that uses the combo boxes. Finally, VBXs are introduced and explained.

Day 19 looks at Multiple Document Interface (MDI) windows. The chapter presents the classes that support MDI-compliant applications and illustrates how to manage MDI-child windows.

Day 20 shows how to use the Application and Class Experts to automatically generate the skeleton of your Windows applications, then modify them in a browser-like atmosphere.

Day 21 describes OLE2 and how it's implemented by Borland's ObjectComponents Framework (OCF). The chapter concentrates on how OCF is integrated into OWL.

Extra Credit Day 1 gives a quick tutorial on some simple debugging techniques. No program is perfect, but this chapter will help you get as close to perfect as possible.

Extra Credit Day 2 describes the common dialog boxes offered by Windows. These help to give a common look to programs when they go to open and save files or print documents. The differences between Windows 3.*x* and Windows 95/Windows NT are discussed.

Extra Credit Day 3 provides an overview of several of the new Windows 95 common controls, including tool tips, progress meters, spinner (or up/down) controls, and tabbed controls.

Extra Credit Day 4 gives an overview of the newly integrated resource editor included in the Borland C++ 5 package.

The book contains Windows programs that illustrate aspects of programming that go beyond the trivial aspects of using various visual controls. Study these programs; they contain techniques and tricks that can enrich your Windows programming. We all learn to program by looking at examples (including nontrivial ones) and by asking questions of our friends.

Note: You can obtain the source code and the project files presented in this book by downloading the files from various online locations:

From CompuServe: go to the SAMS forum. The files can be found in the Sams Programming Library 9.

Via FTP: use anonymous FTP to the ftp.netcom.com site, then take a look in the pub/cr/craiga directory.

On the World Wide Web: if you have access to a Web browser, you can find the source code from my home page, which is located at http://ourworld.compuserve.com/homepages/craiga/

Happy programming!

Who Should Read This Book

You don't need any previous experience in programming to learn Borland C++ with this book. You'll find the numerous examples of syntax and detailed analyses of code an excellent guide as you begin your journey into this rewarding environment. If you have programmed before or have some familiarity with C++, you will see that this book includes many important new features of the Borland product. Whether you are just beginning or need only to learn the latest about Borland C++ 5, this book's clear organization makes doing so fast and easy.

Conventions

 Note: These boxes highlight information that can make your Borland C++ 5 programming more efficient and effective.

 Warning: These boxes focus your attention on problems or negative side effects that can occur in specific situations.

 NEW TERM These boxes provide clear definitions of essential or newly introduced terms.

DO	**DON'T**

DO use the Do/Don't boxes to find a quick summary of a fundamental principle in a lesson.

DON'T overlook the useful information offered here.

This book uses various typefaces to help you distinguish C++ code from regular English. Actual C++ code is typeset in a special monospace font. Placeholders—words or characters used to represent the real words or characters you would type in code—are typeset in *italic monospace*. New or important terms are typeset in *italic*.

In the listings in this book, each real code line is numbered. If you see a code-continuation character ➡ at the beginning of a line, you'll know that the line is really a continuation of the preceding numbered code line (some code lines are too long for the width of the book).

The first week of your journey into learning to write C++ applications starts with an introduction to the Borland C++ 5 environment—the IDE (Integrated Development Environment). The remaining days in this week present the basics of the C++ language itself. You learn about the following:

- [ ] Predefined data types
- [ ] Naming constants, variables, and functions
- [ ] C++ operators and expressions
- [ ] Managing basic input and output (I/O)
- [ ] Making decisions
- [ ] Writing loops
- [ ] Declaring and using arrays

You also will learn about simple user-defined types and pointers along with basic string operations. Thus, this week covers the basic components of the C++ language.

1
2
3
4
5
6
7

Getting Started

Welcome to the world of C++ and Windows programming. Your journey into this exciting world begins today. Most of the information in today's lesson familiarizes you with the Borland C++ Integrated Development Environment (IDE). You will learn about the following topics:

- ☐ The basics and history of C++ programs
- ☐ Reading the Borland C++ documentation
- ☐ Loading and using the Borland C++ IDE
- ☐ EasyWin applications
- ☐ Projects and nodes
- ☐ Typing and running your first C++ program

The Basics of C++ Programs

You don't need any previous experience in programming to learn Borland C++ with this book; however, if you have programmed before, things will be easier. As with other languages, C++ is made up of declarations and statements that specify exact instructions to be executed when the program runs.

C++ was developed by Bjarne Stroustrup at Bell Labs. The language is meant to supersede and build on the popular C language, mainly by adding object-oriented language extensions.

NEW☛ TERM An *object-oriented language* represents the attributes and operations of objects. It's an intuitive way of programming that more closely matches how humans perceive the real world. Although it is possible to write in an object-oriented style with most programming languages, only an object-oriented language enforces the rules of object-oriented coding.

In addition, C++ offers a number of enhancements to C that are not object-oriented. Thus, learning C++ gives you the bonus of becoming very familiar with C. However, unlike C, which has been standardized, C++ is still undergoing the standardization process by the ANSI/ISO committee. As of this writing, it looks like a standard for C++ will be finalized and ratified in 1997.

Programming in C++ requires that you become aware of the supporting libraries, which perform various tasks such as input/output, text manipulation, math operations, file I/O (input/output), and so on. In languages such as BASIC, support for such operations is transparent to programs, meaning that it is automatically available to them. As a result, many programs come across as single components that are independent of any other programming components. By contrast, programming in C++ makes you more aware of a program's dependency on various libraries. The advantage of this language feature is that you are able to select between similar libraries, including ones that you yourself develop. C++ compilers, including Borland C++, use project files and program files. The Borland C++ IDE uses project files to manage the creation and updating of programs.

NEW ☞ *Project files* contain lists of all the files necessary to build one or more applications. This
TERM includes settings that specify what files might be needed in order for another to be
compiled properly. *Program files* contain the source code that creates an application.

Reading the Documentation

Although this book makes a good learning tool, it will always be necessary to refer back to the
original Borland-supplied documentation from time to time. There you will find reference
manuals containing all the functions and all the classes provided by Borland C++, as well as
tutorials for subjects that are beyond the scope of this book.

Like many other applications these days, Borland C++ doesn't automatically come with printed
manuals. Instead, documentation is provided in the form of Windows help files. You can,
however, order printed documentation from Borland for an additional fee.

The Documentation Help Files

All the documentation is in the Windows Help format and can be read with the standard
Windows Help viewer. Some of this documentation is accessible from the IDE's Help menu (to
be described later today) and some is accessible from the Start Menu Program Manager group.
Others require you to locate the file in the Borland C++ Help folder and double-click on it. Table
1.1 lists the help files available with Borland C++ and what is in them.

Table 1.1. List of Borland C++ books.

File Name	Book Title	Contents
BCDOS	*DOS Reference*	A reference to the MS-DOS specific functionality of Borland C++, including BGI
BCERRMSG	*Error Messages and Warnings*	A comprehensive list of the various error and warning messages
BCPP	*Programmer's Guide & Library Reference*	A guide and reference to the compiler and its library routines
BCTOOLS	*Tools and Utilities*	A guide to the various secondary tools

continues

Table 1.1. continued

File Name	Book Title	Contents
BCVDTREF	*Visual Database Tools Help*	Includes the developer's guide and reference to the database tools
BCW	*User's Guide*	A guide to the IDE and its integrated tools
BWCC	*BWCC Reference*	Provides a reference to all the features of Borland's proprietary Windows Common Control look. This is now superseded by the Windows 3D look.
CLASSLIB	*Class Libraries Guide*	A guide to the template class libraries
CTL3D	*Adding 3-D Effects to Code*	An article from Microsoft on using the CTL3D.DLL library
GUIDE	*Win32 Developer's References*	A listing of the various Win32 SDK references
HCW	*Help Author's Guide*	A guide to the Help Author
HW32	*HeapWatch32*	Documentation for the HeapWatch32 utility
KBASE	*Microsoft Knowledge Base*	Displays the Microsoft Knowledge Base of errors in the Windows SDK and OLE
MAPI	*MAPI Programmer's Reference*	Reference for the Messaging API
MC	*Message Compiler for Windows NT*	A guide to the message compiler for Windows NT
MM	*Multimedia Programmer's Reference*	Reference of the multimedia functions in Windows
MSTOOLS	*Microsoft Developer's Tools*	A guide to the Microsoft developer tools included with Borland C++

File Name	Book Title	Contents
OCF	*OCF Help*	Contains reference material for the ObjectComponents Framework
OLE	*OLE 2.0 Programmer's Reference*	Reference of OLE
OLE2VIEW	*OLE 2.0 Object Viewer Application Help*	Documentation for the OLE2VIEW program
OPENGL	*OpenGL Programmer's Reference*	Reference for the OpenGL graphics API
OPENHELP	*Using Online Help*	The main entrance into Borland's online help system
OWL50	*ObjectWindows Help*	Contains the ObjectWindows Programmer's and Reference Guides
RC	*Resource Compiler for Windows NT*	Documentation for the standalone resource compiler
RLMAN	*Resource Localization Manager*	Documentation for the Resource Localization Manager tool
RPC	*Remote Procedure Calls Reference*	A description of Microsoft's RPC strategy
SCRIPT	*Object Scripting Help*	Documenation for the Object Scripting cScript language
SHED	*Using Hotspot Editor*	Instructions for use of the Hotspot Editor
STL	*Standard Template Library*	User's Guide, Tutorial, and Reference Manual for the standard template library
TDWINI	*TDWINI.EXE Information*	Guide to the TDWINI debugger setup program

continues

Table 1.1. continued

File Name	Book Title	Contents
UIGUIDE	*Windows Interface Guidelines*	Microsoft's guidelines for creating Windows interfaces
VBT300	*MicroHelp Custom Controls*	Documentation for the MicroHelp VBX controls included with Borland C++
VFW	*Video for Windows Help*	Documentation on the Video for Windows API
WIN31WH	*Windows 3.1 SDK*	Reference for the Win16 API
WIN32	*Win32 Programmer's Reference*	Reference for the Win32 API
WIN32S	*Win32s Programmer's Reference*	Reference for the Win32s API
WINSIGHT	*WinSight User's Guide*	Guide to the WinSight window information utility
WINSPCTR	*WinSpector User's Guide*	Guide to the WinSpector postmortem utility
WINSYS	*Windows System Classes Reference Guide*	Guide to the Windows system classes supplied by ObjectWindows
WORKSHOP	*Resource Workshop User's Guide*	Guide to the resource editor

One of the most frequent times you will reach for the reference-manual help is when editing a file. By placing the editing cursor over a keyword in the file and pressing F1, you can tell Borland C++ to search the manuals for the entry that describes the particular keyword. It's immensely useful for getting quick help on keywords, including all the information describing their precise usage and limitations.

Loading the Borland C++ IDE

The Borland C++ IDE is the visual interface for the C++ compiler, linker, debugger, and other tools that are used to create, manage, and maintain C++ programs. You can load the IDE by simply selecting the Borland C++ icon in the Start menu or by double-clicking the BCW.EXE program in \BC5\BIN directory.

An Overview of the Borland C++ IDE

The Borland C++ IDE is an MDI-compliant application with the following main components:

- ☐ The frame window with the menu system, minimize, and maximize icons. You can resize, move, maximize, and minimize the main Borland C++ IDE window.

- ☐ The speed bar, which contains special bit-mapped buttons that offer shortcuts to specific commands. The IDE enables you to customize the bit-mapped buttons on the speed bar. In addition, these buttons are context sensitive. Their number and type can change, depending on the current task or active window. The IDE supports tooltips, a nice feature that displays what a bit-mapped button does (the text appears in the status line at the bottom of the window and in a little box that momentarily opens up near the button itself) when you move the mouse over that button.

- ☐ The client area, which contains various windows, such as the editor window, the message window, the variable watch window, the project window, and so on.

- ☐ The status line located at the bottom of the IDE window. This line displays brief online help as you move the mouse over the buttons in the speed bar, offers a brief explanation for the various menu items, displays the cursor location, shows the status of the insert/overwrite mode, and even displays the current time.

Figure 1.1 shows a sample session with the Borland C++ IDE.

Note: Because the IDE is meant to accommodate software developers, many of the options will seem advanced to you if you are a novice programmer. However, you need to be familiar only with the options and their related terms. As you become more experienced, these options and terms will become part of your knowledge as a Borland C++ programmer.

Figure 1.1.
The Borland C++ IDE.

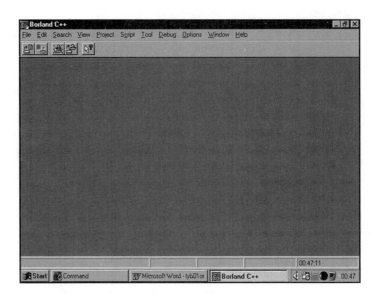

The File Menu

The File menu provides options that enable you to manage files, print text, and exit the IDE. Table 1.2 summarizes the options on the File menu. The File menu also includes a dynamic list of the most recently opened files.

Table 1.2. Summary of the options in the File menu.

Command	Shortcut Keys	Function
New		This has a submenu that enables you to create a new edit window, project file, AppExpert window, or resource
Open...		Loads an existing file into a new edit window or loads a project
Close		Closes the current edit window
Save	Ctrl+K Ctrl+S	Saves the contents of the active edit window
Save as...		Saves the contents of the active edit window using a new filename
Save all		Saves all the opened source-code windows in their respective files
Print...		Prints the contents of a source code window
Print setup...		Sets up the printer

Command	Shortcut Keys	Function
Send...		Sends the file currently being edited via mail
Exit		Exits the IDE

The New Command

The New option enables you to create new files of varying types:

☐ Text Edit opens a new edit window (also known as a source-code window) and assigns it a default associated filename. The default filename of the first new window you open is NONAME00.CPP. Likewise, the default filename of the second new window is NONAME01.CPP, and so on. The newly opened window initially is empty.

☐ Project... creates a new project. On the way, it first stops off at the TargetExpert dialog (shown in Figure 1.2), which enables you to set the various options for the new project, such as what memory model it should use and what version of Windows to use.

☐ AppExpert... invokes the AppExpert utility, which is a valuable and sophisticated tool for rapid program development. Day 20, "The Application and Class Experts," discusses using the AppExpert.

☐ Resource Project... starts the integrated resource editor, enabling you to create such things as dialogs, bit maps, and icons. The resource editor is covered on Extra Credit Day 4.

Figure 1.2.
A sample New Target dialog box.

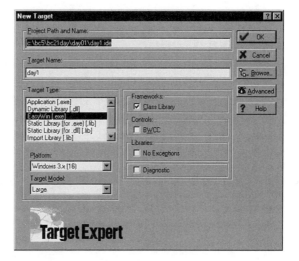

The Open... Option

The Open... option enables you to load the contents of an existing file into a new edit window. In fact, the IDE is capable of loading multiple files. The option invokes the Open a File dialog box, shown in Figure 1.3. The dialog box contains several list-box and combo-box controls that enable you to locate the file and then select it. These controls permit you to choose the drive, directory, and filename wildcards that help you locate the file you seek.

Figure 1.3.
The Open a File dialog box.

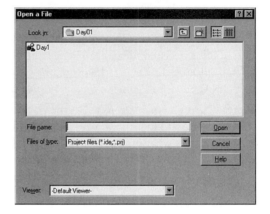

The Close Option

The Close option closes the current source file. This is the same as dismissing the file by clicking on the small x button in the upper-right corner of the window (in Windows 95) or by double-clicking in the upper-left corner of the window.

The Save Option

The Save option assists you in saving the contents of the active edit window to its associated file. If you invoke this option with a new edit window, the Save option invokes the Save File As dialog box, shown in Figure 1.4. This dialog box enables you to optionally specify the nondefault filename, as well as the destination drive and directory. The shortcut keys for the Save option default to Ctrl+K, Ctrl+S; note, however, that they can change if you modify the key mappings (in the Options | Environment menu).

Figure 1.4.
The Save File As dialog box.

The Save As... Option

The Save **A**s... option enables you to save the contents of the active edit window in a file that is different from the currently associated file. In fact, the new filename becomes the new associated file for the active edit window. The Save **A**s... option invokes the Save File As dialog box, shown in Figure 1.4. If you select an existing file, the option displays a message dialog box that asks you whether you want to overwrite the contents of the existing file with those of the active edit window.

The Save All Option

The Save All option writes the contents of all the modified edit windows to their associated files. If the IDE contains new edit windows, this option invokes the Save File As dialog box to save these new windows.

The Print... Option

The **P**rint... option enables you to print the contents of the active edit window. The option displays the Print Options dialog box, shown in Figure 1.5. This dialog box contains check boxes for the following options:

☐ Print a header and page numbers

☐ Print line numbers

☐ Highlight syntax keywords by printing them in bold characters

☐ Use color (if your printer supports colors)

☐ Wrap lines

☐ Left-margin edit-box option

Figure 1.5.
The Print Options dialog box.

The Print Setup... Option

The Print Setup... option enables you to set up your printer using the Print... option before you print. The printer setup option displays the Setup dialog. This is the same dialog box that appears whenever you select Print Setup... from any program.

The Send... Option

The Send... option sends the contents of the current edit window to electronic mail. This is the same option you'll find in any mail-enabled application.

The Exit Option

The Exit option enables you to exit the Borland C++ IDE altogether. The IDE prompts you for any modified edit window that has not been saved.

The Edit Menu

The Edit menu contains options that enable you to edit the text in the edit windows. Table 1.3 summarizes the options in the Edit menu.

Table 1.3. Summary of the options in the Edit menu.

Command	Shortcut Keys	Function
Undo	Ctrl+Z	Undoes the last editing action.
Redo	Shift+Ctrl+Z	Reverses the action of the last Undo option.
Cut	Ctrl+X	Deletes the selected text and copies it to the Clipboard. The previous contents of the Clipboard are lost.
Copy	Ctrl+C	Copies the selected text to the Clipboard. The previous contents of the Clipboard are lost.
Paste	Ctrl+V	Inserts the contents of the Clipboard at the current cursor location.

Command	Shortcut Keys	Function
Clear	Ctrl+Delete	Deletes selected text but does not write it to the Clipboard.
Select all		Selects all the text in the active edit window.
Buffer list...		Displays the Buffer List dialog box.

The Undo Option

The Undo option enables you to reverse the effect of the last editing task and restore the contents of the active edit window. The shortcut keys for this option are Ctrl+Z. This option enables you to quickly and efficiently deal with editing errors.

The Redo Option

The Redo option enables you to reverse the action of the Undo option. The shortcut keys for the Redo option are Shift+Ctrl+Z. The Redo option enables you to switch between two versions of edited source code.

The Cut Option

The Cut option deletes selected text and places it in the Clipboard. The previous contents of the Clipboard are lost. The shortcut keys for the Cut option are Ctrl+X.

The Copy Option

The Copy option copies the selected text into the Clipboard. The previous contents of the Clipboard are lost. The shortcut keys for the Copy option are Ctrl+C.

The Paste Option

The Paste option inserts the contents of the Clipboard at the current insertion point. The contents of the Clipboard remain unaffected. Thus, you can use the Cut and Paste options to move text in the same edit window or across different edit windows. You also can use the Copy and Paste options to duplicate blocks of text in the same edit window or across different edit windows. The shortcut keys for the Paste option are Ctrl+V.

The Clear Option

The Clear option clears the selected text without copying it to the Clipboard. This does not mean that the deleted text is irreversibly lost, because you can use the Undo option to undelete that text. The shortcut keys for the Clear option are Ctrl+Delete.

The Select All Option

The Select All option selects all the text in the active edit window. You can copy this text to the Clipboard by using the Copy option. You can then write the contents of the Clipboard to another edit window using the Paste option.

The Buffer List... Option

The Buffer List... option enables you to examine the list of buffers used with the various edit windows. This option displays the Buffer List dialog box, which enables you to load a buffer into an edit window. The dialog box contains the list of buffers; those that have changed since they were last loaded have the word `modified` (placed in parentheses) after them.

The dialog box is a feature borrowed from the BRIEF editor. In that, you have a list of buffers and a single window; you switch between the different files, changing the currently viewed buffer in the edit window. The IDE's Buffer List dialog box enables you to replace the contents of the current edit window without closing the associated file. If the replaced file is not loaded into another edit window, it is hidden. You may use the buffer list later in order to load the hidden buffer into an edit window.

You can use the Save pushbutton of the Buffer List dialog box to update the file associated with the selected buffer. This action causes the word `modified` to disappear from the selected buffer entry. You also can use the Delete pushbutton to remove the selected buffer from memory, if that buffer is not in an Edit window.

The Search Menu

The Search menu contains options that enable you to locate various types of information, such as text, symbol definitions, function declarations, and program-building errors. Table 1.4 summarizes the options in the Search menu.

Table 1.4. Summary of the options in the Search menu.

Command	Shortcut Keys	Function
Find...	Ctrl+F	Searches for text in the active edit window
Replace...	Ctrl+Q Ctrl+A	Replaces text in the active source-code window
Search again	F3	Repeats the last Find or Replace operation

Command	Shortcut Keys	Function
Browse symbol...	Ctrl+O Ctrl+B	Browses a symbol in any source code that is part of the current project
Locate symbol...		Locates a symbol
Previous message	Alt+F7	Selects the previous program-building message and places the cursor at the offending line in an edit window
Next message	Alt+F8	Selects the next program-building message and places the cursor at the offending line in an edit window

The Find... Option

The Find... option supports searches for text in the active edit window. This option, which has the shortcut keys Ctrl+F, displays the Find Text dialog box, shown in Figure 1.6. This dialog box has the following controls:

- ☐ The **T**ext to find combo-box control, which enables you to type in the search text or to recall recently searched text.
- ☐ The Options check boxes, which include
    - ☐ The Case sensitive check box, which enables you to select case-sensitive or case-insensitive text search.
    - ☐ The Whole words only check box, which enables you to choose between matching entire words or matching any text.
    - ☐ The Regular expression check box, which turns on or off the use of the BRIEF editor's regular expressions feature. Such expressions result in using the text in the Text to find control as the text pattern.
- ☐ The Direction radio-button controls, which enable you to choose between Forward and Backward search.
- ☐ The Scope radio-button controls, which enable you to choose between searching the entire text and limiting the search to the Selected text.
- ☐ The Origin radio-button controls, which enable you to choose between searching the Entire edit window and searching From the cursor position.
- ☐ The OK, Cancel, and Help buttons.

Figure 1.6
The Find Text dialog box.

The Replace... Option

The **R**eplace... option supports replacing text in the active edit window and has the shortcut keys Ctrl+Q Ctrl+A. This option displays the Replace Text dialog box, which looks exactly like the Find... dialog box, except for a few additions. There's a new edit field into which you can enter the text that will be used to replace the found text, there's a new option enabling you to specify whether or not the replacement prompts you for each occurrence, and there's a Change All button that will make changes to all occurrences instead of simply the next one.

The Search Again Option

The **S**earch Again option enables you to repeat the last **F**ind... or **R**eplace... option. The shortcut key for this option is the F3 function key.

The Browse Symbol... Option

The **B**rowse Symbol... option enables you to browse the makeup of a symbol, including classes, functions, and variables. These symbols need not be defined in the active edit window, as long as they are defined in one of the current project's source-code files (your files or the library's included files); the symbols depend upon the symbolic information produced by a compile with debugging on. Figure 1.7 shows a sample symbol-browsing dialog box.

Figure 1.7.
A sample symbol-browsing dialog box.

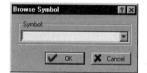

The Locate Symbol... Option

The **L**ocate Symbol... option enables you to find the definition of a symbol. This option displays the Locate Symbol dialog box, which prompts you to enter the name of the symbol you want

to find. The IDE responds by moving to it in an existing edit window or by displaying the function definition in a new edit window, if necessary.

The Previous Message Option

The Previous Message option enables you to zoom in on a source-code line that is associated with the previous message in the Message window. The IDE responds to this option by displaying the edit window that contains the offending source-code line. The shortcut keys for this option are Alt+F7. This is most useful when a compilation fails and displays a number of error messages associated with source-code lines.

The Next Message Option

The Next Message option enables you to zoom in on the source-code line that is associated with the next message in the Message window. The IDE responds to this option by displaying the edit window, which contains the offending source-code line. The shortcut keys for this option are Alt+F8.

The View Menu

The View menu contains options that enable you to view and browse through a wide variety of information. This information goes beyond the declarations in the source-code files of your own project. Table 1.5 summarizes the options in the View menu.

Table 1.5. Summary of the options in the View menu.

Command	Function
ClassExpert	Invokes the ClassExpert utility, which works with project files generated by AppExpert
Project	Displays the Project window
Message	Displays the Message window
Classes	Browses through the classes
Globals	Browses through global data types, constants, and variables
CPU	Displays the CPU window
Process	Displays the Process window
Watch	Selects or opens the Watch window
Breakpoint	Selects or opens the Breakpoints window
Call Stack	Selects or opens the Call Stack window

The ClassExpert Option

The ClassExpert option invokes the ClassExpert utility, which works only with project files created by the AppExpert (both of these topics are discussed on Day 20). This option invokes the ClassExpert window, which has three panes, as follows:

☐ The Classes pane lists the classes involved in the project created using AppExpert. The information in the other two panes is related to the currently selected class in this pane.

☐ The Events pane lists the command notification, control notifications, virtual functions, Windows messages, and other events related to the class selected in the Classes pane.

☐ The source-code window, in which the selected class is defined.

The Project Option

The Project option selects or opens the Project window, which lists the targets and the nodes in the current .IDE file. The Project window displays the files of a target in the form of a tree-like outline. The outline is made up of nodes that you can expand and collapse (if they have child nodes). Each node has a bit map to its left. If the bit-mapped graphic has a + sign, then the node has child nodes that are currently hidden. If you click the + sign, you expand that node, and the IDE replaces the + sign with a – sign. The child nodes without + or – signs have no child nodes of their own.

If you click the right mouse button on a node in the Project window, the IDE displays a floating pop-up menu that enables you to view various components of the project, manage nodes, and edit project-related components.

The project window is discussed in more detail later on today.

The Message Option

The Message option displays, selects, or opens the Message window, which contains the various messages that are output from various portions of the IDE. The Buildtime tab brings up the messages associated with compiling, the Runtime tab brings up the messages associated with running applications, and the Script tab brings up messages associated with the scripting subsystem.

The Classes Option

The Classes option displays the Browsing Objects window, showing a graph of the various classes in the current project and how they are interlinked. Typically, the Browsing Objects window has a vertical and horizontal scroll bar to enable you to scroll through the various classes

involved in the current project. This topic is covered a little later, when there are some classes to browse.

The Globals Option

The **G**lobals option displays the Browsing Globals window, which shows the global data types, constants, variables, and functions. Figure 1.8 shows a sample Browsing Globals window. The window identifies each item by using the following special bit maps:

- ☐ The bit map F signifies that the symbol is a function.
- ☐ The bit map T indicates that the symbol is a data type.
- ☐ The bit map V indicates that the symbol is a variable.
- ☐ The bit map C signals that the symbol is a constant.

The Browsing Globals window contains switches that enable you to filter the viewing of certain global symbols. The window also contains an edit-box control that enables you to type in the name of the symbol you want to find. The edit-box control filters the symbols with every keystroke you enter.

Figure 1.8.
A sample Browsing Globals window.

The CPU Option

The CPU option brings up a window that is used while running and debugging a program. It displays the machine code, registers, flags, and data associated with the lower-level CPU code. It's definitely not for the faint of heart as it displays things in assembly code, but for the experienced programmer it's an invaluable tool for following how a program executes in memory.

The Process Option

The Process option displays a window with a list of the different processes currently running under the IDE. Note that it lists only the programs that were started from within the IDE, and it doesn't list anything else that might be running on the computer.

The Watch Option

The **W**atch option selects or opens the Watch window. This window lists the currently watched variables in your program during debugging. The window displays a check box to the left of each variable. The check box is checked by default to display and update the value in the associated variable. You can uncheck the control to temporarily disable displaying the value of a variable. This task especially is meaningful when the watched variable is not defined in the currently traced function. The Watch window is discussed in Extra Credit Day 1.

The Breakpoint Option

The **B**reakpoint option displays the Breakpoints window, which lists the location and type of breakpoints. A *breakpoint* is a program statement at which the program stops to enable you to inspect its variables. The Breakpoints window displays a list with the following information:

- ☐ A check box denoting the state of the breakpoint (active or inactive)
- ☐ The filename that contains the breakpoint
- ☐ The location where the breakpoint is located (this can be a line number, a filename, a thread ID, and so on)
- ☐ The current state of the breakpoint (verified, unverified, or invalid)
- ☐ The number of passes (that is, the number of times the statement is executed before the program stops at the breakpoint)

If you double-click any entry in the Breakpoints window, the IDE displays the Breakpoints Properties dialog box. This dialog box enables you to edit the breakpoint's data. This dialog box is discussed in Extra Credit Day 1.

The Call Stack Option

The Call **S**tack option displays the Call Stack window, which lists the pending program and the DLL functions that were called (and not yet returned) when the program reached the current breakpoint or the current single-stepped line. The DLL functions are referenced by the name of the DLL library, followed by the address of the function. Again, this is a debugging-related function and will be covered in Extra Credit Day 1.

The Project Menu

The Project menu offers options that manage a project to build an executable program or a library. Table 1.6 summarizes the options in the Project menu.

Table 1.6. Summary of the options in the Project menu.

Command	Shortcut Keys	Function
Open project...		Opens an existing project and closes the current project
Close project		Closes the current project
New **t**arget...		Creates a new target in the current project
Compile	Alt+F9	Compiles the file in the active edit window
Make all	F9	Updates the project files by compiling and linking the necessary source-code files
Build all		Unconditionally compiles and links all of the project source-code files
Generate makefile		Creates a makefile based upon the current project

The Open Project... Option

The **O**pen Project... option enables you to open a new project and automatically close the current one. This option displays the Open Project File dialog box, which resembles the File Open dialog box. The Project File dialog box enables you to specify the drive, directory, and filename wildcards involved in selecting the .IDE or .PRJ project files. The .PRJ project files from previous versions of Borland C++ can still be loaded for backward compatibility; they are converted automatically to .IDE files.

The Close Project Option

The Close Project option closes the current project and its edit windows.

The New Target... Option

The New **T**arget... option enables you to add another target to the project. The option first displays the Add Target dialog box, which enables you to enter the name and type of the target. The target type may be Standard or SourcePool. If you select the Standard target type, the IDE invokes the Add Project dialog box. If you choose the SourcePool target type, the IDE quietly adds a SourcePool target node. The Project window reflects the addition of the new target and indicates its type.

A source-pool target contains a set of nodes that are not built in the project. Instead, source pools play the role of templates for creating reference copies, which allow different targets to employ common source code.

The Compile Option

The Compile option compiles the source code in the active edit window. The option displays the Compile Status dialog box, which informs you of the files being compiled, the number of lines, the number of warnings, and the number of errors. When the compilation process ends, the Message window displays general messages for the compilation steps and includes warning and error messages generated by the compiler, linker, and other tools. The shortcut key for this option is Alt+F9.

The Make All Option

The Make All option updates the project's target by compiling and linking only those files that have been changed since the previous program make or build operations. The option also uses the Compile Status dialog box to display the progress of the compilation and linking steps. After this process is terminated, the Message window displays messages that reflect the progress of compiling and linking, along with any warning and error messages. The shortcut key for this option is F9.

The Build All Option

The Build All option is similar to the Make All option, except that it systematically recompiles and links all of the project's files.

The Generate Makefile Option

The Generate Makefile option creates a makefile out of the current project. A makefile is similar to a project, except that it's stored in a textual format and is meant to be used from the command-line prompt.

The Script Menu

The Script menu enables you to manipulate the Object Scripting that controls a good portion of the IDE. Table 1.7 summarizes the options in the Script menu. A full description of Object Scripting and the cScript language can be found in the online help files.

Table 1.7. Summary of the options in the Script menu.

Command	Shortcut Keys	Function
Run...		Enables you to run a specific cScript command
Commands...		Lists the available cScript commands
Modules...		Lists the cScript modules

Command	Shortcut Keys	Function
Compile File		Compiles a cScript file that's loaded in the active edit window
Run File		Runs a cScript file that's loaded in the active edit window

The Tool Menu

The Tool menu provides you with access to several programming utilities. The IDE Tools... option in the Options menu enables you to customize the list of programming tools that appear in the Tool menu. Table 1.8 summarizes the default options in the Tool menu.

Table 1.8. Summary of the default options in the Tool menu.

Command	Shortcut Keys	Function
Turbo Debugger		Invokes the standalone debugger
Grep		Runs the Grep utility on the currently selected nodes
WinSight		Invokes the WinSight utility to monitor Windows messages
CodeGuard Config		Configures the options available in CodeGuard

The Debug Menu

The Debug menu provides you with options that enable you to manage debugging and executing your C or C++ source code. Table 1.9 summarizes the options in the Debug menu. Extra Credit Day 1 offers a short tutorial on some simple debugging techniques.

Table 1.9. Summary of the options in the Debug menu.

Command	Shortcut Keys	Function
Run	Ctrl+F9	Runs the program of the current target. If necessary, this option also compiles and links the project source-code files.
Load...		Loads a program to debug.

continues

Table 1.9. continued

Command	Shortcut Keys	Function
Attach...		Attaches to a currently running program for debugging.
Run to...		Runs a program to a specific location.
Pause process		Pauses the program and switches to the debugger.
Reset this process		Resets a program so that when stepping into it or running it again, it will start at the beginning.
Terminate process	Ctrl+F2	Stops a program.
Source at execution point		Tries to locate the source code corresponding to the current execution location.
Add breakpoint...		Brings up the Add Breakpoint dialog.
Breakpoint Options...		Enables you to set breakpoint options.
Add Watch...	Ctrl+F5	Opens the Watch Properties dialog box to add a variable to watch.
Evaluate...	Ctrl+F7	Evaluates an expression and modifies the value in a variable.
Inspect...	Alt+F5	Inspects the contents of a variable.

The Options Menu

The Options menu enables you to fine-tune the operations of the compiler, linker, editor, and all the other components of the IDE. Table 1.10 summarizes the options in the Options menu.

Table 1.10. Summary of the options in the Options menu.

Command	Function
Project...	Inspects and edits the setting of the current project.
Environment...	Views and edits the setting of the IDE.

Command	Function
Tools...	Adds, deletes, or modifies tools in the Tool commands.
Style Sheets...	Edits the options style sheets.
Save...	Configures to save the project, desktop, and environment.

The Project... Option

The Project... option displays the dialog box with the title Project Options, as shown in Figure 1.9. The Project Option dialog box contains a list of topics on the left side and a set of controls on the right. Those controls are changed according to the topic selected in the left list. Following are the Project Options topics:

☐ The Directories topic enables you to specify the directories for the include, library, and source-code files, as well as the paths for intermediate and final files.

☐ The Compiler topic enables you to fine-tune the compiling of C and C++ source code, specify the preprocessor definitions, manage the inclusion of debug information, and manage precompiled header files.

☐ The 16-bit Compiler topic and the 32-bit Compiler topic enable you to manage the relative platform-specific options of the compiler.

☐ The C++ Options topic assists you in determining how the C++ compiler interprets your source code to manage new and old C++ language features.

☐ The Optimizations topic enables you to fine-tune some of the performance options available in the compiler.

☐ The Messages topic enables you to determine the type of messages emitted during the creation of the program. The options in the Message topic enable you to choose anything from a very strict to a very relaxed level of warnings and errors.

☐ The Linker topic enables you to control the creation of .OBJ and .LIB files, which are united into the executable .EXE files.

☐ The Librarian section enables you to combine a set of .OBJ files into a .LIB file and control this process.

☐ The Resources section enables you to specify the target Windows version in order to create the right type of .RES compiled resource file and how it is bound to the .EXE.

☐ The Make section offers options that control the integrated make process.

Figure 1.9.
A sample session with the Project Options dialog box.

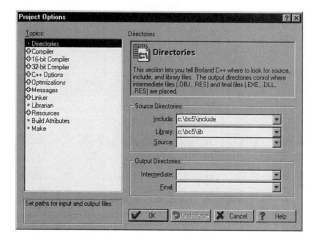

The Environment... Option

The Environment... option displays the Environment Options dialog box, shown in Figure 1.10, which enables you to customize various aspects of the IDE. These aspects are organized and controlled by the following sections that appear in the dialog box:

☐ The Browser topic enables you to determine the default filters for the Browser. In addition, the topic enables you to request the creation of new windows as you traverse through the hierarchy of classes.

☐ The Editor topic controls the operations of the IDE's text editor. The Editor's subtopics enable you to select the default text editor (which is similar to WordStar), select the IDE classical text editor, emulate the BRIEF editor, emulate the Epsilon editor, or customize various aspects of the current text editor.

☐ The Syntax Highlighting topic enables you to determine both the color and style used by the editor to display the source code. The syntax topic offers a few predefined sets of colors and styles.

☐ The Speedbar section enables you to customize the location and contents of the speedbar.

☐ The Scripting option enables you to modify the behavior of the scripting engine, including which scripts to run when the IDE is first run and where to look for script files.

☐ The Process Control section enables you to control the build process. You can also specify how much information should be displayed during the build and which priority should be used.

☐ The Preferences section provides options related to saving various IDE components, such as the editor files, the environment, the desktop, and the project. The section also provides options to specify which parts of the desktop to save.

☐ The Fonts topic lets you specify how text should be displayed in various windows within the IDE.

☐ The Project View section provides options that determine the type of information to include in the Project window—code size, data size, location, name, number of lines, node type, and so on.

☐ The Debugger topic enables you to set the arguments and source directory for debugging programs as well as set debugging behavior and where errors and messages appear.

☐ The Resource Editors section lets you set various preferences with respect to the integrated resource editor. You can also install various control (VBX) libraries.

Figure 1.10.

A sample session with the Environment Options dialog box.

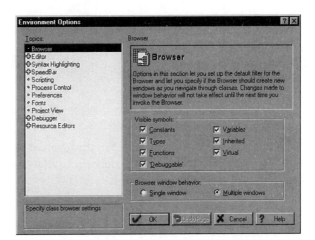

The Tools... Option

The Tools... option enables you to add new menu items to the Tool menu and to delete items from that menu. Figure 1.11 shows the Tools dialog box, which contains a Tools list box that shows you the available tools. If you click the Edit pushbutton, the dialog box displays the Tools Options dialog box, as shown in Figure 1.12. The latter dialog box enables you to specify the name of the tool, along with its path, command line, menu text, and help hint (which appears in the status line).

Figure 1.11.
The Tools dialog box.

Figure 1.12.
*The Tool Options
dialog box.*

Note that most of the tools displayed in the list are actually internal tools and don't appear in the Tool menu. Some of the listed tools can be added to the menu if desired; however, many wouldn't make sense there.

The Style Sheets... Option

The Style Sheets... option displays the Style Sheets dialog box, shown in Figure 1.13, which enables you to select a configuration for the compile and runtime settings for a project. Each style sheet is a predefined collection of settings that can be affiliated with a node.

Figure 1.13.
The Style Sheets dialog box.

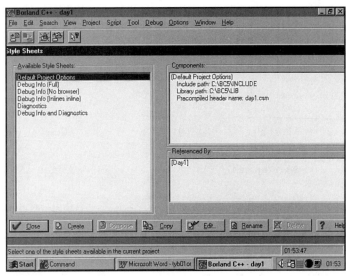

The Save... Option

The **S**ave... option enables you to specify to automatically save the desktop, environment, and project file. This option invokes the Save Options dialog box, which offers check boxes for saving these three IDE components.

The Window Menu

The Window menu offers options to manage windows in the IDE client area. These options, which are summarized in Table 1.11, enable you to arrange, close, minimize, and restore some or all of the windows. In addition to the standard options, the Window menu also lists the current windows.

Table 1.11. Summary of the options in the Window menu.

Command	Shortcut Keys	Function
Cascade	Shift+F5	Cascades the windows in the client area of the IDE.
Tile **h**orizontal	Shift+F4	Tiles the windows horizontally on the client area of the IDE.

continues

Table 1.11. continued

Command	Shortcut Keys	Function
Tile vertical		Tiles the windows vertically on the client area of the IDE.
Arrange icons		Arranges the icons in the client area of the IDE.
Close all		Closes all windows—debugger windows, browser windows, or editor windows.
Minimize all		Minimizes all windows, debugger windows, browser windows, or editor windows.
Restore all		Restores all windows, debugger windows, browser windows, or editor windows.

The Help Menu

The Help menu provides you with the kind of online help you may have gotten from other software. Table 1.12 summarizes the options in the Help menu.

Table 1.12. Summary of the options in the Help menu.

Command	Function
Contents	Displays the table of contents for the online help system.
Keyword search	Displays help regarding the keyword on which the cursor is situated.
Keyboard	Displays information about the mapping of the keyboard.
Using help	Displays information to assist you in using the online help system.
Windows API	Takes you to the Windows API reference mentioned earlier.
OWL API	Opens up the OWL reference mentioned earlier.
About...	Displays information regarding the software version and copyright.

You can also use the F1 key to obtain context-sensitive help regarding whatever is currently active in the IDE (such as an edit or project window or a dialog box). This context-sensitive help may actually be the most important tool in the whole IDE, letting you find help on topics as you need it.

The EasyWin Applications

Microsoft Windows is a complicated environment. Applications are responsible for creating windows, providing support for mouse events, and all sorts of other things. Before windowing environments came about, programs ran in simple console environments like that found in standard MS-DOS. When a program is run, it has simple input from the keyboard and simple output directly to the screen on a character-by-character basis. Although the interface isn't very pretty, it's good for writing simple programs without having to worry about all the many features required for a full-windowed program.

The Borland C++ IDE enables you to build a special kind of program, called an EasyWin application, that provides a simple window that acts like an old-style console program. The programs in Days 1 through 11 of this book are EasyWin applications that enable you to focus on learning C++ using a console interface and input/output procedure. The EasyWin window is the standard input and output for C++ programs (compiled as EasyWin applications). The EasyWin window has a simple menu with few options and a few selections.

It should be noted that EasyWin supports only 16-bit programs. In order to get the simple console type of application that allows easy input and output in a 32-bit environment, you can set the TargetExpert to compile a Win32 console application. This is the default type of application created when you use the command-line tools to compile your programs. The problem with this sort of program, however, is that when you invoke it from Windows, it will simply close its window when it's finished running. This means that any output in which you might have been interested will disappear from the screen before you have a chance to view it. On the other hand, you can run these console applications from an MS-DOS shell window by typing its name on the command line.

To create an EasyWin application, perform the following steps:

1. Load the Borland C++ IDE.
2. Choose the File menu from the menu bar.
3. Select the **N**ew popup menu and then the Project... command to invoke the New Project dialog box.
4. Enter the path and name of the .IDE project file in the topmost edit box. The dialog box echoes the pathname (as you type it) in the Target name edit box (that is, it makes the program name match the name of the project). You need to edit the target name if the name of the program does not match the name of the .IDE project file. You can use the Browse pushbutton to select the directory that will contain the project files.

5. Select the EasyWin [.exe] item in the Target type list box.

6. Click the Advanced pushbutton to invoke the Advanced Options dialog box. Select the check box labeled .cpp Node. This selection causes the IDE to insert the .CPP node for the EasyWin source-code file. This dialog also enables you to add or remove an .RC or .DEF module. Because these are useful only for real Windows applications and not for EasyWin, make sure these two options are unchecked. Close the Advanced Options dialog box by clicking on the OK button.

7. Click the OK pushbutton to create the new project file.

8. The IDE displays the Project window, which lists the nodes for the various programs. When you first create a project file, the Project window will have only one node.

9. Click the main node to view the files contained in that node. The nodes of EasyWin programs contain only one file—a .CPP file, which has the source code. Double-click the .CPP file to request editing the file. Initially, the source window for the .CPP file is empty.

10. Enter the source code for the EasyWin program (such as that shown in Listing 1.1).

11. Press the Ctrl+F9 keys to compile, link, and run the EasyWin program. You can also do this by clicking the speedbar button with the lightning bolt. The compiler flags any errors and lists them in the Message window. If the EasyWin program is correct, the IDE will launch it.

Introduction to Projects and Nodes

When you create a new project or load an old one from disk, the Borland C++ IDE creates a Projects window at the bottom of the IDE. This window contains all the nodes and subnodes needed for the application.

NEW☞ TERM A *node* is the term used to describe the various items found in the project window. These nodes each have specific rules associated with them that the IDE uses to decide how to build applications. Furthermore, each node may, in turn, depend on one or more nodes for compilation. This means that before any particular node can be dealt with, the nodes on which it depends must already have been dealt with successfully. The dependencies are represented by a hierarchy of lines connecting differently indented nodes.

You can add more than one program to an .IDE file. I suggest that you group the separate programs of each of the first twelve days in .IDE files named for their respective days, such as DAY1.IDE, DAY2.IDE, and so on. Grouping related program files in a single project saves disk space because the .IDE files are not small; the fewer .IDE files you create, the more disk space you will save.

To add another target to an existing .IDE file, follow these steps:

1. Load the Borland C++ IDE.
2. Choose the Project menu from the menu bar.
3. Select the New **T**arget command to invoke the New Target dialog box.
4. Enter the name of the new target and click the OK pushbutton.
5. The IDE displays the New Project dialog box. Simply click the OK pushbutton to add a new target node in the Project window. All the changes you made earlier, including those made in the Advanced dialog, are remembered from last time.
6. The IDE displays the Project window, which lists the new nodes for the new target.

This last step just adds a new top-level target to the project with a single .CPP file for its main source code. You can add more nodes as dependencies to any target by selecting that node, clicking the right mouse button, and selecting the Add Node option from the resulting pop-up menu. A dialog box entitled Add to Project List appears and enables you to set the filename of the new node.

You also should note that some nodes have either a plus or a minus sign associated with them. This operates in much the same way as the File Manager's folder bit maps. A plus sign means there are node dependencies that have been hidden in order to help clean up the display. By clicking on the bit map, the plus sign will change to a minus sign, and the node will expand to show its dependencies. Clicking on the node's bit map again will collapse the display and change the minus back into a plus.

It can be extremely useful to have multiple files in conjunction with a single application. Eventually, when you start writing full-fledged Windows applications on Day 12, you're going to see some rather large programs. Putting all the source code for the program in a single file can get extremely unwieldy, so splitting up that source code into multiple files can make life for the programmer much easier. You can find more about this on Day 12, and then later on Day 20 when the AppExpert and its output are discussed.

Your First C++ Program

The first C++ program presented in this book displays a one-line greeting message. This simple program enables you to see the very basic components of a C++ program.

Listing 1.1 contains the source code for the program HELLO.CPP with numbered lines. *Do not* enter the line numbers when you type the program. These line numbers serve as reference only. This simple program displays the string `Hello Programmer!` Carry out the following steps to create and run this first C++ program:

1. Load the Borland C++ IDE if it is not already loaded.

2. Choose the File menu from the menu bar.

3. Select the **N**ew popup menu and then the Project command to invoke the New Project dialog box.

4. Type **c:\bc5\bc21day\day1\day1.ide** in the edit box requesting the Project path and name. (Note that this assumes you installed Borland C++ 5 in the default c:\bc5 location; change the path accordingly to correspond with your installation.) The dialog box now shows the name **day1** in the Target name edit box. You want to change that to **hello**.

5. Select the EasyWin [.exe] item in the Target type list box.

6. Click the Advanced pushbutton to invoke the Advanced Options dialog box. Select the check box labeled .cpp Node and make sure the RC and DEF options are turned off. Close the Advanced Options dialog box.

7. Click the OK pushbutton to create the new project file. The IDE displays the Project window, which lists the node for the hello program.

8. Click the plus sign to the left of the hello.exe node to view the hello.cpp node. Double-click the hello.cpp node to invoke the IDE editor.

9. Enter in the new window the program shown in Listing 1.1.

10. Choose the **S**ave command in the File menu.

11. Press the Ctrl+F9 keys to compile, link, and run the HELLO.EXE program.

> **Note:** With minor modifications (such as the name of the .IDE file and the name of the program), the preceding steps can be used for all the program examples in the book that you type in yourself; the IDE files are all provided for you if you obtain the source code as described in the introduction.

When an EasyWin program ends, the runtime system alters the title of the program's window to include the word **Inactive**. To close the program's window, select the **C**lose command from the system menu, or simply press Alt+F4.

Listing 1.1. Source code for the program HELLO.CPP.

```
1: // A trivial C++ program that says hello
2:
3: #include <iostream.h>
4:
5: int main()
6: {
```

```
7:    cout << "Hello Programmer!";
8:    return 0;
9: }
```

The output of the program appears in Figure 1.14. Notice that the caption of the output window starts with the word Inactive to indicate that the program has terminated.

Figure 1.14.

The output of the HELLO.EXE program.

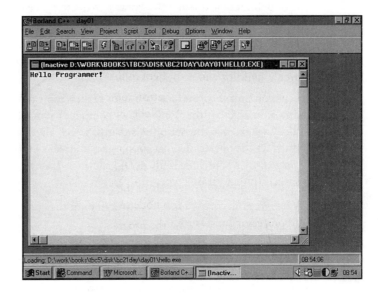

Examine the short code of the C++ program and notice the following characteristics:

☐ C++ uses the // characters for comments that go to the end of the line. C++ also supports the C-style comments that begin with the /* characters and end with the */ characters. Line 1 contains a comment that briefly describes the program.

NEW☞ TERM *Comments* are remarks that you put in the program to explain or clarify certain parts of the program. The compiler ignores comments but the programmer relies on them to figure out what is meant in a program, especially if the code hasn't been looked at in a long time.

☐ The C++ program has no reserved keywords that declare the end of a program. In fact, C++ uses a rather simple scheme for organizing a program. This scheme supports two levels of code: global and single-level functions. In addition, the function main, which starts on line 5, plays a very special role because runtime execution begins with this function. Therefore, there can be only a single function main in a C++ program. You can place the function main anywhere in the code.

☐ The C++ strings and characters are enclosed in double and single quotes, respectively. Thus, `'A'` is a single character, whereas `"A"` is a string that has only one character. Mixing C++ single-character strings and characters is not allowed.

NEW☞ TERM *Strings* can have any number of characters, including no characters. A string without any characters is called the empty string.

☐ C++ defines blocks using the { and } characters. See examples on lines 6 and 9, respectively.

☐ Every statement in a C++ program must end with a semicolon (;). When looking at other code, it might appear that there are exceptions to this rule, but there really aren't, and this will be discussed later on.

☐ C++ contains the `#include` compiler preprocessor directive. An example of this is on line 3, instructing the Borland C++ compiler to include the IOSTREAM.H header file. C++ extends the notion of streams, which already exists in C. IOSTREAM.H provides the operations that support basic stream input and output. The C++ language does not include built-in I/O routines. Instead, the language relies on libraries specializing in various types of I/O.

NEW☞ TERM A *compiler directive* is a special instruction for the compiler and will be described in "The Preprocessor" on Day 2.

A header file contains the declarations of constants, data types, variables, and function prototypes.

A stream is a sequence of data flowing from one part of a computer to another.

☐ The C++ program outputs the string `Hello Programmer!` to the standard output stream `cout`, which is the EasyWin window. In addition, the program uses the output operator, `<<`, to send the emitted string to the output stream.

☐ The function `main` must return a value that reflects the error status of the C++ program. Returning the value `0` signals to the operating system that the program terminated normally with no errors.

Exiting the IDE

To exit the IDE, choose the Exit command from the File menu.

1

Summary

Today's lesson introduced you to a tremendous amount of material about the Borland C++ IDE and presented you with the first C++ program. You learned these basics:

- [ ] C++ programs are modular and rely on standard and custom libraries.

- [ ] Reference information is available via the help system, which is available via the top menu; through pop-up menus, when the right mouse button is clicked; and by pressing either F1 or Ctrl+F1.

- [ ] The two ways to load the Borland C++ IDE are by selecting the Borland C++ icon from the Windows 95 Start menu or double-clicking the BCW.EXE file.

- [ ] The Borland C++ IDE is a versatile environment for developing, maintaining, and debugging C and C++ programs and libraries for Windows applications.

- [ ] The File menu manages the creation of new files, the opening of files, the saving of files, printing, and exiting the IDE.

- [ ] The Edit menu offers options to perform popular editing operations (such as undo, cut, copy, and paste).

- [ ] The Search menu enables you to find and replace text, as well as to browse through symbols, locate functions, and visit the offending source-code lines.

- [ ] The View menu enables you to view a wide variety of information. Among the viewable information are the project nodes, compiler and linker messages, the hierarchy of the project classes, global symbols, watched variables, the stack of called functions, and the CPU registers.

- [ ] The Project menu provides options to create, open, close and manage a project. The project options enable you to compile and link related source-code files.

- [ ] The Debug menu offers options that enable you to debug and single-step in the source code from within the IDE and watch the values of variables in the Watch window.

- [ ] The Tool menu enables quick access to a variety of Windows programming tools, such as the Turbo Debugger, the message-tracing WinSight utility, and your own tools.

- [ ] The Options menu enables you to fine-tune various aspects of your project—environment, tools, and project style sheets.

- [ ] The Window menu is for managing, arranging, closing, and restoring the windows in the IDE desktop.

☐ The Help menu provides you with the online help.

☐ EasyWin applications are Windows applications providing special windows that act as standard input and output devices. EasyWin applications enable you to write DOS-like programs.

☐ New projects are easy to create by setting certain options on a simple dialog box.

☐ Borland C++ Project files enable you to create multiple targets and to have these targets contain multiple files.

☐ The first C++ program in this book is a simple greeting program that illustrates the basic components of a C++ program. These components include comments, the `#include` directive, and the `main` function.

☐ You exit the IDE through the Exit selection on the File menu.

Q&A

Q Does C++ use line numbers?

A No. I am using line numbers in the listings in this book only for the sake of reference. It's useful when typing in a program to compare the current line your editor says you're on with the line number the book says you should be on.

Q Does the IDE's editor monitor what I type?

A Yes, it does. In fact, when you type a C++ keyword, the IDE quickly colors that keyword.

Q What happens if I forget to type the second double quote in the first program?

A The compiler tells you that there is an error in the program. You need to add the second double quote and build the project.

Q How do I delete all occurrences of some text in the currently edited window?

A Use the Replace option in the Edit menu and specify nothing for the replacement string, or use the Edit menu's Cut and Clear commands.

Workshop

The Workshop provides quiz questions to help you solidify your understanding of the material covered and exercises to provide you with experience in using what you've learned. Try to understand the quiz and exercise answers before continuing on to the next day's lesson. (Answers are provided in Appendix A.)

Quiz

1. What is the output of the following program?

```
1: // quiz program #1
2:
3: #include <iostream.h>
4:
5: int main()
6: {
7:    cout << "C++ in 21 Days?";
8:    return 0;
9: }
```

2. What is the output of the following program?

```
1: // quiz program #2
2:
3: #include <iostream.h>
4:
5: int main()
6: {
7:    // cout << "C++ in 21 Days?";
8:    return 0;
9: }
```

3. What is wrong with the following program?

```
1: // quiz program #3
2:
3: #include <iostream.h>
4:
5: int main()
6: {
7:    cout << "C++ in 21 Days?"
8:    return 0;
9: }
```

Exercise

Write a program that displays the message I am a C++ Programmer.

The C++ Preprocessor, Variables, and Operators

Day 1 presented the Borland IDE and a simple C++ program. Today you will focus on the basic components of C++ programs, including data types, variables, constants, and functions. You will learn about the following topics:

☐ The predefined data types in Borland C++ 5

☐ Naming items in Borland C++ 5

☐ The `#include` directive

☐ Declaring variables

☐ Declaring constants

☐ Arithmetic operators and expressions

☐ Increment operators

☐ Arithmetic assignment operators

☐ Typecasting and data conversion

☐ Relational operators and conditional expressions

☐ Bit-manipulating operators

☐ The comma operator

Predefined Data Types in Borland C++ 5

Borland C++ 5 offers the `bool`, `int`, `char`, `float`, `double`, and `void` data types to represent Booleans, integers, characters, single-precision floating-point numbers, double-precision floating-point numbers, and valueless data, respectively. C++ uses the `void` type with a function's returned values to indicate that the function does not yield a significant result—that is, the function acts as a procedure. Functions are described in more detail on Day 5.

C++ adds more flexibility to data types by supporting data type modifiers. The type modifiers are as follows: `signed`, `unsigned`, `short`, and `long`. Table 2.1 shows the predefined data types in C++ (and includes the type modifiers), along with their sizes and ranges. Notice that `int` and `unsigned int` are system dependent.

NEW☛
TERM   A *data type modifier* alters the precision and range of values.

Table 2.1. Predefined data types in C++.

Data Type	Byte Size	Range	Examples
bool	1	false to true	true, false
char	1	−128 to 127	'A','!'
wchar_t	2	−32768 to 32767	L'A',L'!'
signed char	1	−128 to 127	23
unsigned char	1	0 to 255	200,0x1A
int	2 or 4	Depends on platform: −32768 to 32767 for 16-bit, −2147483647 to 2147483647 for 32-bit	3000
unsigned int	2 or 4	Depends on platform: 0 to 65535 for 16-bit, 0 to 4294967295 for 32-bit	0xFFFF, 65535
short int	2	−32768 to 32767	100
unsigned short int	2	0 to 65535	0xFF, 40000
long int	4	−2147483648L to 2147483647L	0xFFFFL, -123456L
unsigned long int	4	0L to 4294967295L	123456L
float	4	3.4E−38 to 3.4E+38 and −3.4E−38 to −3.4E+38	2.35, -52.354, 1.3e+10
double	8	1.7E−308 to 1.7E+308 and −1.7E−308 to −1.7E+308	12.354, -2.5e+100, -78.32544
long double	10	3.4E−4932 to 1.1E+4932 and −1.1E−4932 to −3.4E+4932	8.5e-3000

NEW☞ TERM C++ supports *hexadecimal numbers.* Such numbers begin with the characters 0x, followed by the hexadecimal value. For example, the number 0xff is the hexadecimal equivalent of the decimal number 255.

Naming Items in Borland C++ 5

Borland C++ 5 requires you to observe the following rules with identifiers:

☐ The first character must be a letter or an underscore (_).

☐ Subsequent characters can be letters, digits, or underscores.

☐ The maximum length of an identifier is 32 characters by default (that can be changed in the compiler options).

☐ Identifiers are case-sensitive in C++. Thus, the names rate, RATE, and Rate refer to three different identifiers.

☐ Identifiers cannot be reserved words, such as int, double, or static, to name just a few.

The following are examples of valid identifiers:

```
X
x
aString
DAYS_IN_WEEK
BinNumber0
bin_number_0
bin0Number2
_length
```

And here are some invalid ones:

```
123aNumber
const
NoSpaces Allowed
NorAre*Most+Symbols
```

DO	DON'T

DO use descriptive names that have a reasonable length.

DON'T use identifier names that are too short or too long. Short names yield poor readability, and long names are prone to typographical errors. Some notable exceptions would be with iterators used in loops (to be explained on Day 3). In those cases, a simple i or ix often is used. Also, quickie-type temporary variables are often just a single character, such as a simple s for a string.

The Preprocessor

A long time ago, on a computer far, far away, compilers were a lot simpler than they are today. Back then, compilers required multiple passes through the source code in order to successfully create the machine code that could run on the computer. In those days, the preprocessor was an integral part of the compiling process. The preprocessor would do a quick run through the code in order to bring extra files together and to process macros.

The instructions meant for the preprocessor alone were called *directives*, and although the preprocessor as a separate entity doesn't really exist in the same way today, the terminology has survived. In C and C++, all directives must begin with a number sign (sometimes called sharp or pound—#) on the far left of a line followed by the directive name. There are a number of directives (most of them meant to control how the compiler operates), but the most important ones are #include and #define.

The *#include* Directive

The C++ program in Day 1 contains an #include directive. This directive tells the compiler to include the text of a file as if you have typed that text yourself. Thus, the #include directive is a better alternative than cutting text from one file and pasting it in another file. Instead, one can create a header file that includes the common code and then simply include it in all the relevant programs.

It is vitally important, however, to recognize the difference between including a header file and separating code out into separate source files that later combine into the final target. After a variable is created in memory, another creation is illegal. Therefore, if you actually create a variable in a header file, then include it in two different source files that combine into a single target, you will get compiler errors informing you of duplicate symbols. Typically, the only things that get placed in a header file are macro definitions, structure definitions, type definitions, and function prototypes. All of these will be described in time.

Syntax

The *#include* Directive

The general syntax for the #include directive is

```
#include <filename>
#include "filename"
```

The filename represents the name of the included file. The two forms differ in how the #include directive searches for the included file. The first form searches for the file in the special directory for included files. The second form extends the search to involve the current directory before searching the include directory.

Examples

```
#include <iostream.h>
#include "string.h"
```

The *#define* Directive

The #define directive is what creates macro definitions. The most common of these is a simple substitution type of macro: you tell the preprocessor to substitute every occurrence of a particular text pattern with another. In these cases, the compiler proper never really sees what you originally typed into the source code, but rather its substitution.

The other, slightly less common usage for the #define directive is to create macros that involve some sort of substitution via parameters. This is similar to functions that will be described on Day 5, except, again, the compiler proper never even sees the original source code, but rather is shown only the substitution. Because of that similarity, they will be described then.

The *#define* Directive

The general syntax for the #define directive is

```
#define constantName constantValue
```

The #define directive causes the preprocessor to perform text substitution to replace the macro-based constants with their values. This text-replacement step occurs before the compiler processes the statements in the source file. Consequently, the compiler never sees the macro-based constants themselves, only what they expand to.

Examples

```
#define ASCII_A 65
#define DAYS_IN_WEEK 7
```

Note the tendency for macros to be in all uppercase. This merely is a convention that has survived from the original C macros, but it helps to keep the macros separate from other parts of the program and makes them easier to pick out from all the other code.

Declaring Variables

Declaring variables requires you to state the data type and name of the variable. The word *variable* indicates that you can alter the data of these data containers.

NEW☞
TERM   *Variables* are identifiers used to store and recall information.

In order to help in understanding variables, imagine that there are a number of cardboard boxes, and they are each made to hold only a certain type of object. These objects are called `int`s and `char`s, and so on. You can have any number of any type of box, but you need to have one for each object you want to store; you cannot store an object without a box. So, for example, if you wanted to hold on to an `int`, you would need to have the appropriate type of variable into which you could store the number. Then, when you want to use that number later on, you can just refer to the box to find out what's in it.

Syntax

Declaring Variables

The general syntax for declaring variables is

```
type variableName;
type variableName = initialValue;
type var1 [= initVal1], var2 [= initVal2], ...;
```

Examples

```
int j;
double z = 32.314;
long fileSize, diskSize, totalFileSize = 0;
```

C++ enables you to declare a list of variables (each variable having the same type) in a declarative statement, such as the following:

```
int j, i = 2, k = 3;
double x = 3.12;
double y = 2 * x, z = 4.5, a = 45.7;
```

The initializing values may contain other variables defined earlier.

DO	DON'T

DO remember to use descriptive names for your variables. If you continually use single-letter names for your variables, you're going to have a hard time figuring out what you meant if you ever have to come back to the code.

DON'T declare variables within the same program unit with names that are different in character case (such as `rate` and `Rate`). This can be frightfully confusing when going back over your code later on, and it can be downright sadistic to someone else if they ever have to read your code.

Look at a simple example that uses variables. Listing 2.1 shows the source code for the program VAR.CPP. The program declares four variables, two of which are initialized during their declarations. The program then assigns values to the uninitialized variables and displays the contents of all four variables. Create the project DAY2.IDE (in the directory \BC5\BC21DAY\DAY2) and include the VAR.CPP file as a node. Compile and run the VAR.EXE program.

Listing 2.1. Source code for the program VAR.CPP.

```
1:  // C++ program that illustrates simple variables
2:
3:  #include <iostream.h>
4:
5:  int main()
6:  {
7:      int i, j = 2;
8:      double x, y = 355.0 / 113;
9:
10:     i = 3 * j;
11:     cout << "i = " << i << endl
12:          << "j = " << j << endl;
13:
14:     x = 2 * y;
15:     x = x * x;
16:     cout << "y = " << y << endl
17:          << "x = " << x << endl;
18:     return 0;
19: }
```

Here is a sample session with the program in Listing 2.1.

```
i = 6
j = 2
y = 3.14159
x = 39.4784
```

The program uses the #include directive on line 3 to include the stream I/O header file IOSTREAM.H; it is this header file that defines the code necessary for output. The function main appears on line 5. The function contains the declarations of the int-typed variables i, j on line 7, and the double-typed variables x and y on line 8. The declarations initialize the variables j and y. The statement on line 10 multiplies the value in variable j (which is 2) by 3 and stores the result in variable x. The stream output statement on lines 11 and 12 displays the values of variables i and j. The statement includes strings that label the output.

The statement on line 14 doubles the value in variable y and stores it in variable x. The statement on line 15 squares the value in variable x and assigns the result back to variable x. This statement uses the variable x on both sides of the equal sign. The stream output statement on lines 16 and 17 displays the values in variables x and y. The statement on line 18 returns 0 as the result of function main.

Declaring Constants

Many languages, such as BASIC (the more recent implementations), Modula-2, Ada, C, Pascal, and C++, support constants. No one can deny that constants enhance the readability of a program by replacing numeric constants with identifiers that are more descriptive. Moreover, using constants enables you to change the value of a program parameter by merely changing the value of that parameter in one location. This capability is more convenient and less prone to generate the errors that may occur when you employ your text editor to replace certain numbers with other numbers.

NEW☞ TERM *Constants* are identifiers that are associated with fixed values. C++ offers constants in two varieties: *macro-based* and *formal.* The macro-based constants are inherited from C and use the #define compiler directive.

Syntax

The Formal Constant

The general syntax for the formal constant is

```
const dataType constantName = constantValue;
```

The dataType item is an optional item that specifies the data type of the constant values.

Examples

```
const unsigned char ASCII_A = 65;
const int DAYS_IN_WEEK = 7;
const char FIRST_DISK_DRIVE = 'A';
```

DO	DON'T

DO use uppercase names for constants. This naming style enables you to determine quickly if an identifier is a constant.

DON'T assume that other people who read your code will know what embedded numbers mean. As a matter of fact, don't even assume *you* will know what embedded numbers mean when you read the code again several months or more down the road. Use declared constants to enhance the readability of your programs.

Using Macro-Based Constants

Now consider an example that uses macro-based constants. Listing 2.2 shows the source code for the program CONST1.CPP. The program prompts you to enter the number of hours, minutes, and seconds since midnight. The program then calculates and displays the total number of seconds since midnight. Add the CONST1.CPP file as a node in the project file DAY2.IDE, and then compile and run the CONST1.EXE program.

Listing 2.2. Source code for the program CONST1.CPP.

```
1:  // C++ program that illustrates constants
2:
3:  #include <iostream.h>
4:
5:  #define SEC_IN_MIN 60
6:  #define MIN_IN_HOUR 60
7:
8:  int main()
9:  {
10:     long hours, minutes, seconds;
11:     long totalSec;
12:
13:     cout << "Enter hours: ";
14:     cin >> hours;
15:     cout << "Enter minutes: ";
16:     cin >> minutes;
17:     cout << "Enter seconds: ";
18:     cin >> seconds;
19:
20:     totalSec = ((hours * MIN_IN_HOUR + minutes) *
21:                  SEC_IN_MIN) + seconds;
22:
23:     cout << endl << endl << totalSec << " seconds since midnight";
24:     return 0;
25: }
```

Here is a sample session with the program in Listing 2.2.

```
Enter hours: 10
Enter minutes: 0
Enter seconds: 0


36000 seconds since midnight
```

The program uses the #include directive on line 3 to include the header file IOSTREAM.H; in addition to providing the definitions necessary for output, IOSTREAM.H also is required for input. Lines 5 and 6 contain the #define directive that declares the macro-based constants SEC_IN_MIN and MIN_IN_HOUR. Both constants have the value 60, but each value has a different meaning. The function main, which starts at line 8, declares four long-typed variables: hours, minutes, seconds, and totalSec.

The function uses pairs of statements to output the prompting messages and receive input. Line 13 contains the stream output statement that prompts you for the number of hours. Line 14 contains the stream input statement. The identifier cin is the name of the standard input stream and uses the input operator >> to read data from the keyboard and store it in the variable hours.

The input and output statements on lines 15 through 18 perform a similar task of prompting for input and obtaining keyboard input.

Lines 20 and 21 contain a statement that calculates the total number of seconds since midnight and stores the result in the variable totalSec. The statement uses the macro-based constants MIN_IN_HOUR and SEC_IN_MIN. As you can see, using these constants enhances the readability of the statement, compared to using the number 60 in place of both constants. Line 23 contains a stream output statement that displays the total number of seconds since midnight (stored in the variable totalSec), followed by qualifying text to clarify the output.

2

Using Formal Constants

Now look at a new version of the program—one that uses the formal C++ constants. Listing 2.3 shows the source code for the program CONST2.CPP. This program works like the CONST1.CPP program. Add the CONST2.CPP file as a node in the project file DAY2.IDE. Compile and run the CONST2.EXE program.

Note: At this point, it is assumed that you are familiar with the process of creating the .CPP source file, creating the .IDE project file, and adding .CPP files as nodes in the project file. From now on, creating these files will not be mentioned, unless there is a special set of source files in a project.

Listing 2.3. Source code for the program CONST2.CPP.

```
1:  // C++ program that illustrates constants
2:
3:  #include <iostream.h>
4:
5:  const int SEC_IN_MIN = 60; // global constant
6:
7:  int main()
8:  {
9:      const int MIN_IN_HOUR = 60; // local constant
10:
11:     long hours, minutes, seconds;
12:     long totalSec;
13:
14:     cout << "Enter hours: ";
15:     cin >> hours;
16:     cout << "Enter minutes: ";
17:     cin >> minutes;
18:     cout << "Enter seconds: ";
19:     cin >> seconds;
```

continues

Listing 2.3. continued

```
20:
21:    totalSec = ((hours * MIN_IN_HOUR + minutes) *
22:                 SEC_IN_MIN) + seconds;
23:
24:    cout << endl << endl << totalSec << " seconds since midnight";
25:    return 0;
26: }
```

Here is a sample session with the program in Listing 2.3.

```
Enter hours: 1
Enter minutes: 10
Enter seconds: 20

4220 seconds since midnight
```

The programs in Listings 2.2 and 2.3 are similar. The difference between them is how they declare their constants. In Listing 2.3, the formal C++ constant syntax is used to declare the constants. In addition, the constant `SEC_IN_MIN` on line 5 is declared outside the function `main`. This type of declaration makes the constant global; that is, if there were another function in the program, it would be able to use the constant `SEC_IN_MIN`. By contrast, the constant `MIN_IN_HOUR` is declared inside the function `main`. Thus, the constant `MIN_IN_HOUR` is local to the function `main`.

Operators and Expressions

The manipulation of data involves expressions made up of operands and operators. C++ supports several kinds of operators and expressions.

NEW☞ TERM *Operators* are special symbols that take the values of operands and produce a new value.

If you've taken any simple algebra in school, you will recognize the types of things that are described in this section. They're mostly extensions of the familiar equations you were taught.

Arithmetic Operators

Table 2.2 shows the C++ arithmetic operators. These are used in arithmetic expressions, the textbook example of which looks something like "z = y + x." The variables y and x are operands, and the + is an operator. The result of the expression is dependent upon the data types of the operands and is stored in z. The compiler carries out floating-point or integer division, depending on the operands. If both operands are integer expressions, the compiler yields the code for an integer division. If either or both operands are floating-point expressions, the compiler generates code for floating-point division.

Table 2.2. C++ arithmetic operators.

C++ Operator	Purpose	Data Type	Example
+	Unary plus	Numeric	`x = +y + 3;`
-	Unary minus	Numeric	`x = -y;`
+	Add	Numeric	`z = y + x;`
-	Subtract	Numeric	`z = y - x;`
*	Multiply	Numeric	`z = y * x;`
/	Divide	Numeric	`z = y / x;`
%	Modulus	Integers	`z = y % x;`

Look at an example that uses the mathematical operators with integers and floating-point numbers. Listing 2.4 shows the source code for program OPER1.CPP. The program performs the following tasks:

☐ Prompts you to enter two integers (one integer per prompt)

☐ Applies the +, -, *, /, and % operators to the two integers, storing the results in separate variables

☐ Displays the results of the integer operations

☐ Prompts you to enter two floating-point numbers (one number per prompt)

☐ Applies the +, -, *, and / operators to the two numbers, storing the results in separate variables

☐ Displays the result of the floating-point operations

Type

Listing 2.4. Source code for the program OPER1.CPP.

```
1:  // Simple C++ program to illustrate simple math operations
2:
3:  #include <iostream.h>
4:
5:  int main()
6:  {
7:      int int1, int2;
8:      long long1, long2, long3, long4, long5;
9:      float x, y, real1, real2, real3, real4;
10:
11:     cout << endl << "Type first  integer: ";
12:     cin >> int1;
13:     cout << "Type second integer: ";
14:     cin >> int2;
15:     cout << endl;
16:     long1 = int1 + int2;
```

continues

Listing 2.4. continued

```
17:    long2 = int1 - int2;
18:    long3 = int1 * int2;
19:    long4 = int1 / int2;
20:    long5 = int1 % int2;
21:    cout << int1 << " + " << int2 << " = " << long1 << endl;
22:    cout << int1 << " - " << int2 << " = " << long2 << endl;
23:    cout << int1 << " * " << int2 << " = " << long3 << endl;
24:    cout << int1 << " / " << int2 << " = " << long4 << endl;
25:    cout << int1 << " % " << int2 << " = " << long5 << endl;
26:    cout << endl << endl;
27:    cout << "Type first  real number: ";
28:    cin >> x;
29:    cout << "Type second real number: ";
30:    cin >> y;
31:    cout << endl;
32:    real1 = x + y;
33:    real2 = x - y;
34:    real3 = x * y;
35:    real4 = x / y;
36:    cout << x << " + " << y << " = " << real1 << endl;
37:    cout << x << " - " << y << " = " << real2 << endl;
38:    cout << x << " * " << y << " = " << real3 << endl;
39:    cout << x << " / " << y << " = " << real4 << endl;
40:    cout << endl << endl;
41:    return 0;
42: }
```

Here is a sample session with the program in Listing 2.4.

```
Type first  integer: 10
Type second integer: 5

10 + 5 = 15
10 - 5 = 5
10 * 5 = 50
10 / 5 = 2
10 mod 5 = 0


Type first  real number: 1.25
Type second real number: 2.58

1.25 + 2.58 = 3.83
1.25 - 2.58 = -1.33
1.25 * 2.58 = 3.225
1.25 / 2.58 = 0.484496
```

The program in Listing 2.4 declares a set of int-typed, long-typed, and float-typed variables in the function main. Some of these variables store your input, and others store the results of the mathematical operations. The output statement on line 11 prompts you to enter the first integer. The input statement on line 12 obtains your input and stores it in the variable int1. Lines 13 and 14 perform a similar operation to prompt you for the second integer and store it in variable int2.

The program performs the integer math operation on lines 16 through 20 and stores the results of these operations in variables long1 through long5. These variables were declared as long-typed to guard against possible numeric overflow. The output statements on lines 21 through 25 display the integer operands, the operators used, and the results.

The output statement on line 27 prompts you to enter the first floating-point number. The input statement on line 28 obtains your input and stores it in the variable x. Lines 29 and 30 perform a similar operation to prompt you for the second floating-point number and to store it in variable y.

NEW☛ TERM   A floating-point number also is known as a *real number* and is used for numbers that require a decimal point.

The program performs the floating-point math operation on lines 32 through 35 and stores the results of these operations in variables real1 through real4. The output statements on lines 36 through 39 display the operands, the operators used, and the results.

Arithmetic Expressions

The simplest types of expressions are the ones that contain literals, such as

```
-12
34.45
'A'
"Hello"
```

NEW☛ TERM   In general terms, an *arithmetic expression* is part of a program statement that contains a value.

The literal constants -12 and 34.45 are the simplest arithmetic expressions. The next level of arithmetic expressions includes single variables or constants, such as

```
DAYS_IN_WEEK // a constant
i
x
```

Yet another level of arithmetic expressions contains a single operator with numbers, constants, and variables as operands. Following are a few examples:

```
355 / 113
4 * i
45.67 + x
```

More advanced arithmetic expressions contain multiple operators, parentheses, and even functions, such as

```
(355 / 113) * square(radius)
PI * square(radius)
((2 * x - 3) * x + 2) * x - 5
(1 + x) / (3 - x)
```

The order of executing the operators is discussed at the end of today's lesson, after other types of operators are introduced.

Increment Operators

C++ supports the special increment and decrement operators.

NEW☞ *Increment* (++) and *decrement* (--) *operators* enable you to increment and decrement,
TERM respectively, the value stored in a variable by 1.

Increment Operators

The general syntax for the increment operators is

```
variable++   // post-increment
++variable   // pre-increment
```

Examples

```
lineNumber++;
++index;
```

Decrement Operators

The general syntax for the decrement operators is

```
variable--   // post-decrement
--variable   // pre-decrement
```

Examples

```
lineNumber--;
--index;
```

This general syntax demonstrates that there are two ways to apply the ++ and -- operators. Placing these operators to the left of their operand changes the value of the operand *before* the operand contributes its value in an expression. Likewise, placing these operators to the right of their operands alters the value of the operand *after* the operand contributes its value in an expression. If the ++ or -- operators are the only operators in a statement, there is no practical distinction between using the pre- or post- forms.

Following are a few simple examples:

```
int n, m, t = 5;

t++; // t is now 6, same effect as ++t
--t; // t is now 5, same effect as t--
n = 4 * t++; // t is now 6 and n is 20
t = 5;
m = 4 * ++t; // t is now 6 and m is 24
```

The first statement uses the post-increment ++ operator to increment the value of variable t. If you write ++t instead, you get the same result when the statement finishes executing. The second statement uses the pre-decrement operator. Again, if you write t-- instead, you get the same result. The next statement uses the post-increment ++ operator in a simple math expression. This statement multiplies 4 by the current value of t (that is, 5), assigns the result of 20 to the variable n, and then increments the value in variable t to 6. The last two statements show a different outcome. The statement first increments the value in variable t (the value in variable t becomes 6), then performs the multiplication, and finally assigns the result of 24 to the variable m.

Look at a simple program that illustrates this feature of the increment operator. Listing 2.5 shows the source code for the program OPER2.CPP. The program requires no input from you; it simply displays two integers whose values were obtained using the increment operator.

Listing 2.5. Source code for the program OPER2.CPP.

```
1:  // C++ program illustrates the feature of the increment operator.
2:  // The ++ or -- may be included in an expression.  The value
3:  // of the associated variable is altered after the expression
4:  // is evaluated if the var++ (or var--) is used, or before
5:  // when ++var (or --var) is used.
6:
7:  #include <iostream.h>
8:
9:  int main()
10: {
11:     int i, k = 5;
12:
13:     // use post-incrementing
14:     i = 10 * (k++); // k contributes 5 to the expression
15:     cout << "i = " << i << endl << endl; // displays 50 (= 10 * 5)
16:
17:     k--; // restores the value of k to 5
18:
19:     // use pre-incrementing
20:     i = 10 * (++k); // k contributes 6 to the expression
21:     cout << "i = " << i << endl << endl; // displays 60 (= 10 * 6)
22:     return 0;
23: }
```

Here is a sample session with the program in Listing 2.5.

```
i = 50

i = 60
```

The program in Listing 2.5 has the function main, which declares two int-typed variables, i and k. The function initializes the variable k by assigning it the value 5. Line 14 contains a statement that applies the post-increment operator to the variable k. Consequently, the statement multiplies 10 by the initial value in k, 5, and assigns the product, 50, to variable i. After assigning the result to variable i, the program increments the value in variable k. The output statement on line 15 displays the value in variable i. The statement on line 17 decrements the value in variable k back to 5. The statement on line 20 applies the pre-increment operator to the variable k. Therefore, the program first increments the value in variable k (from 5 to 6) and then multiplies 10 by the updated value in k. The program assigns the result of the multiplication, 60, to the variable i. The output statement on line 21 displays the current value of variable i.

Assignment Operators

As a programmer, you often may come across statements that look similar to the following:

```
IndexOfFirstElement = IndexOfFirstElement + 4;
GraphicsScaleRatio = GraphicsScaleRatio * 3;
CurrentRateOfReturn = CurrentRateOfReturn / 4;
DOSfileListSize = DOSfileListSize - 10;
```

In these, the variable that receives the result of an expression also is the first operand. (Of course, the addition and multiplication are commutative operations, meaning the assigned variable can be either operand with these operations.) Notice the use of relatively long names; this is to remind you of your need to shorten the expression without making the names of the variables shorter.

NEW☛ C++ offers special *assignment operators* that merge with simple math operators. These
TERM enable you to use a shorthand notation for affecting a single operand.

You can write the following statements:

```
IndexOfFirstElement += 4;
GraphicsScaleRatio *= 3;
CurrentRateOfReturn /= 4;
DOSfileListSize -= 10;
```

Notice that the name of the variable appears only once. In addition, notice that the statements use the operators +=, *=, /=, and -=. Table 2.3 shows the arithmetic assignment operators.

Table 2.3. Arithmetic assignment operators.

Assignment Operator	Long Form	Example
x += y	x = x + y	x += 12;
x -= y	x = x - y	x -= 34 + y;
x *= y	x = x * y	scale *= 10;
x /= y	x = x / y	z /= 34 * y;
x %= y	x = x % y	z %= 2;

Look at a program that applies the assignment operators to integers and floating-point numbers. Listing 2.6 shows the source code for the program OPER3.CPP. The program performs the following tasks:

☐ Prompts you to enter two integers (one integer per prompt)

☐ Applies a set of assignment and increment operators to the two integers

☐ Displays the new values of the integers

☐ Prompts you to enter two floating-point numbers (one number per prompt)

☐ Applies a set of assignment and increment operators to the two numbers

☐ Displays the new values of the floating-point numbers

 Listing 2.6. Source code for the program OPER3.CPP.

```
1:  // C++ program to illustrate math assignment operators
2:
3:  #include <iostream.h>
4:
5:  int main()
6:  {
7:      int i, j;
8:      double x, y;
9:
10:     cout << "Type first  integer: ";
11:     cin >> i;
12:     cout << "Type second integer: ";
13:     cin >> j;
14:     i += j;
15:     j -= 6;
16:     i *= 4;
17:     j /= 3;
18:     i++;
19:     j--;
20:     cout << "i = " << i << endl;
21:     cout << "j = " << j << endl;
22:
23:     cout << "Type first  real number: ";
24:     cin >> x;
25:     cout << "Type second real number: ";
26:     cin >> y;
27:     // abbreviated assignments also work with doubles in C++
28:     x += y;
29:     y -= 4.0;
30:     x *= 4.0;
31:     y /=  3.0;
32:     x++;
33:     y--;
34:     cout << "x = " << x << endl;
35:     cout << "y = " << y << endl;
36:     return 0;
37: }
```

Here is a sample session with the program in Listing 2.6.

```
Type first  integer : 55
Type second integer : 66
i = 485
j = 19
Type first  real number : 2.5
Type second real number : 4.58
x = 29.32
y = -0.806667
```

The program in Listing 2.6 contains the function main, which declares two int-typed variables (i and j) and two double-typed variables (x and y) on lines 7 and 8, respectively.

The output statement on line 10 prompts you to enter the first integer. The input statement on line 11 receives your input and stores it in the variable i. Lines 12 and 13 are similar to lines 10 and 11—they prompt you for the second integer and store it in variable j.

The program manipulates the values in variables i and j using the statements on lines 14 through 19. On line 14, the program uses the += operator to increment the value in variable i by the value in variable j. Line 15 uses the -= operator to decrement the value in variable j by 6. Line 16 applies the *= operator to multiply the value in variable i by 4 and assign the result back to variable i. Line 17 utilizes the /= operator to divide the value in variable j by 3 and store the result in j. Lines 18 and 19 apply the increment and decrement operators to variables i and j, respectively. The output statements on lines 20 and 21 display the contents of variables i and j, respectively.

The output statement on line 23 prompts you to enter the first floating-point number. The input statement on line 24 receives your input and saves it in the variable x. Lines 25 and 26 are similar to lines 23 and 24; they prompt you for the second floating-point number and store it in variable y.

The program manipulates the values in variable x and y using the statements on lines 28 through 33. On line 28, the program uses the += operator to increment the value in variable x by the value in variable y. Line 29 uses the -= operator to decrement the value in variable y by 4. Line 30 applies the *= operator to multiply the value in variable x by 4 and to save the result back to x. Line 31 utilizes the /= operator to divide the value in variable y by 3 and to store the result in y. Lines 32 and 33 apply the increment and decrement operators to variables x and y, respectively. The output statements on lines 34 and 35 display the contents of variables x and y, respectively.

The *sizeof* Operator

Frequently, your programs need to know the byte size of a data type or of a variable. C++ provides the sizeof operator, which takes an argument of either a data type or the name of a variable (scalar, array, structure, and so on).

The *sizeof* Operator

The general syntax for the `sizeof` operator is

```
sizeof({variable_name ¦ data_type})
sizeof {variable_name ¦ data_type}
```

The `sizeof` operator is typically used for determining how large a structure or class is (you'll find out about these starting on Day 4; suffice to say now that these are constructs consisting of multiple variables of different types all grouped together) prior to writing it out to a file. The `sizeof` operator will total up all the components of the object in question and return the total size. The operator can, however, be used on simple variables and data types.

Examples

```
int sizeDifference = sizeof(double) - sizeof(float);
int intSize = sizeof int;
```

DO	DON'T

DO use `sizeof` with the name of the variable rather than its data type. This approach is safer because, if you alter the data type of the variable, the `sizeof` operator still returns the correct answer. By contrast, if you use the `sizeof` operator with the data type of the variable and later alter the variable's type, you create a bug if you do not update the argument of the `sizeof` operator.

DON'T use numeric constants to represent the size of a variable. This approach often causes errors.

Listing 2.7 contains the source code for the program SIZEOF.CPP. The program displays two similar tables that indicate the sizes of the `short int`, `int`, `long int`, `char`, and `float` data types. The program displays the first table by applying the `sizeof` operators to variables of these types. The program displays the second table by directly applying the `sizeof` operator to the data types.

Type

Listing 2.7. Source code for the program SIZEOF.CPP.

```
1:  // Simple program that returns the data sizes using the sizeof()
2:  // operator with variables and data types.
3:
4:  #include <iostream.h>
5:
6:  int main()
7:  {
8:      short int aShort;
9:      int anInt;
```

continues

Syntax

Listing 2.7. continued

```
10:    long aLong;
11:    char aChar;
12:    float aReal;
13:
14:    cout << "Table 1. Data sizes using sizeof(variable)" << endl
15:         << endl;
16:    cout << "    Data type         Memory used" << endl;
17:    cout << "                        (bytes)" << endl;
18:    cout << "-----------------    ----------" << endl;
19:    cout << "      short int       " << sizeof(aShort) << endl;
20:    cout << "       integer        " << sizeof(anInt) << endl;
21:    cout << "    long integer      " << sizeof(aLong) << endl;
22:    cout << "      character       " << sizeof(aChar) << endl;
23:    cout << "        float         " << sizeof(aReal) << endl;
24:    cout << endl << endl << endl;
25:
26:    cout << "Table 2. Data sizes using sizeof(dataType)" << endl
27:         << endl;
28:    cout << "    Data type         Memory used" << endl;
29:    cout << "                        (bytes)" << endl;
30:    cout << "-----------------    ----------" << endl;
31:    cout << "      short int       " <<  sizeof(short int) << endl;
32:    cout << "       integer        " <<  sizeof(int) << endl;
33:    cout << "    long integer      " <<  sizeof(long) << endl;
34:    cout << "      character       " <<  sizeof(char) << endl;
35:    cout << "        float         " <<  sizeof(float) << endl;
36:    cout << endl << endl << endl;
37:
38:    return 0;
39: }
```

Here is a sample session with the program in Listing 2.7.

```
Table 1. Data sizes using sizeof(variable)

    Data type         Memory used
                        (bytes)
-----------------    ----------
      short int          2
       integer           2
    long integer         4
      character          1
        float            4
```

```
Table 2. Data sizes using sizeof(dataType)

    Data type          Memory used
                         (bytes)
- - - - - - - - - - -   - - - - - - -
    short int              2
     integer               2
   long integer            4
    character              1
      float                4
```

Note: The output shows the results of compiling the program as a Windows 3.1 16-bit EasyWin application. If this is compiled as a Windows 95 or Windows NT 32-bit console application, then the size of the integer will be 4, not 2.

The program in Listing 2.7 declares five variables in the function main. Each variable has a different data type and derives its name from its data type. For example, the variable anInt is an int-typed variable, the variable aLong is a long-typed variable, and so on.

The statements on lines 14 through 22 display the table of data sizes. The output statements on lines 19 through 23 use the sizeof operator with the variables.

The statements on lines 26 through 35 also display the table of data sizes. The output statements on lines 31 through 35 use the sizeof operator with the data-type identifiers.

Typecasting

Automatic data conversion of a value from one data type to another compatible data type is one of the duties of a compiler. This data conversion simplifies expressions and eases the frustration of both novice and veteran programmers. With behind-the-scenes data conversion, you do not need to examine every expression that mixes compatible data types in your program. For example, the compiler handles most expressions that mix various types of integers or mix integers and floating-point types. You get a compile-time error if you attempt to do something illegal.

NEW☞ TERM *Typecasting* is a language feature that enables you to specify explicitly how to convert a value from its original data type into a compatible data type. Thus, typecasting instructs the compiler to perform the conversion you want and not the one the compiler thinks is needed.

Typecasting

C++ supports the following forms of typecasting:

```
type_cast(expression)
```

and

```
(type_cast)expression
```

Examples

```
int i = 2;
float a, b;
a = float(i);
b = (float)i;
```

Listing 2.8 shows the source code for the program TYPECAST.CPP. The program declares variables that have the character, integer, and floating-point data types. The program then performs two sets of similar mathematical operations. The first set relies on the automatic conversions of data types, performed by the compiler. The second set of operations uses typecasting to explicitly instruct the compiler on how to convert the data types. The program requires no input—it provides its own data—and it displays the output values for both sets of operations. The program illustrates that the compiler succeeds in generating the same output for both sets of operations.

Listing 2.8. Source code for the program TYPECAST.CPP.

```
1:  // Simple C++ program that demonstrates typecasting
2:
3:  #include <iostream.h>
4:
5:  int main()
6:  {
7:      short shortInt1, shortInt2;
8:      unsigned short aByte;
9:      int anInt;            .
10:     long aLong;
11:     char aChar;
12:     float aReal;
13:
14:     // assign values
15:     shortInt1 = 10;
16:     shortInt2 = 6;
17:     // perform operations without typecasting
18:     aByte = shortInt1 + shortInt2;
19:     anInt = shortInt1 - shortInt2;
20:     aLong = shortInt1 * shortInt2;
21:     aChar = aLong + 5; // conversion is automatic to character
22:     aReal = shortInt1 * shortInt2 + 0.5;
23:
24:     cout << "shortInt1 = " << shortInt1 << endl
25:          << "shortInt2 = " << shortInt2 << endl
```

```
26:              << "aByte = " << aByte << endl
27:              << "anInt = " << anInt << endl
28:              << "aLong = " << aLong << endl
29:              << "aChar is " << aChar << endl
30:              << "aReal = " << aReal << endl << endl << endl;
31:
32:         // perform operations with typecasting
33:         aByte = (unsigned short) (shortInt1 + shortInt2);
34:         anInt = (int) (shortInt1 - shortInt2);
35:         aLong = (long) (shortInt1 * shortInt2);
36:         aChar = (unsigned char) (aLong + 5);
37:         aReal = (float) (shortInt1 * shortInt2 + 0.5);
38:
39:         cout << "shortInt1 = " << shortInt1 << endl
40:              << "shortInt2 = " << shortInt2 << endl
41:              << "aByte = " << aByte << endl
42:              << "anInt = " << anInt << endl
43:              << "aLong = " << aLong << endl
44:              << "aChar is " << aChar << endl
45:              << "aReal = " << aReal << endl << endl << endl;
46:     return 0;
47: }
```

Here is a sample session with the program in Listing 2.8.

```
shortInt1 = 10
shortInt2 = 6
uShort = 16
anInt = 4
aLong = 60
aChar is A
aReal = 60.5


shortInt1 = 10
shortInt2 = 6
uShort = 16
anInt = 4
aLong = 60
aChar is A
aReal = 60.5
```

The program in Listing 2.8 declares the following variables in the function main:

☐ The short-typed variables shortInt1 and shortInt2

☐ The unsigned short-typed variable uShort

☐ The int-typed variable anInt

☐ The long-typed variable aLong

☐ The char-typed variable aChar

☐ The float-typed variable aReal

Lines 15 and 16 assign the integers 10 and 6 to variable shortInt1 and shortInt2, respectively. Lines 18 through 22 perform various mathematical operations and assign the results to variables uShort, anInt, aLong, aChar, and aReal.

> **Note:** C and C++ treat the char type as a special integer. Each char-type literal (such as 'A'), constant, or variable has an integer value that is equal to its ASCII representation. This language feature enables you to store an integer in a char-type variable and treat a char-type data item as an integer. The statement on line 21 adds the integer 5 to the value of the variable aLong and assigns the result, an integer, to the variable aChar. The value of the assigned integer, 65, represents the ASCII code for the letter A.

The output statement on lines 24 through 30 displays the values stored in the variables. Notice that the output for variable aChar is the letter A. If you write the output term for variable aChar as << (int) aChar, you get 65, the ASCII code of the character stored in aChar.

The statements on lines 33 through 37 perform similar operations to the statements on lines 18 through 22. The main difference is that the statements on lines 33 through 37 use typecasting to explicitly instruct the compiler on how to convert the result. The output statement on lines 39 through 45 displays the contents of the variables.

Relational and Logical Operators

Table 2.4 shows the C++ relational and logical operators. Notice that C++ does not spell out the operators AND, OR, and NOT. Rather, it uses single- and dual-character symbols. Also notice that C++ does not support the relational XOR operator.

NEW☞
TERM The *relational operators* (less than, greater than, and equal to) and the *logical operators* (AND, OR, and NOT) are the basic building blocks of decision-making constructs in any programming language.

Table 2.4. C++ relational and logical operators.

C++ Operator	Meaning	Example
&&	Logical AND	if (i > 1 && i < 10)
¦¦	Logical OR	if (c==0 ¦¦ c==9)
!	Logical NOT	if (!(c>1 && c<9))
<	Less than	if (i < 0)

C++ Operator	Meaning	Example
<=	Less than or equal to	`if (i <= 0)`
>	Greater than	`if (j > 10)`
>=	Greater than or equal to	`if (x >= 8.2)`
==	Equal to	`if (c == '\0')`
!=	Not equal to	`if (c != '\n')`
?:	Conditional assignment	`k = (i<1) ? 1 : i;`

Warning: Do *not* use the = operator as the equality relational operator. This common error is a source of logical bugs in a C++ program. You may be accustomed to using the = operator in other languages to test the equality of two data items. In C++, you *must* use the == operator. What happens if you employ the = operator in C++? Do you get a compiler error? The answer is that you may get a compiler warning. Other than that, your C++ program should run. When the program reaches the expression that it is supposed to test for equality, it actually attempts to assign the operand on the right of the = sign to the operand on the left of the = sign. Of course, a session with such a program most likely leads to weird program behavior or even a system hang.

Notice that the last operator in Table 2.4 is the ?: operator. This special operator supports what is known as the conditional expression.

NEW☞
TERM The *conditional expression* is shorthand for a dual-alternative simple if-else statement. (See Day 3 for more information about the if statement.)

For example, the following is an if-else statement that can be compressed into a conditional expression:

```
if (condition)
    variable = expression1;
else
    variable = expression2;
```

The equivalent conditional expression is as follows:

```
variable = (condition) ? expression1 : expression2;
```

The conditional expression tests the condition. If that condition is true, it assigns expression1 to the target variable. Otherwise, it assigns expression2 to the target variable.

Boolean Expressions

Often, you need to use a collection of relational and logical operators to formulate a nontrivial condition. Here are examples of such conditions:

```
x < 0 || x > 11
(i != 0 || i > 100) && (j != i || j > 0)
x != 0 && x != 10 && x != 100
```

NEW *Boolean* (also called *logical*) *expressions* are expressions that involve logical operators and/
TERM or relational operators, the result of which is of type *bool*. It should be noted that all the relational operators produce expressions with *bool* results.

DO	DON'T

DO double-check to avoid Boolean expressions that are either always `true` or always `false`. For example, the expression (x < 0 && x > 10) is always `false`, because no value of x can be negative and greater than 10 at the same time.

DON'T use the = operator to test for equality.

Consider now an example that uses relational and logical operators and expressions. Listing 2.9 shows the source code for the program RELOP.CPP. The program prompts you to enter three integers and then proceeds to perform a battery of tests. The program displays the relational and logical operations, their operands, and their results.

Type **Listing 2.9. Source code for the program RELOP.CPP.**

```
1:  // Simple C++ program that uses logical expressions.
2:  // This program uses the conditional expression to display
3:  // TRUE or FALSE messages.
4:
5:  #include <iostream.h>
6:
7:  const int MIN_NUM = 30;
8:  const int MAX_NUM = 199;
9:
10: int main()
11: {
12:     int i, j, k;
13:     int xor_sum;
14:     bool flag1, flag2, in_range,
15:          same_int, xor_flag;
16:
17:     cout << "Type first  integer: "; cin >> i;
18:     cout << "Type second integer: "; cin >> j;
19:     cout << "Type third  integer: "; cin >> k;
20:
21:     // test for range [MIN_NUM..MAX_NUM]
22:     flag1 = i >= MIN_NUM;
```

```
23:     flag2 = i <= MAX_NUM;
24:     in_range = flag1 && flag2;
25:     cout << endl << i << " is in the range "
26:         << MIN_NUM << " to " << MAX_NUM << ": "
27:         << (in_range ? "TRUE" : "FALSE");
28:
29:     // test if two or more entered numbers are equal
30:     same_int = i == j || i == k || j == k;
31:     cout << endl << "at least two integers you typed are equal: "
32:         << (same_int ? "TRUE" : "FALSE");
33:
34:     // miscellaneous tests
35:     cout << endl << i << " != " << j << ": "
36:         << ((i != j) ? "TRUE" : "FALSE");
37:     cout << endl << "NOT (" << i << " < " << j << "): "
38:         << ((!(i < j)) ? "TRUE" : "FALSE");
39:     cout << endl << i << " <= " << j << ": "
40:         << ((i <= j) ? "TRUE" : "FALSE");
41:     cout << endl << k << " > " << j << ": "
42:         << ((k > j) ? "TRUE" : "FALSE");
43:     cout << endl << "(" << k << " = " << i << ") AND ("
44:         << j << " != " << k << "): "
45:         << ((k == i && j != k) ? "TRUE" : "FALSE");
46:
47:     // NOTE: C++ does NOT support the logical XOR operator for
48:     // boolean expressions.
49:     // add numeric results of logical tests.  Value is in 0 to 2
50:     xor_sum = (k <= i) + (j >= k);
51:     // if xor_sum is either 0 or 2 (i.e. not = 1), it is
52:     // FALSE therefore interpret 0 or 2 as false.
53:     xor_flag = xor_sum == 1;
54:     cout << endl << "(" << k << " <= " << i << ") XOR ("
55:         << j << " >= " << k << "): "
56:         << (xor_flag ? "TRUE" : "FALSE");
57:     cout << endl << "(" << k << " > " << i << ") AND("
58:         << j << " <= " << k << "): "
59:         << ((k > i && j <= k) ? "TRUE" : "FALSE");
60:     cout << endl << endl;
61:     return 0;
62: }
```

Here is a sample session with the program in Listing 2.9.

```
Type first  integer: 55
Type second integer: 64
Type third  integer: 87

55 is in the range 30 to 199: TRUE
at least two integers you typed are equal: FALSE
55 != 64: TRUE
NOT (55 < 64): FALSE
55 <= 64: TRUE
87 > 64: TRUE
(87 = 55) AND (64 != 87): FALSE
(87 <= 55) XOR (64 >= 87): FALSE
(87 > 55) AND(64 <= 87): TRUE
```

Analysis The program in Listing 2.9 declares 2 global constants, MIN_NUM and MAX_NUM, to define a range of numbers used in the logical tests. The function main declares a number of int and bool variables that are used for input and various testing. The statements on lines 17 through 19 prompt you for 3 integers and store them in the variables i, j, and k, respectively.

The statements on lines 22 through 27 involve testing whether the value in variable i lies in the range of MIN_NUM and MAX_NUM. The statement on line 22 tests if the value in i is greater than or equal to the constant MIN_NUM. The program assigns the bool result to the variable flag1. The statement on line 23 tests whether the value in i is less than or equal to the constant MAX_NUM. The program assigns the bool result to the variable flag2. The statement on line 24 applies the && operator to the variables flag1 and flag2, and it assigns the bool result to the variable in_range. The output statement on lines 25 through 27 states what the test is and displays TRUE or FALSE depending on the value in the variable in_range. The statement uses the conditional operator ?: to display the string TRUE if in_range is true and to display the string FALSE if otherwise.

The statements on lines 30 through 32 determine whether at least two of the three integers you entered are equal. The statement on line 30 uses a Boolean expression that applies the == relational operators and the || logical operators. The statement assigns the bool result to the variable same_int. The output statement on lines 31 and 32 states the test and displays the TRUE/FALSE outcome. The output statement uses the conditional operator to display the strings TRUE or FALSE depending on the value in variable same_int.

The statements on lines 35 through 45 perform miscellaneous tests that involve the input values, and they display both the test and the results. Please feel free to alter these statements to conduct different tests.

> **Note:** The statements on lines 50 through 56 perform an XOR test and display the outcome. The program uses a simple programming trick to implement the XOR operator. The statement on line 50 adds the Boolean value of the subexpressions (k <= i) and (j >= k). The result is 0 if both subexpressions are false, 1 if only one of the subexpressions is true, and 2 if both subexpressions are true. Because the XOR operator is true only if either subexpression is true, the statement on line 53 assigns TRUE to the variable xor_flag if the previous value is 1. Otherwise, the statement assigns FALSE to xor_flag. The statements on lines 57 through 59 perform another miscellaneous test.

Bit-Manipulation Operators

C++ is a programming language that is suitable for system development. System development requires bit-manipulating operators.

NEW☞
TERM *Bit-manipulating operators* toggle, set, query, and shift the bits of any integral type, save floating point types (`float` and `double`).

Table 2.5 shows the bit-manipulating operators. Notice that C++ uses the symbols & and ¦ to represent the bitwise AND and OR, respectively. Recall that the && and ¦¦ characters represent the logical AND and OR operators, respectively. In addition to the bit-manipulating operators, C++ supports the bit-manipulating assignment operators, shown in Table 2.6. (Using bit-manipulating operators is a part of advanced programming that involves fiddling with single bits. As a novice C++ programmer, you most likely will not use these operators in the near future.)

Table 2.5. C++ bit-manipulating operators.

C++ Operator	Meaning	Example
&	Bitwise AND	i & 128
¦	Bitwise OR	j ¦ 64
^	Bitwise XOR	j ^ 12
~	Bitwise NOT	~j
<<	Bitwise shift left	i << 2
>>	Bitwise shift right	j >> 3

Table 2.6. C++ bit-manipulating assignment operators.

C++ Operator	Long Form	Example
x &= y	x = x & y	i &= 128
x ¦= y	x = x ¦ y	j ¦= 64
x ^= y	x = x ^ y	k ^= 15
x <<= y	x = x << y	j <<= 2
x >>= y	x = x >> y	k >>= 3

Listing 2.10 contains the source code for the program BITS.CPP. The program requires no input, because it uses internal data. The program applies the ¦, &, ^, >>, and << bitwise operators and displays the results of the bitwise manipulation.

Listing 2.10. Source code for the program BITS.CPP.

```
1:  // C++ program to perform bit manipulations
2:
3:  #include <iostream.h>
4:
5:  int main()
6:  {
7:     int i, j, k;
8:
9:     // assign values to i and j
10:    i = 0xF0;
11:    j = 0x1A;
12:
13:    k = j & i;
14:    cout << j << " AND " << i << " = " << k << endl;
15:
16:    k = j ¦ i;
17:    cout << j << " OR " << i << " = " << k << endl;
18:
19:    k = j ^ 0x1C;
20:    cout << j << " XOR " << 0x1C << " = " << k << endl;
21:
22:    k = i << 2;
23:    cout << i << " shifted left by 2 bits = " << k << endl;
24:
25:    k = i >> 2;
26:    cout << i << " shifted right by 2 bits = " << k << endl;
27:    return 0;
28: }
```

Here is a sample session with the program in Listing 2.10.

```
26 AND 240 = 16
26 OR 240 = 250
26 XOR 28 = 6
240 shifted left by 2 bits = 960
240 shifted right by 2 bits = 60
```

The program in Listing 2.10 declares three int-typed variables, i, j, and k. The statements on lines 10 and 11 assign hexadecimal numbers to the variables i and j, respectively. The statement on line 13 applies the bitwise AND operator to the variables i and j, and it stores the result in variable k. The output statement on line 14 displays the operands, the bitwise operator, and the results. The statement on line 16 applies the bitwise OR operator to the variables i and j, and it saves the result to variable k. The output statement on line 17 displays the operands, the bitwise operator, and the results. The statement on line 19 applies the bitwise XOR operator using the variable j and the hexadecimal integer 0x1C. The output statement on line 20 displays the operands, the bitwise operator, and the results.

The statements on lines 22 through 26 apply the shift-left and shift-right operators to variable i. These operators shift the bits of the variable i by two bits and assign the result to variable k. The effect of the left-shift operator is the same as multiplying the value in the variable i by 4. Similarly, the effect of the right-shift operator is the same as dividing the value in the variable i by 4.

The Comma Operator

The comma operator requires that the program completely evaluate the first expression before evaluating the second expression. Both expressions are located in the same C++ statement. What does "located in the same C++ statement" mean, exactly? Why use this rather unusual operator in the first place? Because the comma operator with its peculiar role does serve a specific and very important purpose in the for loop.

NEW☛
TERM *Loops* are powerful language constructs that enable computers to excel in achieving repetitive tasks. The *comma operator* enables you to create multiple expressions that initialize multiple loop-related variables.

You will learn more about the for loop in Day 3. For now, this example shows you how to apply the comma operator; just pretend it's a semicolon, except that the value of the entire expression is the value of the expression that appears after the last comma.

Operator Precedence and Evaluation Direction

Now that you are familiar with most of the C++ operators (there are a few more that deal with pointers and addresses), you need to know two related aspects: first, the precedence of the C++ operators; and second, the direction (or sequence) of evaluation. Table 2.7 shows the C++ precedence of the C++ operators covered so far and also indicates the evaluation direction.

Table 2.7. C++ operators and their precedence.

Category	Name	Symbol	Evaluation Direction	Precedence
Monadic				
	Post-increment	++	Left to right	2
	Post-decrement	- -	Left to right	2
	Address	&	Right to left	2
	Bitwise NOT	~	Right to left	2
	Typecast	(type)	Right to left	2
	Logical NOT	!	Right to left	2
	Negation	-	Right to left	2
	Plus sign	+	Right to left	2
	Pre-increment	++	Right to left	2
	Pre-decrement	- -	Right to left	2
	Size of data	sizeof	Right to left	2
Multiplicative				
	Modulus	%	Left to right	3
	Multiply	*	Left to right	3
	Divide	/	Left to right	3
Additive				
	Add	+	Left to right	4
	Subtract	-	Left to right	4
Bitwise Shift				
	Shift left	<<	Left to right	5
	Shift right	>>	Left to right	5
Relational				
	Less than	<	Left to right	6
	Less than or equal	<=	Left to right	6
	Greater than	>	Left to right	6
	Greater than or equal	>=	Left to right	6
	Equal	==	Left to right	7
	Not equal	!=	Left to right	7

Category	Name	Symbol	Evaluation Direction	Precedence
Bitwise				
	AND	&	Left to right	8
	XOR	^	Left to right	9
	OR	¦	Left to right	10
Logical				
	AND	&&	Left to right	11
	OR	¦ ¦	Left to right	12
Ternary				
	Conditional expression	.?:	Right to left	13
Assignment				
	Arithmetic	=	Right to left	14
		+=	Right to left	14
		-=	Right to left	14
		*=	Right to left	14
		/=	Right to left	14
		%=	Right to left	14
	Shift	>>=	Right to left	14
		<<=	Right to left	14
	Bitwise	&=	Right to left	14
		¦=	Right to left	14
		^=	Right to left	14
	Comma	,	Left to right	15

Summary

Today's lesson presented the basic components of C++ programs. These components include data types, variables, constants, and expressions. You learned the following basics:

☐ The predefined data types in Borland C++ 5 include the `bool`, `int`, `char`, `float`, `double`, and `void` data types. C++ adds more flexibility to data types by supporting data-type modifiers. These modifiers alter the precision and the range of values. The type modifiers are `signed`, `unsigned`, `short`, and `long`.

☐ Borland C++ 5 identifiers can be up to 32 characters long and must begin with a letter or an underscore. The subsequent characters of an identifier may be a letter, digit, or underscore. C++ identifiers are case sensitive. This 32-character limit, however, can be changed by manipulating the compiler's options.

☐ The `#include` directive is a special instruction to the compiler. The directive tells the compiler to include the contents of the specified file as though you typed it in the current source file.

☐ Declaring constants involves using the `#define` directive to declare macro-based constants or using the `const` keyword to declare formal constants. The formal constants require that you specify the constant's type (the default is `int`, when omitted), the name of the constants, and the associated value.

☐ Declaring variables requires you to state the data type and name of the variable. C++ enables you to initialize a variable when you declare it. You can declare multiple variables in a single declarative statement.

☐ The arithmetic operators include `+`, `-`, `*`, `/`, and `%` (modulus).

☐ The arithmetic expressions vary in complexity. The simplest expression contains a single data item (literal, constant, or variable). Complex expressions include multiple operators, functions, literals, constants, and variables.

☐ The increment and decrement operators come in the pre- and post- forms. C++ enables you to apply these operators to variables that store characters, integers, and even floating-point numbers.

☐ The arithmetic assignment operators enable you to write shorter arithmetic expressions, in which the primary operand also is the variable receiving the result of the expression.

☐ The `sizeof` operator returns the byte size of either a data type or a variable.

☐ Typecasting enables you to force the type conversion of an expression.

☐ Relational and logical operators enable you to build logical expressions.

☐ Boolean expressions combine relational and logical operators to formulate nontrivial conditions. These expressions allow a program to make sophisticated decisions.

☐ The conditional expression offers you a short form for the simple, dual-alternative `if-else` statement.

☐ The bit-manipulation operators perform bitwise AND, OR, XOR, and NOT operations. In addition, C++ supports the `<<` and `>>` bitwise shift operators.

☐ The bit-manipulation assignment operators offer short forms for simple bit-manipulation statements.

Q&A

Q Is there a specific style for naming identifiers?

A There are a few styles that have become popular in recent years. The one used here has the identifier begin with a lowercase character. If the identifier contains multiple words, such as `numberOfElements`, make the first character of each subsequent word an uppercase letter.

Q How does the compiler react when you declare a variable but never assign a value to it?

A The compiler issues a warning that the variable is unreferenced.

Q What is the Boolean expression for checking that the value of a variable, `i`, is in the range of values (for example, defined by variables `lowVal` and `hiVal`)?

A The expression that determines whether the value in variable `i` is located in a range is

```
(i >= lowVal && i <= hiVal)
```

Workshop

The Workshop provides quiz questions to help you solidify your understanding of the material covered and exercises to provide you with experience in using what you've learned. Try to understand the quiz and exercise answers before continuing on to the next day's lesson. Answers are provided in Appendix A.

Quiz

1. Which of the following variables are valid, and which are not? Why?

```
numFiles
n0Distance_02_Line
0Weight
Bin Number
static
Static
```

2. What is the output of the following program?

```
#include <iostream.h>
main()
{
    int i = 3;
    int j = 5;
    double x = 33.5;
    double y = 10.0;
    cout << 10 + j % i << endl;
```

```
        cout << i * i - 2 * i + 5 << endl;
        cout << (19 + i + j) / (2 * j + 2) << endl;
        cout << x / y + y / x << endl;
        cout << i * x + j * y << endl;
        return 0;
    }
```

3. What is the output of the following program?

```
#include <iostream.h>
main()
{
    int i = 3;
    int j = 5;
    cout << 10 + j % i++ << endl;
    cout << -i * i - 2 * i + 5 << endl;
    cout << (19 + ++i + ++j) / (2 * j + 2) << endl;
    return 0;
}
```

4. What is the output of the following program?

```
#include <iostream.h>
main()
{
    int i = 3;
    int j = 5;
    i += j;
    j *= 2;
    cout << 10 + j % i << endl;
    i -= 2;
    j /= 3;
    cout << i * i - 2 * i + j << endl;
    return 0;
}
```

5. What is the output of the following program?

```
#include <iostream.h>
main()
{
    int i = 5;
    int j = 10;
    cout << ((i < j) ? "TRUE" : "FALSE") << endl;
    cout << ((i > 0 && j < 100) ?  "TRUE" : "FALSE") << endl;
    cout << ((i > 0 && i < 10) ? "TRUE" : "FALSE") << endl;
    cout << ((i == 5 && i == j) ? "TRUE" : "FALSE") << endl;
    return 0;
}
```

Exercises

1. Use the conditional operator to find the greater of two integers.

2. Use the conditional operator to find the smaller of two integers.

3. Use the conditional operator to find the absolute value of an integer.

4. Use the conditional operator to assign true to the bool variable isOdd if an integer is an odd number and false if otherwise.

The Decision-Making Constructs and Loops

Different programming languages offer varying support for decision-making constructs. Some languages provide only simple decision-making constructs, whereas others offer more sophisticated constructs.

NEW TERM *Decision-making constructs* allow your applications to examine conditions and choose courses of action.

Another facet of the decision-making constructs in C++ are the loops that perform repetitive tasks. They allow the computer to do something repeatedly without forcing the programmer to type in the same stuff over and over, changing things only slightly for each version.

Today's lesson looks at the decision-making constructs and loops in C++ and covers the following topics:

- [ ] The single-alternative `if` statement
- [ ] The dual-alternative `if-else` statement
- [ ] The multiple-alternative `if-else` statement
- [ ] The multiple-alternative `switch` statement
- [ ] Nested decision-making constructs
- [ ] The `try`, `catch`, and `throw` statements
- [ ] The `for` loop statement
- [ ] The `do-while` loop statement
- [ ] The `while` loop statement
- [ ] Skipping iterations
- [ ] Exiting loops
- [ ] Nested loops

Decision-Making Constructs

Today's lesson starts with decision-making constructs. These are methods by which an application can perform different tasks based on differing conditions. For example, if a program asks the user whether or not to continue an action, the program needs to be able to actually continue (or not continue) based on the user's input. These are the first of the decision-making constructs.

The Single-Alternative *if* Statement

Unlike many programming languages, C++ does not have the keyword then in any form of the `if` statement. This language feature may lead you to ask how the `if` statement separates the tested

condition from the executable statements. The answer is that C++ has you enclose the tested condition in parentheses.

NEW🖝 An `if` statement is a *single-alternative* statement.
TERM

The Single-Alternative *if* Statement

The general syntax for the single-alternative `if` statement is

```
if (condition)
    statement;
```

for a single executable statement, and

```
if (condition)
    {
    <sequence of statements>
    }
```

for a sequence of executable statements.

Examples

```
if (numberOfLines < 0)
    numberOfLines = 0;

if ((height - 54) < 3)
    {
    area = length * width;
    volume = area * height;
    }
```

C++ uses the open and close braces {} to define a block of statements. Figure 3.1 shows the flow in a single-alternative `if` statement.

Figure 3.1.
The program flow in the single-alternative if statement.

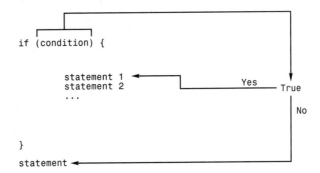

Listing 3.1 shows a program with a single-alternative `if` statement. The program prompts you to enter a nonzero number and stores the input in the variable x. If the value in x is not zero, the program displays the reciprocal of x.

Type

Listing 3.1. Source code for the program IF1.CPP.

```
1: // Program that demonstrates the single-alternative if statement
2:
3: #include <iostream.h>
4:
5: int main()
6: {
7:     double x;
8:     cout << "Enter a non—zero number: ";
9:     cin >> x;
10:    if (x != 0)
11:        cout << "The reciprocal of " << x
12:            << " is " << (1/x) << endl;
13:    return 0;
14: }
```

Here is a sample session with the program in Listing 3.1.

```
Enter a non-zero number: 25
The reciprocal of 25 is 0.04
```

The program in Listing 3.1 declares the double-typed variable x in the function main. The output statement on line 8 prompts you to enter a nonzero number. The input statement on line 9 stores your input in variable x. The if statement on line 10 determines whether x does not equal zero. If this condition is true, the program executes the output statement on lines 11 and 12. This statement displays the value of x and its reciprocal, 1/x. If the tested condition is false, the program skips the statements on lines 11 and 12 and resumes at the statement on line 13.

The Dual-Alternative *if-else* Statement

In the *dual-alternative* form of the if statement, the else keyword separates the statements that are used to execute each alternative.

NEW The *dual-alternative* if-else statement provides two alternate courses of action based on
TERM the Boolean value of the tested condition.

The Dual-Alternative *if-else* Statement

Syntax

The general syntax for the dual-alternative if-else statement is

```
if (condition)
    statement1;
else
    statement2;
```

for a single executable statement in each clause, and

```
if (condition)
```

```
   {
   <sequence #1 of statements>
   }
else
   {
   <sequence #2 of statements>
   }
```

for a sequence of executable statements in both clauses.

Example

```
if (moneyInAccount > withdraw)
   {
   moneyInAccount -= withdraw;
   cout << "You withdrew $" << withdraw << endl;
   cout << "Balance is $" << moneyInAccount << endl;
   }
else
   {
   cout << "Cannot withdraw $" << withdraw << endl;
   cout << "Account has $" << moneyInAccount << endl;
   }
```

Figure 3.2. shows the program flow in the dual-alternative if-else statement.

Look at an example that uses the dual-alternative if-else statement. Listing 3.2 contains the source code for the program IF2.CPP. The program prompts you to enter a letter and then determines whether you actually entered a letter or some other character. The program output classifies your input as either a letter or a nonletter character.

Figure 3.2.
The program flow in the dual-alternative if-else statement.

Listing 3.2. Source code for the program IF2.CPP.

```
 1:  // Program that demonstrates the dual-alternative if statement
 2:
 3:  #include <iostream.h>
 4:  #include <ctype.h>
 5:
 6:  int main()
 7:  {
 8:      char c;
 9:      cout << "Enter a letter: ";
10:      cin >> c;
11:      // convert to uppercase
12:      c = toupper(c);
13:      if (c >= 'A' && c <= 'Z')
14:          cout << "You entered a letter" << endl;
15:      else
16:          cout << "Your input was not a letter" << endl;
17:      return 0;
18: }
```

Here is a sample session with the program in Listing 3.2.

```
Enter a letter: g
You entered a letter
```

The program in Listing 3.2 declares the char-typed variable c on line 8. The output statement on line 9 prompts you to enter a letter. The input statement on line 10 obtains your input and stores it in variable c. The statement on line 12 converts the value in the variable to uppercase by calling the function toupper (prototyped in the CTYPE.H header file). This character-case conversion simplifies the tested condition in the if-else statement on line 13. The if-else statement determines if the variable c contains a character in the range of 'A' to 'Z'. If this condition is true, the program executes the output statement on line 14. This statement displays a message stating that you have entered a letter. Alternatively, if the tested condition is false, the program executes the else clause on line 16. This statement displays a message stating that your input was not a letter.

Potential Problems with the *if* Statement

There is a potential problem with the dual-alternative if statement. This problem occurs when the if clause includes another single-alternative if statement. In this case, the compiler considers that the else clause pertains to the nested if statement. (A nested if statement is one that is contained in another if statement and/or else clause. You learn more about nesting in the next section.) Here is an example.

```
if (i > 0)
   if (i == 10)
      cout << "You guessed the magic number";
else
   cout << "Number is out of range";
```

In this code fragment, when the variable i is a positive number other than 10, the code displays the message Number is out of range. The compiler treats these statements as though the code fragment meant

```
if (i > 0)
    if (i == 10)
        cout << "You guessed the magic number";
    else
        cout << "Number is out of range";
```

To correct this problem, enclose the nested if statement in a statement block:

```
if (i > 0)
    {
    if (i == 10)
        cout << "You guessed the magic number";
    }
else
    cout << "Number is out of range";
```

The Multiple-Alternative *if-else* Statement

C++ enables you to nest if-else statements to create a multiple-alternative form. This alternative gives a lot of power and flexibility to your applications.

NEW☞ The *multiple-alternative* if-else statement contains nested if-else statements.
TERM

Syntax

The Multiple-Alternative *if-else* Statement

The general syntax for the multiple-alternative if-else statement is

```
if (tested_condition1)
    statement1; ¦ { <sequence #1 of statement> }
else if (tested_condition2)
    statement2; ¦ { <sequence #2 of statement> }
...
else if (tested_conditionN)
    statementN; ¦ { <sequence #N of statement> }
[else
    statementN+1; ¦ { <sequence #N+1 of statement> }]
```

Example

```
char op;

int opOk = 1;
double x, y, z;
cout << "Enter operand1 operator operand2: ";
cin >> x >> op >> y;
if (op == '+')
    z = x + y;
else if (op == '-')
    z = x - y;
```

```
else if (op == '*')
   z = x * y;
else if (op == '/' && y != 0)
   z = x / y;
else
   opOk = 0;
```

The multiple-alternative if-else statement performs a series of cascaded tests until one of the following occurs:

☐ One of the conditions in the if clause or in the else if clauses is true. In this case, the accompanying statements are executed.

☐ None of the tested conditions are true. The program executes the statements in the catch-all else clause (if there is an else clause).

Figure 3.3 shows the program flow in the multiple-alternative if-else statement.

Figure 3.3.

The program flow in the multiple-alternative if-else statement.

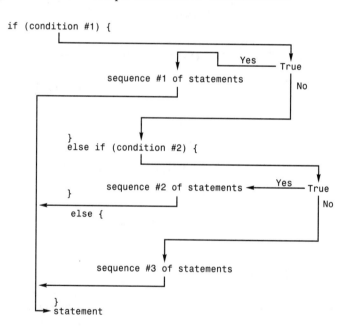

Consider the following example. Listing 3.3 shows the source code for the program IF3.CPP. The program prompts you to enter a character and uses the multiple-alternative if-else statement to determine whether your input is one of the following:

☐ An uppercase letter

☐ A lowercase letter

☐ A digit

☐ A nonalphanumeric character

Type Listing 3.3. Source code for the IF3.CPP program.

```
1: // Program that demonstrates the multiple-alternative if statement
2:
3: #include <iostream.h>
4:
5: int main()
6: {
7:     char c;
8:     cout << "Enter a character: ";
9:     cin >> c;
10:    if (c >= 'A' && c <= 'Z')
11:        cout << "You entered an uppercase letter" << endl;
12:    else if (c >= 'a' && c <= 'z')
13:        cout << "You entered a lowercase letter" << endl;
14:    else if (c >= '0' && c <= '9')
15:        cout << "You entered a digit" << endl;
16:    else
17:        cout << "You entered a non-alphanumeric character" << endl;
18:    return 0;
19: }
```

Here is a sample session with the program in Listing 3.3.

```
Enter a character: !
You entered a non-alphanumeric character
```

The program in Listing 3.3 declares the char-typed variable c on line 7. The output statement on line 8 prompts you to enter a character. The input statement on line 9 obtains your input and stores it in variable c. The multiple-alternative if-else statement tests the following conditions:

☐ On line 10, the if statement determines whether the variable c contains a letter in the range of 'A' to 'Z'. If this condition is true, the program executes the output statement on line 11. This statement confirms that you entered an uppercase letter. The program then resumes at line 18.

☐ If the condition on line 10 is false, the program jumps to the first else if clause on line 12. There the program determines whether the variable c contains a letter in the range of 'a' to 'z'. If this condition is true, the program executes the output statement on line 13. This statement confirms that you entered a lowercase letter. The program then resumes at line 18.

☐ If the condition on line 12 is false, the program jumps to the second else if clause on line 14. There the program determines whether the variable c contains a digit. If this condition is true, the program executes the output statement on line 15. This statement confirms that you entered a digit. The program then resumes at line 18.

☐ If the condition on line 14 is false, the program jumps to the catch-all else clause on line 16 and executes the output statement on line 17. This statement displays a message telling you that your input was neither a letter nor a digit.

The *switch* Statement

The switch statement offers a special form of multiple-alternative decision making. It enables you to examine the various values of an integer-compatible expression and choose the appropriate course of action.

Syntax

The *switch* Statement

The general syntax for the switch statement is

```
switch (expression)
    {
    case constant1_1:
[   case constant1_2: ...]
        <one or more statements>
        break;
    case constant2_1:
[   case constant2_2: ...]
        <one or more statements>
        break;
...
    case constantN_1:
[   case constantN_2: ...]
        <one or more statements>
        break;
    default:
        <one or more statements>
        break;
    }
```

Example

```
ok = true;
switch (op)
    {
    case '+':
        z = x + y;
        break;
    case '-':
        z = x - y;
        break;
    case '*':
        z = x * y;
        break;
    case '/':
        if (y != 0)
            z = x / y;
        else
            ok = false;
        break;
    default:
        ok = false;
break;
    }
```

Following are the rules for using a switch statement:

1. The switch requires an integer-compatible value. This value may be a constant, variable, function call, or expression. The switch statement does not work with floating-point data types.

2. The value after each case label *must* be a constant.

3. C++ does not support case labels with ranges of values. Instead, each value must appear in a separate case label.

4. The end of a case statement is typically marked with a break. This causes execution to resume at the first statement that occurs after the switch. If you don't include a break, then execution will continue with the next case statement. This is actually sometimes desirable, but mostly you'll want to use the break. Alternatively, you could use a return statement instead of a break. This will cause the current function (to be described in more detail on Day 5) to terminate; if the current function is main, then the program will end.

5. The default clause is a catch-all clause, but not necessary if you want to check for only a specific set of circumstances.

6. The set of statements in each case label or grouped case labels need not be enclosed in open and close braces.

Note: The lack of single case labels with ranges of values makes it more appealing to use a multiple-alternative if-else statement if you have a large contiguous range of values.

Figure 3.4 shows the program flow in the multiple-alternative switch statement.

Look at an example that uses the switch statement. Listing 3.4 contains the source code for the program SWITCH.CPP that you can obtain by editing Listing 3.3. The new program performs the same task of classifying your character input, this time using a switch statement.

 Listing 3.4. Source code for the SWITCH.CPP program.

```
1:  // Program demonstrates the multiple-alternative switch statement
2:
3:  #include <iostream.h>
4:
5:  int main()
6:  {
7:      char c;
8:      cout << "Enter a character: ";
9:      cin >> c;
10:     switch (c)
```

Listing 3.4. continued

```
11:        {
12:        case 'A':
13:        case 'B':
14:        case 'C':
15:        case 'D':
16:        // other case labels
17:            cout << "You entered an uppercase letter" << endl;
18:            break;
19:        case 'a':
20:        case 'b':
21:        case 'c':
22:        case 'd':
23:        // other case labels
24:            cout << "You entered a lowercase letter" << endl;
25:            break;
26:        case '0':
27:        case '1':
28:        case '2':
29:        case '3':
30:        // other case labels
31:            cout << "You entered a digit" << endl;
32:            break;
33:        default:
34:            cout << "You entered a non-alphanumeric character" << endl;
35:            break;
36:        }
37:     return 0;
38: }
```

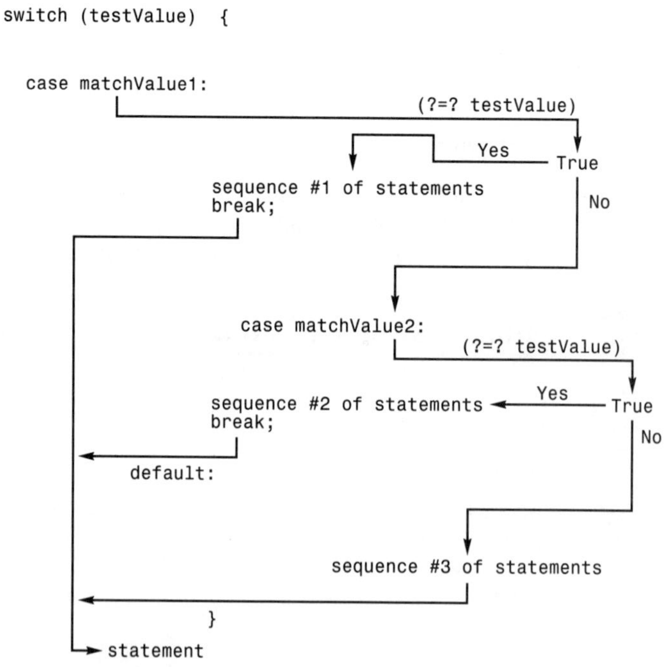

Figure 3.4.

The program flow in the multiple-alternative switch statement.

Here is a sample session with the program in Listing 3.4.

```
Enter a character: 2
You entered a digit
```

The program in Listing 3.4 declares the char-typed variable c. The output statement on line 8 prompts you to enter a character. The statement on line 9 stores your input in variable c. The switch statement starts at line 10. Lines 12 through 15 contain the case labels for the letters A through D. I omitted the case labels for the rest of the uppercase letters to keep the program short. If the character in variable c matches any of the values on lines 12 through 15, the program executes the output statement on line 17. This statement confirms that you entered an uppercase letter. (Because I reduced the number of case labels, the program executes the statement on line 17 only if you enter one of the letters A through D.) The break statement on line 18 causes the program flow to jump to line 37, past the end of the switch statement.

If the character in variable c does not match any of the case labels on lines 12 through 15, the program resumes at line 19 where it encounters another set of case labels. These labels are supposed to represent lowercase characters. As you can see, I reduced the number of labels to shorten the program. If the character in variable c matches any value on lines 19 through 22, the program executes the output statement on line 24. This statement confirms that you entered a lowercase letter. (Because I reduced the number of case labels, the program executes the statement on line 24 only if you enter one of the letters a through d.) The break statement on line 25 causes the program flow to jump to line 37, past the end of the switch statement.

If the character in variable c does not match any of the case labels on lines 19 through 22, the program resumes at line 26, where it encounters another set of case labels. These labels are supposed to represent digits. Again, you can see that I reduced the number of labels to shorten the program. If the character in variable c matches any value on lines 26 through 29, the program executes the output statement on line 31. This statement confirms that you entered a digit. (Because I reduced the number of case labels, the program executes the statement on line 31 only if you enter one of the digits 0 to 3.) The break statement on line 32 causes the program flow to jump to line 37, past the end of the switch statement.

If the character in variable c does not match any case label on lines 26 through 29, the program jumps to the catch-all clause on line 33. The program executes the output statement on line 34. This statement tells you that you entered a nonalphanumeric character.

Nested Decision-Making Constructs

Often you need to use nested decision-making constructs to manage nontrivial conditions. Nesting decision-making constructs enables you to deal with complicated conditions using a divide-and-conquer approach. The outer-level constructs help you to test preliminary or more general conditions. The inner-level constructs help you deal with more specific conditions.

Listing 3.5 shows the source code for the program IF4.CPP. The program prompts you to enter a character. Then the program determines if your input is an uppercase letter, a lowercase letter, or a character that is not a letter. The program displays a message that classifies your input.

Type **Listing 3.5. Source code for the program IF4.CPP.**

```
1:  // Program that demonstrates the nested if statements
2:
3:  #include <iostream.h>
4:
5:  int main()
6:  {
7:      char c;
8:      cout << "Enter a character: ";
9:      cin >> c;
10:     if ((c >= 'A' && c <= 'Z') || (c >= 'a' && c <= 'z'))
11:         if (c >= 'A' && c <= 'Z')
12:             cout << "You entered an uppercase letter" << endl;
13:         else
14:             cout << "You entered a lowercase letter" << endl;
15:     else
16:         cout << "You entered a non-letter character" << endl;
17:     return 0;
18: }
```

Here is a sample session with the program in Listing 3.5.

```
Enter a character: a
You entered a lowercase letter
```

The program in Listing 3.5 declares the char-typed variable c. The output statement in line 8 prompts you to enter a character. The statement in line 9 stores your input in variable c. The program uses nested if-else statements that begin at lines 10 and 11. The outer if-else statement determines whether the variable c contains a letter. If the tested condition is true, the program executes the inner if-else statement in line 11. Otherwise, the program resumes at the else clause of the outer if-else statement and executes the output statement in line 16. This statement tells you that your input was not a letter.

The program uses the inner if-else statement to further examine the condition of the outer if-else statement. The if-else statement in line 11 determines whether the variable c contains an uppercase letter. If this condition is true, the program executes the output statement in line 12. Otherwise, the program executes the else clause statement in line 14. These output statements tell you whether you entered an uppercase or a lowercase letter. After executing the inner if-else statement, the program jumps to line 17, past the end of the outer if-else statement.

Exception Handling

Exception handling was introduced into the ANSI/ISO C++ standard as a way of letting a program deal with unexpected problems that might occur, and also as a means of presenting a universal method of specifying errors. Before exceptions, it sometimes was difficult to tell when something was supposed to be an error and when it was supposed to be a valid number. This especially was true with the return values from functions, which is discussed on Day 5, and with class constructors, which is discussed on Day 8.

The exception mechanism revolves around placing the statements that might generate a runtime error in a special block—the try block. This block is followed by one or more catch blocks that identify and handle the errors generated in the try block.

The *try* and *catch* Blocks

The syntax for the try and catch blocks is

```
try
    {
    // place code that may generate an exception
    }
catch(T1 [X1])
    {
    // handle exception type T1
    }
[catch(T2 [X2])
    {
    // handle exception type T2
    }]
[other catch blocks]
[catch(...)
    {
    // handle remaining types of exceptions
    }]
```

The types T1 and T2 are special types that support user-defined exceptions. The parameter X1 can have the type T1, T1&, const T1, and const T1&. The parameter X2 can have the same variations for type T2. The last catch block uses the ellipsis (three dots) to indicate that it is a catch-all block.

```
try
    {
    // Do something to a file
    DoSomething("filename.ext");
    }
catch(char* str)
    {
    cout << "Couldn't " << str << endl;
    }
catch(...)
    {
    cout << "Unknown exception" << endl;
    }
```

95

The preceding example has a try block that attempts to call a function to manipulate a file called FILENAME.EXT (functions are discussed on Day 5). This function *throws* (that is, generates) an exception. The catch block handles the char* exception type by displaying an error message that contains the message generated by the exception. The last catch block uses an ellipsis (...) rather than actually specifying a type to handle. This enables you to handle exceptions you didn't expect; any exception for which you don't actually specify the type gets handled in this all-encompassing block. You should note some similarity with the default section of a switch statement.

NEW☞
TERM
An *exception* is a runtime error. To *throw an exception* means to generate a runtime error.

C++ enables you to define your own exception types, using structures or classes (discussed on Day 4). An exception type can be an empty structure or object if you need only the name of the structure or object type. If you want to provide more information related to the nature of the exception, the exception type can include data members and member functions that support manipulating the exception state.

The last component of handling exceptions deals with throwing them. C++ supplies the keyword throw, which throws an exception.

The *throw* Keyword

Syntax

The syntax for the throw keyword is

```
throw(exceptionInstance);
```

The exceptionInstance is an instance of an exception structure or class.

Example

```
try
    {
    int rslt;
    if (!(rslt = DoSomething(filename)))
        throw "do something";
    if (!UseRslt(rslt))
        throw "use result";
    if (rslt >= 100)
        throw rslt;
    }
catch(char* str)
    {
    cout << "Couldn't " << str << endl;
    }
catch(int i)
    {
    cout << "Result was too high: " << i << endl;
    }
```

The preceding function throws the exception instances whenever it encounters an error. Note the use of the `char*` type. This is a pointer to a character, which is one of the ways that C++ can handle strings. Pointers are discussed in more detail on Day 4, and strings are discussed in depth on Day 7.

Loops

Loops are employed in order to get C++ to do things repeatedly. Rather than have the programmer type in the same code over and over again, each time modifying it slightly so that it will perform actions in sequence, you can use a loop to perform the repetition automatically.

The *for* Loop

The `for` loop in C++ is a versatile loop because it offers both fixed and conditional iterations. The latter feature of the `for` loop deviates from the typical use of the `for` loop in other programming languages, such as Pascal and BASIC. Whereas these other languages allow you to use only straight integers and go from a single starting point to a single ending point, C++ enables you to specify more complex operations.

3

The *for* Loop

The general syntax for the `for` loop statement is

```
for (<initialization of loop control variables>;
     <loop continuation test>;
     <modification of loop control variables, often an increment or decrement>)
```

Example

```
for (i = 0; i < 10; i++)
   cout << "The current count is " << i << "." << endl;
```

The `for` loop statement has three components, each of which is optional. The first component initializes the loop control variables. (C++ enables you to use more than one loop control variable.) The second part of the loop is the condition that determines whether the loop makes another iteration (sort of like an `if` statement without the actual `if` keyword). The last part of the `for` loop is the clause that modifies the loop control variables; often this simply is an increment and/or decrement operation.

> **Note:** The C++ `for` loop enables you to declare the loop control variables. Such variables exist in the scope of the loop only. Those of you familiar with earlier versions of C++ may remember that the control variables once existed immediately outside of the loop as well. As of the most recent ANSI/ISO C++, this has been changed so that things like the following are now possible:

```
int i = 5;
cout << "i starts at " << i << endl;
for (int i = 0; i < 10; ++i)
    cout << "Step #" << i + 1 << endl;
cout << "i ends at " << i << endl;
```

The output of that code snippet looks like this:

```
i starts at 5
Step #1
Step #2
Step #3
Step #4
Step #5
Step #6
Step #7
Step #8
Step #9
Step #10
i ends at 5
```

Listing 3.6 contains the source code for the program FOR1.CPP. The program prompts you to define a range of integers by specifying the lower- and upper-bounds. The program then calculates the sum of the integers, as well as the average value, in the range you specify.

Listing 3.6. Source code for the program FOR1.CPP.

```
1:  // Program calculates a sum and average of a range of
2:  // integers using a for loop
3:
4:  #include <iostream.h>
5:
6:  int main()
7:  {
8:      int count = 0;
9:      double sum = 0.0;
10:     int first, last, temp;
11:
12:     cout << "Enter the first integer: ";
13:     cin >> first;
14:     cout << "Enter the last integer: ";
15:     cin >> last;
16:     if (first > last)
17:         {
18:         temp = first;
19:         first = last;
20:         last = temp;
21:         }
22:     for (int i = first; i <= last; i++)
23:         {
24:         count++;
25:         sum += (double)i;
```

```
26:        }
27:    cout << "Sum of integers from "
28:         << first << " to " << last << " = "
29:         << sum << endl;
30:    cout << "Average value = " << sum / count << endl;
31:    return 0;
32: }
```

Here is a sample session with the program in Listing 3.6.

```
Enter the first integer: 1
Enter the last integer: 100
Sum of integers from 1 to 100 = 5050
Average value = 50.5
```

The program in Listing 3.6 declares a collection of int-typed and double-typed variables in function main. The function initializes the summation variables, count and sum, to 0. The input and output statements on lines 12 through 15 prompt you to enter the integers that define a range of values. The program stores these integers in the variables first and last. The if statement on line 16 determines whether the value in variable first is greater than the value in variable last. If this condition is true, the program executes the block of statements on lines 18 through 20. These statements swap the values in variables first and last, using the variable temp as a swap buffer. Thus, the if statement ensures that the integer in variable first is less than or equal to the integer in variable last.

The program carries out the summation using the for loop on line 22. The loop declares its own control variable, i, and initializes it with the value in the variable first. The loop continuation condition is i <= last. This condition indicates that the loop iterates as long as i is less than or equal to the value in the variable last. The loop increment component is i++, which increments the loop control variable by 1 for every iteration. The loop contains two statements. The first statement increments the value in the variable count. The second statement adds the value of i (after typecasting it to double) to the variable sum.

> **Note:** You can rewrite the for loop to move the first loop statement to the loop increment component.
>
> ```
> for (int i = first; i <= last; i++, count++)
>     sum += (double)i;
> ```
>
> Notice the use of the comma in the last part of the for statement. This is the most common place in which this C++ feature is used, to allow for multiple statements where only one is normally allowed. Although it has no bearing upon this instance, note that the value of the expression i++, count++ is the same as simply count++.

The output statement on lines 27 through 30 displays the sum and average of integers in the range you specified.

To illustrate the flexibility of the for loop, you can create the program FOR2.CPP, shown in Listing 3.7, by editing the program FOR1.CPP.

 Listing 3.7. Source code for the program FOR2.CPP.

```
1:  // Program calculates a sum and average of a range of
2:  // integers using a for loop
3:
4:  #include <iostream.h>
5:
6:  int main()
7:  {
8:      int count = 0;
9:      double sum = 0.0;
10:     int first, last, temp;
11:
12:     cout << "Enter the first integer: ";
13:     cin >> first;
14:     cout << "Enter the last integer: ";
15:     cin >> last;
16:     if (first > last)
17:         {
18:         temp = first;
19:         first = last;
20:         last = temp;
21:         }
22:     cout << "Sum of integers from "
23:          << first << " to " << last << " = ";
24:     for (; first <= last;)
25:         {
26:         count++;
27:         sum += (double)first++;
28:         }
29:     cout << sum << endl;
30:     cout << "Average value = " << sum / count << endl;
31:     return 0;
32: }
```

Here is a sample session with the program in Listing 3.7.

```
Enter the first integer: 10
Enter the last integer: 100
Sum of integers from 10 to 100 = 5005
Average value = 55
```

The FOR1.CPP and FOR2.CPP programs perform the same tasks and interact identically with the user. The changes made are on lines 22 through 29. Instead of using a predefined loop control variable, you use first, the variable that marks the beginning of the loop. Since this is

going to be changed by the loop, lines 22 and 23 make sure to use it as output for the user first before any modifications begin. Then, the for loop on lines 24 through 28 just uses first instead of i. Note that, since first is already initialized to the starting point, there's no need to do so again in the first for expression. In addition, I removed the loop increment component and compensated for it by applying the post-increment operator to the variable first on line 27.

Open Loops Using the *for* Loops

When you were introduced to the C++ for loop, you learned that the three components of the for loop are optional. In fact, C++ permits you to leave *all* three components empty.

NEW☞ TERM   When you leave the three components of a loop empty, the result is an *open loop*.

It is worthwhile to point out that other languages, such as ADA and Modula-2, do support formal open loops and provide mechanisms to exit these loops. C++ permits you to exit from a loop in the following four ways:

- ☐ The break statement causes the program execution to resume after the end of the current loop in much the same way as it can be used to cause execution to resume outside of a switch statement. Use the break statement when you want to exit a for loop and resume with the remaining parts of the program.

- ☐ The return statement will return from the current function (including main). You'll learn more about return and functions on Day 5.

- ☐ The throw statement causes an exception to be thrown. This is used when an error has occurred and you can't continue with the rest of the program without some sort of error handler. But take care when using this method; exceptions really are only meant to be used in dire circumstances—in the case of some error, for example.

- ☐ In very extreme cases, the exit function (declared in the STDLIB.H header file) enables you to exit the program. Use the exit function in the direst of emergencies when there isn't even any hope of recovering from an error. This will stop iteration and exit the program.

Consider the following example. Listing 3.8 contains the source code for the program FOR3.CPP. The program uses an open loop to prompt you repeatedly for a number. The program takes your input and displays it along with its reciprocal value. Then the program asks you whether you want to calculate the reciprocal of another number. If you type in the letter Y or y, the program performs another iteration. Otherwise, the program ends. If you continue to type Y or y for the latter prompt, the program keeps running—at least until the computer breaks down!

Listing 3.8. Source code for the program FOR3.CPP.

```
1:  // Program that demonstrates using the
2:  // for loop to emulate an infinite loop.
3:
4:  #include <iostream.h>
5:  #include <ctype.h>
6:
7:  int main()
8:  {
9:      char ch;
10:     double x, y;
11:
12:     // for loop with empty parts
13:     for (;;)
14:         {
15:         cout << endl << "Enter a number: ";
16:         cin >> x;
17:         // process number if non-zero
18:         if (x != 0)
19:             {
20:             y = 1 / x;
21:             cout << "1/" << x << " = " << y << endl;
22:             cout << "More calculations? (Y/N) ";
23:             cin >> ch;
24:             if (toupper(ch) != 'Y')
25:                 break;
26:             }
27:         else
28:             // display error message
29:             cout << "Error: cannot accept 0" << endl;
30:         }
31:     return 0;
32: }
```

Here is a sample session with the program in Listing 3.8.

```
Enter a number: 5
1/5 = 0.2
More calculations? (Y/N) y

Enter a number: 12
1/12 = 0.0833333
More calculations? (Y/N) y

Enter a number: 16
1/16 = 0.0625
More calculations? (Y/N) n
```

The program in Listing 3.8 declares the char-typed variable ch and two double-typed variables, x and y. The function main uses the for loop, on line 13, as an open loop by eliminating all three loop components. The output statement on line 15 prompts you to enter a number. The input statement on line 16 obtains your input and stores it in variable x. The if-else statement on

line 18 determines if the value in variable x is not zero. If this condition is true, then the program executes the block of statements on lines 20 through 25. Otherwise, the program executes the else clause statement on line 29. This statement displays an error message.

The statement on line 20 assigns the reciprocal of the value in variable x to variable y. The output statement on line 21 displays the values in variables x and y. The output statement on line 22 prompts you for more calculations, and requires a Y/N (in either uppercase or lowercase) type of answer. The input statement on line 23 stores your single-character input in variable ch. The statement on line 24 converts your input into uppercase, using the function toupper (prototyped in the CTYPE.H header file) and determines whether the character is not the letter Y. If this condition is true, the program executes the break statement on line 25. This statement causes the program execution to exit the open loop and to resume at line 31.

The *do-while* Loop

The do-while loop in C++ is a conditional loop that tests the iteration condition at the end of the loop. Therefore, the do-while loop iterates at least once.

NEW☞
TERM
A *conditional loop* iterates as long as a condition is true. This condition is tested at the end of the loop in a do-while loop and at the beginning of a regular while loop.

The *do-while* Loop

The general syntax for the do-while loop is

```
do
   {
   <sequence of statements>
   } while (condition);
```

Example

The following loop displays the squares of 2 to 10:

```
int i = 2;
do
   {
   cout << i << "^2 = " << i * i << endl;
   } while (++i < 11);
```

Listing 3.9 shows the source code for the program DOWHILE.CPP, which is essentially the same as the FOR3.CPP program—except you can replace the clumsy open for loop with a more appropriate do-while loop.

 Listing 3.9. Source code for the program DOWHILE.CPP.

```
1:  // Program that demonstrates using the
2:  // do-while loop
```

Listing 3.9. continued

```
3:
4:  #include <iostream.h>
5:  #include <ctype.h>
6:
7:  int main()
8:  {
9:      char ch;
10:     double x, y;
11:
12:     do              // do-while loop to perform calculations
13:         {
14:         do          // do-while loop to collect a number
15:             {
16:             cout << endl << "Enter a number: ";
17:             cin >> x;
18:             if (x == 0)
19:                 cout << "Error: cannot accept 0" << endl;
20:             } while (x == 0);
21:         y = 1 / x;
22:         cout << "1/" << x << " = " << y << endl;
23:         cout << "More calculations? (Y/N) ";
24:         cin >> ch;
25:         } while (toupper(ch) == 'Y');
26:     return 0;
27: }
```

The differences between DOWHILE.CPP and FOR3.CPP are rather minimal; they mainly consist of replacing the for loops with do-while loops. First, the outer loop is changed so that it no longer acts as an open for loop. Although open for loops have their uses, they're few and far between; this solution is much more elegant. Here you start the loop on line 12 with the do statement, then finish it on line 25 with the while statement. Notice that you do this while statement as a replacement for the if statement of the previous program that would execute a break in the case of the user typing y or Y.

An addition to the program is the inner do-while loop on lines 14 through 20, which continually asks the user for a number until it gets something that isn't 0.

The *while* Loop

The while loop in C++ is another conditional loop that iterates as long as a condition is true. Thus, the while loop may not iterate if the tested condition is initially false.

The *while* Loop

Syntax

The general syntax of the while loop is

```
while (condition)
    statement; ¦ { sequence of statements }
```

Example

```
// Calculates x to the n power
double pwr = 1;
while (n-- > 0)
    pwr *= x;
cout << x << "^" << n << " = " << pwr << endl;
```

Look at the next example. Listing 3.10 shows the source code for the program WHILE.CPP. This program performs the same operations as the program FOR1.CPP, shown in Listing 3.6. The two programs interact with the user in the same way and yield the same results.

 Listing 3.10. Source code for the program WHILE.CPP.

```
1:  // Program calculates a sum and average of a range of
2:  // integers using a for loop
3:
4:  #include <iostream.h>
5:
6:  int main()
7:  {
8:      int count = 0;
9:      double sum = 0.0;
10:     int first, last, temp;
11:
12:     cout << "Enter the first integer: ";
13:     cin >> first;
14:     cout << "Enter the last integer: ";
15:     cin >> last;
16:     if (first > last)
17:         {
18:         temp = first;
19:         first = last;
20:         last = temp;
21:         }
22:     cout << "Sum of integers from "
23:          << first << " to " << last << " = ";
24:     while (first <= last)
25:         {
26:         count++;
27:         sum += (double)first++;
28:         }
29:     cout << sum << endl;
30:     cout << "Average value = " << sum / count << endl;
31:     return 0;
32: }
```

Here is a sample session with the program in Listing 3.10.

```
Enter the first integer: 1
Enter the last integer: 100
Sum of integers from 1 to 100 = 5050
Average value = 50.5
```

The only difference between Listings 3.10 and 3.6 occurs on line 22, where the for loop is replaced with a while loop. This actually makes more sense than the previous for loop. If the only thing you have for a for loop is the conditional expression, it's likely that what you really want is a while loop.

Skipping Loop Iterations

C++ enables you to jump to the end of a loop and resume the next iteration using the continue statement. This programming feature permits your loop to skip iteration for special values that may cause runtime errors.

Syntax

The *continue* Statement

The general form for using the continue statement is

```
<loop-start clause>
    {
    // sequence #1 of statements
    if (skipCondition)
        continue;
    // sequence #2 of statements
    } <loop-end clause>
```

Example

```
double x, y;
for (int i = -10; i < 11; i++)
    {
    x = i;
    if (i == 1)
        continue;
    y = 1/sqrt(x * x - 1);
    cout << "1/sqrt(" << (x*x-1) << ") = " << y << endl;
    }
```

This form shows that the evaluation of the first sequence of statements in the for loop gives rise to a condition tested in the if statement. If that condition is true, then the if statement invokes the continue statement to skip the second sequence of statements in the for loop.

Look at an example. Listing 3.11 shows the source code for the program FOR4.CPP. The program simply runs through a quick for loop, displaying each number in turn. In order to demonstrate the continue statement, the middle part of the list has been skipped.

Type

Listing 3.11. Source code for the program FOR4.CPP.

```
1:  // Program that demonstrates using the continue statement
2:  // to skip iterations.
3:
4:  #include <iostream.h>
```

```
5:   #include <math.h>
6:
7:   int main()
8:   {
9:     for (int i = 0; i < 10; ++i)
10:       {
11:       if (i >= 4 && i <= 6)
12:         continue;
13:       cout << "Step #" << i << endl;
14:       }
15:     return 0;
16: }
```

Here is a sample session with the program in Listing 3.11.

```
Step #0
Step #1
Step #2
Step #3
Step #7
Step #8
Step #9
```

The program in Listing 3.11 should be relatively self-explanatory. Line 9 starts off the for loop, running from 0 to 9. Line 11 checks to see if the current iteration number is between 4 and 6, and then continue on line 12 if so. Finally, line 13 outputs the current iteration number to the user. Notice in the sample output how the numbers skip from 3 to 7.

Exiting Loops

C++ supports the break statement to exit a loop. The break statement makes the program resume after the end of the current loop, just as it does for the switch statement.

The *break* Statement

The general form for using the break statement in a loop is

```
<start-loop clause>
    {
    // sequence #1 of statements
    if (exitLoopCondition)
        break;
    // sequence #2 of statements
    } <end-loop clause>
// sequence #3 of statements
```

Example

```
// calculate the factorial of n
factorial = 1;
for (int i = 1; ; i++)
```

107

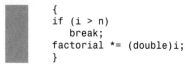

```
{
if (i > n)
   break;
factorial *= (double)i;
}
```

This form shows that the evaluation of the first sequence of statements in the `for` loop gives rise to a condition tested in the `if` statement. If that condition is `true`, then the `if` statement invokes the `break` statement to exit the loop altogether. The program execution resumes at the third sequence of statements.

For a good example that uses the `break` statement, I recommend that you reexamine the FOR3.CPP program in Listing 3.8.

Nested Loops

Nested loops enable you to contain repetitive tasks as part of other repetitive tasks. C++ enables you to nest any type of loop to just about any level needed. Nested loops frequently are used to process arrays (which are covered in Day 6). For a good example that uses nested loops, reexamine the DOWHILE.CPP program in Listing 3.9.

Summary

Today's lesson presented the various decision-making constructs and loops in C++, including the following:

☐ The single-alternative `if` statement, such as

```
if (tested_condition)
   statement; | { <sequence of statements> }
```

☐ The dual-alternative `if-else` statement, such as

```
if (tested_condition)
   statement1; | { <sequence #1 of statements> }
else
   statement1; | { <sequence #1 of statements> }
```

☐ The multiple-alternative `if-else` statement, such as

```
if (tested_condition1)
   statement1; | { <sequence #1 of statement> }
else if (tested_condition2)
   statement2; | { <sequence #2 of statement> }
...
else if (tested_conditionN)
   statementN; | { <sequence #N of statement> }
[else
   statementN+1; | { <sequence #N+1 of statement> }]
```

☐ The multiple-alternative `switch` statement, such as

```
switch (caseVar)
```

```
    {
    case constant1_1:
    case constant1_2:
    <other case labels>
        <one or more statements>
        break;
    case constant2_1:
    case constant2_2:
    <other case labels>
        <one or more statements>
        break;
    ...
    case constantN_1:
    case constantN_2:
    <other case labels>
        <one or more statements>
        break;
    default:
        <one or more statements>
        break;
    }
```

You also learned about the following topics:

☐ The `if` statements require you to observe the following two rules:

1. The tested condition must be enclosed in parentheses.

2. Blocks of statements are enclosed in pairs of open and close braces.

☐ Nested decision-making constructs enable you to deal with complex conditions using a divide-and-conquer approach. The outer-level constructs help you in testing preliminary or more general conditions. The inner-level constructs assist in handling more specific conditions.

☐ The `try`, `catch`, and `throw` statements enable you to use exception handling for error control.

☐ The `for` loop in C++ has the following general syntax:

```
for (<initialization of loop>;
    <loop continuation test>;
    <increment/decrement of loop control variables>)
```

The `for` loop contains three components: the loop initialization, loop continuation condition, and the increment/decrement of the loop variables.

☐ The conditional `do-while` loop has the following general syntax:

```
do
    {
    sequence of statements
    } while (condition);
```

The `do-while` loop iterates at least once.

☐ The conditional `while` loop has the following general syntax:

```
while (condition)
    statement; | { sequence of statements }
```

The `while` loop might not iterate if its tested condition is initially false.

☐ The `continue` statement enables you to jump to the end of the loop and resume with the next iteration. The advantage of the `continue` statement is that it uses no labels to direct the jump.

☐ Open loops are `for` loops with empty components. The `break` statement enables you to exit the current loop and resume program execution at the first statement that comes after the loop. The `exit` function (declared in STDLIB.H) enables you to make a critical loop exit by halting the C++ program altogether.

☐ Nested loops enable you to contain repetitive tasks as part of other repetitive tasks. C++ enables you to nest any kind of loop to just about any level needed.

Q&A

Q Does C++ impose any rules for indenting statements in the clauses of an `if` statement?

A No. The indentation is purely up to you. Typical indentations range from two to four spaces. Using indentations makes your listings much more readable. Following is the case of an `if` statement with unindented clause statements:

```
if (i > 0)
j = i * i;
else
j = 10 - i;
```

Compare the readability of that listing with this indented version:

```
if (i > 0)
    j = i * i;
else
    j = 10 - i;
```

The indented version is much easier to read; it's easy to tell where the `if` and the `else` statements are. Furthermore, if you start playing with nested loops, indenting appropriately will make a major difference in the readability of the code.

Q What are the rules for writing the condition of an `if-else` statement?

A There are two schools of thought. The first recommends that you write the condition so that it is more often `true` than not. The second school recommends avoiding negative expressions (those that use the relational operator `!=` and the Boolean operator `!`). Programmers in this camp translate this `if` statement,

```
if (i != 0)
    j = 100 / i;
else
    j = 1;
```

into the following equivalent form,

```
if (i == 0)
    j = 1;
else
    j = 100 \ i;
```

even though the likelihood of variable i storing 0 might be very low.

In the end, it comes down to something of a "religious" argument, as many things in programming do. Which you do on your own may be one thing, but when working with a group of others, you may find the different ways all converging and even sometimes confusing.

Q How do I handle a condition such as the following, which divides by a variable that can possibly be zero?

```
if (i != 0 && 1/i > 1)
    j = i * i;
```

A C++ does not always evaluate the entire tested condition. This partial evaluation occurs when a term in the Boolean expression renders the entire expression false or true, regardless of the values of the other terms. In this case, if variable i is 0—the runtime system does not evaluate the term 1/i > 1. This is because the term i != 0 is false and would render the entire expression false, regardless of what the second term yields. This is referred to as a short-circuit Boolean expression.

Q Is it really necessary to include an else or default clause in multiple-alternative if-else and switch statements?

A Programmers highly recommend the inclusion of these catch-all clauses to ensure that the multiple-alternative statements handle all conditions. However, they are not technically required for a program to compile.

Q How can a while loop simulate a for loop?

A Here is a simple example.

```
int i;                            int i = 1;
for (i = 1; i <= 10; i +=2)       while (i <= 10)
    {                                 {
    cout << i << endl;                cout << i << endl;
    }                                 i += 2;
                                      }
```

The while loop needs a leading statement that initializes the loop control variable. Also notice that the while loop uses a statement inside it to alter the value of the loop control variable.

Q How can a while loop simulate a do-while loop?

A Here is a simple example.

```
i = 1;                            i = 1;
do                                while (i <= 10)
    {                                 {
    cout << i << endl;                cout << i << endl;
    i += 2;                           i += 2;
    } while (i <= 10);                }
```

The two loops have the same condition in their `while` clauses. Note, however, that if the loop is designed in such a way that it doesn't necessarily know the initial value of i, it could have different effects if, for example, i starts out as 11. The loop on the left would run through once, whereas the loop on the right would never make it through a single iteration.

Q How can the open `for` loop emulate the `while` and `do-while` loops?

A The open `for` loop emulates the other C++ loops by placing the loop-escape `if` statement near the beginning or end of the loop. Here is how the open `for` loop emulates a sample `while` loop:

```
i = 1;                      i = 1;
while (i <= 10)             for (;;)
    {                           {
                                if (i > 10) break;
    cout << i << endl;              cout << i << endl;
    i += 2;                     i += 2;
    }                           }
```

Notice that the open `for` loop uses a loop-escape `if` statement as the first statement inside the loop. The condition tested by the `if` statement is the logical reverse of the `while` loop condition. Here is a simple example showing the emulation of the `do-while` loop:

```
i = 1;                      i = 1;
do                          for (;;)
    {                           {
    cout << i << endl;          cout << i << endl;
    i += 2;                     i += 2;
                                if (i > 10) break;
    } while (i <= 10);          }
```

The open `for` loop uses a loop-escape `if` statement right before the end of the loop. The `if` statement tests the reverse condition as the `do-while` loop.

Please take note, however, that these examples are rather crude and inelegant. One would never use an open `for` loop in this manner. Rather, one might skip one of the three clauses inside the `for` loop's parentheses (such as the initialization clause, if the control variable already has been initialized). Open `for` loops are more often used in cases where exiting the loop would be a rare occurrence, such as if one were accepting and processing a user's keystrokes but exiting when the Esc key is encountered.

Q In nested `for` loops, can I use the loop control variable of the outer loops as part of the range of values for the inner loops?

A Yes. Not only does C++ not prohibit such use, it actually is rather quite common. Here is a simple example.

```
for (int i = 1; i <= 100; i += 5)
    for (int j = i; j <= 100; j++)
        cout << i * j << endl;
```

Q Does C++ restrict nesting of the various types of loops?

A No. You can nest any combination of loops in a C++ program.

Workshop

The Workshop provides quiz questions to help you solidify your understanding of the material covered and exercises to provide you with experience in using what you've learned. Try to understand the quiz and exercise answers before continuing on to the next day's lesson. (Answers are provided in Appendix A.)

Quiz

1. Simplify the following nested `if` statements by replacing them with a single `if` statement:

   ```
   if (i > 0)
      if (i < 10)
         cout << "i = " << i << endl;
   ```

2. Simplify the following `if` statements by replacing them with a single `if-else` statement:

   ```
   if (i > 0)
      {
      j = i * i;
      cout << "j = " << j << endl;
      }
   if (i < 0)
      {
      j = 4 * i;
      cout << "j = " << j << endl;
      }
   if (i == 0)
      {
      j = 10 + i
      cout << "j = " << j << endl;
      }
   ```

3. True or false? The following `if` statements perform the same tasks as the subsequent `if-else` statement:

   ```
   if (i < 0)
      {
      i = 10 + i;
      j = i * i;
      cout << "i = " << i << endl;
      cout << "j = " << j << endl;
      }
   if (i >= 0)
      {
      k = 4 * i + 1;
      cout << "k = " << k << endl;
      }
   ```

```
if (i < 0)
    {
    i = 10 + i;
    j = i * i;
    cout << "i = " << i << endl;
    cout << "j = " << j << endl;
    }
else
    {
    k = 4 * i + 1;
    cout << "k = " << k << endl;
    }
```

4. Simplify the following if-else statement:

```
if (i > 0 && i < 100)
    j = i * i;
else if (i > 10 && i < 50)
    j = 10 + i;
else if (i >= 100)
    j = i;
else
    j = 1;
```

5. What is wrong with the following if statement?

```
if (i > (1 + i * i))
    {
    j = i * i
    cout << "i = " << i << " and j = " << j << endl;
    }
```

6. What is wrong with the following loop?

```
i = 1;
while (i < 10)
    {
    j = i * i - 1;
    k = 2 * j - i;
    cout << "i = " << i << endl;
    cout << "j = " << j << endl;
    cout << "k = " << k << endl;
    }
```

7. What is the output of the following for loop?

```
for (int i = 5; i < 10; i + 2)
    cout << i - 2 << endl;
```

8. What is the output of the following for loop?

```
for (int i = 5; i < 10; )
    cout << i - 2 << endl;
```

9. What is wrong with the following code?

```
for (int i = 1; i <= 10; i++)
    for (i = 8; i <= 12; i++)
        cout << i << endl;
```

10. Where is the error in the following loop?

```
i = 1;
while (i > 0)
   {
   cout << i << endl;
   i++;
   }
```

11. The factorial of a number is the product of the sequence of integers from 1 to that number. The following general equation defines the factorial (which uses the symbol !):

```
n! = 1 * 2 * 3 * ... * n
```

Following is a C++ program that calculates the factorial of a number. The problem is that for whatever positive value you enter, the program displays a 0 value for the factorial. Where is the error in the program?

```
int n;
double factorial;
cout << "Enter positive integer: ";
cin >> n;
for (int i = 1; i <= n; i++)
   factorial *= i;
cout << i << "! = " << factorial << endl;
```

Exercises

1. Write the program SWITCH2.CPP, which implements a simple four-function calculator. The program should prompt you for the operand and the operator, and display both the input and the result. Include error checking for bad operators and for the attempt to divide by zero.

2. Write the program FOR5.CPP, which uses a for loop to compute the average of a list of numbers. The program should first ask for the number of entries the user will make, then gather the numbers, add them together, and divide by the total number of entries made.

3. Write the program WHILE2.CPP, which uses a while loop to do the same thing as the FOR5.CPP program in the preceding exercise.

4. Write the program DOWHILE2.CPP, which uses a do-while loop to do the same as the last two programs (FOR5.CPP and WHILE2.CPP).

User-Defined
Types and Pointers

Creating user-defined data types is one of the necessary features of a modern programming language. Today's lesson looks at the enumerated data types and structures that enable you to better organize your data. In addition, this lesson discusses using pointers with simple variables, arrays, structures, and dynamic data. Today, you will learn about the following topics:

- [ ] The type definition using `typedef`
- [ ] Enumerated data types
- [ ] Structures
- [ ] Unions
- [ ] Reference variables
- [ ] Pointers to existing variables
- [ ] Simple arrays
- [ ] Pointers to arrays
- [ ] Pointers to structures
- [ ] Using pointers to access and manage dynamic data
- [ ] Far pointers

Type Definition in C++

C++ offers the `typedef` keyword, which enables you to define new data-type names as aliases of existing types.

The *typedef* Keyword

The general syntax for using `typedef` is

```
typedef knownType newType;
```

Examples

```
typedef unsigned word;
typedef unsigned char byte;
```

The `typedef` keyword defines a new type from a known one. You can use `typedef` to create aliases that shorten the names of existing data types, or to define names of data types that are more familiar to you or that better describe how the data type is used. The second of the preceding examples illustrates this use of `typedef`. You also can use `typedef` to define the name of an array type.

An Array Type Name

The general syntax for defining the name of an array type is

```
typedef baseType arrayTypeName[arraySize];
```

The `typedef` statement defines the `arrayTypeName`, whose basic type and size are `baseType` and `arraySize`, respectively.

Examples

```
typedef double vector[10];
typedef double matrix[10][30];
```

Thus, the identifiers `vector` and `matrix` are names of data types.

In a way, you can think of `typedef`s as a special kind of C++ macro, similar to the preprocessor `#define` statement. The difference is that, whereas a macro tells C++ to do a straight substitution of one set of text for another, the `typedef` creates a brand-new type that can be used just like any other type. Examine the following code fragment:

```
unsigned char aChar;
typedef unsigned char byte;
byte aByte;
```

The fragment starts by declaring the variable `aChar` of type `unsigned char`. This is something you've seen before, and you should be familiar with it by now. The second line creates a new type called `byte`. Now remember, this isn't just a synonym for `unsigned char`, but rather it's a brand new type—as if the compiler itself included `byte` in its repertoire of basic types. The third line then declares the variable `aByte` of type `byte` just as if `byte` had always been a part of C++. You should take special note that `aChar` and `aByte` are completely different types. Sure, `aByte` is of type `byte`, which has been defined to be of type `unsigned char`, and `aChar` is also of type `unsigned char`, but the two variables are still considered to be completely separate types.

Enumerated Data Types

The rule to follow with enumerated data types is that, although the enumerated identifiers must be unique, the values assigned to them need not be unique.

NEW☞
TERM An *enumerated type* defines a list of unique identifiers and associates values with these identifiers.

An Enumerated Type

The general syntax for declaring an enumerated type is

```
enum enumType { <list of enumerated identifiers> };
```

Examples

```
enum YesNo { no, yes, dontCare, maybe };
enum weekday { Sunday, Monday, Tuesday,
               Wednesday, Thursday, Friday, Saturday };
```

Following is an example of declaring an enumerated type:

```
enum CPUtype { i8088, i80286, i80386, i80486, i80586 };
```

C++ associates integer values with the enumerated identifiers. For example, in this type, the compiler assigns 0 to i8088, 1 to i80286, and so on.

C++ is very flexible in declaring an enumerated type. First, the language enables you to explicitly assign a value to an enumerated identifier. Following is an example:

```
enum weekday { Sunday = 1, Monday, Tuesday, Wednesday,
               Thursday, Friday, Saturday };
```

This declaration explicitly assigns 1 to the enumerated identifier Sunday. The compiler then assigns the next integer, 2, to the next identifier, Monday, and so on. C++ enables you to explicitly assign a value to each member of the enumerated list. Moreover, these values need not be unique. Following are some examples of the flexibility in declaring enumerated types in C++:

```
// explicit value assignment for every list member
enum colors { black = 1, red = 2, blue = 3, green = 5,
              yellow = 7, white = 11 };

// intermittent value assignment
enum colors { black = 1, red, blue, green = 5,
              yellow = 7, white = 11 };

// duplicate values
enum CPUtype { i8088 = 0, i80286 = 2,
               i80386DX = 3, i80386SX = 3,
               i80486DX = 4, i80486SX = 4 };

enum choiceType { false, true, dontCare = 0 };
```

In the last example, the compiler associates the identifier false with 0 by default. However, the compiler also associates the value 0 with dontCare because of the explicit assignment.

C++ enables you to declare variables that have enumerated types in the following ways:

☐ The declaration of the enumerated type may include the declaration of the variables of that type. The general syntax is

```
enum enumType { <list of enumerated identifiers> }
             <list of variables>;
```

Following is an example:

```
enum weekDay { Sun = 1, Mon, Tue, Wed, Thu, Fri, Sat }
                recycleDay, payDay, movieDay;
```

☐ The separate declaration of the enumerated type and its variables includes multiple statements to declare the type and the associated variables separately. The general syntax is

```
enum enumType { <list of enumerated identifiers> };
enumType var1, var2, ..., varN;
```

Listing 4.1 shows the source code for the program ENUM.CPP. The program implements a simple one-line, four-function calculator that performs the following tasks:

☐ Prompts you to enter a number, an operator (+, −, *, or /), and a number.

☐ Performs the requested operation, if valid.

☐ Displays the operands, the operator, and the result, if the operation was valid; otherwise, displays an error message that indicates the type of error. (You either entered a bad operator or attempted to divide by 0.)

Listing 4.1. Source code for the program ENUM.CPP.

```
1:  // C++ program that demonstrates enumerated types
2:
3:  #include <iostream.h>
4:
5:  enum mathError { noError, badOperator, divideByZero };
6:
7:  int main()
8:  {
9:      double x, y, z;
10:     char op;
11:     mathError error = noError;
12:
13:     cout << "Enter a number, an operator, and a number: ";
14:     cin >> x >> op >> y;
15:
16:     switch (op)
17:        {
18:        case '+':
19:           z = x + y;
20:           break;
21:        case '-':
22:           z = x - y;
23:           break;
24:        case '*':
25:           z = x * y;
26:           break;
27:        case '/':
28:           if (y != 0)
29:              z = x / y;
30:           else
```

continues

Listing 4.1. continued

```
31:                error = divideByZero;
32:            break;
33:        default:
34:            error = badOperator;
35:            break;
36:        }
37:
38:    if (error == noError)
39:        cout << x << " " << op << " " << y << " = " << z << endl;
40:    else
41:        switch (error)
42:            {
43:            case noError:
44:                cout << "No error" << endl;
45:                break;
46:            case badOperator:
47:                cout << "Error: invalid operator" << endl;
48:                break;
49:            case divideByZero:
50:                cout << "Error: attempt to divide by zero" << endl;
51:                break;
52:            }
53:    return 0;
54: }
```

Here is a sample session with the program in Listing 4.1.

```
Enter a number, an operator, and a number: 355 / 113
355 / 113 = 3.14159
```

The program in Listing 4.1 declares the enumerated type mathError on line 5. This data type has three enumerated values: noError, badOperator, and divideByZero.

The function main declares the double-typed variables x, y, and z on line 9 to represent the two operands and the result, respectively. In addition, the function declares the char-typed variable op to store the requested operation, and the enumerated variable error to store the error status. The function initializes the variable error with the enumerated value noError.

The output statement on line 13 prompts you to enter the operands and the operator. The statement on line 14 stores your input in variables x, op, and y, in that order. The function uses the switch statement starting on line 16 to examine the value in variable op and perform the requested operation. The case labels provide the values for the four supported math operations. The last case label contains an if statement that detects the attempt to divide by zero. If this is true, then the else clause statement assigns the enumerated value divideByZero to the variable error.

The catch-all default clause on line 33 handles invalid operators. The statement on line 34 assigns the enumerated value badOperator to the variable error.

The `if` statement starting on line 38 determines whether the variable `error` contains the enumerated value `noError`. If this condition is `true`, then the program executes the output statement on line 39. This statement displays the operands, the operator, and the result. Otherwise, the program executes the `else` clause—a `switch` statement that determines the nature of the error and displays an appropriate message.

Structures

C++ supports structures, and these members can be predefined types or other structures.

NEW ☛ *Structures* enable you to define a new type that logically groups several fields or members
TERM together.

Syntax

A Structure

The general syntax for declaring a structure is

```
struct structTag
{
    <list of members>
};
```

Examples

```
struct point
{
    double x;
    double y;
};

struct rectangle
{
    point upperLeftCorner;
    point lowerRightCorner;
};

struct circle
{
    point center;
    double radius;
};
```

Once you define a `struct` type, you can use that type to declare variables. Following are examples of declarations using structures that were declared in the syntax box:

```
point p1, p2, p3;
```

You also can declare structured variables when you define the structure itself:

```
struct point
{
    double x;
    double y;
} p1, p2, p3;
```

NEW
TERM Untagged structures enable you to declare structure variables without defining a name for their structures.

> **Note:** Interestingly, C++ permits you to declare untagged structures. For example, the following structure definition declares the variables p1, p2, and p3 but omits the name of the structure:
>
> ```
> struct
> {
>     double x;
>     double y;
> } p1, p2, p3;
> ```

C++ enables you to declare and initialize a structured variable. Here is an example:

```
point pt = { 1.0, -8.3 };
```

Accessing the members of a structure uses the dot operator. Following are a few examples:

```
p1.x = 12.45;
p1.y = 34.56;
p2.x = 23.4 / p1.x;
p2.y = 0.98 * p1.y;
```

> **Note:** This method of initializing a struct is the old C way of doing things. C++ has a better way: by using a constructor. This can work because structs are actually just special forms of classes. The class and its constructor are covered on Day 8.

Listing 4.2 shows the source code for the program STRUCT.CPP. The program prompts you for two sets of coordinates that define a rectangle. The rectangle is defined by the x and y coordinates of its upper-left and lower-right corners. The program then calculates and displays the area of the rectangle.

Listing 4.2. Source code for the program STRUCT.CPP.

```
1:  // C++ program that demonstrates structured types
2:
3:  #include <iostream.h>
```

```
 4:  #include <math.h>
 5:
 6:  struct point
 7:  {
 8:     double x;
 9:     double y;
10:  };
11:
12:  struct rect
13:  {
14:     point ulc; // upper left corner
15:     point lrc; // lower right corner
16:     double area;
17:  };
18:
19:  int main()
20:  {
21:     rect r;
22:     double length, width;
23:
24:     cout << "Enter (X Y) coordinate for ULC of rectangle: ";
25:     cin >> r.ulc.x >> r.ulc.y;
26:     cout << "Enter (X Y) coordinate for LRC of rectangle: ";
27:     cin >> r.lrc.x >> r.lrc.y;
28:     length = fabs(r.ulc.x - r.lrc.x);
29:     width = fabs(r.ulc.y - r.lrc.y);
30:     r.area = length * width;
31:     cout << "The rectangle has an area of " << r.area << endl;
32:     return 0;
33:  }
```

Here is a sample session with the program in Listing 4.2.

```
Enter (X Y) coordinate for ULC of rectangle: 0 0
Enter (X Y) coordinate for LRC of rectangle: 15 5
The rectangle has an area of 75
```

The program in Listing 4.2 includes the header files IOSTREAM and MATH.H. Line 6 contains the declaration of structure point, which is made up of two double-typed members: x and y. This structure models a two-dimensional point. Line 12 contains the declaration of structure rect, which models a rectangle. The structure contains two point-typed members, ulc and lrc, and the double-typed member area. The members ulc and lrc represent the coordinates for the upper-left and lower-right corners that define a rectangle. The member area stores the area of the rectangle.

The function main declares the rect-typed array r and the double-typed variables length and width. It then gathers the upper-left and lower-right coordinates of the rectangle on lines 24 through 27. Note how the first dot operator gives access to the members of rect, and then an additional dot is used on the ulc and lrc members to get access to the members of point. Length and width are then computed on lines 28 and 29, and those values are used to set the rectangle's area member on line 30. Line 31 displays the result.

Unions

The size of a union is equal to the size of its largest member.

Unions are special structures that store members with shared address spaces.
TERM

Syntax

Unions

The general syntax for unions is

```
union unionTag
{
    type1 member1;
    type2 member2;
    ...
    typeN memberN;
};
```

Example

```
union Long
{
    struct
        {
        unsigned short lo;
        unsigned short hi;
        } w;
    long l;
};

Long l;
l.l = 0x12345678L;
cout << hex << l.l << endl;
cout << hex << l.w.lo << endl;
cout << hex << l.w.hi << endl;
```

The union `Long` stores either the structure `w` (which contains two unsigned short integers that each require two bytes) or a four-byte long integer. In addition, the union `Long` enables you to access the lower or higher words (two-byte integers) of a long integer. The output of the previous code fragment is

```
12345678
5678
1234
```

Unions offer an easy alternative for quick data conversion. Unions were more significant in the recent past, when the price of computer memory was much higher and it was feasible to use unions to consolidate memory. Accessing union members involves the dot access operators, just as in structures.

Reference Variables

C++ supports *reference variables*. You can manipulate the referenced variable by using its alias. As a novice C++ programmer, your initial use of reference variables will most likely be limited. As you advance in using C++, you will discover how reference variables can implement programming tricks that deal with advanced class design. This book discusses only the basics of reference variables.

NEW☞   *Reference variables* are aliases to the variables they access.
TERM

A Reference Variable

The general syntax for declaring a reference variable is

```
type& refVar(aVar);
type& refVar = aVar;
```

The refVar is the reference variable that is initialized when declared. You must ensure that a reference variable is initialized or assigned a value before it gets used.

Examples

```
int x = 10, y = 3;
int& rx(x);
int& ry = y; // take the reference
```

Here is a simple example that shows a reference variable at work. Listing 4.3 shows the source code for the program REFVAR.CPP. The program displays and alters the values of a variable using either the variable itself or its reference. The program requires no input.

Type   **Listing 4.3. Source code for the program REFVAR.CPP.**

```
1: // C++ program that demonstrates reference variables
2:
3: #include <iostream.h>
4:
5: int main()
6: {
7:     int x = 10;
8:     int& rx = x;
9:
10:    // display x using x and rx
11:    cout << "x contains " << x << endl;
12:    cout << "x contains (using the reference rx) "
13:         << rx << endl;
14:
15:    // alter x and display its value using rx
16:    x *= 2;
17:    cout << "x contains (using the reference rx) "
18:         << rx << endl;
19:
```

continues

Listing 4.3. continued

```
20:    // alter rx and display value using x
21:    rx *= 2;
22:    cout << "x contains " << x << endl;
23:    return 0;
24: }
```

Here is a sample session with the program in Listing 4.3.

```
x contains 10
x contains (using the reference rx) 10
x contains (using the reference rx) 20
x contains 40
```

The program in Listing 4.3 declares the int-typed variable x and the int-typed reference variable rx. The program initializes the variable x with 10 and the reference variable rx with the variable x.

The output statement on line 11 displays the value in variable x using the variable x itself. By contrast, the output statement on lines 12 and 13 displays the value in variable x using the reference variable rx.

The statement on line 16 doubles the integer in variable x. The output statement on lines 17 and 18 displays the new value in variable x using the reference variable rx. As the output shows, the reference variable accurately displays the updated value in variable x.

The statement on line 21 doubles the value in variable x by using the reference variable rx. The output statement on line 22 displays the updated value in variable x using variable x. Again, the output shows that the variable x and the reference variable rx are synchronized.

Overview of Pointers

Each piece of information, both code and data, in the computer's memory resides at a specific address and occupies a specific number of bytes. When you run a program, your variables reside at specific *addresses*. With a high-level language such as C++, you are not concerned about the actual address of every variable. That task is handled transparently by the compiler and the runtime system. Conceptually, each variable in your program is a *tag* for a memory address. Manipulating the data using the tag is much easier than dealing with actual numerical addresses, such as 0F63:01AF4.

NEW⟟ An *address* is a memory location. A *tag* is the variable's name.
TERM

Going back to the box analogy (in Day 2), imagine that your computer's memory is just a large number of tiny boxes. Now, imagine that when you declare a variable, you're really just setting aside a box to hold the value of that variable. But what if you weren't so much interested in what

that box contained, but rather you wanted to know just where that box was in memory? You would create a pointer to that box. Creating a pointer is just declaring another variable, but the value that can be found in the pointer's box really is just the address of another variable's box. Regard Figure 4.1 as it relates to the following code snippet:

```
int myInt = 42;
int *pInt = &myInt;
```

Figure 4.1.

Memory depicted by boxes.

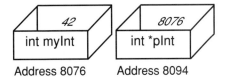

The variable myInt has been declared, which created a box for it, and the value 42 has been placed into it. That box happens to be at memory address 8076. When the pointer pInt was declared, another box was created at another memory address. In this particular case, that memory happens to be 8094. It's important to note that the memory addresses will not necessarily be next to each other, as in this case. When pInt was declared, it was initialized with the address (that's what the & means) of myInt. So, the memory address at which myInt resides was placed inside of pInt's box. pInt is a variable of its own, but its value just happens to be the address of another variable. Note that it is entirely possible, at this point, to declare yet another box, and have that be a pointer to pInt; this would be called a *pointer to a pointer*.

C++ and its parent C are programming languages that also are used for low-level systems programming. In fact, many programmers regard C as a high-level assembler. Low-level system programming requires that you work frequently with the addresses of data. This is where pointers, in general, come into play. Knowing the address of a piece of data enables you to set and query its value.

NEW☞ A *pointer* is a special variable that stores the address of another variable or information.
TERM

Warning: Pointers are very powerful language components. They also can be dangerous if used carelessly, because they may hang your system. This malfunction occurs when the pointer hasn't been set up yet. Don't forget that simply declaring something doesn't automatically give it any value. Until you've set the value of a pointer (with the address of another variable), that pointer is just referring to something random in memory, and if you use that pointer, you could get some really weird results.

Pointers to Existing Variables

In this section, you learn how to use pointers to access the values in existing variables. C++ requires that you associate a data type (including void) with a declared pointer. The associated data type may be a predefined type or a user-defined structure.

Syntax

A Pointer

The general syntax for declaring a pointer is

```
type* pointerName;
type* pointerName = pointerVariable;
type* pointerName = &variable;
```

The & operator is the address-of operator (this is not the reference operator, which also uses the & symbol) and is used to take the address of a variable. The address-of operator returns the address of a variable, structure, function, and so on. By contrast, the reference operator creates an alias to a variable using another variable.

Example

```
int* intPtr; // pointer to an int
double* realPtr; // pointer to a double
char* aString; // pointer to a character
long lv;
long* lp = &lv;
```

You also can declare nonpointers in the same lines that declare pointers.

```
int *intPtr, anInt;
double x, *realPtr;
char *aString, aKey;
```

> **Note:** C++ allows you to place the asterisk character right after the associated data type. You should not interpret this type of syntax to mean that every other identifier appearing in the same declaration is automatically a pointer.
>
> ```
> int* intPtr; // pointer to an int
> double* realPtr; // pointer to a double
> char* aString; // pointer to a character
> int *intP, j; // intP is a pointer to int, j is an int
> double *realPtr,   // both identifiers
>        *doublePtr; // are pointers to doubles
> ```

DO	DON'T

DO initialize a pointer before you use it, just as you do with ordinary variables. In fact, the need to initialize pointers is even more pressing—using uninitialized pointers invites trouble that can lead to unpredictable program behavior or a system hang. Whenever you see a General Protection Fault (a GPF) in a program, it usually is caused by using a pointer that has not been initialized properly.

DON'T assume that uninitialized pointers are harmless.

After a pointer contains the address of a variable, you can access the value in that variable using the * operator followed by the name of the pointer. For example, if px is a pointer to the variable x, then you can use *px to access the value in variable x.

DO	DON'T

4

DO include the * operator to the left of a pointer to access the variable whose address is stored in the pointer.

DON'T forget to use the * operator. Without it, a statement ends up manipulating the address in the pointer instead of the data at that address.

Following is a simple example that shows a pointer at work. Listing 4.4 shows the source code for the program PTR1.CPP. The program displays and alters the values of a variable using either the variable itself or its pointer. The program requires no input.

Listing 4.4. Source code for the program PTR1.CPP.

```
1:  // C++ program that demonstrates pointers to existing variables
2:
3:  #include <iostream.h>
4:
5:  int main()
6:  {
7:    int x = 10;
8:    int* px = &x;
9:    // display x using x and px
10:   cout << "x contains " << x << endl;
11:   cout << "x contains (using the pointer px) "
12:        << *px << endl;
13:   // alter x and display its value using *px
14:   x *= 2;
15:   cout << "x contains (using the pointer px) "
```

continues

Listing 4.4. continued

```
16:        << *px << endl;
17:    // alter *px and display value using x
18:    *px *= 2;
19:    cout << "x contains " << x << endl;
20:    return 0;
21: }
```

Here is a sample session with the program in Listing 4.4.

```
x contains 10
x contains (using the pointer px) 10
x contains (using the pointer px) 20
x contains 40
```

The program in Listing 4.4 declares the int-typed variable x and the int-typed pointer px. The program initializes the variable x with 10 and the pointer px with the address of variable x.

The output statement on line 10 displays the value in variable x using the variable x. By contrast, the output statement on lines 11 and 12 displays the value in variable x using the pointer px. Notice that the statement uses *px to access the value in variable x.

The statement on line 14 doubles the integer in variable x. The output statement on lines 15 and 16 displays the new value in variable x using the pointer px. As the output shows, the pointer accurately displays the updated value in variable x.

The statement on line 18 doubles the value in variable x by using the pointer px. Notice that the assignment statement uses *px on the left side of the = operator to access the variable x. The output statement on line 19 displays the updated value in variable x using variable x. Again, the output shows that the variable x and the pointer px are synchronized.

A Short Introduction to Arrays

An *array* is one of the most useful components in a programming language. It enables the programmer to store a number of data items in a single location. The single-dimensional array is the simplest kind of array. In a single-dimensional array, each variable is individually accessed using a single index.

**NEW☞
TERM** An *array* is a group of values that share the same name (the name of the array) and are stored sequentially in memory.

A Single-Dimensional Array

The general syntax for declaring a single-dimensional array is

```
type arrayName[numberOfElements];
```

The number between the two square brackets signifies the number of elements in the array. In order to access the individual elements of the array, you use a similar construct: the array name followed by the index number inside of square brackets.

C++ requires you to observe the following rules in declaring single-dimensional arrays:

- ☐ The lower bound of a C++ array is set at 0. C++ does not allow you to override or alter this lower bound.
- ☐ Declaring a C++ array entails specifying the number of members. Keep in mind that the number of members is equal to the upper bound plus one.

The valid range of indices for this form extends between `0` and `numberOfElements - 1`.

Examples

```
int intArray[10];
char name[31];
double x[100];
```

An array can be thought of as a row of boxes that are all at sequential addresses. By specifying an index, you are specifying which of the boxes in the array to access. A `0` means to access the very first box, a `1` the next box over, and so on.

Using a single-dimensional array involves stating both its name and the valid index in order to access one of its members. Depending on where the reference to an array element occurs, it can either store or recall a value. Following are the simple rules to remember:

- ☐ Assign a value to an array element before accessing that element to recall data. Otherwise, you get garbage data.
- ☐ Use a valid index. This is of paramount importance, because trying to access an array with an invalid index is like using an uninitialized pointer; it can lead to strange behavior in your program and GPFs in Windows.

DO	DON'T
DO make reasonable checks for the indices that access the arrays.	
DON'T assume that indices are always valid.	

The following is a simple example of accessing arrays:

```
double nums[5];
for (int i = 0; i < 5; ++i)
    {
    cout << "Enter number " << i << ": ";
    cin >> nums[i];
    }
cout << "You entered the following numbers: " << endl;
for (i = 0; i < 5; ++i)
    cout << "  nums[" << i << "] is " << nums[i] << endl;
```

Pointers to Arrays

C++ and its parent language, C, support a special use for the names of arrays. The compiler interprets the name of an array as the address of its first element. Thus, if x is an array, the expressions &x[0] and x are equivalent. In the case of a matrix—call it mat—the expressions &mat[0][0] and mat also are equivalent. This aspect of C++ and C makes them work as high-level assembly languages. Once you have the address of a data item, you've got its number, so to speak. Your knowledge of the memory address of a variable or an array enables you to manipulate its contents using pointers.

NEW☞   A *program variable* is a label that tags a memory address. Using a variable in a program
TERM   means accessing the associated memory location by specifying its name (or tag, if you prefer). In this sense, a variable becomes a name that points to a memory location—a pointer.

C++ enables you to use a pointer to access the various elements of an array. When you access the element x[i] of array x, the compiled code performs two tasks. First, it obtains the base address of the array x (that is, where the first array element is located). Second, it uses the index i to calculate the offset from the base address of the array. This offset equals i multiplied by the size of the basic array type.

```
address of element x[i] = address of x + i * sizeof(basicType)
```

Looking at the preceding equation, assume that you have a pointer ptr that takes the base address of array x.

```
ptr = x; // pointer ptr points to address of x[0]
```

You now can substitute x with ptr in the equation and come up with the following:

```
address of element x[i] = ptr + i * sizeof(basicType)
```

In order for C++ and C to be high-level assemblers, they simplify the use of this equation by absolving it from having to explicitly state the size of the basic array type. Thus, you can write the following:

```
address of element x[i] = ptr + i
```

This equation states that the address of element x[i] is the expression (ptr + i).

The PTR2.CPP program in Listing 4.5 illustrates the use of pointers to access one-dimensional arrays. This program calculates the average value for data in an array. The program begins by prompting you to enter the number of data points and the data itself. The program then calculates the average of the data in the array and displays the average value.

 Listing 4.5. Source code for the program PTR2.CPP.

```
1:   // C++ program that demonstrates the use of pointer with
2:   // one-dimensional arrays.  Program calculates the average
3:   // value of the data found in the array.
4:
5:   #include <iostream.h>
6:
7:   const int MAX = 30;
8:
9:   int main()
10: {
11:     double x[MAX];
12:     // declare pointer and initialize with base
13:     // address of array x
14:     double *realPtr = x; // same as = &x[0]
15:     double sum = 0.0, mean;
16:     int n, count;
17:     // obtain the number of data points
18:     do
19:       {
20:       cout << "Enter number of data points [2 to "
21:          << MAX << "]: ";
22:       cin >> n;
23:       cout << endl;
24:       } while (n < 2 ¦¦ n > MAX);
25:
26:     // prompt for the data
27:     for (int i = 0; i < n; i++)
28:       {
29:       cout << "X[" << i << "]: ";
30:       // use the form *(x+i) to store data in x[i]
31:       cin >> *(x + i);
32:       }
33:
34:     count = n;
35:     for (int i = 0; i < n; i++)
36:       // use the form *(realPtr + i) to access x[i]
37:       sum += *(realPtr + i);
38:     mean = sum / count;
39:     cout << endl << "Mean = " << mean << endl << endl;
40:     return 0;
41: }
```

Here is a sample session with the program in Listing 4.5.

```
Enter number of data points [2 to 30]: 5
```

135

```
X[0]: 1
X[1]: 2
X[2]: 3
X[3]: 4
X[4]: 5

Mean = 3
```

The program in Listing 4.5 declares the double-typed array x to have MAX elements. In addition, the program declares the pointer realPtr and initializes it using the array x. Thus, the pointer realPtr stores the address of x[0], which is the first element in array x.

The program uses the pointer for *(x + i) in the input statement on line 31. Thus, the identifier x works as a pointer to the array x. Using the expression *(x + i) accesses the element number i of array x, just as does using the expression x[i].

The program uses the pointer realPtr in the for loop on line 37. The expression *(realPtr + i) is the equivalent of *(x + i), which in turn is equivalent to x[i]. Thus, the for loop uses the pointer realPtr with an offset value, i, to access the elements of array x.

The Pointer Increment/Decrement Method

The preceding C++ program maintains the same address in the pointer realPtr. Employing pointer arithmetic with the for loop index i, you can write a new program version that increments the offset to access the elements of array x. C++ provides you with another choice that enables you to access sequentially the elements of an array without the help of an explicit offset value. The method merely involves using the increment or decrement operator with a pointer. Simply initialize the pointer to the base address of an array and then use the ++ operator to access the next array element. Following is a modified version of the preceding program, a version that uses the pointer increment method. Listing 4.6 shows the source code for the PTR3.CPP program.

Listing 4.6. Source code for the program PTR3.CPP.

```
1:  // C++ program that demonstrates the use of pointers with
2:  // one-dimension arrays.  The average value of the array
3:  // is calculated.  This program modifies the previous version
4:  // in the following way:  the realPtr is used to access the
5:  // array without any help from any loop control variable.
6:  // This is accomplished by 'incrementing' the pointer, and
7:  // consequently incrementing its address.  This program
8:  // illustrates pointer arithmetic that alters the pointer's
9:  // address.
10:
11: #include <iostream.h>
12:
```

```
13: const int MAX = 30;
14:
15: int main()
16: {
17:     double x[MAX];
18:     double *realPtr = x;
19:     double sum = 0.0, mean;
20:     int n, count;
21:
22:     do
23:        {
24:        cout << "Enter number of data points [2 to "
25:              << MAX << "]: ";
26:        cin >> n;
27:        cout << endl;
28:        } while (n < 2 || n > MAX);
29:
30:     for (int i = 0; i < n; i++)
31:        {
32:        cout << "X[" << i << "]: ";
33:        // increment pointer realPtr after taking its reference
34:        cin >> *realPtr++;
35:        }
36:
37:     // restore original address by using pointer arithmetic
38:     realPtr -= n;
39:     count = n;
40:     for (int i = 0; i < n; i++)
41:        // increment pointer realPtr after taking a reference
42:        sum += *(realPtr++);
43:     mean = sum / count;
44:     cout << endl << "Mean = " << mean << endl << endl;
45:     return 0;
46: }
```

Here is a sample session with the program in Listing 4.6.

```
Enter number of data points [2 to 30]: 5

X[0]: 10
X[1]: 20
X[2]: 30
X[3]: 40
X[4]: 50

Mean = 30
```

The program in Listing 4.6 initializes the realPtr pointer to the base address of array x, on line 18. The program uses the realPtr pointer in the keyboard input statement on line 34. This statement uses *realPtr++ to store your input in the currently accessed element of array x and then to increment the pointer to the next element of array x. When the input loop terminates, the pointer realPtr points past the tail of array x. To reset the pointer to the base address of array x, the program uses the assignment statement on line 38. This statement uses pointer arithmetic to decrease the current address in pointer realPtr by n times sizeof(double). The statement resets the address in the pointer `realPtr` to access the array element `x[0]`. The program uses the same incrementing method to calculate the sum of data in the second `for` loop on line 42.

Take special note of the statements on lines 34 and 42. Note how one uses parentheses and the other doesn't. Each statement performs equivalently; they get the address of the pointer ready, increment the variable that holds that address, then pass the original address to the `*` operator to access the data. Although the second method (which uses the parentheses) is far easier to read, you may very well encounter code written by others that doesn't use them.

Pointers to Structures

C++ supports declaring and using pointers to structures. Assigning the address of a structured variable to a pointer of the same type uses the same syntax as with simple variables. After the pointer has the address of the structured variable, it needs to use the `->` operator to access the members of the structure.

Accessing Structure Members

The general syntax for a pointer to access the members of a structure is

```
structPtr->aMember
```

Example

```
struct point
{
    double x;
    double y;
};

point p;
point* ptr = &p;

ptr->x = 23.3;
ptr->y = ptr->x + 12.3;
```

Here is a sample program that uses pointers to structures. Listing 4.7 shows the source code for the program PTR4.CPP. The program prompts you for four sets of coordinates that define four rectangles. Each rectangle is defined by the x and y coordinates of the upper-left and lower-right corners. The program calculates the area of each rectangle, sorts the rectangles by area, and displays the rectangles in the order of their areas.

Type

Listing 4.7. Source code for the program PTR4.CPP.

```
1:  // C++ program that demonstrates pointers to structured types
2:
3:  #include <iostream.h>
4:  #include <stdio.h>
```

```
 5:  #include <math.h>
 6:
 7:  const int MAX_RECT = 4;
 8:
 9:  struct point
10:  {
11:      double x;
12:      double y;
13:  };
14:
15:  struct rect
16:  {
17:      point ulc; // upper left corner
18:      point lrc; // lower right corner
19:      double area;
20:      int id;
21:  };
22:
23:  typedef rect rectArr[MAX_RECT];
24:
25:  int main()
26:  {
27:      rectArr r;
28:      rect temp;
29:      rect* pr = r;
30:      rect* pr2;
31:      double length, width;
32:
33:      for (int i = 0; i < MAX_RECT; i++, pr++)
34:          {
35:          cout << "Enter (X,Y) coord. for ULC of rect. #"
36:              << i + 1 << ": ";
37:          cin >> pr->ulc.x >> pr->ulc.y;
38:          cout << "Enter (X,Y) coord. for LRC of rect. #"
39:              << i + 1 << ": ";
40:          cin >> pr->lrc.x >> pr->lrc.y;
41:          pr->id = i;
42:          length = fabs(pr->ulc.x - pr->lrc.x);
43:          width = fabs(pr->ulc.y - pr->lrc.y);
44:          pr->area = length * width;
45:          }
46:
47:      pr -= MAX_RECT; // reset pointer
48:      // sort the rectanges by areas
49:      for (int i = 0; i < (MAX_RECT - 1); i++, pr++)
50:          {
51:          pr2 = pr + 1; // reset pointer pr2
52:          for (int j = i + 1; j < MAX_RECT; j++, pr2++)
53:              if (pr->area > pr2->area)
54:                  {
55:                  temp = *pr;
56:                  *pr = *pr2;
57:                  *pr2 = temp;
58:                  }
59:          }
```

continues

Listing 4.7. continued

```
60:
61:    pr -= MAX_RECT - 1; // reset pointer
62:    // display rectangles sorted by area
63:    for (int i = 0; i < MAX_RECT; i++, pr++)
64:        cout << "Rect #" << pr->id + 1 << " has area "
65:             << pr->area << endl;
66:    return 0;
67: }
```

Here is a sample session with the program in Listing 4.7.

```
Enter (X,Y) coord. for ULC of rect. #1: 1 1
Enter (X,Y) coord. for LRC of rect. #1: 2 2
Enter (X,Y) coord. for ULC of rect. #2: 1.5 1.5
Enter (X,Y) coord. for LRC of rect. #2: 3 4
Enter (X,Y) coord. for ULC of rect. #3: 1 2
Enter (X,Y) coord. for LRC of rect. #3: 5 8
Enter (X,Y) coord. for ULC of rect. #4: 4 6
Enter (X,Y) coord. for LRC of rect. #4: 8 4
Rect #1 has area 1
Rect #2 has area 3.75
Rect #3 has area 8
Rect #4 has area 24
```

The program in Listing 4.7 declares the pointers pr and pr2 on lines 29 and 30, respectively. These pointers access the structure of type rect. The program initializes the pointer pr with the base address of array r.

The first for loop, which begins on line 33, uses the pointer pr to access the elements of array r. The loop increment part contains the expression pr++, which uses pointer arithmetic to make the pointer pr access the next element in array r. The input statements on lines 37 and 40 use the pointer pr to access the members ulc and lrc. Notice that the statements use the pointer access operator -> to allow pointer pr to access the members ulc and lrc. The statements on lines 41 through 44 also use the pointer pr to access the members id, ulc, lrc, and area, using the -> operator.

The statement on line 47 resets the address stored in pointer pr by MAX_RECT units (that is, MAX_RECT * sizeof(double) bytes). The nested loops on lines 49 through 59 use the pointers pr and pr2. The outer for loop increments the address in pointer pr by one before the next iteration. The statement on line 51 assigns pr + 1 to the pointer pr2. This statement gives the pointer pr2 the initial access to the element i + 1 in array r. The inner for loop increments the pointer pr2 by 1 before the next iteration. Thus, the nested for loops use the pointers pr and pr2 to access the elements of array r. The if statement on line 53 uses the pointers pr and pr2 to access the area member in comparing the areas of various rectangles. The statements on line 55 through 57 swap the elements of array r, which are accessed by pointers pr and pr2. Notice that the statements use *pr and *pr2 to access an entire element of array r.

The statement on line 61 resets the address in the pointer pr by subtracting MAX_RECT - 1. The last for loop also uses the pointer pr to access and display the members id and area of the various elements in array r.

This program illustrates that you can completely manipulate an array using pointers only. They are powerful and versatile.

Pointers and Dynamic Memory

The programs presented thus far create the space for their variables at compile time. When the programs start running, the variables have their memory spaces preassigned. There are many applications in which you need to create new variables during the program execution. You need to allocate the memory space dynamically for these new variables at runtime. The designers of C++ have chosen to introduce new operators, which are not found in C, to handle the dynamic allocation and deallocation of memory. These new C++ operators are new and delete. While the C-style dynamic memory functions malloc, calloc, and free are still available, you should use the operators new and delete. These operators are more aware of the type of dynamic data that is created than are functions malloc, calloc, and free. Also, the standard C functions for creating and deleting dynamic memory won't handle class constructors and destructors (which are discussed on Day 8).

Syntax

The *new* and *delete* Operators

The general syntax for using the new and delete operators in creating dynamic variables is

```
pointer = new type;
delete pointer;
```

The operator new returns the address of the dynamically allocated variable. The operator delete removes the dynamically allocated memory accessed by a pointer. If the dynamic allocation of operator new fails, it throws an exception of type xalloc (declared in the EXCEPT.H header file). Therefore, you should make sure that you enclose your dynamic memory allocations in try blocks if you suspect trouble.

Example

```
try
   {
   int *pint;
   pint = new int;
   *pint = 33;
   cout << "Pointer pint stores " << *pint << endl;
   delete pint;
   }
catch(xalloc&)
   {
   cout << "Couldn't allocate memory." << endl;
   }
```

A Dynamic Array

To allocate and deallocate a dynamic array, use the following general syntax:

```
arrayPointer = new type[arraySize];
delete[] arrayPointer;
```

The operator new returns the address of the dynamically allocated array. If the allocation fails, the operator throws an xalloc exception. The operator delete removes the dynamically allocated array that is accessed by a pointer.

Example

```
try
    {
    const int MAX = 10;
    int* pint;
    pint = new int[MAX];
    for (int i = 0; i < MAX; i++)
        pint[i] = i * i;
    for (i = 0; i < MAX; i++)
        cout << *(pint + i) << endl;
    delete [] pint;
    }
catch(xalloc&)
    {
    cout << "Couldn't allocate memory." << endl;
    }
```

DO   DON'T

DO maintain access to dynamic variables and arrays at all times. Such access does not need the original pointers that were used to create these dynamic variables and arrays. Here is an example:

```
int* p = new int;
int* q;
*p = 123;
q = p; // q now also points to 123
p = new int; // create another dynamic variable
*p = 345; // p points to 345 whereas q points to 123
cout << *p << " " << *q << " " << (*p + *q) << "\n";
delete p;
delete q;
```

DON'T forget to delete dynamic variables and arrays when you're done using them. If you do, there is the potential of a "memory leak." This is the condition when memory seems to keep getting lower in your system for no apparent reason. It means that something has allocated memory without freeing it.

Using pointers to create and access dynamic data can be illustrated with the next program, PTR5.CPP (Listing 4.8). This program calculates the average value for data in an array. It begins by prompting you to enter the actual number of data and validates your input. Then it prompts you for the data and calculates the average of the data in the array. Next, it displays the average value.

 Listing 4.8. Source code for the program PTR5.CPP.

```
1:   // C++ program that demonstrates the pointers to manage
2:   // dynamic data
3:
4:   #include <except.h>
5:   #include <iostream.h>
6:
7:   const int MAX = 30;
8:
9:   int main()
10:  {
11:      double* x;
12:      double sum = 0, mean;
13:      int *n, count;
14:
15:      try { n = new int; }
16:      catch(xalloc&) { return 1; }
17:
18:      do      // obtain number of data points
19:          {
20:          cout << "Enter number of data points [2 to "
21:          << MAX << "]: ";
22:          cin >> *n;
23:          cout << endl;
24:          } while (*n < 2 || *n > MAX);
25:      // create tailor-fit dynamic array
26:      try { x = new double[*n]; }
27:      catch(xalloc&)
28:          {
29:          delete n;
30:          return 1;
31:          }
32:      // prompt user for data
33:      for (int i = 0; i < *n; i++)
34:          {
35:          cout << "X[" << i << "]: ";
36:          cin >> x[i];
37:          }
38:
39:      // calculate sum of observations
40:      count = *n;              // initialize summations
41:      for (int i = 0; i < *n; i++)
42:          sum += *(x + i);
43:
44:      mean = sum / count; // calculate the mean value
45:      cout << endl << "Mean = " << mean << endl << endl;
```

continues

Listing 4.8. continued

```
46:    // deallocate dynamic memory
47:    delete n;
48:    delete[] x;
49:    return 0;
50: }
```

Here is a sample session with the program in Listing 4.8:

```
Enter number of data points [2 to 30]: 5

X[0]: 1
X[1]: 2
X[2]: 3
X[3]: 4
X[4]: 5

Mean = 3
```

The program in Listing 4.8 uses two pointers for dynamic allocations. Line 11 declares the first pointer, which is used to allocate and access the dynamic array. Line 13 declares the pointer to create a dynamic variable.

The statement on line 15 uses the operator new to allocate the space for a dynamic int variable. The statement returns the address of the dynamic data to the pointer n. The catch statement on line 16 determines whether the dynamic allocation failed. If so, the function main exits and returns an exit code of 1 (to flag an error). This is actually somewhat contrived, though; it will be a very rare occasion where you allocate only a single integer.

The do-while loop on lines 18 through 24 prompts you to enter the number of data points. The statement on line 22 stores your input in the dynamic variable accessed by pointer n. The statement uses the pointer reference *n for this access. The while clause also uses *n to access the value in the dynamic variable. In fact, all the statements in the program access the number of data points using the pointer reference *n.

The statement on line 26 creates a dynamic array using the operator new. The statement creates a dynamic double-typed array with the number of elements that you specify. This feature demonstrates the advantage of using dynamic allocation to create custom-fit arrays. The catch statement on line 27 determines whether the allocation of the dynamic array was successful. If not, the statements on lines 28 and 29 deallocate the dynamic variable accessed by pointer n and exit the function with a return value of 1.

The for loop on lines 33 through 37 prompts you to enter values for the dynamic array. The statement on line 36 stores your input to the element i of the dynamic array. Notice that the statement uses the expression x[i] to access the targeted element. This form resembles that of static arrays. C++ treats the expression x[i] as equivalent to *(x + i). In fact, the program uses

the latter form in the second `for` loop on line 42. The statement on line 42 accesses the elements in the dynamic array using the form `*(x + i)`.

The last statements in function `main` delete the dynamic variable and array. The statement on line 47 deallocates the space for the dynamic variable accessed by pointer `n`. The statement on line 48 deletes the dynamic array accessed by pointer `x`.

Far Pointers

The architecture of processors, such as the family of Intel 80x86, features segmented memory. Each segment is 64 kilobytes (KB) in size. Using segments has advantages and disadvantages. This storage scheme supports two types of pointers: *near pointers* and *far pointers.*

NEW☞ TERM Within a *segment* you can use near pointers to access data in the same segment. The pointers store only the offset address in the segment and, thus, require fewer bytes to store their address. By contrast, far pointers store the segment and offset addresses and, thus, they require more space. 16-bit Windows applications use far pointers.

To declare far pointers, insert the keyword `__far` (or sometimes `_far`) between the type and the name of the pointer.

It's important to note that far pointers are extremely nonportable. That is, they apply only to applications written for the IBM PC and compatible computers, and only then when in 16-bit mode, such as MS-DOS or Windows 3.1. If you write programs for Windows NT, Windows 95, or any other 32-bit version of Windows, you will be able to ignore far pointers completely; in fact, the `__far` and `_far` keywords are illegal when in 32-bit mode. This 32-bit mode is also sometimes referred to as the *flat* model.

You also should note that making the distinction between near and far pointers really makes sense only when compiling in something other than the large memory model (changeable in the Project dialog box accessible from the Options menu in the IDE). I strongly recommend that when you write programs in 16-bit mode, you always compile in large model and never leave it. The memory savings you get from using other memory models is minimal compared to the potential for bugs and consternation in mixing and matching far and near pointers.

Summary

Today's lesson introduced you to user-defined data types and covered the following topics:

☐ You can use the `typedef` statements to create alias types of existing types and define array types. The general syntax for using `typedef` is

```
typedef knownType newType;
```

4

☐ Enumerated data types enable you to declare unique identifiers that represent a collection of logically related constants. The general syntax for declaring an enumerated type is

```
enum enumType { <list of enumerated identifiers> };
```

☐ Structures enable you to define a new type that logically groups several fields or members. These members can be predefined types or other structures. The general syntax for declaring a structure is

```
struct structTag
{
    <list of members>
};
```

☐ Unions are a form of variant structures. The general syntax for unions is

```
union unionTag
{
    type1 member1;
    type2 member2;
    ...
    typeN memberN;
};
```

☐ Reference variables are aliases of the variables that they reference. To declare a reference variable, place the & after the data type of the reference variable or to the left of the variable's name.

☐ Pointers are variables that store the addresses of other variables or data. C++ uses pointers to offer flexible and efficient manipulation of data and system resources.

☐ Pointers to existing variables use the & operator to obtain the addresses of these variables. Armed with these addresses, pointers offer access to the data in their associated variables. To access the value by using a pointer, use the * operator followed by the name of the pointer.

☐ Arrays are groups of values stored in a list with the same name, and they're useful for holding on to collections of the same type of data.

☐ Pointers access the elements of arrays by being assigned the base address of a class. C++ considers the name of an array as equivalent to the pointer of the base address. For example, the name of the array a is treated as &a[0]. Pointers can be used to sequentially traverse the elements of an array to store and/or recall values from these elements.

☐ Pointers to structures manipulate structures and access their members. C++ provides the -> operator in order to allow a pointer access to the members of a structure.

☐ Pointers can create and access dynamic data by using the operators new and delete. These operators enable you to create dynamic variables and arrays. The new operator assigns the address of the dynamic data to the pointer used in creating and accessing the data. The operator `delete` reclaims the space of dynamic data when that information is no longer needed.

☐ Far pointers are pointers that store both the segment and the offset addresses of an item. Near pointers store only the offset address of an item. Far pointers require more storage than near pointers.

Q&A

Q Does C++ support pointers to the predefined type `void`?

A Yes, `void*` pointers are considered typeless pointers and can be used to copy arbitrary data.

Q Because C++ pointers (including `void*` pointers) have types, can I use typecasting to translate the data accessed by the general-purpose `void*` pointers to non-`void*` pointers?

A Yes. C++ enables you to typecast pointer references, such as

```
void* p = data;
long *lp = (long*)p;
```

The pointer `lp` uses the typecast to translate the data it accesses.

Q What happens if I delete a dynamic array by using the delete operator without following it with the empty brackets?

A The effect of deleting an array with a plain `delete` operator is undefined. Expect the plain `delete` operator to leave orphaned dynamic memory and cause memory leaks.

Q Can a structure contain a pointer to itself?

A Yes. Many structures that model dynamic data structures use this type of declaration. For example, the following structure models the nodes of a dynamic list with pointer-based links:

```
struct listNode
{
   dataType data;
   listNode *next;
};
```

Q Does C++ allow the declaration of a pointer-to-structure type before declaring the structure?

A Yes. This feature makes declaring nodes of dynamic data structures possible.

Q Does C++ allow pointers that access the addresses of other pointers?

A Yes, C++ supports pointers-to-pointers (also called *double pointers*). To declare such pointers, use two * characters, as shown in the following example, which declares the double pointer p:

```
int x;
int *px = &x;
int **p = &px;
```

The expression *p accesses the pointer px, and the expression **p accesses the variable x.

Workshop

The Workshop provides quiz questions to help you solidify your understanding of the material covered and exercises to provide you with experience in using what you've learned. Try to understand the quiz and exercise answers before continuing on to the next day's lesson. Answers are provided in Appendix A.

Quiz

1. What is the error in the following statements?

```
enum State { on, off };
enum YesNo { yes, no };
enum DiskDriveStatus { on , off };
```

2. True or false? The declaration of the following enumerated type is incorrect.

```
enum YesNo { no = 0, No = 0, yes = 1, Yes = 1 };
```

3. What is the problem with the following program?

```
#include <iostream.h>
int main()
{
  int *p = new int;
  cout << "Enter a number : ";
  cin >> *p;
  cout << "The square of " << *p << " = " << (*p * *p);
  return 0;
}
```

Exercises

1. Assume that a word is an unsigned short and is two bytes and that a byte is an unsigned char is one byte (shouldn't be too hard, because it's true). Create a union that stores a word but allows you to easily access the individual bytes of that word.

2. Define a structure that can be used to model a dynamic array of integers. The structure should have a member to access the dynamic data and a member to store the size of the dynamic array. Call the structure intArrStruct.

3. Given an index of ix, how many different ways can you think of to access that particular element of the structure in question 2?

Functions

Today you will be introduced to a vital aspect of C++: functions. Functions provide a way of compartmentalizing parts of a program into more easily accessible pieces, which helps to keep different aspects of a program logically separated. You will learn the following about functions:

- ☐ Declaring and prototyping functions
- ☐ Local variables in functions
- ☐ Static variables in functions
- ☐ Macro expansion
- ☐ Inline functions
- ☐ Exiting functions
- ☐ Default arguments
- ☐ Passing arguments by reference
- ☐ Recursive functions
- ☐ Function overloading

Declaring and Prototyping Functions

Most programming languages use functions and procedures. C++ does not support formal procedures. Instead, all C++ routines are functions, and a procedure is implemented as a function with a `void` return type.

**NEW☞
TERM**   *Functions* are the primary building blocks that conceptually extend the C++ language to fit your custom programs. You could think of each function as a small routine that gets a small, very specific piece of a job done.

Syntax

Declaring and Defining Functions

The general form for the ANSI C style of defining and declaring functions (which is maintained by C++) is

```
returnType functionName(typedParameterList)
{
    statementBody
}
```

Examples

```
double sqr(double y)
{ return y * y; }
```

```
char prevChar(char c)
{
   return c - 1;
}
```

Remember the following rules when declaring and defining C++ functions:

- [ ] The return type of the C++ function appears before the function's name.

- [ ] If the parameter list is empty, you still use empty parentheses. C++ also allows you the option of using the void keyword to explicitly state that there are no parameters, but this is a throwback to the C language. I mention the void keyword here only so that you can recognize old code you might encounter that has been updated from C.

- [ ] The typed parameter list consists of a list of typed parameters that use the following general format:

   `[const] type1 parameter1, [const] type2 parameter2, ...`

   This format shows that the individual parameter is declared like a variable—you state the type first and then the parameter's identifier. The list of parameters in C++ is comma-delimited. In addition, you cannot group a sequence of parameters that have exactly the same data type. You must declare each parameter explicitly. If a parameter has the const keyword, the compiler makes sure that the function does *not* alter the arguments of that parameter.

- [ ] The body of a C++ function is enclosed in braces ({}). There is no semicolon after the closing brace.

- [ ] C++ supports passing arguments either by value or by reference. By default, parameters pass their arguments by value. Consequently, the functions work with a copy of the data, preserving the original data. To declare a reference parameter, insert the & character after the data type of the parameter. A reference parameter becomes an alias to its arguments. Any changes made to the reference parameter also affect the original variable used as the argument. The general form for reference parameters is

   `[const] type1& parameter1, [const] type2& parameter2, ...`

   If a parameter has the const keyword, the compiler makes sure that the function does not alter the arguments of that parameter. (Yes, there are good reasons for passing arguments by const reference, and they are discussed later in this chapter.)

- [ ] C++ supports local constants, data types, and variables. Although these data items can appear in nested block statements, C++ does not support nested functions.

- [ ] The return keyword returns the function's value, if any.

☐ If the function's return type is void, you do not have to use the return statement, unless you need to provide an exit route in the middle of the function. In the latter case, the return statement doesn't take any parameters; there's no value to return.

NEW☛ C++ dictates that you either declare or define a function before you use it. Declaring a **TERM** function, commonly called *prototyping*, lists the function name, return type, and the number and type of its parameters. Including the name of the parameter is optional. You then need to place a semicolon after the close parenthesis instead of a statement block. C++ requires that you declare a function if you call it before you define it.

The following is a simple example of prototyping:

```
// prototype the function square
double sqr(double);

int main()
{
    cout << "5^2 = " << sqr(5) << "\n";
    return 0;
}

double sqr(double z)
{ return z * z; }
```

Notice that the declaration of function sqr contains only the type of its single parameter. This is a common practice; however, I discourage it. Placing the name of parameters in prototypes makes figuring out the purpose of a function easier, especially if it's been a while since you wrote the function and can't remember exactly what it's supposed to do.

Typically, the declaration of a function is global. You may, however, prototype a function within another function from where it will be called. This technique conceals the prototype from other functions.

Calling a function requires you to supply its parameters with arguments. The arguments are mapped onto the parameters by the sequence in which the parameters are declared. The arguments must be data types that match or are compatible with those of the parameters. For example, you may have a function volume, defined as follows:

```
double volume(double length, double width, double height)
{
    return length * width * height;
}
```

To call the function volume, you need to supply three double-typed arguments or arguments with compatible types (which, in this case, are all of numeric data types). Here are a number of sample calls to the function volume:

```
double len = 34, width = 55, ht = 100;
int i = 3;
long j = 44;
unsigned k = 33;

cout << volume(len, width, ht) << endl;
cout << volume(1, 2, 3) << endl;
cout << volume(i, j, k) << endl;
cout << volume(len, j, 22.3) << endl;
```

> **Note:** C++ enables you to discard the result of a function. This type of function call is used when the focus is on what the function does rather than its return value. In this case, you're using the function in much the same way as Pascal and other languages use procedures.

What Is a Parameter?

You might have an easier time of things if you understand better how parameters are passed into functions. Normally, when you list a variable in the parameter list of a function, it's the same thing as if you'd just declared a new variable inside the function itself, and then assigned to it the value that was passed into the function. It's similar to creating a copy of that original value and then using it in the function. Because of this copying action, changing the value of a parameter in a function has no effect on whatever was passed to the function from the caller. For example:

```
void foo(int parm)
{
    ++parm;
}

int main()
{
    int value = 5;
    foo(value);
    cout << value << endl;
    return 0;
}
```

The output of this program will be 5. Although the function foo changes the value of the parameter passed, this has no effect whatsoever on the original variable that was passed. In order to change the value of the original variable, you can use a reference parameter. A reference parameter works just like the reference variables you learned about on Day 4. So let's rewrite that last example:

```
void foo(int& parm)          // takes a reference to an int
{
    ++parm;
}

int main()
{
    int value = 5;
    foo(value);
    cout << value << endl;
    return 0;
}
```

The output of the new program will be 6. The variable value is initially set to 5, but then when it's passed to foo, it is assigned to the reference variable parm, which is then incremented. Since this is a reference variable, it's not really holding the value 5, but rather it refers to the original variable value that holds that value of 5. When parm is incremented, it's really value that gets incremented.

In the old-style C functions, it was common to pass a pointer to an object in order to get the same result that C++ accomplishes with reference variables. If you have to look at other peoples' code, you may very well see this style of programming. You will also see it when calling into third-party DLLs while doing Windows programming or when you use Windows calls directly without using OWL. Windows programming will be discussed later on in this book. A quick rewrite of our simple example will show you how pointers can be used to manipulate parameters:

```
void foo(int* parm)       // takes a pointer to an int
{
    ++*parm;              // make sure to use the *
}

int main()
{
    int value = 5;
    foo(&value);          // pass the address of the variable
    cout << value << endl;
    return 0;
}
```

Note that this is all much more cumbersome than simply using reference variables; you're forced to pay more attention to what you're using and when to use the appropriate notations, and so on.

Another great use for reference parameters is to pass some larger objects to a function. When you're copying the contents of something such as an int or a pointer, which are going to be only a few bytes, there's no problem with copying their contents. When it comes to passing something such as a structure, however, you could start copying a tremendous amount of data. Some structures can be in the kilobyte range or larger. If you were to copy its contents every time you passed it to a function, it is conceivable that you could slow down your system enough to notice it even in real-time.

The solution, of course, is to pass the structure by reference. Now, rather than copying the entire contents of the structure, you are copying only a few bytes to create the reference to the original structure, which is much more manageable. However, you create a new problem when you do this; the target function is now capable of changing the contents of the passed structure.

Using *const* in Arguments

The const type modifier comes to the rescue here. So far, I've only really discussed it with respect to creating constant variables. It's best to use it as a modifier of such types as pointers and references. By specifying a function's argument as a const reference, not only are you preventing the copying of a potentially huge structure, you also are preventing the function from modifying the contents of that structure. The function can look at the structure and use anything inside of it; it's just not allowed to modify any part of it.

Syntax

The *const* Argument Modifier

The general syntax for using the const modifier in function parameters is

```
returnType functionName(const argType &arg)
```

Example

```
struct userInfo
{
    int age;
    char name[150];    // Should be big enough for most names
}

void processUserInfo(const userInfo& ui)
{
    if (ui.age < 18)
        {
        cout << "You're too young to be using this function." << endl;
        return;
        }
    if (ui.age < 21)
        ui.age = 21;        // -=*> !!!ERROR!!! <*=-
}
```

Note the line with the comment about the error. Whereas the compiler will have absolutely no problems with processUserInfo checking to make sure the passed user is old enough, the compiler will stop with an error when it encounters this rogue function trying to arbitrarily change the person's age. So much for getting a fake ID.

Now, after all this argument for passing structures by reference rather than by value, let me just say that there's nothing wrong with passing a smaller structure by value. If there are only a few members in it and it doesn't take up much memory on its own, then there's no reason why you shouldn't just pass it right on in. It can be good, however, to get into the habit of just passing structures by reference all the time.

The Declaration of Exceptions Thrown by a Function

Syntax

The syntax for declaring functions that can or cannot throw exceptions is

```
[returnType] functionName([parameterList]);
```

The preceding syntax declares that the function `functionName` can throw any type of exception.

```
[returnType] functionName([parameterList]) throw();
```

The preceding syntax declares that the function `functionName` should *not* throw an exception.

```
[returnType] functionName([parameterList])
throw(exceptionTypeList);
```

The preceding syntax declares that the function `functionName` can throw an exception only if it's listed in the comma-delimited exception type list, `exceptionTypeList`.

Examples

```
void parse();
void calc() throw();
void input() throw(TFileErr, TMemoryErr);
```

The declaration of function `parse` states that the function can throw any type of exception. By contrast, the declaration of function `calc` states that the function cannot throw any type of exception. The declaration of function `input` states that the function can throw only the exceptions of type `TFileErr`, `TMemoryErr`.

C++ requires that you declare the `throw` clause in both the declaration and the definition of a function.

Local Variables in Functions

Good structured-programming techniques foster the notion that functions should be as independent and as reusable as possible. Consequently, functions can have their own data types, constants, and variables to give them this independence.

NEW **TERM** The *local variable* in a function exists only when that function is called. Once the function terminates, the runtime system removes the local variables. Consequently, local variables lose their data between function calls. In addition, the runtime system applies any initialization to local variables every time the host function is called.

DO	DON'T

DO use local variables to store and alter the values of parameters that are declared with the const clause.

DON'T declare a local variable to have the same name as a global variable that you need to access in the function. Using the same name hides the global version, making it difficult to use and very confusing.

Listing 5.1 increments a parameter five times.

 Listing 5.1. Source code for the program LOCAL.CPP.

```
1:  // C++ program to demonstrate local variables
2:
3:  #include <iostream.h>
4:
5:  void increment(int start)
6:  {
7:      int ix;
8:
9:      for (ix = start; ix < start + 5; ++ix)
10:         cout << ix << endl;
11: }
12:
13: int main()
14: {
15:     increment(23);
16:     return 0;
17: }
```

The output from the program in Listing 5.1 looks like the following:

```
23
24
25
26
27
```

The program in Listing 5.1 declares two functions—namely, increment on line 5 and main on line 13. The function increment takes as its parameter start and uses it as the base in a short for loop that increments the local variable ix. The function main simply calls increment with a start value of 23.

There's something to note here. All along you've seen these programs that always started with main and were then enclosed by its statement block. When it comes right down to it, main is just another function, no different from any other except for its special name. When a program starts up, it always begins by calling the main function. As a matter of fact, without the main function, a program won't compile properly.

Static Variables in Functions

In Listing 5.1, the local variable in the function increment loses its value once the function terminates. C++ enables you to declare a local variable that retains its value simply by placing the static keyword to the left of its data type. Static variables usually are initialized. This initialization is performed once, when the host function is called for the first time.

NEW☞
TERM A number of programming techniques require maintaining the values of local variables between function calls. These special local variables are called *static variables*. They're sort of like global variables, in that they are always around, but they can be accessed only from within the function in which they're declared—they are local to that function.

When the host function terminates, the static variables maintain their values. The compiler supports this language feature by storing static variables in a separate memory location that is maintained while the program is running. You can use the same names for static variables in different functions. This duplication does not confuse the compiler because it keeps track of which function owns which static variables.

Listing 5.2 uses a function with static variables to maintain a moving average. The program supplies its own data and calls that function several times in order to obtain and display the current value of the moving average.

Listing 5.2. Source code for the program STATIC.CPP.

```
1:  // C++ program that illustrates static local variables
2:
3:  #include <iostream.h>
4:
5:  double average(double x)
6:  {
7:    static double count = 0;
```

```
8:    static double sum = 0;
9:
10:   ++count;
11:   sum += x;
12:   return sum / count;
13: }
14:
15: int main()
16: {
17:   cout << "average = " << average(1) << endl;
18:   cout << "average = " << average(2) << endl;
19:   cout << "average = " << average(4) << endl;
20:   cout << "average = " << average(10) << endl;
21:   cout << "average = " << average(11) << endl;
22:   return 0;
23: }
```

Here is a sample session with the program in Listing 5.2.

```
average = 1
average = 1.5
average = 2.33333
average = 4.25
average = 5.6
```

The program in Listing 5.2 declares the function average, which contains static local variables. Lines 7 and 8 declare the static variables count and sum, respectively. The function initializes both static variables with 0. Note that this initialization occurs only once, before the function is even called for the first time. Later calls to average will simply bypass those initialization parts and move right on to the statement on line 10, which increments the variable count. The statement on line 11 adds the value of parameter x to the variable sum. Line 12 returns the updated average, obtained by dividing sum by count.

The function main issues a series of calls to function average. The stream output statements in lines 17 through 21 display the updated average. These results are possible thanks to the static local variables count and sum in function average. If static variables were not supported by C++, you would need to resort to using global variables—a highly questionable programming choice.

The *#define* Statement Revisited

It is now time to come back to the #define statement. It was mentioned on Day 2 that the #define statement was really creating macros, and then I went over the simple macro substitution in which a single identifier was replaced with another. Actually, macros also can take parameters in much the same way as regular functions, but you first must take a little care.

Parameters in the *#define* Macro

The syntax for the #define function with parameters is

```
#define macroName(arg1, arg2, ..., argN) substitution
```

The substitution expression can be anything, and doesn't even need to make use of the parameters given to the macro name (it's common to turn off a macro simply by defining it as blank, with no substitution expression). It also is important to note that there are no types involved here; the parameters are just names that are to be used in the substitution expression. Furthermore, be very careful to not put a semicolon on the end of the substitution expression. The following is the classic example of how to use a macro to figure out the smallest (min) and greatest (max) of two variables:

```
#define min(n1, n2) (((n1) < (n2)) ? (n1) : (n2))
#define max(n1, n2) (((n1) > (n2)) ? (n1) : (n2))
```

Note all the parentheses used in that last example. In order to help understand that, remember that arguments passed to regular functions get stored in brand-new variables: the ones declared within the function definition's parentheses. In a macro's case, the arguments are really just substitutions; no new declarations are made and no variables are copied. To expand on the previous example, the following shows a before and after picture, comparing the original source code to what the preprocessor produces for the compiler to use:

```
#define min(n1, n2) (((n1) < (n2)) ? (n1) : (n2))
double num1 = 50, num2 = 5, rslt;
rslt = min(num1 / 2, num2 * 2);
```

Now take a look at that last line when the preprocessor is done with it:

```
rslt = (((50 / 2) < (5 * 2)) ? (50 / 2) : (5 * 2));
```

First, note that if there had been a semicolon at the end of the first line, there would have been two at the end of the final result because the last line of the original source line that calls min has a semicolon at its end.

Finally, look at what that expression would have looked like without all the parentheses in the original macro definition.

```
rslt = 50 / 2 < 5 * 2 ? 50 / 2 : 5 * 2;
```

Which operator is doing what to what else? By placing the parentheses, you ensure that if an expression is used as an argument (rather than just a simple variable or constant), it won't confuse the compiler when the preprocessor is done with the substitutions.

> **Note:** This min and max example looks very useful, but you shouldn't actually
> bother to define them in any of your programs. These two functions are defined in
> the STDLIB.H standard header file. Furthermore, they're defined in such a way as
> to do type checking on the arguments. They will be revisited again when I talk
> about templates.

Inline Functions

Using functions requires the overhead of calling them, passing their arguments, and returning
their results. While macros get around this problem, they have the added problem of being only
macros, and they lose all the advantages of local variables, and so on, that are available in full-
fledged functions. C++ enables you to use *inline functions* that expand into their statements.
Thus, inline functions offer faster execution time—especially helpful where speed is critical—
at the cost of expanding the code.

Syntax

The *inline* Function

The general syntax for the inline function is

```
inline returnType functionName(typedParameterList)
{ statementBlock; }
```

Examples

```
inline double cube(double x)
{ return x * x * x; }

inline char nextChar(char c)
{ return c + 1; }
```

5

The alternative to using inline functions is to use the #define directive to create macro-based
pseudofunctions. Many C++ programmers strongly recommend foregoing this method in favor
of inline functions. The justification for this is that inline functions provide type checking;
macros created with the #define directive do not. However, this lack of type checking is exactly
what makes macros so appealing: one can write a single macro that will act on many different
types of data by expanding the same code in place for each instance.

Also, because the parameters to an inline function are used as if they were sent into a real
function, rather than expanded in a macro, there is less risk of side effects. Regard the min macro,
again, and a dangerous use of it:

```
#define min(n1, n2) (((n1) < (n2)) ? (n1) : (n2))
int num1 = 5, num2 = 10;
rslt = min(++num1, num2);
```

The last line expands to the following:

```
rslt = (((++num1) < (num2)) ? (++num1) : (num2);
```

Note that both `rslt` and `num1` will end up with the value of 7. This is because `num1` is incremented twice: once in the comparison and once in the result portion of the `?:` operator. An inline function would increment `num1` only once before executing the contents of the function.

There is a middle ground that allows for macro-like expansion of full-fledged functions. These are called templates and are explained on Day 10.

DO	**DON'T**

DO start by declaring inline functions as ordinary functions when you develop your programs. Non-inline functions are easier to debug. Once your program is working, insert the inline keyword where needed.

DON'T use inline functions on anything really large. Again, it's important to stress that inline functions are expanded as if they were typed directly at the location from where they are called. There also are some restrictions on what the compiler will let you do within an inline function; but, if you put the `inline` keyword on something the compiler doesn't like, it will just give you a warning and ignore the `inline` keyword. Your program will still compile and run just fine.

DON'T declare inline functions with many statements. The increase in .EXE program size may not be acceptable.

A simple example of a program that uses inline functions, Listing 5.3 contains the source code for the program INLINE1.CPP. This program prompts you for a number, and then calculates and displays the square and cube values for your input.

Listing 5.3. Source code for the program INLINE.CPP.

```
1:  // C++ program that illustrates inline functions
2:
3:  #include <iostream.h>
4:
5:  inline double sqr(double x)
6:  {
7:    return x * x;
8:  }
9:
10: inline double cube(double x)
```

```
11: {
12:    return x * x * x;
13: }
14:
15: int main()
16: {
17:    double x;
18:
19:    cout << "Enter a number: ";
20:    cin >> x;
21:    cout << "square of " << x << " = " << sqr(x) << endl
22:         << "cube of " << x << " = " << cube(x) << endl;
23:    return 0;
24: }
```

Here is a sample session with the program in Listing 5.3.

```
Enter a number: 2.5
square of 2.5 = 6.25
cube of 2.5 = 15.625
```

The program in Listing 5.3 declares the inline functions sqr and cube on lines 5 and 10, respectively. Each function heading starts with the keyword inline. The other aspects of the inline functions resemble short normal functions. The function main calls the functions sqr and cube on lines 21 and 22 to display the square and cube values, respectively.

Note that short functions like these, which don't do much more than a simple operation on one or more parameters, are the ideal candidate for making an inline function. These are short operations that make sense to type in directly, but it makes more sense semantically to separate them out into subfunctions that are easily identified and called. In order to keep the overhead of calling a function just to get something simple done, you can make that function inline and it acts just as if you'd typed it in the first place.

Exiting Functions Prematurely

Usually you make an early exit from a function because particular conditions do not allow you to proceed with executing the statements in that function. C++ provides the return statement to exit from a function. If the function has the void type, you then employ the statement return and include no expression after the return. By contrast, if you exit a non-void function, the return statement should produce a value that indicates the purpose for exiting the function.

Default Arguments

Default arguments are a language feature that is quite simple and yet very powerful. When you omit the argument of a parameter that has a default argument, that argument is used automatically.

Note: C++ permits you to assign default arguments to the parameters of a function.

Using default arguments requires that you follow these rules:

☐ After you assign a default argument to a parameter, you must do so for all subsequent parameters in the same parameter list. You cannot randomly assign default arguments to parameters. This rule means that the parameter list can be divided into two sublists: the leading parameters, which do not have default arguments, and the trailing parameters, which do.

☐ The caller of the function must provide an argument for every parameter that has no default argument.

☐ The caller may omit the argument for a parameter that has a default argument.

☐ Once you omit the argument for a parameter with a default argument, the arguments for all subsequent parameters must also be omitted.

Note: The best way to list the parameters with default arguments is to locate them according to the likelihood of using their default arguments. Place the least-likely-to-be-used arguments first and the most-likely-to-be-used arguments last.

A simple example that uses a function with default arguments, Listing 5.4 shows the source code for the program DEFARGS.CPP. The program prints out a message as said by a particular speaker.

Type

Listing 5.4. Source code for the program DEFARGS.CPP.

```
1:  // C++ program that illustrates default arguments
2:
3:  #include <iostream.h>
4:
5:  void message(const char* msg, const char* name = "Keith")
6:  {
7:      cout << name << " says \"" << msg << '\"' << endl;
8:  }
9:
10: int main()
11: {
12:     message("Hi there!");
```

```
13:     message("Hi yourself!", "Kevin");
14:     return 0;
15: }
```

Here is the output of the program in Listing 5.4.

```
Keith says "Hi there!"
Kevin says "Hi yourself!"
```

The program is short, but sweet. It begins by declaring and defining on line 5 the function message, which takes two parameters: msg and name. Note that the second argument name is set equal to "Keith". This means that if no argument is supplied by the caller, then name should be set to a default value. Line 7 is just a straightforward output statement that uses the parameters to the function to display a line of text.

Now compare lines 12 and 13 of function main. The first call to message doesn't bother to supply the second parameter to the function, and if you compare that call with the first line of output from the program, you'll see that Keith got his name mentioned. On the second call to message, the second parameter *is* set, and now Kevin has a stab at a response.

Default arguments are incredibly useful tools. There will be many instances where you've got a number of parameters that need to be changed occasionally, but will usually be a certain value. In these cases, it makes sense to give those parameters default arguments, making the calls to the function easier.

Recursive Functions

There are many problems that can be solved by breaking them down into simpler and similar problems. Such problems are solved using recursion.

NEW☞ TERM *Recursive functions* are functions that obtain a result and/or perform a task by calling themselves. However, each successive call to a function uses up a little more of the system's limited resources, so these recursive calls must be limited in order to avoid exhausting the memory resources of the computer. Consequently, every recursive function must examine a condition that determines the end of the recursion.

NEW☞ TERM Possibly the easiest example of a recursive function is the mathematical *factorial function*. A factorial of a number N is the product of all the integers from 1 to N, with the exclamation point (!) as the mathematical symbol for the factorial function.

The mathematical equation for a factorial is

```
N! = 1 * 2 * 3 * ... * (N-2) * (N-1) * N
```

The recursive version of this equation is

```
N! = N * (N-1)!
(N-1)! = (N-1) * (N-2)!
(N-2)! = (N-2) * (N-3)!
...
2! = 2 * 1!
1! = 1
```

Recursion entails looping to obtain a result. Most recursive solutions have alternate, nonrecursive solutions. In some cases, the recursive solutions are more elegant than the nonrecursive ones. The factorial function is an example of a mathematical function that can be implemented using either recursion or a nonrecursive, straightforward loop.

The general rule is that recursion can save a lot of code space; there are fewer source lines to deal with, the size of the resulting executable program is smaller, and the actual source code is often easier to read. The disadvantage is one of speed. Recursive functions are usually (though not always) slower than their nonrecursive functions. When you've got a problem that can be solved with either method, you should weigh the different advantages of each before deciding how to write the code—or, if you don't have a deadline breathing down your neck, you could try both and do some tests before deciding which one you like best.

DO	**DON'T**
DO include a decision-making statement in a recursive function to end the recursion. **DON'T** use recursion unless its advantages significantly outweigh the alternate, nonrecursive solution.	

Look at an example that implements the recursive factorial function. Listing 5.5 shows the source code for the program FACTOR.CPP. The program prompts you to enter a positive integer. The program then displays the factorial of that number.

Listing 5.5. Source code for the program FACTOR.CPP.

```
1:  // C++ program that uses a recursive function
2:
3:  #include <iostream.h>
4:
5:  const int MIN = 1;
6:  const int MAX = 30;
7:
8:  double factorial(double f)
```

```
 9:  {
10:     if (f > 1)
11:         return f * factorial(f - 1);
12:     else
13:         return f;
14:  }
15:
16:  int main()
17:  {
18:     int x;
19:
20:     do
21:        {
22:        cout << "Enter an integer between "
23:             << MIN << " and " << MAX << ": ";
24:        cin >> x;
25:        } while (x < MIN || x > MAX);
26:     cout << x << "! = " << factorial(x) << endl;
27:     return 0;
28:  }
```

Here is a sample session with the program in Listing 5.5.

```
Enter an integer between 1 and 30: 5
5! = 120
```

The program in Listing 5.5 starts on lines 5 and 6 with the definition of the constants MIN and MAX, respectively. The first is defined because the factorial function doesn't really work well for numbers less than 1. The second is defined because, as you can test for yourself, it doesn't take a large number to make an extremely large factorial. I chose 30 to keep things relatively under control.

The factorial function starts on line 8. It's a simple function that takes a double as an argument and returns the same. Line 11 is where the actual recursion occurs. You call factorial with f - 1, thus calling yourself. On the previous line, 10, is the check to see if it's time to stop the recursion. Since you're only going down to 1, you want to skip the recursive call to yourself if you've reached the end. If you didn't have this check, you'd just keep calling yourself over and over again, hanging the program and eventually overflowing a part of memory as too many instances of the function would have started. Line 13 simply returns your total if you've reached the end of the recursion.

The main function has a simple loop on lines 20 through 25 that gets a number, making sure it's in the right range. Then line 26 calls the factorial function with the number to use. Note that the user enters an int, but the factorial function takes a double as its parameter. This is another example of the automatic casting of integers to floating-point types. I'd like to remind you again that you cannot go the other way (a floating-point number automatically cast to an integer).

5

Function Overloading

Function overloading is a language feature in C++ that has no parallel in C, Pascal, or BASIC. This feature enables you to declare multiple functions that have the same name but different parameter lists. The function's return type is not part of what's called the function signature, because C++ enables you to discard the result type. Consequently, the compiler cannot distinguish between two functions with the same parameters and different return types when these return types are omitted.

NEW
TERM   A parameter list is also referred to as a *function signature*.

> **Warning:** Using default arguments with overloaded functions may duplicate the signature for some of the functions (when the default arguments are used). The C++ compiler can detect this ambiguity and generate a compile-time error.

DO	DON'T
DO use default arguments to reduce the number of overloaded functions.	
DON'T use overloaded functions to implement different operations.	

The real power of overloaded functions is in the capability to define several versions of the same routine that are capable of acting with different types of data. Look at a simple program that uses overloaded functions. Listing 5.6 contains the source code for the program OVERLOAD.CPP. The program performs the following tasks:

☐ Declares variables that have the `char`, `int`, and `double` types, and initializes them with values

☐ Displays the initial values

☐ Invokes overloaded functions that increment the variables

☐ Displays the updated values stored in the variables

Listing 5.6. Source code for the program OVERLOAD.CPP.

```
1:  // C++ program that illustrates function overloading
2:
```

```
3:   #include <iostream.h>
4:
5:   // inc version for int types
6:   void inc(int& i)
7:   {
8:       i = i + 1;
9:   }
10:
11:  // inc version for double types
12:  void inc(double& x)
13:  {
14:      x = x + 1;
15:  }
16:
17:  // inc version for char types
18:  void inc(char& c)
19:  {
20:      c = c + 1;
21:  }
22:
23:  int main()
24:  {
25:      char c = 'A';
26:      int i = 10;
27:      double x = 10.2;
28:
29:      // display initial values
30:      cout << "c = " << c << endl
31:           << "i = " << i << endl
32:           << "x = " << x << endl;
33:      // invoke the inc functions
34:      inc(c);
35:      inc(i);
36:      inc(x);
37:      // display updated values
38:      cout << "After using the overloaded inc function" << endl;
39:      cout << "c = " << c << endl
40:           << "i = " << i << endl
41:           << "x = " << x << endl;
42:      return 0;
43:  }
```

5

Here is a sample session with the program in Listing 5.6:

```
c = A
i = 10
x = 10.2
```

After using the overloaded inc function:

```
c = B
i = 11
x = 11.2
```

The program in Listing 5.6 declares three versions of the overloaded void function inc. The first version of function inc has an int-typed reference parameter, i. The function increments the parameter i by 1. Because the parameter i is a reference to its arguments, the action of function inc(int&) affects the argument outside the scope of the function. The second version of function inc has a double-typed reference parameter, x. The function increments the parameter x by 1. Because the parameter x is a reference to its arguments, the action of function inc(double&) affects the argument beyond the scope of the function. The third version of function inc has a char-typed reference parameter, c. The function increments the parameter c by 1. The reference parameter affects its arguments outside the scope of the function.

The function main declares the variables c, i, and x to have the char, int, and double types, respectively. The function also initializes the variables c, i, and x using the values 'A', 10, and 10.2, respectively. The statement on lines 30 through 32 displays the initial values in variables c, i, and x. The function main invokes the overloaded function inc on lines 34 through 36. The call to function inc on line 34 ends up calling the function inc(char&) because the argument used is a char-typed variable. The call to function inc on line 35 results in calling the function inc(int&) because the argument used is an int-typed variable. The call to function inc on line 36 invokes the function inc(double&) because the argument used is a double-typed variable. The output statement on lines 39 through 41 displays the updated values in variable c, i, and x.

Summary

Today's lesson presented the various C++ operators and discussed how to use these operators to manipulate data. You learned the following:

☐ The general form for defining functions is

```
returnType functionName(parameterList)
{
    <declarations of data items>

    <function body>
    return returnValue;
}
```

You need to prototype a function if it is used by a client function before the prototyped function is defined. The general form for prototyping functions is

```
returnType functionName(parameterList);
```

You can omit the name of the parameters from the parameter list.

☐ Passing arguments with references can allow the function to modify the original variables, and it also can allow for smaller amounts of memory to be copied when a structure is passed as an argument.

☐ The const type modifier can be extremely useful in preventing arguments that have been passed by reference from being accidentally modified by a function.

□ Functions can specify a restricted list of exceptions that they will throw. The general
      form for defining this is

      ```
      returnType functionName(parameterList) throw(exceptionList)
      ```

    □ Local variables in a function support the implementation of highly independent
      functions. Declaring local variables is similar to declaring global variables.

    □ Static variables in functions are declared by placing the keyword `static` before the
      data type of the variables. Static variables are local variables that retain their values
      between function calls. In most cases, you need to initialize static variables. These
      initial values are assigned to the static variables the first time the program calls the host
      function.

    □ Macros enable you to create simple expressions that are capable of working on many
      different types of data because of their independence from the actual type-checking
      parts of the C++ compiler.

    □ Inline functions enable you to expand their statements in place, similar to macro-
      based pseudofunctions. Unlike these pseudofunctions, however, inline functions
      perform type checking.

    □ You exit functions with the `return` statement. `void` functions do not need to include
      an expression after the `return` keyword.

    □ Default arguments enable you to assign default values to the parameters of a function.
      When you omit the argument of a parameter that has a default argument, that
      argument is used automatically.

    □ Recursive functions are functions that obtain a result and/or perform a task by calling
      themselves. The number of recursive calls must be limited to avoid exhausting the
      memory resources of the computer. Consequently, every recursive function must
      examine a condition that determines the end of the recursion.

    □ Function overloading enables you to declare multiple functions that have the same
      name but different parameter lists (the parameter list is also called the function
      signature). The function's return type is not part of the function signature, because
      C++ enables you to discard the result type.

Q&A

Q Can C++ functions declare nested functions?

A No. Nested functions would actually add a lot of overhead at runtime.

Q When can I use static global variables?

A You can use them whenever you want. When the `static` keyword is applied to a
      global variable (although I still recommend that you never have any global variables in
      the first place), it tells the compiler to not make it visible to any other source file. This

prevents the same variable from being accessed from different nodes of the same project.

Q What is the memory resource used in managing calls to recursive functions?

A The runtime system uses the stack to store intermediate values, including the ones generated by calls to recursive functions. As with other memory resources, stacks have a limited space. Consequently, recursive calls with long sequence or memory-consuming arguments drain the stack space and cause runtime errors or stack over-flows.

NEW☞
TERM A *stack* is a memory location where information is inserted and removed on a last-in-first-out (LIFO) priority. This means that when you retrieve information from the stack (called pop), it's the most recent thing you put onto it (called push).

Workshop

The Workshop provides quiz questions to help you solidify your understanding of the material covered and exercises to provide you with experience in using what you've learned. Try to understand the quiz and exercise answers before continuing on to the next day's lesson. Answers are provided in Appendix A.

Quiz

1. What is the output of the following program? What can you say about the function swap?

```
#include <iostream.h>

void swap(int i, int j)
{
    int temp = i;
    i = j;
    j = temp;
}

int main()
{
    int a = 10, b = 3;
    swap(a, b);
    cout << "a = " << a << " and b = " << b;
    return 0;
}
```

2. What is the output of the following program? What can you say about the function swap?

```
#include <iostream.h>
```

```
void swap(int& i, int& j)
{
   int temp = i;
   i = j;
   j = temp;

}

int main()
{
   int a = 10, b = 3;
   swap(a, b);
   cout << "a = " << a << " and b = " << b;
   return 0;
}
```

3. What is the problem with the following overloaded functions?

```
void inc(int& i)
{
   i = i + 1;
}

void inc(int& i, int diff = 1)
{
   i = i + diff;
}
```

4. Where is the error in the following function?

```
double volume( double length,
               double width = 1,
               double height )
{
   return length * width * height
}
```

5. Where is the error in the following function?

```
void inc(int& i, int diff = 1)
{
   i = I + diff;
}
```

6. What is the error in the following program, and how can you correct it?

```
#include <iostream.h>

int main()
{
   double x = 5.2;

   cout << x << "^2 = " << sqr(x);
   return 0;
}

double sqr(double x)
{ return x * x ; }
```

7. Can you use the conditional operator to write the recursive factorial function?

Exercise

Create the program OVERLOD2.CPP by adding a second parameter with default arguments to the overloaded inc functions in the program OVERLOAD.CPP. The new parameter should represent the increment value, with a default argument of 1.

6

Arrays

Arrays are among the most utilized data structures. They enable programs to store data for later processing. Most popular programming languages support static arrays. Many languages, like C++, also support dynamic arrays.

Today, you will learn about the following topics related to static arrays:

- ☐ Using single-dimensional arrays
- ☐ Initializing single-dimensional arrays
- ☐ Declaring single-dimensional arrays as function parameters
- ☐ Sorting arrays
- ☐ Searching arrays
- ☐ Declaring multidimensional arrays
- ☐ Using multidimensional arrays
- ☐ Initializing multidimensional arrays
- ☐ Declaring multidimensional arrays as function parameters

Using Single-Dimensional Arrays

On Day 4, I provided a very simple example of using a single-dimensional array. Today, let's look at a slightly more involved example. Listing 6.1 shows the source code for the program AVERAGE1.CPP. The program uses a thirty-element numeric array and calculates its average. The program performs the following tasks:

- ☐ Prompts you to enter the number of actual data points (this value must lie in the range of valid numbers indicated by the prompting message)
- ☐ Prompts you to enter the data for the array elements
- ☐ Calculates the average of the data in the array
- ☐ Displays the average value

Type

Listing 6.1. Source code for the program AVERAGE1.CPP.

```
 1:  // C++ program that demonstrates the use of one-dimension
 2:  // arrays.  The average value of the array is calculated.
 3:
 4:  #include <iostream.h>
 5:
 6:  const int MAX = 30;
 7:
 8:  int main()
 9:  {
10:      double array[MAX];
11:      int num_elem;
```

```
12:
13:     // obtain number of data points
14:     do
15:        {
16:        cout << "Enter number of data points [2 to "
17:             << MAX << "]: ";
18:        cin >> num_elem;
19:        cout << endl;
20:        } while (num_elem < 2 || num_elem > MAX);
21:
22:     // prompt user for data
23:     for (int ix = 0; ix < num_elem; ix++)
24:        {
25:        cout << "array[" << ix << "]: ";
26:        cin >> array[ix];
27:        }
28:
29:     // Now get the average
30:     double sum = 0;
31:     for (int ix = 0; ix < num_elem; ++ix)
32:        sum += array[ix];
33:     cout << endl << "Average: " << sum / num_elem << endl;
34:     return 0;
35: }
```

Here is a sample session with the program in Listing 6.1.

```
Enter number of data points [2 to 30]: 5

array[0]: 12.5
array[1]: 45.7
array[2]: 25.6
array[3]: 14.1
array[4]: 68.4

Average: 33.26
```

The program in Listing 6.1 declares the global constant MAX as the size of the array used in the program. The function main declares the double-typed array array, on line 10, to have MAX elements. The function also declares a nonarray variable num_elem on line 11. The array variable will hold the contents of the entered numbers, where as num_elem will hold the number of items actually entered.

The do-while loop, located on lines 14 through 20, obtains the number of data points that the user wants to store in array. The output statement on lines 16 and 17 prompts for the number of data points. The output indicates the range of valid numbers, which is 2 to MAX. The statement on line 18 obtains the input and stores it in the variable num_elem, then the while clause validates your input. The clause determines if the value in num_elem is less than 2 or is greater than MAX. If this condition is true, the do-while loop iterates again to obtain a correct input value.

The for loop statement, on lines 23 through 27, prompts you to enter the data. The loop uses the control variable ix and iterates from 0 to num_elem - 1, in increments of 1. The output statement on line 25 prompts for the indicated array element. The input statement on line 26 obtains the input and stores it in the element array[ix].

The statement on line 30 declares a new variable sum, which will be used to hold the total of all the elements in the array. Line 31 starts the for loop with a simple iteration that runs from 0 to the end of the array, as set in num_elem, then line 32 actually adds the current element to the grand total in sum. Finally, the average is taken on line 33 in the middle of the output statement by dividing the number of elements in the array into its total.

Note: The program in Listing 6.1 shows how to use a for loop to process the elements of an array. The loop-continuation test uses the < operator and the value beyond the last valid index. You can use the <= operator followed by the last index. For example, you can write the data-input loop as

```
22:     // prompt user for data
23:     for (ix = 0; ix <= (num_elem — 1); i++)
24:         {
25:         cout << "array[" << ix << "]: ";
26:         cin >> array[ix];
27:         }
```

This form is not popular, however, because it requires an additional operator, whereas the condition ix < num_elem does not.

DO	DON'T

DO write the loop-continuation expression so that it uses the minimum number of operators. This approach reduces the code size and speeds up loop execution.

DON'T use the <= operator in the loop-continuation condition, unless using the operator helps you write an expression that minimizes the number of operations or makes the purpose of the loop clearer.

Initializing Single-Dimensional Arrays

C++ enables you to initialize arrays and is flexible about the initialization. You need to enclose the list of initializing values in a pair of open and close braces ({ }). The list is comma-delimited and may continue on multiple lines. If there are fewer items in the initializing list than there are array elements, the compiler assigns 0 to the balance of the array elements. By contrast, if the list of initializing values has more items than the number of array elements, the compiler flags a compile-time error.

The next program, Listing 6.2, modifies the last program to supply data internally. Consequently, it eliminates the steps that prompt you for the number of data points and the data itself. The program simply displays the array elements (obtained from the initialization list) and the average value for the data. Although this program does not interact with the user, it offers a version that stores data in the source code. You can edit the program periodically to add, edit, and delete data before recalculating a new average value.

Listing 6.2. Source code for the program AVERAGE2.CPP.

```
1:  // C++ program that demonstrates the use of one-dimension
2:  // arrays.  The average value of the array is calculated.
3:  // The elements of the array are pre-assigned.
4:
5:  #include <iostream.h>
6:
7:  const int MAX = 10;
8:
9:  int main()
10: {
11:     double array[MAX] = { 12.2, 45.4, 67.2, 12.2, 34.6, 87.4,
12:                           83.6, 12.3, 14.8, 55.5 };
13:     int num_elem = MAX;
14:
15:     double sum = 0;
16:     for (int ix = 0; ix < num_elem; ++ix)
17:         {
18:         sum += array[ix];
19:         cout << "array[" << ix << "]: " << array[ix] << endl;
20:         }
21:     cout << endl << "Average: " << sum / num_elem << endl;
22:     return 0;
23: }
```

Here is a sample session with the program in Listing 6.2.

```
array[0]: 12.2
array[1]: 45.4
array[2]: 67.2
array[3]: 12.2
array[4]: 34.6
array[5]: 87.4
array[6]: 83.6
array[7]: 12.3
array[8]: 14.8
array[9]: 55.5

Average: 42.52
```

Now, focus on the initialization of array in Listing 6.2. Line 11 contains the declaration of array and its initialization. The initializing list, which runs to line 12, is enclosed in a pair of braces and has comma-delimited values. The statement on line 13 declares the variable num_elem and initializes it to MAX. The rest of the program resembles parts of the program in Listing 6.1.

If you are somewhat dismayed by the fact that you have to count the exact number of initializing values, then I have some good news for you: C++ enables you to size an array automatically by using the number of items in the corresponding initializing list. Consequently, you don't need to place a number in the square brackets of the array, and you can let the compiler do the work for you.

DO	**DON'T**
DO include dummy values in the initializing list, if the initialized array needs to expand later. **DON'T** rely on counting the number of items in the initializing list to provide the data for the number of array elements.	

In order to use this feature, simply modify lines 11 through 13 to read as follows:

```
double array[] = { 12.2, 45.4, 67.2, 12.2, 34.6, 87.4,
                   83.6, 12.3, 14.8, 55.5 };
int num_elem = sizeof(array) / sizeof(array[0]);
```

Note that you aren't using MAX anymore, so you can go ahead and delete line 7. The interesting part now is how num_elem is set. This is accomplished by first determining the size of the array. Unfortunately, this doesn't simply give the number of elements in the array, but rather the number of bytes of memory used. In order to get the number of elements, you must divide the total size of the array by the size of an individual element. You can use this method to obtain the size of any array of any data type.

Array Parameters in Functions

C++ enables you to declare function parameters that are arrays. In fact, C++ permits you to be either specific or general about the size of the array parameter. You can specify the size of the array in the parameter declaration, or you can use empty brackets with the array parameter.

A Fixed-Array Parameter

The general syntax for declaring a fixed-array parameter is

```
type parameterName[arraySize]
```

Examples

```
int minArray(int arr[100]);
void sort(unsigned dayNum[7]);
```

An Open-Array Parameter

The general syntax for declaring an open-array parameter is

```
type parameterName[]
```

Examples

```
int minArray(int arr[], int num_elem);
void sort(unsigned dayNum[], int num_elem);
```

Note in these examples how each function has an extra parameter that is used to hold the number of elements in the array. This is because the function doesn't really know how many elements there are in the array, and it needs to be told with an extra parameter.

DO	DON'T
DO use open-array parameters in functions.	
DON'T forget to check the upper bound of an open-array parameter in general-purpose functions.	

Look at a simple example. Listing 6.3 shows the source code for the program MINMAX.CPP. The program performs the following tasks:

6

☐ Prompts you to enter the number of data points, which ranges from 2 to 10

☐ Prompts you to enter the integer values for the arrays

☐ Displays the smallest value in the array

☐ Displays the largest value in the array

Listing 6.3. Source code for the program MINMAX.CPP.

```
1:  // C++ program that determines the largest
2:  // and smallest elements of arrays
3:
```

continues

Listing 6.3. continued

```
4:   #include <iostream.h>
5:
6:   const int MIN = 2;
7:   const int MAX = 10;
8:
9:   int getNumPoints(int low, int high)
10: {
11:     int numPoints;
12:     do
13:         {
14:         cout << "Enter number of data points ["
15:             << low << " to "
16:             << high << "]: ";
17:         cin >> numPoints;
18:         } while (numPoints < low ¦¦ numPoints > high);
19:     return numPoints;
20: }
21:
22: int findMin(int array[], int size)
23: {
24:     int small = array[0];
25:     for (int i = 1; i < size; i++)
26:         if (array[i] < small)
27:             small = array[i];
28:     return small;
29: }
30:
31: int findMax(int array[], int size)
32: {
33:     int big = array[0];
34:     for (int i = 1; i < size; i++)
35:         if (array[i] > big)
36:             big = array[i];
37:     return big;
38: }
39:
40: int main()
41: {
42:     int array[MAX], num_elem;
43:
44:     num_elem = getNumPoints(MIN, MAX);
45:
46:     // Prompt user for data
47:     for (int i = 0; i < num_elem; i++)
48:         {
49:         cout << "array[" << i << "]: ";
50:         cin >> array[i];
51:         }
52:
53:     cout << "Smallest value in array is "
54:         << findMin(array, num_elem) << endl
55:         << "Biggest value in array is "
56:         << findMax(array, num_elem) << endl;
57:     return 0;
58: }
```

Here is a sample session with the program in Listing 6.3.

```
Enter number of data points [2 to 10]: 5
arr[0]: 55
arr[1]: 69
arr[2]: 47
arr[3]: 85
arr[4]: 14
Smallest value in array is 14
Biggest value in array is 85
```

The program in Listing 6.3 declares the global constants MIN and MAX, on lines 6 and 7. These constants are used to limit the number of data points the user can enter. To help with the description of the program, I'm going to jump to function main starting on line 40. It begins by declaring the array of integers array with a dimension of MAX and the integer num_elem, then line 44 calls the helper function getNumPoints with MIN and MAX as parameters, assigning the result to num_elem. I'll go over getNumPoints momentarily.

Now that the program knows how many data points to use, it runs through a loop on lines 47 through 51 to obtain these data points, storing them in the array. Finally, the helper functions findMin and findMax are called from the cout statement that starts on line 53. In each case, array and num_elem are passed as parameters to specify the name of the array to search and the number of elements in that array.

Jumping back to line 9, you encounter the function getNumPoints. It takes two parameters: low and high. The former represents the lowest number allowed for input, and the latter is the highest. From there you see a now-familiar loop that keeps asking for a number until it's between the two limits specified in the function's parameters. Up until now you've seen bits of code like this embedded in the main function, but it's actually an often-used and useful bit of code. When you have some code that you can imagine being useful in a generic way, it's a good idea to separate that code out to its own function, making it as generic as possible.

Next are the two functions findMin, which starts on line 22, and findMax, which starts on line 31. These functions are almost identical except that one loops through the passed array, searching for the lowest element of the array (line 26 of findMin), and the other searches for the highest element (line 35 or findMax). You should note that each function accepts not only the array as a parameter but also the number of elements in that array. This is because there's no way to know the number of elements in an array without explicitly storing that value in a separate variable.

An important lesson to learn here is how you can write subordinate functions that do all the dirty work for you, while the main part of the program simply calls these functions in the appropriate sequence with the appropriate parameters to get the job done. A case in point is how the findMin and findMax functions do all the searching of an array for the smallest and largest elements, whereas the main function simply calls those from an output statement.

Sorting Arrays

Sorting and searching are the most common nonnumerical operations for arrays. Sorting an array typically arranges its elements in ascending order. The process uses parts or all of the value in each element to determine the precedence of the elements in the array. Searching for data in sorted arrays is much easier than in unordered arrays.

Computer scientists have spent much time and effort studying and creating methods for sorting arrays. A comprehensive discussion of these methods is beyond the scope of this book. I will only mention that some favorite array-sorting methods include the QuickSort, Shell-Metzner sort, heap sort, and the Comb sort. The QuickSort method is the fastest method, in general, but requires some operational overhead. The Shell-Metzner and Comb sort methods do not require similar overhead. The example in this section uses a simpler sort method called the Bubble sort. It is by no means the fastest or the most efficient, but it's much easier to understand and follow.

Look at a program that sorts an array of integers. Listing 6.4 shows the source code for the program SORT.CPP. The program performs the following tasks:

- [ ] Prompts you to enter the number of data points
- [ ] Prompts you to enter the integer values for the array
- [ ] Displays the elements of the unordered array
- [ ] Displays the elements of the sorted array

 Listing 6.4. Source code for the program SORT.CPP.

```
1:  // C++ program that sorts arrays using the Bubble sort method
2:
3:  #include <iostream.h>
4:
5:  const int MIN = 2;
6:  const int MAX = 10;
7:
8:  int getNumPoints(int low, int high)
9:  {
10:    int numPoints;
11:    do
12:      {
13:      cout << "Enter number of data points ["
14:           << low << " to "
15:           << high << "]: ";
16:      cin >> numPoints;
17:      } while (numPoints < low || numPoints > high);
18:    return numPoints;
19: }
20:
21: void inputArray(int intArr[], int num)
22: {
23:    // prompt user for data
```

```
24:     for (int i = 0; i < num; i++)
25:         {
26:         cout << "array[" << i << "]: ";
27:         cin >> intArr[i];
28:         }
29: }
30:
31: void showArray(int intArr[], int num)
32: {
33:     for (int i = 0; i < num; i++)
34:         {
35:         cout.width(5);
36:         cout << intArr[i] << " ";
37:         }
38:     cout << endl;
39: }
40:
41: void bubbleSort(int intArr[], int num)
42: {
43:     for (int i = 1; i < num; ++i)
44:         for (int j = 0; j <= i; ++j)
45:             if (intArr[i] < intArr[j])
46:                 {
47:                 int temp = intArr[i];
48:                 intArr[i] = intArr[j];
49:                 intArr[j] = temp;
50:                 }
51: }
52:
53: int main()
54: {
55:     int arr[MAX];
56:     int num_elem;
57:
58:     num_elem = getNumPoints(MIN, MAX);
59:     inputArray(arr, num_elem);
60:     cout << "Unordered array is:" << endl;
61:     showArray(arr, num_elem);
62:     bubbleSort(arr, num_elem);
63:     cout << endl << "Sorted array is:" << endl;
64:     showArray(arr, num_elem);
65:     return 0;
66: }
```

6

Here is a sample session with the program in Listing 6.4.

```
Enter number of data points [2 to 10]: 10
arr[0]: 55
arr[1]: 68
arr[2]: 74
arr[3]: 15
arr[4]: 28
arr[5]: 23
arr[6]: 69
arr[7]: 95
```

```
arr[8]: 22
arr[9]: 33
Unordered array is:
    55    68    74    15    28    23    69    95    22    33

Sorted array is:
    15    22    23    28    33    55    68    69    74    95
```

The program in Listing 6.4 declares the constants MIN and MAX on lines 5 and 6. The constant MAX defines the size of the array used in the program, whereas MIN defines the minimum number of data points allowed for that array. These two values are used in main on line 58 in the call to getNumPoints. This is the same function from MINMAX.CPP that obtains the number of data points to use in the array.

The next function is inputArray starting on line 21. This contains a bit of code that you should recognize from MINMAX.CPP; it obtains the actual data points to be stored in the array. Note how it's been pulled out into a rather generic function that takes an array and the number of data points as parameters. This function can now be simply copied into future programs that need to obtain array elements.

Note: The function inputArray illustrates that C++ functions treat array parameters as if they were references to their arguments, because these parameters affect the values in the arguments beyond the scope of the functions. What's really happening is that the base address of the array is being passed to the function rather than the whole array itself. As you learned earlier, when a function receives a pointer to something, the function ends up manipulating the original object. This makes the manipulation of arrays by functions very easy.

The function showArray, starting on line 31, displays the meaningful data in an array. It's a rather simple function that simply iterates through the array and outputs the contents of each array element, separated by a space, on the same line. You should note the statement on line 35 that sets the output width to 5. This width says that any integer that's output will take up five spaces. If the number isn't wide enough on its own (if it doesn't already have five digits), it will be padded with spaces before the number so that it takes up five characters in the output.

The next function, bubbleSort, starts on line 41. It sorts the elements of an array using the Bubble sort method. This function, as do all the others in this program that manipulate an array, takes two parameters: the open-array parameter intArr and the parameter num. The Bubble sort method can be thought of as a bubble that slowly works its way to the top of the array, sorting values as it goes. There's a main loop that runs the length of the array, and then an inner loop that starts at the beginning and goes on up to the current location of the outer loop, exchanging values it determines to be out of place. A great way to get a feel for how this works would be to

insert a call to showArray in the function so that you can watch as values percolate into their appropriately sorted positions.

> **Note:** The function bubbleSort illustrates how array parameters can pass data to and from a function. The function bubbleSort receives a pointer to an unordered array, sorts it, and returns to the function's caller with the pointer now pointing at the newly sorted array. The compiler supports this feature by passing a copy of the address of the array to the function. Thus, the function need not explicitly return the array because it is working with the original data and not a copy.

The function main performs the various program tasks by calling the functions mentioned earlier. The function declares the array arr and the simple variable num_elem on lines 55 and 56. The statement on line 58 calls function getNumPoints to obtain the number of data points the user wants to store in the array. The statement assigns the result of the function to variable num_elem. The statement on line 59 then fills in the array by calling inputArray. The output statement on line 60 displays a message indicating that the program is about to display the elements of the unordered array, then it goes ahead and displays that array on line 61. The statement on line 62 calls the function bubbleSort to sort the elements in array arr. The output statement on line 63 displays a message indicating that the program is about to display the elements of the sorted array, then displays that array on line 64.

Searching Arrays

Searching arrays is another important nonnumerical operation. Because arrays can be sorted or unordered, there is a general category of search methods for each. The simplest search method is the *linear search method.* This will work on any array, no matter what order the elements are in. Another rather simple (and certainly more efficient) method is the versatile *binary search method.* Unfortunately, however, the binary search works only on sorted arrays.

NEW☞ TERM The *linear search method* sequentially examines the array elements, looking for an element that matches the search value. If the sought value is not in the array, the linear search method will have examined all of the array's elements.

NEW The *binary search method* takes advantage of the order in the array. Instead of using brute
TERM force by starting at the beginning and moving on through the entire array element by
element in its search, the binary search can start in the middle. If the element it finds in the
middle matches the search element, then it can stop right there. If the match fails, however, the
search can then decide on which side of the failed match to continue the search. Depending upon
whether or not the search element is greater than or less than the last check, the search can limit
the rest of its search to either all the numbers above or below the last check. This eliminates a
full half of the array right there. When the search continues with the other half, the same method
is applied on that smaller portion, dividing it in half again. This is where the binary search gets
its name: from always dividing the search by two.

All told, if the search value has no match in the examined array, the binary method makes far
fewer examinations than the linear search method. The binary search method is the most
efficient general-purpose search method for sorted arrays.

DO	DON'T
DO use the unordered-array search method when you are not sure that the array is sorted.	
DON'T use sorted-array search methods with unordered arrays. The results of such searches are not reliable.	

Look at a program that searches an array of integers. Listing 6.5 shows the source code for the
program SEARCH.CPP. I created this program by adding functions and operations to the
program SORT.CPP. The program performs the following tasks:

1. Prompts you to enter the number of data points.

2. Prompts you to enter the integer values for the array.

3. Displays the elements of the unordered array.

4. Asks you if you want to search for data in the unordered array. (If you type characters
   other than **Y** or **y**, the program resumes at step 8.)

5. Prompts you for a search value.

6. Displays the search outcome. (If the program finds a matching element, it displays the
   index of that element; otherwise, the program tells you that it found no match for the
   search value.)

7. Resumes at step 4.

8. Displays the elements of the sorted array.

9. Asks you if you want to search for data in the unordered array. (If you type characters other than **Y** or **y** the program ends.)

10. Prompts you for a search value.

11. Displays the search outcome. (If the program finds a matching element, it displays the index of that element; otherwise, the program tells you that it found no match for the search value.)

12. Resumes at step 9.

 Listing 6.5. Source code for the program SEARCH.CPP.

```cpp
1:   // C++ program that searches arrays using the linear
2:   // and binary searches methods
3:
4:   #include <ctype.h>
5:   #include <iostream.h>
6:   #include <stdlib.h>
7:
8:   typedef int (*SearchFunc)(int,int[],int);
9:
10:  const int MIN = 2;
11:  const int MAX = 10;
12:  const int NOT_FOUND = -1;
13:
14:  // Prompt user for number of array elements
15:  int getNumPoints(int low, int high)
16:  {
17:      int numPoints;
18:      do
19:          {
20:          cout << "Enter number of data points ["
21:               << low << " to "
22:               << high << "]: ";
23:          cin >> numPoints;
24:          } while (numPoints < low || numPoints > high);
25:      return numPoints;
26:  }
27:
28:  // Prompt user for array data
29:  void inputArray(int intArr[], int num)
30:  {
31:      for (int i = 0; i < num; i++)
32:          {
33:          cout << "array[" << i << "]: ";
34:          cin >> intArr[i];
35:          }
36:  }
37:
```

 6

continues

Listing 6.5. continued

```
38:    // Display the contents of an array
39:    void showArray(int intArr[], int num)
40:    {
41:        for (int i = 0; i < num; i++)
42:            {
43:            cout.width(5);
44:            cout << intArr[i] << " ";
45:            }
46:        cout << endl;
47:    }
48:
49:    // Linear search routine
50:    int linearSearch(int searchVal, int intArr[], int num)
51:    {
52:        for (int i = 0; i < num; ++i)
53:            if (searchVal == intArr[i])
54:                return i;
55:        return NOT_FOUND;
56:    }
57:
58:    // Recursive binary search sub-function
59:    int binSearch(int searchVal, int intArr[], int low, int high)
60:    {
61:        int middle = (low + high) / 2;
62:
63:        if (low > high)
64:            return NOT_FOUND;
65:        else if (searchVal == intArr[middle])
66:            return middle;
67:        else if (searchVal > intArr[middle])
68:            return binSearch(searchVal, intArr, middle + 1, high);
69:        else
70:            return binSearch(searchVal, intArr, low, middle - 1);
71:    }
72:
73:    // Main entry point for binary search
74:    int binarySearch(int searchVal, int intArr[], int n)
75:    {
76:        return binSearch(searchVal, intArr, 0, n - 1);
77:    }
78:
79:    // Check for continuing search
80:    bool shouldSearch(const char* searchType)
81:    {
82:        char ch;
83:
84:        cout << "Search in " << searchType << " array? (Y/N) ";
85:        cin >> ch;
86:        return tolower(ch) == 'y';
87:    }
88:
89:    // Manage the search test
90:    void searchArray( int intArr[],
91:                        int num,
```

```
 92:                    const char* searchType,
 93:                    SearchFunc search )
 94: {
 95:    int searchVal, index;
 96:    char ch;
 97:
 98:    while (shouldSearch(searchType))
 99:       {
100:       cout << "Enter search value: ";
101:       cin >> searchVal;
102:       index = search(searchVal, intArr, num);
103:       if (index != NOT_FOUND)
104:          cout << "Found matching element at index " << index << endl;
105:       else
106:          cout << "No match found" << endl;
107:       }
108: }
109:
110: // Compare two integers
111: int intCmp(const void* item1, const void* item2)
112:{
113:    return *(int*)item1 - *(int*)item2;
114: }
115:
116: int main()
117: {
118:    int arr[MAX];
119:    int num_elem;
120:
121:    num_elem = getNumPoints(MIN, MAX);
122:    inputArray(arr, num_elem);
123:
124:    cout << "Unordered array is:" << endl;
125:    showArray(arr, num_elem);
126:    searchArray(arr, num_elem, "unordered", linearSearch);
127:
128:    qsort(arr, num_elem, sizeof(arr[0]), intCmp);
129:    cout << endl << "Sorted array is:" << endl;
130:    showArray(arr, num_elem);
131:    searchArray(arr, num_elem, "sorted", binarySearch);
132:    return 0;
133: }
```

6

Here is a sample session with the program in Listing 6.5.

```
Enter number of data points [2 to 10]: 5
arr[0]: 85
arr[1]: 41
arr[2]: 55
arr[3]: 67
arr[4]: 48
Unordered array is:
    85    41    55    67    48
Search in unordered array? (Y/N) y
Enter search value: 55
```

```
Found matching element at index 2
Search in unordered array? (Y/N) y
Enter search value: 41
Found matching element at index 1
Search in unordered array? (Y/N) n

Sorted array is:
    41    48    55    67    85
Search in sorted array? (Y/N) y
Enter search value: 55
Found matching element at index 2
Search in sorted array? (Y/N) y
Enter search value: 67
Found matching element at index 3
Search in sorted array? (Y/N) n
```

The program in Listing 6.5 begins with the definition of the function pointer SearchFunc, which is then used to pass the name of a function as a parameter to another function. This allows the program to specify a number of different sorting methods as functions, and then just pass those functions to other controlling functions.

NEW☞ TERM A *function pointer* is exactly what the name implies: it is a pointer to a function. It's most useful when you want to store a list of functions in an array or pass a function to a function.

One of the most common methods of defining a function pointer is to first create a type for it with a typedef statement that takes the following form:

```
typedef <returnType> (*<funcType>)(<parameterList>);
```

Take the example from line 8 of Listing 6.5, which defines a function pointer type resembling the functions that start on lines 50 and 74.

The two constants MIN and MAX, declared on lines 10 and 11, are identical to the previous listings and are used in this program in the same way. The constant NOT_FOUND, declared on line 12, is used as a return value from the search functions when they are unable to locate the search criteria.

The three functions getNumPoints, inputArray, and showArray are all identical to their definitions in earlier listings, so I will skip them and move on to the linearSearch function. This is very simplistic and merely takes a value to be searched, the array in which to search, and the number of elements in the array. The code itself just runs through a quick for loop that compares searchVal with each element in intArr, returning the index if it's found. If the for loop exits without finding a match, then NOT_FOUND is returned to signify the lack of success.

The binary search routine binSearch that starts on line 59 is a little more complicated. Instead of just taking the number of elements in the array as parameters, this takes both the lower and upper bounds to search in variables low and high, respectively. From there starts the recursive

function (see Day 5 for more information on recursive functions) that first makes sure on line 63 the search area is valid; if low is greater than high, then you've reached the end of your search and line 64 returns NOT_FOUND to signify failure. Line 65 checks to see if the middle element of the search area matches your criteria. If so, then line 66 returns that index. If you haven't yet found a match, then lines 67 through 70 figure out on which side of the middle element your search criteria will be found and then recursively call the binSearch function with the new search area to be checked.

The binarySearch function that starts on line 74 merely calls the binary search function binSearch that starts on line 59. This entry point is used because the standard search function normally takes only the number of elements, whereas the binary search requires a lower and upper bounds. So line 76 simply calls the real binary search function with a lower bound of 0, the beginning of the array, and an upper bound of n - 1, the highest element of the array.

The function shouldSearch that starts on line 80 is a function whose sole purpose is to ask the user whether or not he or she wishes to perform a search. It would normally be embedded in the code that needs it, but in this program, the particular function that uses it does so twice. Because of this, I can make things a little easier by removing that duplicated code and placing it in a single function. To help make it as generic as possible, shouldSearch takes a character array sortType that holds the type of sort to be performed and then uses this when asking the user whether or not to perform the search.

Now comes searchArray, which manages the actual search. You should note that it takes as parameters the array, the number of elements in that array, the type of search (so that it can be passed to shouldSearch) and the function pointer search to be used for the search itself. The function just loops so long as the function shouldSearch reports that the user wants to perform a search, then prompts the user for a value to use in the search. Line 102 shows how to use the function pointer: just call search as if it were a regular function name. The rest of searchArray just reports on the results of the call to search.

The intCmp function that starts on line 111 may seem a little mysterious at first. It takes two void* arguments, converts them to int* and then returns the difference between what they point to. The difference is a way of determining whether one item is greater or less than the other. I'll describe what this function is used for in a moment.

The main function is just about what you'd expect by now. It calls all the functions created so far in their appropriate order. Note on lines 126 and 131 how just the names of the linearSearch and binarySearch functions are passed as the final parameter to searchArray. This helps to illustrate the rule that a function's name is really just a function pointer, and it becomes a function *call* only when you place the open and close parentheses after its name.

You might have noticed that, although the array gets sorted, you haven't actually written any sort routine. This is because C++ provides a sort routine for you. It's called `qsort`, and it implements the Quicksort method. Line 128 shows how the `qsort` function is called; you pass it the array, the number of elements in the array, the size of each element in the array, and a pointer to a function that can be used to determine the order of each item in the array—in this case `intCmp`. I use `sizeof(arr[0])` here instead of `sizeof(int)` because it makes it easier to change the type of elements in the array later on if I feel like it.

The *qsort* Function

The general syntax for the `qsort` function is

```
void qsort(void* base, size_t num_elems, size_t width,
        int (*fcmp)(const void* elem1, const void* elem2) );
```

The first parameter `base` is the base of the array to be sorted, `num_elems` is the number of elements in the array to be sorted, `width` is the size of each element in the array, and `fcmp` is a pointer to a function that knows how to compare the individual elements of the array. The comparison function receives two `const void*` parameters, which it will then need to convert into the appropriate type for comparison. The return value of the comparison function is interpreted by `qsort` as follows:

Comparison	`fcmp` Return Value
`*elem1 < *elem2`	an integer less than 0
`*elem1 == *elem2`	0
`*elem1 > *elem2`	an integer greater than 0

In the comparison, the less-than symbol means the left element should appear before the right element in the final, sorted sequence. If you wish to reverse this order, then you should exchange the return value from `fcmp` between the greater-than and less-than comparisons.

While I'm at it, now that you've seen how they work, you should know that both the linear and binary search are also included with the C++ language.

The *lfind* and *bsearch* Functions

The general syntax of the `lfind` and `bsearch` functions are

```
void* lfind(const void* key, void* base, size_t* num, size_t* width,
        int (*fcmp)(const void* elem1, const void* elem2) );
void* bsearch(const void* key, void* base, size_t* num, size_t* width,
        int (*fcmp)(const void* elem1, const void* elem2) );
```

You'll first note that the two functions are identical in parameters. The `key` parameter is a pointer to the element to be searched for, `base` is the base of the array, `num` is the number of elements in the array, `width` represents the size of each element in the array, and `fcmp` is a pointer to a function that is used to compare the individual elements. Like the fcmp function from qsort, this version takes pointers to the elements to be compared and then returns an integer that's either less than, greater than, or equal to 0, depending upon the relationship of the two elements being compared.

The functions return a pointer to the actual element in the array, rather than an index into the array. If the element doesn't actually exist in the array, the function returns 0. If you wish to obtain the index in the array, you can use the following format.

```
index = (searchRslt - arrayBase) / sizeof(arrayBase[0]);
```

You might also be interested in the lsearch function. It looks exactly like the lfind and bsearch functions, but if it doesn't find the key in the array, it adds that element to the array. Thus, the return value of this function will always be nonzero.

It is very important to realize that all the various sorting and searching functions built into C++ require the array to be contiguous. This means that all the elements of the array must be next to each other with no gaps. So far, that's all you've worked with, but there are other ways of storing lists of items than just simple arrays. One of the most common is a linked list, in which each element of the list is created as needed and so is not necessarily next to any of the other elements in the list. The built-in search and sort mechanisms will not work on these types of data structures.

Multidimensional Arrays

In a *multidimensional array*, each additional dimension provides an additional access attribute. Two-dimensional arrays (or matrices, if you prefer) are the most popular type of multidimensional array. Three-dimensional arrays are used less frequently than matrices, and so on.

NEW☞ TERM   *Multidimensional arrays* are supersets of the single-dimensional arrays.

6

Two-Dimensional and Three-Dimensional Arrays

The general syntax for declaring two-dimensional and three-dimensional arrays is

```
type array [size1][size2];
type array [size1][size2][size3];
```

As with simple arrays, each dimension has a lower bound index of 0, and the declaration defines the number of elements in each dimension.

Examples

```
double matrixA[100][10];
char table[41][22][3];
int index[7][12];
```

It is important to understand how C++ stores the elements of a multidimensional array. Most compilers store these elements in a contiguous fashion (that is, as one long array). The runtime code calculates where a sought element is located in that long array. To explain the storage scheme of multidimensional arrays, I'll start by employing a convention for referencing the indices of the different dimensions. The following specifies the dimension numbering and the concept of high- and low-order dimensions. Following is a six-dimensional array, an extreme case that is a good example:

```
     1     2    3    4    5    6    ←  dimension number
M   [20]  [7]  [5]  [3]  [2]  [2]
higher dimension order →
```

The first element of the array M is M[0][0][0][0][0][0] and is stored at the first memory location of array M. The array M is stored in a contiguous block of 8,400 elements ($20 \times 7 \times 5 \times 3 \times 2 \times 2$). The location in that contiguous block stores the element at index 1 in the highest dimension number, dimension 6 (that is, M[0][0][0][0][0][1]). The location of the next elements in the contiguous block stores the subsequent elements in dimension 6 until the upper limit of dimension 6 is reached. Reaching this limit bumps the index of dimension 5 by 1 and resets the index of dimension 6 to 0. This process is repeated until every element in a multidimensional array is accessed. You can compare this storage scheme to looking at a gasoline pump meter when refueling your car; the right digits turn the fastest, and the left digits turn the slowest.

Here is another example that uses a three-dimensional array, M[3][2][2].

```
M[0][0][0]      <— the starting memory address
M[0][0][1]      <— 3rd dimension is filled
M[0][1][0]
M[0][1][1]      <— 2nd and 3rd dimensions are filled
M[1][0][0]
M[1][0][1]      <— 3rd dimension is filled
M[1][1][0]
M[1][1][1]      <— 2nd and 3rd dimensions are filled
M[2][0][0]
M[2][0][1]      <— 3rd dimension is filled
M[2][1][0]
M[2][1][1]      <— all dimensions are filled
```

Consider an example that illustrates basic matrix manipulation. Listing 6.6 shows the source code for the MATRIX1.CPP program. The program manages a matrix that contains up to 10 columns and 30 rows and performs the following tasks:

☐ Prompts you to enter the number of rows

☐ Prompts you to enter the number of columns

☐ Prompts you to enter the matrix elements

☐ Calculates and displays the average for each column in the matrix

Type Listing 6.6. Source code for the program MATRIX1.CPP.

```
1:  // C++ program that demonstrates the use of two-dimension arrays.
2:  // The average value of each matrix column is calculated.
3:
4:  #include <iostream.h>
5:
6:  const int MIN_COL = 1;
7:  const int MAX_COL = 10;
8:  const int MIN_ROW = 2;
9:  const int MAX_ROW = 30;
10:
11: // Prompt user for number of array elements
12: int getNumPoints(const char* elemType, int low, int high)
13: {
14:     int numPoints;
15:     do
16:         {
17:         cout << "Enter number of "
18:              << elemType << " ["
19:              << low << " to "
20:              << high << "]: ";
21:         cin >> numPoints;
22:         } while (numPoints < low ¦¦ numPoints > high);
23:     return numPoints;
24: }
25:
26: int main()
27: {
28:     double matrix[MAX_ROW][MAX_COL];
29:     double sum, average;
30:     int rows, cols;
31:
32:     // get the number of rows and columns
33:     rows = getNumPoints("rows", MIN_ROW, MAX_ROW);
34:     cols = getNumPoints("columns", MIN_COL, MAX_COL);
35:
36:     // get the matrix elements
37:     for (int i = 0; i < rows; i++)
38:         {
39:         for (int j = 0; j < cols; j++)
40:             {
41:             cout << "matrix[" << i << "][" << j << "]: ";
42:             cin >> matrix[i][j];
43:             }
44:         cout << endl;
45:         }
46:
47:     // obtain the sum of each column
48:     for (int j = 0; j < cols; j++)
49:         {
```

continues

197

Listing 6.6. continued

```
50:        sum = 0.0;                    // initialize sum
51:        for (int i = 0; i < rows; i++)
52:            sum += matrix[i][j];
53:        average = sum / rows;
54:        cout << "Average for column " << j
55:             << " = " << average << endl;
56:        }
57:    return 0;
58: }
```

Here is a sample session with the program in Listing 6.6.

```
Enter number of rows [2 to 30]: 3
Enter number of columns [1 to 10]: 3
matrix[0][0]: 1
matrix[0][1]: 2
matrix[0][2]: 3

matrix[1][0]: 4
matrix[1][1]: 5
matrix[1][2]: 6

matrix[2][0]: 7
matrix[2][1]: 8
matrix[2][2]: 9

Average for column 0 = 4
Average for column 1 = 5
Average for column 2 = 6
```

The program in Listing 6.6 declares the global constants MIN_COL, MAX_COL, MIN_ROW, and MAX_ROW on lines 6 through 9. These constants define the dimensions of the matrix that is created in the program, much like the simple MIN and MAX were used in previous listings.

The function getNumPoints that begins on line 12 is similar to the previous versions from previous examples, except this time I've added a character pointer that contains a description of the type of data for which the number of points is being requested. This is because you're going to want to use this function to obtain the number of points for both the rows and the columns of the matrix. You can see how this is used on lines 33 and 34, where the function is called from main.

Line 37 shows the beginning of the loop that obtains the elements of the matrix. This would normally be in a function, like previous examples, except I'm using a multidimensional array here, and you haven't yet learned how to pass one to a function (it's different from a simple one-dimensional array). This just iterates through two nested loops: one that counts off the rows, then one inside that goes through each of the elements in the columns of each row.

Finally, the bit starting on line 48 actually performs the averaging of the columns. You simply run through a for loop starting on line 48 that iterates through the columns, then run through the for loop starting on line 51 that adds up the entry from each row in the columns.

As you can see, accessing the multidimensional arrays is pretty much just the same as accessing single-dimensional arrays, except that there are more brackets in which you need to put a number or variable.

Initializing Multidimensional Arrays

C++ enables you to initialize a multidimensional array in a manner similar to single-dimensional arrays. You need to use a list of values that appear in the same sequence in which the elements of the initialized multidimensional array are stored. Now you realize the importance of understanding how C++ stores the elements of a multidimensional array; without this knowledge, you would have no idea in what order you would need to have your initialized data. The previous C++ program was modified to use an initializing list that internally supplies the program with data. Consequently, the program does not prompt you for any data. Rather, the program displays the values of the matrix and the average for its columns. Listing 6.7. shows the source code for the MATRIX2.CPP program.

Listing 6.7. Source code for the program MATRIX2.CPP.

```
1:  // C++ program that demonstrates the use of two-dimension arrays.
2:  // The average value of each matrix column is calculated.
3:
4:  #include <iostream.h>
5:
6:  const int MAX_COL = 3;
7:  const int MAX_ROW = 3;
8:
9:  int main()
10: {
11:     double matrix[MAX_ROW][MAX_COL] =
12:        {  1, 2, 3,      // row #1
13:           4, 5, 6,      // row #2
14:           7, 8, 9       // row #3
15:        };
16:     double sum, average;
17:     int rows = MAX_ROW, cols = MAX_COL;
18:
19:     // display the matrix elements
20:     cout << "Matrix is:" << endl;
21:     for (int i = 0; i < rows; i++)
22:        {
23:        for (int j = 0; j < cols; j++)
24:           {
25:           cout.width(4);
```

continues

199

Listing 6.7. continued

```
26:            cout.precision(1);
27:            cout << matrix[i][j] << " ";
28:            }
29:        cout << endl;
30:        }
31:    cout << endl;
32:
33:    // obtain the sum of each column
34:    for (int j = 0; j < cols; j++)
35:        {
36:        sum = 0.0;                // initialize sum
37:        for (int i = 0; i < rows; i++)
38:            sum += matrix[i][j];
39:        average = sum / rows;
40:        cout << "Average for column " << j
41:             << " = " << average << endl;
42:        }
43:    return 0;
44: }
```

Here is a sample session with the program in Listing 6.7.

```
Matrix is:
1    2    3
4    5    6
7    8    9

Average for column 0 = 4
Average for column 1 = 5
Average for column 2 = 6
```

The program in Listing 6.7 declares the matrix `matrix` and initializes its elements with a list of values. Notice that the program declares the constants `MAX_COL` and `MAX_ROW` with values that match the size of the initialized matrix. The declaration statement on lines 12 through 14 shows the elements assigned to each row. The function `main` also initializes the variables `rows` and `columns` with the constants `MAX_ROW` and `MAX_COL`, respectively. The function performs this initialization for two reasons. First, the program no longer prompts you to enter values for the variables `rows` and `columns`. Second, the program is working with a custom-fit size for matrix `matrix`.

The program uses the nested `for` loops on lines 21 through 30 to display the elements of the matrix. The second pair of nested `for` loops on lines 34 through 42 calculates the average for each matrix column with the same method as Listing 6.6.

Multidimensional Array Parameters

C++ enables you to declare function parameters that are multidimensional arrays. As with single-dimensional arrays, C++ enables you either to be specific or general about the size of the array

parameter. In the latter case, however, you can generalize only the first dimension of the array. If you want an array parameter to accept arrays of a fixed dimension, you can specify the size of each dimension of the array in the parameter declaration.

A Fixed-Array Parameter

The general syntax for declaring a fixed-array parameter is

```
type parameterName[dim1Size][dim2Size]...
```

Examples

```
int minMatrix(int intMat[100][20], int rows, int cols);
void sort(unsigned mat[23][55],
          int rows, int cols, int colIndex);
```

An Open-Array Parameter

The general syntax for declaring an open-array parameter is

```
type parameterName[][dim2Size]...
```

Examples

```
int minMat(int intMat[][100], int rows, int cols);
void sort(unsigned mat[][55],
          int rows, int cols, int colIndex);
```

Listing 6.8 shows the source code for the program MATRIX3.CPP. The program performs the same tasks as program MATRIX1.CPP in Listing 6.6. Program MATRIX3.CPP is created by editing program MATRIX1.CPP and placing each program task in a separate function.

Type **Listing 6.8. Source code for the program MATRIX3.CPP.**

```
 1:  // C++ program that demonstrates the use of two-dimension arrays.
 2:  // The average value of each matrix column is calculated.
 3:
 4:  #include <iostream.h>
 5:
 6:  const int MIN_COL = 1;
 7:  const int MAX_COL = 10;
 8:  const int MIN_ROW = 2;
 9:  const int MAX_ROW = 30;
10:
11:  // Prompt user for number of array elements
12:  int getNumPoints(const char* elemType, int low, int high)
13:  {
14:      int numPoints;
15:      do
```

continues

Listing 6.8. continued

```
16:        {
17:          cout << "Enter number of "
18:               << elemType << " ["
19:               << low << " to "
20:               << high << "]: ";
21:          cin >> numPoints;
22:        } while (numPoints < low || numPoints > high);
23:     return numPoints;
24: }
25:
26: // get the matrix elements
27: void inputMatrix(double matrix[][MAX_COL], int rows, int cols)
28: {
29:     for (int i = 0; i < rows; i++)
30:        {
31:          for (int j = 0; j < cols; j++)
32:             {
33:               cout << "matrix[" << i << "][" << j << "]: ";
34:               cin >> matrix[i][j];
35:             }
36:          cout << endl;
37:        }
38: }
39:
40: // obtain the sum of each column
41: void showAverage(double matrix[][MAX_COL], int rows, int cols)
42: {
43:     double sum, average;
44:
45:     for (int j = 0; j < cols; j++)
46:        {
47:          sum = 0.0;                // initialize sum
48:          for (int i = 0; i < rows; i++)
49:             sum += matrix[i][j];
50:          average = sum / rows;
51:          cout << "Average for column " << j
52:               << " = " << average << endl;
53:        }
54: }
55:
56: int main()
57: {
58:     double matrix[MAX_ROW][MAX_COL];
59:     int rows, cols;
60:
61:     // get the number of rows and columns
62:     rows = getNumPoints("rows", MIN_ROW, MAX_ROW);
63:     cols = getNumPoints("columns", MIN_COL, MAX_COL);
64:
65:     inputMatrix(matrix, rows, cols);
66:     showAverage(matrix, rows, cols);
67:
68:     return 0;
69: }
```

Here is a sample session with the program in Listing 6.8.

```
Enter number of rows [2 to 30]: 3
Enter number of columns [1 to 10]: 3
matrix[0][0]: 10
matrix[0][1]: 20
matrix[0][2]: 30

matrix[1][0]: 40
matrix[1][1]: 50
matrix[1][2]: 60

matrix[2][0]: 70
matrix[2][1]: 80
matrix[2][2]: 90

Average for column 0 = 40
Average for column 1 = 50
Average for column 2 = 60
```

The differences between the programs in Listing 6.8 and Listing 6.6 are in the functions inputMatrix and showAverage. Their algorithms are identical to the equivalent code in Listing 6.6, except now they're in functions, and the main function calls them on lines 65 and 66.

Summary

Today's lesson covered various topics related to arrays, including single-dimensional and multidimensional arrays. You learned the following:

☐ The initializing of single-dimensional arrays can be carried out while declaring them. The initializing list of data is enclosed in braces and contains comma-delimited data. C++ enables you to include fewer data than the size of the array. In this case, the compiler automatically assigns zeros to the elements that you do not explicitly initialize. In addition, C++ enables you to omit the explicit size of the initialized array and instead use the number of initializing items as the number of array elements.

☐ Declaring single-dimensional arrays as function parameters takes two forms. The first one deals with fixed-array parameters, whereas the second one handles open-array parameters. Fixed-array parameters include the size of the array in the parameter. Arguments for this type of parameter must match the type and size of the parameter. Open-array parameters use empty brackets to indicate that the arguments for the parameters can be of any size.

☐ Sorting arrays is an important array operation. Sorting arranges the elements of an array in either ascending or descending order. Sorted arrays are much easier to search. For sorting arrays, the built-in qsort Quicksort method is very efficient.

☐ Searching arrays involves locating an array element that contains the same data as the search value. Searching methods either are geared toward unsorted or sorted arrays.

The linear search method is used for unsorted arrays, and the binary search method is used for sorted arrays.

☐ Declaring multidimensional arrays requires you to state the data type of the array elements, the name of the array, and the size of each dimension (enclosed in separate brackets). The lower index of each dimension is 0. The upper bound of each dimension in an array is equal to the dimension size minus one.

☐ Using multidimensional arrays requires you to state the array's name and to include valid indices. Each index must be enclosed in a separate set of brackets.

☐ The initializing of multidimensional arrays can be carried out while declaring them. The initializing list of data is enclosed in braces and contains comma-delimited data. C++ enables you to include fewer data than the total size of the array. In this case, the compiler automatically assigns zeros to the elements that you do not explicitly initialize.

☐ The declaration of multidimensional arrays as function parameters takes two forms. The first one deals with fixed-array parameters, whereas the second one handles parameters with an open first dimension. Fixed-array parameters include the size of each dimension in the array parameter. Arguments for this type of parameter must match the type and sizes of the parameter. Open-array parameters use empty brackets for only the first dimension to indicate that the arguments for the parameters have varying sizes for the first dimensions. The other dimensions of the arguments must match those of the array parameter.

Q&A

Q Does C++ permit me to alter the size of an array?

A No. C++ does not allow you to redimension arrays.

Q Can I declare arrays with the basic type `void` (for example, `void array[81];`) to create buffers?

A No. C++ does not allow you to use the `void` type with an array, because the `void` type has no defined size. Use the `char` or `unsigned char` type to create an array that works as a buffer.

Q Does C++ allow me to redeclare an array?

A Not really, but C++ enables you to declare a new version of the array in a new statement block in order to change its basic type, the number of dimensions, and its size. Here is an example:

```cpp
#include <iostream.h>
const MAX = 100;
const MAX_ROWS = 100;
const MAX_COLS = 20;

int main()
{
    // declare variables here
    {
        double x[MAX];
        // declare other variables

        // statements to manipulate the single-dimensional
        // array x
    }
    {
        double x[MAX_ROWS][MAX_COLS];
        // declare other variables

        // statements to manipulate the matrix x
    }
    return 0;
}
```

The function main declares the array x in the first nested statement block. When program execution reaches the end of that block, the runtime system removes the array x and all other variables declared in that block. Then the function redeclares x as a matrix in the second block. When program execution reaches the end of the second block, the runtime system removes the matrix x and all other variables declared in that block.

Q **Are arrays limited to the predefined types?**

A Not at all. C++ enables you to create arrays using user-defined types.

Workshop

The Workshop provides quiz questions to help you solidify your understanding of the material covered and exercises to provide you with experience in using what you've learned. Try to understand the quiz and exercise answers before continuing on to the next day's lesson. Answers are provided in Appendix A.

Quiz

1. What is the output of the following program?

```cpp
#include <iostream.h>
const int MAX = 5;
int main()
{
    double x[MAX];
    x[0] = 1;
    for (int i = 1; i < MAX; i++)
        x[i] = i * x[i-1];
    for (int i = 0; i < MAX; i++)
        cout << "x[" << i << "] = " << x[i] << endl;
    return 0;
}
```

2. What is the output of the following program?

```cpp
#include <iostream.h>
const int MAX = 5;
int main()
{
    double x[MAX];
    for (int i = 0; i < MAX; i++)
        x[i] = i * i;
    for (int i = 0; i < MAX; i++)
        cout << "x[" << i << "] = " << x[i] << endl;
    return 0;
}
```

3. Where is the error in the following program?

```cpp
#include <iostream.h>
const int MAX = 5;
int main()
{
    double x[MAX];
    x[0] = 1;
    for (int i = 0; i < MAX; i++)
        x[i] = i * x[i-1];
    for (int i = 0; i < MAX; i++)
        cout << "x[" << i << "] = " << x[i] << endl
    return 0;
}
```

Exercise

Write the program SEARCH2.CPP by editing program SEARCH.CPP and replacing the search functions `linearSearch` and `binarySearch` with the C++ `lfind` and `bsearch` functions.

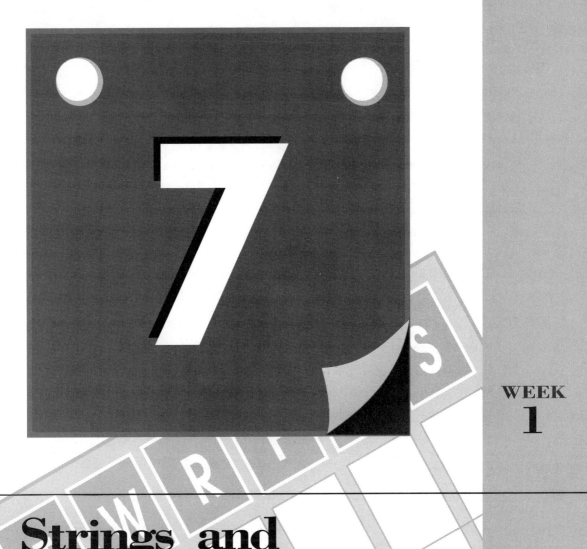

7

Strings and
Managing I/O

Today you will learn a little more about basic console input/output (I/O). C++, like its parent language C, does not define I/O operations that are part of the core language. Instead, C++ and C rely on I/O libraries to provide the needed console I/O support. Such libraries are mainly aimed at non-GUI (graphical user interface) environments such as MS-DOS. These libraries usually work with EasyWin applications, which is why they are of interest in this book. Because the primary goal here is to teach you how to write Windows programs, however, discussion of these console I/O libraries is kept to a minimum. Today's lesson looks at a small selection of input and output operations and functions that are supported by the STDIO.H and IOSTREAM.H header files.

The examples presented so far have been predominantly numeric, with a few that involve character manipulation. You may have grown suspicious about the absence of strings in all of these examples. On Day 10 you will learn about the special C++ `string` class that makes strings into a more usable type. Today's lesson discusses C++ strings as they are inherited from C.

You will learn about the following topics:

- ☐ Formatted stream output
- ☐ Stream input
- ☐ The `printf` function
- ☐ Strings in C++
- ☐ String input
- ☐ Using the standard string library
- ☐ Assigning strings
- ☐ Obtaining the length of strings
- ☐ Concatenating strings
- ☐ Comparing strings
- ☐ Converting strings
- ☐ Reversing the characters in a string
- ☐ Locating characters
- ☐ Locating substrings

Formatted Stream Output

C++ brings with it a family of extensible I/O libraries. The language designers recognized that the I/O functions in STDIO.H, inherited from C, have their limitations when dealing with classes (you learn more about classes on Day 8). Consequently, C++ provides the notion of

streams. Recall that streams, which already exist in C, are a sequence of data flowing from part of a computer to another. In the programs presented thus far, you have seen the extractor operator << working with the standard output stream, cout. You also saw the inserter operator >> and the standard input stream, cin. In this section, you are introduced to the stream functions width and precision, which help in formatting the output. The C++ stream libraries have many more functions to additionally fine-tune the output.

The width function specifies the width of the output. The general form for using this function with the cout stream is

```
cout.width(widthOfOutput);
```

The precision function specifies the number of digits for floating-point numbers. The general form for using this function with the cout stream is

```
cout.precision(numberOfDigits);
```

Look at an example. Listing 7.1 contains the source code for the program OUT1.CPP. The program, which requires no input, displays formatted integers, floating-point numbers, and characters using the width and precision stream functions.

Type   **Listing 7.1. Source code for the program OUT1.CPP.**

```
1:   // Program illustrates C++ formatted stream output
2:   // using the width and precision functions
3:
4:   #include <iostream.h>
5:
6:   int main()
7:   {
8:       int       anInt     = 67;
9:       unsigned char aByte = 128;
10:      char      aChar     = '@';
11:      float     aSingle   = 355.0;
12:      double    aDouble   = 1.130e+002;
13:
14:      // display sample expressions
15:      cout.width(3); cout << int(aByte) << " + ";
16:      cout.width(2); cout << anInt << " = ";
17:      cout.width(3); cout << (aByte + anInt) << endl;
18:
19:      cout.precision(4); cout << aSingle << " / ";
20:                         cout << aDouble << " = ";
21:      cout.precision(5); cout << (aSingle / aDouble) << endl;
22:
23:      cout << "The character in variable aChar is "
24:           << aChar << endl;
25:      return 0;
26:  }
```

7

Here is the output from the program in Listing 7.1.

```
128 + 67 = 195
355 / 113 = 3.1416
The character in variable aChar is @
```

The program in Listing 7.1 declares a set of variables that have different data types. The statements on lines 15 through 17 use the stream function width to specify the output width for the next item displayed by a cout statement. Notice that it takes six statements to display three integers. In addition, notice that on line 15 the program uses the expression int(aByte) to typecast the unsigned char type into an int. Without this type conversion, the contents of the variable aByte appear as a character rather than a number. If you use the stream output to display integers that have default widths, you can indeed replace the six stream-output statements with a single one. Note that the width automatically is reset after each output, which is why you need to set it to the same value multiple times.

Lines 19 through 21 contain the second set of stream-output statements for the floating-point numbers. The statements on these lines contain the stream function precision to specify the total number of digits to display. It takes five C++ statements to output three floating-point numbers. Once more, if you use the stream output to display numbers that have default widths, you can replace the five stream-output statements with a single one. Note that the precision is *not* reset after each output, so the output on line 20 is still using a precision of 4.

Stream Input

Like the standard output stream, C++ offers the standard input stream, cin. This input stream can read predefined data types, such as int, unsigned, long, and char. Typically, you use the inserter operator >> to obtain input for the predefined data types. The programs presented so far use the >> operator to enter a single item. C++ streams enable you to chain the >> operator to enter multiple items. In the case of multiple items, you need to observe the following rules:

1. Enter a space between two consecutive numbers to separate them.

2. Entering a space between two consecutive chars is optional.

3. Entering a space between a char and a number (or vice versa) is necessary only if the char is a digit.

4. The input stream ignores spaces.

5. You can enter multiple items on different lines. The stream-input statements are not fully executed until they obtain all the specified input.

Look at a program that illustrates both the input of multiple items and different combinations of data types. Listing 7.2 shows the source code for the program IN.CPP. The program performs the following tasks:

☐ Prompts you to enter three numbers

☐ Calculates the sum of the three numbers

☐ Displays the sum and the average of the three numbers you entered

☐ Prompts you to type in three characters

☐ Displays your input

☐ Prompts you to enter a number, a character, and a number

☐ Displays your input

☐ Prompts you to enter a character, a number, and a character

☐ Displays your input

Type **Listing 7.2. Source code for the program IN.CPP.**

```
1:  // Program to illustrate standard stream input
2:
3:  #include <iostream.h>
4:
5:  int main()
6:  {
7:      double x, y, z, sum;
8:      char c1, c2, c3;
9:
10:     cout << "Enter three numbers separated by a space: ";
11:     cin >> x >> y >> z;
12:     sum = x + y + z;
13:     cout << "Sum of numbers = " << sum << endl
14:          << "Average of numbers = " << sum / 3 << endl;
15:     cout << "Enter three characters: ";
16:     cin >> c1 >> c2 >> c3;
17:     cout << "You entered characters '" << c1
18:          << "', '" << c2 << "', and '"
19:          << c3 << "'" << endl;
20:     cout << "Enter a number, a character, and a number: ";
21:     cin >> x >> c1 >> y;
22:     cout << "You entered " << x << " " << c1 << " " << y << endl;
23:     cout << "Enter a character, a number, and a character: ";
24:     cin >> c1 >> x >> c2;
25:     cout << "You entered " << c1 << " " << x << " " << c2 << endl;
26:
27:     return 0;
28: }
```

Here is a sample session with the program in Listing 7.2.

```
Enter three numbers separated by a space: 1 2 3
Sum of numbers = 6
Average of numbers = 2
Enter three characters: ABC
You entered characters 'A', 'B', and 'C'
```

```
Enter a number, a character, and a number: 12A34.4
You entered 12 A 34.4
Enter a character, a number, and a character: A3.14Z
You entered A 3.14 Z
```

The program in Listing 7.2 declares four `double`-typed variables and three `char`-typed variables. The output statement on line 10 prompts you to enter three numbers. The input statement on line 11 obtains your input and stores the numbers in variables x, y, and z. You need to enter a space character between any two numbers. You also can enter each number on a separate line. The statement stores the first number you enter in variable y, the second number in variable y, and the third one in variable z. This sequence is determined by the sequence in which these variables appear on line 11. The statement on line 12 calculates the sum of the values in variables x, y, and z. The output statement on lines 13 and 14 displays the sum and average of the numbers that you entered.

The output statement on line 15 prompts you to enter three characters. The input statement on line 16 obtains your input and sequentially stores the characters in variables c1, c2, and c3. Your input need not separate the characters with a space. Thus, you can type in characters such as **1A2**, **Bob**, and **1   D   d**. The output statement on lines 17 through 19 displays the characters that you type, separated by spaces and enclosed in single quotes.

The output statement on line 20 prompts you to enter a number, a character, and a number. The input statement on line 21 sequentially stores your input in variables x, c1, and y. You need to type a space between the character and either of the numbers only if the character can be interpreted as part of either number. For example, if you want to enter the number 12, the dot character, and the number 55, type **12 . 55**. The spaces around the dot ensure that the input stream does not consider it as a decimal part of either floating-point number. The output statement on line 22 displays the values you entered, separated by spaces.

The output statement on line 23 prompts you to enter a character, a number, and a character. The input statement on line 24 sequentially stores your input in variables c1, x, and c2. You need to enter a space between the characters and the number only if the characters can be interpreted as part of the number. For example, if you want to enter the character -, the number 12, and the digit 0, type **- 12 0**. The output statement on line 25 displays the values you entered, separated by spaces.

The *printf* Function

When reading through other people's programs, you may often come across the `printf` function. This is the original standard output statement from C. As C++ is a superset of C, this function is carried over. There are still a number of C++ programmers who prefer the older `printf` over the newer I/O streams that come with C++, so it's likely you'll encounter it. In addition, there are a few powerful features of the `printf` function that can sometimes make it desirable over the newer streams. The function is prototyped in the header file STDIO.H.

The *printf* Function

The general syntax for the `printf` statement is as follows:

```
int printf(const char* format[, argument, ...]);
```

The parameter `format` is a character array that contains the text to be output. In addition to that parameter can be optional additional arguments to the function. Whether or not any additional arguments are needed and what their types might be is determined by whether or not the contents of the `format` character array contain any formatting instructions that require parameters of their own.

The `printf` function offers much power and presents formatted controls. The first step to formatting is the use of special escape sequences that enable you to incorporate special characters. These escape sequences all begin with the backslash character (\) and are shown in Table 7.1.

The `printf` function also enables you to incorporate variable values in its output with the use of formatting instructions. The general syntax for the individual formatting instruction is

```
% [flags] [width] [.precision] [F ¦ N ¦ h ¦ l ¦ L] <type character>
```

The `flags` options indicate the output justification, numeric signs, decimal points, and trailing zeros. In addition, these flags also specify the octal and hexadecimal prefixes. Table 7.2 shows the options for the flags in the format string of the `printf` function.

The `width` option indicates the minimum number of displayed characters. The `printf` function uses zeros and blanks to pad the output if needed. When the width number begins with a `0`, the `printf` function uses leading zeros, instead of spaces, for padding. When the `*` character appears instead of a width number, the `printf` function obtains the actual width number from the function's argument list. The argument that specifies the required width must come before the argument that actually is being formatted. The following is an example that displays the integer 2 using 3 characters, as specified by the second argument of `printf`:

```
printf("%*d", 3, 2);
```

The `precision` option specifies the maximum number of displayed characters. If you include an integer, the *precision* option defines the minimum number of displayed digits. When the `*` character is used in place of a precision number, the `printf` function obtains the actual precision from the argument list. The argument that specifies the required precision must come before the argument that is actually being formatted. The following is an example that displays the floating-point number 3.3244 using 10 characters, as specified by the third argument of `printf`:

```
printf("%7.*f", 10, 3.3244);
```

The `F`, `N`, `h`, `l`, and `L` options are size options used to overrule an argument's default size. The `F` and `N` options are used in conjunction with far and near pointers, respectively. The `h`, `l`, and `L` options are used to indicate a `short int`, a `long`, or a `long double`, respectively.

Table 7.1. The escape sequence.

Sequence	Decimal Value	Hex Value	Task
\a	7	0x07	Bell
\b	8	0x08	Backspace
\f	12	0x0C	Form-feed
\n	10	0x0A	New line
\r	13	0x0D	Carriage return
\t	9	0x09	Horizontal tab
\v	11	0x0B	Vertical tab
\\	92	0x5C	Backslash
\'	44	0x2C	Single quote
\"	34	0x22	Double quote
\?	63	0x3F	Question mark
\0			1 to 3 digits for octal value
\Xhhh and \xhhh		0xhhh	Hexadecimal value

The `printf` function requires that you specify a data type character with each `%` format code. Table 7.2 shows the options for the flags in the format string of `printf`. Table 7.3 shows the data type characters used in the format string of `printf`.

Table 7.2. Options for the flags in the format string of the `printf` function.

Format Option	Outcome
-	Justifies to the left within the specified field
+	Displays the plus or minus sign of a value
blank	Displays a leading blank if the value is positive; displays a minus sign if the value is negative
#	No effect on decimal integers; displays a leading 0X or 0x for hexadecimal integers, a leading zero for octal integers, and the decimal point for reals

Table 7.3. Data type characters used in the format string of printf.

Category	Type Character	Outcome
Character	c	Single character
	d	Signed decimal int
	i	Signed decimal int
	o	Unsigned octal int
	u	Unsigned decimal int
	x	Unsigned hexadecimal int; the set of numeric characters used is 01234567890abcdef (note the lowercase letters)
	X	Unsigned hexadecimal int; the set of numeric characters used is 01234567890ABCDEF (note the uppercase letters)
Pointer	p	Displays only the offset for near pointers as 0000; displays far pointers as SSSS:0000
Pointer to int	n	
Real	f	Displays signed value in the format [-]dddd.dddd
	e	Displays signed scientific value in the format [-]d.dddde[+¦-]ddd
	E	Displays signed scientific value in the format [-]d.ddddE[+¦-]ddd
	g	Displays signed value using either the f or e formats, depending on the value and the specified precision
	G	Displays signed value using either the f or E formats, depending on the value and the specified precision
String pointer	s	Displays characters until the null terminator of the string is reached

Note: Although the function `printf` plays no role in the output of Windows applications, its sister function, `sprintf`, does. Instead of sending output to the screen, `sprintf` creates a string of characters that contains the formatted image of the output. The `sprintf` function looks exactly the same as the `printf` function except for the addition of a single parameter at the beginning of the parameter list: a pointer to the string into which `sprintf` should create the formatted output.

Consider a simple example. Listing 7.3 shows the source code for the program OUT2.CPP. This program was created by editing the OUT1.CPP in Listing 7.1. The new version displays formatted output using the `printf` function. The program displays the same floating-point numbers using three different sets of format code.

Listing 7.3. Source code for the program OUT2.CPP.

```
1:  // Program that uses printf for formatted output
2:
3:  #include <stdio.h>
4:
5:  int main()
6:  {
7:      int       anInt     = 67;
8:      unsigned char aByte = 128;
9:      char      aChar     = '@';
10:     float     aSingle   = 355.0;
11:     double    aDouble   = 1.130e+002;
12:
13:     printf("%3d + %2d = %3d\n",
14:             aByte, anInt, aByte + anInt );
15:
16:     printf("Output uses the %%lf format:\n");
17:     printf("   %6.4f / %6.4lf = %7.5lf\n",
18:             aSingle, aDouble, aSingle / aDouble );
19:
20:     printf("Output uses the %%le format:\n");
21:     printf("   %6.4e / %6.4le = %7.5le\n",
22:             aSingle, aDouble, aSingle / aDouble );
23:
24:     printf("Output uses the %%lg format:\n");
25:     printf("   %6.4g / %6.4lg = %7.5lg\n",
26:             aSingle, aDouble, aSingle / aDouble );
27:
28:     printf("The character in variable aChar is %c\n", aChar);
29:     printf("The ASCII code of %c is %d\n", aChar, aChar);
30:     return 0;
31: }
```

Here is a sample session with the program in Listing 7.3.

```
128 + 67 = 195
Output uses the %lf format
   355.0000 / 113.0000 = 3.14159
Output uses the %le format
   3.5500e+002 / 1.1300e+002 = 3.14159e+00
Output uses the %lg format
      355 /    113 =  3.1416
The character in variable aChar is @
The ASCII code of @ is 64
```

The program in Listing 7.3 declares a collection of variables with different data types. The output statement on lines 13 and 14 displays integers using the %d format control. Table 7.4 shows the effect of the various format controls in the printf statement on line 13. Notice that the printf function converts the first item in output from an unsigned char to an int.

Table 7.4. Effects of the various format controls in the printf statement at line 16.

Format Control	Item	Data Type	Output
%3d	aByte	unsigned char	Integer
%2d	anInt	int	Integer
%3d	aByte + anInt	int	Integer

The output statement starting on line 17 displays the variable aSingle, the variable aDouble, and the expression aSingle / aDouble using the format controls %6.4f, %6.4lf and %7.5lf. These controls specify precision values of 4, 4, and 5 digits, respectively, and minimum widths of 6, 6, and 7 characters, respectively. The last two format controls indicate that they display a double-typed value.

The output statement starting on line 21 is similar to that on line 17. The main difference is that the printf on line 21 uses the e format rather than the f format. Consequently, the three items in the printf statement appear in scientific notation.

The output statement on line 25 is similar to that on line 17. The main difference is that the printf on line 25 uses the g format instead of the f format. Consequently, the first two items in the printf statement appear with no decimal places because they are whole numbers.

The output statement on line 28 displays the contents in the variable aChar using the %c format control. The output statement on line 29 displays the contents of variable aChar twice: once as a character and once as an integer (or, to be more exact, the ASCII code of a character). The printf function on line 29 performs this task by using the %c and %d format controls, respectively.

C++ Character Arrays: An Overview

C++ has a special class (again, we'll get into classes on Day 8) for manipulating strings, but the parent language C doesn't. Instead, C regards strings as arrays of characters that end with the ASCII 0 null character ('\0'). Because of this, a tremendous amount of code currently in existence uses these character arrays. Furthermore, despite the new string class provided by C++, those old character arrays still have their uses. You should try not to get too confused when the term string is used to describe these character arrays as well as the C++ strings that act more like what you might expect from a language such as BASIC. The rest of this chapter examines how to use and abuse character arrays.

NEW The '\0' character also is called the *null terminator*. Strings that end with the null
TERM terminator sometimes are called *ASCIIZ strings*, with the letter Z standing for zero, the ASCII code of the null terminator. You also will see this character referred to as the NUL character, as that's the ASCII name for it.

The null terminator *must* be present in all strings and taken into account when declaring space for a string. When you declare a string variable as an array of characters, be sure to reserve an extra character for the null terminator. The advantage of using the null terminator is that you can create strings that are not restricted by any limit imposed by the C++ implementation. In addition, ASCIIZ strings have very simple structures.

> **Note:** The lesson in Day 4 discusses how pointers can access and manipulate the elements of an array. C and C++ make extensive use of this programming feature in manipulating the characters of a string.

DO	**DON'T**
DO include an extra character for the null terminator when specifying the size of a string. **DON'T** declare a string variable as a single-character array. Such a variable is useless.	

String Input

The programs presented thus far display string literals in output stream statements; C++ supports stream output for strings as a special case for a non-predefined data type. (You can say the support came by popular demand.) String output using string variables uses the same operator and syntax. With string input, the input operator >> does not work well because strings often contain spaces that are ignored by the input operator. Instead of the input operator, you need to use the getline function. This function reads up to a specified number of characters.

The *getline* Function

The general syntax for the overloaded getline function is

```
istream& getline(signed char* buffer,
                 int size,
                 char delimiter = '\n');

istream& getline(unsigned char* buffer,
                 int size,
                 char delimiter = '\n');

istream& getline(char* buffer,
                 int size,
                 char delimiter = '\n');
```

The parameter buffer is a pointer to the string receiving the characters from the stream. The parameter size specifies the maximum number of characters to read. The parameter delimiter specifies the delimiting character that causes the string input to stop before reaching the number of characters specified by parameter size. The parameter delimiter has the default argument of '\n', which means that input will end when that character is reached; in the case of a person typing, this character will manifest itself when the person presses the Enter key.

Example

```
#include <iostream.h>
int main()
{
    char name[80];
    cout << "Enter your name: ";
    cin.getline(name, sizeof(name) - 1);
    cout << "Hello " << name << ", how are you?";
    return 0;
}
```

Using the STRING.H Library

The community of C programmers has developed the standard string library STRING.H, which contains the most frequently used string-manipulation functions. The STDIO.H and IOSTREAM.H header file prototype functions also support string I/O. The ANSI/ISO C++ committee has also developed a C++-style string class. This class models strings more in line with the way Pascal and BASIC use them. (You learn more about classes on Day 8 and the C++ string class on Day 11.) The next sections present several (but by no means all) of the functions that are prototyped in the STRING.H header file.

Some of the string functions in STRING.H have more than one version. The extra versions that prepend the characters _f, f, or _ to the function name work with strings that are specifically accessed using far pointers. Because of this, these functions don't appear in the flat, 32-bit memory model of the Borland compiler.

Assigning Strings

C++ supports two methods for assigning strings. You can assign a string literal to a string variable when you initialize it. This method is simple and requires using the = operator and the assigning string.

Syntax

Initializing a String

The general syntax for initializing a string is

```
char stringVar[stringSize] = stringLiteral;
```

Example

```
char aString[81] = "Borland C++ 5 in 21 days";
char name[] = "René Kinner";
```

The second method for assigning one ASCIIZ string to another actually is just a function that copies the contents of one array to the other, being mindful of the null character on the end of the string—the function strcpy. This function assumes that the copied string ends with a null character and stops copying when it's reached.

Syntax

The *strcpy* Function

The prototype for the function strcpy is

```
char* strcpy(char* target, const char* source)
```

The function copies the characters from string source to string target. The function *assumes* that the target string has enough space to contain the source string.

Example

```
char name[41];
strcpy(name,"Borland C++ 5");
```

The variable `name` contains the string `"Borland C++ 5"`.

The function `strdup` enables you to copy the characters to another string and allocate required space in the target string.

The *strdup* Function

The prototype for the function `strdup` is

```
char* strdup(const char* source)
```

The function copies the characters in the source string and returns a pointer to the duplicate string.

Example

```
char* string1 = "The reign in Spain";
char* string2;

string2 = strdup(string1);
```

This example copies the contents of `string1` into `string2` after allocating the memory space for `string2`.

Note: Because `strdup` allocates memory for the new string, you will have to remember to free it later on. This is a nasty "gotcha" that catches a lot of programmers, both novice and expert.

The string library also offers the function `strncpy` to support copying a specified number of characters from one string to another.

The *strncpy* Function

The prototype for the function `strncpy` is

```
char* strncpy(char* target, const char* source, size_t num);
```

The function copies *num* characters from the `source` string to the `target` string. Note that the function doesn't perform any character truncation or padding.

7

Example

```
char str1[] = "Pascal";
char str2[] = "Hello there";

strncpy(str1, str2, 5);
```

The variable `str1` now contains the string `"Hellol"`. Note how the `'l'` from the original string is still in there after the part that was copied.

Using `strncpy` often is preferred over using `strcpy`. The reason, of course, is to make sure that you don't copy more from the source string than there is room for in the target string. If, for example, the target was created with room for only 20 characters and then you do a `strcpy` that moves 40 characters, you run the risk of corrupting memory and causing those nifty Windows GPFs.

> **Note:** Using pointers to manipulate strings is a new idea to many novice C++ programmers. In fact, you can use pointers to manipulate the trailing parts of a string by assigning the address of the first character to manipulate. For example, if you declare the string `str1` as follows:
>
> ```
> char str1[41] = "Hello World";
> char str2[41];
> char* p = str1;
>
> p += 6; // p now points to substring "World" in str1
> strcpy(str2, p);
> cout << str2 << endl;
> ```
>
> the output statement displays the string `"World"`. This example shows how using pointers can incorporate an offset number of characters.

The Length of a String

Many string operations require information about the number of characters in a string. The STRING.H library offers the function `strlen` to return the number of characters, excluding the null terminator, in a string.

The *strlen* Function

The prototype for the function strlen is

```
size_t strlen(const char* string)
```

The function strlen returns the number of characters in the parameter string. The result type size_t has a typedef of an unsigned int type.

Example

```
char str[] = "1234567890";
size_t i;
i = strlen(str);
```

These statements assign 10 to the variable i.

Concatenating Strings

Often, you build a string by concatenating two or more strings. The function strcat enables you to concatenate one string to another.

NEW☞
TERM   When you *concatenate* strings, you join or link them together.

The *strcat* Function

The prototype for the function strcat is

```
char* strcat(char* target, const char* source)
```

The function appends the contents of the source string to the target string and returns the pointer to the target string. The function *assumes* that the target string can accommodate the characters of the source string.

Example

```
char string[81];
strcpy(string, "Borland");
strcat(string," C++ 5")
```

The variable string now contains "Borland C++ 5".

The function strncat concatenates a specified number of characters from the source string to the target strings.

7

Syntax

The *strncat* Function

The prototype for the function strncat is

```
char* strncat(char* target, const char* source, size_t num)
```

The function appends *num* characters of the source string to the target string and returns a pointer to the target string.

Example

```
char str1[81] = "Hello I am ";
char str2[41] = "Keith Thompson";

strncat(str1, str2, 5);
```

The variable str1 now contains "Hello I am Keith".

DO	DON'T

DO use the function strncat to control the number of concatenated characters in order to make sure you don't exceed the capacity of the target string.

DON'T assume that the target string is always adequate to store the characters in the source string.

Look at a program that uses the getline, strlen, and strcat functions. Listing 7.4 contains the source code for the program STRING1.CPP. The program performs the following tasks:

☐ Prompts you to enter a string; your input should not exceed 40 characters

☐ Prompts you to enter a second string; your input should not exceed 40 characters

☐ Displays the number of characters in each of the strings you enter

☐ Concatenates the second string to the first one

☐ Displays the concatenated strings

☐ Displays the number of characters in the concatenated strings

☐ Prompts you to enter a search character

☐ Prompts you to enter a replacement character

☐ Displays the concatenated string after replacing all the occurrences of the search character with the replacement character

Type Listing 7.4. Source code for the program STRING1.CPP.

```cpp
1:  // C++ program that demonstrates C-style strings
2:
3:  #include <iostream.h>
4:  #include <string.h>
5:
6:  const unsigned MAX1 = 40;
7:  const unsigned MAX2 = 80;
8:
9:  int main()
10: {
11:     char smallStr[MAX1+1];
12:     char bigStr[MAX2+1];
13:     char findChar, replChar;
14:
15:     cout << "Enter first string:" << endl;
16:     cin.getline(bigStr, MAX2);
17:     cout << "Enter second string:" << endl;
18:     cin.getline(smallStr, MAX1);
19:
20:     cout << "String 1 has " << strlen(bigStr)
21:          << " characters" << endl;
22:     cout << "String 2 has " << strlen(smallStr)
23:          << " characters" << endl;
24:
25:     // concatenate bigStr to smallStr
26:     strcat(bigStr, smallStr);
27:     cout << "Concatenated strings are:" << endl
28:          << bigStr << endl;
29:     cout << "New string has " << strlen(bigStr)
30:          << " characters" << endl;
31:
32:     // get the search and replacement characters
33:     cout << "Enter search character: ";
34:     cin >> findChar;
35:     cout << "Enter replacement character: ";
36:     cin >> replChar;
37:
38:     // replace characters in string bigStr
39:     for (int i = 0; i < strlen(bigStr); i++)
40:       if (bigStr[i] == findChar)
41:         bigStr[i] = replChar;
42:
43:     // display the updated string bigStr
44:     cout << "New string is:" << endl
45:          << bigStr;
46:     return 0;
47: }
```

7

Here is a sample session with the program in Listing 7.4.

```
Enter first string:
The rain in Spain stays
Enter second string:
 mainly in the plain
String 1 has 23 characters
String 2 has 20 characters
Concatenated strings are:
The rain in Spain stays mainly in the plain
New string has 43 characters
Enter search character : a
Enter replacement character : A
New string is:
The rAin in SpAin stAys mAinly in the plAin
```

The program in Listing 7.4 includes the STRING.H header file for the string manipulation functions. Lines 6 and 7 declare the global constants MAX1 and MAX2, which are used to size a small string and a slightly less small string, respectively. The function main declares two strings, smallStr and bigStr. Line 11 declares the variable smallStr to store MAX1+1 characters. (The extra space is for the null character.) Line 12 declares the variable bigStr to store MAX2+1 characters. Line 13 declares the char-typed variable findChar and replChar.

The output statement on line 15 prompts you to enter the first string. The statement on line 16 uses the stream input function getline to obtain your input and to store it in variable bigStr. The function call specifies that you can enter up to MAX2 characters. The output statement on line 17 prompts you to enter the second string. The statement on line 18 uses the stream input function getline to obtain your input and to store it in the variable smallStr. The function call specifies that you can enter up to MAX1 characters.

The output statements on lines 20 through 23 display the number of characters in variables bigStr and smallStr, respectively. Each output statement calls function strlen and passes it a string variable.

The statement on line 26 concatenates the string in the variable smallStr to the variable bigStr. The output statement on lines 27 and 28 displays the updated string bigStr. The output statement on lines 29 and 30 displays the number of characters in the updated string variable bigStr. This statement also uses the function strlen to obtain the number of characters.

The statement on line 33 prompts you to enter the search character. The statement on line 34 obtains your input and stores it in variable findChar. The statement on line 35 prompts you to enter the replacement character. The statement on line 36 obtains your input and stores it in variable replChar.

The for loop on lines 39 to 41 translates the characters in string bigStr. The loop uses the control variable i and iterates, in increments of 1, from 0 to strlen(bigStr). The if statement on line 40 determines whether character number i in bigStr matches the character in variable findChar. If this condition is true, the program executes the statement on line 41 to assign the character in variable replChar to character number i in variable bigStr. This loop shows how you can manipulate the contents of a string variable by accessing each character in that string.

The output statement on lines 44 and 45 displays the updated string bigStr.

String Comparison

Because strings are arrays of characters, you can't just simply use the == or != operators (or > and <, for that matter) to test for equality. The STRING.H library provides a set of functions to compare strings. These functions compare the characters of two strings using the ASCII value of each character. The functions are strcmp, stricmp, strncmp, and strnicmp.

In general, all the comparison functions return 0 if the two strings compare equally, a negative value if the second string in the comparison is greater, or a positive value if the first string is greater.

The function strcmp performs a case-sensitive comparison of two strings, using every character possible.

Syntax

The *strcmp* Function

The prototype for the function strcmp is

```
int strcmp(const char* str1, const char* str2);
```

The function compares strings *str1* and *str2*. The integer result indicates the outcome of the comparison.

```
< 0   when str1 is less than str2
= 0   when str1 is equal to str2
> 0   when str1 is greater than str2
```

Example

```
char string1[] = "Borland C++ 5";
char string2[] = "BORLAND C++ 5";
int i;

i = strcmp(string1, string2);
```

The last statement assigns a positive number to the variable i, because the string in variable string1 is greater than the string in variable string2 (lowercase actually is greater than uppercase in ASCII).

The function stricmp performs a case-insensitive comparison between two strings, using every character possible.

7

Syntax

The *stricmp* Function

The prototype for the function stricmp is

```
int stricmp(const char* str1, const char* str2);
```

The function compares strings *str1* and *str2* without making a distinction between upper- and lowercase characters. The integer result indicates the outcome of the comparison.

```
< 0   when str1 is less than str2
= 0   when str1 is equal to str2
> 0   when str1 is greater than str2
```

Example

```
char string1[] = "Borland C++ 5";
char string2[] = "BORLAND C++ 5";
int i;

i = stricmp(string1, string2);
```

The last statement assigns 0 to the variable i because the strings in variables string1 and string2 differ only in their cases.

The function strncmp performs a case-sensitive comparison on specified leading characters in two strings.

Syntax

The *strncmp* Function

The prototype for the function strncmp is

```
int strncmp(const char* str1, const char* str2, size_t num);
```

The function compares the *num* leading characters in two strings, *str1* and *str2*. The integer result indicates the outcome of the comparison, as follows:

```
< 0   when str1 is less than str2
= 0   when str1 is equal to str2
> 0   when str1 is greater than str2
```

Example

```
char string1[] = "Borland C++";
char string2[] = "Borland Pascal";
int i;

i = strncmp(string1, string2, 9);
```

This assigns a negative number to the variable i because "Borland C" is less than "Borland P".

The function `strnicmp` performs a case-insensitive comparison on specified leading characters in two strings.

The *strnicmp* Function

The prototype for the function `strnicmp` is

```
int strnicmp(const char* str1, const char* str2, size_t num);
```

The function compares the *num* leading characters in two strings, *str1* and *str2*, regardless of the character case. The integer result indicates the outcome of the comparison, as follows:

```
< 0  when str1 is less than str2
= 0  when str1 is equal to str2
> 0  when str1 is greater than str2
```

Example

```
char string1[] = "Borland C++";
char string2[] = "BORLAND Pascal";
int i;

i = strnicmp(string1, string2, 7);
```

This assigns 0 to the variable i because the strings "Borland" and "BORLAND" differ only in the case of their characters.

Look at an example that compares strings. Listing 7.5 creates an array of strings and initializes it with data. Then the program displays the unordered array of strings, sorts the array, and displays the sorted array.

Listing 7.5. Source code for the program STRING2.CPP.

```
1:  // C++ program that demonstrates comparing strings
2:
3:  #include <iostream.h>
4:  #include <string.h>
5:
6:  const unsigned STR_SIZE = 40;
7:  const unsigned ARRAY_SIZE = 11;
8:
9:  int main()
10: {
11:     char strArr[STR_SIZE][ARRAY_SIZE] =
12:         { "California", "Virginia", "Alaska", "New York",
13:           "Michigan", "Nevada", "Ohio", "Florida",
14:           "Washington", "Oregon", "Arizona" };
15:
16:     cout << "Unordered array of strings is:" << endl;
17:     for (int i = 0; i < ARRAY_SIZE; i++)
18:         cout << strArr[i] << endl;
```

continues

Listing 7.5. continued

```
19:    cout << endl;
20:
21:    // Use the Bubble sort method to sort the array
22:    for (int i = 0; i < ARRAY_SIZE; ++i)
23:       for (int j = 0; j < i; ++j)
24:          if (strcmp(strArr[i], strArr[j]) < 0)
25:             {
26:             char temp[STR_SIZE];
27:             strcpy(temp, strArr[i]);
28:             strcpy(strArr[i], strArr[j]);
29:             strcpy(strArr[j], temp);
30:             }
31:
32:    cout << "Sorted array of strings is:" << endl;
33:    for (int i = 0; i < ARRAY_SIZE; i++)
34:       cout << strArr[i] << endl;
35:    return 0;
36: }
```

Here is a sample session with the program in Listing 7.5.

```
Unordered array of strings is:
California
Virginia
Alaska
New York
Michigan
Nevada
Ohio
Florida
Washington
Oregon
Arizona

Sorted array of strings is:
Alaska
Arizona
California
Florida
Michigan
Nevada
New York
Ohio
Oregon
Virginia
Washington
```

The program in Listing 7.5 declares the global constants STR_SIZE and ARRAY_SIZE on lines 6 and 7. The constant STR_SIZE specifies the size of each string, whereas the constant ARRAY_SIZE indicates the number of strings in the array used by the program. The function main declares the array strArr (actually, the variable strArr is a two-dimensional matrix of characters) to have

`ARRAY_SIZE` elements and `STR_SIZE` characters per elements. Notice that the declaration states the size of each string in the first dimension and the size of the array in the second dimension. The function also initializes the array `strArr`.

The output statements on lines 16 through 19 display a title and then the elements of `strArr` before the nested `for` loops starting on line 22 sort the array with the Bubble sort routine. Finally, the output statements on line 32 through 34 display the sorted array.

Converting Strings

The STRING.H library offers the functions `_strlwr` and `_strupr` to convert the characters of a string to lowercase and uppercase, respectively. Note that these functions are more commonly called `strlwr` and `strupr` (without the leading underscore character) in C textbooks. I'm showing it with the leading underscore because it's not an ANSI/ISO standard function (probably because it's so trivial to write it on your own), but it's useful enough to mention here.

Syntax

The *_strlwr* Function

The prototype for the function `_strlwr` is

```
char* strlwr(char* source)
```

The function converts the uppercase characters in the string *source* to lowercase. Other characters are not affected. The function also returns the pointer to the string *source*.

Example

```
char str[] = "HELLO THERE";

_strlwr(str);
```

The variable `str` now contains the string `"hello there"`.

Syntax

The *_strupr* Function

The prototype for the function `_strupr` is

```
char* strupr(char* source)
```

The function converts the lowercase characters in the string *source* to uppercase. Other characters are not affected. The function also returns the pointer to the string *source*.

Example

```
char str[] = "Borland C++ 5";
_strupr(str);
```

The variable `str` now contains the string `"BORLAND C++ 5"`.

7

DO	**DON'T**

DO make copies for the arguments of functions _strlwr and _strupr if you need the original arguments later in a program.

DON'T always assume that applying the function _strlwr and then the function _strupr (or vice versa) to the same variable will succeed in restoring the original characters in that variable. For example, think about what would happen if you tried converting the string "Hello, Kevin" to uppercase and then back to lowercase.

Reversing Strings

The STRING.H library offers the function strrev to reverse the characters in a string.

Syntax

The *strrev* Function

The prototype for the function strrev is

```
char* strrev(char* str)
```

The function reverses the order of the characters in string str and returns the pointer to the string str.

Example

```
char str[] = "Hello";

strrev(str);
cout << str;
```

This displays "olleH".

Look at a program that manipulates the characters in a string. Listing 7.6 shows the source code for the program STRING3.CPP. The program performs the following tasks:

- [ ] Prompts you to enter a string
- [ ] Displays your input
- [ ] Displays the lowercase version of your input
- [ ] Displays the uppercase version of your input
- [ ] Displays the character you typed, in reverse order
- [ ] Displays a message that your input has no uppercase character, if this is true
- [ ] Displays a message that your input has no lowercase character, if this is true
- [ ] Displays a message that your input has symmetrical characters, if this is true

Type Listing 7.6. Source code for the program STRING3.CPP.

```
1:   // C++ program that demonstrates manipulating the
2:   // characters in a string
3:
4:   #include <iostream.h>
5:   #include <string.h>
6:
7:   const unsigned STR_SIZE = 40;
8:
9:   int main()
10: {
11:     char str1[STR_SIZE+1];
12:     char str2[STR_SIZE+1];
13:     bool isLowerCase, isUpperCase, isSymmetrical;
14:
15:     cout << "Enter a string: ";
16:     cin.getline(str1, STR_SIZE);
17:     cout << "Input: " << str1 << endl;
18:
19:     strcpy(str2, str1);          // copy str1 to str2
20:     strlwr(str2);                // convert to lowercase
21:     isLowerCase = (strcmp(str1, str2) == 0) ? true : false;
22:     cout << "Lowercase: " << str2 << endl;
23:
24:     strupr(str2);                // convert to uppercase
25:     isUpperCase = (strcmp(str1, str2) == 0) ? true : false;
26:     cout << "Uppercase: " << str2 << "\n";
27:
28:     strcpy(str2, str1);          // copy str1 to str2
29:     strrev(str2);                // reverse characters
30:     isSymmetrical = (strcmp(str1, str2) == 0) ? true : false;
31:     cout << "Reversed: " << str2 << endl;
32:
33:     if (isLowerCase)
34:         cout << "Your input has no uppercase letters" << endl;
35:     if (isUpperCase)
36:         cout << "Your input has no lowercase letters" << endl;
37:     if (isSymmetrical)
38:         cout << "Your input has symmetrical characters" << endl;
39:     return 0;
40: }
```

Here is a sample session with the program in Listing 7.6.

```
Enter a string: level
Input: level
Lowercase: level
Uppercase: LEVEL
Reversed: level
Your input has no uppercase letters
Your input has symmetrical characters
```

The program in Listing 7.6 declares the string variables str1 and str2 in the function main. Each string stores STR_SIZE + 1 characters (including the null terminator). The function also declares the Boolean flags isLowerCase, isUpperCase, and isSymmetrical.

The statement on lines 15 through 16 prompts you to enter a string, then gets that string into str1 with the input function getline. The output statement on line 17 echoes your input.

The statement on line 19 copies the characters in variable str1 to variable str2, then the statement on line 20 calls the function strlwr to convert the characters in variable str2 to all lowercase. The program manipulates the characters of variable str2, while maintaining the original input in variable str1. The statement on line 21 calls the function strcmp to compare the characters in str1 and str2. The two strings can be equal only if your input has no uppercase characters. The statement uses the conditional operator to set the flag isLowerCase to true if the above condition is true. Otherwise, the statement assigns false to the flag isLowerCase. The output statement on line 22 displays the characters in variable str2.

The statement on line 24 calls the function strupr and supplies it the argument str2. This function call converts any lowercase character in variable str2 into uppercase. The statement on line 25 calls the function strcmp to compare the characters in str1 and str2 in a similar manner to line 21 and assigns the result to isUpperCase. The two strings can be equal only if your input has no lowercase characters. The output statement on line 26 displays the characters in variable str2.

To display the original input in reverse order, the program calls the function strcpy to copy the characters of variable str1 to variable str2 once more. The statement on line 29 calls the function strrev and passes it the argument str2. The statement on line 30 calls the function strcmp to compare the characters in str1 and str2 and stores its result in isSymmetrical. The two strings can be equal only if your input has symmetrical characters. The output statement on line 31 displays the characters in variable str2.

The program uses the if statements on lines 33, 35, and 37 to report the status of the flags isLowerCase, isUpperCase, and isSymmetrical, respectively.

Locating Characters

The STRING.H library offers a number of functions for locating characters in strings. These functions include strchr, strrchr, strspn, strcspn, and strpbrk. These functions enable you to search for characters and simple character patterns in strings.

The function strchr locates the first occurrence of a character in a string.

The *strchr* Function

The prototype for the function strchr is

```
char* strchr(const char* target, int c)
```

The function locates the first occurrence of character c in the string target. The function returns the pointer to the character in string target that matches the specified pattern c. If character c does not occur in the string target, the function yields a 0.

Example

```
char str[81] = "Borland C++ 5";
char* strPtr;

strPtr = strchr(str, '+');
```

The pointer strPtr points to the substring "++ 5" in string str.

The function strrchr locates the last occurrence of a character in a string.

The *strrchr* Function

The prototype for the function strrchr is

```
char* strrchr(const char* target, int c)
```

The function locates the last occurrence of pattern c in the string target. The function returns the pointer to the character in string target that matches the specified pattern c. If character c does not occur in the string target, the function yields a 0.

Example

```
char str[81] = "Borland C++ 5 is here";
char* strPtr;

strPtr = strrchr(str, '+');
```

The pointer strPtr points to the substring "+ 5 is here" in string str.

The function strspn yields the number of characters in the leading part of a string that match any character in a pattern of characters.

7

The *strspn* Function

The prototype for the function strspn is

```
size_t strspn(const char* target, const char* pattern)
```

The function returns the number of characters in the leading part of the string target that matches any character in the string pattern.

Example

```
char str[] = "Borland C++ 5";
char substr[] = "narlBo ";
int index;

index = strspn(str, substr);
```

This statement assigns 8 to the variable `index` because the characters in `substr` found a match in each of the first eight characters of `str`.

The function `strcspn` scans a string and yields the number of leading characters in a string that is totally void of the characters in a substring.

The *strcspn* Function

The prototype for the function `strcspn` is

```
size_t strcspn(const char* str1, const char* str2)
```

The function scans `str1` and returns the length of the leftmost substring that is totally void of the characters of the substring `str2`.

Example

```
char strng[] = "The rain in Spain";
int i;

i = strcspn(strng, " in");
```

This example assigns 3 (the location of the first space) to the variable `i`.

The function `strpbrk` searches a string for the first occurrence of any character in a pattern of characters.

The *strpbrk* Function

The prototype for the function `strpbrk` is

```
char* strpbrk(const char* target, const char* pattern)
```

The function searches the `target` string for the first occurrence of *any character* among the characters of the string `pattern`. If the characters in the pattern do not occur in the string `target`, the function yields a `0`.

Example

```
char* str = "Hello there how are you";
char* substr = "hr";
char* ptr;
```

```
ptr = strpbrk(str, substr);
cout << ptr << endl;
```

This displays "here how are you", because the 'h' is encountered in the string before the 'r'.

Locating Strings

The STRING.H library offers the function strstr to locate a substring in a string.

The *strstr* Function

The prototype for the function strstr is

```
char* strstr(const char* str, const char* substr);
```

The function scans the string str for the first occurrence of a string substr. The function yields the pointer to the first character in string str that matches the parameter substr. If the string substr does not occur in the string str, the function yields a 0.

Example

```
char str[] = "Hello there! how are you";
char substr[] = "how";
char* ptr;

ptr = strstr(str, substr);
cout << ptr << endl;
```

This displays "how are you" because the string search matched "how". The pointer ptr points to the rest of the original string, starting with "how".

DO	DON'T

DO use the function strrev before calling the function strstr if you want to search for the last occurrence of a string.

DON'T forget to reverse both the main and the search strings when using the strrev function to locate the last occurrence of the search string.

The string library also provides the function strtok, which enables you to break down a string into substrings based on a specified set of delimiting characters.

NEW☞
TERM
Substrings are sometimes called *tokens*.

The *strtok* Function

The prototype for the function strtok is

```
char* strtok(char* target, const char* delimiters);
```

The function breaks down the target string into tokens, each delimited by the characters found in delimiters. A string supplies the set of delimiter characters. The following example shows how this function works in returning the tokens in a string. The function strtok modifies the string target by inserting '\0' characters after each token. (Make sure that you store a copy of the original target string in another string variable.)

Example

```
#include <stdio.h>
#include <string.h>

int main()
{
    char* str = "(Base_Cost+Profit) * Margin";
    char* tkn = "+* ()";
    char* ptr = str;

    printf("%s\n", str);
    // the first call looks normal
    ptr = strtok(str, tkn);
    printf("\nThis is broken into: %s", ptr);
    while (ptr)
        {
        // must make first argument a 0 character
        if ((ptr = strtok(0, tkn)) != 0)
            printf(", %s", ptr);
        }
    printf("\n");
    return 0;
}
```

This example displays the following when the program is run:

```
(Base_Cost+Profit) * Margin
```

```
This is broken into Base_Cost, Profit, Margin
```

Look at an example that searches for characters and strings. Listing 7.7 shows the source code for the program STRING4.CPP. The program performs the following tasks:

- [ ] Prompts you to enter the main string
- [ ] Prompts you to enter the search string
- [ ] Prompts you to enter the search character
- [ ] Displays a character ruler and the main string
- [ ] Displays the indices where the search string occurs in the main string
- [ ] Displays the indices where the search character occurs in the main string

Listing 7.7. Source code for the program STRING4.CPP.

```
1:  // C++ program that demonstrates searching for
2:  // characters and strings
3:
4:  #include <iostream.h>
5:  #include <string.h>
6:
7:  const unsigned STR_SIZE = 40;
8:
9:  int main()
10: {
11:     char mainStr[STR_SIZE+1];
12:     char subStr[STR_SIZE+1];
13:     char findChar;
14:     char *p;
15:     int index;
16:     int count;
17:
18:     cout << "Enter a string: ";
19:     cin.getline(mainStr, STR_SIZE);
20:     cout << "Enter a search string: ";
21:     cin.getline(subStr, STR_SIZE);
22:     cout << "Enter a search character: ";
23:     cin >> findChar;
```

continues

Listing 7.7. continued

```
24:
25:    cout << "            1         2         3         4" << endl;
26:    cout << "012345678901234567890123456789012345678 90" << endl;
27:    cout << mainStr << endl;
28:    cout << "Searching for string " << subStr << endl;
29:    p = strstr(mainStr, subStr);
30:    count = 0;
31:    while (p)
32:       {
33:       count++;
34:       index = p - mainStr;
35:       cout << "Match at index " << index << endl;
36:       p = strstr(++p, subStr);
37:       }
38:    if (count == 0)
39:       cout << "No match for substring in main string" << endl;
40:
41:    cout << "Searching for character " << findChar << endl;
42:    p = strchr(mainStr, findChar);
43:    count = 0;
44:    while (p)
45:       {
46:       count++;
47:       index = p - mainStr;
48:       cout << "Match at index " << index << endl;
49:       p = strchr(++p, findChar);
50:       }
51:    if (count == 0)
52:       cout << "No match for search character in main string" << endl;
53:    return 0;
54: }
```

Here is a sample session with the program in Listing 7.7.

```
Enter a string: here, there, and everywhere
Enter a search string: here
Enter a search character: e
            1         2         3         4
012345678901234567890123456789012345678 90
here, there, and everywhere
Searching for string here
Match at index 0
Match at index 7
Match at index 23
Searching for character e
Match at index 1
Match at index 3
Match at index 8
Match at index 10
Match at index 17
Match at index 19
Match at index 24
Match at index 26
```

The program in Listing 7.7 declares the strings `mainStr` and `subStr` to represent the main and search strings, respectively. The program also declares the variable `findChar` to store the search character. In addition, the program declares the character pointer `p` and the `int`-typed variables `index` and `count`.

The statements on line 18 through 23 obtain a string in `mainStr`, a search string in `subStr`, and a search character in `findChar`. Then, on lines 25 and 26, a weird construct is printed out that acts as a ruler showing where the index values occur in the string that was entered and is then printed out by line 27.

Line 29 performs an initial search of `mainStr` for `subStr` with the `strstr` function, storing the result in `p`. Line 30 initializes the `count` to 0, and then lines 31 through 37 run through a loop that continues to display the matching indices so long as the subsequent searches (that occur on line 36) come up with a new match. An interesting thing to note is how the index into the array is obtained on line 34 by subtracting the original string's address from the address of the pointer obtained in the search. You should also take careful note of how line 36 increments the result pointer before using it again in the search. This prevents the search from stopping at the same position as the previous search when it finds the exact same match as before. Lines 38 and 39 inform the user if no match was found.

The output statement on line 41 informs you that the program is now searching for the character you specified in the main string. The process of searching for the character in `findChar` is very similar to searching for the string `subStr`. The main difference is that searching for a character involves the function `strchr`.

Summary

Today's lesson examined the basic input and output operations and functions that are supported by the IOSTREAM.H and STDIO.H header files, as well as the C++ strings and their manipulation by functions that are declared in the STRING.H header file. You learned the following:

☐ Formatted stream output uses the `precision` and `width` functions to provide some basic formatting output.

☐ Standard stream input supports the insert operator `>>` to obtain input for the pre-defined data types in C++.

☐ The format codes involved in the format string of the `printf` function allow the `printf` function to control the appearance of the output and even perform type conversion.

☐ Character array strings in C++ end with the null character (the ASCII `0` character).

☐ String input requires the use of the `getline` stream input function. This function requires that you specify the input variable, the maximum number of input characters, and the optional line delimiter.

☐ The STRING.H header file contains the standard string library for the C language. This library contains many versatile functions that support copying, concatenating, converting, reversing, and searching for strings.

☐ C++ supports two methods for assigning strings. The first method assigns a string to another when you declare the latter string. The second method uses the functions `strcpy` and `strncpy` to assign one string to another at any stage in the program. The string library also offers the function `strdup` to copy a string and allocate the needed space.

☐ The function `strlen` returns the length of a string.

☐ The `strcat` and `strncat` functions enable you to concatenate two strings. The function `strncat` enables you to specify the number of characters to concatenate.

☐ The functions `strcmp`, `stricmp`, `strncmp`, and `strnicmp` enable you to perform various types of string comparisons. The function `strcmp` performs a case-sensitive comparison of two strings, using every character possible. The function `stricmp` is a version of the function `strcmp` that performs a case-insensitive comparison. The function `strncmp` is a variant of function `strcmp` that uses a specified number of characters in comparing the strings. The function `strnicmp` is a version of function `stricmp` that also uses a specified number of characters in comparing the strings.

☐ The functions `strlwr` and `strupr` convert the characters of a string into lowercase and uppercase, respectively.

☐ The function `strrev` reverses the order of characters in a string.

☐ The functions `strchr`, `strrchr`, `strspn`, `strcspn`, and `strpbrk` enable you to search for characters and simple character patterns in strings.

☐ The function `strstr` searches for a string in another string. The function `strtok` enables you to break down a string into smaller strings that are delimited by a set of characters that you specify.

Q&A

Q Why is it that I can chain `>>` or `<<` operators?

A Each of these operators returns a special stream data type that can be the input for another similar stream operator.

Q Why can't I use the console stream I/O operators in Windows applications?

A Windows applications have a fundamentally different way of interacting with you. When an EasyWin program (which emulates a non-GUI, MS-DOS application)

executes an input statement, it goes into a special mode where it monitors the keyboard input. By contrast, Windows programs (which are GUI applications) are always monitoring the mouse (its movements and its button clicks) and the keyboard, and reporting the current status to the part of Windows that monitors such events. The vast differences between GUI and non-GUI applications render non-GUI input functions useless in GUI applications.

Q Can a statement initialize a pointer using a string literal?

A Yes. The compiler stores the characters of the string literal in memory and assigns its address to that pointer. Here is an example.

```
const char* p = "I am a small string";
```

Be aware, however, that some compilers may put these strings into a part of memory that is read-only, so you will not be able to modify them. That's why the example assigns a `const char*` instead of a regular `char*`.

Q Can a statement declare a constant pointer to a literal string?

A Yes. This kind of declaration resembles the one mentioned previously. Because the statement declares a constant pointer, however, you cannot overwrite the characters of the initializing string literal (you will get a compile-time error). Here is an example.

```
const char* p = "Version 1.0";
```

Use the `const char*` pointer to store fixed messages and titles.

Q Can a statement declare an array of pointers to a set of string literals?

A Yes. This is the easiest method of using an array of pointers to access a collection of messages, titles, or other types of fixed strings. Here is an example.

```
char* mainMenu[] = { "File", "Edit", "Search", "View",
                     "Debug", "Options", "Windows", "Help"};
```

Thus, the element `mainMenu[0]` accesses the first string, `mainMenu[1]` accesses the second string, and so on.

Q How can I use `strcmp` to compare strings, starting at a specific number of characters?

A Add the offset value to the arguments of the function `strcmp`. Here is an example.

```
char s1[41] = "Borland C++ 5";
char s2[41] = "BORLAND Pascal";
int offset = 7;
int i;
i = strcmp(str1 + offset, str2 + offset);
```

Q How can I use `strncmp` to compare a specific number of characters in two strings, starting at a specific character?

A The solution to this is exactly the same as the solution to the previous question, just with a different function: add the offset value to the arguments of the function `strncmp`. Here is an example.

```
char s1[41] = "Borland C++ 5";
char s2[41] = "BORLAND Pascal";
int offset = 7;
int num = 3;
int i;
i = strncmp(str1 + offset, str2 + offset, num);
```

Workshop

The Workshop provides quiz questions to help you solidify your understanding of the material covered and exercises to provide you with experience in using what you've learned. Try to understand the quiz and exercise answers before continuing on to the next day's lesson. Answers are provided in Appendix A.

Quiz

1. What is wrong with the following statement?

   ```
   cout << "Enter a number " >> x;
   ```

2. What happens in the following statement?

   ```
   cout << "Enter three numbers: ";
   cin >> x >> y >> x;
   ```

3. Where is the error in the following program?

   ```
   #include <iostream.h>
   #include <string.h>
   const int MAX = 10;
   int main()
   {
       char s1[MAX+1];
       char s2[] = "12345678901234567890123 4567890";
       strcpy(s1, s2);
       cout << "String 1 is " << s1 << endl
            << "String 2 is " << s2;
       return 0;
   }
   ```

4. How can you fix the program in the last question using the function strncpy instead of strcpy?

5. What is the value assigned to variable i in the following statements?

   ```
   char s1[] = "Borland C++";
   char s2[] = "Borland Pascal";
   int i;
   i = strcmp(s1, s2);
   ```

6. What is the value assigned to variable i in the following statements?

   ```
   char s1[] = "Borland C++";
   char s2[] = "Borland Pascal";
   int offset = strlen("Borland");
   int i;
   ```

```
i = strcmp(s1 + offset, s2 + offset);
```

7. True or false? The following function correctly returns `true` if a string does not contain lowercase characters, and yields `false` if otherwise.

```cpp
bool hasNoLowerCase(const char* s)
{
    bool rslt;
    char* s2 = new char[strlen(s)+1];
    strcpy(s2, s);
    strupr(s2);
    rslt = strcmp(s, s2) == 0;
    delete s2;
    return rslt;
}
```

Exercises

1. Write the program OUT3.CPP, which displays a table of square roots for whole numbers in the range of 2 to 10. Use the MATH.H header file to import the `sqrt` function, which calculates the square root of a `double`-typed argument. Employ the format controls `%3.0lf` and `%3.4lf` to display the number and its square root, respectively.

2. Write the program OUT4.CPP, which prompts you for an integer and displays the hexadecimal and octal equivalent forms. Use the `printf` format controls to perform the conversion between decimal, hexadecimal, and octal numbers.

3. Write your own version of the function `strlen`. Use a `while` loop and a character-counting variable to obtain the function result.

4. Write another version of the function `strlen`. This time, use a `while` loop and a local pointer to obtain the function result.

5. Write the program STRING5.CPP, which uses the function `strtok` to break down the string `"2*(X+Y)/(X+Z) — (X+10)/(Y—5)"` into three sets of tokens, using the token delimiter strings `"+—*/ ()"`, `"( )"`, and `"+—*/ "`.

Each week in this book is accompanied with a game example to help you get a better idea of how to make use of the lessons learned. Thus far, however, you haven't learned enough to look at the game examples supplied with Borland C++. For this week, you take a look at a simple example that you can type in. The next two weeks address more interesting fare.

This week's example is a simple number-guessing game (shown in Listing R1.1). The program selects a number at random between 1 and 1,000 and prompts you to enter a number in that range. If your input is greater than the secret number, then the program tells you that your guess was higher. By contrast, if your input is less than the secret number, then the program tells you that your guess was lower. If you guess the secret number, the game ends with your victory. The program gives you up to 10 guesses.

You might be interested to know that in Extra Credit 2, you will see a full Windows version of this program written with the ObjectWindows Library. (Never mind that its real intent is to demonstrate a type of input dialog).

Listing R1.1. Source code for program GUESS.CPP.

```cpp
1: #include <ctype.h>
2: #include <iostream.h>
3: #include <stdlib.h>
4:
5: int main()
6: {
7:     int guess = 0, number, count;
8:     char tryagain;
9:
10:     randomize();
11:     cout << "The object of the game is to guess a number between" << endl
12:          << "1 and 1000.  You will be allowed 10 guesses, after" << endl
13:          << "which you will have lost." << endl;
14:     do
15:         {
16:         number = random(1000) + 1;
17:         for (count = 1; (guess != number) && (count <= 10); ++count)
18:             {
19:             cout << "Please enter try #" << count << ": ";
20:             cin >> guess;
21:             if (guess < number)
22:                 cout << "   You're too low." << endl;
23:             else if (guess > number)
24:                 cout << "   You're too high." << endl;
25:             else
26:                 cout << "   Congratulations!  Pip pip!  Good show, and all
    _that!" << endl;
27:             }
28:         if (count > 10)
29:             cout << "   Too bad.  The number was " << number << "." << endl;
30:         cout << "Would you like to try again? ";
31:         cin >> tryagain;
32:         cout << endl;
33:         } while (tolower(tryagain) == 'y');
34:     return 0;
35: }
```

Here is a sample session with the program in Listing R1.1.

```
The object of the game is to guess a number between
1 and 1000.  You will be allowed 10 guesses, after
which you will have lost.
Please enter try #1: 500
You're too low.
Please enter try #2: 750
You're too high.
Please enter try #3: 625
You're too high.
Please enter try #4: 570
You're too high.
Please enter try #5: 530
You're too low.
```

```
Please enter try #6: 550
You're too low.
Please enter try #7: 560
You're too high.
Please enter try #8: 555
You're too low.
Please enter try #9: 557
You're too low.
Please enter try #10: 559
Too bad.  The number was 558.
Would you like to try again? n
```

The first thing done by the program in Listing R1.1 is to initialize the random number generator with a call to the `randomize` function. This initializes the random number seed, allowing the program to come up with a different random number each time it's run. (If `randomize` was not called, the program would always use the same secret numbers, and the game would become rather boring.) The program then tells the user the object of the game.

Line 14 is the start of the main `do-while` loop. Lines 30 and 31 ask the user whether he or she wants to play the game again, and the conclusion of the loop on line 33 repeats if the user types Y. Note the use of the `tolower` function that enables the user to type the response in either upper- or lowercase. You then do a conversion to the case against which you want to check.

Line 16 sets the secret number via the `random` function. Because the `random` function returns a number from 0 to one less than its argument, you use 1,000 for the parameter and then add one immediately afterward to make the range 1 to 1,000. The `for` loop that starts on line 17 initializes the `count` variable to 1, and then has a clause that checks two things: that the current guess isn't correct and that the user hasn't run out of guesses. The final clause in the `for` statement increments the count.

Lines 19 and 20 perform the simple task of retrieving a guess from the user. After that, on lines 21 through 26, the program checks the user's guess against the secret number and lets the user know of his or her proximity in rough terms (can't make it too easy!). Note that if the user guesses correctly, the `for` loop will automatically terminate. If the user makes it out of the loop without guessing the number, then the program lets the user know what that secret number was on line 29.

There is a bug in this program, however. It's rather subtle, and you might not find it immediately. Try mentally running through the code in the case where the user is guessing for the last time (count is 10) and he or she actually gets the right answer. The `if` statement will print out the congratulatory message, and then the `for` loop will exit. Line 28 is designed to tell if the user has exited the loop because he or she ran out of guesses. This works in most cases as it's written; in this case, however, the program is going to assume that the user failed because the count has run out. In order to fix things, you should change line 28 to read `if (guess != number)`.

2

The second week continues teaching you about the C++ language. The topics start with the object-oriented programming (OOP) parts of C++. You learn about classes, components, and the rules for using these components. In addition, you learn about basic file I/O using the C++ stream library. Day 11 introduces you to the string class, which supports strings using C++ classes; you also learn about templates and how they're used in the Standard Template Library. Day 12 begins your introduction to the ObjectWindows Library (OWL), which enables you to create full-fledged Windows applications. From there you will be taken through some of the basics of Windows programs, including basic windows, controls, and dialog boxes.

Object-Oriented Programming and C++ Classes

Classes provide C++ with object-oriented programming (OOP) constructs. Today's lesson, which marks an important milestone for learning C++, introduces you to building individual classes as well as class hierarchy. You learn about the following topics:

- ☐ The basics of object-oriented programming
- ☐ Declaring base classes
- ☐ Constructors
- ☐ Destructors
- ☐ Declaring a class hierarchy
- ☐ Virtual functions
- ☐ Friend functions
- ☐ Operators and friend operators

Basics of Object-Oriented Programming

We live in a world of objects. Each object has its attributes and operations. Some objects are more animated than others. You can categorize objects into classes. For example, an orange is an object that belongs to the class of fruit, or a CASIO Data Bank watch is an object that belongs to the class of watches.

NEW ☛ *Object-oriented programming* (OOP) uses the notions of real-world objects to develop
TERM applications.

You also can relate individual classes in a class hierarchy. The class of CASIO Data Bank watches is part of the watch class hierarchy that might also include a Swatch or a Rolex. The basics of OOP include classes, objects, methods, inheritance, and polymorphism.

NEW ☛ A *class* defines a category of objects. Each *object* is an instance of a class.
TERM

Classes and Objects

An object shares the same attributes and functionality of other objects in the same class. Typically, an object has a unique state, defined by the current values of its attributes. The

functionality of a class determines the operations that are possible for the class instances. C++ calls the attributes of the class *data members* and calls the operations of the class *member functions*. Classes encapsulate data members and member functions.

Going back to the CASIO watch example, you can note that the buttons in the watch represent the member functions of the class of CASIO watches, whereas the display represents a data member. You can click certain buttons to edit the date and/or time. In OOP terms, the member functions alter the state of the object by changing its data members.

Messages and Methods

Object-oriented programming models the interaction with objects as events where requests are sent to an object or between objects. The object receiving a request responds by invoking the appropriate method (that's the member function in C++). C++ does not explicitly foster the notion of requests and methods, as do other OOP languages such as SmallTalk. However, some find it easier to discuss invoking member functions using the term "request." The terms *methods* and *member functions* are equivalent.

NEW☞ TERM The *request* is what is done to an object. The *method* is how the object responds to the incoming request.

NEW☞ TERM A *member function*, when you get right down to it, is just a regular function that's been embedded in a class definition. If you want to call it, you need to specify it within the context of that class.

The thing that makes a member function so special is its relationship with the class that encloses it. During the function's execution, it has access to all the data of its class, and it doesn't need to specify the name of the class. This is done with the help of a hidden parameter that's passed to each and every member function. The hidden parameter is called the this pointer, and it's a special pointer to the instance of the class itself. Whenever a function accesses any of the member data in its class, the lower level of the compiler generates code that uses the this pointer. If you need to explicitly access a pointer to the instance of the class that's called your function, you can use this.

Inheritance

In object-oriented languages, you can derive a class from another one.

NEW☞ TERM With *inheritance*, the derived class (also called the *descendant class*) inherits the data members and member functions of its *parent* and *ancestor classes*. The term *base* class is also used to describe the parents in the hierarchy.

Deriving a class refines the parent class by appending new attributes and new operations. The derived class typically declares new data members and new member functions. In addition, the derived class can override inherited member functions when the operations of these functions are not suitable for the derived class.

To apply the concept of inheritance to the CASIO Data Bank watch, consider the following possible scenario. Suppose that the watch manufacturer decides to create a CASIO Data Comm watch that offers the same features as the CASIO Data Bank plus a beeper! Rather than redesigning the new model (that is the new class, in OOP terms) from scratch, the CASIO engineers start with the existing design of the CASIO Data Bank and build on it. This process may well add new attributes and operations to the existing design and alter some existing operations to fit the new design. Thus, the CASIO Data Comm model inherits the attributes and the operations of the CASIO Data Bank model. In OOP terms, the class of CASIO Data Comm watches is a descendant of the class of CASIO Data Bank watches.

Polymorphism

The OOP feature of polymorphism allows the instances of different classes to react in a particular way to a function invocation. For example, in a hierarchy of graphical shapes (point, line, square, rectangle, circle, ellipse, and so on), each shape has a Draw function that is responsible for properly responding to a request to draw that shape.

NEW☞ TERM *Polymorphism* enables the instances of different classes to respond to the same function in ways that are appropriate to each class.

Declaring Base Classes

C++ enables you to declare a class that encapsulates data members and member functions. These functions alter and/or retrieve the values of the data members as well as perform related tasks.

Syntax

A Base Class

The general syntax for declaring a base class is

```
class className
{
private:
    <private data members>
    <private constructors>
    <private member functions>
protected:
    <protected data members>
    <protected constructors>
    <protected member functions>
public:
    <public data members>
    <public constructors>
    <public destructor>
    <public member functions>
};
```

Example

```
class point
{
protected:
    double x;
    double y;
public:
    point(double xVal, double yVal);
    double getX();
    double getY();
    void assign(double xVal, double yVal);
    point& assign(point& pt);
};
```

The Sections of a Class

The previous syntax shows that the declaration involves the keyword class. C++ classes offer three levels of visibility for the various members (that is, both data members and member functions):

☐ The private section

☐ The protected section

☐ The public section

NEW☞
TERM In the private section, only the member functions of the class can access the private members. Descendant classes are denied access to private members of its base classes. In the protected section, only the member functions of the class and its descendant classes

can access members. The public section specifies members that are visible to the member functions of the class, class instances, member functions of descendant classes, and pretty much anyone else who might be interested.

The following rules apply to the various class sections:

1. The class sections can appear in any order.

2. The class sections may appear more than once.

3. If no class section is specified, the C++ compiler treats the members as private.

4. You should avoid placing data members in the public section unless such a declaration significantly simplifies your design. Data members typically are placed in the protected section to allow their access by member functions of descendant classes.

5. Use member functions to set and/or query the values of data members. The members that set the data members assist in performing validation and updating other data members, if need be.

6. The class may have multiple constructors.

7. The class can have only one destructor, which must be declared in the public section.

8. The member functions (as well as the constructors and destructors) that have multiple statements are defined outside the class declaration. The definition may reside in the same file that declares the class. This is similar to the difference between prototyping and defining regular functions.

NEW◆ *Constructors* are special members that don't have any return type and must have the same
TERM name as the host class. They're called when class instances are created. Destructors are
called when class instances are removed.

> **Note:** It should be mentioned at this point that classes and structures really are the same—with one single difference. A class, without specifying a protection level, starts out with private. A structure starts out with public. All the rules you are used to for putting data in and manipulating structures apply to classes.

In software libraries, the definition of the member functions referred to in rule 8 typically resides in a separate source file (.H and .CPP files). When you define a member function, you must qualify the function name with the class name. The syntax of such a qualification involves using

the class name followed by two colons (::) and then the name of a function. For example, consider the following class:

```
class point
{
protected:
   double x;
   double y;
public:
   point(double xVal, double yVal);
   double getX();
   // other member functions
};
```

The definitions of the constructor and member functions are

```
point::point(double xVal, double yVal)
{
   // statements
}

double point::getX()
{
   // statements
}
```

After you declare a class, you can use the class name as a type identifier to declare class instances. The syntax resembles declaring variables.

Listing 8.1 shows the source code for the program RECT.CPP. The program prompts you to enter the length and width of a rectangle (which is an object). The program then displays the length, width, and area of the rectangle you specified.

Listing 8.1. Source code for the program RECT.CPP.

```
1:  // C++ program that illustrates a class
2:
3:  #include <iostream.h>
4:
5:  class rectangle
6:  {
7:  private:
8:     double length;
9:     double width;
10: public:
11:    rectangle()                          { assign(0, 0); }
12:    rectangle(double Len, double Wide)   { assign(Len, Wide); }
13:    double Length()                      { return length; }
14:    double Width()                       { return width; }
15:    double Area()                        { return length * width; }
16:    void assign(double Len, double Wide);
17: };
18:
19: void rectangle::assign(double Len, double Wide)
```

continues

Listing 8.1. continued

```
20: {
21:     length = Len;
22:     width = Wide;
23: }
24:
25: int main()
26: {
27:     rectangle rect;
28:     double len, wide;
29:
30:     cout << "Enter length of rectangle: ";
31:     cin >> len;
32:     cout << "Enter width of rectangle: ";
33:     cin >> wide;
34:     rect.assign(len, wide);
35:     cout << "Rectangle length = " << rect.Length() << endl
36:          << "           width  = " << rect.Width() << endl
37:          << "           area   = " << rect.Area() << endl;
38:     return 0;
39: }
```

Here is a sample session with the program in Listing 8.1.

```
Enter length of rectangle: 10
Enter width of rectangle: 12
Rectangle length = 10
          width  = 12
          area   = 120
```

The program in Listing 8.1 declares the class `rectangle`, which models a rectangle. The class has two `double`-typed data members, `length` and `width`, which store the dimensions of a rectangle. In addition, the class has two constructors: the default constructor and the nondefault constructor. The class also defines the member functions `Length`, `Width`, `Area`, and `assign`.

NEW☞ The *default constructor* doesn't take any parameters (or all its parameters have default
TERM values) and is used whenever an instance of that class is declared that doesn't take any parameters. If an instance is declared that does take parameters, the appropriate *nondefault constructor* is called.

The function `Length`, defined in the class declaration, simply returns the value in member `length`. The function `Width`, also defined in the class declaration, merely returns the value in member `width`. The function `Area`, defined in the class declaration, simply returns the value of the result of multiplying the members `length` and `width`.

The member function `assign`, defined outside the class declaration, assigns the arguments for its parameters `Len` and `Wide` to the data members `length` and `width`, respectively. The implementation of this function is simplified by not checking for negative values.

The function main declares rect as an instance of class rectangle and declares the double-typed variables len and wide. Note that there are no parameters used in the declaration (just as you're used to from all the other declarations you've done so far), but you should also note that you *could've* used some parameters to automatically specify the length and witdh of the rectangle. This would have been done with a line like the following:

```
rectangle rect(10, 20);
```

This would have called the rectangle::rectangle(double,double) function rather than the rectangle::rectangle() function and consequently assigned the parameters to length and width from the outset.

The statements on lines 30 through 33 prompt for and then retrieve values for len and wide. The function main uses these values in a call to the assign member function. The arguments of the call are variables len and wide.

The output statement on lines 35 through 37 displays the length, width, and area of the object rect. This statement calls the member functions Length, Width, and Area of the object rect.

Constructors

C++ constructors and destructors work automatically to guarantee the appropriate creation and removal of class instances.

Syntax

Constructors

The general syntax for constructors is

```
class className
{
public:
    className(); // default constructor
    className(const className& c); // copy constructor
    className(<parameter list>); // another constructor
};
```

Example

```
class point
{
protected:
    double x;
    double y;
public:
    point();
    point(double xVal, double yVal);
    point(const point& pt);
```

```
    double getX();
    double getY();
    void assign(double xVal, double yVal);
    point& assign(point& pt);
};

int main()
{
    point p1;
    point p2(10, 20);
    point p3(2);
    p1.assign(p2));
    cout << p1.getX() << " " << p1.getY() << endl;
    cout << p2.getX() << " " << p2.getY() << endl;
    cout << p3.getX() << " " << p3.getY() << endl;
    return 0;
}
```

NEW☞ A *copy constructor* enables you to create class instances by copying the data from existing
TERM instances.

C++ has the following features and rules regarding constructors:

1. The name of the constructor must be identical to the name of its class.

2. You must not include any return type, not even void.

3. A class can have any number of constructors, including none. In the latter case, the
   compiler automatically creates one for that class.

4. The default constructor is the one that either has no parameters or possesses a parameter list where all the parameters use default arguments. Here are two examples.

```
// class use parameterless constructor
class point1
{
protected:
    double x;
    double y;
public:
    point1();
    // other member functions
};

// class use constructor with default arguments
class point2
{
protected:
    double x;
    double y;
```

```
public:
    point(double xVal = 0, double yVal = 0);
    // other member functions
};
```

5. The *copy constructor* enables you to create a class instance using an existing instance. Here is an example.

```
class point
{
protected:
    double x;
    double y;
public:
    point();
    point(double xVal, double yVal);
    point(const point& pt);
    // other member functions
};
```

6. The declaration of a class instance (which includes function parameters and local instances) involves a constructor. Which constructor is called? The answer depends on how many constructors you have declared for the class and how you declared the class instance. For example, consider the following instances of the last version of the class `point`:

```
point p1;          // involves the default constructor
point p2(1.1, 1.3); // uses the second constructor
point p3(p2);       // uses the copy constructor
```

Because instance p1 specifies no arguments, the compiler uses the default constructor. The instance p2 specifies two floating-point arguments. Consequently, the compiler uses the second constructor. The instance p3 has the instance p2 as an argument. Therefore, the compiler uses the copy constructor to create instance p3 from instance p2.

DO	DON'T

DO declare copy constructors, especially for classes that model dynamic data structures. These constructors perform what is called a *deep copy*, which includes the dynamic data. By default, the compiler creates what are called *shallow copy* constructors, which copy the data members only. A shallow copy, therefore, will copy any members that contain pointers to data, but it won't copy the data itself.

DON'T rely on the shallow copy constructor to copy instances for classes having members that are pointers.

Destructors

C++ classes may contain destructors that automatically remove class instances.

Destructors

The general syntax for destructors is

```
class className
{
public:
    className(); // default constructor
    // other constructors
    ~className();
    // other member function
};
```

Example

```
class String
{
protected:
    char *str;
    int len;

public:
    String();
    String(const String& s);
    ~String();
    // other member functions
};
```

C++ has the following features and rules regarding destructors:

1. The name of the destructor must begin with a tilde (~). The rest of the destructor name must be identical to the name of its class.

2. You must not include any return type, not even void.

3. A class can have no more than one destructor. In addition, if you omit the destructor, the compiler automatically creates one for you.

4. The destructor cannot have any parameters.

5. The runtime system automatically invokes a class destructor when the instance of that class goes out of scope, or when the instance is explicitly deleted.

Examples of Constructors and Destructors

Look at a program that typifies the use of constructors and destructors. Listing 8.2 contains the source code for the ARRAY.CPP program. The program performs the following tasks:

☐ Creates a dynamic array (the object)

☐ Assigns values to the elements of the dynamic array

☐ Displays the values in the dynamic array

☐ Removes the dynamic array

 Listing 8.2. Source code for the ARRAY.CPP program.

```
1:  // Program demonstrates constructors and destructors
2:
3:  #include <iostream.h>
4:
5:  const unsigned MIN_SIZE = 4;
6:
7:  class Array
8:  {
9:  protected:
10:     double *dataPtr;
11:     unsigned sz;
12:
13: public:
14:     Array(unsigned size = MIN_SIZE);
15:     Array(const Array& a);
16:     ~Array()
17:        { delete[] dataPtr; }
18:     unsigned Size() const
19:        { return sz; }
20:     void store(double x, unsigned index)
21:        { if (index < sz) dataPtr[index] = x; }
22:     double recall(unsigned index)
23:        {
24:        if (index < sz)
25:            return dataPtr[index];
26:        return -1;
27:        }
28: };
29:
30: Array::Array(unsigned size)
31: {
32:     sz = (size < MIN_SIZE) ? MIN_SIZE : size;
33:     dataPtr = new double[sz];
34: }
35:
36: Array::Array(const Array& a)
37: {
38:     sz = a.sz;
39:     dataPtr = new double[sz];
40:     for (int i = 0; i < sz; i++)
41:         dataPtr[i] = a.dataPtr[i];
42: }
43:
44: int main()
45: {
46:     Array Arr(10);
```

continues

Listing 8.2. continued

```
47:    double x;
48:    // assign data to array elements
49:    for (unsigned i = 0; i < Arr.Size(); i++)
50:        Arr.store((double)(i * i), i);
51:    // display data in the array element
52:    cout << "Array Arr has the following values:" << endl;
53:    for (int i = 0; i < Arr.Size(); i++)
54:        cout << "Arr[" << i << "] = " << Arr.recall(i) << endl;
55:    return 0;
56: }
```

Here is a sample session with the program in Listing 8.2.

```
Array Arr has the following values:
Arr[0] = 0
Arr[1] = 1
Arr[2] = 4
Arr[3] = 9
Arr[4] = 16
Arr[5] = 25
Arr[6] = 36
Arr[7] = 49
Arr[8] = 64
Arr[9] = 81
```

The program in Listing 8.2 declares the global constant MIN_SIZE on line 5, which specifies the minimum size of dynamic arrays. The program also declares the class Array starting on line 7. The class has two data members, dataPtr and sz. The member dataPtr is the pointer to the array's dynamically allocated elements, and the member sz stores the number of elements in an instance of class Array.

The class declares a default constructor on line 14. (The constructor actually has a parameter with the default value MIN_SIZE.) The program defines that default constructor on lines 30 through 34. The default argument for the parameter size specifies the number of array elements. The statement on line 32 assigns the greater value of parameter size and the constant MIN_SIZE to the data member sz. The statement on line 33 allocates the dynamic space for the array by using the operator new. The statement assigns the base address of the dynamic array to the member dataPtr.

The class also declares a copy constructor. Because there is allocated data involved, it's wise to have this constructor in order to make sure the contents of that data are copied properly. Line 39 allocates the same amount of space as the old Array, and then proceeds to copy the old contents into the new space on lines 40 and 41.

The destructor -Array removes the dynamic space of the array by applying the operator delete to the member dataPtr.

The member function Size, defined in the class declaration, returns the value in data member sz.

The function store, defined in the class declaration, stores the value passed by parameter x at the element number specified by the parameter index. The implementation of this function is made a little safer by eliminating the possibility of the index being out of range.

The function recall, defined in the class declaration, returns the value in the element specified by the parameter index. The implementation of this function also checks to make sure that index is valid.

The function main declares the object Arr as an instance of class Array. The declaration, located on line 46, specifies that the instance has 10 elements. The function also declares the double-typed variable x. The for loop on lines 49 through 50 stores values in the instance Arr by calling the member function Array::store.

The output statement on line 52 comments on the output of the for loop on lines 53 and 54. The loop uses the control variable i and iterates from 0 to Arr.Size() -1, in increments of 1. The output statement in line 53 displays the element in instance Arr by calling the member function recall with the argument i.

Declaring a Class Hierarchy

The power of the OOP features of C++ comes from the fact that you can derive classes from existing ones. A descendant class inherits the members of its ancestor classes (that is, parent class, grandparent class, and so on) and also can override some of the inherited functions. Inheritance enables you to reuse code in descendant classes.

A Derived Class

The general syntax for declaring a derived class is

```
class className : [<protection>] parentClass
{
<friend classes>

private:
    <private data members>
    <private constructors>
    <private member functions>

protected:
    <protected data members>
    <protected constructors>
    <protected member functions>
```

```
public:
    <public data members>
    <public constructors>
    <public destructor>
    <public member functions>

<friend functions and friend operators>
};
```

Example

The following example shows the class Rectangle and its descendant, the class Box:

```
class Rectangle
{
protected:
    double length;
    double width;
public:
    Rectangle(double len, double wide);
    double getLength() const;
    double getWidth() const;
    double assign(double len, double wide);
    double calcArea();
};

class Box : public Rectangle
{
protected:
    double height;

public:
    Box(double len, double wide, double height);
    double getHeight() const;
    assign(double len, double wide, double height);
    double calcVolume();
};
```

The class lineage is indicated on the first line of the class declaration with a colon followed by the optional protection modifier (which can be either public, protected, or private) and then the name of the parent class. When you include the keyword public, you allow the instances of the descendant class to access the public members of the parent and other ancestor classes. By contrast, when you omit the keyword public or use the private keyword, you deprive the instance of the descendant class from accessing the members of the ancestor classes.

A descendant class inherits the data members of its ancestor classes. C++ has no mechanism for removing unwanted inherited data members—you're basically stuck with them. By contrast, C++ enables you to override inherited member functions. You see more about this topic later in today's lesson. The descendant class declares new data members, new member functions, and overriding member functions. Again, you can place these members in the private, protected, or public sections, as you see fit in your class design.

DO	DON'T

DO reduce the number of constructors by using default argument parameters.

DO use member functions to access the values in the data members. These member functions enable you to control and validate the values in the data members.

DON'T declare all the constructors of a class protected unless you want to force the client programmers (that is, those programmers that use the class) to use the class by declaring its descendants with public constructors.

DON'T declare the data members in the public section. This gives the class users a way to bypass any validation or other security you might have built into the member functions.

Look at an example that declares a small class hierarchy. Listing 8.3 shows the source code for the CIRCLE.CPP program. This program declares classes that contain a hierarchy of two simple geometric shapes: a circle and a cylinder. The program requires no input. Instead, it uses internal data to create the geometric shapes and to display their dimensions, areas, and volume.

Listing 8.3. Source code for the CIRCLE.CPP program.

```
1:  // Program demonstrates a small hierarchy of classes
2:
3:  #include <iostream.h>
4:  #include <math.h>
5:
6:  const double pi = 4 * atan(1);
7:
8:  inline double sqr(double x)
9:  {
10:    return x * x;
11: }
12:
13: class Circle
14: {
15: protected:
16:    double radius;
17:
18: public:
19:    Circle(double radiusVal = 0) : radius(radiusVal) {}
20:    void setRadius(double radiusVal)
21:       { radius = radiusVal; }
22:    double Radius() const
23:       { return radius; }
24:    double Area() const
25:       { return pi * sqr(radius); }
26:    void showData();
27: };
```

continues

Listing 8.3. continued

```
28:
29: class Cylinder : public Circle
30: {
31: protected:
32:    double height;
33:
34: public:
35:    Cylinder(double heightVal = 0, double radiusVal = 0)
36:       : height(heightVal), Circle(radiusVal) {}
37:    void setHeight(double heightVal)
38:       { height = heightVal; }
39:    double Height() const
40:       { return height; }
41:    double Area() const
42:       { return 2 * Circle::Area() +
43:               2 * pi * radius * height; }
44:    void showData();
45: };
46:
47: void Circle::showData()
48: {
49:    cout << "Circle radius   = " << Radius() << endl
50:         << "Circle area     = " << Area() << endl << endl;
51: }
52:
53: void Cylinder::showData()
54: {
55:    cout << "Cylinder radius = " << Radius() << endl
56:         << "Cylinder height = " << Height() << endl
57:         << "Cylinder area   = " << Area() << endl << endl;
58: }
59:
60: int main()
61: {
62:    Circle circle(1);
63:    Cylinder cylinder(10, 1);
64:
65:    circle.showData();
66:    cylinder.showData();
67:    return 0;
68: }
```

Here is a sample session with the program in Listing 8.3.

```
Circle radius     = 1
Circle area       = 3.14159

Cylinder radius   = 1
Cylinder height   = 10
Cylinder area     = 69.115
```

The program in Listing 8.3 declares the classes Circle and Cylinder. The class Circle models a circle, whereas the class Cylinder models a cylinder.

The `Circle` class declares a single data member, `radius`, to store the radius of the circle. The class also declares a constructor and a number of member functions. The constructor assigns a value to the data member `radius` when you declare a class instance. Notice that the constructor uses a new syntax to initialize the member `radius`. Whenever a constructor is called, it can call a base class's constructor and any member data after a colon. In this case, the member data `radius` is "created" by calling it with a parameter of `radiusVal`, thus initializing it to the new value.

The functions `setRadius` and `Radius` serve to set and query the value in member `radius`, respectively. The function `Area` returns the area of the circle. The function `showData` displays the radius and area of a class instance.

The class `Cylinder`, a descendant of `Circle`, declares a single data member, `height`, to store the height of the cylinder. The class inherits the member `radius` needed to store the radius of the cylinder. The `Cylinder` class declares a constructor and a number of member functions. The constructor assigns values to the `radius` and `height` members when creating a class instance. Notice the use of the new syntax to initialize the members—member `height` is initialized, and member `radius` is initialized by invoking the constructor of class `Circle` with the argument `radiusVal`. The functions `setHeight` and `Height` serve to set and query the value in member `height`, respectively. The class uses the inherited functions `setRadius` and `Radius` to manipulate the inherited member `radius`. The function `Area`, which overrides the inherited function `Circle::Area()`, returns the surface area of the cylinder. Notice that this function explicitly invokes the inherited function `Circle::Area()`. The function `showData` displays the radius, height, and area of a class instance.

I would also like to point out that the declarations of the functions `Area`, `Height`, and `Area` on lines 24, 39, and 41 end with the keyword `const`. Using the keyword `const` in this way tells the compiler that the member function cannot change any data member. This feature mainly is aimed at teams of programmers where the team manager sets the specifications for the class and determines which member functions can alter the values of data members.

The function `main` declares the instance `circle`, of class `Circle`, and assigns 1 to the circle's radius. In addition, the function also declares the instance `cylinder`, of class `Cylinder`, and assigns 10 and 1 to the circle's `height` and `radius`, respectively. The function then informs member function `showData` of the instances `circle` and `cylinder`.

Mutable Data Members

I just mentioned that the placement of `const` on the end of a member function definition keeps the member function from modifying any of the member data in the class. There is, however, a way around that with the `mutable` keyword.

The *mutable* Keyword

The general syntax of the mutable keyword is as follows:

```
mutable <type> <variable>;
```

The mutable keyword is used to make certain data member variables changeable even when a member function is declared with the const specifier.

Example

```cpp
#include <iostream.h>
class A {
   mutable int count;
   mutable const int* iptr;
   int last;
public:
   int func(int i = 0) const  // Promises not to change data
      {
      count = i++;  // But count can be changed.
      iptr = &i;    // And so can iptr
      last = i;     // But not this: ERROR ERROR ERROR
      return count;
      }
};
```

The mutable keyword can be especially useful for such things as internal reference counts that really have no bearing upon what the user of the class might see or have need to know. By specifying mutable on certain data members, you can specify const on the member functions as appropriate and still change the data that needs to be modified.

Virtual Functions

As mentioned previously, polymorphism is an important object-oriented programming feature. Consider the following simple classes and the function main:

```cpp
#include <iostream.h>
class X
{
public:
   double A(double x) { return x * x; }
   double B(double x) { return A(x) / 2; }
};

class Y : public X
{
public:
   double A(double x) { return x * x * x; }
};

int main()
{
```

```
    Y y;
    cout << y.B(3) << endl;
    return 0;
}
```

Class X contains functions A and B, where function B calls function A. Class Y, a descendant of class X, inherits function B, but overrides function A. The intent here is to have the inherited function X::B call function Y::A in order to support polymorphic behavior. What is the program output? The answer is 4.5 and not 13.5! Why? The answer lies in the fact that the compiler resolves the expression Y.B(3) by using the inherited function X::B, which in turn calls function X::A. Therefore, function Y:A is left out and the program fails to support polymorphic behavior.

C++ fixes this problem and supports polymorphic behavior by offering virtual functions.

NEW☞ *Virtual functions,* which are bound at runtime, are declared by placing the keyword virtual
TERM before the function's return type.

After you declare a function virtual, you can override it only with functions in descendant classes. These overriding functions must have the same parameter list. Virtual functions can override nonvirtual functions in base classes. Note that once a function is declared as virtual in a specific class, all descendants of that class will regard the function as virtual, whether or not the virtual keyword is used.

Virtual Functions

The general syntax for declaring virtual functions is

```
class className1
{
    // member functions
    virtual returnType functionName(<parameter list>);
};

class className2 : public className1
{
    // member functions
    virtual returnType functionName(<parameter list>);
};
```

Example

This example shows how virtual functions can successfully implement polymorphic behavior in classes X and Y:

```
#include <iostream.h>
class X
{
```

```
public:
    virtual double A(double x) { return x * x; }
    double B(double x) { return A(x) / 2; }
};

class Y : public X
{
public:
    virtual double A(double x) { return x * x * x; }
};

main()
{
    Y y;
    cout << y.B(3) << endl;
    return 0;
}
```

This example displays 13.5, the correct result, because the call to the inherited function X::B is resolved at runtime by calling Y::A.

DO	**DON'T**
DO use virtual functions when you have a callable function that implements a class-specific behavior. Declaring such a function as virtual ensures that it provides the correct response that is relevant to the associated class.	
DON'T declare a member function as virtual by default. Virtual functions have some additional overhead.	

Look at an example. Listing 8.4 shows the source code for the program VIRTUAL.CPP. The program creates a square and a rectangle and displays their dimensions and areas. No input is required.

Listing 8.4. Source code for the program VIRTUAL.CPP.

```
1:  // Program demonstrates virtual functions
2:
3:  #include <iostream.h>
4:
5:  class Square
6:  {
7:  protected:
8:      double length;
9:
10: public:
11:     Square(double len)    { length = len; }
12:     double Length()       { return length; }
13:     virtual double Width() { return length; }
```

```
14:     double Area()              { return Length() * Width(); }
15: };
16:
17: class Rectangle : public Square
18: {
19: protected:
20:     double width;
21:
22: public:
23:     Rectangle(double len, double wide)
24:         : Square(len), width(wide) {}
25:     virtual double Width() { return width; }
26: };
27:
28: int main()
29: {
30:     Square square(10);
31:     Rectangle rectangle(10, 12);
32:
33:     cout << "Square has length = " << square.Length() << endl
34:          << "        and area   = " << square.Area() << endl;
35:     cout << "Rectangle has length = "
36:          << rectangle.Length() << endl
37:          << "            and width   = "
38:          << rectangle.Width() << endl
39:          << "            and area    = "
40:          << rectangle.Area() << endl;
41:     return 0;
42: }
```

Here is a sample session with the program in Listing 8.4.

```
Square has length = 10
        and area    = 100
Rectangle has length = 10
          and width  = 12
          and area   = 120
```

The program in Listing 8.4 declares the classes Square and Rectangle to model squares and rectangles, respectively. The class Square declares a single data member, length, to store the length (and width) of the square. The class declares a constructor with the parameter len, which passes arguments to the member length. The class also declares the functions Length, Width, and Area. Both functions Length and Width return the value in member length. Notice that the class declares function Width as virtual. The function Area returns the area of the rectangle, calculated by calling the functions Length and Width. I invoke these functions rather than use the data member length in order to demonstrate how the virtual function Width works.

The program then declares class Rectangle as a descendant of class Square. The class Rectangle declares the data member width and inherits the member length. These members enable the class to store the basic dimensions of a rectangle. The class constructor has the parameters len and wide. Notice that the constructor invokes the constructor Square and supplies it with the argument len. The constructor initializes the data member width with the value of parameter wide.

The class Rectangle declares the virtual function Width. This version returns the value in data member width. The class inherits the member functions Length and Area without bothering to change them because their implementation is adequate for the Rectangle.

The function main declares the object square as an instance of class Square. The instance square has a length of 10. The function main also declares the object rectangle as an instance of class Rectangle with a length of 10 and a width of 12.

The output statement on lines 33 and 34 displays the length and area of the instance square. The statement calls Length and Area in order to obtain the sought values. The instance square invokes the function Area, which in turn calls the functions Square::Length and Square::Width.

The output statement on lines 35 through 40 displays the length, width, and area of the instance rectangle. The statement calls Length, Width, and Area. The instance responds by calling the inherited function Square::Length, the virtual function Rectangle::Width, and the inherited function Square::Area. The latter function calls the inherited function Square::Length and the virtual function Rectangle::Width to correctly calculate the area of the rectangle.

DO	**DON'T**

DO declare your destructor as virtual. This ensures polymorphic behavior in destroying class instances. In addition, I highly recommend that you declare a copy constructor and an assignment operator for each class.

DON'T forget that you inherit virtual functions and destructors in the descendant class. You need not declare shell functions and destructors that simply call the corresponding member of the parent class.

The Rule for Virtual Functions

The rule for declaring a virtual function is "once virtual, always virtual." In other words, after you declare a function to be virtual in a class, any descendant class that overrides the virtual function must do so using another function that has the same parameter list. If the descendant class fails to use the same parameter list, the base class's version of the virtual function will be inaccessible to the descendant class (and any of its descendants). At first, this rule seems to lock you in. This limitation certainly is true for object-oriented programming languages that support virtual functions but not overloaded functions. In the case of C++, the workaround is interesting. You can declare nonvirtual and overloaded functions that have the same name as the virtual function, but bear a different parameter list. Moreover, you cannot inherit nonvirtual member functions that share the same name with a virtual function. Here is a simple example that illustrates the point.

```
#include <iostream.h>
class A
{
public:
    A() {}
    virtual void foo(char c)
        { cout << "virtual A::foo() returns " << c << endl; }
};

class B : public A
{
public:
    B() {}
    void foo(const char* s)
        { cout << "B::foo() returns " << s << endl; }
    void foo(int i)
        { cout << "B::foo() returns " << i << endl; }
    virtual void foo(char c)
        { cout << "virtual B::foo() returns " << c << endl; }
};

class C : public B
{
public:
    C() {}
    void foo(const char* s)
        { cout << "C::foo() returns " << s << endl; }
    void foo(double x)
        { cout << "C::foo() returns " << x << endl; }
    virtual void foo(char c)
        { cout << "virtual C::foo() returns " << c << endl; }
};

int main()
{
    A Aobj;
    B Bobj;
    C Cobj;

    Aobj.foo('A');
    Bobj.foo('B');
    Bobj.foo(10);
    Bobj.foo("Bobj");
    Cobj.foo('C');
    Cobj.foo(144.123);
    Cobj.foo("Cobj");
    return 0;
}
```

This code declares three classes—A, B, and C—to form a linear hierarchy of classes. Class A declares function foo(char) as virtual. Class B also declares its own version of the virtual function foo(char). In addition, class B declares the nonvirtual, overloaded functions foo(const char*) and foo(int). Class C, the descendant of class B, declares the virtual function foo(char) and the nonvirtual and overloaded functions foo(const char*) and foo(double). Notice that class C must declare the `foo(const char*)` function if it needs the function because it cannot inherit the member function `B::foo(const char*)`. C++ supports a different function inheritance scheme when an overloaded function and virtual function are involved. The function `main` creates an instance for each of the three classes and involves the various versions of the member function `foo`.

Friend Functions

C++ allows member functions to access all the data members of a class. In addition, C++ grants the same privileged access to friend functions. The declaration of friend functions appears in the class and begins with the keyword `friend`. Other than using the special keyword, friend functions look very much like member functions—except they cannot access the befriended class automatically, because that requires the hidden `this` pointer. Given a pointer to an instance of the befriended class, however, the function can access all parts of the class. When you define friend functions outside the declaration of their befriended class, you need not qualify the function names with the name of the class.

**NEW☞
TERM** *Friend functions* are ordinary functions that have access to all data members of one or more classes.

Syntax

Friend Functions

The general form of friend functions is

```
class className
{
public:
    className();
    // other constructors

friend returnType friendFunction(<parameter list>);
};
```

Example

```
class String
{
protected:
    char *str;
    int len;

public:
    String();
    ~String();
```

```
      // other member functions
   friend String& append(String& str1, String& str2);
   friend String& append(const char* str1, String& str2);
   friend String& append(String& str1, const char* str2);
   };
```

Friend classes can accomplish tasks that are awkward, difficult, and even impossible with member functions.

Look at a simple example for using friend functions. Listing 8.5 contains the source code for the FRIEND.CPP program. This program internally keeps track of the memory needed to store a character array. It's a first pass at creating a string class.

Listing 8.5. Source code for the FRIEND.CPP program.

```
1:  // Program demonstrates friend functions
2:
3:  #include <iostream.h>
4:  #include <string.h>
5:
6:  class String
7:  {
8:  public:
9:      String(const char* Str = 0);
10:     String(const String& Str);
11:     virtual ~String();
12:
13:     char* Array() { return str; }
14:     void Assign(const String& Str);
15:
16:     friend String add(const String& s1, const String& s2);
17:
18:  private:
19:     char* str;
20:     int   num;
21:  };
22:
23:  String::String(const char* Str)
24:  {
25:      str = 0;
26:      num = Str ? strlen(Str) : 0;
27:      if (num > 0)
28:          {
29:          str = new char[num + 1];
30:          strcpy(str, Str);
31:          }
32:  }
33:
34:  String::String(const String& Str)
35:  {
36:      Assign(Str);
37:  }
38:
39:  String::~String()
```

continues

Listing 8.5. continued

```
40: {
41:     delete[] str;
42: }
43:
44: void String::Assign(const String& Str)
45: {
46:     delete[] str;
47:     str = 0;
48:     num = Str.num;
49:     if (num > 0)
50:         {
51:         str = new char[num + 1];
52:         strcpy(str, Str.str);
53:         }
54: }
55:
56: String add(const String& s1, const String& s2)
57: {
58:     String newstr;
59:
60:     newstr.num = s1.num + s2.num;
61:     if (newstr.num > 0)
62:         {
63:         newstr.str = new char[newstr.num + 1];
64:         strcpy(newstr.str, s1.str);
65:         strcat(newstr.str, s2.str);
66:         }
67:     return newstr;
68: }
69:
70: int main()
71: {
72:     String s1("Kevin");
73:     String s2(" Hay");
74:     String s3;
75:
76:     s3.Assign(add(s1, s2));
77:     cout << "\"" << s1.Array() << "\" + \"" << s2.Array()
78:         << "\" = \"" << s3.Array() << "\"" << endl;
79:     return 0;
80: }
```

Here is a sample session with the program in Listing 8.5.

```
"Kevin" + " Hay" = "Kevin Hay"
```

The program in Listing 8.5 declares the class String, which makes a first attempt at modeling the kind of string that Pascal and BASIC programmers are used to. C++ offers a string class (which will be covered on Day 11), but it doesn't hurt to try building a simple model now to help demonstrate a few other C++ concepts.

The String class has two constructors, the first of which takes a character array (a standard C string). This character pointer defaults to the value of 0, thus letting the constructor act as a default constructor. The other constructor is a copy constructor, which takes a reference to another instance of a String and then copies its contents into the one being constructed. The destructor is declared as virtual to make sure it gets called properly in any derived version. I, personally, make it a practice to always declare my destructors as virtual to be sure I don't make a mistake later on.

Next are the member functions Array, which is used to get a character array version of String, and Assign, which is used to change the contents of the String. There's also a friend function in there called add, which takes two separate Strings and combines them, returning the result. In the private section you will see the two data members str and num, which hold a pointer to the internal character array and the number of items in that array, respectively.

The first constructor starts its definition on line 23. It begins by initializing the str member to 0, just in case the passed Str parameter is 0. The strlen function is used to assign the length of the parameter to num so long as the passed Str parameter is nonzero, and then, if that value is greater than zero, a new character array is created for str, into which the contents of the parameter Str are copied.

The second constructor, starting on line 34, is the copy constructor, which is useful for creating copies of objects. As a matter of fact, C++ will often make use of copy constructors in hidden ways. For example, the return value from the add function in this example is a String. In order to create that object from the local version that's actually returned from the function, C++ creates a new object, calling the copy constructor to initialize the new instance. In this case, the copy constructor makes use of the Assign member function to do all the dirty work.

The destructor that starts on line 39 fairly simply gets rid of the memory that's been allocated so far. Note how useful this feature of classes is. This has just now caused a pointer that's been dynamically allocated to be automatically freed when the class that allocated it goes out of scope. It makes cleanup much easier when you don't have to worry so much about it. Of course, you have to make sure you remember to put that delete statement in the destructor.

The Assign member function that starts on line 44 takes another String as a parameter. First, before it can change the current value of the internal str data member, it must free the memory that it's already using. Then, it's a simple matter of copying the contents of the passed Str into a newly allocated array.

The add function that starts on line 56 is also rather simple. First it declares a new String to hold the result, then manually creates the room for the new information before copying in the old strings. Note that this function, though not a member function of String, is able to access the internal member data that would normally be hidden to a nonfriend function. Also note that, although it's able to access these members, it must first preface them with the appropriate class name. add isn't a member function, but rather a separate function that only has the privilege of getting at the internal data, not the access.

Putting it all together in the main function, three little strings are declared, two of them preinitialized with a name. Line 76 then calls the member function Assign to set s3's value to the result of the function add. This is all then displayed for the user starting on line 77.

Operators and Friend Operators

The last program used a member function and a friend function to implement some functions that are implemented in regular types via operators such as = and +. The approach is typical in C and Pascal because these languages do not support user-defined operators. By contrast, C++ enables you to declare operators and friend operators. These operators include +, -, *, /, %, ==, !=, <=, <, >=, >, +=, -=, *=, /=, %=, [], (), <<, and >>. Consult a C++ language reference book for more details on the rules of using these operators. C++ treats operators and friend operators as special member functions and friend functions.

Operators and Friend Operators

The general syntax for declaring operators and friend operators is

```
class className
{
public:
    // constructors and destructor
    // member functions

    // unary operator
    returnType operator operatorSymbol();
    // binary operator
    returnType operator operatorSymbol(operand);
    // unary friend operator
    friend returnType operator operatorSymbol(operand);
    // binary operator
    friend returnType operator operatorSymbol(firstOperand,
                                              secondOperand);
};
```

Example

```
class String
{
protected:
    char *str;
    int num;

public:
    String();
    ~String();
    // other member functions
    // assignment operator
    String& operator =(String& s);
    String& operator +=(String& s);
```

```
       // concatenation operators
       friend String& operator +(String& s1, String& s2);
       friend String& operator +(const char* s1, String& s2);
       friend String& operator +(String& s1, const char* s2);
       // relational operators
       friend int operator >(String& s1, String& s2);
       friend int operator =>(String& s1, String& s2);
       friend int operator <(String& s1, String& s2);
       friend int operator <=(String& s1, String& s2);
       friend int operator ==(String& s1, String& s2);
       friend int operator !=(String& s1, String& s2);
};
```

The functions you write use the operators and friend operators just like predefined operators. Therefore, you can create operators to support the operations of classes that model, for example, complex numbers, strings, arrays, and matrices. These operators enable you to write expressions that are far more readable than expressions that use named functions.

Look at an example. Listing 8.6 contains the source code for the OPERATOR.CPP program. This program was created by modifying and expanding Listing 8.5. The new program replaces some of the previous functions with operators.

 Listing 8.6. Source code for the OPERATOR.CPP program.

```
1:  // Program demonstrates operators
2:
3:  #include <iostream.h>
4:  #include <string.h>
5:
6:  class String
7:  {
8:  public:
9:      String(const char* Str = 0);
10:     String(const String& Str);
11:     virtual ~String();
12:
13:     operator const char*()    { return str; }
14:     String& operator=(const String& Str);
15:
16:     friend String operator+(const String& s1, const String& s2);
17:
18: private:
19:     char* str;
20:     int   num;
21: };
22:
23: String::String(const char* Str)
24: {
25:     str = 0;
26:     num = Str ? strlen(Str) : 0;
27:     if (num > 0)
28:         {
29:         str = new char[num + 1];
30:         strcpy(str, Str);
```

continues

Listing 8.6. continued

```
31:            }
32: }
33:
34: String::String(const String& Str)
35: {
36:     operator=(Str);
37: }
38:
39: String::~String()
40: {
41:     delete[] str;
42: }
43:
44: String& String::operator=(const String& Str)
45: {
46:     delete[] str;
47:     str = 0;
48:     num = Str.num;
49:     if (num > 0)
50:         {
51:         str = new char[num + 1];
52:         strcpy(str, Str.str);
53:         }
54:     return *this;
55: }
56:
57: String operator+(const String& s1, const String& s2)
58: {
59:     String newstr;
60:
61:     newstr.num = s1.num + s2.num;
62:     if (newstr.num > 0)
63:         {
64:         newstr.str = new char[newstr.num + 1];
65:         strcpy(newstr.str, s1.str);
66:         strcat(newstr.str, s2.str);
67:         }
68:     return newstr;
69: }
70:
71: int main()
72: {
73:     String s1("Kevin");
74:     String s2(" Hay");
75:     String s3;
76:
77:     s3 = s1 + s2;
78:     cout << "\"" << s1 << "\" + \"" << s2
79:          << "\" = \"" << s3 << "\"" << endl;
80:     return 0;
81: }
```

Here is a sample session with the program in Listing 8.6.

```
"Kevin" + " Hay" = "Kevin Hay"
```

The only differences in this version from that of Listing 8.5 is that I've replaced a number of the functions with operator equivalents. The obvious ones are on line 14 and line 16. I've simply replaced Assign with operator= and add with operator+. An additional complexity is that, because of the standard definition for the operator= function, I had to add a return value to the function that returns a reference to the object being assigned. This should always be the object itself, and so I return the this pointer on line 54.

The interesting conversion is the operator const char* on line 13. C++ not only enables you to override and define the standard operators, but it also enables you to define conversion operators. Whenever a default conversion to const char* is required, this function will automatically get called. Take care, though; if you have more than one conversion type, it may confuse the compiler if there can ever be any ambiguity between which one might be needed in a given situation. For this reason, some OOP purists often discourage the use of these types of operator functions.

Again, everything is brought together in the main function, only this time it's a lot easier to read and looks like the String class was just another type like an int or a double. The program illustrates that you can use operators and friend operators to write code that is more readable and supports a higher level of abstraction.

Summary

Today's lesson introduced you to C++ classes and discussed the following topics:

- ☐ The basics of object-oriented programming include classes, objects, methods, inheritance, and polymorphism.

- ☐ You declare base classes to specify the various private, protected, and public members. C++ classes contain data members and member functions. The data members store the state of a class instance, and the member functions query and manipulate that state.

- ☐ Constructors and destructors support the automatic creation and removal of class instances. Constructors are special members that must have the same name as the host class. You may declare any number of constructors, or none at all. In the latter case, the compiler creates one for you. Each constructor enables you to create a class instance in a different way. There are two special types of constructors: the default constructor and the copy constructor. In contrast to constructors, C++ enables you to declare only one destructor, and it must be parameterless. The runtime system automatically invokes the constructor and destructor when a class instance comes into and goes out of its scope.

- ☐ Declaring a class hierarchy enables you to derive classes from existing ones. The descendant classes inherit the members of their base classes. C++ classes are able to override inherited member functions by defining their own versions. If you override a nonvirtual function, you may declare the new version using a different parameter list. By contrast, you cannot alter the parameter list of an inherited virtual function.

☐ Virtual member functions enable your classes to support polymorphic behavior. Such behavior offers a response that is suitable for each class in a hierarchy. After you declare a function virtual, you can override it only with a virtual function in a descendant class. All versions of a virtual function in a class hierarchy must have the same signature.

☐ Friend functions are special nonmember functions that may access protected and private data members. These functions enable you to implement operations that are more flexible than those offered by member functions.

☐ Operators and friend operators enable you to support various operations, such as addition, assignment, and indexing. These operators enable you to offer a level of abstraction for your classes. In addition, they assist in making the expressions that manipulate class instances more readable and more intuitive.

Q&A

Q What happens if I declare the default, copy, and other constructors as protected?

A Client programs are unable to create instances of that class. However, client programs can use that class by declaring descendant classes with public constructors.

Q Can I chain methods to an instance?

A Yes, you can, as long as the chained member functions return a reference to the same class that was invoked. For example, if you have a class String with the following member functions:

```
String& upperCase();
String& reverse();
String& mapChars(char find, char replace);
```

you can write the following statement for the instance of class String s:

```
s.upperCase().reverse().mapChar(' ', '+');
```

Q What happens if a class relies on the copy constructor, which is created by the compiler, to copy instances of a class that has pointers?

A These constructors perform a bit-by-bit copy. Consequently, the corresponding pointer members in both instances end up with the address to the same dynamic data. This kind of duplication is a recipe for trouble!

Q Can I create an array of instances?

A Yes, you can. However, the accompanying class must have a default constructor. The instantiation of the array uses the constructor mentioned previously.

8

Q Can I use a pointer to create an instance of class?

A Yes, you need to use the operators `new` and `delete` to allocate and deallocate the dynamic space for the instance. Here is an example using the class `Complex`. Don't forget that the `->` operator is used to access members of classes or structures when you use pointers to those classes or structures.

```
Complex* pC;
pC = new Complex;
// manipulate the instance accessed by pointer pC
delete pC;
```

   or

```
Complex* pC = new Complex;
// manipulate the instance accessed by pointer pC
delete pC;
```

Workshop

The Workshop provides quiz questions to help you solidify your understanding of the material covered and exercises to provide you with experience in using what you've learned. Try to understand the quiz and exercise answers before continuing on to the next day's lesson. Answers are provided in Appendix A.

Quiz

1. Where is the error in the following class declaration?

```
class String {
    char *str;
    unsigned len;
    String();
    String(const String& s);
    String(unsigned size, char = ' ');
    String(unsigned size);
    String& assign(String& s);
    ~String();
    unsigned getLen() const;
    char* getString();
    // other member functions
};
```

2. Where is the error in the following class declaration?

```
class String {
protected:
    char *str;
    unsigned len;
public:
```

287

```
        String();
        String(const char* s);
        String(const String& s);
        String(unsigned size, char = ' ');
        String(unsigned size);
        ~String();
        // other member functions
    };
```

3. True or false? The following statement, which creates the instance s based on the preceding declaration of class `String`, is correct:

```
s = String("Hello Borland C++");
```

4. Looking at the program OPERATOR.CPP, if you change the declarations of the instances in function `main` to the following, will the program still compile?

```
String s1 = String("Kevin");
String s2 = String(" Hay");
String s3 = s1;
```

Exercise

Create the program OARRAY.CPP from OPERATOR.CPP by replacing the individual instances s1 to s3 with s, an array of instances.

9

Namespaces

Namespaces provide a way of resolving conflicts between similar names and keeping logical sections of code separate. Runtime type information (RTTI) gives C++ programs the ability to dynamically determine the types of variables and do type-safe conversions.

Today you also will learn about templates, the C++ version of a type-checking macro. Hand in hand with templates, you also learn about the Standard Template Library that comes with Borland C++ 5. The Standard Template Library is a useful set of classes for manipulating collections of data.

In today's chapter you will learn about the following:

- [ ] Namespaces
- [ ] Runtime type information
- [ ] Templates
- [ ] The Standard Template Library
- [ ] The Borland Class Libraries

Namespaces

When you start to build up large libraries of useful routines and classes, conflicts in names start to appear. One library might want to use the type `window` to represent something used to look through a wall in a house, another might want to use the term to represent something visible on a computer, and yet another library might want to use `Window` to represent something visible on a completely different computer.

Previously, such conflicts were resolved by prepending these type names with words to represent which version of the type name was represented. Using the examples from the previous paragraph, these type names might be `house_window`, `pc_window`, and `mac_window`. This works, of course, but it becomes quite cumbersome when typing these names out over and over again, and the resulting code starts to look really ugly and hard to read.

What C++ needed was a way of separating these types in such a way that one could refer to them in a more logical manner. This is accomplished with namespaces.

NEW☞
TERM
A *namespace* is a grouping of code into a named section. This is similar to how code can be broken up among different functions—except one doesn't call a namespace; rather, one declares its use.

Syntax

Declaring A Namespace

The general syntax for declaring a namespace is as follows:

```
namespace namespaceName
{
    <statements, declarations, etc.>
}
```

The use of a namespace can solve the window problem in a logical, more easily readable format. To solve the previous example, you could place the same window type in three separate namespaces: house, pc, and mac. This would be done in something similar to the following:

```
namespace house
{
    class window;
}

namespace pc
{
    class window;
}

namespace mac
{
    class window;
}
```

As you can see, there's really very little to declaring a namespace. Basically, you just wrap a section of code in a namespace declaration. As a matter of fact, namespaces are open. That is to say, you can declare one section of code in a namespace, then elsewhere you can declare a completely different section of code in the same namespace. Both of these sections of code will be considered to be in the same namespace. For example:

```
namespace fnorky
{
    void foo();
    int bar();
} // end of namespace fnorky

const char* mars();
const char* jupiter();

namespace fnorky
{
    int wankel();
    int rotary();
    int engine();
} // end of namespace fnorky
```

The function declarations for `foo`, `bar`, `wankel`, `rotary`, and `engine` are all members of the namespace `fnorky`. Of all the preceding function declarations, only the two function definitions `mars` and `jupiter` are not members of the namespace `fnorky`. These latter two are said to be in the global scope, whereas the other five are said to be in the scope of namespace `fnorky`.

The ANSI/ISO committee that is currently working on the standard for C++ has decreed that libraries should be placed in namespaces to help keep them separate and eliminate potential name conflicts. The Standard Template Library (described later today) is currently the only part of Borland C++ that is in a namespace, though other pieces are scheduled to be placed in one later. The most glaring example of a library that deserves its own namespace is the Object Window Library (OWL), which I begin discussing on Day 12. It isn't in a namespace for Borland C++ 5 due to backwards compatibility; there is a lot of existing code that doesn't know anything about namespaces, and if OWL were to be placed in there immediately for this release, a lot of code would cease to function properly. Expect future releases of Borland C++ to fold more and more of their libraries into namespaces.

Using Namespaces

After you've placed things inside a namespace, you won't be able to use it unless you let the compiler know that you want to make use of the namespace. The simplest method is to just treat the namespace entries in the same way as you would a class member; that is to say, you use the scope operator (`::`). You can place the namespace name in front of the `::` and the member of the namespace after, as follows:

```
int rslt = fnorky::bar();
```

If you're planning on using a particular function or data object from a namespace, it can start to get quite cumbersome typing the name of the namespace each time it's needed. This is where the `using` directive comes in.

Syntax

The *using* Directive

The general syntax for the `using` directive is as follows:

```
using namespaceName::namespaceMember;
```

Example

```
using fnorky::engine;
int rslt1 = engine();
int rslt2 = engine();
```

After you've declared the `using` directive, the object you've specified is usable for the duration of the current scope. This means that if you use the directive outside of any function, then the directive has a global scope, and you can use the object at any point after the declaration. If, however, you use the directive inside a function (or, indeed, between any two curly braces that specify a scope), then the specified object is usable for the duration of the function. For example:

```
using fnorky::wankel;

int myFunc()
{
    using fnorky::engine;

    wankel();   // Legal: fnorky::wankel declared globally
    rotary();   // ILLEGAL: fnorky::rotary not yet declared
    engine();   // Legal: fnorky::engine declared locally
}

int myOtherFunc()
{
    using fnorky::rotary;

    wankel();   // Legal: fnorky::wankel declared globally
    rotary();   // Legal: fnorky::rotary declared locally
    engine();   // ILLEGAL: fnorky::engine not declared anymore
}
```

In addition to the using directive, there is a using declaration (take careful note of how similar the two terms are). The using declaration is meant as a transition measure to let programmers get used to the namespaces that are actually very new to C++.

The *using* Declaration

The general syntax of the using declaration is as follows:

```
using namespace namspaceName;
```

Example

```
using namespace fnorky;

int w = wankel();
int r = rotary();
int e = engine();
```

After you've placed the using declaration in your code, you can make use of everything contained in the particular namespace; no further qualification is needed. The using declaration, as the using directive, is good for the duration of the current scope. If you use the declaration outside of a function, everything in that file can make use of the namespace, but if you use the declaration inside a function or between any other set of curly braces, the namespacc will be usable only until the matching end brace.

Namespace Aliases

One problem with namespaces is that you don't want to make their names too small. If you use small names only for your namespaces, then you're liable to have conflicts between different people all wanting to use, say, the same three-letter acronym for something. On the other hand, it's rather cumbersome to keep using large names when writing the programs that make use of the namespaces.

```
namespace TeachYourselfBorlandC5
{
    void func1();
    void func2();
    void func3();
}

void myFunc()
{
    TeachYourselfBorlandC5::func1();
    TeachYourselfBorlandC5::func2();
    TeachYourselfBorlandC5::func3();
}
```

You'd soon wear down the tips of your fingers if you had to type that over and over again. The solution is to use namespace aliases.

The Namespace Alias

The general syntax of a namespace alias is as follows:

```
namespace namespaceAlias = originalNamespace;
```

Example

```
void myFunc()
{
    namespace tyb5 = TeachYourselfBorlandC5;
    tyb5::func1();
    tyb5::func2();
    tyb5::func3();
}
```

With namespace aliases, you can give long, descriptive names to any namespace that you might have to pass out into the world; the end user can make up an alias if they so desire.

Member Function Overloading

Witness a common problem in C++:

```
class Base
{
public:
   void func(char);
};

class Derived : public Base
{
public:
   void func(int);  // hides func(char)
};

void useClass(Derived& d)
{
   d.func('c');  // calls Derived::func(int)
}
```

Because the `Base::func` member function wasn't declared as virtual, the `Derived::func` member function hides the base class's version. This means that the `useClass` function will call the wrong version of `func`. Namespaces provide a solution. Compare the following code to the last example:

```
class Base
{
public:
   void func(char);
};

class Derived : public Base
{
public:
   void func(int);    // hides func(char)
   using Base::func; // bring Base::func into Derived
};

void useClass(Derived& d)
{
   d.func('c');  // calls Base::func(char)
}
```

And now you've got the desired result.

Resolving Ambiguity

Namespaces can also help to resolve some ambiguities. It is possible to create some situations in which the compiler might have difficulty deciding what you want, situations in which you can create ambiguity. Examine the following:

```
class Base1
{
public:
    void func(int);
};

class Base2
{
public:
    void func2(double);
};

class Derived : public Base1, public Base2
{
public:
    void watusi()
        {
        func(1);     // ERROR: which func should be used?
        func(1.0);  // ERROR: which func should be used?
        }
};
```

In this case the compiler can't decide which base class's version of func to use. They both have the same importance as far as the compiler is concerned. The solution is to redo Derived so that it contains the definitions for both versions of func:

```
class Derived : public Base1, public Base2
{
public:
    using Base1::func;
    using Base2::func;

    void watusi()
        {
        func(1);
        func(1.0);
        }
};
```

Now Derived has its own declarations for the func member functions. As far as the compiler is concerned, those two different versions are a part of the Derived itself, and so the compiler has no trouble finding which one to use inside watusi.

Runtime Type Information

Runtime type information (RTTI) provides a means of identifying and retrieving information about C++ objects. The basic idea behind the process is simple: there's a single, built-in operator, `typeid`, that returns a reference to an object of type `typeinfo` (defined in the TYPEINFO.H header file). This `typeinfo` object can then be compared to other `typeinfo` objects for equality. You can also get the name of the object from `typeinfo`'s member function `name`.

There is one major restriction, however. In order to keep things simple for the compiler writers and in order to keep code size small, `typeid` works only on objects that have virtual functions in them. Most of the time objects have virtual functions in them; if for no other reason, the destructor is usually virtual to guard against potential problems with derivation.

The *typeid* Operator

The general syntax of the `typeid` operator is as follows:

```
const typeinfo& id = typeid(typeName);
const typeinfo& id = typeid(objName);
```

Example

```
class Flibble {};
Flibble var;

const typeinfo& id1 = typeid(Flibble);
const typeinfo& id2 = typeid(var);
if (id1 == id2)
    cout << "id1 and id2 are equal" << endl;
```

This example prints out the text stating the equality of id1 and id2.

The most important thing to note from the example in the syntax box is how the two `typeinfo` references can be compared for equality. This is the prime use for `typeid`: determining whether or not two objects are of the same type.

The other, more infrequent use for the `typeinfo` object is to obtain a textual name for a type. This is done with the `name` member function.

The *typeinfo::name* Member Function

The general syntax for the `typeinfo::name` member function is as follows:

```
const char* name = typeid(<typeName or objName>).name();
```

Example

```cpp
#include <iostream.h>

class A {};
class B : public A {};
class C : public A {};

void foo(const A& a)
{
    cout << typeid(a).name() << endl;
}

int main()
{
    B b;
    foo(b);
    return 0;
}
```

When compiled and run, this example will print out B.

The `name` member function is actually not used all that often. It's most useful when you need to put in diagnostic statements of some kind that will print the name of an object into a log file or debugging monitor.

Type-Safe Casting

The type information embedded in objects for RTTI means more than just being able to compare the types of two objects together. It also provides a means for type-safe casting. You will recall from Day 2 the discussion of type casting and how you can convert one type of object to another with the following syntax:

```
(type_cast)expression
```

This is extremely useful, but it can be also be extremely dangerous. There can be times when you might try to blindly cast one object into another when the two objects just aren't compatible. Examine the following:

```cpp
struct Narf
{
    int myInt;
};

struct Zort
{
    char myStr[25];
};
```

```
void Poit(Narf* arg)
{
   Zort* ptr = (Zort*)arg;
   cout << ptr->myStr;
}
```

Note how different those two structures Narf and Zort are. But then notice how Poit just blindly casts its parameter into the other type. C++ will compile this code with no problems, but when you try to run things you'll end up with some nasty problems.

The solution is to introduce some new methods of type casting:

- ☐ dynamic_cast
- ☐ static_cast
- ☐ const_cast
- ☐ reinterpret_cast

These enable you to be a little more specific about how you perform your type casting. Each has a specific use for changing the types of objects.

The *dynamic_cast* Operator

The dynamic_cast operator provides for safe conversions from one type of pointer or reference to another. It does this by making use of the runtime type information embedded in classes to make sure that the requested cast should be allowed. If the conversion is allowed, the operator returns the requested type. If the conversion isn't allowed, then the operator returns a 0.

The *dynamic_cast* Operator

The general syntax of the dynamic_cast operator is as follows:

```
dynamic_cast<newType*>(origPtr);
dynamic_cast<newType&>(origRef);
```

The first version converts the origPtr variable to a newType pointer. If the cast is not allowed, dynamic_cast returns 0. The second version converts the origRef variable to a newType reference. If the cast is not allowed, dynamic_cast throws an exception of type Bad_cast. Because dynamic_cast requires type information to be embedded in the objects being converted, only classes with virtual functions can be used. The cast is generally used for traversing class hierarchies—in other words, converting from a base class to a derived class.

One thing to pay careful attention to here is the use of the angle brackets (< >) instead of the standard parentheses used elsewhere in the language. This was done, in part, to help make the RTTI version of the cast stand out against the other method of casting.

Example

```
void func(TWindow* win)
{
   TDialog* dlg = dynamic_cast<TDialog*>(win);
   if (dlg)
      {
      // treat as a TDialog
      }
   else
      {
      // treat as ordinary TWindow
      }
}
```

It's important to note that the dynamic_cast operator converts only between either pointers or references. The most common usage is with pointers.

The *static_cast, const_cast,* and *reinterpret_cast* Operators

The static_cast operator doesn't make use of the type information embedded in classes. Instead, it's meant as one of the replacements for the standard type casting inherited from the C programming language. It was introduced into the language, as were the reinterpret_cast and const_cast operators, for the express purpose of making the programmer think first about the cast and to make certain types of casting easier to locate in source code through searching.

The *static_cast* Operator

The general syntax of the static_cast operator is as follows:

```
static_cast<newType>(varName);
```

This operator is generally used in the same places as dynamic_cast, but usually when there's not type information to verify the conversion. Typically, it's used to convert from a base class type to a derived type.

The *const_cast* Operator

The general syntax for the const_cast operator is as follows:

```
const_cast<newType>(varName);
```

The const_cast operator is used for those occasions when you need to remove an object's constness. The newType must be the exact same type as varName, except without the const modifier.

Example

```
extern char* doSomething (char*, char);
char* doSomething(const char* str, char ch)
{
    return strchr(const_cast<char*>(str), ch);
}
```

This example adds a safer version of the doSomething function, assuming that doSomething doesn't actually change the contents of str.

Syntax

The *reinterpret_cast* Operator

The general syntax for the reinterpret_cast operator is as follows:

```
reinterpret_cast<newType>(varName);
```

This is used for all other types of casting not covered by the previous three. It's meant as the catch-all conversion operator. Take careful note of how this can be just as dangerous as the old C-style casting.

Templates

It is common for a language to have many functions, each of which does the same thing but for different data types. Wouldn't it be nice if you could tell the compiler, "Here's what I want to do; you figure out how to do it?" C++ has a feature that can do this, called a template.

NEW☞ A *template* is a method for telling the compiler the algorithm to use to perform a function.
TERM

The compiler handles the details of the function for the data type being used. Both global functions and classes can be programmed as templates.

When programming a template, you provide a name to use as the symbol for the unknown data type and write the code using that symbol.

Here is a function defined as a template:

```
// return the lowest of 3 values
template <class T> const T& Low(const T& a, const T& b, const T& c)
{
    if (a < b)
        {
        if (a < c)
            return a;
        }
    else if (b < c)
        return b;
    return c;
}
```

The first line of the function is what identifies it as a template. The word `template` in the function definition is followed by the characters <class, a symbol to use for the type, and then by a >. Although a single character is most often used for the symbol, it can be any legal C++ name.

This template function is used as any other function would be. For example, this returns the lowest of three C++ string items.

```
string s1("6543");
string s2("5432");
string s3("4321");
cout << Low(s1, s2, s3) << endl;
```

Although use of the word `class` is required when defining a template, templates are not limited to having classes as arguments. They can be used as fundamental data types also. `Low(1, 2, 3);`, for example, uses integers and is a valid call of the `Low` function.

A class can be defined in terms of templates. The syntax for doing this is the same as with the preceding function, but some changes are required when declaring instances of the class.

```
template <class TypeSymbol> class ArrayType
{
protected:
    TypeSymbol *items;
    int        numItems;
public:
    ArrayType(const TypeSymbol& firstItem);
    ~ArrayType();
    int AddItem(TypeSymbol& toAdd);
    TypeSymbol& operator [] (int index);
};
```

When you declare an instance of this class, the compiler must know which data type is to be used with this class. The declaration for `iArray` shows this, as the angle brackets enclose the type to use.

```
ArrayType<int> iArray(1);
```

Look at Listing 9.1 and the program TEMPLATE.CPP, which is an example of using templates. It implements a template class that can hold up to five items, gives them values, and prints them to the screen. Versions of the class are used for `float` and `integer` types. It also uses a template function that is not in a class; that function reports the size of the data type.

 Listing 9.1. Source code for the program TEMPLATE.CPP.

```
1:  #include <iostream.h>
2:  #include <typeinfo.h>
3:
4:  template <class X> class ArrayType
5:  {
6:  public:
7:      ArrayType(int capacity);
8:      ~ArrayType()        { delete[] items; }
9:
```

```
10:    bool InRange(int n)      { return (n >= 0) && (n < numItems); }
11:    int Capacity()           { return maxItems; }
12:    bool AddItem(X& toAdd);
13:    X& operator[](int index) { return items[index]; }
14:
15: protected:
16:    int maxItems; // maximum number of items this will hold
17:    int numItems; // number of items it is holding now
18:    X  *items;    // array of items
19: };
20:
21: template <class X> ArrayType<X>::ArrayType(int capacity)
22: {
23:    maxItems = capacity;
24:    items = new X[capacity];
25:    numItems = 0;
26: }
27:
28: template <class a> bool ArrayType<a>::AddItem(a& toAdd)
29: {
30:    if (numItems >= maxItems)
31:       return false;
32:    items[numItems++] = toAdd;
33:    return true;
34: }
35:
36: template <class SomeType> size_t Size(const SomeType&)
37: {
38:    return sizeof(SomeType);
39: }
40:
41: template <class D, class X> void Report(D& d, X& x)
42: {
43:    cout << typeid(D).name() << " has space for " << d.Capacity()
44:         << " items.  Each item uses " << Size(x)
45:         << " bytes." << endl;
46:    for (int i = 0; d.InRange(i); i++)
47:       cout << "\t" << typeid(D).name() << "[" << i << "] "
48:            << d[i] << endl;
49: }
50:
51: int main()
52: {
53:    int             iVal;
54:    float           fVal;
55:    ArrayType<int>   iArray(3);
56:    ArrayType<float> fArray(5);
57:
58:    for (iVal = 0, fVal = 0.0; iVal < 10; ++iVal, fVal += 1.11)
59:       {
60:       iArray.AddItem(iVal);
61:       fArray.AddItem(fVal);
62:       }
63:    Report(iArray, iArray[0]);
64:    cout << endl;
65:    Report(fArray, fArray[0]);
66:    return 0;
67: }
```

When you run this example, the results are as follows:

```
ArrayType<int> has space for 3 items.  Each item uses 2 bytes.
        ArrayType<int>[0] 0
        ArrayType<int>[1] 1
        ArrayType<int>[2] 2

ArrayType<float> has space for 5 items.  Each item uses 4 bytes.
        ArrayType<float>[0] 0
        ArrayType<float>[1] 1.11
        ArrayType<float>[2] 2.22
        ArrayType<float>[3] 3.33
        ArrayType<float>[4] 4.44
```

Beginning with line 4, the template class is defined. The symbol X is declared to be used for the type and is used within the body of the definition wherever the type name is needed.

The X is valid only within the block to which the `template` word refers. It is not related to what is used in other blocks. On line 28, a is used as the symbol for the type, and although the `AddItem` function with which it is used is a member of the `ArrayType` class that uses an X in its template, there is no confusion. The compiler is content to use a for the function block.

The inline functions `InRange`, `Capacity`, `operator[]`, and `~ArrayType` don't need a separate `template` word applied to them, because they are contained in the same one that is used for the class. Both `ArrayType` (line 21) and `AddItem` (line 28) need `template` in their definition, because the lines of code for them are not located within the class and are not covered by the class use of the keyword `template`.

Line 36 has a template function that is neither a class nor a class member. The syntax of C++ still requires the word `class` in the angle brackets that come after the `template` keyword. `SomeType` is used as the type symbol, but X or any other valid C++ name would work as well. The calling argument to `Size` is described as a type without a variable name applied to it. Unlike C, C++ does not require that a variable name be placed there; the `Size()` function needs to know only the type, not an actual variable.

The function `Report` (line 52) has an interesting variation on the template system. Two dummy type names are provided, and both types are used by the function. When called from lines 63 and 65, the function makes calls to `Capacity` and `InRange`. If the data type for the d calling argument in `Report` did not have functions with those names, an error would be generated.

`Report` calls the `typeid` function and the `name` member function of the `typeinfo` object that's returned. This is a good example of how RTTI can be used to present the user of a program with diagnostic information.

The `main` function starts on line 51. On lines 55 and 56 it declares two instances of `ArrayType`: one that will hold up to three items of type `int`, and one that will hold up to five items of type `float`.

Between lines 58 and 62, the items in the two classes are initialized. Ten initializations are done for each, relying on the AddItem function to detect and ignore initializations following those that have already filled the class to capacity.

Lines 63 and 65 call the Report function to tell some things about the classes. Report uses the Capacity member function of the class to print the maximum number of items it can hold. It also calls Size (line 44) to show the number of bytes used for each member.

Lines 46 through 48 then perform a for loop to display the data members of each class, stopping when the InRange function returns false.

This example is a bit contrived in order to illustrate using templates. For container classes that you can use for general arrays and so on, the Standard Template Library provides a multitude of better choices.

The Standard Template Library

A number of data structures for holding on to data have been developed over the years. These various structures are referred to as *containers*, and the ANSI/ISO C++ committee has approved a particular implementation of those structures developed by Hewlett-Packard called the Standard Template Library (STL). In addition to the containers, the STL also provides numerous algorithms for acting on these containers, such as search functions, sort functions, and various other manipulative functions.

There's a very large amount of stuff in the STL, so much so that there's not enough room here to list all of it (indeed, the STL deserves a book of its own). But behind its design are a few underlying concepts that can be extremely helpful in understanding its makeup. The first of these is the abstract concept of a container and an iterator.

NEW☞
TERM A *container* is an object into which other objects may be stored, such as an array. An *iterator* is the mechanism by which the objects in a container may be accessed. For example, in a standard array, you use an index to access the members of the array; this index is the iterator.

These containers and iterators are all implemented with templates (hence the name of the library). As you saw with the example for the templates in the previous section, implementing a container with templates allows it to work for all sorts of objects.

The other underlying concept of the STL concerns the algorithms that, rather than being folded into the containers themselves, are kept separate and general enough to be useful to all the containers equally.

The best way to describe the STL is to give an example. Listing 9.2 shows an example of using the list container, which provides a linked list of objects.

Type

Listing 9.2. Source code for the program STLLIST.CPP.

```cpp
1:  #include <iostream.h>
2:  #include <list>
3:  #include <string>
4:
5:  using namespace std;
6:
7:  // Create some typedefs to make things easier
8:  // later on when we create the list and its
9:  // iterator.
10: //
11: typedef list<string>           strList;
12: typedef list<string>::iterator strIter;
13:
14: int main()
15: {
16:     strList myList;
17:
18:     // Add some strings
19:     //
20:     myList.insert(myList.end(), "first");
21:     myList.insert(myList.end(), "second");
22:     myList.insert(myList.end(), "third");
23:     myList.insert(myList.end(), "fourth");
24:     myList.insert(myList.end(), "fifth");
25:     myList.push_front("Head");      // add at beginning
26:     myList.push_back("Tail");       // add at ending
27:
28:     // Print out the list
29:     //
30:     for (strIter iter = myList.begin(); iter != myList.end(); ++iter)
31:         cout << *iter << endl;
32:     cout << endl;        // Add a blank line
33:
34:     // Get rid of one of the entries
35:     //
36:     myList.erase(find(myList.begin(), myList.end(), "third"));
37:
38:     // Now show what's left...in reverse
39:     //
40:     strIter iter = myList.end();
41:     --iter;
42:     for (int ix = myList.size(); ix > 0; --iter, --ix)
43:         cout << *iter << endl;
44:
45:     return 0;
46: }
```

Output

Here is the output produced by Listing 9.2.

```
Head
first
second
third
fourth
```

```
fifth
     Tail

     Tail
     fifth
     fourth
     second
     first
     Head
```

Analysis The first item of interest in this program occurs on lines 2 and 3. I'm sure you've noticed that so far, all the included header files have had a `.h` appended to the ends of their names. The STL, on the other hand, doesn't use any extensions for its header files. Line 2 includes the header file that defines the `list` container and iterator, and line 3 includes the file that defines the `string` class. The `string` class will be described in great detail on Day 11, but for now you can just think of it as a way to encapsulate all the intricacies of the character arrays used so far.

Lines 11 and 12 create the `strList` and `strIter` types in order to help make the code a little more readable. As can be seen from all that goes into creating these two new types, it would be quite cumbersome to continually require typing out the whole definition of the list container and iterator.

The next interesting bit of code spans lines 20 through 24. These lines call the `insert` member function of the list container. The arguments to this particular version of the `insert` member function (there are a few others) are the location in the container at which to insert the new item, and the new item itself. In order to append the items to the end of the list, the list's `end` member function is called. This returns an iterator that points to the end of the list.

Lines 25 and 26 are a little more straightforward, though maybe a little confusingly named. The `push_front` and `push_back` member functions take one argument, the object to add to the container, and add items to the beginning and ending of the container, respectively.

Lines 30 and 31 give a good example of using an iterator. You'll notice how similar these lines look to previous code you've seen that iterates through an array. In this case, a `strIter` is created and assigned to the iterator returned by the container's `begin` member function. Then the `for` loop continues so long as the iterator doesn't equal the one returned by the list's `end` member function. Note how the iterator is incremented just as integers are incremented in standard array code; the iterators can be similarly decremented. Line 31 shows how to use the iterator to access the contents of the list to which it points. Just use an asterisk to dereference the iterator as if it were a pointer; this returns the object currently being pointed to by the iterator.

The `erase` member function used on line 36 should be reasonably obvious in that it takes a single parameter: an iterator pointing to the location in the list to be removed. In this particular case, the iterator is obtained by calling the `find` algorithm. The parameters to this are iterators pointing at the beginning and ending of the list, and then the object for which to search.

Lines 40 through 43 iterate backward through the container to print the list in reverse. The method it uses should be rather obvious by now. The only new part of this is the use of the `size` member function—a member function I'm sure you could have guessed existed. Because the

307

`begin` member function returns an iterator that points to the beginning of the container and `end` returns an iterator that points to just past the ending of the container, you have to use the size of the container and a second iterator (`ix`) to move backward.

The Class Libraries

Before the STL was created, Borland created its own container libraries. They're not quite as elegant as the STL, but they do get the job done. Table 9.1 shows the types of containers provided with the Borland C++ compiler. Originally, that job was most useful in the ObjectWindows Library. As of this version, the Borland Class Libraries are still used for the ObjectWindows Library, but they are expected to be replaced by the STL. For now, though, it makes sense to discuss the Class Libraries so that you can be familiar with existing code that uses them. When writing your own code that needs to use containers, you should use the STL.

Table 9.1. Borland C++ Class Library containers.

Container	Header File	Usage
Array	arrays.h	Mimics the standard C++ arrays in which objects are contained in a contiguous block of memory, but with the addition of being expandable in size after they already have been declared.
Association	assoc.h	Stores a key value with each object, enabling you to use the key to locate and retrieve the object.
Bag	bags.h	This is the least structured of all the containers in that it just stores objects in any order.
Binary search tree	binimp.h	Binary trees are a method of storing sorted data in an easy-to-search way. Objects are stored in such a way that each object can have up to two children. The child on the "left" of the parent must be less than the parent, and the "right" child greater than the parent.
Dequeue	deques.h	Contains a "train" of objects; you store objects at either end of the container and then access them in the order in which they were stored. As you access either end of the container, the objects are removed.
Dictionary	dict.h	Simple storage of objects as they're added to the container.

Container	Header File	Usage
Double-linked list	dlistimp.h	A double-linked list contains objects in noncontiguous memory. Traversing the list involves following pointers in each entry that point to the previous and next entries in the list.
Hash table	hashimp.h	This is similar to an association container, except that the associated keys (the hash values) are calculated based on the object being stored rather than specified directly.
Queue	queues.h	Queues allow objects to be stored in one end and retrieved from the other end. This sometimes is referred to as a FIFO (First In, First Out) container.
Set	sets.h	Sets are similar to bags in that they store objects in an unordered format, but sets can contain only one of any object.
Single-linked list	listimp.h	Single-linked lists, like double-linked lists, contain objects that aren't stored in contiguous memory. Single-linked list entries, however, contain only a pointer to the next entry and no pointer to the previous.
Stack	stacks.h	A stack is a way of storing objects one on top of each other, so that the most recently added object will be the one that can be retrieved. This sometimes is referred to as a LIFO (Last In, First Out) container.
Vector	vectimp.h	Vectors contain objects in contiguous memory. It usually is used simply as a storage method for the other classes.

Each of these types of classes has several different versions. These different versions are created to reflect the differing conditions in which they are used. In order to help the programmer distinguish between the different versions of each class, there is a standard set of characters that are used at the beginning of class names (see Table 9.2). By looking at the classes provided and decoding the abbreviation characters, you can deduce the differences of the container.

Table 9.2. Container class name abbreviations.

Abbreviation	Meaning	Description
T	Class Library prefix	All Borland-supplied classes (including OWL, which is described starting on Day 12) start with this letter.
M	User-supplied memory management	The programmer must supply to the container a class that will handle the memory management for the contained objects.
I	Indirect	The container holds a pointer to the object rather than to the object itself.
C	Counted	The container keeps a running count of the number of objects stored within it.
S	Sorted	The container sorts its objects. In order to achieve this, the objects must have valid comparison operators.

Each container has specific iterators associated with it. Although each iterator can have any number of functions, there are a few that are common among all the iterators (see Table 9.3).

Table 9.3. Common container iterator member functions.

Function	Description
constructor	The constructor typically takes one argument: a reference to the specific container for which it is to manipulate. The constructor initializes the iterator to point at the "beginning" of the container. (Note that the term "beginning" doesn't apply very well to some containers.)
current	This returns the object currently being pointed to by the iterator.
restart	This restarts the iterator to point at the "beginning" of the list.
operator int	When you need to know whether a container has been completely traversed, you can just compare it to 0, which will invoke a conversion operator. If the iterator is equal to 0, then the "end" of the container has been reached.
operator++	Obviously, traversing a container involves incrementing its iterator, and this is the function that does it. Just use the regular ++ increment operator.

Again, space constraints prevent me from providing a full list of all the various classes in the class libraries; there are a great number of them. Instead, I will present one example that goes through using a double-linked list for storing strings in LIST.CPP shown in Listing 9.3. This is just a rewrite of Listing 9.2, this time using the Class Libraries instead of the STL.

Type **Listing 9.3. Source code for the program BORLIST.CPP.**

```
1:  #include <cstring.h>
2:  #include <classlib\dlistimp.h>
3:  #include <iostream.h>
4:
5:  // Create some typedefs to make things easier
6:  // later on when we create the list and its
7:  // iterator.
8:  //
9:  typedef TDoubleListImp<string> strList;
10: typedef TDoubleListIteratorImp<string> strIter;
11:
12: int main()
13: {
14:     strList list;
15:
16:     // Add some strings
17:     //
18:     list.Add("first");
19:     list.Add("second");
20:     list.Add("third");
21:     list.Add("fourth");
22:     list.Add("fifth");
23:     list.AddAtHead("Head");    // Add at Head
24:     list.AddAtTail("Tail");    // Add at Tail
25:
26:     // Print out the list
27:     //
28:     strIter i(list);
29:     while (i != 0)
30:         {
31:         cout << i.Current() << endl;
32:         ++i;
33:         }
34:     cout << endl;       // Add a blank line
35:
36:     // Get rid of one of the entries
37:     //
38:     list.Detach("third");
39:
40:     // Now show what's left in reverse
41:     //
42:     for (i.RestartAtTail(); i != 0; --I)
43:         cout << i.Current() << endl;
44:
45:     return 0;
46: }
```

9

311

Here is the output produced by Listing 9.3.

```
Head
fifth
fourth
third
second
first
Tail

Tail
first
second
fourth
fifth
Head
```

 Taking a look at the program, you can see on lines 9 and 10 that two `typedefs` are used to create easy access to the new template list and iterator. The names for these template classes can become rather long, so it's a common practice to create shorter `typedefs` of the more complicated names for easier typing and identification during programming.

On line 14 is a declaration for the list itself. As you can see, it's a fairly simple line with no special parameters needed for the constructor. Immediately following this are some calls to the class member functions `Add`, `AddAtHead`, and `AddAtTail`. These are passing literal strings that are, in turn, being passed to the `string` constructor, which then is passed to the various add routines. The template nature of the Class Libraries means that each container class is specially made to match the type of its contained objects, so the `Add` functions take `string` parameters and passing a literal string just creates a `string` object to be added to the container.

Note the `AddAtHead` and `AddAtTail` functions on lines 23 and 24. The normal `Add` function actually adds items to the head of the list by default, as you can see in the output where the `"Head"` string is displayed next to the `"fifth"` string. Using `AddAtHead` and `AddAtTail` allows for finer control of where objects are placed in the list.

NEW☞
TERM The *head* and *tail* of a linked list are the beginning and ending, respectively. Because there's no real sense of a 0 index or a maximum size, it's necessary to keep track of the beginning and ending of the list differently.

You should note a major difference between the Borland Class Library and the STL when it comes to their list-addition member functions. In the STL, you used an `insert` member function that required a specific location in the list at which to insert the new data; the Class Library, however, has an `Add` member function that automatically inserts data items at the head of the list. The STL doesn't supply any generic function like the Class Library's `Add`.

Next, on line 28, you can see how an iterator is instantiated with the list to which it should be associated. Following this, you can see how the iterator is used to traverse the list, displaying each item in turn and then displaying an additional blank line in preparation for the next list.

On line 38, the string `"third"` is removed from the list. Note that it isn't necessary to search for the item before detaching it; the container automatically searches for the requested item and then removes it.

Starting on line 42, another method of traversing the list is shown: a `for` loop. Here you use the initializing portion of the `for` loop expression to restart the iterator at the list's tail, and you then decrement the iterator as you traverse the list backwards. Note how the output shows the contents of the list in reverse order from which its contents were initially added.

Altogether, the class libraries provide for a very easy method of using powerful data structures. Many versions of these automatically sort items as they are added to the containers, and some provide very fast searching mechanisms. Take some time to read the documentation for a full list of the various containers provided by the class libraries.

Summary

This chapter presented namespaces, runtime type information, templates, and a glimpse at the Standard Template Library and Class Libraries. You should now be familiar with the following:

☐ Namespaces can be used to separate sections of C++ code to help prevent naming conflicts.

☐ Runtime type information (RTTI) can help you determine the compatibility of different types. RTTI also delineates type casting, helping to remove the ambiguity and danger of the standard method.

☐ C++ templates can be used with functions and classes to work with any kind of data type. You define a template with "generic" arguments and use a template giving specific arguments. The compiler generates code appropriate to the actual argument types.

☐ Creating an instance of a template class requires that you specify the type(s) as part of the class name.

☐ The Standard Template Library (STL) provide a rich set of easy-to-use classes for creating containers. These containers can store objects in a variety of useful formats.

☐ The Borland Class Libraries are also available for creating containers.

Q&A

Q Can I use templates with my own structures and classes, or am I limited to using C++'s built-in types?

A Templates can use any type, as in the following example:

```
template <class T> const T& Dump(const T& objectToDump);
```

```
int a = 100;

struct {
    int p;
    long q;
    double r;
} b;

Dump(a);
Dump(b);
```

Q Can I create a template with more than one type?

A Yes. Just separate the types with commas, as in the following example:

```
template <class Form, class Printer> class SpecialFormPrinter
{
    ...
};

InsuranceFormLaserPrinter = new SpecialFormPrinter<InsuranceForm,
➥LaserPrinter>;
```

Q Can I create a double-linked list that automatically sorts the items added to it?

A No and yes. In the STL, there are no lists that automatically sort entries as they're inserted, but the `list` container has a `sort` member function that sorts its contents. In the Borland Class Libraries, use the `TSDoubleListImp` and `TSDoubleListIteratorImp` classes to create and traverse lists that are automatically sorted.

Workshop

The Workshop provides quiz questions to help you solidify your understanding of the material covered and exercises to provide you with experience in using what you've learned. Try to understand the quiz and exercise answers before continuing on to the next day's lesson. Answers are provided in Appendix A.

Quiz

1. True or false? RTTI makes for safer type usage.
2. True or false? Templates let you use any type, including your own classes, without ever having to provide any extra code.

Exercise

Write a program that uses the STL `queue` container to store some number of items determined by the user. When the user is finished, the program should replay the user's entries.

WEEK
2

Basic Stream
File I/O

Today's lesson introduces you to file I/O (input/output) operations using the C++ stream library. You have a choice of using file I/O functions in the STDIO.H file or in the C++ stream library. Each of these two I/O libraries offers a lot of power and flexibility. Today's lesson presents basic and practical operations that enable you to read and write data to files. You learn about the following topics:

☐ Common stream I/O functions

☐ Sequential stream I/O for text

☐ Sequential stream I/O for binary data

☐ Random access stream I/O for binary data

The C++ Stream Library

The C++ stream I/O library (also known as the iostream library) is made up of a hierarchy of classes that are declared in several header files. The IOSTREAM.H header file used thus far is only one of these. The other one that will be of interest in this chapter is FSTREAM.H. The file IOSTREAM.H supports the basic input and output stream classes. The FSTREAM.H file contains definitions that support the basic file input and output stream classes. There are additional stream library files that offer even more specialized stream I/O.

Common Stream I/O Functions

This section presents stream I/O member functions that are common to both sequential and random access I/O. These member functions include `open`, `close`, `good`, and `fail`, in addition to the operator `!`.

The `open` member function enables you to open a file stream for input, for output, for append, and for both input and output. The function also permits you to specify whether the related I/O is binary or text.

Note: When dealing with file I/O, it's vitally important to know the difference between *text mode* and *binary mode*. Text mode is for text files, in which one deals with lines of readable text. Binary mode is used for anything else, especially files that are stored in formats most humans would find difficult to read.

There are some special quirks about text-mode files that you should take extra special care to remember. The first is that the EOF character code (ASCII 26 or Ctrl+Z) is considered to mark the end of the file. In text mode, when the EOF character is encountered, the low-level C++ system automatically seeks to the end of the file; you won't be able to read anything past the special character. This can be a problem when that character is embedded in the middle of a file.

Another quirk of text mode involves how lines of text are interpreted. Each line ends with an end-of-line (EOL) sequence. On PCs and compatible machines, this EOL sequence is represented by two ASCII codes: CR (ASCII 13 or Ctrl+M) and LF (ASCII 10 or Ctrl+J). This CRLF sequence is used when the function for reading in or writing out a line of text is used, automatically being inserted or removed as appropriate. It should also be noted that on most other systems (notably UNIX and Macintosh), the EOF sequence is merely the LF character.

The *open* Member Function

The prototype for the open function is

```
void open(const char* filename,
          int mode,
          int m = filebuf::openprot);
```

The parameter `filename` specifies the name of the file to open. The parameter `mode` indicates the I/O mode. Following is a list of arguments for parameter `mode` that are exported by the FSTREAM.H header file:

in	Open stream for input
out	Open stream for output
ate	Set stream pointer to the end of the file
app	Open stream for append mode
trunc	Truncate file size to 0 if it already exists
nocreate	Raise an error if the file does not already exist
noreplace	Raise an error if the file already exists
binary	Open in binary mode

Example

```
// open stream for input
fstream f;
f.open("\\AUTOEXEC.BAT", ios::in);

// open stream for output
fstream f;
f.open("\\AUTOEXEC.OLD", ios::out);

// open stream for binary input and output
fstream f;
f.open("INCOME.DAT", ios::in | ios::out | ios::binary);
```

Note: The file stream classes offer constructors that include the action of (and have the same parameters as) the member function open.

The `close` member function closes the stream and recovers the resources involved. These resources include the memory buffer used in the stream I/O operations.

Syntax

The *close* Member Function

The prototype for the `close` function is

```
void close();
```

Example

```
fstream f;
// open stream
f.open("\\AUTOEXEC.BAT", ios::in);
// process file
// now close stream
f.close();
```

The C++ stream library includes a set of basic functions that check the error status of a stream operation. These functions include the following:

1. The `good()` function returns a nonzero value if there is no error in a stream operation. The declaration of function `good` is

   ```
   int good();
   ```

2. The `fail()` function returns a nonzero value if there is an error in a stream operation. The declaration of function `fail` is

   ```
   int fail();
   ```

3. The overloaded operator `!` is applied to a stream instance to determine the error status.

The C++ stream libraries offer additional functions to set and query other aspects and types of stream errors.

Sequential Text Stream I/O

The functions and operators involved in sequential text I/O are simple. You already have been exposed to most of them in earlier lessons. The functions and operators include the following:

☐ The stream extractor operator << writes strings and characters to a stream.

☐ The stream inserter operator >> reads characters from a stream.

☐ The getline function reads strings from a stream.

The *getline* Member Function

The prototypes for the member function getline are

```
istream& getline(char* buffer,
                 int size,
                 char delimiter = '\n');

istream& getline(signed char* buffer,
                 int size,
                 char delimiter = '\n');

istream& getline(unsigned char* buffer,
                 int size,
                 char delimiter = '\n');
```

The parameter buffer is a pointer to the string receiving the characters from the stream. The parameter size specifies the maximum number of characters to read. The parameter delimiter specifies the delimiting character, which causes the string input to stop before reaching the number of characters specified by parameter size. The parameter delimiter has the default argument of '\n'.

Example

```
fstream f;
char textLine[MAX];
f.open("\\CONFIG.SYS", ios::in);
while (!f.eof())
   {
   f.getline(textLine, MAX);
   cout << textLine << endl;
   }
f.close();
```

Look at an example. Listing 10.1 shows the source code for the program TRIM.CPP. The program performs the following tasks:

☐ Prompts you to enter the name of an input text file.

☐ Prompts you to enter the name of an output text file. (The program detects if the names of the input and output files are the same, and if so, prompts you again for a different output filename.)

☐ Reads the lines from the input file and removes any trailing spaces from these lines.

☐ Writes the lines to the output file and also to the standard output window.

Listing 10.1. Source code for the TRIM.CPP program.

```cpp
1:  // C++ program that demonstrates sequential file I/O
2:
3:  #include <iostream.h>
4:  #include <fstream.h>
5:  #include <string.h>
6:
7:  const unsigned LINE_SIZE = 128;
8:  const unsigned NAME_SIZE = 64;
9:
10: void trimStr(char* s)
11: {
12:     int i = strlen(s) - 1;
13:     // locate the character where the trailing spaces begin
14:     while (i >= 0 && s[i] == ' ')
15:         i--;
16:     s[i + 1] = '\0';        // truncate string
17: }
18:
19: void getInputFilename(char* inFile, fstream& f)
20: {
21:     bool ok;
22:
23:     do
24:         {
25:         ok = true;
26:         cout << "Enter input file: ";
27:         cin.getline(inFile, NAME_SIZE);
28:         f.open(inFile, ios::in);
29:         if (!f)
30:             {
31:             cout << "Cannot open file " << inFile << endl << endl;
32:             ok = false;
33:             }
34:         } while (!ok);
35: }
36:
37: void getOutputFilename(char* outFile, const char* inFile,
38:                        fstream& f)
39: {
40:     bool ok;
41:
42:     do
43:         {
44:         ok = true;
45:         cout << "Enter output file: ";
46:         cin.getline(outFile, NAME_SIZE);
47:         if (stricmp(inFile, outFile) != 0)
48:             {
49:             f.open(outFile, ios::out);
50:             if (!f)
51:                 {
52:                 cout << "File " << outFile << " is invalid" << endl << endl;
53:                 ok = false;
54:                 }
55:             }
```

```
56:       else
57:           {
58:           cout << "Input and output files must be different!" << endl;
59:           ok = false;
60:           }
61:       } while (!ok);
62: }
63:
64: void processLines(fstream& fin, fstream& fout)
65: {
66:     char line[LINE_SIZE + 1];
67:
68:     // loop to trim trailing spaces
69:     while (fin.getline(line, LINE_SIZE))
70:         {
71:         trimStr(line);
72:         fout << line << endl;    // write line to output file
73:         cout << line << endl;    // echo to output window
74:         }
75: }
76:
77: int main()
78: {
79:     fstream fin, fout;
80:     char inFile[NAME_SIZE + 1], outFile[NAME_SIZE + 1];
81:
82:     getInputFilename(inFile, fin);
83:     getOutputFilename(outFile, inFile, fout);
84:     processLines(fin, fout);
85:     // close streams
86:     fin.close();
87:     fout.close();
88:     return 0;
89: }
```

Here is a sample session with the program in Listing 10.1.

```
Enter input file: sample.txt
Enter output file: sample.out
This is line 1
This is line 2
This is line 3
This is line 4
```

The program in Listing 10.1 declares no classes and, instead, focuses on using file streams to input and output text. The program declares the functions trimStr, getInputFilename, getOutputFilename, processLines, and the requisite main.

The function trimStr shaves the trailing spaces in the strings passed by parameter s. The function declares the local variable i and assigns it the index of the character just before the null terminator. The function uses the while loop starting on line 14 to perform a backward scan of the characters in string s for the first nonspace character. The statement on line 16 assigns the null terminator character to the character located right after the last nonspace character in the string s.

The function getInputFilename obtains the input filename and opens its corresponding input file stream. The parameter inFile passes the name of the input file to the function caller. The reference parameter f passes the opened input stream to the function caller. The function getInputFilename declares the local flag ok. The function uses the do-while loop on lines 23 through 34 to obtain a valid filename and to open that file for input. Line 25 contains the first statement inside the loop, which initializes ok to the value true. The output statement on line 26 prompts you for the input filename; line 27 then gets it with a call to getline, storing the result in inFile. The statement on line 28 tries to open the input file using the stream parameter f. The open statement uses the ios::in value to indicate that the stream is to be opened for text input. If the call to open failed, then the if statement on line 29 will catch this and let the user know of the failure to open the file while ok is set to false. With ok set to false, the do-while loop will repeat and keep asking the user for a filename until it's successful at opening a file.

The function getOutputFilename is similar to getInputFilename in that it attempts to obtain a filename from the user and then open it. This time, however, the file is opened for writing, and the name of the file is first compared with the name that was used for the input file. If the user enters the same name for both the input and output files, the check for which is on line 47, this function complains and makes the user try again.

The function processLines reads lines from the input file stream, trims them, and then writes them to the output file stream. The parameters fin and fout pass the input and output file streams, respectively. The function declares the local string variable line and uses the while loop on lines 69 through 74 to process the text lines. The while clause contains the call to function getline, which reads the next line in the input stream fin and assigns the input line to variable line. The result of function getline causes the while loop to stop iterating when there are no more input lines. The contents of the loop simply call the trimStr function and then send the line to both fout and cout. Note how the command for both obtaining the line of text from a file and for sending it out to a file are exactly the same as those you've been using for obtaining text from and sending it out to the screen itself. That's because the cout and cin you've been using are really just streams that have been opened automatically and directed at the screen.

The function main is, as usual with all the support functions already written, fairly simple. It just declares the file stream variables fin and fout, then some inFile and outFile to hold the names of those file streams. Then the input file and output file are opened in getInputFilename and getOutputFilename. Finally, processLine trims and copies the contents of the file, and the member function close is called for each of the streams.

Sequential Binary File Stream I/O

The C++ stream library offers the overloaded stream member functions write and read for sequential binary file stream I/O. The member function write sends multiple bytes to an output stream. This function can write any variable or instance to a stream.

The *write* Member Function

The prototypes for the overloaded member function write are

```
ostream& write(const char* buff, int num);
ostream& write(const signed char* buff, int num);
ostream& write(const unsigned char* buff, int num);
```

The parameter buff is the pointer to the buffer that contains the data to be sent to the output stream. The parameter num indicates the number of bytes in the buffer that are sent to the stream.

Example

```
const MAX = 80;
char buff[MAX+1] = "Hello World!";
int len = strlen(buffer) + 1;
fstream f;
f.open("CALC.DAT", ios::out | ios::binary);
f.write((const unsigned char*)&len, sizeof(len));
f.write((const unsigned char*)buff, len);
f.close();
```

This example opens up the file CALC.DAT, writes out an integer containing the number of bytes in a string, then writes out that string to the file before closing it.

The member function read receives multiple bytes from an input stream. This function can read any variable or can read from a stream.

The *read* Member Function

The prototypes for the overloaded member function read are

```
istream& read(char* buff, int num);
istream& read(signed char* buff, int num);
istream& read(unsigned char* buff, int num);
```

The parameter buff is the pointer to the buffer that receives the data from the input stream. The parameter num indicates the number of bytes to read from the stream.

Example

```
const MAX = 80;
char buff[MAX+1];
int len;
fstream f;
f.open("CALC.DAT", ios::in | ios::binary);
f.read((const unsigned char*)&len, sizeof(len));
f.read((const unsigned char*)buff, len);
f.close();
```

This example retrieves the information written out in the previous example.

Look at an example that performs sequential binary stream I/O. Listing 10.2 shows the source code for the program ARRAY.CPP. The program declares a class that models dynamic

numerical arrays. The stream I/O operations enable the program to read and write both the individual array elements and an entire array in binary files. The program creates the arrays arr1, arr2, and arr3 and then performs the following tasks:

☐ Assigns values to the elements of array arr1. (This array has 10 elements.)

☐ Assigns values to the elements of array arr3. (This array has 20 elements.)

☐ Displays the values in array arr1.

☐ Writes the elements of array arr1 to the file ARRAY1.DAT, one element at a time.

☐ Reads the elements of arr1 from the file into the array arr2, one at a time. (The array arr2 has 10 elements—the same size as array arr1.)

☐ Displays the values in array arr2.

☐ Displays the values in array arr3.

☐ Writes the elements of array arr3 to file ARRAY3.DAT in one swoop.

☐ Reads, in one swoop, the data in file ARRAY3.DAT and stores them in array arr1.

☐ Displays the values in array arr1. (The output shows that array arr1 now has the same size and data as array arr3.)

Type

Listing 10.2. Source code for the ARRAY.CPP program.

```
1:   // C++ program that demonstrates sequential binary file I/O
2:
3:   #include <iostream.h>
4:   #include <fstream.h>
5:
6:   const unsigned MIN_SIZE = 10;
7:   const double BAD_VALUE = -1.0e+30;
8:
9:   class Array
10:  {
11:  public:
12:     Array(unsigned Size = MIN_SIZE);
13:     virtual ~Array()                      { delete[] dataPtr; }
14:
15:     unsigned getSize() const              { return size; }
16:     double& operator[](unsigned index)    { return *getPtr(index); }
17:
18:     bool writeElem(fstream& os, unsigned index);
19:     bool readElem(fstream& is, unsigned index);
20:     bool writeArray(const char* filename);
21:     bool readArray(const char* filename);
22:
23:  protected:
24:     void resize(unsigned Size);
25:     double* getPtr(unsigned index)
26:        { return (index < size) ? (dataPtr + index) : &badValue; }
27:
28:  private:
```

```
29:     Array(const Array&);
30:
31:     double *dataPtr;
32:     unsigned size;
33:     double badValue;
34: };
35:
36: Array::Array(unsigned Size)
37:     : badValue(BAD_VALUE)
38: {
39:     size = (Size < MIN_SIZE) ? MIN_SIZE : Size;
40:     dataPtr = new double[size];
41: }
42:
43: bool Array::writeElem(fstream& os, unsigned index)
44: {
45:     if (index >= size)
46:         return false;
47:     os.write((unsigned char*)getPtr(index), sizeof(double));
48:     return os.good();
49: }
50:
51: bool Array::readElem(fstream& is, unsigned index)
52: {
53:     if (index >= size)
54:         return false;
55:     is.read((unsigned char*)getPtr(index), sizeof(double));
56:     return is.good();
57: }
58:
59: bool Array::writeArray(const char* filename)
60: {
61:     fstream f(filename, ios::out | ios::binary);
62:
63:     if (f.fail())
64:         return false;
65:     f.write((unsigned char*)&size, sizeof(size));
66:     f.write((unsigned char*)dataPtr, size * sizeof(double));
67:     f.close();
68:     return f.good();
69: }
70:
71: bool Array::readArray(const char* filename)
72: {
73:     fstream f(filename, ios::in | ios::binary);
74:     unsigned sz;
75:
76:     if (f.fail())
77:         return false;
78:     f.read((unsigned char*)&sz, sizeof(sz));
79:     resize(sz);
80:     f.read((unsigned char*)dataPtr, size * sizeof(double));
81:     f.close();
82:     return f.good();
83: }
```

continues

Listing 10.2. continued

```
84:
85:  void Array::resize(unsigned Size)
86:  {
87:     if (size != Size)
88:         {
89:         delete[] dataPtr;
90:         dataPtr = new double[Size];
91:         size = Size;
92:         }
93:  }
94:
95:  void dispArray(const char* arrName, Array& arr)
96:  {
97:     cout << "Array " << arrName
98:          << " has the following values:" << endl;
99:     for (int i = 0; i < arr.getSize(); i++)
100:        cout << arr[i] << "  ";
101:    cout << endl << endl;
102: }
103:
104: int main()
105: {
106:    const unsigned SIZE1 = 10;
107:    const unsigned SIZE2 = 20;
108:    Array arr1(SIZE1), arr2(SIZE1), arr3(SIZE2);
109:    char* filename1 = "array1.dat";
110:    char* filename2 = "array3.dat";
111:    fstream f(filename1, ios::out | ios::binary);
112:
113:    // assign values to array arr1 and arr3
114:    for (unsigned i = 0; i < arr1.getSize(); i++)
115:        arr1[i] = 10 * i;
116:    for (unsigned i = 0; i < arr3.getSize(); i++)
117:        arr3[i] = i;
118:
119:    dispArray("arr1", arr1);       // display arr1
120:
121:    // write elements of array arr1 to the stream
122:    for (unsigned i = 0; i < arr1.getSize(); i++)
123:        arr1.writeElem(f, i);
124:    f.close();
125:
126:    // reopen the stream for input
127:    f.open(filename1, ios::in | ios::binary);
128:    for (unsigned i = 0; i < arr1.getSize(); i++)
129:        arr2.readElem(f, i);
130:    f.close();
131:
132:    dispArray("arr2", arr2);       // display arr2
133:    dispArray("arr3", arr3);       // display arr3
134:    arr3.writeArray(filename2);    // write arr3 to file ARRAY3.DAT
135:    arr1.readArray(filename2);     // read arr1 from file ARRAY3.DAT
136:    dispArray("arr1", arr1);       // display arr1
137:
```

```
138:     return 0;
139: }
```

Here is a sample session with the program in Listing 10.2.

```
Array arr1 has the following values:
0   10   20   30   40   50   60   70   80   90

Array arr2 has the following values:
0   10   20   30   40   50   60   70   80   90

Array arr3 has the following values:
0   1   2   3   4   5   6   7   8   9   10   11   12   13   14   15   16   17   18   19

Array arr1 has the following values:
0   1   2   3   4   5   6   7   8   9   10   11   12   13   14   15   16   17   18   19
```

10

The program in Listing 10.2 declares a version of class `Array` that resembles the one in Day 8, Listing 8.2. The main difference is that here I use the `operator[]` to replace both the member functions `store` and `recall`. This operator checks for valid indices and returns the value in member `badIndex` if the argument is out of range. In addition to `operator[]`, I added the member functions `writeElem`, `readElem`, `writeArray`, and `readArray` to perform sequential binary file stream I/O, I also added the functions `resize` and `getPtr` as helper functions to change the size of the array and to return a pointer to the appropriate element in the array, respectively.

Also note the copy constructor on line 29, and especially that it isn't actually defined anywhere. This is a trick that can be used to prevent other functions or classes from automatically copying it when you know that it would be a Bad Thing (in this case because of the dynamic data, the contents of which would need to be copied).

The function `writeElem`, defined on lines 43 through 49, writes a single array element to an output stream. The parameter `os` represents the output stream. The parameter `index` specifies the array element to write. The function `writeElem` yields `true` if the argument for the index is valid and if the stream output proceeds without any error. After `writeElem` writes an array element, the internal stream pointer advances to the next location.

The function `readElem`, defined on lines 51 through 57, reads a single array element from an input stream. The parameter `is` represents the input stream. The parameter `index` specifies the array element to read. The function `readElem` returns `true` if the argument for the index is valid and if the stream input proceeds without any error. After the `readElem` reads an array element, the internal stream pointer advances to the next location.

The functions `writeElem` and `readElem` permit the same class instance to write and read data elements, respectively, from multiple streams.

The function `writeArray`, defined on lines 59 through 69, writes all the elements of the array to a binary file. The parameter `filename` specifies the name of the output file. The function opens an output stream and writes the value of the data member `size` and then writes the elements of

the dynamic array. The `writeArray` function returns `true` if it successfully writes the array to the stream. Otherwise, it yields `false`. The function opens a local output stream by using the stream function `open` and supplying it with the filename and I/O mode argument. The I/O mode argument is the expression `ios::out | ios::binary`, which specifies that the stream is opened for binary output only. The function makes two calls to the stream function `write`—the first to write the data member `size`, and the second to write the elements of the dynamic array.

The function `readArray`, defined on lines 71 through 83, reads all the elements of the array from a binary file. The parameter `filename` specifies the name of the input file. The function opens an input stream and reads the value of the data member `size` and then reads the elements of the dynamic array. The `readArray` function returns `true` if it successfully reads the array to the stream. Otherwise, the function yields `false`. The function opens a local input stream by using the stream function `open` and supplying it the filename and I/O mode arguments. The I/O mode argument is the expression `ios::in | ios::binary`, which specifies that the stream is opened for binary input only. The function makes two calls to the stream function `read`—the first to read the data member `size`, and the second to read the elements of the dynamic array. Another feature of function `readArray` is that it resizes the instance of class `Array` to accommodate the data from the binary file by calling the member function `resize`. This means that a dynamic array accessed by the class instance may either shrink or expand, depending on the size of the array stored on file.

The `resize` member function that starts on line 65 is really very simple. It checks to see if the requested size is the same as what's already been set. If not, the memory allocated by the original `dataPtr` is freed, then a new memory area is created to match the new size. This new size is then set in the `size` member data.

The `dispArray` function would normally be a member function, but I decided to make it a regular function just this once in order to better demonstrate how the use of the `operator[]` function enables anyone who uses the `Array` to access its members in exactly the same way they'd access the members of a standard array. In this case, there's a simple `for` loop that runs through the elements of the passed `arr` and displays its contents.

Finally we get to the function `main` on line 104. As usual, it mostly just runs through the functions that have already been created to perform the following tasks:

☐ Declares, on line 108, three instances of class `Array`—namely, `arr1`, `arr2`, and `arr3`. (The first two instances have the same dynamic array size, specified by the constant `SIZE1`, whereas instance `arr3` has a larger size, specified by the constant `SIZE2`.)

☐ Declares, on line 111, the file stream `f` and opens it (using a stream constructor) to access file ARRAY1.DAT in binary output mode.

☐ Uses the `for` loops on lines 114 and 116 to arbitrarily assign values to the instance `arr1` and `arr3`, respectively.

- ☐ Displays the elements of instance arr1 on line 119.
- ☐ Writes the elements of array arr1 to the output file stream f, using the for loop on line 122 to call the writeElem member function with the output file stream f and the loop control variable i.
- ☐ Closes the output file stream by calling the close member function of the output file stream f.
- ☐ Opens, on line 127, the file stream f to access the data file ARRAY1.DAT. (This time, the message open specifies a binary input mode.)
- ☐ Reads the elements into arr2 (which has not yet been assigned any values) from the input file stream f, using the for loop on line 128.
- ☐ Closes the input file stream on line 130.
- ☐ Displays the elements of instance arr2 and arr3 on lines 132 and 133.
- ☐ Writes the entire contents of arr3 by calling the writeArray member function. (The writeArray member function has the filename argument of ARRAY3.DAT.)
- ☐ Reads the array in file ARRAY3.DAT into instance arr1, calling the member function readArray and supplying the filename argument of ARRAY3.DAT.
- ☐ Displays the new elements of instance arr1.

Random-Access, File-Stream I/O

Random-access, file-stream operations also use the stream member functions read and write that were presented in the preceding section. The stream library offers a number of stream-seeking functions to enable you to move the stream pointer to any valid location. The member function seekg is one such function.

The *seekg* Member Function

The prototypes for the overloaded member function seekg are

```
istream& seekg(long pos);
istream& seekg(long offset, seek_dir dir);
```

The parameter pos in the first version specifies the absolute byte position in the stream. In the second version, the parameter offset specifies a relative offset, based on the argument for parameter dir. Following are the arguments for the latter parameter:

ios::beg	From the beginning of the file
ios::cur	From the current position of the file
ios::end	From the end of the file

Example

```
const BLOCK_SIZE = 80;
char buff[BLOCK_SIZE] = "Hello World!";
fstream f("CALC.DAT", ios::in ¦ ios::out ¦ ios::binary);
f.seekg(3 * BLOCK_SIZE); // seek block # 4
f.read((const unsigned char*)buff, BLOCK_SIZE);
cout << buff << endl;
f.close();
```

NEW☞
TERM   A *virtual array* is a disk-based array that stores fixed-size strings on disk. You can think of it as a regular array that, instead of storing its elements in memory, stores its elements in a disk file.

Look at an example that uses random-access, file-stream I/O. Listing 10.3 shows the source code for the program VIRTUAL.CPP and implements a virtual array. The program performs the following tasks:

☐ Uses an internal list of names to create a virtual array object.

☐ Displays the elements in the unordered virtual array object.

☐ Sorts the elements of the virtual array object; this process requires random-access I/O.

☐ Displays the elements in the sorted virtual array object.

 Listing 10.3. Source code for the VIRTUAL.CPP program.

```
1:    // C++ program that demonstrates random-access binary file I/O
2:
3:    #include <iostream.h>
4:    #include <fstream.h>
5:    #include <stdlib.h>
6:    #include <string.h>
7:
8:    const unsigned MIN_SIZE = 5;
9:    const unsigned STR_SIZE = 31;
10:   const double BAD_VALUE = -1.0e+30;
11:
12:   class VmArray
13:   {
14:   public:
15:      VmArray(unsigned Size, const char* filename);
16:      ~VmArray()                  { f.close(); }
17:
18:      unsigned getSize() const    { return size; }
19:      bool setElem(const char* str, unsigned index);
20:      bool getElem(char* str, unsigned index);
21:      void BubbleSort();
22:      void display();
23:
24:   protected:
25:      fstream f;
```

```
26:     unsigned size;
27:     double badIndex;
28: };
29:
30: VmArray::VmArray(unsigned Size, const char* filename)
31:     : badIndex(BAD_VALUE)
32: {
33:     size = max(MIN_SIZE, Size);
34:     f.open(filename, ios::in | ios::out | ios::binary);
35:     if (f.good())
36:         {
37:         // fill the file stream with empty strings
38:         char s[STR_SIZE+1] = "";
39:         f.seekg(0);
40:         for (unsigned i = 0; i < size; i++)
41:             f.write((unsigned char*)s, sizeof(s));
42:         }
43: }
44:
45: bool VmArray::setElem(const char* str, unsigned index)
46: {
47:     if (index >= size)
48:         return false;
49:     f.seekg(index * (STR_SIZE+1));
50:     f.write((unsigned char*)str, (STR_SIZE+1));
51:     return f.good();
52: }
53:
54: bool VmArray::getElem(char* str, unsigned index)
55: {
56:     if (index >= size)
57:         return false;
58:     f.seekg(index * (STR_SIZE+1));
59:     f.read((unsigned char*)str, (STR_SIZE+1));
60:     return f.good();
61: }
62:
63: void VmArray::BubbleSort()
64: {
65:     for (int i = 1; i < size; ++i)
66:         for (int j = 0; j <= i; ++j)
67:             {
68:             char strI[STR_SIZE+1], strJ[STR_SIZE+1];
69:             getElem(strI, i);
70:             getElem(strJ, j);
71:             if (strcmp(strI, strJ) < 0)
72:                 {
73:                 setElem(strJ, i);
74:                 setElem(strI, j);
75:                 }
76:             }
77: }
78:
79: void VmArray::display()
80: {
```

continues

Listing 10.3. continued

```
81:      char str[STR_SIZE+1];
82:      for (unsigned i = 0; i < getSize(); ++i)
83:          {
84:          getElem(str, i);
85:          cout << str << endl;
86:          }
87:  }
88:
89:  int main()
90:  {
91:      char* data[] = { "Michigan", "California", "Virginia", "Main",
92:                       "New York", "Florida", "Nevada", "Alaska",
93:                       "Ohio", "Maryland" };
94:      VmArray arr(10, "arr.dat");
95:
96:      // assign values to array
97:      for (unsigned i = 0; i < arr.getSize(); i++)
98:          arr.setElem(data[i], i);
99:
100:     cout << "Unsorted arrays is:" << endl;
101:     arr.display();
102:
103:     arr.BubbleSort();
104:     cout << endl << "Sorted arrays is:" << endl;
105:     arr.display();
106:     return 0;
107: }
```

Here is a sample session with the program in Listing 10.3.

```
Unsorted arrays is:
Michigan
California
Virginia
Maine
New York
Florida
Nevada
Alaska
Ohio
Maryland

Sorted arrays is:
Alaska
California
Florida
Maine
Maryland
Michigan
Nevada
New York
Ohio
Virginia
```

The program in Listing 10.3 declares the class VmArray. This class models a disk-based dynamic array that stores all its elements in a random-access binary file. Notice that the class declares an instance of class fstream and that there is no pointer to a dynamic array. The class declares a constructor, a destructor, and a number of member functions.

The class constructor has two parameters, Size and filename. The parameter Size specifies the size of the virtual array. The parameter filename names the binary file that stores the elements of a class instance. The constructor opens the stream f using the stream function open and supplies it the argument of parameter filename and the I/O mode expression ios::in ¦ ios::out ¦ ios::binary. This expression specifies that the stream is opened for binary input and output mode (that is, random-access mode). If the constructor successfully opens the file stream, it proceeds to fill the file with empty strings. The class destructor performs the simple task of closing the file stream f.

The functions setElem and getElem support the random access of array elements. These functions use the stream function seekg to position the stream pointer at the appropriate array element. The setElem function then calls the stream function write to store an array element (supplied by the parameter str). By contrast, the function getElem calls the stream function read to retrieve an array element (returned by the parameter str). Both functions return bool results that indicate the success of the I/O operation.

The VmArray class also declares the BubbleSort function to sort the elements of the virtual array. This function uses the getElem and setElem member functions to access and swap the array elements. Then, finally, the last member function display runs through the elements of the virtual array and sends them to the screen.

The function main performs the following relevant tasks:

☐ Declares the instance arr, of class VmArray. (This instance stores 10 strings in the binary file ARR.DAT.)

☐ Assigns random values to the elements of instance arr using the for loop on lines 97 and 98.

☐ Displays the unsorted elements of instance arr by calling the member function display.

☐ Sorts the array by calling BubbleSort.

☐ Displays the sorted elements of instance arr.

Summary

Today's lesson provided a brief introduction to the C++ stream I/O library and discussed the following topics:

☐ Common stream functions include open, close, good, fail, and the operator !. The function open opens a file for stream I/O and supports alternate and multiple I/O modes. The function close shuts down a file stream. The functions good and fail indicate the success or failure, respectively, of a stream I/O operation.

☐ C++ enables you to perform sequential stream I/O for text, using the operators << and >> as well as the stream function getline. The operator << is able to write characters and strings (as well as the other predefined data types). The operator >> is suitable for obtaining characters. The function getline enables your applications to read strings from the keyboard or from a text file.

☐ Sequential stream I/O for binary data uses the stream functions write and read to write and read data from any types of variable.

☐ Random-access stream I/O for binary data uses the seekg function in conjunction with the functions read and write. The seekg function enables you to move the stream pointer to either absolute or relative byte locations in the stream.

Q&A

Q How can I emulate the random access of lines in a text file?

A First, read the lines in the file as text, obtain the length of the lines (plus the two characters for the end of each line), and store the cumulative length in a special array. (Call it something like lineIndex.) This array stores the byte location where each line starts. The last array element should store the size of the file. To access line number i, use the seek or seekg function to locate the offset value in lineIndex[i]. The size of line number i is equal to lineIndex[i+1]-lineIndex[i].

Q How do I write a general-purpose routine to copy between an input and an output file stream?

A You need to use the stream function gcount() to obtain the number of bytes actually read in the last unformatted stream input. The following is the function copyStream:

```
void copyStream(fstream& fin, fstream& fout,
                unsigned char* buffer, int buffSize)
{
   int n;
   while (fin.read(buffer, buffSize))
      {
      n = fin.gcount();
      fout.write(buffer, n);
      }
}
```

Workshop

The Workshop provides quiz questions to help you solidify your understanding of the material covered and exercises to provide you with experience in using what you've learned. Try to understand the quiz and exercise answers before continuing on to the next day's lesson. Answers are provided in Appendix A.

Quiz

1. True or false? The stream I/O functions read and write are able to correctly read and write any data type.

2. True or false? The stream I/O functions read and write are able to correctly read and write any data type, as long as the type has no pointer members.

3. True or false? The seek and seekg functions expand the file when you supply them an index that is one or more bytes beyond the current end of file.

4. True or false? The arguments of the functions seek and seekg require no range checking.

Exercise

Create the program VSEARCH.CPP by modifying the program VIRTUAL.CPP. The class VmArray in VSEARCH.CPP should have the function binSearch, which conducts a binary search on the members of the sorted array. Add a loop at the end of the function main to search in the array arr, using the unordered data of the initializing list. (The members of this list are accessed using the pointer data.)

The Standard Template Library's *string* Class

On Day 7, you learned about strings and the functions in STRING.H that work with them. The Standard Template Library (STL) provides a more powerful method of dealing with strings— the string class. This class conforms to the string class from the ANSI/ISO C++ standards committee and is prototyped in the header file STRING.

> **Note:** This chapter describes the string class as it is implemented by the STL. Prior to the STL, however, Borland C++ provided its own string class prototyped in the CSTRING.H header file. This file still exists in Borland C++ 5, and you may come across older code that uses the old string class, but you should use the new STL version for all new work you do.

C-style strings are powerful, but they require control of many low-level items such as allocation sizes and pointer offsets. The STL string class is designed to increase the power available above that of C strings, but without need for low-level concerns.

At the end of today's lesson, you will be familiar with the following:

- [ ] Benefits of the STL string class
- [ ] I/O with the STL string class
- [ ] Comparing strings
- [ ] Searching for "tokens"
- [ ] Controlling how string class comparisons are done
- [ ] Searching for substrings inside of larger strings
- [ ] Mixed operations with C-style strings and the string class

Benefits of the STL *string* Class

The programmer can design a class that inherits from the string class. The newly designed class can use all the power of the string class, as well as whatever else needs to be added.

The result is an object-oriented program design, which is easier to write and maintain. The following shows how the STL string class provides solutions to C-string difficulties.

Table 11.1. C-String difficulties and STL string class solutions.

C-String Difficulty	STL `string` Class Solution

C-string functions have obscure names, which makes it difficult to find the function you want.	Operators such as `!=` or `=` are used when possible. When function names are used, they sound like what they do, such as the following:
	
	`strcmp versus ==`
	`strcpy versus =`
	`strstr versus find`
	`strlwr versus to_lower`

No variable or function reports the allocated size of a C string. When copying to a string, the programmer must remember the allocated size or allocate a new string large enough to hold the string or strings that he or she wants to store.	The STL `string` class handles allocations and knows the allowed size. Operations are checked against the current size, and the allocated size is increased when necessary.
When allocating memory for a string, an additional byte must be allocated for the terminating `\0` character. Forgetting to do this is a common error.	Terminating characters are automatically provided.
Comparisons using C-style strings must be done with a call to a function such as `strcmp`. A frequent error is when the programmer uses logical operators, such as `=` or `<`, for C strings, receiving a result that tells of the relationship between the address of the strings in memory rather than of the strings themselves.	Source code to compare STL `strings` can be written as if comparing integers, because familiar comparison operators (such as `==`, `=!`, and so on) are provided. An explicit function call is not needed to do a comparison.
Parsing strings into words or finding substrings in C-style strings involves many lines of code with calls to functions such as `strtok`, the use of which is complicated and detail-intensive.	This work and the consequent debugging are now unnecessary. Powerful functions are in the `string` class to do such common tasks. For example, read next word (token) from the keyboard, a file, or from another string is done with a call to `read token`. It can be set to skip leading spaces or leave them in the string.

continues

Table 11.1. continued

C String Difficulty	STL string Class Solution
When an allocation error is made, other memory outside the string array is altered. When that memory is a critical area, it often will cause the program to crash or the computer to lock up.	Exception handling is done by the class. It traps allocation failures and errors, terminating the program safely.

The *string* Class Header File STRING

The string class is actually based on a template class called basic_string. The implementation details of the class are rather complex and really aren't all that important to the discussion in this book. It's a good thing to keep this fact in mind, however; when compiling programs that contain errors in expressions that make use of string, the error message will get really long and rather complex. Most of that complexity will be due to the long name of the basic_string definition.

Note: All programs that use the string class must include the header file STRING.

NEW TERM npos is used as a value to indicate that no position is specified. It is declared in a kind of convoluted fashion, but the upshot is equivalent to the following:

```
const size_t npos = size_t(-1);
```

The size_t type is defined as an unsigned.

Constructors and Copy Constructors

What follows is a list of the public constructors for the string class that can be used to create a new string object instance:

```
string();
string(const string& s);
string(const string& s,  size_t startIndex,
       size_t numChars = npos);
string(const char*  cp);
string(const char*  cp, size_t numChars);
```

```
string(size_t numChars, char c);
string(const char*   begin, const char* end);

string copy() const; // Note: There are other copy() functions below

string& operator=(const string& s);
string& operator=(const char* s);
string& operator=(char c);
```

Comparing

As stated earlier, the string class provides easier methods of comparison than the strcmp style functions. The following are the comparison operators defined by the string class:

```
bool operator== ( const string& s1, const string& s2 );
bool operator== ( const string& s,  const char   *cp );
bool operator== ( const char   *cp, const string& s );

bool operator!= ( const string& s1, const string& s2 );
bool operator!= ( const string& s,  const char   *cp );
bool operator!= ( const char   *cp, const string& s );

bool operator>  ( const string& s1, const string& s2 );
bool operator>  ( const string& s,  const char   *cp );
bool operator>  ( const char   *cp, const string& s );

bool operator<  ( const string& s1, const string& s2 );
bool operator<  ( const string& s,  const char   *cp );
bool operator<  ( const char   *cp, const string& s );

bool operator<= ( const string& s1, const string& s2 );
bool operator<= ( const string& s,  const char   *cp );
bool operator<= ( const char   *cp, const string& s );

bool operator>= ( const string& s1, const string& s2 );
bool operator>= ( const string& s,  const char   *cp );
bool operator>= ( const char   *cp, const string& s );

int compare( const string& s, size_t startIndex = 0,
             size_t numChars = npos ) const;
int compare( char* s, size_t startIndex = 0 ) const;
int compare( char* s, size_t startIndex,
             size_t numChars ) const;
```

Concatenating Strings

The string class provides simpler methods of concatenating strings than using the strcat style of functions. Several of these are implemented as operators, whereas others are implemented with the append member function for adding on to the end of a string.

```
string operator+ ( const string& s1, const string& s2 );
string operator+ ( const string& s,  const char *cp );
string operator+ ( const char*   cp, const string& s );
```

```
string operator+ ( const string& s,  char c );
string operator+ ( char          c,  const string& s );

string& operator+= ( const string& s );
string& operator+= ( const char*   cp );
string& operator+= ( char          c );

string& append( const string& s,  size_t startIndex = 0,
                size_t numChars = npos );
string& append( const char*   cp );
string& append( const char*   cp, size_t startIndex );
string& append( size_t numChars, char c );
```

Inserting Characters into a String

The insert member function enables you to insert other strings into the middle of a string object.

```
string& insert( size_t startInsertAt, const string& s,
                size_t startIndex = 0, size_t numChars = npos );
string& insert( size_t startInsertAt, const char* cp );
string& insert( size_t startInsertAt, const char* cp,
                size_t numChars );
string& insert( size_t startInsertAt, size_t numChars, char c );
```

Removing Characters from Within a String

There are two member functions for removing characters from within a string. The replace member function replaces characters in a string with the contents of another string. The remove member function removes characters from the string.

```
string& replace( size_t removeFrom, size_t removeCount,
                 const string& s,   size_t startReplacePosition = 0,
                 size_t replaceCount = npos );
string& replace( size_t removeFrom, size_t removeCount,
                 const char* cp );
string& replace( size_t removeFrom, size_t removeCount,
                 const char* cp, size_t replaceCount );
string& replace( size_t removeFrom, size_t removeCount,
                 size_t numChars, char c );

string& remove( size_t startIndex = 0, size_t numChars = npos );
```

Addressing Individual Characters in a String

When dealing with regular C-string arrays, it's possible to manipulate single characters within the string by using the array operators [ ]. The STL string object defines the bracket operators to perform the same function.

Note in the following syntax that one of these operators returns a reference to the specified character rather than just the character itself. This means that you can assign new characters to that position in the string in the same way you would with a C-string array.

In addition to the bracket operators, at is provided for a more primitive method of getting and changing characters in a string object.

```
char  operator[] ( size_t index ) const;
char& operator[] ( size_t index );

char  at( size_t index ) const;
char& at( size_t index );
```

Getting a Substring from Within a String

The string class provides a method for obtaining a substring from within a string:

```
string substr( size_t startIndex = 0, size_t numChars = npos ) const;
```

Searching Within a String

Some of the more useful features of the string class are its member functions that enable you to search the contents of a string. The basic member functions are find, find_first_of, find_first_not_of, find_last_of, and find_last_not_of.

```
size_t find             ( const string& s, size_t startIndex = 0 ) const;
size_t find             ( const char* cp, size_t startIndex,
                          size_t numCPChars ) const;
size_t find             ( const char* cp, size_t startIndex = 0 ) const;
size_t find             ( char c, size_t startIndex = 0 ) const;

size_t rfind            ( const string& s, size_t startIndex = npos ) const;
size_t rfind            ( const char* cp, size_t startIndex,
                          size_t numCPChars ) const;
size_t rfind            ( const char* cp, size_t startIndex = npos ) const;
size_t rfind            ( char c, size_t startIndex = npos ) const;

size_t find_first_of    ( const string& s, size_t startIndex = 0 ) const;
size_t find_first_of    ( const char* cp, size_t startIndex,
                          size_t numCPChars ) const;
size_t find_first_of    ( const char* cp, size_t startIndex = 0 ) const;
size_t find_first_of    ( char c, size_t startIndex = 0 ) const;

size_t find_last_of     ( const string& s, size_t startIndex = npos ) const;
size_t find_last_of     ( const char* cp, size_t startIndex,
                          size_t numCPChars ) const;
size_t find_last_of     ( const char* cp, size_t startIndex = npos ) const;
size_t find_last_of     ( char c, size_t startIndex = npos ) const;

size_t find_first_not_of   ( const string& s, size_t startIndex = 0 ) const;
size_t find_first_not_of   ( const char* cp, size_t startIndex,
                          size_t numCPChars ) const;
```

```
size_t find_first_not_of    ( const char* cp, size_t startIndex = 0 ) const;
size_t find_first_not_of    ( char c, size_t startIndex = 0 ) const;

size_t find_last_not_of     ( const string& s, size_t startIndex = npos ) const;
size_t find_last_not_of     ( const char* cp, size_t startIndex,
                            size_t numCPChars ) const;
size_t find_last_not_of     ( const char* cp, size_t startIndex = npos ) const;
size_t find_last_not_of     ( char c, size_t startIndex = npos ) const;
```

Reading the Length

In order to get the length of a C-style string, you use the `strlen` function. The `string` class supplies the `length` member function to obtain the length of the string.

```
size_t length() const;
```

Copying to a C-Style String

Although using the `string` class is very useful, occasionally it still may be necessary to use a C-style string array. The `copy` member function copies the contents of a `string` object into a standard character array.

```
size_t copy( char *cb, size_t numChars );
```

There's also a special member function called `c_str`, which returns a constant pointer to a C-style character array.

```
const char* c_str() const;
```

This member function is most useful when you need to use a C-style string as a parameter to a function.

I/O Operations

There are a number of functions for getting strings to interact with input and output streams.

```
ostream& operator<< ( ostream& os, const string& s );
istream& operator>> ( istream& is, string& s );
istream& getline( istream& is, string& s, char c );
```

Syntax

Declaring a String

You can declare variables of `string` class type (called *instances of the class* or *class instances*). You also can declare pointers or references to a class instance. Any of these can be initialized in the same statement that declares the variable. A string can be declared with an optional initial value.

```
using namespace std;
```

```
string Str1;
string Str2 = "String 2";
string Str3("String 3");
```

A string pointer or reference also can be allocated with an optional initial value.

```
string *pStr4 = new string;
string *pStr5 = new string("String 5");
string *pStr6;
string &rStr7 = * new string("String Reference");

pStr6 = new string("A New String Is Constructed");
```

Before anything else, you should note the first line that includes the STL namespace std. If this is not done, the compiler will come back with all sorts of errors to let you know that it has absolutely no idea what you're talking about when you try to use string. You should always remember that anything defined in the STL is defined in the std namespace.

Str1, Str2, and Str3 are strings. Str1 has not been given an initial value so it begins as an empty string (as ""). Str2 is set to a value, but the initialization is done with an assignment statement on the same line; you should note that it calls the same constructor as that for Str3. Str3 takes advantage of the class constructor argument to set the initial value without the perceived additional step of assigning it.

pStr4, pStr5, and pStr6 are not strings. They are pointers to strings; they each can hold the address of a string.

pStr4 and pStr5 are assigned the address of a string by a call to the function new. The string to which pStr4 points is empty, and the one to which pStr5 points contains "String 5".

pStr6 begins as pointing to nothing in particular. The assignment statement creates a string with new, initializes it to the given value, and places the address into pStr6.

Bug Busters

Be careful not to use items such as pStr6 until they have been assigned a valid address. Forgetting this is a common programming mistake that can be difficult to track down. Always check that all pointers have been initialized before being used.

The rStr7 is a reference to a string. You can think of it as a pointer to a string, which can be handled in source code as if it were a string.

When new is called to initialize rStr7, a * is placed before it. As new returns a pointer and a reference is treated as an actual string, the * indicates to use the item at the address contained in the pointer. However, you should note very carefully that this reference is pointing at some dynamically allocated memory. As always, you need to make very sure that you have a call somewhere to free the memory or you'll run into memory leaks.

Reading and Comparing Strings

In C, to copy the contents of one string to another, you place the addresses of the source and destination C strings as calling arguments to the `strcpy` function. The string class defines an `=` operator, so you need only do an assignment, just as with an integer.

Assigning Strings

You can assign one string to another using the equals sign (=).

```
string str = initialString;
```

Example

```
string string1 = "First String";
string string2 = "Second String";

string2 = string1;
```

This places the characters `"First String"` into `string2`. The old contents of `string2` are lost.

As was the case with an assignment statement, the class provides familiar operators for use in performing comparisons. Operators such as `==` and `<` free you from calling and interpreting the results of the `strcmp` function used for C-style strings. In cases where you want to save the comparison results, a `strcmp`-like function that returns the same kind of positive integer, zero, or negative integer is available. The name is a bit easier to remember than `strcmp`: it's called `compare`.

Comparing Strings

Strings can be compared directly as if comparing integers. Old-style strings can also be compared to STL strings in this fashion.

The following comparison operators are supplied for strings:

```
==   <=   >=   <   >   !=
```

Example

```
char oldstyle[] = "OLD STYLE STRING";
string newstyle = "new style string";

if (oldstyle < newstyle)
    cout << "oldstyle is lower in value than newstyle" << endl;
```

The message will be displayed because capital letters have smaller values than lowercase letters. The line

```
int compare( const string &compareTo, size_t startIndex = 0,
             size_t numChars = npos ) const;
```

returns a positive value if the string is greater than `compareTo`, and a negative value if it is less. If the two strings are equal, then zero is returned. Although using `<`, `>` and `==` to compare strings is easy, `compare` provides a value that can be saved for use later.

The familiar `cin >>`, `getline`, and `cout <<` syntax works well with C++ strings. Because the stream classes also handle file I/O, this works with disk files as well.

Syntax

Reading and Writing Strings

Normal I/O streams functions are provided for the C++ string class. The `cin`, `cout`, and file I/O are supported.

Example

```
string textLine;

cin >> textLine;    // Get input from stdin.
// If "the word" is entered, textLine will become "the"

getline(cin, textLine, '\n');
// If "the word" is entered, textLine will become "the word"


ifstream inputFile;
ofstream outputFile;

inputFile.open("FileName.Txt");
outputFile.open("FileName.Out");

getline(inputFile, textLine, '\n');
// textLine now contains the first line from the file

outputFile << textLine << endl;
// the string is now stored in the output disk file
```

Just as with C-style strings, a C++ string can be addressed as if it were an array with an index within square brackets. Readers who have migrated from BASIC or FORTRAN might be pleased to learn that parentheses also can be used.

Examining Individual Characters

STL strings can be accessed as arrays just as is done with C strings. Remember that the first element is `stringName[0]`. If the value contained in `stringVar` is `"0123456789"`, then `cout << stringVar[7];` prints a 7 to the screen.

For those of you whose first love was FORTRAN or another language that uses parentheses for array subscripts, you can use them as well; `cout << stringVar(7);` also prints a 7.

The following example is a small program using some of the previously mentioned syntax. References are used so that the code is more readable.

Three strings are created. The program reads strings from the keyboard and reports on how they compare. Entering a string of end ends the program. Because comparison defaults to being case-sensitive, a value of END will not end the program.

Listing 11.1 contains a program that reads and compares C++ string class strings.

 Listing 11.1. Source code for the program STRING.CPP.

```
1:  #include <iostream.h>
2:  #include <string>
3:
4:  using namespace std;
5:
6:  int main()
7:  {
8:      string s1, s2, message;
9:
10:     for (;;)        // run this loop forever
11:         {
12:         cout << "Enter two lines of text, \"end\" to end program" << endl;
13:
14:         getline((istream&)cin, s1, '\n');  // read a line into s1 from the
                                               // keyboard
15:         if (s1 == "end")        // If ending the program is requested
16:             break;              // break out of the loop
17:
18:         getline((istream&)cin, s2, '\n');  // read a line into s2
19:         if (s2 == "end")        // If ending the program is requested
20:             break;              // break out of the loop
21:
22:         if (s1 == s2)
23:             message = "The strings are equal";
24:         else if (s1 > s2)
25:             message = "The first string is greater";
26:         else
27:             message = "The second string is greater";
28:
29:         cout << message << endl << endl; // report the result
30:         }
31:     return 0;
32: }
```

 Note: As of this writing, the preceding will not execute unless you switch from dynamic to static mode.

Here is a sample session with the example program.

```
Enter two lines of text, "end" to end program
this
that
The first string is greater
```

```
Enter two lines of text, "end" to end program
that
this
The second string is greater

Enter two lines of text, "end" to end program
those
those
The strings are equal

Enter two lines of text, "end" to end program
end
```

Line 8 declares the string variables s1, s2, and message. On lines 14 and 18, a full line of text is read into strings. Remember that the getline function removes the end-of-line character from the input. After each call to getline, the string is compared to "end" to see if the user has requested an end to the program. If so, then the break statement is issued, which terminates the loop that would otherwise continue forever.

Line 22 starts the comparisons of the two entered strings, and the variable message is assigned text that reflects the result of the comparisons. This message is then output to the screen on line 29.

String Search, Substitution, and File I/O

The string class provides powerful tools for searching within strings and substituting parts of strings (substrings). REPLACE.CPP manipulates the text in a file, substituting alternative text for words and placing this new text in an output file. Listing 11.2 contains the source code for the program REPLACE.CPP.

 Listing 11.2. Source code for the program REPLACE.CPP.

```
1:  #include <fstream.h>
2:  #include <string>
3:
4:  using namespace std;
5:
6:  short ProcessFile(const string& toFind, const string& replaceWith)
7:  {
8:      size_t   foundPos;      // Position in string where found
9:      string   buffer;        // Holds a line of input data from the file
10:     short    startPos;      // Position in string to start search
11:     bool     replaced;      // Set to true if replacement has been done
12:     short    numFound = 0;  // Number of replacements that were made
13:     ifstream inFile("\\BC5\\README.TXT");
14:     ofstream outFile("README.NEW");
15:
16:     while (inFile)                      // While data left in input file
```

continues 349

Listing 11.2. continued

```
17:          {
18:          getline((istream&)inFile, buffer, '\n');    // Read one line
19:          replaced = false;                    // Init flag and position
20:          startPos = 0;
21:
22:          do
23:             {
24:             foundPos = buffer.find(toFind, startPos);
25:             if (foundPos != string::npos)        // If a match is found
26:                {
27:                buffer.replace(foundPos, toFind.length(), replaceWith);
28:                ++numFound;
29:                replaced = true;
30:                startPos = foundPos + replaceWith.length();
31:                }
32:             } while (foundPos != string::npos);
33:
34:          outFile << buffer << endl;       // Copy line to the output file
35:
36:          if (replaced)
37:             cout << buffer << endl;       // Show modified lines on screen
38:          }
39:
40:      inFile.close();
41:      outFile.close();
42:      cout << endl;
43:      return numFound;
44: }
45:
46: int main()
47: {
48:      string    toFind;
49:      string    replaceWith;
50:
51:      cout << "Enter the word to find: ";
52:      cin >> toFind;
53:
54:      cout << "Enter replacement word: ";
55:      cin >> replaceWith;
56:
57:      if (toFind != replaceWith)
58:         cout << ProcessFile(toFind, replaceWith)
59:              << " words were replaced" << endl;
60:      else
61:         cout << "Error: Find and Replace words are the same" << endl;
62:      return 0;
63: }
```

SAMS PUBLISHING

> **Note:** As with the program preceding this one, you should switch from dynamic to static to avoid a runtime error.

Here is an example session with the REPLACE application.

```
Enter the word to find: important
Enter replacement word: unimportant
This README file contains unimportant information about BORLAND C++.
This section lists the unimportant new features of Borland C++ 5.0.
This section contains unimportant information that may not be found in

3 words were replaced
```

This program uses the STL string class to take the README.TXT file, which came with Borland C++ 5, and to create a new file, README.NEW, in which it has substituted some words. When run, it asks for the word to find and the word to replace it.

The main program is small. It acquires the toFind and replaceWith strings from the user. Then, so long as they're not the same (not much point in doing a replace if the replacement text is the same as the original text), ProcessFile is called on line 58 and the returned count of replaced words is printed on line 59.

Number of Characters in a String

Syntax

Each string class variable has a member function called length that reports the length of the string in characters. The return value is an unsigned. The name size_t is defined by the language standards groups, so that it can be set to whatever is appropriate for the current machine. With Borland C++ 5, size_t is defined as an unsigned. The stringVar.length(); returns the same value as strlen(stringVar.c_str());.

The loop that starts on line 16 and ends on line 38 is where the real work of ProcessFile is done. With each pass through the loop, a line of text is read from the input file into the string variable buffer (line 18).

The variable replaced acts as a detector to remember if any words have been replaced on a line and is set to false. The startPos is the starting position for searching the line and is set to the beginning of the line (to zero).

Syntax

Searching Within a String

The following `string` member function searches for a match with the `toFind` string. The return value is the index of where the match occurred, or `string::npos` if no match is found.

```
size_t find(const string &toFind, size_t startAt = 0);
```

The function specifies that, instead of beginning at the start of the string, the search will begin at position `startAt` in the string. Note how the default value for `startAt` is the beginning of the string. Remember that the first character of an array in C or C++ is array index zero. Because of that, if `startAt` were 2, then the third character is where the search would begin.

The `do-while` loop from lines 22 through 32 processes a single line of text from the input file. Starting in character position `startPos`, it searches the string for a match with the `toFind` string. If successful, the `find` function returns the starting character position in `buffer` of the matching characters. On line 25, the position found is compared against the predefined symbol `string::npos`, whose value is used to indicate that no position in the string matches the search string.

Lines 27 through 30 execute only if a match is found. The call to `replace` causes `toFind.length()` characters beginning at position `foundPos` to be deleted and the contents of the string `replaceWith` to be inserted in their place.

Syntax

String Class I/O

The `getline` member function using the C++ `string` class is declared for input and output file streams. The `>>` and `<<` input and output operators also are provided for file operations with this class.

```
istream &getline(istream& is, string& s, char delim);
operators >> and <<
```

Syntax

Changing Part of a C++ String

The `replace` function, a member function of the C++ `string` class, is overloaded to have many forms. The one used in Listing 11.2 is defined as follows:

```
string &replace(size_t       startPos,
                size_t       deleteLength,
                const string &replaceWith,
                size_t       replaceFrom = 0,
                size_t       replaceLength = npos);
```

This will remove `deleteLength` characters from the string starting at `startPos` and then replace those characters with `replaceWith`. It will only use `replaceLength` characters starting at `replaceFrom` from `replaceWith` when it inserts the new string.

If the string to be modified is too short to remove the requested number of characters, then the characters from startPos to the end of the string are removed.

"Steven Smith", for example, could be searched for and "Steven" replaced with "George" from the string "George Jones".

The replaceFrom argument specifies the starting position in the replacement string to begin in substituting characters. If there are no replaceLength characters in the replacement string, then the number found in the string is used.

The replaceLength defaults to the value npos, which will use all remaining characters in the string.

The following two lines, for example, perform the same function:

```
replace(startPos, deleteLen, replaceWith, 0, string::npos);
replace(startPos, deleteLen, replaceWith);
```

Line 34 executes independently of having done any replacements and writes the possibly altered string to the new file. Lines 36 and 37 detect whether any replacements have been done and, if so, write the changed string to the screen.

Lines 40 through 43 perform the clean-up actions of closing files and returning the number of replacements that have been made.

There also are more useful functions in the string class.

Other C++ *string* Class Functions

The following append member function adds characters to the end of a string:

```
string& append(const string &fromStr size_t startPos = 0,
               size_t numChars = npos);
```

This places the characters of fromStr, starting with startPos and continuing for numChars characters, to the end of the string.

Example

```
string firstString("ABC");
string secondString("DEF");

firstString.append(secondString); // firstString is now "ABCDEF"
```

Note that another way to append characters to the end of a string is to use the += operator. The same appending operations could have been done with the following:

```
firstString += secondString;
```

Often it will be necessary to just pass a string object as if it were a C-style string array. The string class provides the c_str member function, which simply returns a const char* to a C-style version of the string.

You can use find to determine whether or not a substring exists within another string. After you determine that a substring exists within a string object, it can be useful to determine where in that string the substring can be found. This is done with the find_first_of function.

```
size_t find_first_of(const string &s, size_t startAt = 0) const;
```

This returns the position of the first character found in the string, which is one of the characters in the string s passed to the function. The search begins at startAt. If nothing is found, then it returns string::npos.

In addition to finding the first position in a string at which another string begins, it is also possible to find the first position that isn't a part of another string. This is done with the find_first_not_of member function.

```
size_t find_first_not_of(const string &s, size_t startAt = 0) const;
```

This returns the first character *not* in the calling argument, or string::npos if nothing is found.

The find_last_of and find_last_not_of member functions are very similar to their find_first equivalents, except that they search starting at the end of the string and work backwards.

```
size_t find_last_of(const string &s, size_t startAt = npos) const;
size_t find_last_not_of(const string &s, size_t startAt = npos) const;
```

These are called in exactly the same manner as the corresponding find_first type functions, and they return the same type of information except that they work backwards.

When you want to delete characters from a string, you use the remove member function.

```
string &remove(size_t startAt = 0, size_t howMany = npos);
```

This removes howMany characters from a string, starting at position startAt. The stringVar.remove(4); statement is the same as stringVar[4] = '\0';.

Summary

This chapter presented the C++ string class, templates, and a glimpse at the class library. You should now be familiar with the following:

☐ The string class handles allocation and manipulation of strings without need for the low-level issues necessary when working with C-style strings.

☐ When declaring a string variable, the initial value can be placed in parentheses immediately after (as in string myStr("Init Value");). When you assign a new value to it, any necessary size adjustment is handled for you.

☐ Simple comparison operators can be used with the `string` class. There is no need to call functions such as `strcmp` or `strncmp`.

☐ C++ templates can be used with functions and classes to work with any kind of data type. You define a template with "generic" arguments and use a template giving specific arguments. The compiler generates code appropriate to the actual argument types.

☐ Creating an instance of a template class requires that you specify the type(s) as part of the class name.

☐ The class libraries provide a rich set of easy-to-use classes for creating containers. These containers can store objects in a variety of useful formats.

Q&A

Q Can I get the value of a character in a string as I can in C?

A Yes, and in the same way. If `strC` is a C-style array and `strCpp` is a C++ string class and both are set to `"ABC"`, then both `strC[1]` and `strCpp[1]` are equal to the character `'B'`.

Q What happens if I assign a `char` to a string index that is beyond the end of an array?

A In C, when you write to a character that is past the end of an array, the character is stored in the position where it would have been, had the array been large enough. If that memory contains critical information, the computer could lock up—but only after it has run further, destroying the symptoms of where the problem occurred.

With a C++ string, when you write past the end of the array, the overwrite is detected and the exception-handling system is called. If running a DOS program, the program ends with an `Abnormal program termination` error. If you were stepping through the program with a debugger, the error would be displayed at the line where it occurred, not elsewhere.

Q What happens if I copy to a string and the size is larger than has been allocated?

A The C++ string class detects that and expands the array to fit. If you were using C-style strings, a DOS `Abnormal termination` would be presented or an equivalent complaint would be shown by Windows. If debugging, the debugger would stop at the line where the problem occurred, telling you of the problem.

Q I found a function that operates on C-style strings and does what I want. How can I use it with C++ `string` class items?

A Use the `c_str` function. For example, if `strCpp` is a C++ string, then `strlen(strCpp.c_str());` will find the length of the string.

Workshop

The Workshop provides quiz questions to help you solidify your understanding of the material covered and exercises to provide you with experience in using what you've learned. Try to understand the quiz and exercise answers before continuing on to the next day's lesson. Answers are provided in Appendix A.

Quiz

1. Which header file must be included to use the STL `string` class?
2. How is a `string` class variable declared?
3. How do you compare a `string` to a C-style string?
4. Which `string` class function will find and replace text in one call?
5. To read the second character in a `string`, which array index is used?
6. Declare a `string` named `myString` with an initial value of `12`.
7. Assuming that you have two `string` class variables, `s1` and `s2`, and that `s1` contains `"11"` and `s2` contains `"2112"`, what is the result of the following code lines?

    a. `s1 + s2;`

    b. `s2.contains(s1);`

    c. `s1 > s2`

    d. `s2.find(s1, 0);`

Exercises

1. Write a line of code that declares a C-style string of value `12`, and another that declares a C++ string class variable with the same value.
2. Write a function that accepts a reference to a string as its calling argument and writes that string to the computer screen.
3. Modify the function written for the previous exercise to perform a loop, writing all the characters from the string, one per pass through the loop, and to return the size of the string.
4. Write a function that calls `strrev`, which reverses the characters in a C-style string, to reverse the characters contained in a C++ string class variable.

Programming Windows with OWL5

ObjectWindows version 5 (or OWL5) is included with Borland C++ 5. It is a C++ library that shortens the time and effort needed to develop a Windows program. OWL uses a feature of the C++ language called *templates.* Today, you will learn about the following:

☐ OWL and basic Windows issues

☐ Hungarian notation

☐ The basic structure of OWL

☐ Windows messages and OWL

☐ Developing a real OWL program, complete with resources, menus, and screen writing

OWL and Windows Issues

Although using OWL means that you need not worry about many of the details of Windows, you still need some knowledge of how Windows does things and especially of some of the symbols used in Windows programs.

Under DOS or EasyWin, there can be only one program running at a time (with the exception of TSR programs, such as Print). That program owns the screen, keyboard, and mouse. Under Windows, several programs can be running at a time, and normally each one has screen, keyboard, and mouse I/O capability. To force these programs to cooperate, Windows enforces strict conditions on program structure, handling each task almost as if it were a function in a larger application of which Windows itself is the main program.

Windows administers a communication channel called the *message loop,* which acts as a type of "party line" by which it communicates with all the executing tasks. When a task writes to the screen or the user provides some keyboard or mouse input, Windows gathers up the information and calls a function in whichever task it has decided should receive the appropriate message.

The complexity of having independently executing functions for each of your program's screen windows, along with a main program that never calls any of them directly, is what OWL addresses. The problem is that no interface library can totally hide what is underneath. Windows uses an extensive set of macros that substitute for data types and other items. Table 12.1 lists some of the more important ones. You might want to put a bookmark at this page so that you can refer back to it.

Table 12.1. Some common Windows macro names.

Macro	Meaning	Equivalent
TRUE	Used for function return values	1 or true
FALSE	Used for function return values	0 or false

Macro	Meaning	Equivalent
NULL	A null pointer, as in the C language	0
UINT	An unsigned integer value (this is a 16-bit value in Win16 and a 32-bit value in Win32)	unsigned int
BYTE	An unsigned 8-bit value	unsigned char
WORD	An unsigned 16-bit value	unsigned short
DWORD	An unsigned 32-bit value	unsigned long
LONG	A signed 32-bit value	long
VOID	As a function return, it means that it returns nothing; as a pointer, it means that the data type it points to is not specified	void
LPSTR	Long pointer to a string	char far*
LPCSTR	Long pointer to a constant string	const char far*
HANDLE	A generic handle to some form of Windows item	void*
HWND	A handle to a window	*not applicable*
PASCAL	Specifies that the function to which it applies uses the Pascal calling method; most Windows API functions use this calling convention because it allows Pascal programs to use the API and because it is a slightly more efficient method of passing parameters to a function (the reasons for which are beyond the scope of this book)	pascal
WPARAM	A word parameter, used to define a data type as a calling argument to a function	UINT
LPARAM	A long parameter, used to define a data type as a calling argument to a function	LONG
LRESULT	Used to define the data type a function returns	LONG
HINSTANCE	Handle to the instance or copy of the program that is currently running	*not applicable*

12

You should take careful notice of the TRUE and FALSE macros. These were implemented by Microsoft before the bool type was added to the C++ language. Because of this, all of Windows is riddled with the BOOL type, which is really just an int. OWL, however, uses bool instead; it hides the Windows BOOL type. As a matter of fact, because TRUE is defined to be 1 and FALSE is defined to be 0, you can simply use bool in any call to a Windows function that asks for a BOOL. C++ will automatically convert it to an int for you.

Hungarian Notation

Microsoft has been developing Windows since the early 1980s. At its inception, the ANSI standard for C compilers did not exist, and type-checking was minimal. Microsoft programmers adopted a naming convention for variables that had the data type indicated as the first few characters of the variable name. It was called *Hungarian notation* because its inventor was from Hungary.

With the introduction of the ANSI C standard with its stronger type-checking, and especially with C++, a strongly typed language, Hungarian notation is no longer needed; still, it is not uncommon.

In a variable name such as lpszFilename, the lpsz means long pointer to zero-terminated string. Many programmers feel confident that they would know a variable called Filename is a string without having to add lpsz to the name. Because Windows documentation uses Hungarian notation, however, it is important to have some feel for what the leading characters in the names are, so Table 12.2 shows the prefixes used in Hungarian notation. Nonetheless, your program will run as well without them as with them.

Table 12.2. Hungarian notation prefixes.

Prefix	Data Type
c	char
by	BYTE (unsigned char)
n	short or int
i	int
x, y	short (used as *x* coordinate or *y* coordinate)
cx, cy	short (used as *x* or *y* length; the c stands for "count")
b	BOOL (int)
w	UINT (unsigned int) or WORD (unsigned short)
l	LONG (long)

Prefix	Data Type
dw	DWORD (unsigned long)
fn	function pointer
s	C string (character array)
sz	C string terminated by 0 byte

The Differences Between Win16 and Win32

When Windows first came out, it was meant to run on the most advanced PC processor available at the time: a simple IBM XT compatible. With the advancement of the processor (starting with Windows 3.1), the operating system eventually came to work only on machines with a 80386 or better in what is referred to as enhanced mode. This is a 16-bit addressing mode wherein the processor still needs to use two 16-bit registers in order to address memory.

Then came Windows NT and 32-bit addressing. This version of Windows finally used the full processing power of the PC in a 32-bit mode where memory is addressed. This was great news, except that now there were two versions of Windows along with two different versions of many API functions—and many inconsistencies between the two versions. Windows 3.1 came to be known as using the Win16 API, and Windows NT came to be known as using the Win32 API.

Windows 95 is the attempt to synthesize many of these two worlds into a single Win32 interface. Windows NT is still separate and still has its place, but at least now there's a single Win32 API that remains the same between the two operating systems. You need only write to the Win32 API and make sure to check the results of your attempts; the functions to get things done are the same across both operating systems, but the ones that don't mean anything in one will simply return an error result to inform of this fact.

However, there is still a great deal of "legacy code" out there that is written to the Win16 API. Because both of the more recent versions of Windows still support that old API in special modes (though Windows NT doesn't always do as good a job as Windows 95), the old Win16 code is going to last for a while yet.

The most important difference between Win16 and Win32 is the fact that Win32 has a lot more functionality and a far richer API than Win16; there are some things you can do with Win32 that just don't exist in the older API. Another difference is that some functions have changed their signatures. But the real gotcha is in the whole messaging system.

12

Windows works at a very basic level with the passing of messages between the various programs that are running. Each message takes two parameters used to pass specific data pertaining to it. In Win32, one of those parameters changed from being 16 bits to 32 bits. With the extra room in the parameter, Microsoft decided it could cram more information into it.

Luckily, Borland has kept OWL up to date with the changes. If you use OWL instead of writing to Windows directly, you will be able to ignore many of those differences. In fact, it's possible to write a program and then just recompile it, depending upon which version of Windows you wish to target. Since Win32 is what everything is moving toward and Win16 is being phased out, this book is geared toward the Win32 API.

The Basic Structure of OWL

OWL has groups of classes, each of which addresses a certain phase of Windows programming. The structure uses multiple inheritance to allow classes to encapsulate those combinations of functionality they need.

Event Handling: *TEventHandler*

The programmer does little with this directly. The functions it provides are available in many of the other program groups because of C++ inheritance. It manages the messages that constantly flow in a Windows program.

Streamable or Persistent Objects: *TStreamableBase*

This is actually part of the regular class library and not an OWL class. It allows a class to be viewed as a stream and saved to memory or disk for later use in the current run of the program or at another time that the program is run. This is exotic for small programs but is of great value in more advanced programs, such as those using the document-view architecture.

Module Management: *TModule* and *TApplication*

TModule and TApplication are in the module management group. TModule is responsible for loading and unloading DLLs, whereas TApplication is responsible for initializing the program, managing it while it runs, and handling the tasks that are needed when the program ends.

Window Management: *TWindow*

TWindow is the base window class and inherits from TEventHandler and TStreamableBase. There are various types of windows that you might want to use in your program, and they all build on TWindow:

- ☐ TFrameWindow is a simple framed window with menu capability.

- ☐ TDecoratedFrame adds capabilities to use other items, such as status bars and tool bars.

- ☐ TMDIFrame, TMDIChild, and TDecoratedMDIFrame are Multiple Document Interface (MDI) classes used to present multiple windows in a single application.

Other functional groups are provided for the graphics, menu handling, dialog boxes, printing, and exception handling.

A Sample OWL Program

Our first OWL program displays only a window with a title. You have to press Alt+F4 or open the system menu and select Close to end it.

This program has two elements: a class to manage the window, and a class to manage the application.

A class called MainApp is derived from TApplication, the class that manages the startup, the continuing message handling, and the ending tasks. TApplication has a virtual function called InitMainWindow. In MainApp, you overload that function and provide your own. Within the function, you make a call setting the main window to a frame window with your window title.

Windows applications normally do not start with a function called main. Instead, they use a function that is declared as follows:

```
int PASCAL WinMain(HINSTANCE hInstance, HINSTANCE hPrevInstance,
                   LPSTR lpszCmdLine, int cmdShow);
```

OWL allows a main function similar to what you're used to with other C and C++ programs, as follows:

```
int OwlMain(int argc, char *argv[]);
```

> **Note:** On the first day, when EasyWin was described, it was mentioned that when a so-called real Windows program was created, the EasyWin flag needed to be turned off in the IDE's option screens. Because OWL applications are considered real Windows applications, you will need to access the IDE's TargetExpert by clicking in the Project window on the appropriate EXE node, then clicking on the

right mouse button and selecting the option from the pop-up menu. A dialog box will appear with a list box titled Target Type. You need to select the Application [.exe] item in this list box and then click the OK button.

Listing 12.1. FIRST.CPP, a first OWL program.

```
1:  #include <owl\framewin.h>
2:  #include <owl\applicat.h>
3:
4:  class MainApp : public TApplication
5:  {
6:  public:
7:     MainApp() : TApplication() {}
8:     void InitMainWindow();        // overload TApplication function
9:  };
10:
11: void MainApp::InitMainWindow()
12: {
13:    SetMainWindow(new TFrameWindow(0, "First OWL Program"));
14: }
15:
16: int OwlMain(int, char **)
17: {
18:    return MainApp().Run();
19: }
```

Figure 12.1 shows what the first OWL program does.

Figure 12.1.
The minimalist OWL program.

`OwlMain` begins on line 16. It calls the `Run` function, and OWL's default processing does the rest. (`Run` is a function within `TApplication`.)

The "magic" of how this operates is hidden in how the classes are set up. `MainApp` calls the constructor for `TApplication` on line 7, inside its own constructor. That triggers default processing for all maintenance functions except the `InitMainWindow` function, which has been overloaded by declaring a member function of the same name on line 8.

On line 13, the `InitMainWindow` function calls `SetMainWindow` to allocate a `TFrameWindow` and link the application with this window object. The same line allocates the `TFrameWindow` by calling new for it and passes the window caption to it in the constructor call.

The two header files that are included are for `TFrameWindow` (FRAMEWIN.H) and `TApplication` (APPLICAT.H). A Windows program should have a .DEF file to tell the linker what to do with the segments and stack. Borland C++ supplies one for you, \BC5\LIB\DEFAULT.DEF, and it was used for this program. It should be added to the list in your project file by following the instructions for project management on Day 1, or you can just leave it out altogether. If a .DEF file isn't specified explicitly, the default file will be used, but you'll always receive a warning in the message window that no .DEF file was specified and that the default was used. Personally, I don't supply the .DEF file unless I'm working on a large project that needs to have the settings of the .DEF file changed. Check the online help for more information on the contents of the .DEF file.

Windows Messages and OWL

The Windows system calls the function in your program that it has logged as the handling function for an open window. Several calling arguments are passed to the function, one of which is called the message. The other calling parameters are `WPARAM` and `LPARAM`. What they mean varies depending upon the message.

Messages are all named with `#define` macros. Two of the more common ones are

`WM_CHAR`, which reports a normal key is pressed. The `WPARAM` argument contains the value of the key. The `LPARAM` argument contains the number of times it has been pressed in the lower 16 bits, and has an array of bit flags in the upper 16 bits to indicate other data about the keyboard. You can access those values with the `HIWORD` and `LOWORD` macros that extract the upper 16 bits and the lower 16 bits, respectively.

`WM_SIZE`, which says the window size has changed. The `WPARAM` argument contains a value defining the type of size change, such as if it has been minimized. The `LPARAM` argument has the new width in the lower 16 bits and the new height in the upper 16 bits.

It's important to know just how integral the messaging system is to Windows. All Windows programs work by having their windows respond to input in the form of messages from the system. These messages can represent such things as user input or lower-level system operations that affect the running of a program. In between the processing of messages, most Windows programs tend to lie dormant, waiting for the next message that needs attention.

The normal processing of Windows messages is through a single function, and that function would traditionally have a huge switch statement to parse which messages it would support. Then the WPARAM and LPARAM parameters would have to be fiddled with in order to retrieve the pertinent information associated with each message. It's cumbersome and difficult to program, especially when a large number of messages need to be processed.

There are a tremendous number of Windows messages—well over 500. It should be noted here that you usually don't have to handle very many of them. This is due, in large part, to the fact that OWL handles those messages that absolutely *must* be handled, and the rest are needed only when you're doing something that specifically calls for those messages.

OWL provides two macros and an array of functions that know about Windows messages and their associated data. When an event occurs for which Windows calls the OWL window procedure, OWL parses the information from the calling arguments and calls any function you may have provided to handle that event. This relieves you of deciphering the information stored in the WPARAM and LPARAM parameters, and it also lets you compartmentalize your code into separate member functions that respond only to specific messages. You know the name to use for the functions because they are derived from the name of the message, such as the following:

Windows Message	Event-Handler Function Name
WM_CHAR	void EvChar(uint key, uint repeat, uint flags);
WM_SIZE	void EvSize(uint sizeType, TSize& newSize); TSize is a structure with an x and a y member called cx and cy, respectively. It holds the new dimensions of the window.

In the OWL handlers, the other calling parameters are said to be "cracked"—broken down into more easily understood parameters and not buried in the middle of a parameter value. The cracking of messages avoids many common code bugs. OWL's handling of the repetitive overhead needed by each message avoids many more bugs.

The way you tell OWL that you have supplied an event handler is done with two macros and a declaration. Within your class derived from TWindow, you declare the function itself. Also within the class definition, you place a macro to tell it that the overloading of functions is being done. In a typical class definition, those lines would look like the following:

```
class BaseWindow : public TWindow
{
protected:
    void EvChar(uint key, uint repeatCount, uint flags);
```

```
    :
public:
    :
DECLARE_RESPONSE_TABLE(BaseWindow);
};
```

Later in the code, you define the response table with one entry for each function that you need.

```
DEFINE_RESPONSE_TABLE1(BaseWindow, TWindow)
    EV_WM_CHAR,
    EV_WM_SIZE,
END_RESPONSE_TABLE;
```

The macro used here is DEFINE_RESPONSE_TABLE1 because there is only one immediate class from which BaseWindow inherits. Were there two classes, then DEFINE_RESPONSE_TABLE2 would be used and the second class also would be listed as an argument to the macro. Macros are available for up to three inherited classes.

The Windows message name has EV_ placed in front of it to help in the macro parsing, but otherwise it is the same name as the message.

As described on Day 1, a helpful feature of the Borland C++ IDE is that if the cursor is placed on a name such as EvChar and Ctrl+F1 is pressed, the online Help will display the function, its calling arguments, and an explanation of what each argument means.

A Real OWL Program: Resources, Menus, and Screen Writing

A demonstration that only puts a window on the screen is not very useful. Menus and screen writing have been added to the next example. It demonstrates techniques for handling normal Windows messages and messages from menus.

Menus are a feature that you can add to a window. The Windows system runs them for you, returning a number corresponding to the user selection. The message that Windows sends in response to a menu selection is WM_COMMAND, with the WPARAM parameter set to the value of the selected item. Because the selections in a menu that you create would not be part of the operating system, OWL has no built-in detection for them. What it does have is an EV_COMMAND macro that enables you to specify response functions for nonstandard events.

There are three source files involved in adding a menu to an application. The source file for the program is involved, but you also need a resource file.

Resources are predefined items that will be added to the executable as a last step. As the program is already compiled and linked when they are added, this arrangement enables resources to be more easily changed—a great advantage when changing a menu from English to German, for example. Because resource files normally have the file extension .RC, they often are called .RC files.

The third file involved is a header file listing the macros used for menu selections, along with their number equivalents. By including the same header file in the source code and the .RC file, any changes in the selection numbers will track through to the C++ compilation as well as to the resource compiler's handling of the .RC file. As you did with DEFAULT.DEF, add the name REAL.RC to the IDE project file list. Listing 12.2 shows a resource file.

 Listing 12.2. REAL.RC, a resource file.

```
1:  #include "real.rh"
2:
3:  MENU_1 MENU
4:  {
5:     POPUP "&File"
6:        {
7:           MENUITEM "&Clear",  CM_CLEAR
8:           MENUITEM "E&xit",   CM_FILEEXIT
9:        }
10:    MENUITEM "&About",  CM_ABOUT
11: }
```

Figure 12.2 shows what it looks like.

Figure 12.2.
From REAL.RC, a resource file.

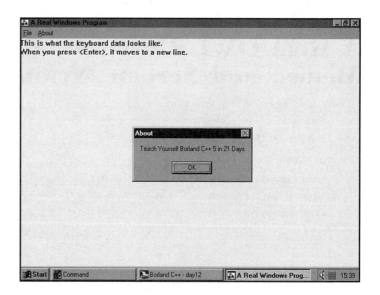

Later you will use Resource Workshop to create .RC files containing menus and other items. For now, there is little value in using that tool unless you have some feel for what is being created with it, so this text file is what you will use instead.

On line 3, the MENU_1 item is introduced without having been referenced in the header file or the source file. With the available information, the resource compiler will make it a text string. You can take advantage of this name string in the program when you load a menu identified as MENU_1.

Line 5 starts defining a pop-up menu. A *pop-up* is a menu that, when selected, opens to display more menu selections. It does not return a value, although the newly shown selections often do. The first pop-up item in the menu is given the name &File. The & character flags the F as special. In the menu it will be shown underlined, and pressing Alt+F will cause it to be selected.

The pop-up contains two menu items on lines 7 and 8. A menu item does return a value to the program. In this case, the displayed names for the menu items are Clear and Exit, with the C and x underlined. You can use the C and X keys to select these items when the pop-up is opened. If Clear is selected, CM_CLEAR is returned. The following header file assigns the number 1125 to CM_CLEAR, but the program doesn't care what that number is. All it cares about is whether or not it receives a message with the WPARAM set equal to whatever the macro CM_CLEAR stands for.

On line 9, the curly brace after E&xit ends the pop-up. Following that on line 10 is another menu item selection for &About. If selected, the value CM_ABOUT will be sent to the program, which will display an About box that tells the name of the program.

When the program is running, OWL doesn't have any knowledge of what the CM_CLEAR, CM_FILEEXIT, or CM_ABOUT values accompanying a WM_COMMAND message are, so it ignores them. You can change this with additions to the response table, which tells OWL what to do with those messages.

Along with predefined messages such as WM_SIZE and WM_CHAR, you can use the EV_COMMAND macro to say that you have a command message you want OWL to crack. It is used as follows:

```
DEFINE_RESPONSE_TABLE1(BaseWindow, TWindow)
    EV_WM_CHAR,
    EV_WM_SIZE,
    EV_COMMAND(CM_ABOUT, CmAbout),
END_RESPONSE_TABLE;
```

The function is expected to take no parameters and return no value—in other words, void CmAbout(). OWL programmers commonly use a certain way of naming such functions, and if you follow that convention, your code will be more understandable to others and you will be getting used to the same type of naming that is used in the documentation that came with Borland C++. To name the function, delete any underscores and capitalize the first letter of each word. For example, CM_ABOUT becomes CmAbout(). Windows event handlers drop the WM_ entirely and put Ev at the beginning of the name; thus WM_CHAR becomes EvChar. Remember that event handlers usually take some parameters. When you use one, look it up in the online Help to check that you have the arguments correct.

REAL.CPP writes to the screen what you have typed. OWL provides an entire class, called TEdit, which can edit and capture your input far better than REAL.CPP does. This and other controls will be covered in later chapters. This example's writing to the screen is meant to illustrate how one paints a window under Windows, which is very different than under DOS or EasyWin.

 NEW☞ TERM Windows uses an item called a *device context*, also called a *DC*. A DC is a structure containing information about a device such as a screen, a printer, or a block of memory.

You can write to anything for which you have asked Windows to provide a DC. Windows has only a limited number of DC blocks, so they are handled by requesting one, using it, and then calling Windows to free it for other uses. Forgetting to release DCs can result in Windows apparently stopping. With OWL, you needn't worry unless requesting a DC yourself. OWL automatically checks out a DC when it's time to paint the screen and returns it afterward. OWL expands upon this by placing the device context into a class called TDC along with functions that use DCs. Those functions already know what device you are writing to when you call them. Listing 12.3 shows a header file.

Type

Listing 12.3. REAL.RH, a header file.

```
1: #define CM_CLEAR    1125
2: #define CM_FILEEXIT 1126
3: #define CM_ABOUT     1127
```

REAL.RH does not get listed in the compiler's project file. The compiler will discover what header files are used by itself via the #include preprocessor directive.

Listing 12.4 shows the source code for a program that uses a menu, accepts keyboard input, and writes the input to the screen.

Type

Listing 12.4. REAL.CPP, a real OWL program.

```
1:   #include <owl\framewin.h>
2:   #include <owl\applicat.h>
3:   #include <owl\dc.h>
4:   #include <mem.h>
5:
6:   #include "real.rh"
7:
8:   const int maxLines = 25;
9:   const int maxWidth = 80;
10:  const int maxData = maxLines * (maxWidth + 1);
11:
12:  class BaseWindow : public TWindow
13:  {
14:  public:
15:      BaseWindow(TWindow *parent = 0);
```

```
16:      ~BaseWindow()    { delete[] linePtrs[0]; }
17:
18:  protected:
19:      int   currentLine;          // line being typed in now
20:      int   lineLen[maxLines];    // length of each line
21:      char *linePtrs[maxLines];   // string for each line
22:      bool  isMinimized;          // true if window is an icon
23:      TSize windowSize;           // structure with size in pixels
24:
25:      void EvChar(uint key, uint repeatCount, uint flags);
26:      void Paint(TDC& dc, bool, TRect&);
27:      void EvSize(uint sizeType, TSize& size);
28:
29:      void CmAbout();
30:      void CmClear();
31:
32:      // Menu choice, end the program
33:      void CmFileExit() { PostQuitMessage(0); }
34:  DECLARE_RESPONSE_TABLE(BaseWindow); // says we'll have a
35:  };                                  // response table
36:
37:  DEFINE_RESPONSE_TABLE1(BaseWindow, TWindow)
38:      EV_WM_CHAR,
39:      EV_WM_SIZE,
40:      EV_COMMAND( CM_ABOUT,    CmAbout),
41:      EV_COMMAND( CM_FILEEXIT, CmFileExit),
42:      EV_COMMAND( CM_CLEAR,    CmClear),
43:  END_RESPONSE_TABLE;
44:
45:  class MyApp : public TApplication
46:  {
47:  public:
48:      MyApp() : TApplication() {}
49:
50:      void InitMainWindow();
51:  };
52:
53:  BaseWindow::BaseWindow(TWindow *parent)
54:  {
55:      int lineNum;
56:
57:      Init(parent, 0, 0);
58:      linePtrs[0] = new char[maxData]; // allocate edit buffer
59:      lineLen[0] = currentLine = 0;
60:
61:      // apportion the buffer out to the line pointer array
62:      for (lineNum = 1; lineNum < maxLines; ++lineNum)
63:          {
64:          linePtrs[lineNum] = linePtrs[lineNum - 1] + maxWidth;
65:          lineLen[lineNum] = 0;
66:          }
67:  }
68:
69:  // Menu choice, display an About box,
70:  // use a message box to do it
```

continues

Listing 12.4. continued

```
71:   void BaseWindow::CmAbout()
72:   {
73:       MessageBox("Teach Yourself Borland C++ 5 in 21 Days", "About");
74:   }
75:
76:   // Menu choice, clear the display
77:   void BaseWindow::CmClear()
78:   {
79:       for (int lineNum = 0; lineNum < maxLines; ++lineNum)
80:           lineLen[lineNum] = 0;    // empty all lines
81:
82:       currentLine = 0;             // move back to top line
83:       Invalidate();                // window is invalid, repaint
84:   }
85:
86:   // this is called whenever the window changes size
87:   void BaseWindow::EvSize(uint sizeType, TSize& size)
88:   {
89:       if (sizeType == SIZE_MINIMIZED)  // if shrunk to icon
90:           isMinimized = true;
91:       else
92:           {
93:           windowSize = size;           // save window size
94:           isMinimized = false;
95:           }
96:   }
97:
98:   // called when time to update (paint) the screen
99:   void BaseWindow::Paint(TDC& dc, bool, TRect&)
100: {
101:     int   lineNum;          // line number to write
102:     int   yPos;             // vertical position on screen
103:     int   displayedLines;   // number of linePtrs in this window
104:     TSize textSize;         // used to get char height in pixels
105:
106:     if (isMinimized)        // don't write to an icon
107:         return;
108:
109:     // get char sizes so that height is saved
110:     textSize = dc.GetTextExtent("W", 1);
111:     displayedLines = windowSize.cy / textSize.cy;
112:
113:     if (displayedLines > maxLines)
114:     displayedLines = maxLines;
115:
116:     for (lineNum = yPos = 0; lineNum < displayedLines; ++lineNum)
117:         {
118:         if (lineLen[lineNum] > 0)  // if any text on the line
119:         dc.TextOut(0, yPos, linePtrs[lineNum], lineLen[lineNum]);
120:
121:         yPos += textSize.cy;   // adjust screen line position
122:         }
123: }
124:
```

```
125: // called when a normal key is pressed
126: void BaseWindow::EvChar(uint key, uint repeatCount, uint)
127: {
128:     bool invalidDisplay = false;
129:     bool eraseBackground = false;
130:
131:     while (repeatCount--)
132:         {
133:         if ((key >= ' ') && (key <= '~')) // if a printable key
134:             {
135:             if (currentLine >= maxLines)    // if buffer full
136:                 {
137:                 MessageBeep(-1);            //    complain
138:                 break;
139:                 }
140:             else                           // else
141:                 {                          //    add char
142:                 linePtrs[currentLine][lineLen[currentLine]] = (char) key;
143:
144:                 if (++lineLen[currentLine] >= maxWidth)
145:                     ++currentLine;
146:
147:                 invalidDisplay = true;
148:                 }
149:             }
150:         else if (key == '\b')  // rubout, delete char
151:             {
152:             if (currentLine >= maxLines)
153:                 break;
154:             else if (lineLen[currentLine] == 0)
155:                 {
156:                 if (currentLine > 0)
157:                     --currentLine;
158:                 }
159:             else
160:                 --lineLen[currentLine];
161:
162:             invalidDisplay = eraseBackground = true;
163:             }
164:         else if (key == '\r') // if carriage return (Enter key)
165:             ++currentLine;
166:         }
167:
168:     if (currentLine >= maxLines)
169:         currentLine = maxLines - 1;
170:
171:     if (invalidDisplay)                  // if buffer has changed
172:         Invalidate(eraseBackground); //    force window repaint
173: }
174:
175: void MyApp::InitMainWindow()
176: {
177:     SetMainWindow(new TFrameWindow(0, "A Real Windows Program",
178:                   new BaseWindow()));
179:     GetMainWindow()->AssignMenu("MENU_1");
```

continues

Listing 12.4. continued

```
180: }
181:
182: int OwlMain(int, char **)
183: {
184:     return MyApp().Run();
185: }
```

Before running this application, you may want to get a feel for how it looks by examining Figure 12.2.

The next thing you should do is go through the program and look at all the functions used. There are quite a few minor functions used throughout this book, and I simply can't list the definitions for all of them. This book's intent is to teach you the programming principles that will enable you to create programs on your own. In order to get comprehensive definitions of various functions, you should go to the online help and look them up, just as you would a dictionary for English.

As with the first program, this begins in OwlMain. Line 184 calls the constructor for MyApp, and then calls Run.

The constructor is declared on line 48. It in turn calls the constructor for TApplication. Line 50 has a function called InitMainWindow that overloads the virtual function of the same name in the inherited class.

TApplication's constructor calls InitMainWindow (lines 175 through 180). That function makes two calls to new, creating a base window and then a frame window to handle the items on the base window's borders. The GetMainWindow call on the next line assigns the menu to the main window. From then on, the application runs on its own, with Windows driving it by way of messages about menu selections and keyboard events.

The response table on lines 37 through 43 declares response functions for a character being entered, a window size change, and any of the three menu selections. Also, BaseWindow's inheritance chain includes a virtual function called Paint, which has been overloaded.

The data in the BaseWindow class is for keyboard input. Such input causes EvChar on line 126 to be called. The calling arguments are the value of the key, the number of times it has been entered since you were last called, and a flag's variable that you don't use. The repeat count is important because a long process, such as saving a disk file, could allow the keyboard to insert several keys into the keyboard buffer.

This function passes through a loop as many times as the repeat count directs, adding keys to the keyboard buffer. When a line is full, it skips to the next line and begins entering there. If the buffer is full, the computer beeps at you (line 137).

If the user chooses the Backspace button, it deletes the last character entered (if one exists). The end of the function calls `Invalidate`, a function that tells Windows that the whole window must be updated. The `eraseBackground` variable is set to `true` only if a character is deleted. This minimizes screen blinking.

In response to the `Invalidate` call, Windows sends the window procedure a message to paint the window. In the process, it sets things up and calls `Paint`.

`Paint` gets the text size. Fonts in Windows often are of variable width, but the measurement you are interested in is the vertical, which doesn't vary. You also calculate the number of displayable lines. It's a waste of time to paint more than that, because additional lines won't be placed on the screen.

A loop starting on line 116 passes through each line, writing any data in it to the screen. Note that `linePtrs[lineNum]` is an array of characters, not a string. No `'\0'` has been placed at the end. It relies on the `lineLen` array to handle how long the string is.

Note the `TDC` argument to `Paint`. That is the device context you are to use in writing the screen. OWL has assigned it and will delete it after your function ends.

If you grab the corner of the window with the mouse cursor and resize it, `EvSize` from line 87 will be called. If the application is minimized (shrunk to an icon), it merely sets a flag and returns. If it is not minimized, it captures the window dimensions into the `TSize` structure called `windowSize` for later use by the `Paint` function.

Menu operation is straightforward. Select any menu item and OWL calls the corresponding function. The `CmClear` function (starting on line 77) sets the line length for all strings to zero and moves the current line number to point at the first line (`linePtrs[0]`). It then invalidates the window so that `Paint` will be called. When called with no arguments, `Invalidate` defaults to `true` so the background will also be erased.

`CmAbout` calls a message box—a built-in Windows function—to show the name of the book.

`CmFileExit` on line 33 calls a true Windows function, `PostQuitMessage`. This function ends the program, and the return value is the function argument.

Summary

Today's lesson introduced you to Borland's ObjectWindows Library application framework and discussed the following topics:

☐ Windows requires special programming techniques because it allows multiple programs to run at the same time (unlike DOS).

12

☐ Windows communicates with programs via messages, and programs receive and process these messages in their message loop.

☐ Windows defines several shorthand names for common types of variables.

☐ Hungarian notation is a style of naming variables to indicate the type of data they hold, and it helps in preventing bugs caused by mixing incompatible types. It's somewhat old-fashioned, as C++ implements very strong C++ type checking, but Windows still uses some of its notations.

☐ OWL consists of groups of classes used to represent Windows structures, including event handling, module management, and window management.

☐ OWL processes Windows messages by executing the appropriate functions found in a window object's response table. OWL also "cracks" the parameters that Windows sends into more meaningful values.

☐ Adding a menu to a window requires that you create a menu resource, tell OWL to load it, and process the menu items using the EV_COMMAND macro.

Q&A

Q I have a DOS program I'd like to port to Windows. Do I have to rewrite it to use Windows techniques like message loops?

A Yes. It won't be a Windows program if it doesn't follow Windows rules. However, you can use Borland C++'s EasyWin library, which enables you to use DOS-style input and output functions. The result is a Windows program that looks like a DOS program.

Q The shorthand type names like DWORD and LPCSTR are confusing. Can't I just use the normal C++ types?

A Yes, you can, but you have to make sure you do everything exactly the same. For example, everywhere you would normally use LPCSTR, make sure you use const char far *. Although learning the types takes some time, it usually is worth the extra effort, if only in saving the time it takes to type!

Q What function in my program is called first?

A DOS programs start at the main function, which has arguments for the command-line parameters. Windows instead looks for a WinMain function, with several arguments for instance handles, command-line parameters, and main window sizes. OWL simplifies it by providing an OwlMain function that takes the same parameters as main does.

Q Do I have to use a resource editor like Resource Workshop to create my resources?

A No. Resource files (with a .RC extension) are text files, so you can create and edit them with any text editor. However, Resource Workshop greatly simplifies editing resources, especially graphical ones.

Workshop

The Workshop provides quiz questions to help you solidify your understanding of the material covered and exercises to provide you with experience in using what you've learned. Try to understand the answers before continuing on to the next day's lesson. Answers are provided in Appendix A.

Quiz

1. True or false? The underlying Windows types, such as WORD and UINT, will never change.
2. True or false? Even though an OWL program is quite different from a program written in C, it still is a normal Windows program.

Exercise

Create the program REAL2.CPP by using the TWindow::MessageBox function to display a message when the user types an invalid key.

Basic Windows

The most relevant aspect of the Windows environment, as the name suggests, is the use of windows. Windows are the holders of information. The application is responsible for maintaining information when you resize, move, or use existing scroll bars. In today's lesson, you learn about the following:

- ☐ Creating read-only text windows
- ☐ Scrolling through text using scroll bars
- ☐ Changing the scroll-bar metrics (units, line size, page size, and ranges)
- ☐ Optimizing the `Paint` member function

Creating a Read-Only Text Window

Day 12 presented a number of menu-driven OWL applications. However, there was very little explanation concerning how information was displayed in windows. This section presents an OWL application that displays read-only text in its windows. The basic notion of the application is similar to that of the read-only online Help windows.

The purpose of the program is to demonstrate how to display text and maintain that text after one or more of the following has occurred:

- ☐ Resizing the window
- ☐ Minimizing, restoring, or maximizing the window
- ☐ Moving a window or dialog box over the text area

The main tools to implement the application's features are the member functions `TDC::TextOut` and `TWindow::Paint`. The function `TDC::TextOut` draws a character string on the specified display. The text appears in the currently selected font and at the specified window coordinates.

NEW☞ TERM A *font* is a description of the type of characters used to display text. This description includes what the characters look like (called the *typeface*) as well as their size (referred to as their *point size*). Some common typefaces are *Arial* and *Times New Roman*, both of which come with Windows. Also, such things as italic and bold characters are described by fonts.

The *TextOut* Function

Syntax

The declarations for the overloaded `TDC` member function `TextOut` are

```
bool TextOut(int x, int y, const char far* str, int count = -1);
bool TextOut(const TPoint& p, const char far* str, int count = -1);
```

The x and y parameters identify the window location where the first character appears. The `str` parameter points to the string to be displayed in the window. The `count` parameter indicates the leading number of characters of `str` to display. The argument for the last parameter is usually the size of the displayed string argument. Note that this has a default of -1, which means to display all the characters of `str`. In the second version of the function `TextOut`, the x and y parameters are replaced by a reference to a `TPoint` structure. The function returns a nonzero value when successful and 0 when it fails.

Example

```
char s[81] = "Hello";
string str("Guten Tag!");
TPoint pt(10, 20);
dc.TextOut(20, 10, s);
dc.TextOut(pt, str.c_str());
```

As expected, the function `TDC::TextOut` displays text once. This means that altering the viewing area of the window or moving another window over the displayed text erases that text. What is needed is a mechanism that updates the display of text in the window. Consider the member function `TWindow::Paint`. This function enables you to display and maintain the contents of a window (both text and graphics). The versatility of the function `TWindow::Paint` comes from the fact that it responds to a `WM_PAINT` message whenever Windows determines that the window needs repainting. This repainting feature includes the initial creation of the window. Consequently, the versatility of `TWindow::Paint` includes setting the initial display as well as maintaining it.

Note: You need to declare your own version of the `Paint` member function in your derived window class. The code you place inside your version of the `Paint` function determines which information appears, remains, and disappears.

In the case of this OWL application, the same information is displayed from start to finish. The general form of the `Paint` member function is

```
void MyWindow::Paint(TDC& dc, bool erase, TRect& rect)
{
   // declarations

   // statements using the TextOut member function
   // e.g.
   //     dc.TextOut(x, y, s, strlen(s));
}
```

The parameter dc that is passed to the `Paint` member function is referred to as the device context, and it's the link to the display of the window. The `dc.TextOut` function can be used as needed to place text on the window. Interestingly, if you come across a C-coded Windows application that uses the `TextOut` API function, you note that a similar text output requires initializing the device-context object and then promptly releasing it once it has finished its task. These steps are performed automatically by the `TWindow::EvPaint` function, which in turn calls the `Paint` function.

I briefly introduced device contexts (DCs) on Day 12. A DC is the place in which all output goes. Anything that needs to be painted, such as text or graphics, must go onto DCs. These DCs can directly represent physical pixels on the screen, or they can be memory DCs. Memory DCs typically are used as temporary space in which to create such things as bit maps before actually putting them on the screen by copying to another DC.

Now look at the code for the OWL application. Listing 13.1 contains the script for the resource file READONLY.RC. This resource file defines a menu with a single menu item, Exit, to exit the application. Listing 13.2 shows the source code for the READONLY.CPP program.

Create the directory DAY13 as a subdirectory of \BC5\BC21DAY and store all the project's files in the new directory. The project's DAY13.IDE file should contain the files READONLY.CPP and READONLY.RC.

Compile and run the application. Notice that the lines of text appear when the window is created. Alter the window by resizing it, minimizing it, and then restoring it to normal. The lines of text are always visible (or at least a portion of them) as long as the upper-left portion of the screen is not obscured by another window. You also can click the left mouse button to display a message box. Drag that message box over the text lines and release the mouse. Then, drag the message box away from the text location. What do you see? The text lines reappear; `Paint` is constantly at work.

Listing 13.1. Script code for READONLY.RC.

```
1: #include <windows.h>
2: #include <owl\window.rh>
3:
4: EXITMENU MENU LOADONCALL MOVEABLE PURE DISCARDABLE
5: BEGIN
6:     MENUITEM "E&xit", CM_EXIT
7: END
```

Listing 13.2. Source code for READONLY.CPP.

```
1: #include <owl\applicat.h>
2: #include <owl\dc.h>
3: #include <owl\framewin.h>
4: #include <owl\window.h>
5: #include <owl\window.rh>
6: #include <stdio.h>
7:
```

```
 8:  const MAX_LINES = 30;
 9:
10: class TMyWindow : public TWindow
11: {
12: public:
13:    TMyWindow(TWindow* parent = 0);
14:
15: protected:
16:    bool CanClose();
17:
18:    void CmExit();
19:    void EvLButtonDown(uint, TPoint&);
20:
21:    void Paint(TDC&, bool, TRect&);
22:
23:    DECLARE_RESPONSE_TABLE(TMyWindow);
24: };
25: DEFINE_RESPONSE_TABLE1(TMyWindow, TWindow)
26:    EV_WM_LBUTTONDOWN,
27:    EV_COMMAND(CM_EXIT, CmExit),
28: END_RESPONSE_TABLE;
29:
30: class TMyApp : public TApplication
31: {
32: public:
33:    TMyApp() : TApplication() {}
34:
35:    void InitMainWindow()
36:       {
37:       SetMainWindow(new TFrameWindow(  0,
38:                            "A Simple Read-Only Text Window",
39:                            new TMyWindow ));
40:       GetMainWindow()->AssignMenu("EXITMENU");
41:       }
42: };
43:
44: TMyWindow::TMyWindow(TWindow* parent)
45: {
46:    Init(parent, 0, 0);
47: }
48:
49: bool TMyWindow::CanClose()
50: {
51:    return IDYES == MessageBox("Want to close this application?",
52:                            "Query",
53:                            MB_YESNO | MB_ICONQUESTION );
54: }
55:
56: void TMyWindow::CmExit()
57: {
58:    SendMessage(WM_CLOSE);
59: }
60:
61: void TMyWindow::EvLButtonDown(uint, TPoint&)
62: {
63:    MessageBox( "You clicked the left button!",
```

continues

Listing 13.2. continued

```
64:                    "Mouse Click Event",
65:                    MB_OK );
66: }
67:
68: void TMyWindow::Paint(TDC& dc, bool /*erase*/, TRect& /*rect*/)
69: {
70:     char s[81];
71:     bool ok = true;
72:     int y = 0;
73:
74:     for (int i = 0; i < MAX_LINES && ok; ++i)
75:         {
76:         sprintf(s, "This is line number %d", i);
77:         ok = dc.TextOut(0, y, s);
78:         y += dc.GetTextExtent(s, lstrlen(s)).cy;
79:         }
80: }
81:
82: int OwlMain(int, char *[])
83: {
84:     return TMyApp().Run();
85: }
```

Figure 13.1 shows a sample session with the program READONLY.EXE.

Figure 13.1.

A sample session with the program READONLY.EXE.

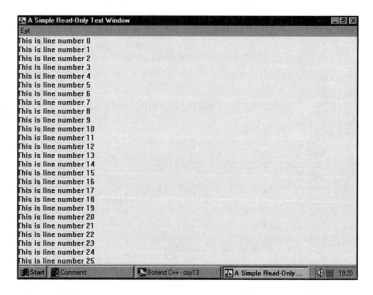

Listing 13.2 shows the source code for the READONLY.CPP program file. The part of the program that is relevant to this application is the TMyWindow class and its member functions, declared on lines 10 through 28. The window class declares a constructor and three member

functions, namely `EvLButtonDown`, `CmClose`, and `Paint`. The constructor creates a window on line 37 with the title `"A Simple Read-Only Text Window"` that has default size and location, and that uses the EXITMENU menu resource.

The main point of interest is the `Paint` function that starts on line 68. The function declares the constant `MAX_LINES`, the string variable s, and the `bool`-typed variable ok. The `Paint` function displays the lines using the `for` loop on lines 74 through 79. Each loop iteration executes three statements. The first statement calls the `sprintf` function (prototyped in the STDIO.H header file) to create the image of a formatted output and store it in the variable s. The next statement calls the DC's `TextOut` member function, which places the formatted output on the window. Notice the first two arguments of the `TextOut` function. They are 0 for parameters x and y. These values result in displaying the text, starting with the left margin of the window. The next function called is the DC's `GetTextExtent` member function. This is used to determine the height of the text and any line spacing, and to use that information by adding it to the y variable so that the next time through the loop, the next line is placed appropriately below the previous line.

Scrolling Through Text

One of the versatile features of windows is the capability to scroll information, if that information cannot be contained in the current viewing portion of the window. The scroll bars are the visual components of a window that assist in scrolling through the window's contents. Recall that a window can have a vertical scroll bar, horizontal scroll bar, or both. A scroll bar has an arrow box at each end and a scroll thumb. The arrow boxes enable you to scroll the window's contents to either end or to either side. In today's lesson, you learn about scrolling windows that contain text drawn using device-context objects.

NEW☞ The *scroll thumb* serves two purposes. First, it shows where you are relative to the entire
TERM width or length of the viewed information. Second, when you drag the thumb with the mouse, you can move to a specific portion of the viewed information.

The scrolling effect mentioned at the beginning of today's lesson is supported by a visual interface and an internal "engine." You can easily include the visual scroll bars in a window by incorporating the `WS_VSCROLL` and `WS_HSCROLL` styles in the `Attr.Style` member data from the window's constructor. To create a window with both vertical and horizontal scroll bars, for example, use the following statement:

```
// both vertical and horizontal scroll bars
Attr.Style |= WS_VSCROLL | WS_HSCROLL;
```

The `WS_VSCROLL` and `WS_HSCROLL` constants add the visual aspect of the scroll bars. The functionality is supported by overriding the `EvVScroll`, `EvHScroll`, and `EvSize` functions, and then adjusting your `Paint` function to take advantage of any scrolling changes. OWL provides an integrated class that does just this, called `TScroller`. An object of this class, when assigned the `TWindow`'s `Scroller` member function, provides scrolling by working with the `TWindow` class to automatically sense the setting of the scroll bars, and it adjusts the window's viewport accordingly.

NEW☞ The *viewport* is that portion of the window that is visible at any one time. It is possible to
TERM paint on a window outside of the visible portion, but that will be *clipped* from view. By adjusting the viewport's origin, the clipped region will change, and offsets within the window will be adjusted accordingly. For example, given a standard window, when a string of text is drawn at (`10,10`), the text will appear offset down and to the right of the upper-left corner of the window. By adjusting the viewport origin to begin at (`10,10`), drawing that same text at the same location now will make it appear in the upper-left corner.

The constructor for the `TScroller` class looks like this.

```
TScroller(TWindow* window, int xUnit, int yUnit,
          long xRange, long yRange);
```

The `window` parameter is a pointer to the window for which the `TScroller` object is being created. The `xUnit` and `yUnit` parameters specify how many device units to scroll in each direction. In the case of textual information, this usually is going to be the size of a single character, so that scrolling goes by lines. Note, however, that because most fonts in Windows are variable (each of the characters is of a differing width), the horizontal unit tends to be the average width of all the characters. Finally, the `xRange` and `yRange` parameters specify how many scrolling positions exist. For example, a `yRange` of `20` would mean that the down arrow on the scroll bar could be clicked 20 times.

It is easy to add an additional `include` file at the top,

```
#include <owl\scroller.h>
```

and the following two lines to the constructor of the `TMyWindow` class from the last example:

```
Attr.Style ¦= WS_VSCROLL ¦ WS_HSCROLL;
Scroller = new Tscroller(this, 7, 16, 20, MAX_LINES - 1);
```

If you add those two lines and recompile, you will find that your window now has scroll bars on the bottom and right side, and you can scroll to the right 20 columns and down as many lines as are drawn (minus one, so at least one of the lines stays on-screen). The two more interesting functions of the `TScroller` class are the `VScroll` and `HScroll` member functions.

Manually Scrolling with *TScroller*

The declarations of TScroller's VScroll and HScroll member functions are

```
void VScroll(uint scrollEvent, int thumbPos);
void HScroll(uint scrollEvent, int thumbPos);
```

The scrollEvent specifies the scrolling request. Table 13.1 shows the predefined constants for the various scrolling requests. The thumbPos parameter specifies the position of the thumb box when the argument for scrollEvent is either SB_THUMBPOSITION or SB_THUMBTRACK.

Example

```
Scroller->VScroll(SB_LINEDOWN, 0);
Scroller->HScroll(SB_THUMBPOSITION, 23);
```

Table 13.1. Predefined constants for vertical scrolling requests.

Value	Meaning
SB_BOTTOM	Scroll to the bottom
SB_ENDSCROLL	End scroll
SB_LINEDOWN	Scroll one line down
SB_LINEUP	Scroll one line up
SB_PAGEDOWN	Scroll one page down
SB_PAGEUP	Scroll one page up
SB_THUMBPOSITION	Scroll to the nPos position
SB_THUMBTRACK	Drag the scroll thumb box to the nPos position
SB_TOP	Scroll to the top

In the preceding short example, the 7 and 16 are approximations of a character's width and height. They will work when using the default font on most standard VGA screens, but you will run into problems when you try to use different fonts or when you run on screens that use a smaller font (such as an 800×600 or 1024×768 screen). The solution is to figure out the size of the font beforehand and set the scroll units accordingly.

A Scrolling Window

This section presents a program that defines general scrollable windows. TEXTSIZE.EXE has two main menu items: Exit and Char Sets. The second menu item is a pop-up menu that has five selections: 8, 10, 14, 20, and 26. These options produce text lines in the specified point size, thus changing the line spacing and maximum number of lines. The text fonts are the same for all five sets. The application also supports the cursor-movement keys to scroll the text. The

13

Home and End keys scroll vertically to the top and bottom, respectively. Similarly, the PgUp and PgDn keys scroll up and down one page. The up- and down-arrow keys scroll one line at a time. The left- and right-arrow keys scroll horizontally by pages.

This program illustrates two main aspects of scrolling windows:

☐ Declaring a scrolling window class with additional member functions that manage the assignment, access, and use of scrolling-related data

☐ Using assigned values to control vertical scrolling, and relying on the current window metrics to control the horizontal scrolling

Look at the code for the general text scroller window application. Listings 13.3 and 13.4 show the header file TEXTSIZE.H and the resource file TEXTSIZE.RC, respectively. Listing 13.5 contains the source code for the TEXTSIZE.CPP program.

 Listing 13.3. Source code for TEXTSIZE.H.

```
1:  #define  CM_HEIGHT8    (WM_USER + 100)
2:  #define  CM_HEIGHT10   (WM_USER + 101)
3:  #define  CM_HEIGHT14   (WM_USER + 102)
4:  #define  CM_HEIGHT20   (WM_USER + 103)
5:  #define  CM_HEIGHT26   (WM_USER + 104)
```

 Listing 13.4. Script code for TEXTSIZE.RC.

```
1:  #include <windows.h>
2:  #include <owl\window.rh>
3:  #include "textsize.h"
4:
5:  EXITMENU MENU LOADONCALL MOVEABLE PURE DISCARDABLE
6:  BEGIN
7:      MENUITEM "E&xit", CM_EXIT
8:      POPUP "&Char Heights"
9:      BEGIN
10:        MENUITEM "&8", CM_HEIGHT8
11:        MENUITEM "1&0", CM_HEIGHT10
12:        MENUITEM "1&4", CM_HEIGHT14
13:        MENUITEM "&20", CM_HEIGHT20
14:        MENUITEM "2&6", CM_HEIGHT26
15:     END
16: END
```

 Listing 13.5. Source code for TEXTSIZE.CPP.

```
1:  #include <owl\applicat.h>
2:  #include <owl\dc.h>
3:  #include <owl\framewin.h>
4:  #include <owl\scroller.h>
```

```
 5:  #include <owl\window.h>
 6:  #include <owl\window.rh>
 7:  #include <stdio.h>
 8:
 9:  #include "textsize.h"
10:
11:  const MAX_LINES = 30;
12:
13:  class TMyWindow : public TWindow
14:  {
15:  public:
16:      TMyWindow(TWindow* parent = 0);
17:      ~TMyWindow();
18:
19:  protected:
20:      virtual void SetupWindow();
21:
22:      bool CanClose();
23:
24:      void CmExit();
25:      void CmHeight8();
26:      void CmHeight10();
27:      void CmHeight14();
28:      void CmHeight20();
29:      void CmHeight26();
30:      void EvKeyDown(uint, uint, uint);
31:      void EvLButtonDown(uint, TPoint&);
32:
33:      void Paint(TDC&, bool, TRect &);
34:
35:  private:
36:      TFont* pFont;
37:
38:      void NewFont(int);
39:
40:      DECLARE_RESPONSE_TABLE(TMyWindow);
41:  };
42:  DEFINE_RESPONSE_TABLE1(TMyWindow, TWindow)
43:      EV_WM_KEYDOWN,
44:      EV_WM_LBUTTONDOWN,
45:      EV_COMMAND(CM_EXIT, CmExit),
46:      EV_COMMAND(CM_HEIGHT8, CmHeight8),
47:      EV_COMMAND(CM_HEIGHT10, CmHeight10),
48:      EV_COMMAND(CM_HEIGHT14, CmHeight14),
49:      EV_COMMAND(CM_HEIGHT20, CmHeight20),
50:      EV_COMMAND(CM_HEIGHT26, CmHeight26),
51:  END_RESPONSE_TABLE;
52:
53:  class TMyApp : public TApplication
54:  {
55:  public:
56:      TMyApp() : TApplication() {}
57:
58:      void InitMainWindow()
59:          {
60:          SetMainWindow(new TFrameWindow(  0,
```

continues

Listing 13.5. continued

```
61:                                "A Simple Read-Only Text Window",
62:                                new TMyWindow ));
63:         GetMainWindow()->AssignMenu("EXITMENU");
64:         }
65: };
66:
67: TMyWindow::TMyWindow(TWindow* parent)
68: {
69:     Init(parent, 0, 0);
70:     Attr.Style |= WS_VSCROLL | WS_HSCROLL;    // Add scroll bars
71:     pFont = NULL;
72: }
73:
74: TMyWindow::~TMyWindow()
75: {
76:     if (pFont)
77:         delete pFont;
78: }
79:
80: void TMyWindow::SetupWindow()
81: {
82:     TWindow::SetupWindow();
83:
84:     // Set up the scroller and font.  Note that
85:     // dummy values of 7 and 16 are used for the
86:     // scroll bar's units, but they'll be reset
87:     // as soon as the font is set.
88:     //
89:     Scroller = new TScroller(this, 7, 16, 20, MAX_LINES - 1);
90:     NewFont(8);                              // Initialize our font
91: }
92:
93: bool TMyWindow::CanClose()
94: {
95:     return IDYES == MessageBox("Want to close this application?",
96:                                "Query",
97:                                MB_YESNO | MB_ICONQUESTION );
98: }
99:
100: void TMyWindow::CmExit()
101: {
102:     SendMessage(WM_CLOSE);
103: }
104:
105: void TMyWindow::CmHeight8()
106: {
107:     NewFont(8);
108: }
109:
110: void TMyWindow::CmHeight10()
111: {
112:     NewFont(10);
113: }
114:
115: void TMyWindow::CmHeight14()
```

```
116: {
117:     NewFont(14);
118: }
119:
120: void TMyWindow::CmHeight20()
121: {
122:     NewFont(20);
123: }
124:
125: void TMyWindow::CmHeight26()
126: {
127:     NewFont(26);
128: }
129:
130: void TMyWindow::EvKeyDown( uint key,
131:                            uint /*repeatCount*/,
132:                            uint /*flags*/ )
133: {
134:     if (Scroller)          // Can't scroll if it ain't there!
135:         switch (key)
136:             {
137:             case VK_HOME:
138:                 Scroller->VScroll(SB_TOP, 0);
139:                 break;
140:             case VK_END:
141:                 Scroller->VScroll(SB_BOTTOM, 0);
142:                 break;
143:             case VK_PRIOR:
144:                 Scroller->VScroll(SB_PAGEUP, 0);
145:                 break;
146:             case VK_NEXT:
147:                 Scroller->VScroll(SB_PAGEDOWN, 0);
148:                 break;
149:             case VK_UP:
150:                 Scroller->VScroll(SB_LINEUP, 0);
151:                 break;
152:             case VK_DOWN:
153:                 Scroller->VScroll(SB_LINEDOWN, 0);
154:                 break;
155:             }
156: }
157:
158: void TMyWindow::EvLButtonDown(uint, TPoint&)
159: {
160:     MessageBox( "You clicked the left button!",
161:                 "Mouse Click Event",
162:                 MB_OK );
163: }
164:
165: void TMyWindow::Paint(TDC& dc, bool /*erase*/, TRect& /*rect*/)
166: {
167:     char s[81];
168:     bool ok = true;
169:     int y = 0;
170:
171:     for (int i = 0; i < MAX_LINES && ok; ++i)
```

13

continues

Listing 13.5. continued

```
172:        {
173:        if (pFont)
174:            dc.SelectObject(*pFont);
175:        sprintf(s, "This is line number %d", i);
176:        ok = dc.TextOut(0, y, s);
177:        y += dc.GetTextExtent(s, lstrlen(s)).cy;
178:        if (pFont)
179:            dc.RestoreFont();
180:        }
181: }
182:
183: void TMyWindow::NewFont(int nHeight)
184: {
185:    if (pFont)
186:        delete pFont;
187:    pFont = new TFont("Arial", nHeight);
188:
189:    // Now reset the scroller's units
190:    if (pFont && Scroller)
191:        {
192:        TClientDC dc(*this);
193:        TEXTMETRIC tm;
194:
195:        dc.SelectObject(*pFont);
196:        dc.GetTextMetrics(tm);
197:        dc.RestoreFont();
198:
199:        Scroller->SetUnits(  tm.tmAveCharWidth,
200:                             tm.tmHeight + tm.tmExternalLeading );
201:
202:        Invalidate();
203:        }
204: }
205:
206: int OwlMain(int, char *[])
207: {
208:    return TMyApp().Run();
209: }
```

Figure 13.2 shows a sample session with the program TEXTSIZE.EXE.

This program is very similar to the first one presented in this chapter. The major differences are the addition of the scroll bars on the right and bottom of the window and the new menu item enabling the user to change the font as it is displayed on-screen.

The TMyWindow class on lines 13 through 51 declares a new data member and a new member function, both private, for use in displaying different point-sized fonts:

☐ The pFont member on line 36 stores a pointer to the font used to display the text. This variable is preset to NULL in the class's constructor on line 71 and initialized in the SetupWindow function on line 90. It then is reset by the user via the menus.

☐ The NewFont function starting on line 183 is used to change the font. It takes an integer value that is used as the point size, and it then creates a TFont object, assigning it to the pFont data member.

☐ The Paint function starting on line 165 first selects the pFont object into the device context before writing to the window. After it's done, it reselects the original font back into the window.

Figure 13.2.

A sample session with the program TEXTSIZE.EXE.

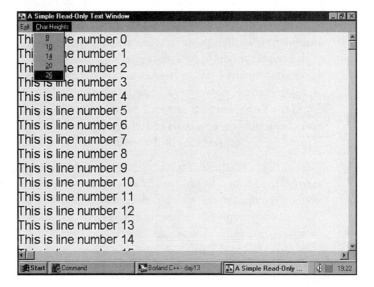

> **Note:** When dealing with windows and selecting objects into device contexts such as fonts or text colors, it's always a good idea to make sure you leave the DC in the same condition as you found it. If you change the font, make sure you change it back to whatever it might have been before you modified it.

Note that the pFont is only preset to NULL in the constructor, but the real initialization occurs in the SetupWindow member function. This is a very important distinction, as creating the font requires the existence of a window.

The *SetupWindow* Member Function

Although the TWindow class has the usual constructor, where things can be initialized as in any other class, it also has the member function SetupWindow for all initializations that rely on an actual window to be there. The SetupWindow function looks like this.

```
void SetupWindow(void);
```

When the `TWindow` class is first created, all that exists is the interface object or C++ object. For many initializations, an actual interface element or Windows object (a window) may need to exist. During the course of the window's initialization, the `SetupWindow` will be called. This function does the actual initialization of the Windows object to which the C++ object is to be connected; this includes the creation of any child windows contained within the window. This is why it is vitally important for any derived versions of `SetupWindow` to call the parent's version. Until the actual `TWindow::SetupWindow` function is called, there will be no Windows object.

This program enables the user to use the keyboard to scroll the window. It does this through a single member function `EvKeyDown` starting on line 130. In this function is a `switch` statement that checks for the keys on the keypad. For each of these, it sends the `Scroller` object the appropriate command (refer to Table 13.1) to scroll the window. The `Scroller` object is closely tied to the `TWindow` object, of which `TMyWindow` is directly descended, so it handles all the dirty work of changing the scroll bars and telling the window to update itself. `Scroller` then calls `Paint` to paint the correct portions of the screen.

In order to enable the user to change the font, the `Char Heights` pop-up menu item has been added with various selections, enabling the user to select specific point sizes for the fonts. The program responds to these menu selections through the various `CmHeightXX` member functions on lines 105 through 128. These functions serve only to call the `NewFont` member function with the appropriate point size, as specified by the user.

Finally, the `NewFont` member function, starting on line 183, handles the creation of the fonts used in painting the window:

☐ First, it checks to see if the `pFont` data member has been set yet. If so, it deletes the old one in preparation for replacing it with a new version, which it does immediately. It allocates a new `TFont` object with the typeface *Arial* and a point size of `nHeight`.

> **Note:** Although it is safe to delete a `NULL` pointer in Borland C++, it still is a good idea to check first, because not all compilers are as safe.

☐ Assuming that the `Scroller` object exists and the creation of `pFont` succeeded, the function proceeds to set the `Scroller` with new values to let it know how big the characters are now. To do this, it first gets a device context from the window and selects the new `pFont` into it. The font's attributes are placed into the `TEXTMETRIC` object, and that information is used in the `TScroller`'s `SetUnits` function.

☐ Finally, because the font you use to paint the window has changed, you need to tell the window to update itself with the new font. This is done with the `Invalidate`

function, which tells the window that its contents are no longer valid and need repainting. Windows automatically tells the window to repaint itself, at which time the Paint function will be entered.

Summary

Today's lesson discussed the mechanics of creating windows that show fixed and scrollable text. The lesson included the following topics:

☐ Read-only text windows that display information are the basis of help screens.

☐ You can write text in a window using the versatile TDC::TextOut member function.

☐ You can create scrollable windows with vertical and horizontal scroll bars. These windows can scroll using either the mouse or the cursor-control keys. The classes of scrollable windows use the TScroller class assigned to the TWindow's Scroller data member, as well as other functions to manage the text metrics.

Q&A

Q Is the member function Paint needed to maintain windows with visual controls such as command buttons?

A No. You need only to write the function Paint to maintain windows that draw text and graphics. In the case of windows with controls, you do not need to declare your own version of function Paint.

Workshop

The Workshop provides quiz questions to help you solidify your understanding of the material covered and exercises to provide you with experience in using what you've learned. Try to understand the quiz and exercise answers before continuing on to the next day's lesson. Answers are provided in Appendix A.

Quiz

1. True or false? The member function Paint redraws the window only when needed.

2. True or false? The TWindow::Scroller data member offers default scrolling features.

3. True or false? Omitting the EvKeyDown member function in program TEXTSIZE.CPP disables the vertical scrolling feature altogether.

Exercise

Experiment with modifying the TEXTSIZE.CPP program by adding cases to the `EvKeyDown` function that will enable the window to scroll horizontally in response to the right- and left-arrow keys being pressed. In addition, you can experiment with adding more `CmHeightXX` member functions and the corresponding menu selections.

OWL Controls

Interacting with Windows applications often involves dialog boxes that contain various types of controls, such as the list box, the edit control (also called edit box), and the pushbutton. These controls can be included in windows or, more frequently, in dialog boxes. Today's lesson and the next three look at the controls as they appear in windows and focus on the basic properties of these controls. Day 15 presents dialog boxes and views how the controls work with these boxes. Today, you learn about the following topics:

☐ The TControl object

☐ Static-text control

☐ Edit control

☐ Pushbutton control

Understanding the various controls and mastering how they behave and interact enables you to implement highly interactive Windows applications. Today's lesson and the two that follow discuss the constructors and relevant member functions for the control classes.

The *TControl* Object

To learn about OWL controls, it's best to start with the TControl object. This object is the base from which all other control objects are derived. Note that you will never have any need to create a TControl object directly, but a discussion of it here helps you to understand the control objects derived from it.

The TControl object is derived from the TWindow class, which means that it has much of the same functionality as the TWindow class. This actually is a direct mapping of the Windows environment, where controls are, indeed, just specialized child windows.

The *TControl* Constructor

The constructors of the TControl class are

```
TControl(TWindow*      parent,
         int           id,
         const char far* title,
         int           x,
         int           y,
         int           w,
         int           h,
         TModule*      module = 0);
TControl(TWindow*      parent,
         int           resourceId,
         TModule*      module = 0);
```

The parent parameter is a pointer to the parent window in which the control will be placed. The id represents the control's ID, which is used in communication between the parent window and

the control itself (more on this later, when specific controls are discussed). Next comes the title of the control. This parameter isn't always displayed by the particular control created, but it's always set. The four parameters x, y, w, and h describe the position and size of the control to be created. Finally, the module parameter specifies the DLL with which the control is associated. This has a default value of 0, and you will rarely find a need to override that; it's mainly used for placing a number of controls in a DLL separate from the main program code being executed.

In the second version of the constructor, instead of all the descriptive information about the control, there is only a single resourceId that identifies the control's ID inside a dialog box that's been loaded from the program's resource section (as defined by an RC file). Dialog boxes and how this constructor is used are discussed on Day 15.

You will see the parameters to this class duplicated repeatedly in the various control classes derived from TControl. Added on to these standard parameters will be other parameters specific to the particular class being created.

The Static-Text Control

The static-text control provides a window or a dialog box with static text. The TStatic class implements the static-text control. Look at the class constructor and members.

NEW☞ TERM *Static text* is text that the application user cannot easily and readily change. Static text does not necessarily mean text etched in stone! In fact, static-text controls allow your OWL applications to alter the text at any time, or you can specify that the text be permanent and unchangeable. The choice ultimately is yours.

The TStatic class, a descendant of TControl (which, in turn, is descended from TWindow), offers static text that is defined by a display area, text to display, and text attributes. Of these three components, you can alter only the displayed text during runtime.

The *TStatic* Constructor

The constructors of the TStatic control are

```
TStatic(TWindow*      parent,
        int           id,
        const char far *title,
        int           x,
        int           y,
        int           w,
        int           h,
        uint          textLen = 0,
        TModule*      module = 0 );
TStatic(TWindow*      parent,
        int           resourceId,
```

14

```
uint        textLen = 0,
TModule*    module = 0 );
```

Example

```
pText = new TStatic(this, -1, "Sample Text", 10, 10, 75, 25);
pText->Attr.Style &= ~SS_LEFT;
pText->Attr.Style |= SS_SIMPLE;
```

The parent parameter specifies the parent window into which the static control will be placed. The id is used to give the static control a unique identifier. A control's ID typically is used when the static text needs to be changed by the application. In the case of a static control, this is a very rare occasion, so the id parameter is usually set to -1. The title sets an initial text string that will appear within the control. The next four parameters—x, y, w, and h—describe the location and size of the control as it will appear within its parent window. The textLen parameter is used for advanced transfer and streaming capabilities, and the module pointer is used for specifying the DLL with which the static control is associated. Note that these last two both have default values of 0, and you will rarely find a need to override that.

In addition to the usual WS_CHILD and WS_VISIBLE styles that go along with all controls, static controls have their own special set of SS_XXX styles, as shown in Table 14.1. Note that the TStatic class automatically includes the SS_LEFT style.

Table 14.1. Values for static text styles.

Value	Meaning
SS_BITMAP	Specifies a bit map is to be displayed in the static control. The given text is the name of a bit map (not a filename) defined elsewhere in the resource file. The style ignores the width and height parameters in the constructor; the control automatically sizes itself to accommodate the bit map (Win32 only).
SS_BLACKFRAME	Designates a box with a frame drawn and the color matching that of the window frame (black, in the default Windows color scheme).
SS_BLACKRECT	Specifies a rectangle filled with the color matching that of the window frame (black, in the default Windows color scheme).
SS_CENTER	Centers the static-text characters; text is wrappable.
SS_CENTERIMAGE	Specifies that, if the bit map or icon is smaller than the client area of the static control, the rest of the client area is filled with the color of the pixel in the top-left corner of the bit map or icon. If the static control contains a single line of text, the text is centered vertically in the client area of the control (Win32 only).

Value	Meaning
SS_ENHMETAFILE	Specifies that an enhanced metafile is to be displayed in the static control. The given text is the name of a metafile. An enhanced metafile static control has a fixed size; the metafile is scaled to fit the static control's client area (Win32 only).
SS_ETCHEDFRAME	Draws the frame of the static control using the EDGE_ETCHED edge style (Win32 only).
SS_ETCHEDHORZ	Draws the top and bottom edges of the static control using the EDGE_ETCHED edge style (Win32 only).
SS_ETCHEDVERT	Draws the left and right edges of the static control using the EDGE_ETCHED edge style (Win32 only).
SS_GRAYFRAME	Specifies a box with a frame that has the same color as the screen background (gray, in the default Windows color scheme).
SS_GRAYRECT	Selects a rectangle filled with the same color as the screen background (gray, in the default Windows color scheme).
SS_ICON	Specifies an icon that is to be displayed in the control. The text is interpreted as the resource name of the icon. (Note that the width and height of the control are ignored as the icon automatically is sized.)
SS_LEFT	Indicates left-justified text; text is wrappable.
SS_LEFTNOWORDWRAP	Indicates left-justified text that cannot be wrapped.
SS_NOPREFIX	Specifies that the ampersand character (&) in the static text string should not be a hot-key-designator character, but rather part of the static-text character.
SS_NOTIFY	Sends the parent window STN_CLICKED, STN_DBLCLK, STN_DISABLE, and STN_ENABLE notification messages when the user clicks or double-clicks the control (Win32 only).
SS_OWNERDRAW	Specifies that the owner of the static control is responsible for drawing the control. The owner window receives a WM_DRAWITEM message whenever the control needs to be drawn (Win32 only).
SS_REALSIZEIMAGE	Prevents a static icon or bit-map control (that is, static controls that have the SS_ICON or SS_BITMAP style) from being resized as it is loaded or drawn. If the icon or bit map is larger than the destination area, the image is clipped (Win32 only).

14

continues

Table 14.1. Values for static text styles.

Value	Meaning
SS_RIGHT	Selects right-justified text that is wrappable.
SS_RIGHTJUST	Specifies that the lower-right corner of a static control with the SS_BITMAP or SS_ICON style is to remain fixed when the control is resized. Only the top and left sides are adjusted to accommodate a new bit map or icon (Win32 only).
SS_SIMPLE	Indicates that the static text characters cannot be altered at runtime and that the static text is displayed on a single line with line breaks ignored.
SS_SUNKEN	Draws a half-sunken border around a static control (Win32 only).
SS_WHITEFRAME	Specifies a box with a frame that has the same color as the window background (white, in the default Windows color scheme).
SS_WHITERECT	Selects a rectangle filled with the same color as the window background (white, in the default Windows color scheme).

The string accessed by the title pointer in the constructor may include the ampersand (&) character to visually specify a hot key. The hot-key character appears as an underlined character. The ampersand should be placed before the hot-key character. If the string contains more than one ampersand character, only the last occurrence is effective. The other occurrences of the ampersand are not displayed and are ignored. To display the & character, you need to specify the SS_NOPREFIX style. The price you pay for using this style is the inability to display a hot-key character.

Now focus on the component of the static-text control that you can change during runtime—namely, the text itself. If you specify the SS_SIMPLE style in the control's Attr.Style data member, you cannot alter its text. In this sense, the instance of TStatic is, indeed, etched in stone. The TStatic class enables you to set, query, and clear the characters of the static text using the GetTextLen, GetText, SetText, and Clear functions.

The *GetTextLen* Function

Syntax

The parameterless GetTextLen member function returns the length of the control's text.

```
int GetTextLen();
```

Example

```
int nLen = pText->GetTextLen();
```

The *GetText* Function

Syntax

The GetText member function enables you to access the static-text characters. The declaration of the function is

```
int GetText(char far* text, int maxChars);
```

The text parameter is a pointer to the string that receives a copy of the static-text characters. The maxChars parameter specifies the maximum number of static-text characters to copy. The function result returns the actual number of characters copied to the string accessed by the pointer text.

Example

```
char s[128];
pText->GetText(s, sizeof(s) - 1);
```

The *SetText* Function

Syntax

The SetText member function overwrites the current static-text characters with those of a new string. The declaration of the function is

```
void SetText(const char far* str);
```

The str parameter is the pointer to the new text for the control. If the new text is an empty string, the SetText function call simply clears the text in the static-text-control instance.

Example

```
pText->SetText("New Text");
```

The *Clear* Function

Syntax

The Clear member function is simply a wrapper that passes an empty string to the SetText member function. The declaration of the function is

```
void Clear();
```

Its existence is there to make code look a little cleaner by enabling you to call the Clear function rather than SetText("");.

14

The Edit Control

The ObjectWindows Library offers the TEdit class that implements an edit control. The edit control enables the user to type in and edit the text in the input dialog box. This section discusses the functionality of class TEdit in more detail, because implementing customized text editors in your OWL application requires you to become quite familiar with the TEdit member functions.

The *TEdit* Class

The TEdit class is derived from the TStatic class and implements a versatile edit control that supports single-line and multiline text, as well as the capability to cut, paste, copy, delete, and clear text. The edit control also can undo the last text changes and exchange text with the Clipboard.

The *TEdit* Constructor

The declarations of the TEdit constructors are

```
TEdit(TWindow*      parent,
      int           id,
      const char far* text,
      int           x,
      int           y,
      int           w,
      int           h,
      uint          textLen = 0,
      bool          multiline = false,
      TModule*      module = 0 );
TEdit(TWindow*      parent,
      int           resourceId,
      uint          textLen = 0,
      TModule*      module = 0 );
```

The parameters to the first constructor are almost identical to the ones for the TStatic constructor. The only difference is the addition of a multiline parameter. This tells whether the edit control should have more than one input line, like a text editor. Unlike the TStatic control, however, it never makes sense to use an invalid number in the id parameter of the TEdit control, as the TEdit control will need to send notification messages back to its parent window.

The second constructor is identical in usage to the second constructor for the TStatic control. It is used to associate a C++ class object with a control loaded with a dialog resource. Again, this will be discussed on Day 15.

Example

```
const IDE_INPUT = 101;
pInput = new TEdit(this, IDE_INPUT, "", 10, 10, 100, 25);
```

The TEdit control also has its own set of special styles, ES_XXX, that can be used to modify its behavior (see Table 14.2). When you create a TEdit object, the ES_LEFT and ES_AUTOHSCROLL are added in automatically. If the multiline parameter is set, then the ES_MULTILINE and ES_AUTOVSCROLL also are automatically set.

Table 14.2. Values for edit-control styles.

Value	Meaning
ES_AUTOHSCROLL	Allows the text to automatically scroll to the right by 10 characters when the user enters a character at the end of the line; when the user presses the Enter key, text scrolls back to the left.
ES_AUTOVSCROLL	Permits the text to scroll up by one page when the user presses the Enter key on the last visible line.
ES_CENTER	Centers the text in a multiline edit control.
ES_LEFT	Justifies the text to the left.
ES_LOWERCASE	Converts into lowercase all the letters that the user types.
ES_MULTILINE	Specifies a multiline edit control that recognizes line breaks (designated by the sequence of carriage return and line-feed characters).
ES_NOHIDESEL	By default, hides the selected text when it loses focus and shows the selection when it gains focus again; prevents edit control from restoring the selected text.
ES_NUMBER	Allows only digits to be entered into the edit control (Win32 only).
ES_OEMCONVERT	Converts the entered text from the Windows character set to the OEM character set and back again. This is useful for controls that receive filenames.
ES_PASSWORD	Displays all characters as asterisks (*) as they are typed. Note that this affects only the display; what the user types is stored accurately in the control.
ES_READONLY	Prevents the user from modifying the contents of the control, although it is still possible to select text in the control.
ES_RIGHT	Justifies the text to the right in multiline edit controls.
ES_UPPERCASE	Converts into uppercase all the letters that the user types.
ES_WANTRETURN	Normally, the Enter key will click the default button. When this style is set in an edit control, however, pressing Enter while editing text will insert a new line. This applies only to multiline edit controls.

Clipboard-Related Editing Functions

The TEdit class includes a set of member functions that handle Clipboard-related text editing commands. These commands are available in typical menu options: Cut, Copy, Paste, Clear, Undo, and Delete. Table 14.3 shows the TEdit member functions and their purposes. These functions work with the Clipboard in the CF_TEXT format.

Table 14.3. TEdit member functions that support Clipboard-related editing menu commands.

Member Function	Purpose
CanUndo	Returns whether an undo operation is possible at the moment. It is used to enable and disable the Undo menu item accordingly.
Cut	Deletes the current selection in the edit control and copies the text to the Clipboard.
Copy	Copies the current selection to the Clipboard.
Paste	Inserts the text from the Clipboard to the current cursor position in the edit control.
Clear	Deletes all the text in the control; this does not affect the Clipboard.
Undo	Undoes the last change made to the text of the edit control.

Query of Edit Controls

The TEdit class has a family of text-query member functions. These functions enable you to retrieve either the entire control text or parts of it, or they permit you to obtain information on the text statistics (number of lines, length of lines, and so on). Two of these functions, GetTextLen and GetText, are inherited directly from the TStatic class. They are used to retrieve the contents of edit controls and are declared and used in the same way as they are in the TStatic class.

Because edit controls allow for both multiple lines and user manipulation, additional functions are used to get text from different lines and to manipulate the selection.

The *GetNumLines* Function

Syntax

The `GetNumLines` member function returns the number of lines in the edit control. The declaration is

```
int GetNumLines() const;
```

Example

```
nLineCount = pEdit->GetNumLines();
```

Note: In the case of multiline edit controls, you should take into account the characters involved in either the soft or hard line breaks.

Hard line breaks use pairs of carriage-return and line-feed characters (`"\r\n"`) at the end of each line. Soft line breaks use two carriage returns and a line feed at line breaks (`"\r\r\n"`).

This information is relevant when you are counting the number of characters to process.

The *GetLineFromPos* Function

Syntax

The `GetLineFromPos` member function returns the line number of a specified character index. Its declaration is

```
int GetLineFromPos(uint charPos) const;
```

If the `charPos` argument is `-1`, then the function will return either of the following two values:

- [ ] If there is selected text, the function yields the line number where the first selected character is located.
- [ ] If there is no selected text, the function returns the line number where the caret is, where character insertion occurs.

Example

```
nLineNum = pEdit->GetLineFromPos(-1);
```

14

Syntax

The *GetLineIndex* Function

The GetLineIndex member function returns the character index of a specific line. The character index is also the size of the text in the edit control up to the specified line number. Its declaration is

```
uint GetLineIndex(int lineNumber) const;
```

The lineNumber parameter specifies the line index. If it is -1, then it represents the current line as represented by the caret, which marks the user's current position. The function returns the number of characters from the first line through to the specified line. If the argument of lineNumber is greater than the actual number of lines, then the function will return -1.

Example

```
nCharIndex = pEdit->GetLineIndex(-1);
```

Syntax

The *GetLineLength* Function

The GetLineLength member function returns the length of a line for a specific line number. Its declaration is

```
int GetLineLength(int lineNumber) const;
```

The lineNumber parameter specifies the line number from which to get the length. If lineNumber is -1, then the function will return one of the following:

- ☐ If no text is selected, the length of the current line is returned.
- ☐ If text is selected, the length of the line minus the length of the currently selected text is returned.

Example

```
nLen = pEdit->GetLineLength(1);
```

Syntax

The *GetSelection* Function

The GetSelection member function returns the starting and ending character positions of the selected text. The starting character position is the index of the first selected character. The ending position is the index of the first character *after* the selected text. The declaration of the function is

```
void GetSelection(uint& startPos, uint& endPos) const;
```

The function fills in the passed startPos and endPos with the corresponding selection locations. If these two values are equal, there is no selected text, because both uints are the character indices to the current position.

Syntax

Example

```
pEdit->GetSelection(start, end);
```

The *GetLine* Function

The GetLine member function returns a line from a multiline edit control. Its declaration is

```
bool GetLine(char far* str, int strSize, int lineNumber) const;
```

The str parameter points to a buffer that is to receive the text of the line; strSize is the number of characters to receive; and lineNumber is the line to retrieve. If there is a problem copying the line or if the line is longer than strSize, the function will return false; otherwise it will return true.

Example

```
char s[128];
pEdit->GetLine(s, sizeof(s) - 1, 22);
```

Altering the Edit Controls

Now focus on the member functions of TEdit that alter the edit control text. The operations of these member functions include writing new text to the control, selecting text, and replacing the selected text.

- ☐ The SetText member function that is inherited from the parent TStatic class acts in the same manner; it overwrites the current edit-control characters with those of a new string.
- ☐ The SetSelection member function defines a block of characters as the new selected text.
- ☐ The Insert member function replaces the selected text with new characters.

Syntax

The *SetSelection* Function

The declaration of the SetSelection function is

```
bool SetSelection(uint startPos, uint endPos);
```

The startPos and endPos parameters define the range of characters that make up the new selected text. If the starting and ending positions are 0 and -1, respectively, then the entire text in the edit control is selected. If startPos is -1, then any selection is removed. The current position is placed at the greater of the two parameters.

Example

```
pEdit->SetSelection(0, -1);
```

The *Insert* Function

The declaration of the Insert function is

```
void Insert(const char far* str);
```

The str parameter is the pointer to the new selected text that replaces the current selection. If there is no selected text, the function simply inserts the text accessed by str at the current insertion point.

Example

```
pEdit->Insert("New Text");
```

Note: You can use the Insert function to delete parts of the edit-control text by first selecting that part and then replacing it with an empty string.

The Pushbutton Control

The *pushbutton control* is, perhaps, psychologically the most powerful control (you never hear about the nuclear list box or the nuclear check box). In a sense, the pushbutton control represents the fundamental notion of a control—you click on the control and something happens. The rest of today's lesson focuses on the aspects of the class TButton that deal with the pushbutton controls.

NEW TERM There basically are two types of pushbutton controls: *default buttons* and *nondefault buttons*. Default buttons have slightly thicker edges than nondefault buttons. Pressing the Enter key is equivalent to clicking the default button in a dialog box. There can be only one default button in a dialog box. You can select a new default button by pressing the Tab key. This feature works only when the buttons are in a dialog box. If a nondialog box window owns a pushbutton control, it can only visually display a default button—the functionality is not supported.

The *TButton* Class

The TButton class, a descendant of TControl, models the Windows pushbutton control.

Syntax

The *TButton* Constructor

The declaration for the TButton constructor is

```
TButton(TWindow*      parent,
        int           id,
        const char far* text,
        int           X,
        int           Y,
        int           W,
        int           H,
        bool          isDefault = false,
        TModule*      module = 0 );
TButton(TWindow* parent, int resourceId, TModule* module = 0);
```

The first seven parameters to this function should now be relatively familiar to you, as they're identical to the ones in both the TStatic and TEdit controls. In fact, you'll find that most of these controls are descendants of the TControl class; the parameters will be virtually the same across the control classes. In this case, the difference is the addition of an isDefault parameter. This parameter specifies whether or not the button is default.

Example

```
pOk = new TButton(this, IDOK, "&OK", 10, 10, 50, 25, true);
pCancel = new TButton(this, IDCANCEL, "&Cancel", 70, 10, 50, 25);
```

In addition to the constructors, TButton declares four additional public functions: GetIsDefPB, SetIsDefPB, GetIsCurrentDefPB, and SetIsCurrentDefPB. These work rather predictably to change a TButton object into a default pushbutton and to query the current status of that quality. The Get*XXX* functions return a bool, and the Set*XXX* functions accept a bool as a parameter.

Handling Button Messages

When you click a button, the control sends the BN_CLICKED notification message to its parent window. The parent window responds to this message by invoking a message response member function based on the ID of the button. If you have a button that was created with an ID of IDB_EXIT, for example, the message handler function is

```
// Other declarations
void HandleExitBtn();
// Other declarations

DEFINE_RESPONSE_TABLE1(TMyWindow, TWindow)
   // Other possible message mapping macros
   EV_BN_CLICKED(IDB_EXIT, HandleExitBtn),
   // Other possible message mapping macros
END_RESPONSE_TABLE;
```

This example shows that the message map macro EV_BN_CLICKED is used to map the IDB_EXIT notification message with the HandleExitBtn member function.

14

Manipulating Buttons

You can disable and enable a button by using the `EnableWindow` function, which is inherited from the `TWindow` ancestor. A disabled button has a faded gray caption and does not respond to mouse clicks or keyboard input. The `TWindow::EnableWindow` function lets you enable or disable a button. The function accepts a single argument, a `bool` argument that specifies whether the button is enabled (when the argument is `true`) or disabled (when the argument is `false`). Sample calls to the `EnableWindow` member function are

```
pOk->EnableWindow(false);
pCalculate->EnableWindow(true);
```

You can query the enabled state of a button by using the `bool IsWindowEnabled` function, which takes no arguments. A sample call to `IsWindowEnabled` is

```
// Toggle the enabled state of a button
pButton->EnableWindow(!pButton->IsWindowEnabled());
```

You also can hide and show a button using the `ShowWindow` function. The function takes one argument, either the `SW_HIDE` constant to hide the button or the `SW_SHOW` constant to show the button. Other constant values are defined for this function, but `SW_HIDE` and `SW_SHOW` are the only two that apply to pushbuttons. The `bool IsWindowVisible` function queries the visibility of a button. This function takes no arguments. A sample call to the `ShowWindow` and `IsWindowVisible` functions is

```
// Toggle the visibility of a button
pButton->ShowWindow(pButton->IsWindowVisible() ? SW_HIDE : SW_SHOW);
```

Mr. Calculator

Look at an application that uses static text, single-line edit controls, multiline edit controls, and pushbuttons—*Mr. Calculator*. This nontrivial application implements a floating-point calculator that uses edit controls rather than buttons. This type of interface is somewhat visually inferior to the typical button-populated calculator in Windows applications. This interface, however, can support more mathematical functions without requiring the addition of the buttons for those extra functions. In Mr. Calculator, the calculator is made up of the following controls:

- ☐ Two edit controls for the first and second operands to accept integers, floating-point numbers, and the names of single-letter variables, A to Z.
- ☐ One edit control for the operator, which supports the calculator's four basic math operations and exponentiation (using a caret, ^).
- ☐ One edit control that displays the result of the math operation.
- ☐ One edit control that displays any error messages.

- [ ] One multiline edit control that enables you to store a number in the Result edit control in one of 26 single-letter variables, A to Z. The multiline edit displays the current values stored in these variables and enables you to view and edit these numbers. You can use the vertical scroll bar to inspect the values in the different variables.

- [ ] Multiple-static text controls serve to label the various edit controls. Of particular interest is the static control for the Error Message box. If you click the accompanying static text, the Error Message is cleared of any text.

- [ ] A menu with the single Exit option.

- [ ] A pushbutton with the caption "Calc" that performs the operation specified in the Operator edit control, using the operands in the operand edit controls.

- [ ] A pushbutton with the caption "Store" that stores the contents of the result edit control in the currently selected line of the multiline edit control.

- [ ] A pushbutton with the caption "Exit" that exits the application.

The program supports the following special features for the Store button control:

- [ ] The Store pushbutton is disabled if the application attempts to execute an invalid operator. This feature illustrates an example of disabling a pushbutton when a certain condition arises (in this case, a specific calculation error).

- [ ] The Store pushbutton is enabled if you click the Error Message static text. The same button is enabled when you successfully execute a math operation.

The calculator application demonstrates the following tasks:

- [ ] Using single-line edit controls for simple input
- [ ] Using a multiline edit control to view and edit information
- [ ] Accessing and editing line-oriented text
- [ ] Simulating static text that responds to mouse clicks
- [ ] Using pushbuttons
- [ ] Disabling and enabling pushbuttons

First, compile and run the application to get a good sense for how the calculator application works. Experiment with typing different numeric operands and the supported operators and click the Calc button. Each time, the result appears in the Result box, overwriting the previous result. Try dividing a number by zero to experiment with the error-handling features.

Using the single-letter variables is easy. All of these variables are initialized with 0. Therefore, the first step to using them is to store a nonzero value. Perform an operation and then click inside the Variables edit box. Select the first line that contains the variable A. Now click the Store button and watch the number in the Result box appear in the first line of the Variables edit box. The name of the variable and the colon and space characters that follow reappear with the new text line. Now replace the contents of the Operand1 edit box with the variable A, and then click the Calc button. The Result edit box displays the result of the latest operation.

Listing 14.1 shows the source code for the MRCALC.H header file. The header file declares the command constants for the menu item and the various controls. Listing 14.2 contains the script for the MRCALC.RC resource file. Listing 14.3 contains the source code for the MRCALC.CPP program file.

Type

Listing 14.1. Source code for the MRCALC.H header file.

```
1:  #define IDB_CALC      101
2:  #define IDB_STORE     102
3:  #define IDB_EXIT      103
4:  #define IDE_OPERAND1  104
5:  #define IDE_OPERATOR  105
6:  #define IDE_OPERAND2  106
7:  #define IDE_RESULT    107
8:  #define IDE_ERRMSG    108
9:  #define IDE_VARIABLE  109
```

Type

Listing 14.2. Script for the MRCALC.RC resource file.

```
1:  #include <windows.h>
2:  #include <owl\window.rh>
3:
4:  EXITMENU MENU LOADONCALL MOVEABLE PURE DISCARDABLE
5:  BEGIN
6:      MENUITEM "E&xit", CM_EXIT
7:  END
```

Type

Listing 14.3. Source code for the MRCALC.CPP program file.

```
1:  #include <ctype.h>
2:  #include <math.h>
3:  #include <stdio.h>
4:  #include <owl\applicat.h>
5:  #include <owl\button.h>
6:  #include <owl\edit.h>
7:  #include <owl\framewin.h>
8:  #include <owl\static.h>
9:  #include <owl\window.h>
10: #include <owl\window.rh>
11:
12: #include "mrcalc.h"
13:
14: class TCalcWindow : public TWindow
15: {
16: public:
```

```
17:     TCalcWindow(TWindow* parent = 0);
18:     ~TCalcWindow();
19:
20: protected:
21:     virtual void SetupWindow();
22:     virtual void EvLButtonDown(uint modKeys, TPoint& point);
23:
24:     void CmCalc();
25:     void CmStore();
26:     void CmExit()           { SendMessage(WM_CLOSE); }
27:
28: private:
29:     TStatic  *ErrMsgLabel;
30:     TEdit    *Operand1, *Operator, *Operand2, *Result,
31:              *ErrMsg, *Variable;
32:     TButton  *Store;
33:
34:     double get_number(TEdit* edit);
35:     double get_var(int line);
36:     void put_var(double val);
37:
38:     DECLARE_RESPONSE_TABLE(TCalcWindow);
39: };
40: DEFINE_RESPONSE_TABLE1(TCalcWindow, TWindow)
41:     EV_WM_LBUTTONDOWN,
42:     EV_COMMAND(CM_EXIT, CmExit),
43:     EV_BN_CLICKED(IDB_CALC, CmCalc),
44:     EV_BN_CLICKED(IDB_STORE, CmStore),
45:     EV_BN_CLICKED(IDB_EXIT, CmExit),
46: END_RESPONSE_TABLE;
47:
48: TCalcWindow::TCalcWindow(TWindow* parent)
49: {
50:     Init(parent, 0, 0);
51:
52:     int   wlblspacing = 40,
53:           hlblspacing = 5,
54:           wlbl        = 100,
55:           hlbl        = 20,
56:           wbox        = 100,
57:           hbox        = 30,
58:           wboxspacing = 40,
59:           hboxspacing = 40,
60:           wbtn        = 80,
61:           hbtn        = 30,
62:           wbtnspacing = 30;
63:     int   wlongbox    = 4 * (wbox + wboxspacing);
64:     int   wvarbox     = 2 * wbox,
65:           hvarbox     = 3 * hbox;
66:     int   x0 = 20, y0 = 30;
67:     int   x, y;
68:
69:     // First, create the labels for the edit text boxes.
70:     //
```

continues

415

Listing 14.3. continued

```
71:        x = x0;
72:        y = y0;
73:        new TStatic(this, -1, "Operand1", x, y, wlbl, hlbl);
74:        x += wlbl + wlblspacing;
75:        new TStatic(this, -1, "Operator", x, y, wlbl, hlbl);
76:        x += wlbl + wlblspacing;
77:        new TStatic(this, -1, "Operand2", x, y, wlbl, hlbl);
78:        x += wlbl + wlblspacing;
79:        new TStatic(this, -1, "Result", x, y, wlbl, hlbl);
80:
81:        // Now create the edit text boxes
82:        //
83:        x = x0;
84:        y += hlbl + hlblspacing;
85:        Operand1 = new TEdit(this, IDE_OPERAND1, "", x, y, wbox, hbox);
86:        Operand1->Attr.Style |= ES_UPPERCASE;
87:        x += wbox + wboxspacing;
88:        Operator = new TEdit(this, IDE_OPERATOR, "", x, y, wbox, hbox);
89:        Operator->Attr.Style |= ES_UPPERCASE;
90:        x += wbox + wboxspacing;
91:        Operand2 = new TEdit(this, IDE_OPERAND2, "", x, y, wbox, hbox);
92:        Operand2->Attr.Style |= ES_UPPERCASE;
93:        x += wbox + wboxspacing;
94:        Result = new TEdit(this, IDE_RESULT, "", x, y, wbox, hbox);
95:
96:        // Now create the label and box for the error message
97:        //
98:        x = x0;
99:        y += hbox + hboxspacing;
100:       ErrMsgLabel = new TStatic( this, -1, "Error Message", x, y,
101:                                   wlbl, hlbl );
102:       y += hlbl + hlblspacing;
103:       ErrMsg = new TEdit(this, IDE_ERRMSG, "", x, y, wlongbox, hbox);
104:
105:       // Create the label and box for the single-letter
106:       // variable selection
107:       //
108:       y += hbox + hboxspacing;
109:       new TStatic(this, -1, "Variables", x, y, wlbl, hlbl);
110:       y += hlbl + hlblspacing;
111:       char str[6 * ('Z' - 'A' + 1) + 1];
112:       char* p = str;
113:       for (char ch = 'A'; ch <= 'Z'; ++ch)
114:           p += sprintf(p, "%c: 0\r\n", ch);
115:       Variable = new TEdit(this, IDE_VARIABLE, str, x, y,
116:                            wvarbox, hvarbox, 0, true );
117:
118:       // Finally create some buttons
119:       //
120:       x += wvarbox + wbtnspacing;
121:       new TButton(this, IDB_CALC, "Calc", x, y, wbtn, hbtn);
122:       x += wbtn + wbtnspacing;
123:       Store = new TButton(this, IDB_STORE, "Store", x, y, wbtn, hbtn);
124:       x += wbtn + wbtnspacing;
```

```
125:     new TButton(this, IDB_EXIT, "Exit", x, y, wbtn, hbtn);
126: }
127:
128: TCalcWindow::~TCalcWindow()
129: {
130: }
131:
132: void TCalcWindow::SetupWindow()
133: {
134:     TWindow::SetupWindow();    // Initialize the visual element
135:
136:     // Keep the users out of the destination areas.
137:     //
138:     Result->SetReadOnly(true);
139:     ErrMsg->SetReadOnly(true);
140:     Variable->SetReadOnly(true);
141: }
142:
143: void TCalcWindow::EvLButtonDown(uint /*modKeys*/, TPoint& point)
144: {
145:     TRect rct = ErrMsgLabel->GetWindowRect();
146:     ClientToScreen(point);
147:     if (rct.Contains(point))
148:         {
149:         ErrMsg->SetReadOnly(false);
150:         ErrMsg->Clear();
151:         ErrMsg->SetReadOnly(true);
152:         Store->EnableWindow(true);
153:         }
154: }
155:
156: double TCalcWindow::get_number(TEdit* edit)
157: {
158:     double rslt;
159:     char*  str;
160:     int    size;
161:
162:     if (edit)
163:         {
164:         str = new char[size = edit->GetWindowTextLength() + 1];
165:         edit->GetWindowText(str, size);
166:         if (isalpha(str[0]))
167:             rslt = get_var(tolower(str[0]) - 'a');
168:         else
169:             rslt = atof(str);
170:         delete str;
171:         }
172:     return rslt;
173: }
174:
175: double TCalcWindow::get_var(int line)
176: {
177:     double rslt;
```

continues

417

Listing 14.3. continued

```
178:
179:     int size = Variable->GetLineLength(line) + 1;
180:     char* str = new char[size];
181:     Variable->GetLine(str, size, line);
182:     rslt = atof(str + 3);        // Don't want first 3 chars
183:     delete str;
184:     return rslt;
185: }
186:
187: void TCalcWindow::put_var(double var)
188: {
189:     uint start, end;
190:     Variable->GetSelection(start, end);
191:     if (start != end)
192:         Variable->SetSelection(start, start);
193:     int line = Variable->GetLineFromPos(-1);
194:     int size = Variable->GetLineLength(line) + 1;
195:     char* str = new char[size];
196:     Variable->GetLine(str, size, line);
197:     sprintf(str, "%c: %g", str[0], var);
198:     start = Variable->GetLineIndex(-1);
199:     end = start + Variable->GetLineLength(-1);
200:     Variable->SetSelection(start, end);
201:     Variable->Insert(str);
202:     delete str;
203: }
204:
205: void TCalcWindow::CmCalc()
206: {
207:     double x, y, z = 0;
208:     char   *str, *err = 0;
209:     int    size;
210:
211:     x = get_number(Operand1);
212:     y = get_number(Operand2);
213:
214:     str = new char[size = Operator->GetWindowTextLength() + 1];
215:     Operator->GetWindowText(str, size);
216:     if (str[1] != '\0')
217:         err = "Invalid operator";
218:     else
219:       switch (str[0])
220:           {
221:           case '+':
222:               z = x + y;
223:               break;
224:           case '-':
225:               z = x - y;
226:               break;
227:           case '*':
228:               z = x * y;
229:               break;
230:           case '/':
231:               if (y)
```

```
232:                z = x / y;
233:             else
234:                err = "Division by zero error";
235:             break;
236:          case '^':
237:             if (x > 0)
238:                z = exp(y * log(x));
239:             else
240:                err = "Can't raise power of negative numbers";
241:             break;
242:          default:
243:             err = "Invalid operator";
244:             break;
245:          }
246:      if (!err)
247:          ErrMsg->Clear();
248:      else
249:          ErrMsg->SetWindowText(err);
250:      Store->EnableWindow(!err);
251:      if (!err)
252:          {
253:          char dest[81];
254:          sprintf(dest, "%g", z);
255:          Result->SetWindowText(dest);
256:          }
257:     delete str;
258: }
259:
260: void TCalcWindow::CmStore()
261: {
262:     int size = Result->GetWindowTextLength() + 1;
263:     char* str = new char[size];
264:     Result->GetWindowText(str, size);
265:     put_var(atof(str));
266:     delete str;
267: }
268:
269: class TCalcApp : public TApplication
270: {
271: public:
272:     TCalcApp() : TApplication()
273:         { nCmdShow = SW_SHOWMAXIMIZED; }
274:
275:     void InitMainWindow()
276:         {
277:         SetMainWindow(new TFrameWindow(   0,
278:                                 "Mr. Calulator",
279:                                 new TCalcWindow ));
280:         GetMainWindow()->AssignMenu("EXITMENU");
281:         }
282: };
283:
284: int OwlMain(int, char *[])
285: {
286:     return TCalcApp().Run();
287: }
```

14

Figure 14.1 shows a sample session with the Mr. Calculator program.

Figure 14.1.

A sample session with MRCALC.EXE.

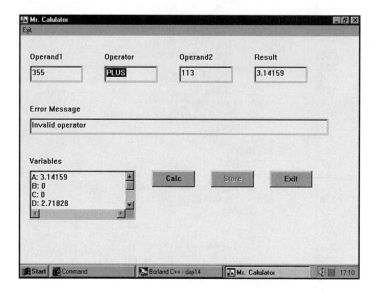

The program in Listing 14.3 contains a number of data members in the TCalcWindow class, each of which is a pointer to a control class. These are the TStatic, TEdit, and TButton controls, declared on lines 29 through 32. In general, there is no real need to keep track of these controls because OWL will automatically take care of deleting them when their corresponding Windows elements are destroyed. If you have some need to access them during their existence, however, you will need a pointer in order to affect them.

Note that as the operand and operator edit boxes are created on lines 83 through 94, they are given the style of ES_UPPERCASE. This style results in automatically converting into uppercase the single-letter variable names that you type in these edit controls.

Usually, controls such as TButton and especially TStatic can be created without bothering to keep a pointer to them; a button will automatically send notifications to its parent and, because static-text controls are usually used as labels, there rarely is a need to keep track of them. In this case, however, you need to keep track of the Store button so that you can enable and disable it according to error conditions. You also need to keep track of the Error Message label so that you can tell when the user has clicked it, at which point you need to clear the error message and reenable the Store button.

In the constructor of TCalcWindow are a number of declarations between lines 52 and 67. These are used when placing the controls as they are created. The declarations define the various widths and heights of the controls as well as the space in between them. As the controls are created, the local variables x and y are updated to the location of the next control.

In the SetupWindow member function of TCalcWindow starting on line 132, the Result, ErrMsg, and Variable edit controls are set to read-only by calling the TEdit::SetReadOnly member function. This is done to prevent the user from modifying the parts of the screen that should be updated only by the program itself. The user can still place the caret in these edit controls, even select text and scroll around in them, but Windows will prevent the user from changing any of the contents.

On lines 111 through 116, the Variable edit box is created somewhat differently from the other edit boxes. First, an elaborate initializing string is made up for it. This string consists of 26 letters ('A' through 'Z'), each followed by a colon, a space, the number 0, and finally the characters "\r\n". This makes up the format of the list box and later will be changed dynamically by the user clicking the Store button.

Secondly, the Variable edit box constructor receives two extra parameters on lines 115 through 116. The first of the two extra parameters, 0, is the same as the default parameter that is used whenever the constructor is called without passing anything for that argument. The next parameter, however, is the one stating that you want a multiline edit control. This automatically sets the control to allow for multiple lines, as well as add the horizontal and vertical scroll bars.

The EvLButtonDown member function starting on line 143 performs a simple task. It checks whether the mouse click occurs in the rectangle occupied by the Error Message static-text control, and it clears the Error Message if so. The function accomplishes this with the following steps:

☐ Obtains the Error Message static-text-control window's rectangle.

☐ Converts the point to be based upon the screen's coordinates instead of the client window's.

☐ Checks to see if the point is contained within the rectangle.

☐ If the point is in the rectangle, then the Error Message edit box has its read-only flag turned off, its contents cleared, and then the read-only flag is turned back on.

☐ The Store pushbutton is enabled.

Because you will have two edit boxes, from which you will want to get either a number or a value associated with a variable, it makes sense to have only one function that performs this action that is called for in each edit box. This is the purpose of the get_number private member function starting on line 156. Its single parameter is a pointer to a TEdit object. From this, the function obtains the text that is stored in that edit box on line 165. If the first character in that edit box is an alphabetic character (checked through the ANSI C function isalpha on line 166), then the private get_var function is called on line 167; otherwise, the contents are converted to a floating point number with the atof function on line 169.

> **Note:** As you've just seen, there's a difference between what's called *screen coordinates* and what's referred to as *client coordinates*. When you deal with coordinates, they're always relative to something. Screen coordinates are relative to the actual screen, meaning that location (0, 0) is at the upper-left corner of the screen. Client coordinates are relative to a specific window, meaning that location (0, 0) is at the upper-left corner of the window. The EvLButtonDown function receives its TPoint object in client coordinates, relative to the window that received the event. When you obtain a window's rectangle, however, you receive that in screen coordinates. In order to do a proper comparison of these two objects, one of them must first be converted to the other form.

The get_var function starting on line 175 is used to obtain the value associated with a specific variable in the Variable edit control. Given a line number, it gets the text from that line in the edit control, and then passes that line—skipping the first three characters (the variable letter, the colon, and the space)—to the atof function for conversion to a floating point number.

The put_var function starting on line 187 changes a variable in the Variable edit box. It does so with the following steps:

1. It checks for a selection in the Variable edit box on lines 190 and 191. If there is one, it removes that selection and sets the current insertion point to the beginning of the selection.

2. Using the GetLineFromPos function, it gets the line of the insertion point on line 193.

3. After creating a string large enough to hold the line, it gets the line and then changes it to include the new value on lines 195 through 197.

4. By passing -1 to the GetLineIndex function on line 198, it obtains the character location of the start of the current line. Adding the length of the line, it gets the start of the next line.

5. Using the SetSelection function on line 200, it selects the current line. It then Inserts the new string on line 201, replacing the current selection.

The CmCalc member function starting on line 205 responds to the notification message emitted by the Calc button. You told the window to have the function called by using the EV_BN_CLICKED macro during the TCalcWindow's response table declaration on line 43. The function performs the following tasks:

1. It obtains the two operands from the Operand1 and Operand2 edit boxes with the get_number private member function on lines 211 and 212.

2. It copies the text in the Operator edit box into the local variable str on line 215.

3. It determines and performs the requested operation by using a `switch` statement on lines 219 through 245, checking the first character of the string for the supported operators +, −, *, / and ^ (power).

4. If at any time an error is detected, the `err` local variable is set to a string describing the error; at the end on line 249, if this variable is nonzero, its value is placed in the Error Message edit box and the Store button is disabled.

The `CmStore` member function, starting on line 260, stores the contents of the Result box in a single-letter variable. The function first obtains the string from the Result edit box by calling the `GetWindowText` function on line 264. Then, the function invokes the private member function `put_var` on line 265 to actually store the result string at the current insertion point in the Variables edit box.

Summary

Today's lesson looked at static-text, edit-box, and pushbutton controls. Using these and other controls animates the Windows applications and provides a more consistent user interface. You learned about the following topics:

☐ You can create static-text controls and manipulate their text at runtime.

☐ Single-line and multiline edit-box controls enable you to type in and edit the text in the input dialog box.

Day 16 presents the grouped controls, the classes for group, check-box, and radio controls. These controls are used to fine-tune the execution of a specified task, such as searching and replacing text in a text editor.

Q&A

Q How do I create a string for a multiline static text control?

A You build a multiline string, such as `"This is\r\na multiline"` (notice the embedded `\r\n` characters, which break the line) and pass it as the third argument to the `TStatic` class's constructor.

Q Why does program MRCALC.CPP use local variables such as x and y to specify the location of a control? Why not replace these variables with numeric constants?

A Using variables, such as x and y, enables you to specify the location of the controls relative to one another. This method enables you to shift controls very easily. By contrast, using numeric constants specifies the absolute values for the control locations. Shifting controls, in this case, means plugging in a new set of numbers.

Q What do .RC resource files compile into?

A The .RC resource files are compiled into .RES files. Also, note that the Resource Workshop is quite capable of saving your various dialog boxes and other resources in an .RES file as well as an .RC file. This precompiled file could then be included in your .IDE file instead of the .RC.

Workshop

The Workshop provides quiz questions to help you solidify your understanding of the material covered and exercises to provide you with experience in using what you've learned. Try to understand the quiz and exercise answers before continuing on to the next day's lesson. Answers are provided in Appendix A.

Quiz

1. True or false? The text for all static-text controls is unchangeable.

2. True or false? The SS_CENTER style centers each line of a multiline static-text control.

3. True or false? A static text control needs an accompanying pointer for access only when the program needs to set or query the text in the control.

4. True or false? Every edit control needs an accompanying pointer for access.

5. True or false? The API Windows function EnableWindow can disable any control.

6. True or false? The Windows messages emitted by a pushbutton can be mapped using the EV_COMMAND map.

Exercises

1. Experiment with the program MRCALC.CPP to add other functions.

2. Experiment with a copy of the program MRCALC.CPP by changing values assigned to the constants that specify the size and spacing of the various controls.

As you end the second week of learning to program with Borland C++ 5, look at the Turbo Blocks example provided with the package. This is a Tetris clone, and it can be found in the BC5\EXAMPLES\OWL\GAMES\BLOCKS directory. The file of most importance, the one with all the C++ source code, is BLOCKS.CPP. Accompanying this example is a BLOCKS.RC file, which contains an About dialog box, the program's menu, and the program's icon. To run this program, open the BLOCKS.IDE file with Borland C++. You'll be able to see the files that make up the project, and you'll be able to build and run the application.

One of the first items in the file is the declaration and definition of the TBlock structure. Notice that, although this is declared as a struct, it includes a member function. You'll remember from Day 8 that structures are really just classes, except a structure's member starts out with the public default, whereas classes start out as private. The TBlock structure declares two data members, size and elements. The first of these two is an indicator of just how large the block is, and the second holds an array of characters that are used to define the actual shape of the block. The rotate member function is used to rotate the shape 90 degrees to the left. Note that four rotations will bring the block back to its initial state, so there's no real need for a function that will rotate to the right: just rotate it to the left three times.

Immediately following the `rotate` member function is the declaration of the global variable `blocks`. This holds the definition of all the blocks that will be used in the game. There also are the global variables `pen` and `brush`, which will be used to draw the blocks in the window. We'll get to those in a bit. Notice, however, that there is one more entry in each of `pen` and `brush` than there is in `blocks`.

Now you start to get into the meat of the program with the `TBlocksWindow` class. This class is a descendant of `TWindow`, and so inherits all the functionality thereof. The first member of the new class is the enumeration `GameState`, which provides values for the different states in which the game can be at any one time: an idle state (no game running), a block dropping (game in progress), paused (the user needs a break), and when lines are flashing or being removed. The next members are data items, each of which is labeled quite well, so I'll skip their descriptions here and instead mention them as they're used.

An interesting member function is `EvEraseBkgnd`. All it does is return `true`, but that has a lot of significance in the Windows world. Normally, when Windows goes to redraw a window (just before sending the `WM_PAINT` message, which triggers the OWL `Paint` member function), it sends the `WM_ERASEBKGND` message. The default response to this message is to completely erase the background of the window. This is normally a Good Thing, but when you're trying to do animation, you don't want the flicker this action creates; the window would briefly clear before being redrawn. So, in order to prevent Windows from performing its default action, you return `true`, thus keeping the window's painting all to yourself.

Next comes the declaration for `SetupWindow`, which starts its definition on line 209. It begins by calling the base class's version (a requirement), then proceeds to set up a timer. Timers are discussed more completely on Day 18, but suffice it to say that this call sets up a Windows timer that will call you back every hundredth of a second with a message that triggers the `EvTimer` member function. The timer is destroyed by the `CleanupWindow` member function, which is called when the window is closed. After the timer is created, `SetupWindow` sets up a memory DC for use in drawing the blocks into the window. When you need to paint fast, it's sometimes best to not take the time to do all sorts of memory allocation and deletion, but to create something once and then use it over and over again as needed.

The `PauseEnabler` member function is called whenever the user tries to use the program's menu. This function allows the program to enable or change the text of the menu item for which it's associated. This association occurs in the response table definition on the line that reads `EV_COMMAND_ENABLE(CM_GAMEPAUSE, PauseEnabler)`. The `PauseEnabler` function disables the menu item if there's no game in progress, and it sets the text of the menu item to reflect whether the user can pause or resume the game in progress.

The constructor begins by loading some user data from an .INI file, then simply resets the size of the window to the size of the board before clearing the board and initializing various data members. The RemoveLines member function is sort of interesting to look at. It initializes one counter to the bottom line of the board, then checks each line to see if it's full of blocks. If so, the function removes that line by copying the contents of all the lines above down by one line, and then clears the top. There's no need to actually remove the full line because the copy operation will cover it up. Note that the while loop doesn't iterate to the previous line if there was a copy operation; if it did, it might skip a full line that had just been copied from its old location down to the current line. Instead, the next iteration of the loop looks at the very same line.

The NewGame member function is a little less interesting. It simply clears the board before creating a new falling block at random. It then sets the game state to that of one in progress and invalidates the window. This last action tells Windows that the window needs to be repainted, and the Paint function will get called in short order. Similarly uninteresting is the ClearBoard member function. It just goes through all the blocks and sets them to 0 while setting the invisible borders to -1 (the latter action is done so it will be easy to tell when a falling block hits it).

The EvTimer function, which is called intermittently by Windows, performs different actions depending on the current game state. If no game is going on, or if the current game is paused, or if the game is in the process of removing lines, the function does nothing. If, however, the game is in progress and a block is dropping, the timer function must act to animate the block. First it increments the dropCount data member, which is used to further subdivide the timer intervals. If either dropCount has reached its maximum value or if the user has asked to drop the current block (signified by the dropping data member), then the function needs to move the block down a line. First, dropCount is reset for the next run-through with the timer. Then, the block's location is moved down a line by incrementing its y component. If the HitTest function returns true, then it signifies that the block has hit something and must be placed onto the board. This is done with the PlaceBlock function. After that, it makes sure to remove lines and start a new block falling. Finally, the window is invalidated to make sure everything gets redrawn properly.

The EvKeyUp and EvKeyDown functions handle keypresses. Rather than wait for the standard keypress that results in an EvChar message, this wants to watch as the keys are actually pressed and held down, and then watch them as they're released. This enables the player to press a key and have it affect the game for the duration of time it is pressed. The various keys do some rather obvious things, such as move the block over to the left or right, if possible, or rotate the block. With the matching sections of both EvKeyDown and EvKeyUp, the dropping data member is set to true as long as the down arrow key is pressed, and then is reset to false the moment it's released.

The HitTest function is actually quite simple. It first sets up a pair of nested loops that runs through the contents of the current block, and then performs a series of three if statements. The first statement checks to make sure that the part of the block it's about to check actually is in range on the board; because pieces don't always take up the whole space of the block, there could be parts that extend off the board. The second test is to see if something already is on the board in the selected location. If so, then it checks the block itself to see if there's a piece of it there as well. If all of these conditions are true, then the function returns that condition.

The NewBlock function sets the currentBlock according to the blockType parameter and the current color accordingly. Because the player could be about to lose, it also checks to see if the new block is hitting something at the top of the screen. If so, it then places the block and ends the game. PlaceBlock simply copies the contents of the current block to the board and then removes any full lines that might exist.

DrawBlock actually paints a block on-screen. First it selects a brush and pen of the appropriate color into the supplied device context. For objects such as rectangles (which is what this function draws), it uses the pen to draw the outline, and uses the brush to fill that in. This makes it quite easy to create those nice-looking segmented squares of which each block is made. After selecting the drawing objects, a pair of nested loops goes through all the elements of the block and puts a rectangle on the DC for each occupied element.

Finally, you get to the Paint function—the workhorse function that is responsible for all the drawing on the window. Here is where that memory DC gets used. The reasoning behind using a memory DC is to minimize any flicker on-screen and make the drawing as smooth as possible. If it were to draw to the screen DC directly, the user might be able to see the drawing process as it happened. By drawing to the memory DC instead, and then copying that memory DC directly to the screen, it makes the whole screen-drawing process happen in one quick step.

First, Paint takes care of the case in which the game is paused. If it allowed users to pause the game and study the screen, the game would become a little easier, and consequently less fair. So, in this case, the DC is cleared with a call to FillRect and then the string " * * P A U S E D * * " is written in the middle. The resulting DC is copied to the screen with the BitBlt function and Paint returns.

If the game isn't paused, Paint goes through the process of drawing the board. It draws a square for each position on the board, doing so in the color that had been assigned to it either during initialization or in the PlaceBlock function. Finally, if the game is in progress, it calls DrawBlock to show the currently falling block. When all this is done, Paint copies the memory DC to the screen.

The rest of the program should look quite familiar to you by now. A TApplication descendant is defined that creates a frame window with our specially defined window as its client. This TBlocksApp object is then instantiated in the OwlMain function and run.

The last week presents topics that cover more aspects of creating Windows applications using various classes in the OWL library. You will learn about dialogs and more complicated Windows controls, including check boxes, radio buttons, list boxes, combo boxes, and scroll bars. You also will learn how to include Visual Basic Controls (VBXs) in your application. These controls make up most of the visual controls that are common to Windows applications. You then will be introduced to MDI applications and OLE 2 applications.

Along with this basic information on Windows programming, you also will be introduced to the Application and Class Experts, features of the Borland C++ IDE that enable you to quickly and easily generate and maintain complex Windows programs.

WEEK
3

Dialog Boxes

Dialog boxes are special pop-up windows containing controls that display information or input data. Windows applications use dialog boxes to exchange information with the user. The nicest feature of dialog boxes is that they can be created with all their controls by using a screen painter (the integrated resource editor), and then accessed simply by loading them in from resources.

Today's lesson looks at the modal and modeless dialog boxes supported by Windows.

NEW☞   *Modal dialog boxes* require you to close them before you can proceed any further with the
TERM   application, because they are meant to perform a critical exchange of data. In fact, modal dialog boxes disable their parent windows while they have the focus. Modeless dialog boxes do not need to be closed to continue using the application. You need merely to click on another of the application's windows to continue.

Today you learn about the following topics:

☐ Constructing instances of the class `TDialog`

☐ Executing a modal dialog box

☐ Transferring control data

☐ Transferring data for modal dialog boxes

☐ Transferring data for modeless dialog boxes

Constructing Dialog Boxes

OWL declares the `TDialog` class to support both modeless and modal dialog boxes. The `TDialog` class, a descendant of `TWindow`, has a class constructor and a number of member functions, including the `Create` and `Execute` functions. The `TDialog` constructor is declared as follows:

```
TDialog(TWindow* parent, TResId resId, TModule* module = 0);
```

The `parent` parameter is a pointer to the parent window. The `resId` parameter describes the dialog box's resource name or ID. The `module` parameter, which normally is left out of calls to the constructor, can be used to specify different locations from which to load the resource (for example, loading from a separate DLL).

The `TResId` class is a method used by OWL to encapsulate the different ways that a resource can be named in an application's resources. For example, one could specify a dialog template as having either a number or a name. The useful `TResId` class has three overloaded constructors. The first one, the default constructor, takes no arguments and initializes the class to a `0` value. The other two constructors look like the following:

```
TResId(LPCSTR resString);
TResId(int resNum);
```

This means that you can easily create a `TResId` by simply passing the appropriate value for the constructor. Also, if you use it as a temporary object, you can have `TDialog` constructors that look something like this:

```
TDialog* errdlg = new TDialog(this, "ErrorDlg");
TDialog* newdlg = new TDialog(this, 101);
```

Note: Using resources to define dialog boxes and their controls enables you to define the location, dimensions, style, and caption of a control outside the Windows application source code. Thus, you can change the resource file, recompile it, and then incorporate it in the .EXE application file without recompiling the source file itself. This approach enables you to develop different resource versions with varying colors, styles, and even languages while maintaining a single copy of the application code. Furthermore, this approach does away with the need to write all that complicated code for creating and placing controls in the constructor of a `TWindow` class.

The Borland C++ package includes an integrated resource editor (the IRE), which enables you to create dialog boxes by drawing the controls in the dialog boxes. The resource editor creates .RC resource files that are then bound to your Windows applications. If you are a novice Windows programmer, first learn about the .RC file and its script. Using the resource editor is easy and intuitive. Knowing about the .RC resource script makes working with the output of the resource editor even easier.

Creating Dialog Boxes

Typically, modal dialog boxes are created and removed more frequently than modeless dialog boxes and much more frequently than windows. Executing modal dialog boxes involves the following steps:

1. Create a dialog box object by using the `TDialog` constructor.

2. Call the `Execute` member function, declared in the class `TDialog`, to display the dialog box. Typically, dialog boxes contain the OK and Cancel pushbuttons, with the OK button as the default button. The OK and Cancel buttons have the predefined IDs of `IDOK` and `IDCANCEL`, respectively. You can use pushbutton controls with different captions other than OK and Cancel; however, you still should use the `IDOK` and `IDCANCEL` with these renamed buttons. Using these IDs enable you to take advantage

of the automatic response to IDOK and IDCANCEL provided by the CmOk and CmCancel member functions defined in the TDialog class. Clicking OK or pressing the Enter key usually signals your acceptance of the current (that is, the default or edited) data in the dialog box. By contrast, clicking the Cancel button signals your dissatisfaction with the current data. Following is the declaration of the Execute function:

```
int Execute();
```

The function returns an integer that represents the outcome. This typically is the value of a pushbutton ID, such as IDOK and IDCANCEL.

3. Compare the result of the Execute function with IDOK (or, less frequently, IDCANCEL). The outcome of this comparison determines the steps to take. Such steps usually involve accessing data that you entered in the dialog-box controls.

Creating modeless dialog boxes takes only a little more effort. First, they must be created dynamically with a call to new. Then its Create and ShowWindow member functions must be called, as in the following:

```
TDialog* pdlg = new TDialog(this, "My Dialog");
pdlg->Create();
pdlg->ShowWindow(SW_SHOW);
```

Unlike modal dialog boxes, the modeless dialog object will not be deleted automatically when the dialog box is closed. Be sure to delete the object when you know the dialog box is gone. This *can* be done automatically, however, if you set the wfDeleteOnClose flag in the window with the following member-function call:

```
pdlg->SetFlag(wfDeleteOnClose);
```

Like the TWindow class, from which much of TDialog's functionality is inherited, the SetupWindow, CanClose, and Destroy member functions support the execution of both modal and modeless dialog boxes. The SetupWindow member function serves to initialize the dialog box and its controls. The declaration of the SetupWindow function is as follows:

```
virtual void SetupWindow();
```

Typically, the SetupWindow function initializes the controls of the dialog box. This initialization usually involves copying data from buffers or data members.

The CanClose function is called whenever the user presses the OK button. Following is the declaration of the CanClose function:

```
virtual bool CanClose();
```

CanClose acts to copy data from the dialog-box controls to data members or buffers after deciding whether it's all right to close the dialog. This function returns either true or false, depending on whether the user is allowed to close the dialog box, given the data entered.

The `Destroy` member function handles the closing of the dialog box. Following is the declaration of `Destroy`:

```
virtual void Destroy(int retValue = IDCANCEL);
```

The `Destroy` function serves to clean up before the dialog box is closed, which may involve closing data files, for example. Usually, the last statement in the `Destroy` member-function definition is a call to the `Destroy` function of its parent class.

The next example is a simple OWL program that uses a dialog box defined in resource files. It also uses resource files to create alternate forms of the same dialog box; the first uses modern English and the second uses old English. The application is simple and is made up of an empty window with a single menu item, Exit. When you click the Exit menu item (or press Alt+X), a dialog box appears and asks you whether you want to exit the application. The dialog box has a title, a message, and two buttons (in fact, I purposely made it so that it resembles the dialog boxes spawned by the `MessageBox` function). The program alternates between the two versions of the dialog box. When you first click the Exit menu, you get the modern English version (with OK and Cancel buttons), shown in Figure 15.1. If you click the Cancel button and then click the Exit menu again, you get the old English version of the dialog box (with Yea and Nay buttons), shown in Figure 15.2. Every time you select the Cancel or Nay button and then click the Exit menu, you toggle between the two versions of the dialog box. To exit the application, click the OK or Yea button, depending on the current dialog-box version.

Listing 15.1 shows the DIALOG1.RC resource file. Listing 15.2 shows the source code for the DIALOG1.CPP program.

Type

Listing 15.1. Script for the DIALOG1.RC resource file.

```
 1: #include <windows.h>
 2: #include <owl\window.rh>
 3:
 4: EXITMENU MENU LOADONCALL MOVEABLE PURE DISCARDABLE
 5: BEGIN
 6:   MENUITEM "E&xit", CM_EXIT
 7: END
 8:
 9: ModernEnglish DIALOG DISCARDABLE LOADONCALL PURE MOVEABLE 20, 50, 200, 100
10: STYLE WS_POPUP | DS_MODALFRAME
11: CAPTION "Message"
12: BEGIN
13:   CTEXT "Exit the application?", -1, 10, 10, 170, 15
14:   DEFPUSHBUTTON "OK", IDOK, 20, 50, 70, 15, WS_VISIBLE | WS_TABSTOP
15:   PUSHBUTTON "Cancel", IDCANCEL, 110, 50, 70, 15, WS_VISIBLE | WS_TABSTOP
16: END
17:
18: OldeEnglish DIALOG DISCARDABLE LOADONCALL PURE MOVEABLE 20, 50, 200, 100
19: STYLE WS_POPUP | DS_MODALFRAME
20: CAPTION "Message"
```

continues

Listing 15.1. continued

```
21: BEGIN
22:    CTEXT "Leavest thou now?", -1, 10, 10, 170, 15
23:    DEFPUSHBUTTON "Yea", IDOK, 20, 50, 70, 15, WS_VISIBLE ¦ WS_TABSTOP
24:    PUSHBUTTON "Nay", IDCANCEL, 110, 50, 70, 15, WS_VISIBLE ¦ WS_TABSTOP
25: END
```

Listing 15.2. Source code for the DIALOG1.CPP program file.

```
1: #include <owl\applicat.h>
2: #include <owl\dialog.h>
3: #include <owl\framewin.h>
4: #include <owl\window.h>
5: #include <owl\window.rh>
6:
7: class TMyWindow : public TWindow
8: {
9: public:
10:    TMyWindow(TWindow* parent = 0);
11:
12:    virtual bool CanClose();
13:
14: protected:
15:    void CmExit();
16:
17:    DECLARE_RESPONSE_TABLE(TMyWindow);
18: };
19: DEFINE_RESPONSE_TABLE1(TMyWindow, TWindow)
20:    EV_COMMAND(CM_EXIT, CmExit),
21: END_RESPONSE_TABLE;
22:
23: TMyWindow::TMyWindow(TWindow* parent)
24:    : TWindow(parent)
25: {
26: }
27:
28: bool TMyWindow::CanClose()
29: {
30:    static bool bFlag = false;
31:
32:    bFlag = !bFlag;
33:    if (bFlag)
34:       return TDialog(this, "ModernEnglish").Execute() == IDOK;
35:    else
36:       return TDialog(this, "OldeEnglish").Execute() == IDOK;
37: }
38:
39: void TMyWindow::CmExit()
40: {
41:    SendMessage(WM_CLOSE);
42: }
43:
44: class TDialogApp : public TApplication
45: {
```

```
46: public:
47:     TDialogApp() : TApplication()
48:         { nCmdShow = SW_SHOWMAXIMIZED; }
49:
50:     void InitMainWindow()
51:         {
52:         SetMainWindow(new TFrameWindow(  0,
53:                             "Simple Dialog Box Tester Application",
54:                             new TMyWindow ));
55:         GetMainWindow()->AssignMenu("EXITMENU");
56:         }
57: };
58:
59: int OwlMain(int, char *[])
60: {
61:     return TDialogApp().Run();
62: }
```

Figure 15.1 shows a sample session.

Figure 15.1.

A sample session with the DIALOG1.EXE application showing the dialog box with modern English wording.

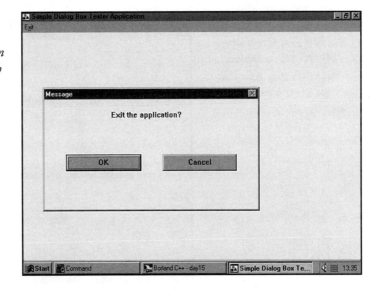

Listing 15.1 shows the script for the DIALOG1.RC resource file, which defines the following resources:

☐ The menu resource, EXITMENU, which displays a single menu with the single item Exit.

☐ The dialog-box resource starting on line 9, ModernEnglish, which has a defined style, caption, and list of child controls. The specified style indicates that the dialog box is a modal pop-up child window. The caption specified on line 11 is the string Message. The dialog box contains three controls: a centered static text (for the dialog-box message), a default OK pushbutton, and an ordinary Cancel button. The OK button has the resource ID of the predefined `IDOK` constant, and the Cancel button has the resource ID of the predefined `IDCANCEL` constant.

☐ The dialog-box resource starting on line 18, `OldeEnglish`, which is similar to the `ModernEnglish` dialog box resource, except that it uses old English wording. The Yea button has the resource ID of the predefined `IDOK` constant. The Nay button has the resource ID of the predefined `IDCANCEL` constant. These buttons are examples of exit buttons with atypical captions.

You should note that the dialog box listed in the .RC file shows a `STYLE` line, where special styles are set for the dialog box. These styles specify different aspects of a window, and there are a tremendous amount of them available for both windows and dialogs (which are special windows). To get a comprehensive list, look in the online help at the entry for the Windows API function `CreateWindow`, which lists all the various styles available for all types of windows.

Figure 15.2 shows a sample session.

Figure 15.2.

A sample session with the DIALOG1.EXE application showing the dialog box with the old English wording.

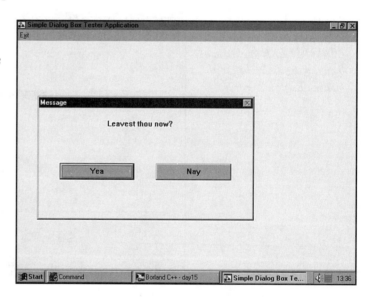

The `CTEXT` keyword specifies centered text. The `DEFPUSHBUTTON` keyword enables you to define a default pushbutton and requires the caption, ID, location, dimensions, and control style of the control. The `PUSHBUTTON` definition is identical to the `DEFPUSHBUTTON` keyword's definition, but it describes an ordinary button instead of a default pushbutton.

Until now, you have been creating resources by manually creating the .RC file. When making dialog boxes from scratch, it is far easier to use the resource editor. This provides an easy

interface by which dialog boxes can be painted on-screen exactly the way you want them to appear when your application is run. Of course, for the rest of this book, it will be easier to type in the .RC file as before, then edit it at will with the resource editor.

Listing 15.2 shows the source code for the DIALOG1.CPP program file. The source code declares two classes: an application class starting on line 44, and a window class starting on line 7. The application uses the standard TDialog class; it does not derive a specialized descendant, because no additional dialog-box functionality is required.

The most relevant member function is CanClose starting on line 28, which responds to the user's request to close the window (triggered by the CmExit function on line 39, which in turn is triggered by the Exit menu choice). The function uses the Boolean static local variable, bFlag, to toggle between the two dialog-box resources ModernEnglish and OldeEnglish. The modern English dialog box is invoked in the following statement:

```
return TDialog(this, "ModernEnglish").Execute() == IDOK;
```

The dialog-box object is executed using the Execute function, disabling the parent window until you click either pushbutton control. The value returned by the Execute member function is compared with the IDOK constant, and the result is returned to the caller to let it know what the user selected, and whether to close the application window.

The instance of the old English version of the dialog box is similarly created, as shown in the following statement:

```
return TDialog(this, "OldeEnglish").Execute() == IDOK;
```

Connecting OWL Objects with Windows Controls

Until now, the constructors for the various controls you have learned have had the same general look of the constructor of the TControl class from which they are descendants. Here's its constructor:

```
TControl( TWindow* parent,
          int id,
          const char far* title,
          int x,
          int y,
          int w,
          int h,
          TModule* module = 0 );
```

Occasionally, there have been additional parameters after the h and before the module parameters, as the various controls needed. These all assume that the controls needed to be created from scratch, including their positions in their parent window.

When creating a dialog box from a resource file, however, these controls are created automatically from the resource script at the same time as the dialog box. In order to have access to the controls from an OWL object, there is a second constructor for each control class that enables you to create an object that has a direct correspondence with the actual Windows control. They're all based on the following constructor for the TControl class:

```
TControl(TWindow* parent, int resourceId, TModule* module = 0);
```

The following are the constructors for creating the various controls that have already been introduced:

```
TStatic( TWindow* parent, int resourceId, uint textLen = 0,
        TModule* module = 0);
TEdit( TWindow* parent, int resourceId, uint textLen = 0,
        TModule* module = 0 );
TButton(TWindow* parent, int resourceId, TModule* module = 0);
```

In addition, there are a number of other controls that will be introduced formally in the next few days. Since I am assuming you are at least marginally familiar with the controls themselves, I will introduce their constructors here so that you can easily create them in your dialog boxes. Note that they all tend to adhere to a common standard, with the exception of parameters specific to certain controls. These parameters will be explained in detail when the control is introduced.

```
TCheckBox( TWindow* parent, int resourceId, TGroupBox* group = 0,
        TModule* module = 0 );
TRadioButton( TWindow* parent, int resourceId, TGroupBox* group = 0,
        TModule* module = 0 );
TGroupBox(TWindow* parent, int resourceId, TModule* module = 0);
TListBox(TWindow* parent, int resourceId, TModule* module = 0);
TComboBox( TWindow* parent, int resourceId, uint textLen = 0,
        TModule* module = 0 );
TScrollBar(TWindow* parent, int resourceId, TModule* module = 0);
```

The control objects, as with the full versions, should be created in a dialog's constructor. The following is an example of creating an OWL object to interface with a window's Cancel button:

```
cancel = new TButton(this, IDCANCEL);
```

Transferring Control Data

Dialog boxes often serve as pop-up windows to request input from the application user. This input often includes a variety of settings that use radio buttons, check boxes, and edit boxes. Because dialog boxes are frequently created, it makes sense to preserve the latest values in the dialog's controls for the next time it appears. The Search and Replace dialog boxes that are found in many Windows editors are typical examples. These dialog boxes remember the settings of all

or some of their controls from the last time the dialog box was executed. You also can use the transfer mechanism as an easy way to set and retrieve data in the dialog box for simple initialization and retrieval purposes.

To implement this feature in dialog boxes, you need a data-transfer mechanism between the dialog box and a buffer. This buffer usually is a data member of the parent window. Therefore, the first step in supporting data transfer is to define a transfer buffer type. The buffer declares the data fields to buffer the controls that transfer their data. These controls typically include the edit box, list box, combo box, scroll bar, check box, and radio button. The static-text, group-box, and pushbutton controls usually have no data to transfer and, therefore, do not enter in the declaration of the data-transfer-buffer type because OWL has them disabled by default. Following is a sample data-buffer type that includes a single instance of each allowable control:

```
struct TAppTransferBuffer
{
    char EditBox[MaxEditLen];
    TListBoxData ListBoxData;
    TComboBoxData ComboBoxData;
    TScrollBarData ScrollBarData;
    uint CheckBox;
    uint RadioButton;
};
```

The buffer structure needs only to include the controls that actually transfer data. You do not need to declare the fields of the buffer structure in any particular order, so long as the OWL controls they match are created in the same order. This sample buffer type includes three special classes that transfer data between dialog boxes and list boxes, combo boxes, and scroll bars. You will see more about these classes later in this section.

Look at the various members of the data-transfer-buffer type:

- [ ] The `EditBox` member assists in moving data between the edit control and the data buffer. The data member defines a character array that should be equal to or greater than the number of characters in the edit control.

- [ ] The `ListBoxData` member helps to transfer data between a list-box control and the data buffer. The `ListBoxData` is an instance of the `TListBoxData` class that OWL provides for keeping track of the contents of a list box, including any selections.

- [ ] The `ComboBoxData` member helps to move data between a combo-box control and the data buffer. The `ComboBoxData` is an instance of the `TComboBoxData` class. This, too, is provided by OWL to keep track of the contents and state of a combo box.

- [ ] The `ScrollBarData` member is an instance of the `TScrollBarData` class that assists in transferring data between a scroll-bar control and the data buffer.

- [ ] The `CheckBox` member stores the current check state of a check box in a `uint` type.

- [ ] The `RadioButton` member stores the current check state of a radio button in a `uint` type.

441

After the transfer buffer has been set up, it needs to be passed to the dialog box so that the OWL `TDialog` class knows to transfer data between the controls and the data buffer. This is done with the `SetTransferBuffer` member function. It is also important to make sure that all the controls represented in the data buffer are created in the `TDialog`'s constructor at the same time as the call to `SetTransferBuffer`.

Data Transfer for Modal Dialog Boxes

The next application is a simple example of transferring data between the controls of a modal dialog box and a buffer. It creates a typical dialog box that is used in replacing characters in a text editor. The dialog box contains the following controls:

- ☐ Find edit box
- ☐ Replace edit box
- ☐ Scope group box that contains the Global and Selected Text radio-button controls
- ☐ Case Sensitive check box
- ☐ The Whole Word check box
- ☐ The OK pushbutton control
- ☐ The Cancel pushbutton control

Note that not all of these controls have been presented yet. They are, however, familiar controls that I'm sure you've seen time and again in various other Windows applications (including Borland C++). All I'm doing with them here is creating OWL interface objects that transfer the settings in and out of them. I'll cover the controls in detail on the following days.

The application has a main menu with the Exit and Dialog menu items. To invoke the dialog box, click the Dialog menu item or press Alt+D. When you invoke the dialog box for the first time, the controls have the following initial values and states:

- ☐ The Find edit box contains the string DOS.
- ☐ The Replace edit box has the string Windows 95.
- ☐ The Global radio button is checked.
- ☐ The Case Sensitive check box is checked.
- ☐ The Whole Word check box is checked.

Type new strings in the edit box and alter the check states of the radio buttons and check boxes. Now, click the OK button (or press Alt+O) to close the dialog box. Invoke the Dialog menu item again to pop up the dialog box. Notice that the controls of the dialog box have the same values and states as when you last closed the dialog box.

Listing 15.3 shows the source code for the DIALOG2.H header file. Listing 15.4 contains the script for the DIALOG2.RC resource file. Listing 15.5 shows the source code for the DIALOG2.CPP program file.

 Listing 15.3. Source code for the DIALOG2.H header file.

```
1: #define CM_DIALOG (WM_USER + 100)
2:
3: #define IDE_FIND        101
4: #define IDE_REPLACE     102
5: #define IDR_GLOBAL      103
6: #define IDR_SELTEXT     104
7: #define IDC_CASE        105
8: #define IDC_WHOLEWORD   106
```

 Listing 15.4. Script for the DIALOG2.RC resource file.

```
1:  #include <windows.h>
2:  #include <owl\window.rh>
3:  #include "dialog2.h"
4:
5:  Search DIALOG DISCARDABLE LOADONCALL PURE MOVEABLE 10, 10, 200, 150
6:  STYLE DS_MODALFRAME | WS_POPUP | WS_VISIBLE | WS_CAPTION |
7:       WS_SYSMENU | DS_3DLOOK
8:  CAPTION "Controls Demo"
9:  BEGIN
10:    LTEXT "Find", -1, 20, 10, 100, 15, NOT WS_GROUP
11:    EDITTEXT IDE_FIND, 20, 25, 100, 15
12:    LTEXT "Replace", -1, 20, 45, 100, 15, NOT WS_GROUP
13:    EDITTEXT IDE_REPLACE, 20, 60, 100, 15
14:    GROUPBOX " Scope ", -1, 20, 80, 90, 50, BS_GROUPBOX
15:    RADIOBUTTON "Global", IDR_GLOBAL, 30, 90, 50, 15,
16:              BS_AUTORADIOBUTTON
17:    RADIOBUTTON "Selected Text", IDR_SELTEXT, 30, 105, 60, 15,
18:              BS_AUTORADIOBUTTON
19:    CHECKBOX "Case Sensitive", IDC_CASE, 20, 130, 80, 15,
20:            BS_AUTOCHECKBOX | WS_TABSTOP
21:    CHECKBOX "Whole Word", IDC_WHOLEWORD, 100, 130, 80, 15,
22:            BS_AUTOCHECKBOX | WS_TABSTOP
23:    DEFPUSHBUTTON "&OK", IDOK, 120, 90, 30, 20
24:    PUSHBUTTON "&Cancel", IDCANCEL, 160, 90, 30, 20
25: END
26:
27: MainMenu MENU LOADONCALL MOVEABLE PURE DISCARDABLE
28: BEGIN
29:    MENUITEM "E&xit", CM_EXIT
30:    MENUITEM "&Dialog", CM_DIALOG
31: END
```

Listing 15.5. Source code for the DIALOG2.CPP program file.

```
1:  #include <cstring.h>
2:  #include <windows.h>
3:  #include <owl\applicat.h>
4:  #include <owl\checkbox.h>
5:  #include <owl\dialog.h>
6:  #include <owl\edit.h>
7:  #include <owl\framewin.h>
8:  #include <owl\radiobut.h>
9:  #include <owl\window.h>
10: #include <owl\window.rh>
11:
12: #include "dialog2.h"
13:
14: const MaxEditLen = 30;
15:
16: struct TTransferBuffer
17: {
18:    char find[MaxEditLen];
19:    char replace[MaxEditLen];
20:    uint global, seltext, csensitive, wholeword;
21: };
22:
23: class TSearchDialog : public TDialog
24: {
25: public:
26:    TSearchDialog( TWindow* parent,
27:                   TTransferBuffer* xfer,
28:                   TModule* module = 0);
29:
30: };
31:
32: TSearchDialog::TSearchDialog( TWindow* parent,
33:                               TTransferBuffer* xfer,
34:                               TModule* module)
35:    : TDialog(parent, "Search", module)
36: {
37:    new TEdit(this, IDE_FIND, MaxEditLen);
38:    new TEdit(this, IDE_REPLACE, MaxEditLen);
39:    new TRadioButton(this, IDR_GLOBAL);
40:    new TRadioButton(this, IDR_SELTEXT);
41:    new TCheckBox(this, IDC_CASE);
42:    new TCheckBox(this, IDC_WHOLEWORD);
43:    SetTransferBuffer(xfer);
44: }
45:
46: class TMyWindow : public TWindow
47: {
48: public:
49:    TMyWindow(TWindow* parent = 0);
50:
51: protected:
52:    void CmExit();
53:    void CmDialog();
```

```
54:
55: private:
56:     TTransferBuffer xfer;
57:
58:     DECLARE_RESPONSE_TABLE(TMyWindow);
59: };
60: DEFINE_RESPONSE_TABLE1(TMyWindow, TWindow)
61:     EV_COMMAND(CM_EXIT, CmExit),
62:     EV_COMMAND(CM_DIALOG, CmDialog),
63: END_RESPONSE_TABLE;
64:
65: TMyWindow::TMyWindow(TWindow* parent)
66:     : TWindow(parent)
67: {
68:     memset(&xfer, 0, sizeof(xfer));
69:     lstrcpy(xfer.find, "DOS");
70:     lstrcpy(xfer.replace, "Windows 95");
71:     xfer.global = BF_CHECKED;
72:     xfer.csensitive = BF_CHECKED;
73:     xfer.wholeword = BF_CHECKED;
74: }
75:
76: void TMyWindow::CmExit()
77: {
78:     SendMessage(WM_CLOSE);
79: }
80:
81: void TMyWindow::CmDialog()
82: {
83:     if (TSearchDialog(this, &xfer).Execute() == IDOK)
84:       {
85:         string msg("Find String: ");
86:         msg += xfer.find;
87:         msg += "\n\nReplace String: ";
88:         msg += xfer.replace;
89:         MessageBox(msg.c_str(), "Dialog Box Data");
90:       }
91:   }
92:
93:   class TDialogApp : public TApplication
94:   {
95:   public:
96:       TDialogApp() : TApplication()
97:         { nCmdShow = SW_SHOWMAXIMIZED; }
98:
99:       void InitMainWindow()
100:         {
101:         SetMainWindow(new TFrameWindow(  0,
102:                             "Modal Dialog Box Data Transfer Tester",
103:                             new TMyWindow ));
104:         GetMainWindow()->AssignMenu("MainMenu");
105:         }
106: };
107:
108: int OwlMain(int, char *[])
```

continues

445

Listing 15.5. continued

```
109: {
110:    return TDialogApp().Run();
111: }
```

Figure 15.3 shows a sample session with the DIALOG2.EXE application.

Figure 15.3.

A sample session with the DIALOG2.EXE application.

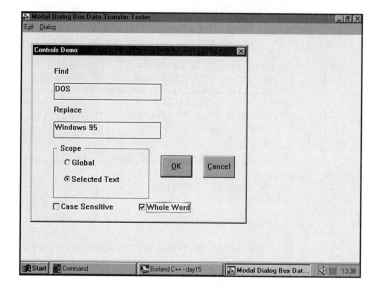

Listing 15.4 contains the script for the DIALOG2.RC resource file. This file defines the resources for the menu and the dialog box, including its controls. In the dialog-box resource definition on lines 21 and 22, the OK and Cancel pushbuttons have the predefined IDOK and IDCANCEL IDs, respectively.

Listing 15.5 shows the source code for the DIALOG2.CPP program file. The program declares the data-transfer type TTransferBuffer starting on line 16 and includes members for the edit boxes, radio buttons, and check boxes.

Starting on line 23, the application declares the TSearchDialog class as a descendant of the TDialog class. Notice that it doesn't have any member data, and the only function declared is its constructor. This constructor starts on line 32 and, in turn, does nothing more than create some OWL interface objects to be associated with the various controls created from the dialog resource. The constructor then makes a call to the SetTransferBuffer function on line 43, passing the xfer parameter along. OWL takes over from here and performs automatically all the transfers between xfer and the actual controls.

Starting on line 43, the TMyWindow class declares its constructor, two functions to respond to the menu, and a data member of type TTransferBuffer. This data member is initialized in the constructor, first with a call to the memset function on line 68. This call fills the xfer data member with zeros. I recommend that you systematically call the memset function to perform a basic initialization of buffers and structures before assigning specific values to them. Then the xfer's data members are set to some initial values. Another way to ensure an empty structure is to provide it with a default constructor that clears all the data members.

Starting on line 81, the CmDialog function, which responds to the Dialog menu item, creates a modal dialog of type TSearchDialog on line 83, passing the xfer data member as a parameter. If the user clicks the OK button to exit this dialog box, it will return IDOK, and the CmDialog function then will build and display a message string that reflects the current Find and Replace text on lines 85 through 89.

Transferring Data for Modeless Dialog Boxes

The method of transferring data from modeless dialog boxes is almost the same as that used for modal dialog boxes. The main difference is that the mechanism that automatically transfers the data between the controls and the transfer buffer is called only when the dialog window is modal. The programmer needs to make the call explicitly in the case of a modeless dialog box. This can be done by overriding the CloseWindow member function in the dialog box's descendant class.

```
void TMyDialog::CloseWindow(int retValue)
{
   TransferData(tdGetData);
   TDialog::CloseWindow(retValue);
}
```

At this point, all the control data will be transferred to the buffer that was sent to the SetTransferBuffer in the dialog box's constructor.

Another possible action might be to have a Send button in the dialog box, with a response function that looks similar to the following:

```
void TMyDialog::CmSend()
{
   TransferData(tdGetData);
   Parent->HandleMessage(WM_COMMAND, IDB_SEND);
}
```

Then, in the dialog box's parent's window class, add a member function to handle the Send button in the same way you did for the dialog class. This function is called automatically when the dialog box simulates the press of the Send button via the call to its parent's HandleMessage function.

Summary

Today's lesson presented you with powerful dialog boxes that serve as input tools. You learned about the following topics:

☐ You can construct instances of class `TDialog` to create modeless or modal dialog boxes.

☐ You can construct instances of the various control classes that give access to the controls created automatically from the dialog resource.

☐ Modal dialog boxes are executed with the `Execute` member function.

☐ The basics of transferring control data include declaring the data-transfer-buffer type, declaring the buffer, creating the controls in a sequence that matches their buffers, and establishing the buffer link with the `SetTransferBuffer` member function.

☐ The first step in supporting data transfer is to define a transfer buffer type. You can transfer data for modal dialog boxes and modeless dialog boxes.

Q&A

Q Does OWL support specialized dialog boxes?

A Yes. OWL has a set of classes that implement dialog boxes for selecting files, selecting colors, selecting fonts, printing, searching/replacing text, and many others. The classes that model these dialog boxes are all descendants of the class `TDialog` and display the common dialog boxes.

Q Is the data-transfer buffer necessary for modeless dialog boxes?

A Not always. You can have an application that pops up multiple modeless dialog boxes and have them communicate with each other directly, without the need of a data-transfer buffer.

Workshop

The Workshop provides quiz questions to help you solidify your understanding of the material covered and exercises to provide you with experience in using what you've learned. Try to understand the quiz and exercise answers before continuing on to the next day's lesson. Answers are provided in Appendix A.

Quiz

1. True or false? You must compile all the .RC files into .RES files before or during the creation of the executable.
2. True or false? The OK and Cancel buttons in a dialog box are optional.
3. True or false? You can create a dialog box with buttons labeled Yes and No.
4. True or false? Nested dialog boxes are not allowed by Windows.
5. True or false? Dialog boxes must always have a nondialog window parent.

Exercises

1. Create a version of the MrCalc application (from Day 14) that uses a dialog box as a standalone window.
2. Use the resource editor to create the dialog-box resource for the DIALOG2 program.

16

Grouped Controls

Windows supports check-box and radio-button controls that act as software switches. These controls appear in typical Search and Replace dialog boxes, and they influence certain aspects of the text search or replacement. These aspects include the scope, direction, and case sensitivity of searching or replacing text. In today's lesson, you learn about the following topics:

- ☐ The check-box control
- ☐ The radio-button control
- ☐ The group control

Today's lesson also shows you how to respond to the messages emitted by these controls as well as how to use the ForEach iterators to manipulate the check-box and radio-button controls.

NEW ☞ The *group control* is a special control that visually and logically groups the check-box and **TERM** radio-button controls.

The Check-Box Control

The check-box control is a special button that toggles a check mark. The control instances appear with a small rectangular button and a title that appears, by default, to the right side of the square. When you click the square, you toggle the control's check mark. Think of the check box as a bool value that can be either true or false. The instances of a check box can appear inside or outside a group box and are not mutually exclusive—toggling any check box does not affect the check state of other check boxes.

> **Note:** Placing check boxes inside groups (inside a dialog box) serves two purposes. First, the group box provides a visual grouping that clarifies the purpose of the check boxes to the application user. Second, you can streamline the notification messages emitted by the check boxes in a group to detect any change in the checked state of the check boxes.

NEW ☞ Windows enables you to specify a check box that can have one of three states: checked, **TERM** unchecked, and *grayed.* The grayed state fills the control's rectangular button with a gray color. This third state can serve to indicate that the check-box control is in an indeterminate (or "don't care") state.

The *TCheckBox* Class

The ObjectWindows Library offers the TCheckBox class, a descendant of TButton, as the class that provides the instances of check-box controls. Day 14 introduced you to the TButton class and discussed the aspects of that class that are related to the pushbutton controls. Because check boxes are really just specialized buttons, much of what applies to buttons also applies to check boxes. By deriving the TCheckBox class from the TButton class, you ensure that TCheckBox inherits much of the parent's functionality. The check-box styles shown in Table 16.1 indicate that there are two basic modes for managing the check state of a check-box control: automatic and nonautomatic (manual, if you prefer). In automatic mode (specified by BS_AUTOCHECKBOX and BS_AUTO3STATE), Windows toggles the check state when you click the control. In manual mode, your application code is responsible for managing the check state of the check box.

Table 16.1. Check-box control styles.

Style	Meaning
BS_CHECKBOX	Specifies a check box with the title to the right of the rectangular button.
BS_AUTOCHECKBOX	Same as BS_CHECKBOX, except the button is automatically toggled when you click it. This is the default setting for the TCheckBox class.
BS_3STATE	Same as BS_CHECKBOX, except that the control has three states: checked, unchecked, and grayed.
BS_AUTO3STATE	Same as BS_3STATE, except the button is automatically toggled when you click it.
BS_LEFTTEXT	Sets the control's title to the left of the button. Note that this is the only style that can be ORed into the style.

The TCheckBox class provides member functions to set and query the state of the check box. The GetCheck member function returns a state of the check-box control and is declared as follows:

```
uint GetCheck() const;
```

The function returns a uint-typed value that represents the check state. A value of BF_UNCHECKED indicates that the control is not checked. A value of BF_CHECKED signals that the control is checked. A value of BF_GRAYED indicates that the control is in an indeterminate state. The latter value is valid for the BS_3STATE and BS_AUTO3STATE styles.

The SetCheck member function enables you to set the check state of a check-box control. The declaration of the SetCheck function is

```
void SetCheck(uint check);
```

The check parameter specifies the new state of the check-box control and should be one of the BF_*XXX* values.

Responding to Check Box Messages

Because check boxes are descendants of TButton with a BS_CHECKBOX or BS_AUTOCHECKBOX style, your OWL application responds to the messages emitted by check boxes in a manner similar to the pushbuttons. The EV_BN_CLICKED macro maps the message sent by the check-box control with the member function that responds to that message.

The Radio Button Control

Radio buttons typically enable you to select from two or more options. This type of control comes with a circular button and a title that appears, by default, to the right of the button. When you check a radio button, a tiny, filled circle appears inside the circular button. Radio buttons need to be placed in group boxes that visually and logically group them. In each group of radio buttons, only one button can be selected at a time. Therefore, radio buttons are mutually exclusive.

The *TRadioButton* Class

OWL applications use the TRadioButton class, a descendant of TCheckBox, to create radio-button controls by specifying BS_RADIOBUTTON or BS_AUTORADIOBUTTON. Table 16.2 contains the radio-button styles. The constructor creates a radio button with the BS_AUTORADIOBUTTON style. Like the check-box controls, the radio buttons use the GetCheck and SetCheck member functions to query and set the state. Unlike the check box, the radio button has only two states: checked and unchecked.

Table 16.2. Radio-button control styles.

Style	Meaning
BS_RADIOBUTTON	Specifies a radio button with the title to the right of the circular button.
BS_AUTORADIOBUTTON	Same as BS_RADIOBUTTON, except the button is automatically toggled when you click it. This is the default style for the TRadioButton class.
BS_LEFTTEXT	Sets the control's title to the left of the button. This is the only style that can be ORed into the style.

The radio-button controls send the same type of notification messages to their parent windows as do the check-box controls. Handling these messages for radio buttons is identical to that of check-box and pushbutton controls.

The Group Control

The group control encloses radio buttons and check boxes. The group box performs the following tasks:

☐ Visually groups radio buttons or check boxes, which makes relating these controls to each other clearer for the application user by placing a box around them. Note that you don't necessarily need controls in a box to get the visual effect.

☐ Logically groups multiple radio buttons so that when you select one radio button, the other buttons in the same group are automatically deselected.

NEW
TERM The group control is a special type of control known as a *container control.*

You can code your OWL application so that the controls inside a group box notify the parent of the group box that you have changed the state of its controls.

The *TGroupBox* Class

Your OWL applications can create group boxes with the `TGroupBox` class, descended from `TControl`. This automatically creates the visual element and provides access via its `SelectionChanged` member function. The declaration of the `SelectionChanged` function is

```
void SelectionChanged(int controlId);
```

When an item in the group is changed, this function is called. By default, the `SelectionChanged` function checks the `TGroupBox`'s `NotifyParent` data member. If it's `true`, then the function notifies the parent window of the group box that one of its selections has changed by sending it a child-ID-based message. By deriving your own version of `TGroupBox` and redefining `SelectionChanged`, you can handle selection changes from the group box itself.

The Widget Selection Application

Here's a short application that demonstrates a possible use for the controls introduced in this chapter. The program shows a sample order form for the World-Wide Widget Wielders company. On it, the user can select one each of Type A, Type B, and Type C widgets. For each of those widget types, there are several different models from which the user can choose. In each case, the different models are disabled so long as the widget type is not checked.

This program illustrates the following:

☐ The basic use of check-box controls

☐ The basic use of radio buttons

☐ Responding to check-box notification messages

☐ Overriding a group box to keep track of changes in radio-button selections

☐ Making initial radio-button selections

Listing 16.1 contains the source code for the WIDGETS.H header file, Listing 16.2 shows the source code for the WIDGETS.RC resource file, and Listing 16.3 shows the WIDGETS.CPP program file.

Listing 16.1. Source code for the WIDGETS.H header file.

```
 1: #define IDC_TYPEA       101
 2: #define IDC_TYPEB       102
 3: #define IDC_TYPEC       103
 4: #define IDR_ETCHED      104
 5: #define IDR_POLISHED    105
 6: #define IDR_WOODGRAIN   106
 7: #define IDR_VARNISHED   107
 8: #define IDR_ENGRAVED    108
 9: #define IDR_MEDIOCRE    109
10: #define IDR_DELUXE      110
11: #define IDG_TYPEA       111
12: #define IDG_TYPEB       112
13: #define IDG_TYPEC       113
```

Listing 16.2. Source code for the WIDGETS.RC resource file.

```
 1: #include "widgets.h"
 2:
 3: WWWW DIALOG 8, 15, 241, 165
 4: STYLE DS_MODALFRAME ¦ WS_POPUP ¦ WS_VISIBLE ¦ WS_CAPTION ¦ WS_SYSMENU
 5: CAPTION "World-Wide Widget Weilders"
 6: FONT 8, "MS Sans Serif"
 7: {
 8:     CHECKBOX "Type A", IDC_TYPEA, 10, 12, 40, 12,
 9:             BS_AUTOCHECKBOX ¦ WS_TABSTOP
10:     CONTROL "", IDG_TYPEA, "static", SS_BLACKFRAME ¦ WS_GROUP,
11:             67, 6, 160, 25
12:     CONTROL "Etched", IDR_ETCHED, "BUTTON", BS_AUTORADIOBUTTON,
13:             77, 12, 60, 12
14:     CONTROL "Polished", IDR_POLISHED, "BUTTON", BS_AUTORADIOBUTTON,
15:             147, 12, 60, 12
16:     CHECKBOX "Type B", IDC_TYPEB, 10, 59, 40, 12,
17:             BS_AUTOCHECKBOX ¦ WS_TABSTOP
```

```
18:    CONTROL "", IDG_TYPEB, "static", SS_BLACKFRAME ¦ WS_GROUP,
19:            67, 48, 160, 34
20:    CONTROL "Wood-Grain", IDR_WOODGRAIN, "BUTTON", BS_AUTORADIOBUTTON,
21:            77, 49, 60, 12
22:    CONTROL "Varnished", IDR_VARNISHED, "BUTTON", BS_AUTORADIOBUTTON,
23:            150, 49, 60, 12
24:    CONTROL "Engraved", IDR_ENGRAVED, "BUTTON", BS_AUTORADIOBUTTON,
25:            77, 68, 60, 12
26:    CHECKBOX "Type C", IDC_TYPEC, 10, 105, 40, 12,
27:             BS_AUTOCHECKBOX ¦ WS_TABSTOP
28:    CONTROL "", IDG_TYPEC, "static", SS_BLACKFRAME ¦ WS_GROUP,
29:            67, 97, 160, 28
30:    CONTROL "Mediocre", IDR_MEDIOCRE, "BUTTON", BS_AUTORADIOBUTTON,
31:            77, 105, 60, 12
32:    CONTROL "Deluxe", IDR_DELUXE, "BUTTON", BS_AUTORADIOBUTTON,
33:            153, 105, 60, 12
34:    DEFPUSHBUTTON "Done", IDOK, 47, 134, 50, 14
35:    PUSHBUTTON "Cancel", IDCANCEL, 144, 134, 50, 14
36: }
```

Type

Listing 16.3. Source code for the WIDGETS.CPP program file.

```
1:     #include <stdio.h>
2:     #include <owl\applicat.h>
3:     #include <owl\button.h>
4:     #include <owl\checkbox.h>
5:     #include <owl\dialog.h>
6:     #include <owl\framewin.h>
7:     #include <owl\groupbox.h>
8:     #include <owl\radiobut.h>
9:     #include <owl\window.h>
10:    #include <owl\window.rh>
11:
12:    #include "widgets.h"
13:
14:    class TMyGroup : public TGroupBox
15:    {
16:    public:
17:       TMyGroup(TWindow*      parent,
18:                int          id,
19:                TModule*     module = 0 )
20:          : TGroupBox(parent, id, module), cur(-1)
21:          { }
22:
23:       LPCSTR GetCurCheck();
24:
25:       virtual void SelectionChanged(int controlId)
26:          { TGroupBox::SelectionChanged(cur = controlId); }
27:
28:    private:
29:       int cur;
```

continues

457

Listing 16.3. continued

```
30:    };
31:
32:    LPCSTR TMyGroup::GetCurCheck()
33:    {
34:        TWindow* w = Parent->ChildWithId(cur);
35:        return w ? w->Title : NULL;
36:    }
37:
38:    class TWidgetDialog : public TDialog
39:    {
40:    public:
41:        TWidgetDialog(TWindow* parent = 0, TModule* module = 0);
42:
43:    protected:
44:        virtual void SetupWindow();
45:
46:        void EnableGroupA(bool enable);
47:        void EnableGroupB(bool enable);
48:        void EnableGroupC(bool enable);
49:
50:        bool BuildStr( LPSTR str,
51:                       LPCSTR name,
52:                       TCheckBox* check,
53:                       TMyGroup* group );
54:
55:        void CmDone();
56:        void CmCancel();
57:        void CmTypeA();
58:        void CmTypeB();
59:        void CmTypeC();
60:
61:    private:
62:        TCheckBox       *TypeA, *TypeB, *TypeC;
63:        TMyGroup        *GroupA, *GroupB, *GroupC;
64:        TRadioButton    *Etched, *Polished,
65:                        *WoodGrain, *Varnished, *Engraved,
66:                        *Mediocre, *Deluxe;
67:
68:        DECLARE_RESPONSE_TABLE(TWidgetDialog);
69:    };
70:    DEFINE_RESPONSE_TABLE1(TWidgetDialog, TDialog)
71:        EV_BN_CLICKED(IDOK, CmDone),
72:        EV_BN_CLICKED(IDCANCEL, CmCancel),
73:        EV_BN_CLICKED(IDC_TYPEA, CmTypeA),
74:        EV_BN_CLICKED(IDC_TYPEB, CmTypeB),
75:        EV_BN_CLICKED(IDC_TYPEC, CmTypeC),
76:    END_RESPONSE_TABLE;
77:
78:    TWidgetDialog::TWidgetDialog(TWindow* parent, TModule* module)
79:        : TDialog(parent, "WWWW", module)
80:    {
81:        TypeA = new TCheckBox(this, IDC_TYPEA);
82:        GroupA = new TMyGroup(this, IDG_TYPEA);
83:        Etched = new TRadioButton(this, IDR_ETCHED, GroupA);
```

```
84:        Polished = new TRadioButton(this, IDR_POLISHED, GroupA);
85:
86:        TypeB = new TCheckBox(this, IDC_TYPEB);
87:        GroupB = new TMyGroup(this, IDG_TYPEB);
88:        WoodGrain = new TRadioButton(this, IDR_WOODGRAIN, GroupB);
89:        Varnished = new TRadioButton(this, IDR_VARNISHED, GroupB);
90:        Engraved = new TRadioButton(this, IDR_ENGRAVED, GroupB);
91:
92:        TypeC = new TCheckBox(this, IDC_TYPEC);
93:        GroupC = new TMyGroup(this, IDG_TYPEC);
94:        Mediocre = new TRadioButton(this, IDR_MEDIOCRE, GroupC);
95:        Deluxe = new TRadioButton(this, IDR_DELUXE, GroupC);
96:    }
97:
98:    void TWidgetDialog::SetupWindow()
99:    {
100:        TDialog::SetupWindow();     // Initialize the visual element
101:
102:        EnableGroupA(false);
103:        EnableGroupB(false);
104:        EnableGroupC(false);
105:    }
106:
107:    void TWidgetDialog::EnableGroupA(bool enable)
108:    {
109:        if (Etched)
110:            Etched->EnableWindow(enable);
111:        if (Polished)
112:            Polished->EnableWindow(enable);
113:    }
114:
115:    void TWidgetDialog::EnableGroupB(bool enable)
116:    {
117:        if (WoodGrain)
118:            WoodGrain->EnableWindow(enable);
119:        if (Varnished)
120:            Varnished->EnableWindow(enable);
121:        if (Engraved)
122:            Engraved->EnableWindow(enable);
123:    }
124:
125:    void TWidgetDialog::EnableGroupC(bool enable)
126:    {
127:        if (Mediocre)
128:            Mediocre->EnableWindow(enable);
129:        if (Deluxe)
130:            Deluxe->EnableWindow(enable);
131:    }
132:
133:    bool TWidgetDialog::BuildStr( LPSTR str,
134:                                  LPCSTR name,
135:                                  TCheckBox* check,
136:                                  TMyGroup* group )
```

continues

Listing 16.3. continued

```
137:    {
138:        bool rslt = false;
139:        if (str && check && check->GetCheck())
140:            {
141:            rslt = true;
142:            LPCSTR groupname;
143:
144:            str += lstrlen(str);     // point to end of str
145:            sprintf(str, "\n   %s: ", name);
146:            if (group && (NULL != (groupname = group->GetCurCheck())))
147:                strcat(str, groupname);
148:            }
149:        return rslt;
150:    }
151:
152:    void TWidgetDialog::CmDone()
153:    {
154:        char            str[256] = "";
155:        int             sels = 0;
156:
157:        strcpy(str, "You have selected the following:");
158:        sels += BuildStr(str, "Widget A", TypeA, GroupA);
159:        sels += BuildStr(str, "Widget B", TypeB, GroupB);
160:        sels += BuildStr(str, "Widget C", TypeC, GroupC);
161:        if (!sels)
162:            strcat(str, "\n   << No selections >>");
163:        MessageBox(str, "Widget Selection", MB_OK);
164:        SendMessage(WM_CLOSE);
165:    }
166:
167:    void TWidgetDialog::CmCancel()
168:    {
169:        SendMessage(WM_CLOSE);
170:    }
171:
172:    void TWidgetDialog::CmTypeA()
173:    {
174:        if (TypeA)
175:            EnableGroupA(TypeA->GetCheck());
176:        if (GroupA && !GroupA->GetCurCheck() && Etched)
177:            Etched->Check();
178:    }
179:
180:    void TWidgetDialog::CmTypeB()
181:    {
182:        if (TypeB)
183:            EnableGroupB(TypeB->GetCheck());
184:        if (GroupB && !GroupB->GetCurCheck() && WoodGrain)
185:            WoodGrain->Check();
186:    }
187:
188:    void TWidgetDialog::CmTypeC()
189:    {
190:        if (TypeC)
```

```
191:         EnableGroupC(TypeC->GetCheck());
192:     if (GroupC && !GroupC->GetCurCheck() && Mediocre)
193:         Mediocre->Check();
194: }
195:
196: class TWidgetApp : public TApplication
197: {
198: public:
199:     TWidgetApp() : TApplication()
200:         { nCmdShow = SW_SHOWMAXIMIZED; }
201:
202:     void InitMainWindow()
203:     {
204:         SetMainWindow(new TFrameWindow(  0,
205:                 "World-Wide Widget Weilders",
206:                 new TWidgetDialog ));
207:     }
208: };
209:
210: int OwlMain(int, char *[])
211: {
212:     return TWidgetApp().Run();
213: }
```

Figure 16.1 shows a sample session with the WIDGETS.EXE program.

Figure 16.1.
A sample session with program WIDGETS.EXE.

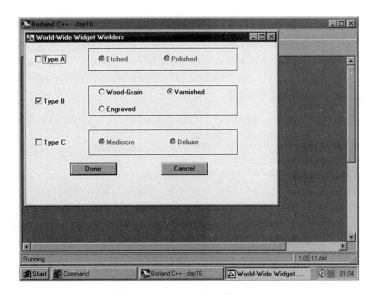

The program starts off on line 14 of Listing 16.3 by declaring a descendant of TGroupBox called TMyGroup. The purpose of this is to keep track of the selections made by the controls contained within it. The class initializes its cur data member to -1 in the constructor on line 20. This signifies that no control has yet been selected inside the group. This value is changed in the overridden `SelectionChanged` member function on line 26. This function, as described earlier, is called whenever a control inside the group is selected. This version of the function simply passes the single parameter along to the parent's version of the function, while assigning the value of that parameter to the `cur` data member. Finally, the `TMyGroup` class defines the `GetCurCheck` member function starting on line 32. This function uses the parent window's `ChildWithId` function to obtain a `TWindow` pointer to the control with the ID recorded in `cur`. If a control was found, then its `Title` data member is returned.

The main dialog `TWidgetDialog` then is declared, starting on line 38. As usual, there is a constructor and a `SetupWindow` member function. The constructor creates all the various controls that are to appear on the screen, starting on line 78: three check boxes, each with a group next to it, and then between two and three radio buttons inside that group. The `SetupWindow` member function that starts on line 98, after calling its parent's version of the function, makes calls to three functions to initially disable the various groups of radio buttons.

Next are the helper functions `EnableGroupA`, `EnableGroupB`, and `EnableGroupC` on lines 107 through 131. These are used to enable and disable whole groups of controls via `TDialog`'s `EnableWindow` member function. They each take a single `bool`-typed `enable` parameter that determines whether the controls are to be enabled or disabled. This parameter is passed directly on to the individual control's `EnableWindow` function.

The two functions `CmDone` and `CmCancel` on lines 152 through 170 come next. They respond to the two buttons Done and Cancel, respectively. In both cases, they send the `WM_CLOSE` message to the main window in order to shut the application down, but the `CmDone` function first creates and displays a message box informing the user of the selections made. It builds this string by doing the following:

1. It fills in the `str` variable on line 157 with an initial string, letting the user know what information follows.

2. The `BuildStr` member function (discussed next) is called for each of the three check boxes and group boxes on lines 158 through 160. The return values of these calls are added to the `sels` variable, and `BuildStr` modifies `str`.

3. After filling up the string with results of the user's selections, the `sels` variable is checked. If it's still `0`, then nothing was selected, and the `str` variable is filled to reflect that on lines 161 and 162. This bit of code works because `true` is defined to be `1` and `false` to be `0`. So, when the `bool` return values from multiple calls to `BuildStr` are added together in `sels`, you're checking to see if any of the return values were `true` without actually caring about which one.

4. The str variable is then sent to the MessageBox function on line 163 for display to the user.

5. Finally, the WM_CLOSE message is sent to the window via the SendMessage function on line 164 to effectively terminate the window and, thus, the program.

The BuildStr member function, starting on line 133, works by taking a destination string in its str parameter, the name of the check box to be reported to the user in the name parameter, and the pointers to the check-box and group controls in the check and group parameters, respectively. The function does the following things:

☐ First, it checks on line 139 to make sure it received valid str and check parameters. It's always a good idea to check parameters before trying to use them to help prevent unwanted bugs in the program. In the same statement, it also calls check's GetCheck function. If that returns true, then the check box has been checked, and you need to start filling in the str parameter.

☐ In order to keep from overwriting the previous contents of the str parameter, str is made to point at its end by adding the value obtained from the lstrlen function on line 144.

☐ The name of the check box is printed into the str, along with some formatting characters on line 145.

☐ If you have a valid group parameter and you are able to get the title of its selected radio button, then that title is concatenated to the str parameter on line 147.

☐ Finally, the result of whether anything was actually added to str is returned on line 149.

The last functions of interest are the CmTypeA, CmTypeB, and CmTypeC member functions on lines 172 through 194. These each respond, in turn, to the Type A, Type B, and Type C check boxes, respectively. In each one, first the appropriate EnableGroupX is called with the check box's check state to either enable or disable the appropriate group's radio buttons. The function then attempts to find out the title of the currently selected radio button. If this value isn't set, then you know that this is the first time the check box has been set, so you initialize the radio buttons by setting the first one with its Check member function.

Summary

Today's lesson discussed the special switch controls: group box, check box, and radio button. You learned the following:

☐ Check-box and radio-button controls act as software switches.

☐ You can set and query the check state for the check-box and radio-button controls.

☐ Notification messages can be sent by these controls to their parent window.

☐ Group controls enclose radio buttons and check boxes.

☐ Switch controls can be selectively manipulated.

Day 17 presents the list-box, and Day 18 presents the scroll-bar and combo-box controls. These controls are value selectors because they enable you to select from a list or range of values.

Q&A

Q The check box has the states BF_UNCHECKED, BF_CHECKED, and BF_GRAYED. What can I use the third state for?

A You can use the BF_GRAYED state as a "don't care" or undetermined state.

Q Does it make any difference if I place check-box controls in a group control?

A Placing check-box controls in a group control affects the logical grouping of such controls as the user sees them. Consequently, this can enhance the interface for the user. However, this makes no difference in how the check box responds to the user; only radio buttons are affected by group boxes.

Workshop

The Workshop provides quiz questions to help you solidify your understanding of the material covered and exercises to provide you with experience in using what you've learned. Try to understand the quiz and exercise answers before continuing on to the next day's lesson. Answers are provided in Appendix A.

Quiz

1. True or false? A check box can replace any two radio buttons in a group control.
2. True or false? You should use radio buttons in a group control when you have three or more options.
3. True or false? A set of check boxes parallels the bits in a byte or word.
4. True or false? Radio buttons, in a group control, are mutually nonexclusive.

Exercise

Expand on program WIDGETS.CPP by adding more widget types and more design types for each widget.

List-Box Controls

List-box controls are input tools that conveniently provide you with items from which to choose. This feature makes list-box controls popular because it absolves you from remembering the list members—especially when computer programs expect exact spelling. Experience with DOS programs has shown that the various DOS utilities displaying lists of files and directories are far easier and friendlier to use than their counterparts that assume the user knows all the names of the files and directories. Using list-box controls gradually has become a routine method for retrieving information. Today's lesson discusses the single-selection and multiple-selection list boxes. You will learn about the following topics:

☐ The list-box control

☐ Handling single-selection list boxes

☐ Handling multiple-selection list boxes

The List-Box Control

List boxes are typically framed and include a vertical scroll bar. When you select an item by clicking it, the selection is highlighted. Microsoft suggests the following guidelines for making a selection:

☐ Use a single mouse click to select a new or an additional item. A separate button control retrieves the selected item.

☐ Use a double-click as a shortcut for selecting an item and retrieving it.

NEW☛
TERM
The *list box* is an input control that permits the application user to select from a list of items.

A list-box control supports multiple selections only if you specify the multiple-selection style when you create the control. Making multiple selections is convenient when you want to process the selected items in a similar manner. For example, selecting multiple files for deletion speeds up the process and reduces the effort you have to make.

The *TListBox* Class

The Borland ObjectWindows Library offers the TListBox class, a descendant of TControl, to implement list-box controls. The TListBox class has a set of member functions that enable you to easily manipulate and query both the contents of the list box and the selected item. As with many other classes in OWL, the class TListBox uses a default constructor to create list-box instances.

The *TListBox* Constructor

Syntax

The declarations of the TListBox constructors are

```
TListBox(TWindow* parent,
         int      id,
         int      x,
         int      y,
         int      w,
         int      h,
         TModule* module = 0 );
TListBox(TWindow* parent, int resourceId, TModule* module = 0);
```

Notice that the TListBox class constructors look very much like the other controls descended from TControl (such as TEdit, TButton, and so on). You specify the control's parent window, its control ID, and its dimensions within that window, or you specify its ID in the dialog box as loaded from a resource file.

17

Example

```
TListBox* pFiles = new TListBox(this, IDL_FILES, 10, 10, 75, 250);
TListBox* pFolders = new TListBox(this, IDL_FOLDERS);
```

Along with the regular WS_*XXX* styles, the list box makes use of the special LBS_*XXX* styles (see Table 17.1). The TListBox class, by default, sets the LBS_STANDARD style. This is equivalent to the WS_BORDER, WS_VSCROLL, LBS_SORT, and LBS_NOTIFY styles. You can remove the LBS_SORT style from the list-box controls to maintain a list of items that is not automatically sorted. Such a list enables you to maintain items in a chronological fashion. You also can use this type of list to maintain the items sorted in descending order (you are responsible for maintaining the list items in that order). Removing the WS_VSCROLL style gives you a list box without the vertical scroll bar. The next section presents a demonstration program that uses this type of list box to implement the synchronized scrolling of multiple list boxes.

Table 17.1. List-box control styles.

Style	Meaning
LBS_DISABLENOSCROLL	Specifies that the list box is to always have a scroll bar that is gray when there is nothing to scroll. Normally, the scroll bar disappears when not needed.
LBS_EXTENDEDSEL	Allows the extension of multiple selections in the list box by using the Shift or Ctrl keys. Using the Shift key selects multiple objects that must be next to each other, and the Ctrl key selects noncontiguous items (they don't need to be next to each other).

continues

Table 17.1. continued

Style	Meaning
LBS_HASSTRINGS	Used in owner-drawn list boxes to have the control maintain a copy of the strings added.
LBS_MULTICOLUMN	Designates a multicolumn list box that scrolls horizontally.
LBS_MULTIPLESEL	Supports multiple selections in a list box.
LBS_NOINTEGRALHEIGHT	Allows showing parts of an item if it doesn't fit within the displayed portion of the list box.
LBS_NOREDRAW	Prevents the list box from being updated when the selection is changed. (You can use the SetRedraw member function to change this at will.)
LBS_NOSEL	Specifies that the list box contains items that can be viewed but not selected (Win32 only).
LBS_NOTIFY	Notifies the parent window when you click or double-click in the list box.
LBS_OWNERDRAWFIXED	Used to specify an owner-drawn list box (a list box for which the application is responsible for drawing, instead of the automatic Windows functions). Specifies that the list box items all will be the same height.
LBS_OWNERDRAWVARIABLE	Specifies an owner-drawn list box that contains items of differing heights.
LBS_SORT	Specifies that the items inserted in the list box be automatically sorted in ascending alphanumeric order.
LBS_STANDARD	Sets the WS_BORDER, WS_VSCROLL, LBS_SORT, and LBS_NOTIFY styles.
LBS_USETABSTOPS	Allows the tab character to be expanded within the list-box control.
LBS_WANTKEYBOARDINPUT	Permits the list-box owner to receive WM_VKEYTOITEM or WM_CHARTOITEM messages when a key is pressed while the list box has the focus (allows the application to manipulate the items in the list box).

The TListBox class enables you to refer to the items in a list box by index. The index of the first item is 0. The TListBox class offers the following member functions to set and query ordinary and selected list members:

☐ The AddString member function adds a string to the list box.

☐ The DeleteString member function removes a list member from a specified position.

☐ The parameterless ClearList member function clears the list of strings in the list-box control in one swoop. This function serves to reset the contents of a list box before building up a new list.

☐ The FindExactString and FindString member functions perform case-insensitive searches for items in the list box. The first searches the list box for an exact match to a string, whereas the second searches for a list-box entry that begins with a string.

☐ The parameterless GetCount member function returns the number of items in the list box. The function returns a negative number if there is an error.

☐ The parameterless GetSelIndex member function returns the position of the selected item in a single-selection list box. If there is no selected item, the function yields a negative value. This function is aimed at single-selection list boxes only.

☐ The GetSel member function returns the selection state of a list-box item, specified by an index.

☐ The parameterless GetSelCount member function returns the number of selected items in the list box. For single-selection list boxes, the number will be either 0 or 1.

☐ The GetSelIndexes member function returns the number and positions of the selected items in a multiple-selection list box.

☐ The GetString member function obtains an item in a list box by specifying its index.

☐ The GetStringLen member function returns the length of a list item specified by its position in the list.

☐ The GetTopIndex member function returns the index of the first visible list-box item.

☐ The InsertString member function inserts a string in a list box.

☐ The SetSelString member function selects a list-box item that matches a search string.

☐ The SetSelItemRange member function enables you to select a range of items in one call.

☐ The SetSelIndex member function chooses a list item as the new selection in a single-selection list box.

☐ The SetSel member function makes or clears a selection in a multiple-selection list box.

☐ The SetTopIndex member function selects the list-box entry that becomes the first visible item in the list-box control.

☐ The DirectoryList member function is a special member function that enables you to automatically insert filenames in a list box.

> **Note:** Many of the TListBox functions return either LB_ERR or LB_ERRSPACE. Note that both of these values are negative, so just checking a return value to see if it's less than 0 is often enough.

The *AddString* Function

The declaration of the AddString member function is

```
int AddString(const char far* str);
```

The str parameter is the pointer to the added string. The function returns the position of the added string in the control. If there is any error in adding the string, the function yields an LB_ERR or LB_ERRSPACE value (out-of-memory error). If the LBS_SORT style is set, then the string is inserted so that the list order is maintained. If the LBS_SORT style is not set, then the added string is inserted at the end of the list.

Example

```
pList->AddString("MS-DOS");
```

The *DeleteString* Function

The declaration of the DeleteString member function is

```
int DeleteString(int index);
```

The index parameter specifies the position of the item to delete. The function returns the number of remaining list members. If errors occur, then DeleteString yields the value LB_ERR.

Example

```
pList->DeleteString(0); //Deletes item 0
```

The *FindExactString* and *FindString* Functions

The declarations of the FindExactString and FindString functions are

```
int FindExactString(const char far* str, int searchIndex) const;
int FindString(const char far* str, int searchIndex) const;
```

In both cases, the searchIndex parameter specifies the index of the first list-box member to be searched, and the str parameter is the pointer to the searched string. The functions search the entire list, beginning with position searchIndex and resuming at the beginning of the list, if needed. The search stops when either a list member matches the search string or the entire list is searched. Passing an argument of 1 to searchIndex forces the functions to start searching from the beginning. The functions return the position of the matching list item, or they yield the LB_ERR value if no match is found or when an error occurs.

The difference between the two functions is that although FindExactString looks for an exact match of the parameter str to an entry in the list box, FindString will stop as soon as it finds an entry that begins with str.

Example

```
int msdos = pList->FindString("MS-DOS", -1);
int anti = pList->FindString("anti", -1);
```

> **Note**: The interesting search method used by FindExactString and FindString enables you to speed up the search by specifying a position that comes closely before the most likely location for a match. For example, if you happen to know where the first item starting with an s is located, and you're searching for something that begins with the same character, you can specify that initial index in an attempt to speed up the search.
>
> The beauty of this method is that if you specify a position that actually is beyond that of the string you seek, you cannot miss finding that string because the function resumes searching at the beginning of the list. Another benefit of FindExactString and FindString is their capability to find duplicate strings.

The *GetSel* Function

The declaration of the function GetSel is

```
bool GetSel(int index) const;
```

The index parameter specifies the index of the queried list-box item. The function returns a true if the item is selected, false if the item is not selected.

Example

```
bool isSel = pList->GetSel(0); //saves state of item 0
```

The *GetSelIndexes* Function

The declaration of the GetSelIndexes function is

```
int GetSelIndexes(int* indexes, int maxCount) const;
```

471

The maxCount parameter specifies the size of the array accessed by the indexes pointer. The indexes parameter is the pointer to an array of integers that stores the positions of the selected items. The function returns the current number of selections. The function yields LB_ERR with single-selection list boxes.

Example

```
int num_items = pList->GetSelCount();
int* items = new int[num_items];
pList->GetSelIndexes(items, num_items);
```

Syntax

The *GetString* Function

The declaration for the GetString function is

```
int GetString(char far* str, int index) const;
```

The index parameter specifies the index of the retrieved item. The first list-box item has the index of 0. The str parameter points to a buffer that receives the retrieved item.

You are responsible for ensuring that the buffer has enough space for the retrieved item (for example, using GetStringLen when allocating a receiving buffer). The function returns the number of characters retrieved from the list box.

Example

```
char* s = 0;
int size = pList->GetStringLen(ix);
if (size > 0)
    {
    s = new char[size + 1];
    pList->GetString(s, ix);
    }
```

Syntax

The *GetStringLen* Function

The declaration of the GetStringLen function is

```
int GetStringLen(int index) const;
```

The parameter index specifies the index of the target list item. The function returns the length of the target item, or the LB_ERR result if an error occurs.

Example

See the example for GetString.

The *InsertString* Function

Syntax

The declaration of the InsertString function is

```
int InsertString(const char far* str, int index);
```

The index parameter specifies the requested insertion position. The str parameter is the pointer to the inserted string. The function returns the actual insertion position, or it yields the LB_ERR value if an error occurs. If the argument for index is 1, then the string is simply appended to the end of the list.

Example

```
pList->InsertString("Windows", 0);
```

Warning: In general, do not use the InsertString member function with list boxes that have the LBS_SORT style set. Using this function with ordered list boxes will most likely corrupt the sort order of the list.

The *SetSelString* Function

Syntax

The declaration of the SetSelString function is

```
int SetSelString(const char far* str, int searchIndex);
```

The parameters and search mechanism of SetSelString are identical to those of FindString. The difference is that SetSelString selects the list-box item that matches the string accessed by parameter str.

Example

```
int ix = pList->SetSelString("MS-DOS", -1);
```

The *SetSelItemRange* Function

Syntax

The declaration of the SetSelItemRange function is

```
int SetSelItemRange(bool select, int first, int last);
```

The select parameter acts as a switch used to select or deselect the range of list-box items defined by parameters of first and last. The number returned is the number of items actually selected between and including first and last.

Example

```
pList->SetSelItemRange(true, 0, 10);
```

The *SetSelIndex* Function

The declaration of the SetSelIndex function is

```
int SetSelIndex(int index);
```

The parameter index specifies the position of the new selection. To clear a list box from any selection, pass a 1 argument as the select parameter. The function returns LB_ERR if an error occurs. This is used for single-selection list boxes.

Example

```
pList-SetSelIndex(-1);      // clear current selection
```

The *SetSel* Function

The declaration of the SetSel function is

```
int SetSel(int index, bool select);
```

The index parameter specifies the list-box item to either select, if select is true, or deselect, if select is false. The function returns LB_ERR if an error occurs. The function result serves only to flag a selection/deselection error. You can use the SetSel function to toggle the selection of multiple items in a multiple-selection list box, one at a time.

Example

```
pList->SetSel(0, true);      // select first item in list
```

The *SetTopIndex* Function

The declaration of the function SetTopIndex is

```
int SetTopIndex(int index);
```

The index parameter specifies the index of the list-box item that becomes the first visible item. This selection scrolls the list box unless the item index is already the first visible item. The function returns LB_ERR if an error occurs. Otherwise, the result is meaningless.

Example

```
pList->SetTopIndex(10);
```

Syntax

The *DirectoryList* Function

The declaration of the DirectoryList function is

```
int DirectoryList(uint attrs, const char far* fileSpec);
```

The attrs parameter specifies the combination of attributes, as shown in Table 17.2. The table also shows the equivalent file-attribute constants that are declared in the DOS.H header file. The fileSpec parameter is the pointer to the filename specification, such as *.*, L*.EXE, or A???.CPP. The return value is the number of files added to the list box.

Example

```
int numFiles = pList->DirectoryList(DDL_ARCHIVE, "CTL*.CPP");
```

17

Table 17.2. Attributes for the attrs parameter in the TListbox::DirectoryList member function.

Attribute Value	Equivalent Constant in DOS.H Header File	Meaning
DDL_ARCHIVE	FA_ARCH or _A_ARCH	File has the archive bit set.
DDL_DIRECTORY	FA_DIREC or _A_SUBDIR	Name indicated by parameter fileSpec also supplies the directory.
DDL_DRIVES		Includes all the drives that match the filename supplied by fileSpec.
DDL_EXCLUSIVE		Exclusive flag (prevents normal files from being included with specified files).
DDL_HIDDEN	FA_HIDDEN or _A_HIDDEN	File is hidden.
DDL_POSTMSGS		Posts messages to the application instead of sending them directly to the list box.
DDL_READONLY	FA_RDONLY or _A_RDONLY	File is read only.
DDL_READWRITE	FA_NORMAL or _A_NORMAL	File can be used for input and output.
DDL_SYSTEM	FA_SYSTEM or _A_SYSTEM	File is system file.

Note that in the preceding table, there are two constants defined in the DOS.H header file for each item. The first is the value defined by Borland; the second is the one defined for the Microsoft compiler. Borland defines these to help with compatibility, making programs more easily portable between the two compilers.

Responding to List-Box Notification Messages

The list-box control emits various types of messages, as shown in Table 17.3. The table also shows the message-mapping macros that are associated with the various command and notification messages. Each type of command or notification message requires a separate member function declared in the control's parent window class.

Table 17.3. List-box notification messages.

Message	Macro	Meaning
WM_COMMAND	EV_COMMAND	The Windows command message through which all the LBN_*xxx* subcommands are passed; they're specified in the wParam parameter.
LBN_DBLCLK	EV_LBN_DBLCLK	A list item is selected with a mouse double-click.
LBN_ERRSPACE	EV_LBN_ERRSPACE	The list box cannot allocate more dynamic memory to accommodate new list items.
LBN_KILLFOCUS	EV_LBN_KILLFOCUS	The list box has lost focus.
LBN_SELCHANGE	EV_LBN_SELCHANGE	A list item is selected with a mouse click.
LBN_SETFOCUS	EV_LBN_SETFOCUS	The list box has gained focus.

The List-Manipulation Tester

The next program demonstrates how to set and query normal and selected strings, and how to set and query the current selection in a single-selection list box—a simple list-manipulation tester. This program focuses on illustrating how to use most of the TListBox member functions presented earlier in this section. The program contains the following controls that offer the indicated test features:

☐ A list-box control

☐ A String Box edit control that enables you to type in and retrieve a list member

☐ An Index Box edit control that enables you to key in and retrieve the position of the current selection

☐ An Add String pushbutton to add the contents of the String Box to the list box (the program does not enable you to add duplicate names; if you attempt to do so, the program displays a warning message)

☐ A Delete String pushbutton to delete the current selection in the list box (the program automatically selects another list member)

☐ The Get Selected String pushbutton that copies the current list selection to the String Box

☐ The Set Selected String pushbutton that overwrites the current selection with the string in the String Box

☐ The Get Selected Index pushbutton that writes the position of the current selection in the Index Box

☐ The Set Selected Index pushbutton that uses the integer value in the Index Box as the position of the new list-box selection

☐ The Get String button that copies the string whose position appears in the Index Box into the String Box

☐ The Exit pushbutton

These controls exercise various aspects of manipulating a sorted list box and its members. The program is coded to retain a current selection and to prevent the insertion of duplicate names.

Listings 17.1, 17.2, and 17.3 show the header file CTLLST.H, the script for the CTLLST.RC resource file, and the source code for the CTLLST.CPP program file, respectively. The resource file contains a single-item menu resource.

Compile and run the program. When the program starts running, it places a set of names in the list box. Experiment with the various pushbutton controls to add, delete, and obtain strings. The program is straightforward and easy to run.

 Listing 17.1. Source code for the CTLLST.H header file.

```
 1: #define IDL_STRINGS      101
 2: #define IDE_STRING       102
 3: #define IDE_INDEX        103
 4: #define IDB_ADD          104
 5: #define IDB_DEL          105
 6: #define IDB_GETSELSTR    106
 7: #define IDB_SETSELSTR    107
 8: #define IDB_GETSELIDX    108
 9: #define IDB_SETSELIDX    109
10: #define IDB_GETSTR       110
11: #define IDB_EXIT         111
```

Type

Listing 17.2. Script for the CTLLST.RC resource file.

```
 1:  #include <windows.h>
 2:  #include <owl\window.rh>
 3:  #include "ctllst.h"
 4:
 5:  EXITMENU MENU LOADONCALL MOVEABLE PURE DISCARDABLE
 6:  BEGIN
 7:    MENUITEM "E&xit", CM_EXIT
 8:  END
 9:
10:  CTLLST DIALOG 7, 18, 288, 209
11:  STYLE DS_MODALFRAME | WS_POPUP | WS_VISIBLE | WS_CAPTION | WS_SYSMENU
12:  CAPTION "Simple List Box Tester Application"
13:  FONT 8, "MS Sans Serif"
14:    {
15:    LTEXT "List Box", -1, 10, 20, 60, 8
16:    LISTBOX IDL_STRINGS, 10, 31, 74, 137, LBS_STANDARD
17:    LTEXT "String Box", -1, 100, 20, 60, 8
18:    EDITTEXT IDE_STRING, 100, 31, 180, 12
19:    LTEXT "Index Box", -1, 100, 63, 62, 8
20:    EDITTEXT IDE_INDEX, 100, 74, 180, 12
21:    PUSHBUTTON "Add String", IDB_ADD, 100, 111, 80, 14
22:    PUSHBUTTON "Delete String", IDB_DEL, 100, 136, 80, 14
23:    PUSHBUTTON "Get Selected String", IDB_GETSELSTR, 100, 161, 80, 14
24:    PUSHBUTTON "Set Selected String", IDB_SETSELSTR, 100, 186, 80, 14
25:    PUSHBUTTON "Get Selected Index", IDB_GETSELIDX, 200, 111, 80, 14
26:    PUSHBUTTON "Set Selected Index", IDB_SETSELIDX, 200, 136, 80, 14
27:    PUSHBUTTON "Get String by Index", IDB_GETSTR, 200, 161, 80, 14
28:    PUSHBUTTON "Exit", IDB_EXIT, 200, 186, 80, 14
29:  }
```

Type

Listing 17.3. Source code for the CTLLST.CPP program file.

```
 1:  #include <stdio.h>
 2:  #include <owl\applicat.h>
 3:  #include <owl\button.h>
 4:  #include <owl\dialog.h>
 5:  #include <owl\edit.h>
 6:  #include <owl\framewin.h>
 7:  #include <owl\listbox.h>
 8:  #include <owl\static.h>
 9:  #include <owl\window.h>
10:  #include <owl\window.rh>
11:
12:  #include "ctllst.h"
13:
14:  class TMyDialog : public TDialog
15:  {
16:  public:
17:    TMyDialog(TWindow* parent = 0, TModule* module = 0);
18:    virtual ~TMyDialog();
19:
```

```
20:    protected:
21:        virtual void SetupWindow();
22:
23:        void CbAdd();
24:        void CbDel();
25:        void CbGetSelStr();
26:        void CbSetSelStr();
27:        void CbGetSelIdx();
28:        void CbSetSelIdx();
29:        void CbGetStr();
30:        void CmExit();
31:
32:    private:
33:        TListBox *list;
34:        TEdit *strbox, *idxbox;
35:
36:        DECLARE_RESPONSE_TABLE(TMyDialog);
37:    };
38:    DEFINE_RESPONSE_TABLE1(TMyDialog, TDialog)
39:        EV_COMMAND(CM_EXIT, CmExit),
40:        EV_BN_CLICKED(IDB_ADD, CbAdd),
41:        EV_BN_CLICKED(IDB_DEL, CbDel),
42:        EV_BN_CLICKED(IDB_GETSELSTR, CbGetSelStr),
43:        EV_BN_CLICKED(IDB_SETSELSTR, CbSetSelStr),
44:        EV_BN_CLICKED(IDB_GETSELIDX, CbGetSelIdx),
45:        EV_BN_CLICKED(IDB_SETSELIDX, CbSetSelIdx),
46:        EV_BN_CLICKED(IDB_GETSTR, CbGetStr),
47:        EV_BN_CLICKED(IDB_EXIT, CmExit),
48:    END_RESPONSE_TABLE;
49:
50:    TMyDialog::TMyDialog(TWindow* parent, TModule* module)
51:        : TDialog(parent, "CTLLST", module)
52:    {
53:        list = new TListBox(this, IDL_STRINGS);
54:        strbox = new TEdit(this, IDE_STRING);
55:        idxbox = new TEdit(this, IDE_INDEX);
56:    }
57:
58:    TMyDialog::~TMyDialog()
59:    {
60:    }
61:
62:    void TMyDialog::SetupWindow()
63:    {
64:        TDialog::SetupWindow();    // Initialize the visual element
65:
66:        // Initialize the list box with some data and
67:        // select the second item
68:        //
69:        if (list)
70:            {
71:            list->AddString("Keith");
72:            list->AddString("Kevin");
73:            list->AddString("Ingrid");
```

continues

Listing 17.3. continued

```
74:             list->AddString("Roger");
75:             list->AddString("Rick");
76:             list->AddString("Beth");
77:             list->AddString("Kate");
78:             list->AddString("James");
79:             list->SetSelIndex(1);
80:             }
81:     }
82:
83:     void TMyDialog::CbAdd()
84:     {
85:         if (strbox && list)
86:             {
87:             char* str;
88:             int size = strbox->GetWindowTextLength() + 1;
89:             if ((size > 1) && (0 != (str = new char[size])))
90:                 {
91:                 strbox->GetWindowText(str, size);
92:                 if (list->FindExactString(str, -1) >= 0)
93:                     MessageBox("Cannot add duplicate names", "Bad Data");
94:                 else
95:                     {
96:                     int ix = list->AddString(str);
97:                     list->SetSelIndex(ix);
98:                     }
99:                 delete str;
100:                }
101:            }
102:    }
103:
104:    void TMyDialog::CbDel()
105:    {
106:        if (list)
107:            {
108:            int ix = list->GetSelIndex();
109:            list->DeleteString(ix);
110:            list->SetSelIndex((ix > 0) ? (ix - 1) : 0);
111:            }
112:    }
113:
114:    void TMyDialog::CbGetSelStr()
115:    {
116:        if (list && strbox)
117:            {
118:            char* str;
119:            int ix = list->GetSelIndex();
120:            if (ix >= 0)
121:                {
122:                if (0 != (str = new char[list->GetStringLen(ix) + 1]))
123:                    {
124:                    list->GetString(str, ix);
125:                    strbox->SetWindowText(str);
126:                    delete str;
127:                    }
```

```
128:              }
129:          }
130:  }
131:
132:  void TMyDialog::CbSetSelStr()
133:  {
134:      if (list && strbox)
135:          {
136:          int ix = list->GetSelIndex();
137:
138:          char* str;
139:          int size = strbox->GetWindowTextLength() + 1;
140:          if ((size > 1) && (0 != (str = new char[size])))
141:              {
142:              strbox->GetWindowText(str, size);
143:              if (list->FindExactString(str, -1) >= 0)
144:                  MessageBox("Cannot add duplicate names", "Bad Data");
145:              else
146:                  {
147:                  list->DeleteString(ix);
148:                  ix = list->AddString(str);
149:                  list->SetSelIndex(ix);
150:                  }
151:              delete str;
152:              }
153:          }
154:  }
155:
156:  void TMyDialog::CbGetSelIdx()
157:  {
158:      if (list && idxbox)
159:          {
160:          char str[15];
161:          sprintf(str, "%d", list->GetSelIndex());
162:          idxbox->SetWindowText(str);
163:          }
164:  }
165:
166:  void TMyDialog::CbSetSelIdx()
167:  {
168:      if (list && idxbox)
169:          {
170:          char* str;
171:          int size = idxbox->GetWindowTextLength() + 1;
172:          if ((size > 1) && (0 != (str = new char[size])))
173:              {
174:              idxbox->GetWindowText(str, size);
175:              list->SetSelIndex(atoi(str));
176:              delete str;
177:              }
178:          }
179:  }
180:
181:  void TMyDialog::CbGetStr()
```

continues

481

Listing 17.3. continued

```
182:    {
183:        if (list && idxbox && strbox)
184:            {
185:            char* str;
186:            int ix = -1;
187:            int size = idxbox->GetWindowTextLength() + 1;
188:            if ((size > 1) && (0 != (str = new char[size])))
189:                {
190:                idxbox->GetWindowText(str, size);
191:                ix = atoi(str);
192:                delete str;
193:                }
194:            if ((ix >= 0) && (0 != (str = new char[list->GetStringLen(ix) + 1])))
195:                {
196:                list->GetString(str, ix);
197:                strbox->SetWindowText(str);
198:                delete str;
199:                }
200:            }
201:    }
202:
203:    void TMyDialog::CmExit()
204:    {
205:        SendMessage(WM_CLOSE);
206:    }
207:
208:    class TListApp : public TApplication
209:    {
210:    public:
211:        TListApp() : TApplication()
212:            { nCmdShow = SW_SHOWMAXIMIZED; }
213:
214:        void InitMainWindow()
215:            {
216:            SetMainWindow(new TFrameWindow(  0,
217:                    "Simple List Box Tester Application",
218:                    new TMyDialog ));
219:            GetMainWindow()->AssignMenu("EXITMENU");
220:            }
221:    };
222:
223:    int OwlMain(int, char *[])
224:    {
225:      return TListApp().Run();
226:    }
```

Figure 17.1 shows a sample session with the CTLLST.EXE application.

Figure 17.1.

A sample session with the CTLLST.EXE application.

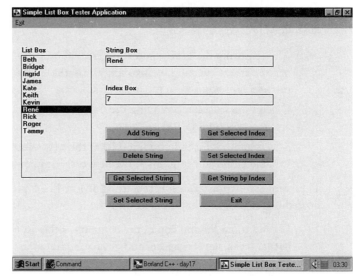

The program in Listing 17.3 declares the dialog class TMyDialog, starting on line 14, which contains a number of data members that are pointers to the controls owned by the main dialog. The class also declares a SetupWindow member function and several member functions that respond to the notification messages emitted by the various pushbutton controls.

The TMyDialog constructor, starting on line 50, performs the creation of interface elements that can connect with the resources loaded in the dialog box. Then the SetupWindow member function initializes the list box, starting on line 62.

The member function CbAdd, starting on line 83, adds the string of the String Box in the list-box control. The function performs the following tasks:

☐ Ensures that the list box and edit box were created properly on line 85

☐ If the String Box edit control isn't empty, the function creates room for copying the contents of the edit control and then places those contents in the str variable on lines 87 through 91

☐ Verifies that the added string does not already exist in the list box, using the FindExactString function on line 92 to detect an attempt to add duplicate strings, and complains with a message box on line 93 if a duplicate is found

☐ Adds the string in str to the list box and assigns the position of the string to the local variable ix using the AddString function on line 96

☐ Makes the added string the current selection by invoking the SetSelIndex function with the argument ix on line 97

The member function `CbDel`, starting on line 104, deletes the current selection by carrying out the following tasks:

☐ After ensuring the `list` pointer was created properly on line 106, obtains the position of the current selection by invoking the `GetSelIndex` function on line 108, and stores the selection position in the local variable `ix`

☐ Deletes the selection by calling the `DeleteString` function and supplying it the argument `ix` on line 109

☐ Selects another list item on line 110 as the new selection at position `ix` - `1` (if the variable `ix` already contains `0`, the new first list item becomes the new selection)

The member function `CbGetSelStr` starting on line 114 copies the current selection to the String Box edit control. The function performs the following tasks:

☐ Creates room for and copies the contents of the list box's current selection using the `GetSelIndex`, `GetStringLen`, and `GetString` functions on lines 118 through 124

☐ Overwrites the contents of the String Box with the characters retrieved from the list box on line 125

The member function `CbSetSelStr`, starting on line 132, overwrites the current selection with the string in the String Box edit control. Because the list maintains sorted items, the replacement string likely has a position different from the original selection. The function performs the following tasks:

☐ Obtains the position of the current selection, using the `GetSelIndex` function, and assigns that value to the local variable `ix` on line 136

☐ Copies the text in the String Box to the newly allocated `str` variable on line 142

☐ Verifies that the string in `str` does not already exist in the list box, using the `FindExactString` function on line 143, displaying a message box if the string already exists on line 144

☐ If the string is new to the list, the function uses the `DeleteString` function to delete the current selection on line 147, uses the `AddString` function to add the string on line 148, and then uses `SetSelIndex` to select the added string on line 149

If the string has a matching list item, the function displays a message informing you that you cannot add duplicate strings in the list box. This warning also appears if you attempt to overwrite the current selection with the same string.

The member function `CbGetSelIdx`, starting on line 156, writes the position of the current selection to the Index Box edit box on line 162. The function uses the `GetSelIndex` function to obtain the sought position on line 161.

The member function CbSetSelIdx, starting on line 166, reads the value in the Index Box edit control and uses that value to set the new current selection. The function uses the SetSelIndex function to make the new selection on line 175.

The member function CbGetStr, starting on line 181, enables you to retrieve the list item whose position appears in the Index Box edit control. The function performs the following tasks:

☐ Copies the characters of the Index Box to an allocated string in the str data member on line 190

☐ Converts the string in str to the int-typed local variable ix on line 191

☐ Copies the characters of the list item at position ix to a reallocated str on line 196

☐ Writes the characters of str to the String Box edit control on line 197

Handling Multiple-Selection Lists

This section demonstrates the use of multiple-selection lists and focuses on getting and setting the selection strings and their indices. There are two modes for making multiple selections in a list box. These modes depend on whether you set the LBS_EXTENDEDSEL style when you create a TListBox instance. Setting this style enables you to quickly extend the range of selected items by holding down the Shift key and clicking the mouse. The disadvantage of this style is that you are committed to selecting blocks of contiguous items in the list box manually (that is, using the mouse or cursor keys). Using the SetSel or SetSelItemRange member functions, you can make your program select noncontiguous items. The user could also use the Ctrl key instead of the Shift key in order to select noncontiguous entries. By contrast, if you do not set the LBS_EXTENDEDSEL style, then you can make dispersed selections easily by clicking the mouse button on the individual items that you want to select. The disadvantage of this selection mode is that you must click every item to select it, including neighboring items. Choose the selection mode that you feel best meets the user-interface requirements for your OWL applications.

The Multiple-Selection List Tester

Figure 17.2 shows a sample session with the XFERLIST.EXE application—a program that demonstrates how to query multiple selections in a list box—and also shows the controls used by that application. Following are the controls used by the test program and the operations they support:

☐ Two multiple-selection list boxes that have the LBS_MULTIPLESEL style selected, but not the LBS_EXTENDEDSEL style

☐ Two pushbuttons, one with the caption <-- and the other with the caption -->, that transfer the selected items of one list box to the other

☐ Static-text controls that label the list boxes

Figure 17.2.

A sample session with the XFERLIST.EXE application.

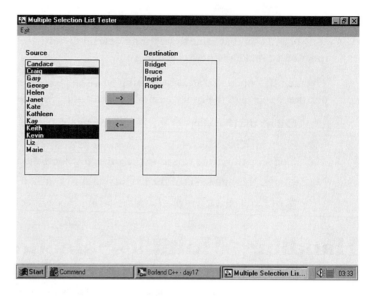

The multiple-selection list tester application basically enables the user to transfer the contents of one list box to the other and then back again. Listings 17.4, 17.5, and 17.6 contain the source code for the XFERLIST.H, XFERLIST.RC, and XFERLIST.CPP files, respectively.

Compile and run the program. The application initializes the list box with many names. Select a few list items in the Source list box and click the --> pushbutton. The selected strings appear in the Destination list box and disappear from the Source list box. Now select a few names in the Destination list box and click the <-- pushbutton. The names move over to the Source list box. When you have finished experimenting with the program, click the Exit menu item.

 Listing 17.4. Source code for the XFERLIST.H header file.

```
1:  #define IDL_SRC    101
2:  #define IDL_DST    102
3:  #define IDB_TOSRC  103
4:  #define IDB_TODST  104
```

 Listing 17.5. Script for the XFERLIST.RC resource file.

```
1:  #include <windows.h>
2:  #include <owl\window.rh>
3:  #include "xferlist.h"
4:
5:  EXITMENU MENU LOADONCALL MOVEABLE PURE DISCARDABLE
6:  BEGIN
7:    MENUITEM "E&xit", CM_EXIT
8:  END
9:
```

```
10: XFERLIST DIALOG 6, 15, 219, 170
11: STYLE DS_MODALFRAME ¦ WS_POPUP ¦ WS_VISIBLE ¦ WS_CAPTION ¦ WS_SYSMENU
12: CAPTION "Multiple Selection List Tester"
13: FONT 8, "MS Sans Serif"
14: {
15: LTEXT "Source", -1, 9, 15, 60, 8
16: LISTBOX IDL_SRC, 9, 27, 78, 130, LBS_STANDARD ¦ LBS_MULTIPLESEL
17: PUSHBUTTON "-->", IDB_TODST, 95, 62, 30, 14
18: PUSHBUTTON "<--", IDB_TOSRC, 95, 92, 30, 14
19: LTEXT "Destination", -1, 135, 15, 60, 8
20: LISTBOX IDL_DST, 135, 27, 78, 130, LBS_STANDARD ¦ LBS_MULTIPLESEL
21: }
```

Type

Listing 17.6. Source code for the XFERLIST.CPP program file.

17

```
1:  #include <owl\applicat.h>
2:  #include <owl\button.h>
3:  #include <owl\dialog.h>
4:  #include <owl\framewin.h>
5:  #include <owl\listbox.h>
6:  #include <owl\static.h>
7:  #include <owl\window.h>
8:  #include <owl\window.rh>
9:
10: #include "xferlist.h"
11:
12: class TMyDialog : public TDialog
13: {
14: public:
15:    TMyDialog(TWindow* parent = 0, TModule* module = 0);
16:    virtual ~TMyDialog();
17:
18: protected:
19:    virtual void SetupWindow();
20:
21:    void CbToDst();
22:    void CbToSrc();
23:    void CmExit();
24:
25: private:
26:    TListBox *src, *dst;
27:
28:    void MoveSels(TListBox* src, TListBox* dst);
29:
30:    DECLARE_RESPONSE_TABLE(TMyDialog);
31: };
32: DEFINE_RESPONSE_TABLE1(TMyDialog, TDialog)
33:    EV_COMMAND(CM_EXIT, CmExit),
34:    EV_BN_CLICKED(IDB_TODST, CbToDst),
35:    EV_BN_CLICKED(IDB_TOSRC, CbToSrc),
36: END_RESPONSE_TABLE;
```

continues

Listing 17.6. continued

```
37:
38:    TMyDialog::TMyDialog(TWindow* parent, TModule* module)
39:        : TDialog(parent, "XFERLIST", module)
40:    {
41:        src = new TListBox(this, IDL_SRC);
42:        dst = new TListBox(this, IDL_DST);
43:    }
44:
45:    TMyDialog::~TMyDialog()
46:    {
47:    }
48:
49:    void TMyDialog::SetupWindow()
50:    {
51:        static char *names[] =
52:            { "Keith", "Bruce", "Kevin", "Bridget", "Kate",
53:              "Kay", "Roger", "Marie", "Kathleen", "Liz",
54:              "Ingrid", "Craig", "George", "Janet", "Gary",
55:              "Helen", "Candace",
56:              NULL };
57:
58:        TWindow::SetupWindow();
59:
60:        if (src)
61:            for (int ix = 0; names[ix]; ++ix)
62:                src->AddString(names[ix]);
63:    }
64:
65:    void TMyDialog::MoveSels(TListBox* src, TListBox* dst)
66:    {
67:        if (src && dst)
68:            {
69:            int *sels, numsels = src->GetSelCount();
70:            if ((numsels > 0) && (0 != (sels = new int[numsels])))
71:                {
72:                int ix;
73:
74:                src->GetSelIndexes(sels, numsels);
75:                for (ix = 0; ix < numsels; ++ix)
76:                    {
77:                    char* str;
78:                    int size = src->GetStringLen(sels[ix]) + 1;
79:                    if ((size > 1) && (0 != (str = new char[size])))
80:                        {
81:                        src->GetString(str, sels[ix]);
82:                        dst->AddString(str);
83:                        delete str;
84:                        }
85:                    }
86:                for (ix = numsels - 1; ix >= 0; --ix)
87:                    src->DeleteString(sels[ix]);
88:
89:                delete sels;
90:                }
```

```
91:          }
92:  }
93:
94:  void TMyDialog::CbToDst()
95:  {
96:      MoveSels(src, dst);
97:  }
98:
99:  void TMyDialog::CbToSrc()
100: {
101:     MoveSels(dst, src);
102: }
103:
104: void TMyDialog::CmExit()
105: {
106:     SendMessage(WM_CLOSE);
107: }
108:
109: class TXferApp : public TApplication
110: {
111: public:
112:     TXferApp() : TApplication()
113:         { nCmdShow = SW_SHOWMAXIMIZED; }
114:
115:     void InitMainWindow()
116:         {
117:         SetMainWindow(new TFrameWindow(  0,
118:                           "Multiple Selection List Tester",
119:                           new TMyDialog ));
120:         GetMainWindow()->AssignMenu("EXITMENU");
121:         }
122: };
123:
124: int OwlMain(int, char *[])
125: {
126:     return TXferApp().Run();
127: }
```

The program in Listing 17.6 works similarly to the other programs presented so far. It declares an application class TXferApp on line 109 and a dialog class TMyDialog on line 12. The dialog class creates a couple of interface controls in its constructor, then does its initialization in the SetupWindow member function.

The TMyDialog dialog class declares two data members, src and dst on line 26, which are pointers to class objects of type TListBox. These are used to access the source and destination list boxes after they are created.

The function MoveSels, starting on line 65, is the main workhorse of the program. It does the following:

☐ It takes two parameters: the source list box src and the destination list box dst.

☐ After making sure it was given valid TListBox pointers, it obtains the number of selections from the source list box on line 69 and creates an array to hold those indices on line 70. It then retrieves those indices and stores them in the newly created sels array on line 74.

☐ The function iterates through the list of selections on lines 75 through 85 and gets a string for each entry with the GetString function on line 80. It then adds this string to the destination list box with the AddString function on line 82.

☐ Finally, the function iterates through the list of selections again, this time backwards, and deletes them from the source list box with the DeleteString function on lines 86 and 87.

Note that when the MoveSels function deletes the selections from the source list box, it does so in reverse order. The reason for this is that, as the function deletes an entry, every item after the now-deleted one in the list box has its index decreased by one. If the function were to delete the strings forwards, then all but the first selection would be incorrect, because the retrieved list becomes out of sync with the list box itself.

The two functions that respond to the buttons, CbToDst on line 94 and CbToSrc on line 99, both call the MoveSels function, and they both pass the same arguments; however, they each pass them in a different order. By doing this, you can use the MoveSels function for both buttons, but have it move the selections between opposite list boxes as the parameters are switched.

Summary

Today's lesson presented the list-box control, which enables an application user to choose from a collection of values. You learned about the following topics:

☐ The single-selection, list-box control provides you with a list of items from which to select. This type of list box enables you to select only one item at a time.

☐ The multiple-selection list box enables you to select multiple items in a list box for collective processing. Setting the LBS_EXTENDEDSEL style when you create the list box enables you to quickly extend the range of selected items by holding down the Shift key and clicking the mouse.

Q&A

Q Can the argument for the fileSpec parameter in function TListBox::DirectoryList contain multiple wildcards, such as "*.CPP *.H"?

A No, the argument list for fileSpec is limited to one filename wildcard.

Q Does OWL support intercepting the messages related to the movement of the thumb box in a list-box control?

A Yes, but the standard ListBox control doesn't have any default notifications for these events. You can intercept the WM_HSCROLL and WM_VSCROLL messages to track the thumb. You'll learn a bit more about scroll bars on Day 18.

Q What is the general approach to implementing a program with two list boxes that scroll simultaneously?

A The general approach is to intercept the WM_HSCROLL and WM_VSCROLL messages in each list box and then adjust the other accordingly. Again, you learn more about handling scroll bars on Day 18.

Q Should I use InsertString in a list box created with the LBS_SORT style?

A No, you shouldn't, because the LBS_SORT style maintains the list-box items in order. Using InsertString corrupts the order in the list box. Instead, use the AddString member function.

Workshop

The Workshop provides quiz questions to help you solidify your understanding of the material covered and exercises to provide you with experience in using what you've learned. Try to understand the quiz and exercise answers before continuing on to the next day's lesson. Answers are provided in Appendix A.

Quiz

1. True or false? The list-box notification message LBN_SETFOCUS is suitable for optional initializing related to selecting a list-box control.

2. True or false? The list-box notification message LBN_KILLFOCUS is suitable for optional validation after you deselect a list-box control.

3. True or false? The list box enables you to detect only the final selection, using the LBN_KILLFOCUS notification.

4. True or false? You should use LBN_SELCHANGE with a special flag to detect mouse double-clicks on a list-box item.

5. True or false? LBS_STANDARD creates a list-box control with unordered items.

Exercise

Modify the XFERLIST program to initialize the source list box with a directory listing, then have it enable and disable the appropriate pushbuttons depending on whether there is anything selected in the corresponding list boxes.

18

Scroll Bars,
Combo Boxes, and
VBX Controls

Day 17 presented list-box controls. Today's lesson presents two somewhat similar controls: the scroll bar and the combo box. The scroll-bar control enables you to select a numeric value quickly, usually in a wide range of values. The combo-box control combines the edit control and the list box, enabling the user to select a value from the list-box component or to enter a new value in the edit-control part.

Today you also will learn about the Visual Basic Controls (VBXs). The VBX interface was designed to provide a standard method of creating custom controls for Visual Basic, allowing third-party vendors to supply interesting, original controls in addition to those supplied by standard Windows. VBXs are wide and varied, and Borland supplies a set of classes to enable the programmer to implement them easily.

You will learn about the following topics:

☐ The scroll-bar control

☐ The combo-box control in its various styles

☐ VBX controls

The Scroll-Bar Control

Windows allows the scroll bar to exist as a separate control as well as to be incorporated in windows, lists, and combo boxes. The scroll-bar control appears and behaves much like the scroll bar of a window. The control has a thumb box that keeps track of the current value; when the user clicks and drags the thumb box, the display can be changed with a fine control. This thumb-box mechanism is supported by the EvVScroll or EvHScroll member functions. In addition, the scroll bar responds to cursor control keys— Home, End, PageUp, and PageDown, for example. This feature is supported by the EvKeyDown member function. The main purpose of the scroll-bar control is to enable you to quickly and efficiently select an integer value in a predefined range of values. Windows, for example, uses scroll bars to fine-tune the color palette, the keyboard rate, and the mouse sensitivity.

The *TScrollBar* Class

The ObjectWindows Library offers the TScrollBar class, a descendant of TControl, as the class that models the scroll-bar controls. The TScrollBar class declares a class constructor and a number of member functions to set and query the control's current position and range of values.

The class constructors appear similar to all the other classes derived from TControl.

The *TScrollBar* Constructor

The declaration of the TScrollBar constructor is

```
TScrollBar( TWindow* parent,
            int id,
            int x,
            int y,
            int w,
            int h,
            bool isHScrollBar,
            TModule* module = 0 );
TScrollBar(TWindow* parent, int resourceId, TModule* module = 0);
```

As with the other control-class constructors, the parent refers to the parent window that contains the control, and id is the identifier used to differentiate the control from others. The x, y, w, and h parameters describe the location and size of the scroll-bar control. The isHScrollBar parameter is used to specify in which direction the scroll bar will be. If the parameter is true, then the scroll bar extends horizontally; false means a vertical scroll bar. The resourceId parameter is used to associate the OWL object with a dialog box's interface element.

Note that the type of scroll bar that appears will be the same regardless of the values specified in the w and h parameters. If you specify a width and height for a vertical scroll bar, but specify true for the isHScrollBar parameter, you'll end up with a very oddly shaped horizontal scroll bar. For this reason, the constructor will automatically set either the width or height of the control if the appropriate parameter is set to 0. When creating a horizontal scroll bar, for example, specifying 0 for the h parameter will give the control a standard height.

There are several styles, described in Table 18.1, that can be used to control the display of the scroll bar with respect to the rectangle you define in the constructor. Only two of them, the SBS_HORZ and SBS_VERT styles, are automatically set, depending on the state of the isHScrollBar parameter.

Example

```
TScrollBar* pThermometer = TScrollBar( this,
                                       IDSB_THERMOMETER,
                                       10, 10, 180, 0,
                                       true );
```

Table 18.1. SBS_XXX styles for the scroll-bar control.

Value	Meaning
SBS_BOTTOMALIGN	Specifies a style used with SBS_HORZ to align the bottom of the scroll bar with the bottom edge of the rectangle specified in the TScrollBar constructor.

continues

Table 18.1. continued

Value	Meaning
SBS_HORZ	Specifies a horizontal scroll bar whose location, width, and height are specified by the parameters in the constructor, if neither SBS_BOTTOMALIGN nor SBS_TOPALIGN is specified.
SBS_LEFTALIGN	Specifies a style used with the SBS_VERT to align the left edge of the scroll bar with the left edge of the rectangle specified in the constructor.
SBS_RIGHTALIGN	Specifies a style used with SBS_VERT to align the right edge of the scroll bar with the right edge of the rectangle specified in the constructor.
SBS_SIZEBOX	Specifies a size box whose location, width, and height are specified by the parameters in the constructor, if neither one of the next two SBS_*XXX* styles is specified.
SBS_SIZEBOXBOTTOMRIGHTALIGN	Specifies a style used with SBS_SIZEBOX to align the lower-right corner of the size box with the lower-right corner of the rectangle specified in the constructor.
SBS_SIZEBOXTOPLEFTALIGN	Specifies a style used with the SBS_SIZEBOX style to align the upper-left corner of the size box with the upper-left corner of the rectangle specified in the constructor.
SBS_SIZEGRIP	Same as SBS_SIZEBOX, but with a raised edge (Win32 only).
SBS_TOPALIGN	Specifies a style used with SBS_HORZ to align the top of the scroll bar with the top edge of the rectangle specified in the constructor.
SBS_VERT	Specifies a vertical scroll bar whose location, width, and height are specified by the parameters in the constructor, if neither SBS_RIGHTALIGN nor SBS_LEFTALIGN is specified.

The TScrollBar class declares a number of member functions. The following are some of the more useful ones:

- The first member function you will most likely use after creating a TScrollBar instance is SetRange. This function enables you to set the range of values for the scroll bar.
- The GetRange member function enables you to query the current range of values for the scroll bar.
- The parameterless GetPosition member function returns the current position of the thumb box.
- The SetPosition member function moves the thumb box to the specified position. OWL makes sure that the newly specified position is kept within the current range.

The *SetRange* Function

Syntax

The declaration of the SetRange function is

```
void SetRange(int min, int max);
```

The arguments for the min and max parameters designate the new range of values for the scroll-bar control.

Example

```
pThermometer->SetRange(32,212);      // Freezing to boiling
```

18

The *GetRange* Function

Syntax

The declaration of the GetRange function is

```
void GetRange(int& min, int& max) const;
```

The parameters min and max are filled in by the GetRange member function with the minimum and maximum of the current range values for the scroll-bar control.

Example

```
int freezing, boiling;
pThermometer->GetRange(freezing, boiling);
```

The *SetPosition* Function

Syntax

The declaration of the member function SetPosition is

```
void SetPosition(int thumbPos);
```

The parameter thumbPos specifies the new thumb-box position.

Example

```
pThermometer->SetPosition(68);      // a comfortable temp
```

Responding to Scroll-Bar Notification Messages

There are several methods by which a program can handle scroll-bar notifications. The first is by creating a descendant class of the TScrollBar class, and then overriding the various member functions that are called in response to the SB_XXX notification messages as listed in Day 16's lesson. The following table associates the notification messages with their corresponding TScrollBar member functions:

Table 18.2. SBS_XXX and TScrollBar member functions.

Notification Message	TScrollBar member function
SB_LINEUP	SBLineUp
SB_LINEDOWN	SBLineDown
SB_PAGEUP	SBPageUp
SB_PAGEDOWN	SBPageDown
SB_THUMBPOSITION	SBThumbPosition
SB_THUMBTRACK	SBThumbTrack
SB_ENDSCROLL	SBEndScroll
SB_TOP	SBTop
SB_BOTTOM	SBBottom

You must remember, however, that when overriding a descendant class's version of a response function, the parent's version must be called first. It is that version that keeps the scroll bar updated. Consider the following example:

```
void TMyScrollBar::SBTop()
{
   TScrollBar::SBTop();      // Make sure our parent gets a chance
   sndPlaySound("TOP.WAV", SND_ASYNC);   // Play a sound
}
```

Another method of responding to scroll-bar notification messages is by intercepting the EvHScroll or EvVScroll member functions in the scroll bar's parent class. There, you can interrogate the scroll bar as to its current position and then act accordingly.

```
void TMyWindow::EvVScroll(uint code, uint pos, HWND hwnd)
{
   TWindow::EvVScroll(code, pos, hwnd);  // Give our parent a chance
   int newpos = scrollbar->GetPosition(); // get the updated position
   switch (code)
      {
      case SB_TOP:
```

```
            sndPlaySound("TOP.WAV", SND_ASYNC);
            break;
        }
}
```

Finally, if one uses the `EV_CHILD_NOTIFY_ALL_CODES` macro when defining the response table to assign a response function to the scroll bar's ID, the assigned function will be called for all notification messages coming from the scroll bar. The response function looks and acts similarly to the `EvXScroll` functions, but in this case it isn't necessary to call the parent's version of the function.

```
DEFINE_RESPONSE_TABLE1(TMyWindow, TWindow)
   EV_CHILD_NOTIFY_ALL_CODES(IDSC_THERMOMETER, EvScrollBar),
END_RESPONSE_TABLE;

void TMyWindow::EvScrollBar(uint code)
{
   switch (code)
      {
      case SB_TOP:
         sndPlaySound("TOP.WAV", SND_ASYNC);
         break;
      }
}
```

The Countdown Timer

The *countdown timer* application contains the following controls:

- [ ] A timer scroll-bar control that has a default range of 0 to 60 seconds
- [ ] Two static-text controls that label the range of values for the timer scroll bar
- [ ] A static-text control to show the current setting of the scroll bar
- [ ] Start and Exit buttons

You can set the number of seconds by using the scroll bar. When you move the scroll-bar thumb box, the current thumb position appears in a static box. To trigger the countdown process, click the Start button. During the countdown, the application decrements the number of seconds in the edit box and moves the scroll bar's thumb box upward. When the countdown ends, the program sounds a beep and restores the scroll bar to its starting value.

The countdown-timer application illustrates the following scroll-bar manipulations:

- [ ] Setting and altering the scroll bar's range of values
- [ ] Moving and changing the scroll bar's thumb-box position (the program illustrates how these tasks are performed internally or with the mouse)
- [ ] Using the scroll bar to supply a value

Listing 18.1 shows the source code for the COUNTDN.H header file, Listing 18.2 shows the source code for the COUNTDN.RC resource file, and Listing 18.3 shows the source code for the COUNTDN.CPP program file.

Listing 18.1. Source code for the COUNTDN.H header file.

```
1:  #define IDB_START    101
2:  #define IDB_EXIT     102
3:  #define IDS_STATUS   103
4:  #define IDSC_TIMER   104
```

Listing 18.2. Source code for the COUNTDN.RC resource file.

```
1:  #include "countdn.h"
2:
3:  COUNTDN DIALOG 6, 15, 272, 182
4:  STYLE DS_MODALFRAME ¦ WS_POPUP ¦ WS_VISIBLE ¦ WS_CAPTION ¦ WS_SYSMENU
5:  CAPTION "Count Down Timer"
6:  FONT 8, "MS Sans Serif"
7:  {
8:    RTEXT "Countdown: ", -1, 42, 20, 52, 8
9:    LTEXT "50", IDS_STATUS, 94, 20, 29, 8
10:   PUSHBUTTON "Start", IDB_START, 19, 65, 30, 20
11:   PUSHBUTTON "Exit", IDB_EXIT, 62, 65, 30, 20
12:   SCROLLBAR IDSC_TIMER, 131, 32, 9, 100, SBS_VERT
13:   LTEXT "0", -1, 145, 33, 13, 8
14:   LTEXT "60", -1, 145, 124, 13, 8
15: }
```

Listing 18.3. Source code for the COUNTDN.CPP program file.

```
1:  #include <stdio.h>
2:  #include <owl\applicat.h>
3:  #include <owl\button.h>
4:  #include <owl\dialog.h>
5:  #include <owl\framewin.h>
6:  #include <owl\scrollba.h>
7:  #include <owl\static.h>
8:  #include <owl\window.h>
9:  #include <owl\window.rh>
10:
11: #include "countdn.h"
12:
13: class TMyDialog : public TDialog
14: {
15: public:
16:    TMyDialog(TWindow* parent = 0, TModule* module = 0);
17:
18: protected:
19:    virtual void SetupWindow();
```

```
20:
21:     void EvTimerBar(uint code);
22:     void CbStart();
23:     void CbExit();
24:
25:  private:
26:     TScrollBar* timerbar;
27:     TStatic*    status;
28:
29:     DECLARE_RESPONSE_TABLE(TMyDialog);
30:  };
31:  DEFINE_RESPONSE_TABLE1(TMyDialog, TDialog)
32:     EV_CHILD_NOTIFY_ALL_CODES(IDSC_TIMER, EvTimerBar),
33:     EV_BN_CLICKED(IDB_START, CbStart),
34:     EV_BN_CLICKED(IDB_EXIT, CbExit),
35:  END_RESPONSE_TABLE;
36:
37:  TMyDialog::TMyDialog(TWindow* parent, TModule* module)
38:     : TDialog(parent, "COUNTDN", module)
39:  {
40:     status = new TStatic(this, IDS_STATUS);
41:     timerbar = new TScrollBar(this, IDSC_TIMER);
42:  }
43:
44:  void TMyDialog::SetupWindow()
45:  {
46:     TWindow::SetupWindow();     // Initialize the visual element
47:
48:     if (timerbar)
49:         {
50:         timerbar->SetRange(0, 60);
51:         timerbar->SetPosition(15);
52:         EvTimerBar(SB_THUMBPOSITION);
53:         }
54:  }
55:
56:  void TMyDialog::EvTimerBar(uint /*code*/)
57:  {
58:     if (status)
59:         {
60:         char text[25];
61:         sprintf(text, "%d", timerbar ? timerbar->GetPosition() : 0);
62:         status->SetText(text);
63:         }
64:  }
65:
66:  void DelaySecs(DWORD dwSecs)
67:  {
68:  #if (WINVER >= 0x0400)
69:     Sleep(dwSecs * 1000L);
70:  #else
71:     DWORD dwTime = GetTickCount() + (dwSecs * 1000L);
72:     while (GetTickCount() < dwTime)
73:         /* Just wait a while. */;
```

continues

Listing 18.3. continued

```
74:    #endif
75:    }
76:
77:    void TMyDialog::CbStart()
78:    {
79:        if (timerbar)
80:            {
81:            // First, let the user know that we're stopping the
82:            // system for a time.
83:            //
84:            ::SetCursor(::LoadCursor(NULL, IDC_WAIT));
85:
86:            int start = timerbar->GetPosition();
87:            for (int ix = start - 1; ix >= 0; —ix)
88:                {
89:                timerbar->SetPosition(ix);
90:                EvTimerBar(SB_THUMBPOSITION);
91:                DelaySecs(1L);           // Wait a sec
92:                }
93:            timerbar->SetPosition(start);
94:            EvTimerBar(SB_THUMBPOSITION);
95:            }
96:    }
97:
98:    void TMyDialog::CbExit()
99:    {
100:       SendMessage(WM_CLOSE);
101:   }
102:
103:   class TCountDownApp : public TApplication
104:   {
105:   public:
106:       TCountDownApp() : TApplication()
107:           { nCmdShow = SW_SHOWMAXIMIZED; }
108:
109:       void InitMainWindow()
110:           {
111:           SetMainWindow(new TFrameWindow(  0,
112:                                "Count Down Timer",
113:                                new TMyDialog ));
114:           }
115:   };
116:
117:   int OwlMain(int, char *[])
118:   {
119:       return TCountDownApp().Run();
120:   }
```

The interesting parts of the program in Listing 18.3 start with the SetupWindow member function starting on line 44. First, make sure to call the parent's version to create the actual visual elements. After making sure the timerbar object was created successfully, its range and position are initialized on lines 50 and 51, and the EvTimerBar member function is called with the

parameter SB_THUMBPOSITION on line 52. Although EvTimerBar doesn't actually make use of the parameter it's passed, you should be sure that you send an accurate value, just in case some future version of this program *does* make use of the parameter.

The EvTimerBar member function that starts on line 56 responds to any notification message that might be sent by the scroll bar, as well as the various times it's called explicitly by the program itself. Its sole purpose at this point is to keep the status static-text box updated with the current position of the scroll bar.

Figure 18.1.

A sample session with the COUNTDN.EXE application.

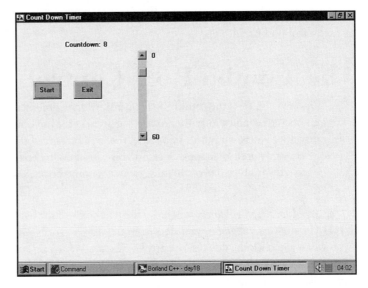

The next function is the nonmember function DelaySecs, starting on line 66. Here's something interesting that shows off some of the differences between the old Win16 API and the newer Win32. What you want to do in this function is simply wait for some number of seconds. You can do this easily by obtaining the number of milliseconds elapsed since Windows was started via the function GetTickCount, adding the number of milliseconds you need to wait, then looping until GetTickCount is greater than or equal to your end time. The problem here is that you completely tie up the machine for the duration of the loop. Win32 provides a function (which doesn't exist in Win16) to go to sleep for a number of milliseconds. While the program is asleep, other programs get a chance to run. So, on line 68 is a check to see if the Windows version is 4.0 or greater. If so, then the function Sleep is used. Otherwise, the other method is employed.

It's the CbStart function that provides the real meat of the program starting on line 77. After ensuring on line 79 that you have a valid pointer to the timerbar object, you set the cursor to the hourglass on line 84. Because you'll be delaying the program for the duration of the countdown, it's polite to let the user know that you are taking over for a while by changing the cursor to the hourglass. As soon as you exit the loop and go back to Windows, the cursor will automatically be changed back to the regular arrow. Note the use of the scope modifier on the calls to SetCursor and LoadCursor. This is used to make sure you get the original Windows functions instead of the TWindow member functions, which behave slightly differently.

On line 86 you initialize the start variable with the current position of the scroll bar and start a countdown to 0 from there. As you count down, you set the scroll bar's position, update the static text box, and then call the DelaySecs function on lines 89 through 91. After the loop is finished, you reset the scroll bar to its original position on line 93 and update the static-text control on line 94.

The Combo-Box Control

Windows supports the combo-box control, which combines an edit box with a list box. Thus, a combo box enables you either to select an item in the list-box component (or part, if you prefer) or to enter your own input. In a sense, the list-box part of the combo box contains convenient or frequently used selections. A combo box, unlike a list box, does not confine you to choosing items in the list box. There are three types of combo boxes: simple, drop-down, and drop-down list.

NEW☛
TERM The *simple combo box* includes the edit box and the list box that are always displayed. The *drop-down combo box* differs from the simple type by the fact that the list box appears only when you click the down scroll arrow. The *drop-down list combo box* provides a drop-down list that appears when you click the down scroll arrow. There is no edit box in this type of combo box.

The *TComboBox* Class

OWL offers the TComboBox class, a descendant of TListBox, to support the combo-box controls. The TComboBox class declares a constructor and a rich set of member functions to support the edit-control components in addition to all the inherited list-box member functions.

The declaration of the constructor is

```
TComboBox( TWindow* parent,
           int     id,
           int     x, int y, int w, in h,
           uint32  style,
```

```
            uint    textLen,
        TModule* module = 0 );
TComboBox(TWindow* parent, int resourceId, uint testLen, TModule* module = 0);
```

The new parameters to this control class are `style` and `textLen`. The `TComboBox` control is the only control class whose constructor takes a parameter for specifying the style. This is because it is the one class in which you will most often want to modify the style. These styles are described in Table 18.3, and only the `CBS_SORT` and `CBS_AUTOHSCROLL` styles are set automatically; anything else you might want must be passed via the `style` parameter. The `textLen` parameter works similarly to the one sent to the `TEdit` class from Day 14. When the combo box has an edit box at the top, this parameter specifies the text length for that box to be `textLen` - 1. Specifying 0 for `textLen` will allow up to 64K of text in the edit box.

Example

```
pcb = new TComboBox(this, 101, 10, 10, 100, 150, CBS_DROPDOWN, 0);
```

The `style` parameter may include either `CBS_SIMPLE` for a simple combo box, `CBS_DROPDOWN` for a drop-down combo box, or `CBS_DROPDOWNLIST` for a drop-down list combo box.

Table 18.3. Combo-box control styles.

Style	Meaning
CBS_AUTOHSCROLL	Automatically scrolls the text in the edit control to the right when you enter a character at the end of the line (removing this style limits the text to the characters that fit inside the rectangular boundary of the edit control).
CBS_DISABLENOSCROLL	Causes the scroll bar of the drop-down, list-box portion of the combo box simply to become disabled and gray when scrolling is not allowed. By default, the scroll bar disappears.
CBS_DROPDOWN	Specifies a drop-down combo box.
CBS_DROPDOWNLIST	Specifies a drop-down list combo box.
CBS_HASSTRINGS	When used with an owner-drawn combo box, it causes the strings added to the combo box to be copied internally by the standard Windows routines. This always is the case when Windows does the drawing of the combo box.
CBS_LOWERCASE	Converts all typed characters to lowercase (Win32 only).
CBS_NOINTEGRALHEIGHT	Tells the combo box that its drop-down, list-box portion need not be truncated to fit the height of its items; partial displays of items may be displayed.

continues

Table 18.3. continued

Style	Meaning
CBS_OEMCONVERT	Allows Windows to convert the character sets as appropriate (useful for filenames).
CBS_OWNERDRAWFIXED	Creates an owner-drawn combo box; the programmer must create routines to display the items in the combo box. All items in the drop-down, list-box portion will be the same height.
CBS_OWNERDRAWVARIABLE	Exactly the same as CBS_OWNERDRAWFIXED, except the display items may be of differing heights.
CBS_SIMPLE	Specifies a simple combo box.
CBS_SORT	Automatically sorts the items in the list box.
CBS_UPPERCASE	Converts all typed characters to uppercase (Win32 only).

The TComboBox class declares member functions to manage the edit-box component and overrides member functions to manage the list-box components. Most of these functions are similar to the corresponding members of the TEdit and TListBox classes.

In addition to the inherited TListBox member functions, the TComboBox class declares some extra member functions to handle the drop-down specifics of the combo-box control. Among these are the following:

☐ The parameterless ShowList and HideList functions, to drop down and roll up the combo box, respectively. Note that these are just wrapper functions that call the version of the ShowList function that takes a bool parameter, ShowList passing true and HideList passing false.

☐ The GetDroppedControlRect member function, to obtain the size of the dropped-down control.

☐ The parameterless GetDroppedState member function, which returns a bool to tell whether the combo box is currently dropped down.

☐ The pair of member functions GetExtendedUI and SetExtendedUI, which get and set the extended user interface for the combo box.

The *GetDroppedControlRect* Function

The declaration of the GetDroppedControlRect function is

```
void GetDroppedControlRect(TRect& Rect) const;
```

When this function is called, the Rect parameter is filled with the screen coordinates of the dropped-down list box.

Example

```
TRect rct;
pcb->GetDroppedControlRect(rct);
```

Although the TComboBox class isn't directly derived from the TEdit class, it has member functions to manipulate the edit control that comes as part of the combo box:

☐ The parameterless GetTextLen member function, which returns an integer specifying the length of the text in the edit box

☐ The GetText and SetText member functions, which modify the edit text

☐ The GetEditSel and SetEditSel member functions, which allow the manipulation of the starting and ending character position (that is, the index of the first selected character and the index of the first selected character that is not in the selected text)

☐ The parameterless Clear member function, which clears the selected text

The *GetText* Function

Syntax

The declaration of the GetText function is

```
int GetText(char far* str, int maxChars) const;
```

The parameter str is a pointer to a buffer into which GetText will copy the contents of the edit box, and maxChars is the maximum number of characters to copy (the size of the input buffer).

Example

```
int len = pcb->GetTextLen() + 1;
char* str = new char[len];
pcb->GetText(str, len);
```

Responding to Combo-Box Notification Messages

The combo-box control emits various types of messages (see Table 18.4). The table also shows the message-mapping macros that are associated with the various command and notification messages. Each type of command or notification message requires a separate member function declared in the control's parent window class.

Table 18.4. Combo-box notification messages.

Message	Macro	Meaning
CBN_CLOSEUP	EV_CBN_CLOSEUP	The combo box has been closed up.
CBN_DBLCLK	EV_CBN_DBLCLK	A combo item is selected with a mouse double-click.
CBN_DROPDOWN	EV_CBN_DROPDOWN	The combo box has been dropped down.
CBN_EDITCHANGE	EV_CBN_EDITCHANGE	The contents of the edit box are changed.
CBN_EDITUPDATE	EV_CBN_EDITUPDATE	The contents of the edit box are updated.
CBN_ERRSPACE	EV_CBN_ERRSPACE	The combo box cannot allocate more dynamic memory to accommodate new list items.
CBN_KILLFOCUS	EV_CBN_KILLFOCUS	The combo box has lost focus.
CBN_SELCHANGE	EV_CBN_SELCHANGE	A combo item is selected or deselected with a mouse click.
CBN_SELENDCANCEL	EV_CBN_SELENDCANCEL	The user has just selected an item and then selected another control or closed the window.
CBN_SELENDOK	EV_CBN_SELENDOK	The user has just clicked a list item or selected an item and closed the list. This is sent before every CBN_SELCHANGE message.
CBN_SETFOCUS	EV_CBN_SETFOCUS	The combo box has gained focus.

Combo Boxes as History-List Boxes

A combo box also can be a history-list box. History-list boxes typically follow these rules of operation:

☐ The combo list box removes the CBS_SORT style to insert the list items in a chronological fashion. New items are inserted at position 0, pushing the older items farther down the list. The oldest item is the one at the bottom of the list.

☐ History-list boxes usually have a limit on the number of items you can insert, to prevent bleeding memory. This conservation scheme requires that the oldest list items be removed after the number of list items reaches a maximum limit.

☐ If the edit control contains a string that does not have an exact match in the accompanying list box, the edit-control string is inserted as a new member at position 0.

☐ If the edit control contains a string that has an exact match in the accompanying list box, the matching list member is moved to position 0, the top of the list. This process involves first deleting the matching list member from its current position and then reinserting it at position 0.

A history list box is really a combo box that manipulates its edit control and list-box items in a certain way. There is no need to derive a descendant of TComboBox to add new member functions, although if you use a history-list box enough, it might make sense to create a descendant class that automates the functionality. Furthermore, for additional functionality, the descendant class could save the history list to disk for future invocations of the program.

The Son of Mr. Calculator Application

This section presents an updated version of the calculator application—*Son of Mr. Calculator*. This new version adds functionality to Day 14's version by using history combo boxes for the operands and result, instead of the standard edit boxes, and uses a simple combo box that contains the list of supported operators and functions. Figure 18.2 shows a sample session with the CALCJR.EXE application.

Figure 18.2.

A sample session with the CALCJR.EXE application.

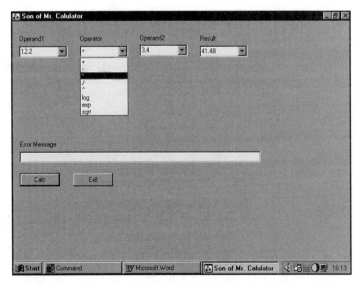

Compile and run the program. Experiment with entering and executing numbers and operators or functions. Notice that combo boxes for the operands and the result fill in their accompanying list boxes in a chronological order. The Operand and Result combo boxes remember the last 30 different operands you entered. In a way, the Result combo box acts as temporary memory.

Listing 18.4 shows the source code for the CALCJR.H header file, Listing 18.5 contains the source code for the CALCJR.RC resource file, and Listing 18.6 contains the source code for the CALCJR.CPP program file. The resource file defines the accelerator keys and menu resources.

Listing 18.4. Source code for the CALCJR.H header file.

```
1:  #define IDB_CALC      101
2:  #define IDB_EXIT      102
3:  #define IDC_OPERAND1  103
4:  #define IDC_OPERATOR  104
5:  #define IDC_OPERAND2  105
6:  #define IDC_RESULT    106
7:  #define IDE_ERRMSG    107
```

Listing 18.5. Source code for the CALCJR.RC resource file.

```
1:  #include "calcjr.h"
2:
3:  CALCJR DIALOG 6, 19, 326, 205
4:  STYLE DS_MODALFRAME | WS_POPUP | WS_VISIBLE | WS_CAPTION | WS_SYSMENU
5:  CAPTION "Son of Mr. Calculator"
6:  FONT 8, "MS Sans Serif"
7:  {
8:    LTEXT "Operand1", -1, 10, 15, 60, 8
9:    LTEXT "Operator", -1, 85, 15, 60, 8
10:   LTEXT "Operand2", -1, 160, 14, 60, 8
11:   LTEXT "Result", -1, 235, 15, 60, 8
12:   COMBOBOX IDC_OPERAND1, 10, 27, 60, 95, CBS_DROPDOWN | WS_TABSTOP
13:   COMBOBOX IDC_OPERATOR, 85, 27, 60, 95, CBS_DROPDOWNLIST | WS_TABSTOP
14:   COMBOBOX IDC_OPERAND2, 160, 26, 60, 95, CBS_DROPDOWN | WS_TABSTOP
15:   COMBOBOX IDC_RESULT, 235, 27, 60, 95, CBS_DROPDOWN | WS_TABSTOP
16:   LTEXT "Error Message", -1, 10, 133, 60, 8
17:   EDITTEXT IDE_ERRMSG, 10, 145, 301, 12
18:   PUSHBUTTON "Calc", IDB_CALC, 10, 169, 50, 15, BS_DEFPUSHBUTTON | WS_TABSTOP
19:   PUSHBUTTON "Exit", IDB_EXIT, 76, 169, 50, 15, WS_TABSTOP
20: }
```

Listing 18.6. Source code for the CALCJR.CPP program file.

```
1:  #include <ctype.h>
2:  #include <math.h>
3:  #include <stdio.h>
4:  #include <owl\applicat.h>
5:  #include <owl\button.h>
6:  #include <owl\dialog.h>
7:  #include <owl\combobox.h>
8:  #include <owl\edit.h>
9:  #include <owl\framewin.h>
10: #include <owl\static.h>
11: #include <owl\window.h>
```

```
12:   #include <owl\window.rh>
13:
14:   #include "calcjr.h"
15:
16:   class THistoryBox : public TComboBox
17:   {
18:   public:
19:      THistoryBox(TWindow* parent,
20:                    int       id,
21:                    int x, int y, int w, int h,
22:                    int       historyLen,
23:                    uint      textLen = 0,
24:                    TModule* module = 0);
25:      THistoryBox(TWindow* parent,
26:                    int       resourceId,
27:                    int       historyLen,
28:                    uint      textLen = 0,
29:                    TModule* module = 0);
30:
31:      void EvKillFocus(THandle);
32:
33:   private:
34:      int history;
35:
36:      DECLARE_RESPONSE_TABLE(THistoryBox);
37:   };
38:   DEFINE_RESPONSE_TABLE1(THistoryBox, TComboBox)
39:      EV_WM_KILLFOCUS,
40:   END_RESPONSE_TABLE;
41:
42:   THistoryBox::THistoryBox(   TWindow* parent,
43:                                int       id,
44:                                int x, int y, int w, int h,
45:                                int       historyLen,
46:                                uint      textLen,
47:                                TModule* module )
48:      : TComboBox(parent, id, x, y, w, h, CBS_DROPDOWN, textLen, module)
49:   {
50:      Attr.Style &= ~CBS_SORT;        // We don't want to sort
51:      history = historyLen;
52:   }
53:
54:   THistoryBox::THistoryBox(   TWindow* parent,
55:                                int       resourceId,
56:                                int       historyLen,
57:                                uint      textLen,
58:                                TModule* module )
59:      : TComboBox(parent, resourceId, textLen, module)
60:   {
61:      Attr.Style |= CBS_DROPDOWN;     // Make sure it's a drop-down
62:      Attr.Style &= ~CBS_SORT;        // We don't want to sort
63:      history = historyLen;
64:   }
65:
66:   void THistoryBox::EvKillFocus(THandle)
```

continues

Listing 18.6. continued

```
67: {
68:     int len = GetTextLen() + 1;
69:     char* str = new char[len];
70:     GetText(str, len);
71:     int ix = FindExactString(str, -1);
72:     if (ix < 0)
73:         {
74:         InsertString(str, 0);
75:         while (GetCount() >= history)
76:             DeleteString(GetCount() - 1);
77:         }
78:     else if (ix > 0)
79:         {
80:         DeleteString(ix);
81:         InsertString(str, 0);
82:         SetSelIndex(0);
83:         }
84:     delete str;
85: }
86:
87: class TCalcJrDialog : public TDialog
88: {
89: public:
90:     TCalcJrDialog(TWindow* parent = 0, TModule* module = 0);
91:
92: protected:
93:     virtual void SetupWindow();
94:
95:     void CmCalc();
96:     void CmExit();
97:
98: private:
99:     TComboBox    *Operator;
100:    THistoryBox *Operand1, *Operand2, *Result;
101:    TEdit        *ErrMsg;
102:
103:    DECLARE_RESPONSE_TABLE(TCalcJrDialog);
104: };
105: DEFINE_RESPONSE_TABLE1(TCalcJrDialog, TDialog)
106:    EV_BN_CLICKED(IDB_CALC, CmCalc),
107:    EV_BN_CLICKED(IDB_EXIT, CmExit),
108: END_RESPONSE_TABLE;
109:
110: TCalcJrDialog::TCalcJrDialog(TWindow* parent, TModule* module)
111:    : TDialog(parent, "CALCJR", module)
112: {
113:    Operand1 = new THistoryBox(this, IDC_OPERAND1, 30);
114:    Operator = new TComboBox(this, IDC_OPERATOR);
115:    Operand2 = new THistoryBox(this, IDC_OPERAND2, 30);
116:    Result = new THistoryBox(this, IDC_RESULT, 30);
117:    ErrMsg = new TEdit(this, IDE_ERRMSG);
118: }
119:
120: void TCalcJrDialog::SetupWindow()
```

```
121: {
122:     TWindow::SetupWindow();     // Initialize the visual element
123:
124:     // Fill up the Operator combo box with a variety
125:     // of operators for our user's computational pleasure.
126:     //
127:     if (Operator)
128:         {
129:         static char* p[] =
130:             { "+", "-", "*", "/", "^", "log", "exp", "sqrt", 0 };
131:         for (int ix = 0; p[ix]; ++ix)
132:             Operator->AddString(p[ix]);
133:         }
134:
135:     // Keep the users out of the error box.
136:     //
137:     if (ErrMsg)
138:         ErrMsg->SetReadOnly(TRUE);
139: }
140:
141: double get_number(TComboBox *numbox)
142: {
143:     double rslt = 0;          // default to 0
144:     char* str;
145:     int size;
146:
147:     if (numbox)
148:         {
149:         str = new char[size = numbox->GetTextLen() + 1];
150:         if (str)
151:             {
152:             numbox->GetText(str, size);
153:             rslt = atof(str);
154:             delete str;
155:             }
156:         }
157:     return rslt;
158: }
159:
160: void TCalcJrDialog::CmCalc()
161: {
162:     double x, y, z = 0;
163:
164:     x = get_number(Operand1);
165:     y = get_number(Operand2);
166:
167:     if (Operator)
168:         {
169:         int   ix = Operator->GetSelIndex();
170:         if (ix >= 0)
171:             {
172:             char* err = 0;
173:
174:             switch (ix)
175:                 {
```

continues

Listing 18.6. continued

```
176:                 case 0:      // + operator
177:                     z = x + y;
178:                     break;
179:                 case 1:      // - operator
180:                     z = x - y;
181:                     break;
182:                 case 2:      // * operator
183:                     z = x * y;
184:                     break;
185:                 case 3:      // / operator
186:                     if (y)
187:                         z = x / y;
188:                     else
189:                         err = "Can't divide by zero.";
190:                     break;
191:                 case 4:      // ^ operator
192:                     if (x > 0)
193:                         z = exp(y * log(x));
194:                     else
195:                         err = "Need positive number to raise power.";
196:                     break;
197:                 case 5:      // log function
198:                     if (x > 0)
199:                         z = log(x);
200:                     else
201:                         err = "Need positive number for log.";
202:                     break;
203:                 case 6:      // exp function
204:                     if (x < 230)
205:                         z = exp(x);
206:                     else
207:                         err = "Need a smaller number for exp.";
208:                     break;
209:                 case 7:      // sqrt function
210:                     if (x >= 0)
211:                         z = sqrt(x);
212:                     else
213:                         err = "Can't do sqrt of negative number.";
214:                     break;
215:                 default:
216:                     err = "Unknown operator";
217:                     break;
218:                 }
219:
220:             if (ErrMsg)
221:                 if (!err)
222:                     ErrMsg->Clear();
223:                 else
224:                     ErrMsg->SetWindowText(err);
225:             if (!err && Result)
226:                 {
227:                 char dest[81];
228:                 sprintf(dest, "%g", z);
```

```
229:                    Result->SetWindowText(dest);
230:                    Result->EvKillFocus(0);     // Force history addition
231:                }
232:            }
233:        }
234: }
235:
236: void TCalcJrDialog::CmExit()
237: {
238:     SendMessage(WM_CLOSE);
239: }
240:
241: class TCalcJrApp : public TApplication
242: {
243: public:
244:     TCalcJrApp() : TApplication()
245:         { nCmdShow = SW_SHOWMAXIMIZED; }
246:
247:     void InitMainWindow()
248:         {
249:         SetMainWindow(new TFrameWindow(  0,
250:                                "Son of Mr. Calulator",
251:                                new TCalcJrDialog ));
252:         }
253: };
254:
255: int OwlMain(int, char *[])
256: {
257:     return TCalcJrApp().Run();
258: }
```

The program in Listing 18.6 begins by declaring, starting on line 16, a descendant of TComboBox called THistoryBox. This descendant declares its constructors, a single member function, and a single data member. The constructor that creates a brand-new control specifies the CBS_DROPDOWN style when calling the parent TComboBox constructor on line 48, and then turns off the CBS_SORT style and initializes the history member data with the historyLen parameter on lines 50 and 51.

The constructor that simply associates the OWL object with the preexisting dialog control works similarly to the other constructor, except this needs to move the CBS_DROPDOWN setting into the constructor's body, rather than the call to the base class's constructor.

The EvKillFocus member function of THistoryBox that starts on line 66 is called in response to the WM_KILLFOCUS Windows message. This message is sent when the user has the focus on a window (the edit box is active or the list box is highlighted) and then clicks on something else. At this time, the function inserts the string of the edit-control part in the list-box part. This insertion occurs only if the string is not already in the list-box part. In this case, the string is inserted at index 0 and becomes the new top-of-the-list item. If the targeted string already is in the list-box part, the function deletes the existing item in the list box and reinserts it at index 0. Thus, the targeted string appears to have moved up to the top of the list-box part.

The TCalcJrDialog's constructor that starts on line 110 does the usual creation of controls. The SetupWindow member function then initializes the Operator combo box by filling its list-box component with the supported operators and functions on lines 129 through 132.

The get_number function, starting on line 141, is used, as in Day 14, to obtain a double value from a control. This time, it receives a TComboBox pointer, gets the contents of its edit box, then uses the atof function to obtain the double value that is returned.

The Calc button causes the CmCalc member function, starting on line 160, to be called. This is the function that does all the following work of the application:

☐ Retrieves the values from the Operand1 and Operand2 combo boxes and places their values in the x and y variables, respectively, on lines 164 and 165.

☐ Obtains the index of the selected operator in the Operator combo box on line 169.

☐ If something is actually selected, a switch statement is used to determine the requested operation or math function, then the case statement performs the requested task and assigns the result to variable z, or sets the err pointer to an appropriate error string.

☐ Sets the Error Message edit box if an error occurred, or clears that same edit box if no error was detected on lines 220 through 224.

☐ If no error occurred, displays the result of the operation or function evaluation in the edit-control box of the Result combo box, then calls its EvKillFocus function directly to have that value inserted into its list-box component on lines 225 through 231.

VBX Controls

VBX is an acronym for *Visual Basic eXchange* and describes the host of controls written to the Visual Basic control format. The VBX interface is rather complex, but OWL makes it easy to use with support classes that can be mixed in to the standard ones you've been using so far. There really are just a few simple steps to using VBX controls:

☐ Declare an instance of the class TBIVbxLibrary. This initializes the VBX subsystem that is required to interface with the VBX controls, and is usually done in the OwlMain function.

☐ Use the mixin class TVbxEventHandler, multiply inheriting from it and the regular interface class (such as TWindow or TDialog) and specifying it when defining the response table.

NEW *Mixin classes* are ones that can add functionality to a base class simply by being
TERM codeclared as a multiply-inherited base class. For example, the following code
snippet adds VBX control functionality to a descendent dialog class by simply adding
`TVbxEventHandler` to the list of base classes:

```
class MyVbxDialog : public TDialog, public TVbxEventHandler
{
    // ... member functions and data go here ...
    DECLARE_RESPONSE_TABLE(MyVbxDialog);
}
```

☐ Use the `EV_VBXEVENTNAME` macro when defining a response table for your interface.

☐ Create OWL objects to connect with the VBX interface elements that appear on the
screen.

Initializing the VBX Subsystem

The initialization and termination of the VBX subsystem occur with calls to two simple
functions: `VBXInit` and `VBXTerm`. Luckily, these two functions are called automatically by the
constructor and destructor of the `TBIVbxLibrary` class. Here is a sample `OwlMain` function in
which this class is declared.

```
int OwlMain(int argc, char* argv[])
{
    TBIVbxLibrary vbxLib;
    return TApplication().Run();
}
```

As you can see, there really isn't all that much to it. The `TBIVbxLibrary`'s constructor does the
initialization, and its destructor shuts down the system when the program closes.

Defining a VBX Response Table

The response table for a dialog box that uses VBX controls looks very much like the ones you've
already created, except for a few additions.

```
DEFINE_RESPONSE_TABLE2(MyVbxDialog, TDialog, TVbxEventHandler)
    // ... other response functions go here ...
    EV_VBX_EVENTNAME(ID_CONTROL1, "DragDrop", EvControl1),
    EV_VBX_EVENTINDEX(ID_CONTROL1, 1, EvControl1),
END_RESPONSE_TABLE;
```

18

Take careful note of the DEFINE_RESPONSE_TABLE2 line. So far, your response tables have been defined with a 1, but because this is multiply inherited from two separate classes, you need to specify this when defining the response table by using a 2. (Note that if this were for a TWindow descendant, then TWindow would have been used in place of TDialog.) Then the response table entries themselves use the EV_VBX_EVENTNAME or EV_VBX_EVENTINDEX macros, which have the following basic definitions:

```
EV_VBX_EVENTNAME(controlID, eventName, EvHandler)
EV_VBX_EVENTINDEX(controlID, eventIndex, EvHandler)
```

The controlId parameter is the typical control ID parameter used in defining other response-table entries; it refers to the ID assigned to the control when it's created by Windows, typically the ID used in the resource file describing the dialog in which the control resides. eventName is a string holding the name of the event itself. VBX controls identify their separate events with both indexes and with string labels; these are what belong here. Finally, the EvHandler is the name of the member function to be called whenever the event occurs, much like you've already defined in earlier response tables.

The response function for a VBX event is rather simple and looks like the following:

```
void EvHandler(VBXEVENT far* event);
```

Because the VBX events have so much information associated with them, they're passed in a structure rather than as individual arguments to the function. Here is the definition of the VBXEVENT structure:

```
struct VBXEVENT
{
    HCTL    Control;
    HWND    Window;
    int     ID;
    int     EventIndex;
    LPCSTR  EventName;
    int     NumParams;
    LPVOID  ParamList;
};
```

Following is the breakdown of the various items in the structure:

- [ ] Control is the handle of the sending VBX control. Be careful not to confuse this with a window control; this is a special handle used to refer to the VBX control alone.

- [ ] Window is a handle to the control window itself.

- [ ] ID is the ID of the VBX control, the same one defined in the resource file, and so on.

- [ ] EventIndex is the event index. All VBX controls have their individual events numbered, and this is the number associated with this particular VBX control's event.

- [ ] EventName is the name of the event. The name is provided, mainly, for the programmer's convenience so the VBX-control authors can more easily communicate the purpose of the event.

- [ ] NumParams is the number of parameters for this event. Each event can have a number of different parameters (VBXEVENT is just a wrapper that describes the event itself) that are encoded in the next structure item.

- [ ] ParamList is a pointer to an array containing the pointers to the parameter values for this event. The number of parameters is defined by the previous parameter, and they are indexed from 0 to NumParams - 1. You need to know the details of the VBX control itself to be able to identify the types of the parameters. These are supplied by the VBX control vendor.

There are two macros that can be used to access the parameters passed in ParamList. Both of them require the parameters up to the one accessed be the same as the one accessed. Here are the two macros.

```
VBX_EVENTARGNUM(event, type, index)
VBX_EVENTARGSTR(event, index)
```

The event parameter is the same as the one passed to an event handler of the type VBXEVENT far*. The type parameter in the first macro should be the type of the argument to retrieve. index is the zero-based number of the argument. Because strings are such a common item to retrieve, VBX_EVENTARGSTR is provided, which already knows the type of argument to access. The types are all based upon Visual Basic types and have C++ equivalents, as shown in Table 18.5.

Table 18.5. VBX argument types.

Basic	C++
Boolean	bool
Control	HCTL
Double	double
Enum	short
Integer	short
Long	long
Single	float
String	HLSTR

Note that the string is referred to as an HLSTR. This is not a standard C++ character array or even a reference to the C++ string class. These are handles to Visual Basic strings, and they need to be accessed with the following special functions:

```
HLSTR   VBXCreateBasicString(LPVOID buffer, USHORT len);
VOID    VBXDestroyBasicString(HLSTR string);
int     VBXGetBasicStringBuf(HLSTR string, LPSTR buffer, int len);
USHORT  VBXGetBasicStringLength(HLSTR string);
ERR     VBXSetBasicString(HLSTR far *string, LPVOID buffer, USHORT len);
```

Based on your previous experiences in this book, I would imagine the functions and how they're used are fairly obvious after reading just the function names. In order, they create strings, destroy them, copy them to a character array, obtain a string's length, and copy a character array into a string. If you need more information, you can check out the online help provided with Borland C++.

The *TVbxControl* OWL Interface Class

When it finally comes time to instantiate an interface object to communicate with the VBX control, you need to use the `TVbxControl` class. The following are the two constructors for this object:

```
TVbxControl(TWindow*        parent,
            int             id,
            const char far* vbxName,
            const char far* vbxClass,
            const char far* title,
            int             x,
            int             y,
            int             w,
            int             h,
            long            initLen = 0,
            void far*       initData = 0,
            TModule*        module = 0);
TVbxControl(TWindow* parent, int resourceId, TModule* module = 0);
```

Notice that the second constructor looks just like all the other constructors used to associate an OWL class with a resource control, and that's just exactly what it is. Looking back at the first constructor, you'll see that many of the parameters are the same as those used to create other controls (`parent`, `id`, `title`, `x`, `y`, `w`, `h`, and `module`). The `vbxName` parameter specifies the filename of the VBX control library, and the `vbxClass` parameter specifies the class name of the control (libraries can contain multiple controls, and the class name enables you to select the particular one in which you're interested).

There are two additional parameters towards the end of the list called `initLen` and `initData`, both of which have default values of `0`. These are used to supply specific information to the VBX control as it is being initialized. This information is control-specific, and its exact makeup needs to be defined by the author of the VBX control.

Unlike the other controls, however, VBX controls have a number of properties that describe their appearance and actions. These properties, like the response functions, are defined by the VBX-control author; you will need to consult the documentation for the specific control you want to use.

After you know which properties you want to manipulate, you can do so with a variety of `GetProp` and `SetProp` functions. There are a substantial number of these overloaded functions, enabling you to access properties of varying types, either by index or name.

Note: As you might have noticed before with the response functions, all VBX controls use both indexes and names together to provide easier access to the programmer.

Here are the general formats of the property manipulation functions:

```
bool GetProp(int propIndex, type& value, int arrayIndex = -1);
bool GetProp(const char far* name, type& value, int arrayIndex = -1);
bool SetProp(int propIndex, type value, int arrayIndex = -1);
bool SetProp(const char far* name, type value, int arrayIndex = -1);
```

Note that I didn't specify a particular type for each of these functions. As stated earlier, these functions are overloaded to accept a number of different types: `int`, `long`, `bool`, `ENUM`, `HPIC`, `float`, `string`, and `COLORREF`. The `arrayIndex` parameter can be used to access different elements of an array property. By default, you access the first property, whether or not there are any more to access.

In addition to the functions for changing the different properties, you can ask the VBX to tell you which properties it contains, and even what the property types are.

```
int GetNumProps();
int GetPropIndex(const char far* name);
void GetPropName(int propIndex, string& str);
int GetPropType(int propIndex);
int GetPropType(char far* name);
bool IsArrayProp(int propIndex);
bool IsArrayProp(char far* name);
```

The `GetNumProps` function returns the number of properties associated with the control, whereas `GetPropName` supplies the name of the indexed control. `GetPropIndex` searches the control's properties for the supplied name and returns the associated index. You can determine a property's type by using the `GetPropType` function. This returns a value that can be checked against one of the macros described in Table 18.6. Checking the `IsArrayProp` function tells you whether or not the specified property is stored as an array.

Table 18.6. VBX property types.

Property Type	Equivalent C++ Type
PTYPE_CSTRING	HSZ
PTYPE_SHORT	short
PTYPE_LONG	LONG
PTYPE_BOOL	bool

continues

521

18

Table 18.6. continued

Property Type	Equivalent C++ Type
PTYPE_COLOR	DWORD or COLORREF
PTYPE_ENUM	BYTE or ENUM
PTYPE_REAL	float
PTYPE_XPOS	LONG (Twips)
PTYPE_XSIZE	LONG (Twips)
PTYPE_YPOS	LONG (Twips)
PTYPE_YSIZE	LONG (Twips)
PTYPE_PICTURE	HPIC
PTYPE_BSTRING	HLSTR

Although this listing of and inquiry of the various properties of a VBX control can be useful, you probably won't have much call for it. Usually you will need to determine the properties beforehand by reading the VBX's documentation, then make use of the properties as described.

Summary

Today's lesson presented the scroll-bar and combo-box controls. These controls share the common factor of being input objects. Also presented were VBX controls. You learned about the following topics:

☐ The scroll-bar control enables you to select quickly from a wide range of integers.

☐ There are various types of combo-box controls: simple, drop-down, and drop-down list.

☐ You can make a history list box out of a drop-down combo box.

☐ VBX controls can be easily controlled with OWL classes and, with a few minor differences, can be treated like ordinary Windows controls.

Q&A

Q Do the scroll bars strictly select integers?

A Yes. However, these integers can be indices to arrays, items in list-box controls, and other integer codes to various attributes such as colors. Therefore, in a sense, the scroll bar can be used to select nonintegers.

Q Can I create a scroll-bar control with an excluded subrange of values?

A No. You may want to use a list-box control instead and have that control list the value numbers.

Workshop

The Workshop provides quiz questions to help you solidify your understanding of the material covered and exercises to provide you with experience in using what you've learned. Try to understand the quiz and exercise answers before continuing on to the next day's lesson. Answers are provided in Appendix A.

Quiz

1. True or false? If you do not include the CBS_AUTOHSCROLL style in creating a combo-list box, you limit the text to the characters that fit inside the rectangular boundary of the edit control.

2. True or false? You can handle the CBN_SELCHANGE notification message to monitor every keystroke in the edit control of a combo box.

3. True or false? Setting CBS_SORT creates a combo box whose list-box items are sorted and unique.

4. True or false? To emulate a history-list box, a combo box must be created without the CBS_SORT style.

5. True or false? A history list may have duplicate items.

6. True or false? COUNTDN.CPP demonstrates how to implement a two-way connection between the current value of a scroll-bar control and the numeric value in a text box.

7. True or false? The range of values for a scroll-bar control is fixed when you create the control.

Exercises

Write a wrapper class to simulate the VBX HLSTR object, allowing programmers to act on it like it was a C++ string.

Write a program that uses a combo box to enable the user to enter the name of a VBX control, then loads that control and stores the property names in a list box. The combo box should have a history of the last ten controls selected.

MDI Windows

The *Multiple Document Interface* (*MDI*) is a standard Windows interface used by many popular Windows applications and utilities, such as Word for Windows, the Windows 3.1 Program Manager, and even the Borland C++ IDE. The MDI interface is also part of the Common User Access (CUA) standard set by IBM. Each MDI-compliant application enables you to open child windows for file-specific tasks such as editing text, managing a database, or working with a spreadsheet. Today, you will learn the following topics on managing MDI windows and objects:

☐ The basic features and components of an MDI-compliant application

☐ Basics of building an MDI-compliant application

☐ The class `TMDIFrame`

☐ The class `TMDIClient`

☐ Building MDI client windows

☐ The class `TMDIChild`

☐ Building MDI child windows

☐ Managing messages in an MDI-compliant application

The MDI Application Features and Components

An MDI-compliant application is made up of the following objects:

☐ The visible *MDI frame window* that contains all other MDI objects. The MDI frame window is an instance of the class `TMDIFrame` or its descendants. Each MDI application has one MDI frame window.

☐ The invisible *MDI client window* that performs underlying management of the MDI child windows that are dynamically created and removed. The MDI client window is an instance of the class `TMDIClient`. Each MDI application has one MDI client window.

☐ The dynamic and visible *MDI child window*. An MDI application dynamically creates and removes multiple instances of MDI child windows. An MDI child window is an instance of `TMDIChild` or its descendant. These windows are located, moved, resized, maximized, and minimized inside the area defined by the MDI frame window. At any given time (and while there is at least one MDI child window), there is only one active MDI child window.

When you maximize an MDI child window, it occupies the area defined by the client area of the MDI frame window. When you minimize an MDI child window, the icon of that window appears at the bottom area of the MDI frame window.

Note: The MDI frame window has a menu that manipulates the MDI child windows and their contents. The MDI child windows cannot have a menu, but they may contain controls. In any other respect, you can think of an MDI child window as an instance of TFrameWindow or its descendants.

Basics of Building an MDI Application

Before discussing in more detail the creation of the various components that make up an MDI application, focus on the basic strategy involved. In the last section, you learned that the basic ingredients for an MDI application are the TMDIFrame, TMDIClient, and TMDIChild (or TMDIChild descendant) classes. The TMDIFrame class supports the creation and handling of the MDI client window as well as menu management.

The MDIClient class focuses on the creation and underlying management of MDI child windows. The TMDIChild class offers the functionality for the MDI child windows.

The *TMDIFrame* Class

ObjectWindows offers the TMDIFrame class, a descendant of TFrameWindow, to implement the MDI frame window of an MDI application. The declaration of the TMDIFrame constructors is as follows:

```
TMDIFrame(const char far* title,
          TResId           menuResId,
          TMDIClient&       clientWnd = *new TMDIClient,
          TModule*          module = 0);
TMDIFrame(THandle frameHandle HWND clientHandle, TModule* module = 0);
```

The first constructor creates a class instance by specifying the title in title, associated menu resource ID in menuResId, and reference to the associated MDI client window in clientWnd. You should note that the client window has a default argument that creates a new window; you will rarely, if ever, override this argument. The second constructor creates a class instance from an existing non-OWL window and has you provide a handle to the frame window in frameHandle and the Windows handle of the client window in clientHandle.

The class TMDIFrame also declares some other public member functions:

```
bool        SetMenu(HMENU newMenu);
TMDIClient* GetClientWindow();
static HMENU FindChildMenu(HMENU menu);
```

The function SetMenu is overloaded from the parent TWindow function. In this case, before replacing the current menu, it looks for the MDI submenu in the frame's menu bar and includes

it with `newMenu`. The function `GetClientWindow` returns a pointer to the associated MDI client window. The function `FindChildMenu` searches for the child menu of an MDI frame's menu bar.

Building MDI Frame Windows

The usual approach for creating the objects that make up an ObjectWindows application starts with creating the application instance and then its main window instance. In the case of an MDI-compliant application, the application's main window is typically a descendant of class `TMDIFrame`. The `InitMainWindow` member function of the application class creates this window. Looking at the first two `TMDIFrame` constructors, you can tell that creating the main MDI window involves a title and menu resource—there is no pointer to a parent window because MDI frame windows have no parent windows. The MDI frame window, unlike most descendants of class `TWindow`, must have a menu associated with it. This menu typically includes the items in Table 19.1, needed to manipulate the MDI children. In addition, the menu of the MDI frame window is dynamically and automatically updated to include the current MDI children.

Table 19.1. The predefined menu commands for manipulating MDI children.

Action	Menu ID Constant
Arrange Icons	`CM_ARRANGEICONS`
Cascade	`CM_CASCASDECHILDREN`
Close All	`CM_CLOSECHILDREN`
Create Window	`CM_CREATECHILD`
Tile	`CM_TILECHILDREN`
Tile Horizontal	`CM_TILECHILDRENHORIZ`

The constructor of the descendant of `TMDIFrame` (call it the application frame class) can, in many cases, simply invoke the parent class constructor. This invocation occurs if the steps taken by the parent class are adequate for creating the MDI frame window instance. When you want to modify the behavior of the application frame class, you need to include the required statements. Such statements might assign initial values to data members declared in the application frame class.

The `SetupWindow` member function invokes the `InitClientWindow` to create the `TMDIClient` instance. You can modify the `SetupWindow` function to automatically create the first MDI child window, for example.

The *TMDIClient* Class

ObjectWindows offers the TMDIClient class, a descendant of TWindow, to implement the MDI client window. The declaration of the TMDIClient constructor is as follows:

```
TMDIClient(TModule* module = 0);
```

As you can see, there's only one parameter, and even that has a default value. It's this simple because it doesn't really need to know all that much; the main frame that has the knowledge is the TMDIFrame window, of which this is merely the client.

The following function will return a pointer to the currently active child window:

```
TMDIChild* GetActiveMDIChild();
```

The next four member functions are useful for performing actions upon all the child windows:

```
bool CloseChildren();
void ArrangeIcons();
void CascadeChildren();
void TileChildren(int tile = MDITILE_VERTICAL);
```

The CloseChildren function does just as it says: closes all the child windows, usually causing them to go away (though you'll notice in the Windows v3.1 Program Manager how the child windows have overridden that functionality to make the windows simply minimize). The ArrangeIcons function puts all the minimized child windows in order at the bottom of the screen. CascadeChildren displays all the child windows in overlapping order from the upper-left corner of the client screen toward the lower-right corner. TileChildren resizes all the child windows so that they can all be displayed on the screen at one time. It does this by setting their sizes approximately equally and ordering them according to the tile parameter, which can be MDITILE_VERTICAL, MDITILEHORIZONTAL, or MDITILE_SKIPDISABLED. Note that these are used only in Win16.

19

The next function is the one that will most often be overridden in descendent versions of TMDIClient:

```
TMDIChild* InitChild();
```

This function is what actually creates a new child window. If you want to have a specialized descendent version of TMDIChild, you will have to override the InitChild function in TMDIClient.

The MDI Child Window Class

The class TMDIChild models the basic operations of all MDI child windows. It's derived from TFrameWindow, and it has the following two public constructors:

```
TMDIChild(TMDIClient&     parent,
         const char far* title = 0,
         TWindow*        clientWnd = 0,
         bool            shrinkToClient = false,
         TModule*        module = 0);
TMDIChild(HWND hWnd, TModule* module = 0);
```

You'll note that there's no difference between these constructors and those offered by the TFrameWindow class, except for the first parameter. It takes a TMDIClient& instead of a TWindow*, and this needs to be the MDI client window. Notice that there is a parameter for specifying a client of the MDI client; this can be used to insert a dialog as the client, as you've seen on previous days.

When it comes right down to it, you can treat the TMDIChild window as if it were any other frame window. It's just that there are a few of the regular functions this has overloaded to provide for the MDI child functionality. They're usually quite transparent, and you can typically ignore what's going on in order to concentrate on your own window processing.

Building MDI Child Windows

Building MDI child windows is similar to building application windows in the programs presented earlier. Following are the differences:

☐ An MDI child window cannot have its own menu. The menu of the MDI frame window is the one that manipulates the currently active MDI child window or all of the MDI children.

Note: The keyboard handler must not be enabled. It actually causes the reverse effect in the MDI children and antagonizes the proper operations of the MDI application.

☐ An MDI child window can have controls—this is unusual but certainly allowed.

Simple Text Viewer

Look at a simple MDI-compliant application. Because MDI applications frequently are used as text viewers and text editors, the next application is presented because it emulates a simple text viewer. I say "emulates" because the application actually displays random text rather than text you can retrieve from a file. This approach keeps the program simple and helps you to focus on implementing the various MDI objects. Figure 19.1 shows a sample session with the MDI1.EXE program. The MDI application has a simple menu containing the Exit and MDI Children items.

Compile and run the application. Experiment with creating MDI children. Notice that the text in odd-numbered MDI child windows is static, whereas the text in even-numbered windows can be edited. This feature is implemented to illustrate how to create a simple form of text viewer and text editor (with no Save option, to keep the example short). Try to tile, cascade, maximize, and minimize these windows. Also test closing individual MDI child windows as well as closing all of the MDI children.

Examine the code that implements this simple MDI application. Listing 19.1 shows the source code for the MDI1.H header file. This file declares the command-message constants and a control-ID constant. Listing 19.2 contains the script for the MDI1.RC resource file. The file defines the menu resource required by the MDI frame window. The menu has two menu items, Exit and MDI Children. The latter menu item is a pop-up menu with several options. The commands, except the option Count Children, use predefined command-message constants. Listing 19.3 shows the source code for the MDI1.CPP program file.

 Listing 19.1. The source code for the MDI1.H header file.

```
1: #define CM_COUNTCHILDREN 101
2: #define ID_TEXT_EDIT     102
```

 Listing 19.2. The script for the MDI1.RC resource file.

```
1:  #include <windows.h>
2:  #include <owl\window.rh>
3:  #include <owl\mdi.rh>
4:  #include "mdi1.h"
5:
6:  MDIMenu MENU LOADONCALL MOVEABLE PURE DISCARDABLE
7:  BEGIN
8:    MENUITEM "E&xit", CM_EXIT
9:    POPUP "&MDI Children"
10:   BEGIN
11:     MENUITEM  "C&reate", CM_CREATECHILD
12:     MENUITEM  "&Cascade", CM_CASCADECHILDREN
13:     MENUITEM  "&Tile", CM_TILECHILDREN
14:     MENUITEM  "Arrange &Icons", CM_ARRANGEICONS
15:     MENUITEM  "C&lose All", CM_CLOSECHILDREN
16:     MENUITEM  "C&ount Children", CM_COUNTCHILDREN
17:   END
18: END
```

19

 Listing 19.3. The source code for the MDI1.CPP program file.

```
1:  // Program to illustrate simple MDI windows
2:
3:  #include <owl\mdi.rh>
```

Listing 19.3. continued

```
 4:   #include <owl\applicat.h>
 5:   #include <owl\framewin.h>
 6:   #include <owl\mdi.h>
 7:   #include <owl\mdichild.h>
 8:   #include <owl\static.h>
 9:   #include <owl\edit.h>
10:   #include <owl\scroller.h>
11:   #include <stdio.h>
12:   #include <string.h>
13:   #include "mdi1.h"
14:
15:   class TMyMDIChild : public TMDIChild
16:   {
17:   public:
18:       TMyMDIChild(TMDIClient& parent, int ChildNum);
19:       virtual ~TMyMDIChild();
20:
21:       virtual bool CanClose();
22:       static void SetExpressClose(bool tf) { ExpressClose = tf; }
23:       static int GetNumChildren()          { return NumChildren; }
24:
25:   protected:
26:       char* add_word(char* str, int& strsize);
27:       char* build_text(char* str, int strsize);
28:
29:   private:
30:       static bool ExpressClose;
31:       static int NumChildren;
32:   };
33:
34:   bool TMyMDIChild::ExpressClose = false;
35:   int TMyMDIChild::NumChildren = 0;
36:
37:   TMyMDIChild::TMyMDIChild(TMDIClient& parent, int ChildNum)
38:       :  TMDIChild(parent)
39:   {
40:       char s[1024];
41:
42:       // set the scrollers in the window
43:       Attr.Style |= WS_VSCROLL | WS_HSCROLL;
44:       Scroller = new TScroller(this, 200, 15, 10, 50);
45:
46:       // set MDI child window title
47:       sprintf(s, "MDI Child #%i", ChildNum);
48:       SetCaption(s);
49:
50:       // build the list of random words
51:       build_text(s, sizeof(s) - 1);
52:
53:       // create a static text object in the child window if the
54:       // ChildNum variable stores an odd number.  Otherwise,
55:       // create an edit box control
56:       if (ChildNum % 2 == 0)
57:           {
```

```
58:        // create an edit box without borders or scroll bars
59:        TEdit* TextBox = new TEdit( this, ID_TEXT_EDIT, s,
60:                                10, 10, 300, 400, 0, true);
61:        TextBox->Attr.Style &= ~WS_BORDER;
62:        TextBox->Attr.Style &= ~WS_VSCROLL;
63:        TextBox->Attr.Style &= ~WS_HSCROLL;
64:        }
65:    else
66:        new TStatic(this, -1, s, 10, 10, 300, 400, strlen(s));
67:    ++NumChildren;
68: }
69:
70: TMyMDIChild::~TMyMDIChild()
71: {
72:    --NumChildren;
73: }
74:
75: bool TMyMDIChild::CanClose()
76: {
77:    return   ExpressClose
78:          || MessageBox( "Close this MDI window?",
79:                         "Query",
80:                         MB_YESNO | MB_ICONQUESTION) == IDYES;
81: }
82:
83: char* TMyMDIChild::add_word(char* str, int& strsize)
84: {
85:    const int LineSize = 45;
86:    static char* wordlist[] =
87:        {
88:        "the", "friend", "saw", "a", "squeaky",
89:        "girl", "drink", "milk", "boy",
90:        "cake", "bread", "family", "swim",
91:        "dinner", "breakfast", "afternoon"
92:        };
93:    char *word = wordlist[random(sizeof(wordlist) / sizeof(char*))];
94:    const char *filler = strlen(str) > 0 ? " " : "";
95:
96:    if (strlen(str) + strlen(filler) + strlen(word) >= LineSize)
97:        filler = "\r\n";
98:    if (strlen(filler) + strlen(word) < strsize)
99:        {
100:       strcat(str, filler);
101:       if (*filler == '\r')
102:           str += strlen(str);
103:       strcat(str, word);
104:       strsize -= strlen(filler) + strlen(word);
105:       }
106:    return str;
107: }
108:
109: char* TMyMDIChild::build_text(char* str, int strsize)
110: {
111:    const int MaxWords = 100;
112:    char *line = str;
```

continues

533

Listing 19.3. continued

```
113:
114:     randomize();            // Initialize random numbers
115:     *line = '\0';           // Start out empty
116:     for (int i = 0; i < MaxWords; ++i)
117:         line = add_word(line, strsize);
118:     return str;
119: }
120:
121: class TMyMDIClient : public TMDIClient
122: {
123: public:
124:     TMyMDIClient() : TMDIClient() {}
125:
126:     virtual TMDIChild* InitChild();    // create a new child
127:     virtual bool CloseChildren();      // close all MDI children
128:
129:     // handle the command for counting the MDI children
130:     void CmCountChildren();
131:
132:     virtual bool CanClose();
133:
134: private:
135:     static int HighMDIIndex;
136:
137:     DECLARE_RESPONSE_TABLE(TMyMDIClient);
138: };
139: DEFINE_RESPONSE_TABLE1(TMyMDIClient, TMDIClient)
140:     EV_COMMAND(CM_COUNTCHILDREN, CmCountChildren),
141: END_RESPONSE_TABLE;
142:
143: int TMyMDIClient::HighMDIIndex = 0;
144:
145: TMDIChild* TMyMDIClient::InitChild()
146: {
147:     return new TMyMDIChild(*this, ++HighMDIIndex);
148: }
149:
150: bool TMyMDIClient::CloseChildren()
151: {
152:     bool result;
153:
154:     TMyMDIChild::SetExpressClose(true);
155:     result = TMDIClient::CloseChildren();
156:     TMyMDIChild::SetExpressClose(false);
157:     HighMDIIndex = 0;
158:     return result;
159: }
160:
161: //  display a message box that shows the number of children
162: void TMyMDIClient::CmCountChildren()
163: {
164:     char msgStr[81];
165:
166:     sprintf(msgStr, "There are %i MDI child windows",
167:             TMyMDIChild::GetNumChildren() );
```

```
168:     MessageBox(msgStr, "Information", MB_OK ¦ MB_ICONINFORMATION);
169: }
170:
171: bool TMyMDIClient::CanClose()
172: {
173:     return MessageBox("Close this application?",
174:                       "Query",
175:                       MB_YESNO ¦ MB_ICONQUESTION) == IDYES;
176: }
177:
178: class TMyApp : public TApplication
179: {
180: public:
181:     TMyApp() : TApplication()
182:         { nCmdShow = SW_SHOWMAXIMIZED; }
183:
184:     virtual void InitMainWindow()
185:         {
186:         SetMainWindow( new TMDIFrame( "Simple MDI Text Viewer",
187:                                       "MDIMenu",
188:                                       *new TMyMDIClient ) );
189:         }
190: };
191:
192: int OwlMain(int, char *[])
193: {
194:     return TMyApp().Run();
195: }
```

Figure 19.1.

*A sample session with the
MDI1.EXE program.*

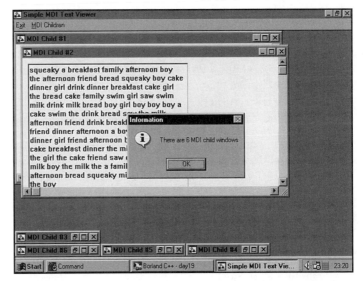

The program in Listing 19.3 starts with the declaration of the TMyMDIChild class as a descendent
of TMDIChild. It overrides the constructor and the CanClose function, then declares the two static

535

functions SetExpressClose and GetNumChildren functions, the two protected functions add_word, and build_text, and the two private static data members ExpressClose and NumChildren. These last two are then defined immediately after the class declaration and set to false and 0, respectively.

The TMyMDIChild constructor starts on line 37, and its first duty is to call its base class's constructor. It then declares a rather large string buffer of 1024 bytes. This will be used to store the text that is to be displayed in the window. Next, on lines 43 and 44, the window is given scroll bars. Lines 47 and 48 change the title of the child window, reflecting the ChildNum parameter.

Line 51 makes a call to build_text, passing the string buffer s and its size. Note that the size has 1 subtracted from it in the call to make sure there's room for the terminating NULL character. After this is done, the control to hold that buffer is created on lines 56 through 66. Line 67 increments the internal counter that holds the number of children active at any one time. This counter is decremented by the destructor on line 72.

The CanClose member function comes next on line 75. This is overridden so as to have the user make sure he wants to close a window before it's actually done. However, in order to make for better automation, the user isn't questioned if the ExpressClose flag is set. This is used when the Close All menu item is selected, thus preventing a number of message boxes from popping up in a row.

The add_word member function starts on line 63. Its purpose is to add a random word to the passed str, so long as the total amount of characters to be added won't go over the strsize length. The main trick of this function is that it pays attention to how many characters can fit on a line and automatically wraps the words to the next line when they won't fit normally. Line 85 contains the definition of the LineSize (here arbitrarily set to 45) and line 86 starts the listing of some words I just threw together. Line 93 picks out a word at random and assigns it to word. Note that, instead of using a constant for the number of words in the array wordlist, I use the formula sizeof(wordlist) / sizeof(char*) to determine the number of elements in the array. This makes it much easier to add and delete words from the list at will.

Line 94 contains the definition of the filler variable, which is initialized to a space. This is used to separate the words as they're appended to str. Line 96 determines if the addition of the filler and the word would go over the line-length limit. If so, then filler is changed to the characters that make a new line. Line 98 makes sure that the additional characters won't go over the total size remaining in the string. If there's room, then first the filler is added. If the filler had been changed to new line earlier, then str is adjusted to its endpoint. That way, future tests for line length won't include all the previous text. Finally, the word itself is added, and strsize is adjusted by the number of characters added. Line 106 returns str so that it can be used in future calls to the function.

You might be wondering why I used a const char* for filler rather than an array. This works here because I never actually copy anything into filler. Rather, I assign it pointers to static

strings that reside in the system. So long as I don't try to modify `filler`, I'm okay. That's why I made it `const`, to make sure that any attempted changes would be caught by the compiler for me.

Starting on line 109, `build_text` is the main entry function for building the text string, but it's far simpler that `add_word`. It simply iterates through a loop that calls `add_word` to build the string, one word at a time.

The `TMyMDIClient` class starts on line 121. It declares a default constructor that simply calls its base class's version. It then overloads the `InitChild`, `CloseChildren`, and `CanClose` member functions while declaring a new `CmCountChildren` function. It also declares the static `HighMDIIndex` data variable and initializes it to 0 on line 143.

Line 147 shows that `InitChild` does nothing more than create a new `TMyMDIChild` and return a pointer to it. `InitChild` passes the incremented value of `HighMDIIndex` in the constructor to help differentiate between the different child windows. `CloseChildren`, starting on line 150, tells the `TMyMDIChild` class to use express closing when it closes its windows for the duration of the call to `TMDIClient::CloseChildren`, then it resets the `HighMDIIndex` value to 0.

The `CmCountChildren` function that starts on line 162 creates a string containing the total number of child windows in existence as reported by `TMyMDIChild::GetNumChildren`. It then displays this string in a message box for the user.

The rest of the program is very much like what you've seen before—except that this time, instead of using `TFrameWindow`, `TMDIFrame` is used on line 186. This simple change is all that's needed to switch the frame window over to an MDI frame.

Revised Text Viewer

Let's expand on the MDI1.EXE program to illustrate other aspects of managing MDI windows. The next application also creates MDI children that contain edit-box controls with random text. However, each MDI child window has the following additional controls:

☐ An Upper Case pushbutton control that converts the text in the MDI child window into uppercase.

☐ A Lower Case pushbutton control that converts the text in the MDI child window into lowercase.

☐ A Can Close check box. Using this box replaces using the confirmation dialog box that appears when you want to close the MDI child window. The check box enables you to predetermine whether the MDI child window can be closed.

The application menu adds a new pop-up menu item, Current MDI Child. This menu item has options that work on the current MDI child window. The commands enable you to clear, convert to uppercase, convert to lowercase, or rewrite the characters in the MDI child window. The new pop-up menu shows how you can manipulate MDI children with custom menus.

Compile and run the application. Create a few MDI children and use their pushbutton controls to toggle the case of characters in these windows. Also use the Current MDI Child commands to further manipulate the text in the currently active MDI child window. Try to close the MDI children with the Can Close check box marked and unmarked. Only the MDI children with the Can Close control checked close individually. Use the Close All option in the MDI Children pop-up menu and watch all of the MDI children close, regardless of the check state of the Can Close control. Figure 19.2 shows a sample session with the MDI2.EXE program.

Listing 19.4 shows the source code for the MDI2.H header file. The file contains the constants for the menu commands and the control IDs. Listing 19.5 contains the script for the MDI2.RC resource file and shows the resource for the expanded menu. Listing 19.6 contains the source code for the MDI2.CPP program file.

Listing 19.4. The source code for the MDI2.H header file.

```
1: #define CM_COUNTCHILDREN 101
2: #define CM_UPPERCASE     102
3: #define CM_LOWERCASE     103
4: #define CM_RESET         104
5: #define CM_CLEAR         105
6: #define IDE_TEXT         106
7: #define IDC_CANCLOSE     107
8: #define IDB_UPPERCASE    108
9: #define IDB_LOWERCASE    109
```

Listing 19.5. The script for the MDI2.RC resource file.

```
1:  #include <windows.h>
2:  #include <owl\window.rh>
3:  #include <owl\mdi.rh>
4:  #include "mdi2.h"
5:
6:  MDIMenu MENU LOADONCALL MOVEABLE PURE DISCARDABLE
7:  BEGIN
8:    MENUITEM "E&xit", CM_EXIT
9:    POPUP "&MDI Children"
10:   BEGIN
11:     MENUITEM  "C&reate", CM_CREATECHILD
12:     MENUITEM  "&Cascade", CM_CASCADECHILDREN
13:     MENUITEM  "&Tile", CM_TILECHILDREN
14:     MENUITEM  "Arrange &Icons", CM_ARRANGEICONS
15:     MENUITEM  "C&lose All", CM_CLOSECHILDREN
16:     MENUITEM  "C&ount Children", CM_COUNTCHILDREN
17:   END
18:   POPUP "&Current MDI Child"
19:   BEGIN
```

```
20:     MENUITEM  "&Clear", CM_CLEAR
21:     MENUITEM  "&Uppercase", CM_UPPERCASE
22:     MENUITEM  "&Lowercase", CM_LOWERCASE
23:     MENUITEM  "&Reset", CM_RESET
24:   END
25: END
```

Listing 19.6. The source code for the MDI2.CPP program file.

```
1:  // Program to illustrate simple MDI windows
2:
3:  #include <owl\mdi.rh>
4:  #include <owl\applicat.h>
5:  #include <owl\button.h>
6:  #include <owl\checkbox.h>
7:  #include <owl\edit.h>
8:  #include <owl\framewin.h>
9:  #include <owl\mdi.h>
10: #include <owl\mdichild.h>
11: #include <owl\scroller.h>
12: #include <owl\static.h>
13: #include <stdio.h>
14: #include <string.h>
15: #include "mdi2.h"
16:
17: class TMyMDIChild : public TMDIChild
18: {
19: public:
20:    TMyMDIChild(TMDIClient& parent, int ChildNum);
21:    virtual ~TMyMDIChild();
22:
23:    virtual bool CanClose();
24:    virtual void SetupWindow()
25:       { TMDIChild::SetupWindow(); CmReset(); }
26:    static void SetExpressClose(bool tf) { ExpressClose = tf; }
27:    static int GetNumChildren()          { return NumChildren; }
28:    void CmClear()                        { textBox->Clear(); }
29:    void CmReset();
30:    void CmLowerCase();
31:    void CmUpperCase();
32:
33: protected:
34:    char* add_word(char* str, int& strsize);
35:    char* build_text(char* str, int strsize);
36:
37: private:
38:    static bool ExpressClose;
39:    static int NumChildren;
40:
41:    TEdit* textBox;
42:    TCheckBox* canClose;
43:
44:    DECLARE_RESPONSE_TABLE(TMyMDIChild);
```

continues

Listing 19.6. continued

```
45:  };
46:  DEFINE_RESPONSE_TABLE1(TMyMDIChild, TMDIChild)
47:    EV_COMMAND(IDB_UPPERCASE, CmUpperCase),
48:    EV_COMMAND(IDB_LOWERCASE, CmLowerCase),
49:    EV_COMMAND(CM_CLEAR, CmClear),
50:    EV_COMMAND(CM_UPPERCASE, CmUpperCase),
51:    EV_COMMAND(CM_LOWERCASE, CmLowerCase),
52:    EV_COMMAND(CM_RESET, CmReset),
53:  END_RESPONSE_TABLE;
54:
55:  bool TMyMDIChild::ExpressClose = false;
56:  int TMyMDIChild::NumChildren = 0;
57:
58:  TMyMDIChild::TMyMDIChild(TMDIClient& parent, int ChildNum)
59:      :  TMDIChild(parent)
60:  {
61:    const int wspacing = 20;
62:    const int hspacing = 10;
63:    const int wbtn = 50 * 3;
64:    const int hbtn = 30;
65:    const int wchk = 200 * 3;
66:    const int hchk = 20;
67:    const int wbox = 200 * 3;
68:    const int hbox = 200 * 3;
69:    const int x0 = 10;
70:    const int y0 = 10;
71:
72:    // set the scrollers in the window
73:    Attr.Style |= WS_VSCROLL | WS_HSCROLL;
74:    Scroller = new TScroller(this, 200, 15, 10, 50);
75:
76:    // set MDI child window title
77:    char str[25];
78:    sprintf(str, "MDI Child #%i", ChildNum);
79:    SetCaption(str);
80:
81:    int x = x0, y = y0;
82:    new TButton(this, IDB_UPPERCASE, "Upper Case",
83:                x, y, wbtn, hbtn, true);
84:    x += wbtn + wspacing;
85:    new TButton(this, IDB_LOWERCASE, "Lower Case",
86:                x, y, wbtn, hbtn, false);
87:    x = x0;
88:    y += hbtn + hspacing;
89:    canClose = new TCheckBox(this, IDC_CANCLOSE, "Can Close",
90:                             x, y, wchk, hchk);
91:    y += hchk + hspacing;
92:    textBox = new TEdit( this, IDE_TEXT, 0,
93:                         x, y, wbox, hbox, 0, true);
94:    textBox->Attr.Style &= ~WS_BORDER;
95:    textBox->Attr.Style &= ~WS_VSCROLL;
96:    textBox->Attr.Style &= ~WS_HSCROLL;
97:    ++NumChildren;
98:  }
99:
```

```
100: TMyMDIChild::~TMyMDIChild()
101: {
102:     --NumChildren;
103: }
104:
105: bool TMyMDIChild::CanClose()
106: {
107:     return ExpressClose || canClose->GetCheck() == BF_CHECKED;
108: }
109:
110: void TMyMDIChild::CmReset()
111: {
112:     char s[1024];
113:     build_text(s, sizeof(s) - 1);
114:     textBox->SetText(s);
115: }
116:
117: void TMyMDIChild::CmLowerCase()
118: {
119:     int size = textBox->GetTextLen() + 1;
120:     char* str = new char[size + 1];
121:     textBox->GetText(str, size);
122:     strlwr(str);
123:     textBox->SetText(str);
124:     delete str;
125: }
126:
127: void TMyMDIChild::CmUpperCase()
128: {
129:     int size = textBox->GetTextLen() + 1;
130:     char* str = new char[size + 1];
131:     textBox->GetText(str, size);
132:     strupr(str);
133:     textBox->SetText(str);
134:     delete str;
135: }
136:
137: char* TMyMDIChild::add_word(char* str, int& strsize)
138: {
139:     const int LineSize = 45;
140:     static char* wordlist[] =
141:         {
142:         "the", "friend", "saw", "a", "squeaky",
143:         "girl", "drink", "milk", "boy",
144:         "cake", "bread", "family", "swim",
145:         "dinner", "breakfast", "afternoon"
146:         };
147:     char *word = wordlist[random(sizeof(wordlist) / sizeof(char*))];
148:     const char *filler = strlen(str) > 0 ? " " : "";
149:
150:     if (strlen(str) + strlen(filler) + strlen(word) >= LineSize)
151:         filler = "\r\n";
152:     if (strlen(filler) + strlen(word) < strsize)
153:         {
154:         strcat(str, filler);
```

continues

19

Listing 19.6. continued

```
155:         if (*filler == '\r')
156:             str += strlen(str);
157:         strcat(str, word);
158:         strsize -= strlen(filler) + strlen(word);
159:         }
160:     return str;
161: }
162:
163: char* TMyMDIChild::build_text(char* str, int strsize)
164: {
165:     const int MaxWords = 100;
166:     char *line = str;
167:
168:     randomize();          // Initialize random numbers
169:     *line = '\0';         // Start out empty
170:     for (int i = 0; i < MaxWords; ++i)
171:         line = add_word(line, strsize);
172:     return str;
173: }
174:
175: class TMyMDIClient : public TMDIClient
176: {
177: public:
178:     TMyMDIClient() : TMDIClient() {}
179:
180:     virtual TMDIChild* InitChild();   // create a new child
181:     virtual bool CloseChildren();     // close all MDI children
182:
183:     // handle the command for counting the MDI children
184:     void CmCountChildren();
185:
186:     virtual bool CanClose();
187:
188: private:
189:     static int HighMDIIndex;
190:
191:     DECLARE_RESPONSE_TABLE(TMyMDIClient);
192: };
193: DEFINE_RESPONSE_TABLE1(TMyMDIClient, TMDIClient)
194:     EV_COMMAND(CM_COUNTCHILDREN, CmCountChildren),
195: END_RESPONSE_TABLE;
196:
197: int TMyMDIClient::HighMDIIndex = 0;
198:
199: TMDIChild* TMyMDIClient::InitChild()
200: {
201:     return new TMyMDIChild(*this, ++HighMDIIndex);
202: }
203:
204: bool TMyMDIClient::CloseChildren()
205: {
206:     bool result;
207:
208:     TMyMDIChild::SetExpressClose(true);
```

```
209:      result = TMDIClient::CloseChildren();
210:      TMyMDIChild::SetExpressClose(false);
211:      HighMDIIndex = 0;
212:      return result;
213: }
214:
215: //  display a message box that shows the number of children
216: void TMyMDIClient::CmCountChildren()
217: {
218:      char msgStr[81];
219:
220:      sprintf(msgStr, "There are %i MDI child windows",
221:             TMyMDIChild::GetNumChildren() );
222:      MessageBox(msgStr, "Information", MB_OK | MB_ICONINFORMATION);
223: }
224:
225: bool TMyMDIClient::CanClose()
226: {
227:      return MessageBox("Close this application?",
228:                          "Query",
229:                          MB_YESNO | MB_ICONQUESTION) == IDYES;
230: }
231:
232: class TMyApp : public TApplication
233: {
234: public:
235:      TMyApp() : TApplication()
236:          { nCmdShow = SW_SHOWMAXIMIZED; }
237:
238:      virtual void InitMainWindow()
239:          {
240:          SetMainWindow( new TMDIFrame( "Simple MDI Text Viewer",
241:                                          "MDIMenu",
242:                                          *new TMyMDIClient ) );
243:          }
244: };
245:
246: int OwlMain(int, char *[])
247: {
248:      return TMyApp().Run();
249: }
```

19

Note: Due to a minor bug in OWL, if you choose Close All after creating a few MDI children, the MDI Children | Create menu becomes disabled. To reenable the menu option, choose the Exit menu and click on No. Then both the Create and Count Children options under MDI Children become enabled.

In general, when Close All is selected, all of the menu items need to be reset back to the way they were when the application started.

Figure 19.2.

A sample session with the MDI2.EXE program.

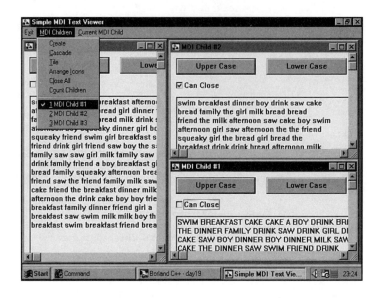

The only thing that's really changed between this program and the one in Listing 19.3 is the implementation of the TMyMDIChild class. The changes start with the addition of five member functions and two data members to the class:

☐ The SetupWindow member function is used to help centralize the function that adds the random text to the child window's text box. It's a simple inline function that calls the base class's SetupWindow to ensure that the Windows objects are properly created and connected with the OWL objects, then it calls the CmReset function to fill in the text box.

☐ The CmClear member function should be rather obvious: it clears the contents of the text box.

☐ CmReset is now the central location for filling in the text box with the random words. It creates the local character array, which is then passed to the build_text function.

☐ CmLowerCase figures out how many characters are in the text box, loads it into a newly created character array, then calls strlwr to convert all its characters to lowercase. The array is then sent back into the text box before being deleted.

☐ CmUpperCase is identical to CmLowerCase except that it calls strupr to convert the characters to uppercase.

☐ The textBox and canClose data members hold pointers to the text box and check-box controls in the child window.

Another major difference in the TMyMDIChild class is the addition of a response table to handle window messages. These are all for the two buttons, the check box, and for all the menu items that need specific responses. Luckily, the function signatures for the menu-response functions and for the control-response functions are the same, so the same function can be used for both responses.

The final difference occurs in the constructor for the TMyMDIChild class. This now creates more than just the text box; it also creates two buttons and a check box. Because there's no need to keep track of the state of the buttons, there's no need to assign them to variables.

> **Note:** The Current MDI Child pop-up menu has four options that manipulate the currently active MDI child window. The command messages emitted by these options are handled by the MDI child window instances and not the MDI frame instance—which is what a window instance normally does regarding its own menu commands. This order of handling the command messages is preferred and makes use of the fact that the menu-based messages do reach the currently active MDI child window first. You can rewrite the program such that the functions CmClear, CmUpperCase, CmLowerCase, and CmReset appear as member functions of class TMyMDIFrame.

Summary

This chapter presented the Multiple Document Interface (MDI), which is an interface standard in Windows. The chapter discussed the following subjects:

☐ The basic features and components of an MDI-compliant application, including the MDI frame window, the invisible MDI client window, and the dynamically created MDI child windows

☐ The basics of building an MDI application

☐ The TMDIFrame class, which manages the MDI client window, the MDI child windows, and the execution of the menu commands

☐ Building MDI frame windows as objects that are owned by the application and that own the MDI client window

☐ The TMDIClient class, which owns the MDI child windows

☐ Building MDI child windows as an instance of a TMDIChild descendant and using customized client windows as instances of TWindow descendants

☐ Managing messages in an MDI-compliant application; the currently active MDI child window has a higher priority for handling menu-based command messages than its parent, the MDI client window

19

Q&A

Q Should each MDI child window have an ID?

A Yes. Associating each MDI child window with an ID gives you more control over managing these windows, especially if they vary in relevance. Thus, you can use the ID to exclude special MDI child windows from collective operations.

Q Can I hide MDI child windows?

A Yes. You can use the inherited member function `TWindow::ShowWindow` to show and hide one MDI child window or more.

Workshop

The Workshop provides quiz questions to help you solidify your understanding of the material covered and exercises to provide you with experience in using what you've learned. Try to understand the quiz and exercise answers before continuing on to the bonus chapters. Answers are provided in Appendix A.

Quiz

1. True or false? MDI child windows can have their own menus.
2. True or false? MDI child windows can be moved outside the area of the frame window.
3. True or false? OWL supports nested MDI child windows.

Exercises

1. Experiment with expanding the vocabulary of programs MDI1.EXE and MDI2.EXE.
2. Add a control that inserts the date and time in MDI child windows of program MDI1.EXE.

The Application and Class Experts

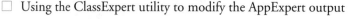
The AppExpert utility is a versatile tool that helps you create project source-code files quickly and systematically. The utility generates functioning skeleton code that you can then customize to meet the needs of your Windows applications. Thus, rather than start from scratch or adapt similar existing code, you can use the AppExpert utility to do much of the systematic work for you, freeing you to concentrate on implementing the code that supports your application's special features. It's like having a consultant inside Borland C++! This chapter focuses on the following topics:

- [ ] Using the AppExpert utility
- [ ] Examining the source-code output generated by selecting some project options in AppExpert
- [ ] Using the ClassExpert utility to modify the AppExpert output

> **Note:** The listings generated by AppExpert were edited to better fit the pages in this book.

Using the AppExpert Utility

To use the AppExpert utility, invoke the AppExpert... option in the File | New menu. The IDE brings up the project file-selection dialog box. This dialog box is similar to the Open a File dialog box. Select an appropriate folder and .IDE filename, or type in the name of a new .IDE file and then click the OK button. If you type in the name of a new .IDE file, the AppExpert utility creates a new project file. On the other hand, if you choose an existing .IDE file, the AppExpert utility merely adds the new target to that project file. Next, the AppExpert utility displays the AppExpert Application Generation Options dialog box (called the AppExpert dialog box for short), as shown in Figure 20.1. This dialog box has three topics in its left-hand list box: Application, Main Window, and MDI Child/View.

> **Note:** It is important to know that the AppExpert dialog box hides and shows different controls based on the currently selected topic or subtopic in the same way as the Options dialog box. As you select different items in the left-hand list box, the options on the right side of the dialog will change.

The Application Topic

Figure 20.1 shows the options of the Application topic. You will be working with these options in this chapter to generate projects with the AppExpert utility. The options of the Application topic are as follows:

- ☐ The choice between an application that supports SDI or MDI child windows, or one that supports a dialog client
- ☐ The use of document and view classes in the text editor
- ☐ A button to expand the Application subtopics

Figure 20.1.

The AppExpert Application Generation Options dialog box.

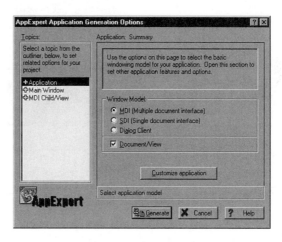

If you click the + sign located to the left of the Application topic, double-click the Application topic itself, or click on the Customize Application button, you expand the Application subtopics. Figure 20.2 shows the options offered by the Application subtopics:

- ☐ Basic Options
- ☐ Advanced Options
- ☐ OLE 2 Options
- ☐ Code Gen Control
- ☐ Admin Options

The Basic Options Subtopic

Figure 20.2 shows the options offered by the Basic Options subtopic. The option choices include the following:

- ☐ The name of the target

☐ The base directory for the target

☐ A number of options for including various features

☐ The option to provide online help with its corresponding help file

Figure 20.2.

The AppExpert dialog box showing the Basic Options subtopic in the Application topic.

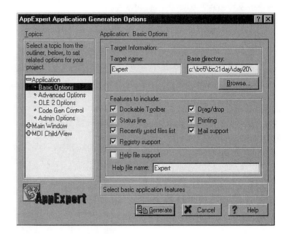

The dialog box offers two edit-box controls for you to enter the target information. In addition, the dialog box shows a Browse pushbutton, which enables you to invoke a dialog box for selecting a new base directory.

The features available for inclusion in your program include the following:

☐ *Dockable Toolbar.* Adds a dockable toolbar to the application.

☐ *Status Line.* Adds a status line at the bottom of the main application window.

☐ *Recently used files list.* Adds a list of the most recently used files to the application's File menu.

☐ *Registry support.* Adds support for using the system registry.

☐ *Drag/Drop.* Adds support for drag and drop.

☐ *Printing.* Adds printer support.

☐ *Mail support.* Adds MAPI support for sending mail.

As for the help file, the AppExpert dialog box contains a check box that enables you to either support or prevent the creation of the help file and an edit box enabling you to set the name of the help file.

The Advanced Options Subtopic

The Advanced Options subtopic is shown in Figure 20.3. These options include the capabilities of selecting the application's startup state and its control style.

Figure 20.3.
The AppExpert dialog box showing the Advanced Options subtopic in the Application topic.

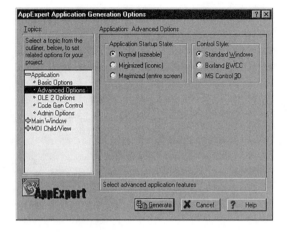

The radio buttons for setting the startup options enable you to have the application automatically minimized or maximized when it starts up, or to start up in the normal manner. The radio buttons for the control styles default to the standard Windows setting, which shows a white background on dialog boxes in Windows 3.*x*. The BWCC style refers to Borland's set of "chiseled steel" dialog boxes with the mottled background and controls with a more three-dimensional appearance. The MS Control 3D appearance is used in standard Microsoft applications, but it isn't needed in Windows 95 or Windows NT as this is the default behavior.

The OLE 2 Options Subtopic

The OLE 2 Options offered by the Application Generator are shown in Figure 20.4. They include the following:

- [ ] Whether an application is an OLE 2 container
- [ ] Whether an application is an OLE 2 server, and whether it's an EXE or a DLL server
- [ ] Whether the application should have automation
- [ ] The server ID to be used in registering the application

The first option is obvious; an application either is or isn't an OLE 2 container. With the server, however, an application may have the OLE 2 server routines reside in either an EXE or a DLL, and the application generator will handle both cases. The automation routines allow one application to be controlled from another. Finally, the server ID is a unique number, guaranteed to be different from all other IDs that might exist. OLE 2 is described in more detail on Day 21.

Figure 20.4.

The AppExpert dialog box showing the OLE 2 Options subtopic in the Application topic.

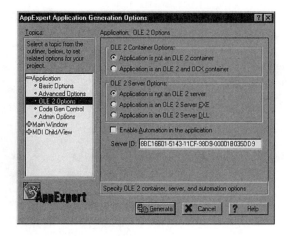

The Code Gen Control Subtopic

The Code Gen Control subtopic offers the options shown in Figure 20.5. When you select this subtopic, the AppExpert dialog box displays the target name and the base directory. In addition, the dialog box offers edit-box controls to select the following:

- ☐ The source directory
- ☐ The header directory
- ☐ The main source file
- ☐ The main header file
- ☐ The application class
- ☐ The About dialog class

The dialog box offers browse buttons for the source and header directory options. If you are running on a system that supports long filenames, you can check the box that will have the AppExpert generate long filenames. In addition, the dialog box presents two radio buttons that enable you to select between verbose or terse comments. The default setting enables verbose comments.

The Admin Options Subtopic

The Admin Options subtopic, shown in Figure 20.6, handles the administrative side of the project. The AppExpert dialog box provides you with edit-box controls to enter the following information:

- ☐ The version number (the default is 1.0)
- ☐ The copyright notice (the dialog box offers a default wording for the copyright notice)

☐ The description (the default description is the target name)

☐ The name of the target author

☐ The name of the company

Figure 20.5.
The AppExpert dialog box showing the Code Gen Control subtopic.

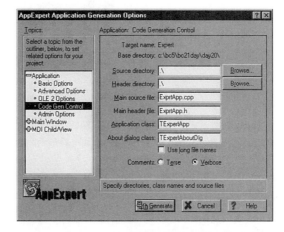

Figure 20.6.
The AppExpert dialog box showing the Admin Options subtopic.

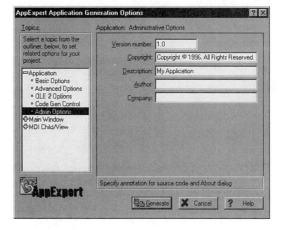

The Main Window Topic

The Main Window topic alters the AppExpert dialog box to offer you options that set the window title and background (see Figure 20.7). The dialog box also presents a box that enables you to set the background color.

Figure 20.7.
The AppExpert dialog box showing the Main Window topic.

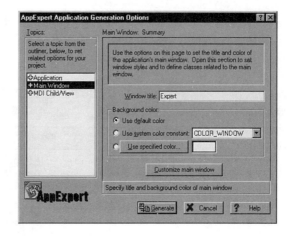

The Main Window topic has the following subtopics:

- ☐ Basic Options
- ☐ SDI Client
- ☐ MDI Client
- ☐ Dialog Client

The Basic Options Subtopic

The Basic Options subtopic in the Main Window topic permits you to select the window style. Figure 20.8 shows the options offered by this subtopic, as follows:

- ☐ *Caption.* Creates a single thin border and a title bar that can display a caption.
- ☐ *Border.* Creates a single thin border that has no title bar.
- ☐ *Max box.* Adds a maximize button to the right side of the title bar that belongs to the application's main window.
- ☐ *Min box.* Adds a minimize button to the right side of the title bar that belongs to the application's main window.
- ☐ *Vertical scroll.* Includes a vertical scroll on the right side of the main window.
- ☐ *Horizontal scroll.* Includes a horizontal scroll on the bottom of the main window.
- ☐ *System menu.* Includes the system-menu button located to the left side of the title bar in the main window. The Caption option must be selected to make this option available.

□ *Visible.* Makes the main window visible.

□ *Disabled.* Disables the main window.

□ *Thick frame.* Displays the main window as a dialog box, with a double border. Consequently, you cannot resize the main window.

□ *Clip siblings.* Protects the sibling windows of the main window.

□ *Clip children.* Ensures that the main window is not painted over by the child windows.

Figure 20.8.
The AppExpert dialog box showing the Basic Options subtopic in the Main Window topic.

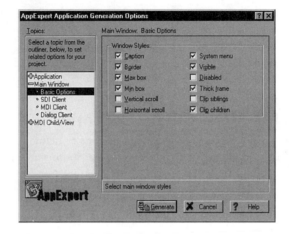

The SDI Client Subtopic

The SDI Client subtopic offers options that define the class, which in turn models the client area of an SDI-compliant main window. These options are effective only if you select the Single Document Interface option in the opening AppExpert dialog box. Figure 20.9 shows the AppExpert dialog box displaying the SDI Client subtopic with the following options:

□ The drop-down combo box that enables you to select the Client/View class.

□ The drop-down combo box that permits you to select the Document class.

□ The three edit boxes to enter the file-type filters. These controls accept the file description, filters, and default extensions.

□ An edit box enabling you to set the name of the SDI view class.

□ Two edit boxes to set the names of the source file and the header file for the SDI class.

Figure 20.9.
The AppExpert dialog box showing the SDI Client subtopic.

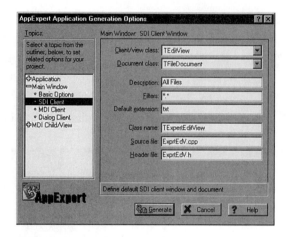

The MDI Client Subtopic

The MDI Client subtopic offers options to define the class that models the client area of an MDI-compliant frame window. These options are effective only if you select the Multiple Document Interface option in the opening AppExpert dialog box. Figure 20.10 shows the AppExpert dialog box displaying the MDI Client subtopic with the following options:

- The name of the MDI client window class
- The source filename
- The header filename

Figure 20.10.
The AppExpert dialog box showing the MDI Client subtopic.

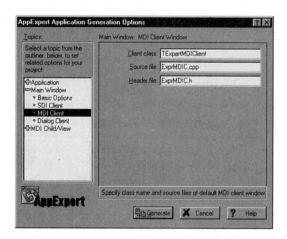

The Dialog Client Subtopic

The Dialog Client subtopic offers options to define the class that models the client area of a dialog frame window. You can select the resource ID of the dialog box to load, and you can select whether to include a menu bar. These options are effective only if you select the Dialog Client option in the opening AppExpert dialog box. Figure 20.11 shows the AppExpert dialog box displaying the Dialog Client subtopic with the following options:

☐ The name of the dialog client-window class

☐ The source filename

☐ The header filename

☐ The resource ID of the dialog box to load into the client

☐ Whether to include a menu bar in the frame

Figure 20.11.
The AppExpert dialog box showing the Dialog Client subtopic.

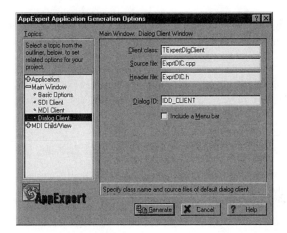

The MDI Child/View Topic

The MDI Child/View topic, shown in Figure 20.12, has options that enable you to specify the following:

☐ The name of the MDI child-window class

☐ The source file that contains the implementation of the MDI child-window class

☐ The header file that contains the declaration of the MDI child-window class

Figure 20.12.

The AppExpert dialog box showing the MDI Child/ View topic.

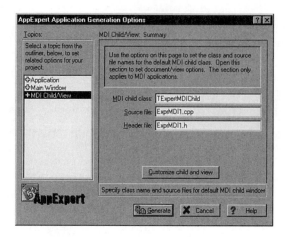

The AppExpert dialog box offers the Customize child and view pushbutton control, which simply invokes the Basic Options subtopic that is discussed next.

The Basic Options Subtopic

The *Basic Options* subtopic offers options to define the class that models the client area of an MDI child window. These options are effective only if you select the Multiple Document Interface option in the opening AppExpert dialog box. Figure 20.13 shows the AppExpert dialog box displaying the Basic Options subtopic with the following options:

☐ The drop-down combo box that enables you to select the MDI Client/View class.

☐ The drop-down combo box that enables you to select the Document class.

☐ The three edit boxes to enter the file-type filters. These controls accept the file description, filters, and default extensions.

☐ The class name, source file, and header file.

Figure 20.13.

The AppExpert dialog box showing the Basic Options subtopic in the MDI Child/ View topic.

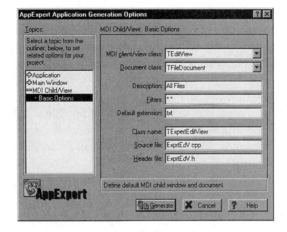

Studying the AppExpert Output

You've just seen that the AppExpert utility offers many options to determine the kind of source code files that can be generated. Now I present an SDI-compliant project generated by altering the AppExpert options. Because the total number of possible source-code listings is rather large, we will focus on a selection of source-code files generated by AppExpert.

Note: Although the AppExpert creates a sizable amount of source code very quickly, you should study the output nonetheless. Acquainting yourself with the output enables you to quickly and efficiently customize the AppExpert output. This approach shortens the overall process of developing your applications. By contrast, not being familiar with the emitted source code will cost you extra time in debugging your programs.

20

The ideal study of the source-code files generated by AppExpert would include varying each of the AppExpert options, one at a time, and covering all of the possible combinations. Because the total number of these combinations is relatively large, we will examine just one set of the possible output source code that is generated. The AppExpert generates a minimally functioning text editor. Please do not interpret the words *minimally functioning* to mean that it's a real dud. In fact, the generated text editors offer an acceptable level of operations, because the various OWL classes used in these editors support these operations. I would like to point out that working with all the different combinations is a good independent exercise. I suggest that you experiment with these various combinations to see what kind of program each combination generates.

The Expert Project

The sample project is EXPERT. This project generates an SDI-compliant text editor with no toolbar, no status line, no drag-and-drop feature support, and no printing-related features. In other words, the EXPERT project is the simplest text editor generated by AppExpert.

When you invoke the AppExpert utility from the IDE Project menu, set the name of the project to Expert. When the AppExpert dialog appears, select the SDI option, deselect the Document/View checkbox, and turn off all the features in the Basic Options section of Application. When the Generate button is pressed, the utility generates the following set of files:

Filename	Description
applsdi.ico	Application icon
expert.apx	AppExpert reference file
expert.ide	IDE project file
exprtabd.cpp	About box source
exprtabd.h	About box header
exprtapp.cpp	Main application source
exprtapp.def	Application definition file
exprtapp.h	Main application header
exprtapp.rc	Resource source
exprtapp.rh	Resource header
exprtedf.cpp	TEditFile descendant class source
exprtedf.h	TEditFile descendant class header
hslider.bmp	Bit map of a horizontal slider's thumb
vsliter.bmp	Bit map of a vertical slider's thumb

The preceding files contains icon, header, definition, resource header, resource, implementation, and IDE files. Look at the .DEF, .H, .RH, .RC, and .CPP files. Build the EXPERT project and experiment with its text-editing features.

Listing 20.1. The contents of the EXPRTAPP.DEF definition file.

```
;--------------------------------------------------------------------
;   Project Expert
;
;   Copyright © 1996. All Rights Reserved.
;
;   SUBSYSTEM:    Expert Module Defintion File
;   FILE:         ExprtApp.def
;   AUTHOR:
;
;--------------------------------------------------------------------

NAME 'Expert'

DESCRIPTION 'Expert Application - Copyright © 1996. All Rights Reserved.'
EXETYPE       WINDOWS
CODE          PRELOAD MOVEABLE DISCARDABLE
DATA          PRELOAD MOVEABLE

; Note: The following are recommended settings for the default
;       AppExpert application when compiled as a 16-bit target.
;
; HEAPSIZE    4096
; STACKSIZE   8192
```

Listing 20.2. The source code for the EXPRTAPP.RH resource header file.

```
//--------------------------------------------------------------------
//   Project Expert
//
//   Copyright © 1996. All Rights Reserved.
//
//   SUBSYSTEM:    Expert Application
//   FILE:         ExprtApp.h
//   AUTHOR:
//
//   OVERVIEW
//   ~~~~~~~~
//   Constant definitions for all resources defined in ExprtApp.rc.
//
//--------------------------------------------------------------------
//#if !defined(exprtapp_rh)   // Sentry use file only if it's not already included.
//#define exprtapp_rh


//
// Application specific definitions:
//
#define IDI_SDIAPPLICATION      1001             // Application icon
```

continues

Listing 20.2. continued

```
#define IDM_SDI                 100            // Menu resource ID and Accelerator
                                              // IDs


//
// CM_FILEnnnn commands (include/owl/editfile.rh except for CM_FILEPRINTPREVIEW)
//
#define CM_FILENEW             24331          // SDI New
#define CM_FILEOPEN            24332          // SDI Open
#define CM_FILECLOSE           24339
#define CM_FILESAVE            24333
#define CM_FILESAVEAS          24334


//
// Window commands (include/owl/window.rh)
//
#define CM_EXIT                24310


//
// CM_EDITnnnn commands (include/owl/window.rh)
//
#define CM_EDITUNDO            24321
#define CM_EDITCUT             24322
#define CM_EDITCOPY            24323
#define CM_EDITPASTE           24324
#define CM_EDITDELETE          24325
#define CM_EDITCLEAR           24326
#define CM_EDITADD             24327
#define CM_EDITEDIT            24328


//
// Search menu commands (include/owl/editsear.rh)
//
#define CM_EDITFIND            24351
#define CM_EDITREPLACE         24352
#define CM_EDITFINDNEXT        24353


//
// Help menu commands.
//
#define CM_HELPABOUT           2009


//
// About Dialogs
//
#define IDD_ABOUT              22000
#define IDC_VERSION            22001
#define IDC_COPYRIGHT          22002
#define IDC_DEBUG              22003
```

```
//
// OWL defined strings
//

//
// Statusbar
//
#define IDS_MODES              32530
#define IDS_MODESOFF           32531

//
// EditFile
//
#define IDS_UNTITLED           32550
#define IDS_UNABLEREAD         32551
#define IDS_UNABLEWRITE        32552
#define IDS_FILECHANGED        32553
#define IDS_FILEFILTER         32554

//
// EditSearch
//
#define IDS_CANNOTFIND         32540


//
// General & application exception messages (include/owl/except.rh)
//
#define IDS_UNKNOWNEXCEPTION   32767
#define IDS_OWLEXCEPTION       32766
#define IDS_OKTORESUME         32765
#define IDS_UNHANDLEDXMSG      32764
#define IDS_UNKNOWNERROR       32763
#define IDS_NOAPP              32762
#define IDS_OUTOFMEMORY        32761
#define IDS_INVALIDMODULE      32760
#define IDS_INVALIDMAINWINDOW  32759
#define IDS_VBXLIBRARYFAIL     32758

//
// Owl 1 compatibility messages
//
#define IDS_INVALIDWINDOW      32709
#define IDS_INVALIDCHILDWINDOW 32708
#define IDS_INVALIDCLIENTWINDOW 32707

//
// TXWindow messages
//
#define IDS_CLASSREGISTERFAIL  32749
#define IDS_CHILDREGISTERFAIL  32748
#define IDS_WINDOWCREATEFAIL   32747
#define IDS_WINDOWEXECUTEFAIL  32746
#define IDS_CHILDCREATEFAIL    32745
```

20

continues

Listing 20.2. continued

```
#define IDS_MENUFAILURE          32744
#define IDS_VALIDATORSYNTAX      32743
#define IDS_PRINTERERROR         32742

#define IDS_LAYOUTINCOMPLETE      32741
#define IDS_LAYOUTBADRELWIN       32740

//
// TXGdi messages
//
#define IDS_GDIFAILURE           32739
#define IDS_GDIALLOCFAIL         32738
#define IDS_GDICREATEFAIL        32737
#define IDS_GDIRESLOADFAIL       32736
#define IDS_GDIFILEREADFAIL      32735
#define IDS_GDIDELETEFAIL        32734
#define IDS_GDIDESTROYFAIL       32733
#define IDS_INVALIDDIBHANDLE     32732


//
// TInputDialog DIALOG resource (include/owl/inputdia.rh)
//
#define IDD_INPUTDIALOG          32514
#define ID_PROMPT                4091
#define ID_INPUT                 4090


//
// TSlider bitmaps (horizontal and vertical) (include/owl/slider.rh)
//
#define IDB_HSLIDERTHUMB         32000
#define IDB_VSLIDERTHUMB         32001


//
// Validation messages (include/owl/validate.rh)
//
#define IDS_VALPXPCONFORM        32520
#define IDS_VALINVALIDCHAR       32521
#define IDS_VALNOTINRANGE        32522
#define IDS_VALNOTINLIST         32523


//#endif  // exprtapp_rh
```

Listing 20.2 shows the source code for the EXPRTAPP.RH resource header file. The file contains the definitions of constants used to manage the following menu commands and resources:

☐ The File menu options

☐ The Edit menu options

- ☐ The Help menu options
- ☐ The About dialog box
- ☐ The edit file messages
- ☐ The general and application exception messages
- ☐ The input dialog box resources
- ☐ The validation messages

Type **Listing 20.3. The source code for the EXPRTAPP.H header file.**

```
//----------------------------------------------------------------------
//   Project Expert
//
//   Copyright © 1996. All Rights Reserved.
//
//   SUBSYSTEM:    Expert Application
//   FILE:         ExprtApp.h
//   AUTHOR:
//
//   OVERVIEW
//   ~~~~~~~~
//   Class definition for TExpertApp (TApplication).
//
//----------------------------------------------------------------------
#if !defined(exprtapp_h)             // Sentry, use file only if it's not already
                                     // included.
#define exprtapp_h

#include <owl/opensave.h>


#include "ExprtApp.rh"              // Definition of all resources.


//
// FrameWindow must be derived to override Paint for Preview and Print.
//
//{{TDecoratedFrame = TSDIDecFrame}}
class TSDIDecFrame : public TDecoratedFrame {
  public:
    TSDIDecFrame(TWindow* parent, const char far* title, TWindow* clientWnd, bool
              ➥trackMenuSelection = false, TModule* module = 0);
    ~TSDIDecFrame();
};    //{{TSDIDecFrame}}


//{{TApplication = TExpertApp}}
class TExpertApp : public TApplication {
  private:
```

20

continues

565

Listing 20.3. continued

```
    public:
      TExpertApp();
      virtual ~TExpertApp();

      TOpenSaveDialog::TData FileData;                 // Data to control open
                                                       //saveas standard dialog.

      void OpenFile(const char* fileName = 0);

//{{TExpertAppVIRTUAL_BEGIN}}
    public:
      virtual void InitMainWindow();
//{{TExpertAppVIRTUAL_END}}

//{{TExpertAppRSP_TBL_BEGIN}}
    protected:
      void CmFileNew();
      void CmFileOpen();
      void CmHelpAbout();
//{{TExpertAppRSP_TBL_END}}
DECLARE_RESPONSE_TABLE(TExpertApp);
};      //{{TExpertApp}}


#endif   // exprtapp_h sentry.
```

Listing 20.3 shows the source code for the EXPRTAPP.H header file. This file declares the text-editor application class `TExpertApp` as a descendant of `TApplication`. The class has public, protected, and private members. The public members include the constructor, destructor, and member function `InitMainWindow`. The protected members include the `Cm` functions that respond to various menu commands. Note the data member `FileData`, an instance of class `TOpenSaveDialog::TData`, which stores the data for the File Open and File Save dialog boxes.

 Listing 20.4. The source code for the EXPRTABD.H header file.

```
//------------------------------------------------------------------------
//   Project Expert
//
//   Copyright © 1996. All Rights Reserved.
//
//   SUBSYSTEM:    Expert Application
//   FILE:         ExprtAbD.h
//   AUTHOR:
//
//   OVERVIEW
//   ~~~~~~~~
//   Class definition for TExpertAboutDlg (TDialog).
//
//------------------------------------------------------------------------
#if !defined(exprtabd_h)              // Sentry, use file only if it's not already
                                      // included.

#define exprtabd_h
```

```
#include <owl/static.h>

#include "ExprtApp.rh"                    // Definition of all resources.


//{{TDialog = TExpertAboutDlg}}
class TExpertAboutDlg : public TDialog {
  public:
    TExpertAboutDlg(TWindow* parent, TResId resId = IDD_ABOUT, TModule* module =
➥0);
    virtual ~TExpertAboutDlg();

//{{TExpertAboutDlgVIRTUAL_BEGIN}}
  public:
    void SetupWindow();
//{{TExpertAboutDlgVIRTUAL_END}}
};     //{{TExpertAboutDlg}}


// Reading the VERSIONINFO resource.
//
class TProjectRCVersion {
  public:
    TProjectRCVersion(TModule* module);
    virtual ~TProjectRCVersion();

    bool GetProductName(LPSTR& prodName);
    bool GetProductVersion(LPSTR& prodVersion);
    bool GetCopyright(LPSTR& copyright);
    bool GetDebug(LPSTR& debug);

  protected:
    uint8 far*  TransBlock;
    void far*   FVData;

  private:
    // Don't allow this object to be copied.
    //
    TProjectRCVersion(const TProjectRCVersion&);
    TProjectRCVersion& operator = (const TProjectRCVersion&);
};

#endif  // exprtabd_h sentry.
```

Listing 20.4. shows the source code for the EXPRTABD.H header file. This header file contains
the declaration of the About dialog box class, TExpertAboutDlg. This class is a descendant of the
class TDialog and declares a constructor, destructor, and the member function SetupWindow.
Whereas many of the generated files will change from project to project, the About dialog source
code will remain fairly constant. The only real difference will be in the name of the dialog box
class, which is derived from the project name.

Listing 20.5. The script for the EXPRTAPP.RC resource file.

```
//---------------------------------------------------------------------------
//  Project Expert
//
//  Copyright © 1996. All Rights Reserved.
//
//  SUBSYSTEM:  Expert Application
//  FILE:       ExprtApp.rc
//  AUTHOR:
//
//  OVERVIEW
//  ~~~~~~~~
//  All resources defined here.
//
//---------------------------------------------------------------------------

#if !defined(WORKSHOP_INVOKED)
# include <windows.h>
#endif
#include "ExprtApp.rh"


IDM_SDI MENU
BEGIN
  POPUP "&File"
  BEGIN
    MENUITEM "&New", CM_FILENEW
    MENUITEM "&Open...", CM_FILEOPEN
    MENUITEM SEPARATOR
    MENUITEM "&Save", CM_FILESAVE, GRAYED
    MENUITEM "Save &As...", CM_FILESAVEAS, GRAYED
    MENUITEM SEPARATOR
    MENUITEM "E&xit\tAlt+F4", CM_EXIT
  END

  MENUITEM SEPARATOR

  POPUP "&Edit"
  BEGIN
    MENUITEM "&Undo\tAlt+BkSp", CM_EDITUNDO, GRAYED
    MENUITEM SEPARATOR
    MENUITEM "Cu&t\tShift+Del", CM_EDITCUT, GRAYED
    MENUITEM "&Copy\tCtrl+Ins", CM_EDITCOPY, GRAYED
    MENUITEM "&Paste\tShift+Ins", CM_EDITPASTE, GRAYED
    MENUITEM SEPARATOR
    MENUITEM "Clear &All\tCtrl+Del", CM_EDITCLEAR, GRAYED
    MENUITEM "&Delete\tDel", CM_EDITDELETE, GRAYED
  END

  POPUP "&Search"
  BEGIN
    MENUITEM "&Find...", CM_EDITFIND, GRAYED
    MENUITEM "&Replace...", CM_EDITREPLACE, GRAYED
    MENUITEM "&Next\aF3", CM_EDITFINDNEXT, GRAYED
  END
```

```
    MENUITEM SEPARATOR

    MENUITEM SEPARATOR

    MENUITEM SEPARATOR


    MENUITEM SEPARATOR

    POPUP "&Help"
    BEGIN
      MENUITEM "&About...", CM_HELPABOUT
    END

END


// Accelerator table for short-cut to menu commands. (include/owl/editfile.rc)
//
IDM_SDI ACCELERATORS
BEGIN
  VK_DELETE, CM_EDITCUT, VIRTKEY, SHIFT
  VK_INSERT, CM_EDITCOPY, VIRTKEY, CONTROL
  VK_INSERT, CM_EDITPASTE, VIRTKEY, SHIFT
  VK_DELETE, CM_EDITCLEAR, VIRTKEY, CONTROL
  VK_BACK,   CM_EDITUNDO, VIRTKEY, ALT
  VK_F3,     CM_EDITFINDNEXT, VIRTKEY
END


// Table of help hints displayed in the status bar.
//
STRINGTABLE
BEGIN
  -1,                "File/document operations"
  CM_FILENEW,        "Creates a new window"
  CM_FILEOPEN,       "Opens a window"
  CM_FILECLOSE,      "Closes the active document"
  CM_FILESAVE,       "Saves the active document"
  CM_FILESAVEAS,     "Saves the active document with a new name"
  CM_EXIT,           "Quits Expert and prompts to save the documents"
  CM_EDITUNDO-1,     "Edit operations"
  CM_EDITUNDO,       "Reverses the last operation"
  CM_EDITCUT,        "Cuts the selection and puts it on the Clipboard"
  CM_EDITCOPY,       "Copies the selection and puts it on the Clipboard"
  CM_EDITPASTE,      "Inserts the Clipboard contents at the insertion point"
  CM_EDITDELETE,     "Deletes the selection"
  CM_EDITCLEAR,      "Clears the active document"
  CM_EDITADD,        "Inserts a new line"
  CM_EDITEDIT,       "Edits the current line"
  CM_EDITFIND-1,     "Search/replace operations"
  CM_EDITFIND,       "Finds the specified text"
  CM_EDITREPLACE,    "Finds the specified text and changes it"
  CM_EDITFINDNEXT,   "Finds the next match"
  CM_HELPABOUT-1,    "Access About"
```

20

continues

Listing 20.5. continued

```
    CM_HELPABOUT,          "About the Expert application"
END


//
// OWL string table
//

// EditFile (include/owl/editfile.rc and include/owl/editsear.rc)
//
STRINGTABLE LOADONCALL MOVEABLE DISCARDABLE
BEGIN
  IDS_CANNOTFIND,        "Cannot find ""%s""."
  IDS_UNTITLED,          "Document"
  IDS_UNABLEREAD,        "Unable to read file %s from disk."
  IDS_UNABLEWRITE,       "Unable to write file %s to disk."
  IDS_FILECHANGED,       "The text in the %s file has changed.\n\nDo you want to
                          save the changes?"
  IDS_FILEFILTER,        "Text files¦*.txt¦AllFiles¦*.*¦"
END


// Exception string resources (include/owl/except.rc)
//
STRINGTABLE LOADONCALL MOVEABLE DISCARDABLE
BEGIN
  IDS_OWLEXCEPTION,      "ObjectWindows Exception"
  IDS_UNHANDLEDXMSG,     "Unhandled Exception"
  IDS_OKTORESUME,        "OK to resume?"
  IDS_UNKNOWNEXCEPTION,  "Unknown exception"

  IDS_UNKNOWNERROR,      "Unknown error"
  IDS_NOAPP,             "No application object"
  IDS_OUTOFMEMORY,       "Out of memory"
  IDS_INVALIDMODULE,     "Invalid module specified for window"
  IDS_INVALIDMAINWINDOW, "Invalid MainWindow"
  IDS_VBXLIBRARYFAIL,    "VBX Library init failure"

  IDS_INVALIDWINDOW,     "Invalid window %s"
  IDS_INVALIDCHILDWINDOW,"Invalid child window %s"
  IDS_INVALIDCLIENTWINDOW,"Invalid client window %s"

  IDS_CLASSREGISTERFAIL, "Class registration fail for window %s"
  IDS_CHILDREGISTERFAIL, "Child class registration fail for window %s"
  IDS_WINDOWCREATEFAIL,  "Create fail for window %s"
  IDS_WINDOWEXECUTEFAIL, "Execute fail for window %s"
  IDS_CHILDCREATEFAIL,   "Child create fail for window %s"

  IDS_MENUFAILURE,       "Menu creation failure"
  IDS_VALIDATORSYNTAX,   "Validator syntax error"
  IDS_PRINTERERROR,      "Printer error"

  IDS_LAYOUTINCOMPLETE,  "Incomplete layout constraints specified in window %s"
  IDS_LAYOUTBADRELWIN,   "Invalid relative window specified in layout constraint in
                          window %s"
```

```
  IDS_GDIFAILURE,        "GDI failure"
  IDS_GDIALLOCFAIL,      "GDI allocate failure"
  IDS_GDICREATEFAIL,     "GDI creation failure"
  IDS_GDIRESLOADFAIL,    "GDI resource load failure"
  IDS_GDIFILEREADFAIL,   "GDI file read failure"
  IDS_GDIDELETEFAIL,     "GDI object %X delete failure"
  IDS_GDIDESTROYFAIL,    "GDI object %X destroy failure"
  IDS_INVALIDDIBHANDLE,  "Invalid DIB handle %X"
END


// General Window's status bar messages. (include/owl/statusba.rc)
//
STRINGTABLE
BEGIN
  IDS_MODES             "EXT¦CAPS¦NUM¦SCRL¦OVR¦REC"
  IDS_MODESOFF          "    ¦    ¦   ¦    ¦   ¦   "
  SC_SIZE,              "Changes the size of the window"
  SC_MOVE,              "Moves the window to another position"
  SC_MINIMIZE,          "Reduces the window to an icon"
  SC_MAXIMIZE,          "Enlarges the window to it maximum size"
  SC_RESTORE,           "Restores the window to its previous size"
  SC_CLOSE,             "Closes the window"
  SC_TASKLIST,          "Opens task list"
  SC_NEXTWINDOW,        "Switches to next window"
END


// Validator messages (include/owl/validate.rc)
//
STRINGTABLE LOADONCALL MOVEABLE DISCARDABLE
BEGIN
  IDS_VALPXPCONFORM     "Input does not conform to picture:\n""%s"""
  IDS_VALINVALIDCHAR    "Invalid character in input"
  IDS_VALNOTINRANGE     "Value is not in the range %ld to %ld."
  IDS_VALNOTINLIST      "Input is not in valid-list"
END


//
// Misc application definitions
//

// Application ICON
//
IDI_SDIAPPLICATION ICON "applsdi.ico"


// About box.
//
IDD_ABOUT DIALOG 12, 17, 204, 65
STYLE DS_MODALFRAME ¦ WS_POPUP ¦ WS_CAPTION ¦ WS_SYSMENU
CAPTION "About Expert"
FONT 8, "MS Sans Serif"
BEGIN
```

continues

Listing 20.5. continued

```
      CTEXT "Version", IDC_VERSION, 2, 14, 200, 8, SS_NOPREFIX
      CTEXT "My Application", -1, 2, 4, 200, 8, SS_NOPREFIX
      CTEXT "", IDC_COPYRIGHT, 2, 27, 200, 17, SS_NOPREFIX
      RTEXT "", IDC_DEBUG, 136, 55, 66, 8, SS_NOPREFIX
      ICON IDI_SDIAPPLICATION, -1, 2, 2, 34, 34
      DEFPUSHBUTTON "OK", IDOK, 82, 48, 40, 14
END


// TInputDialog class dialog box.
//
IDD_INPUTDIALOG DIALOG 20, 24, 180, 64
STYLE WS_POPUP ¦ WS_CAPTION ¦ DS_SETFONT
FONT 8, "Helv"
BEGIN
   LTEXT "", ID_PROMPT, 10, 8, 160, 10, SS_NOPREFIX
   CONTROL "", ID_INPUT, "EDIT", WS_CHILD ¦ WS_VISIBLE ¦ WS_BORDER ¦ WS_TABSTOP ¦
➥ES_AUTOHSCROLL, 10, 20, 160, 12
   DEFPUSHBUTTON "&OK", IDOK, 47, 42, 40, 14
   PUSHBUTTON "&Cancel", IDCANCEL, 93, 42, 40, 14
END


// Slider thumb bitmaps for TSlider and TVSlider (include/owl/slider.rc)
//
IDB_HSLIDERTHUMB BITMAP "hslider.bmp"
IDB_VSLIDERTHUMB BITMAP "hslider.bmp"


// Version info.
//
#if !defined(__DEBUG_)

// Non-Debug VERSIONINFO
//
1 VERSIONINFO LOADONCALL MOVEABLE
FILEVERSION 1, 0, 0, 0
PRODUCTVERSION 1, 0, 0, 0
FILEFLAGSMASK 0
FILEFLAGS VS_FFI_FILEFLAGSMASK
#if defined(BI_PLAT_WIN32)
FILEOS VOS__WINDOWS32
#else
FILEOS VOS__WINDOWS16
#endif
FILETYPE VFT_APP
BEGIN
  BLOCK "StringFileInfo"
  BEGIN
    // Language type = U.S. English(0x0409) and Character Set = Windows,
    // Multilingual(0x04e4)
    BLOCK "040904E4"                // Matches VarFileInfo Translation hex value.
    BEGIN
      VALUE "CompanyName", "\000"
      VALUE "FileDescription", "Expert for Windows\000"
      VALUE "FileVersion", "1.0\000"
```

```
      VALUE "InternalName", "Expert\000"
      VALUE "LegalCopyright", "Copyright © 1996. All Rights Reserved.\000"
      VALUE "LegalTrademarks", "Windows(TM) is a trademark of Microsoft
➡Corporation\000"
      VALUE "OriginalFilename", "Expert.exe\000"
      VALUE "ProductName", "Expert\000"
      VALUE "ProductVersion", "1.0\000"
    END
  END

  BLOCK "VarFileInfo"
  BEGIN
    VALUE "Translation", 0x0409, 0x04e4      // U.S. English(0x0409) & Windows
                                             // Multilingual(0x04e4) 1252
  END
END

#else

// Debug VERSIONINFO
//
1 VERSIONINFO LOADONCALL MOVEABLE
FILEVERSION 1, 0, 0, 0
PRODUCTVERSION 1, 0, 0, 0
FILEFLAGSMASK VS_FF_DEBUG | VS_FF_PRERELEASE | VS_FF_PATCHED | VS_FF_PRIVATEBUILD |
➡VS_FF_SPECIALBUILD
FILEFLAGS VS_FFI_FILEFLAGSMASK
#if defined(BI_PLAT_WIN32)
FILEOS VOS__WINDOWS32
#else
FILEOS VOS__WINDOWS16
#endif
FILETYPE VFT_APP
BEGIN
  BLOCK "StringFileInfo"
  BEGIN
    // Language type = U.S. English(0x0409) and Character Set = Windows,
    // Multilingual(0x04e4)
    BLOCK "040904E4"                    // Matches VarFileInfo Translation hex value.
    BEGIN
      VALUE "CompanyName", "\000"
      VALUE "FileDescription", "Expert for Windows\000"
      VALUE "FileVersion", "1.0\000"
      VALUE "InternalName", "Expert\000"
      VALUE "LegalCopyright", "Copyright © 1996. All Rights Reserved.\000"
      VALUE "LegalTrademarks", "Windows(TM) is a trademark of Microsoft
➡Corporation\000"
      VALUE "OriginalFilename", "Expert.exe\000"
      VALUE "ProductName", "Expert\000"
      VALUE "ProductVersion", "1.0\000"
      VALUE "SpecialBuild", "Debug Version\000"
      VALUE "PrivateBuild", "Built by \000"
    END
  END
```

20

continues

Listing 20.5. continued

```
    BLOCK "VarFileInfo"
    BEGIN
      VALUE "Translation", 0x0409, 0x04e4      // U.S. English(0x0409) & Windows
                                               // Multilingual(0x04e4) 1252
    END
END

#endif
```

Listing 20.5 contains the script for the EXPRTAPP.RC resource file. This file contains the definition of the various menu, accelerator, string, icon, and dialog-box resources.

Listing 20.6. The source code for the EXPRTABD.CPP implementation file.

```
//-------------------------------------------------------------------------
//  Project Expert
//
//  Copyright © 1996. All Rights Reserved.
//
//  SUBSYSTEM:    Expert Application
//  FILE:         ExprtAbD.cpp
//  AUTHOR:
//
//  OVERVIEW
//  ~~~~~~~~
//  Source file for implementation of TExpertAboutDlg (TDialog).
//
//-------------------------------------------------------------------------

#include <owl/pch.h>
#include <stdio.h>
#if defined(BI_PLAT_WIN16)
#include <ver.h>
#endif

#include "ExprtApp.h"
#include "ExprtAbD.h"


TProjectRCVersion::TProjectRCVersion(TModule* module)
{
  uint32  fvHandle;
  uint    vSize;
  char    appFName[255];
  TAPointer<char> subBlockName = new char[255];

  FVData = 0;

  module->GetModuleFileName(appFName, sizeof appFName);
  OemToAnsi(appFName, appFName);
  uint32 dwSize = ::GetFileVersionInfoSize(appFName, &fvHandle);
```

```
    if (dwSize) {
      FVData  = (void far *)new char[(uint)dwSize];
      if (::GetFileVersionInfo(appFName, fvHandle, dwSize, FVData)) {
        // Copy string to buffer so if the -dc compiler switch(Put constant strings
        // in code segments)
        // is on VerQueryValue will work under Win16.  This works around a problem in
        // Microsoft's ver.dll
        // which writes to the string pointed to by subBlockName.
        //
        strcpy(subBlockName, "\\VarFileInfo\\Translation");
        if (!::VerQueryValue(FVData, subBlockName,(void far* far*)&TransBlock,
&vSize)) {
          delete[] FVData;
          FVData = 0;
        }
        else
          // Swap the words so sprintf will print the lang-charset in the correct
          // format.
          //
          *(uint32 *)TransBlock = MAKELONG(HIWORD(*(uint32 *)TransBlock),
LOWORD(*(uint32 *)TransBlock));
      }
    }
}


TProjectRCVersion::~TProjectRCVersion()
{
  if (FVData)
    delete[] FVData;
}


bool TProjectRCVersion::GetProductName(LPSTR& prodName)
{
  uint    vSize;
  TAPointer<char> subBlockName = new char[255];

  if (FVData) {
    sprintf(subBlockName, "\\StringFileInfo\\%08lx\\%s", *(uint32
➥*)TransBlock,(LPSTR)"ProductName");
    return FVData ? ::VerQueryValue(FVData, subBlockName,(void far* far*)&prodName,
&vSize) : false;
  } else
    return false;
}


bool TProjectRCVersion::GetProductVersion(LPSTR& prodVersion)
{
  uint    vSize;
  TAPointer<char> subBlockName = new char[255];

  if (FVData) {
    sprintf(subBlockName, "\\StringFileInfo\\%08lx\\%s", *(uint32
```

continues

Listing 20.6. continued

```
*)TransBlock,(LPSTR)"ProductVersion");
    return FVData ? ::VerQueryValue(FVData, subBlockName,(void far*
➥far*)&prodVersion, &vSize) : false;
  } else
    return false;
}


bool TProjectRCVersion::GetCopyright(LPSTR& copyright)
{
  uint    vSize;
  TAPointer<char> subBlockName = new char[255];

  if (FVData) {
    sprintf(subBlockName, "\\StringFileInfo\\%08lx\\%s", *(uint32
*)TransBlock,(LPSTR)"LegalCopyright");
    return FVData ? ::VerQueryValue(FVData, subBlockName,(void far*
➥far*)&copyright, &vSize) : false;
  } else
    return false;
}


bool TProjectRCVersion::GetDebug(LPSTR& debug)
{
  uint    vSize;
  TAPointer<char> subBlockName = new char[255];

  if (FVData) {
    sprintf(subBlockName, "\\StringFileInfo\\%08lx\\%s", *(uint32
➥*)TransBlock,(LPSTR)"SpecialBuild");
    return FVData ? ::VerQueryValue(FVData, subBlockName,(void far* far*)&debug,
➥&vSize) : false;
  } else
    return false;
}


//{{TExpertAboutDlg Implementation}}


//----------------------------------------------------------
// TExpertAboutDlg
// ~~~~~~~~~~
// Construction/Destruction handling.
//
TExpertAboutDlg::TExpertAboutDlg(TWindow* parent, TResId resId, TModule* module)
:
  TDialog(parent, resId, module)
{
  // INSERT>> Your constructor code here.
}
```

```
TExpertAboutDlg::~TExpertAboutDlg()
{
  Destroy();

  // INSERT>> Your destructor code here.
}


void TExpertAboutDlg::SetupWindow()
{
  LPSTR prodName = 0, prodVersion = 0, copyright = 0, debug = 0;

  // Get the static text for the value based on VERSIONINFO.
  //
  TStatic* versionCtrl = new TStatic(this, IDC_VERSION, 255);
  TStatic* copyrightCtrl = new TStatic(this, IDC_COPYRIGHT, 255);
  TStatic* debugCtrl = new TStatic(this, IDC_DEBUG, 255);

  TDialog::SetupWindow();

  // Process the VERSIONINFO.
  //
  TProjectRCVersion applVersion(GetModule());

  // Get the product name and product version strings.
  //
  if (applVersion.GetProductName(prodName) &&
➥applVersion.GetProductVersion(prodVersion)) {
    // IDC_VERSION is the product name and version number, the initial value of
    // IDC_VERSION is
    // the word Version (in whatever language) product name VERSION product version.
    //
    char buffer[255];
    char versionName[128];

    buffer[0] = '\0';
    versionName[0] = '\0';

    versionCtrl->GetText(versionName, sizeof versionName);
    sprintf(buffer, "%s %s %s", prodName, versionName, prodVersion);

    versionCtrl->SetText(buffer);
  }

  // Get the legal copyright string.
  //
  if (applVersion.GetCopyright(copyright))
    copyrightCtrl->SetText(copyright);

  // Only get the SpecialBuild text if the VERSIONINFO resource is there.
  //
  if (applVersion.GetDebug(debug))
    debugCtrl->SetText(debug);
}
```

20

Listing 20.6 shows the source code for the EXPRTABD.CPP implementation file. This file defines the class `TExpertAboutDlg`, which implements the About dialog box. In addition, the file declares and defines the project resource version class, `TProjectRCVersion`. Look briefly at this class first. The class defines a constructor, destructor, a set of public member functions, and two protected data members. The class `TProjectRCVersion` supports operations that extract the information about the product name, version, and copyright.

The About dialog box class defines the following members:

☐ The constructor simply invokes the constructor of the parent class `TDialog`. The constructor has no executable statements and contains a comment that indicates where to place your code to support additional initialization.

☐ The destructor simply calls the inherited member function `Destroy`. The definition contains a comment that indicates where to place your code to support additional cleanup.

☐ The member function `SetupWindow` is a bit more interesting; it sets up the About dialog box by carrying out the following tasks:

☐ Creates three static-text control objects for the version, copyright, and debug information. The function assigns the addresses of these controls to the local pointers `versionCtrl`, `copyrightCtrl`, and `debugCtrl`. These objects are surrogate objects for the statics created in the dialog resource.

☐ Invokes the `SetupWindow` member function of the parent dialog-box class.

☐ Creates the instance `applVersion` of the class `TProjectRCVersion`.

☐ Calls `applVersion`'s `GetProductName` and `GetProductVersion` to obtain the product name and version. If successful in getting these, the function then sets the `versionCtrl` static-text box with the names.

☐ Calls `applVersion`'s `GetCopyright` to obtain the copyright information from the dialog-box resource. If successful, it then sets the corresponding static-text box.

☐ Assigns the debug information to the debug static-text control if `applVersion`'s `GetDebug` function returns a nonzero value.

 Listing 20.7. The source code for the EXPRTAPP.CPP implementation file.

```
//--------------------------------------------------------------------------
//  Project Expert
//
//  Copyright © 1996. All Rights Reserved.
//
//  SUBSYSTEM:    Expert Application
//  FILE:         ExprtApp.cpp
//  AUTHOR:
//
//  OVERVIEW
//  ~~~~~~~~
```

```
//   Source file for implementation of TExpertApp (TApplication).
//
//---------------------------------------------------------------------------

#include <owl/pch.h>

#include <stdio.h>

#include "ExprtApp.h"
#include "ExprtEdF.h"                         // Definition of client class.
#include "ExprtAbD.h"                         // Definition of about dialog.


//{{TExpertApp Implementation}}


//
// Build a response table for all messages/commands handled
// by the application.
//
DEFINE_RESPONSE_TABLE1(TExpertApp, TApplication)
//{{TExpertAppRSP_TBL_BEGIN}}
  EV_COMMAND(CM_FILENEW, CmFileNew),
  EV_COMMAND(CM_FILEOPEN, CmFileOpen),
  EV_COMMAND(CM_HELPABOUT, CmHelpAbout),
//{{TExpertAppRSP_TBL_END}}
END_RESPONSE_TABLE;


//---------------------------------------------------------
// TExpertApp
//
TExpertApp::TExpertApp() : TApplication("Expert")
{

  // Common file file flags and filters for Open/Save As dialogs.  Filename and
  // directory are
  // computed in the member functions CmFileOpen, and CmFileSaveAs.
  //
  FileData.Flags = OFN_FILEMUSTEXIST ¦ OFN_HIDEREADONLY ¦ OFN_OVERWRITEPROMPT;
  FileData.SetFilter("All Files (*.*)¦*.*¦");
  FileData.DefExt = "txt";

  // INSERT>> Your constructor code here.
}


TExpertApp::~TExpertApp()
{
  // INSERT>> Your destructor code here.
}


//---------------------------------------------------------
// TExpertApp
// ~~~~~
```

continues

Listing 20.7. continued

```
// Application intialization.
//
void TExpertApp::InitMainWindow()
{
  if (nCmdShow != SW_HIDE)
    nCmdShow = (nCmdShow != SW_SHOWMINNOACTIVE) ? SW_SHOWNORMAL : nCmdShow;

  TSDIDecFrame* frame = new TSDIDecFrame(0, GetName(), 0, false);

  // Assign ICON w/ this application.
  //
  frame->SetIcon(this, IDI_SDIAPPLICATION);
  frame->SetIconSm(this, IDI_SDIAPPLICATION);

  // Menu associated with window and accelerator table associated with table.
  //
  frame->AssignMenu(IDM_SDI);

  // Associate with the accelerator table.
  //
  frame->Attr.AccelTable = IDM_SDI;

  SetMainWindow(frame);

  frame->SetMenuDescr(TMenuDescr(IDM_SDI));
}


//--------------------------------------------------------
// TExpertApp
// ~~~~~~~~~~~
// Menu File New command
//
void TExpertApp::CmFileNew()
{
  TExpertEditFile* client = TYPESAFE_DOWNCAST(GetMainWindow()->GetClientWindow(),
➥TExpertEditFile);    // Client window for the frame.
  client->NewFile();
}


//--------------------------------------------------------
// TExpertApp
// ~~~~~~~~~~~
// Menu File Open command
//
void TExpertApp::CmFileOpen()
{
  // Display standard Open dialog box to select a file name.
  //
  *FileData.FileName = 0;

  TExpertEditFile* client = TYPESAFE_DOWNCAST(GetMainWindow()->GetClientWindow(),
➥TExpertEditFile);    // Client window for the frame.
```

```
      if (client->CanClose())
        if (TFileOpenDialog(GetMainWindow(), FileData).Execute() == IDOK)
          OpenFile();
  }


  void TExpertApp::OpenFile(const char* fileName)
  {
    if (fileName)
      strcpy(FileData.FileName, fileName);

    TExpertEditFile* client = TYPESAFE_DOWNCAST(GetMainWindow()->GetClientWindow(),
  ➥TExpertEditFile);      // Client window for the frame.
    client->ReplaceWith(FileData.FileName);
  }


  //{{TSDIDecFrame Implementation}}


  TSDIDecFrame::TSDIDecFrame(TWindow* parent, const char far* title, TWindow*
  ➥clientWnd, bool trackMenuSelection, TModule* module)
  :
    TDecoratedFrame(parent, title, !clientWnd ? new TExpertEditFile(0, 0, 0) :
  ➥clientWnd, trackMenuSelection, module)
  {
    // INSERT>> Your constructor code here.

  }


  TSDIDecFrame::~TSDIDecFrame()
  {
    // INSERT>> Your destructor code here.

  }


  //------------------------------------------------------------
  // TExpertApp
  // ~~~~~~~~~~
  // Menu Help About Expert command
  //
  void TExpertApp::CmHelpAbout()
  {
    // Show the modal dialog.
    //
    TExpertAboutDlg(MainWindow).Execute();
  }


  int OwlMain(int , char* [])
  {
    TExpertApp    app;
    return app.Run();
  }
```

20

Listing 20.7 shows the source code for the EXPRTAPP.CPP implementation file. The listing includes the EXPRTABD.H header file to access the definition of the application and About dialog-box classes. In addition, the listing contains the declaration of a class that models a decorated SDI window frame.

The listing contains the definition of the message-response table for the application class TExpertApp. The table includes a set of EV_COMMAND macros to map the various CM_*XXXX* commands with their respective Cm*XXXX* member functions.

The listing contains the definitions of the following TExpertApp members:

- ☐ The constructor, which performs the following minimal initialization:

  - ☐ Assigns an expression of bitwise ORed OFN_*XXXX* constants to the Flags member of the data member FileData.

  - ☐ Calls the data member FileData's SetFilter member function with a string literal argument that assigns the file-type filters to the member FileData.

  - ☐ Sets the data member FileData's DefExt data member to "txt".

  The preceding assignments initialize the data member FileData to prepare it for the dialog boxes that open and save files. The constructor contains a comment that indicates where to place statements for additional initialization.

- ☐ The destructor merely contains a comment that indicates where to place statements for application clean-up.

- ☐ The member function InitMainWindow initializes the main window by carrying out the following tasks:

  - ☐ Assigns a value to the inherited data member nCmdShow such that the window appears in its normal state.

  - ☐ Creates a new decorated SDI frame window by allocating an instance of class TSDIDecFrame. The function assigns the address of this instance to the local pointer frame.

  - ☐ Assigns the application's icon using the icon resource IDI_SDIAPPLICATION. This involves calling the member functions SetIcon for the large icon and SetIconSm for the small icon of the SDI window accessed by the pointer frame.

  - ☐ Assigns the application's menu from the menu resource IDM_SDI using the frame's AssignMenu member function.

  - ☐ Assigns the accelerator table IDM_SDI to the frame window.

  - ☐ Uses the SetMainWindow member function to set the main window to frame.

  - ☐ Sets the menu descriptor to the IDM_SDI resource.

- ☐ The member function CmFileNew responds to the New menu option by calling the C++ member function NewFile of the window client area accessed by the RTTI statement.

☐ The member function `CmFileOpen` responds to the Open menu option. The function contains nested `if` statements. The outer `if` statement checks to see if the client window can close with a call to the member function `CanClose`. If this returns a nonzero value, the function `CmFileOpen` executes the nested `if` statement. This statement creates a dynamic instance of the class `TFileOpenDialog` and calls its `Execute` member function. The `if` statement compares the result of this function with `IDOK`. If the two values match, the function invokes the member function `OpenFile`.

☐ The member function `OpenFile` performs two simple tasks. The first task assigns the string in the parameter `fileName` to the member `FileName` of data member `FileData`. The second task updates the title of the window with the name of the newly opened file. The function performs this task by calling the client window's `ReplaceWith` member function. The argument of this function is the member `FileName` of the data member `FileData`.

☐ The listing offers the definition of class `TSDIDecFrame`. This class, a descendant of class `TDecoratedFrame`, models the decorated SDI frame window.

☐ The `TExpertApp`'s member function `CmHelpAbout` responds to the Help | About menu option. The function creates a new instance of class `TExpertAboutDlg` to invoke the About dialog box. The function invokes this modal dialog box by calling the `Execute` member function.

Finally, the typical `OwlMain` is presented, in which an `TExpertApp` object is created and run.

Altering AppExpert's Options

As mentioned before, the potential output from the AppExpert is varied. I go over some different output on Day 21 when I use the AppExpert to jump-start the creation of an OLE2 application. In the meantime, you really need to experiment with all the various options.

For one thing, letting the AppExpert generate code for you, and then studying that output, is a great way of figuring out how to get certain things done with Borland C++, such as generating an application that uses a toolbar (there's a check box on the first AppExpert option screen). You see many extra files generated—particularly .BMP files with bit maps—that will be displayed on the buttons in the toolbar. You also will see how the toolbar is set up and used.

20

Invoking ClassExpert

To use the *ClassExpert*, invoke the ClassExpert menu option in the View menu selection. Figure 20.14 shows a sample session with the ClassExpert utility in a project created by AppExpert. The ClassExpert window contains three panes: the Classes pane, the Events pane, and the editor pane. The Classes pane lists the classes in the current project. The Events pane shows an outline of the various messages for the selected class in the Classes pane. These messages include command notifications, control notifications, virtual functions, and Windows messages. The + symbol indicates that an outline item is hiding subitems. The - symbol indicates that the item is expanded. The editor pane is supported by an editor that enables you to enter, edit, and delete statements.

When you select a different class in the Class pane, the contents of the Events pane automatically change to reflect the events available for the newly selected class.

When you expand the outlines in the Events pane, notice check marks to the left of certain outline items. These check marks indicate that the event has a handler in the project's source code. You'll note that some of the big check marks are black and others are gray. The gray ones mean that the item nearby can be expanded to reveal other options with a check mark.

Figure 20.14.

A sample session with the ClassExpert utility.

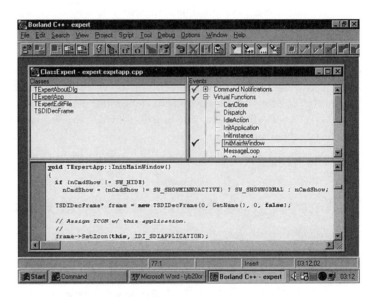

 **Note:** The right mouse button offers versatile, context-sensitive pop-up menus that enable you to perform various tasks. (The pop-up menus are so context-sensitive that they vary not only from one pane to another, but also between one type of selection and another in the same pane.)

The following sections describe how to add new member functions and classes.

Adding New Member Functions

Use the simple SDI-compliant text editor you just finished. First, add an additional menu to the project by right-clicking in either the Classes or Events panes of the ClassExpert. Then, from the pop-up menu, select Edit menu. This new menu should be called Special and should be placed between the Search and Help menus. It should have several separate menu commands in order to support the following features:

☐ *Lowercase.* Converts the selected text (or the entire contents of the file if there is no selected text) to lowercase characters.

☐ *Uppercase.* Converts the selected text (or the entire contents of the file if there is no selected text) to uppercase characters.

☐ *Reverse.* Reverses the characters of the selected text (or the entire contents of the file if there is no selected text).

☐ *Insert Date.* Inserts the current date.

☐ *Insert Time.* Inserts the current time.

☐ *Insert Date/Time.* Inserts the current date and time.

Each of the preceding menu options has an event-handler member function. To create the new application, follow these general steps:

1. Use the Resource editor to add the menu selection Special and its nested menu options Lowercase, UpperCase, Reverse, Insert Date, Insert Time, and Insert Date/Time. (Consult the help files or Bonus Day 5 for more information.) Use the identifiers CM_LOWERCASE, CM_UPPERCASE, CM_REVERSE, CM_INSDATE, CM_INSTIME, and CM_INSDATETIME, respectively, for the menu options. Insert a separator menu item between the first three and last three menu options in the menu selection. When you finish adding the preceding menu items, exit the resource editor and return to the ClassExpert.

2. Before the changes you've made show up in the ClassExpert, you will need to rescan the files. Right-click on the expert.exe target name in the project window (bring up the window if it isn't already visible), go to the Special popup menu, then select Rescan. This will update the internal ClassExpert database with the new identifiers you just added in the resource editor.

3. Use the ClassExpert utility to add the member functions needed to handle the six new menu options. Click on TExpertApp in the Classes pane, and then on the plus sign of the Command Notifications item in the Events pane, to expand that outline item.

20

4. Search for the CM_LOWERCASE identifier, which represents the commands for the new menu option Lowercase.

5. Click in the + symbol located to the left of the identifier CM_LOWERCASE. This action reveals two nested outline items: Command and Command Enable.

6. Select the Command outline and click the right mouse button to access the pop-up menu.

7. Select and invoke the Add Handler menu option. This option prompts you with a simple input dialog box, which requests that you enter the name of the handler member function. Make sure the name is CmLowercase and then click the OK button of the dialog box. The ClassExpert responds by creating the following:

   ☐ The declaration of member function CmLowercase in the declaration of class TExpertApp (located in the header file EXPRTAPP.H)

   ☐ The event response-table macro that links the command CM_LOWERCASE with the member function CmLowercase (located in the source file EXPRTAPP.CPP)

   ☐ The empty definition of member function CmLowercase (located in the source file EXPRTAPP.CPP)

8. Repeat Steps 4 through 7 for the other CM_*XXX* constants that handle the remaining new menu options. Specify the member functions CmInsertDate, CmInsertDateTime, CmInsertTime, CmUppercase, and CmReverse to handle the Windows commands CM_INSDATE, CM_INSDATETIME, CM_INSTIME, CM_UPPERCASE, and CM_REVERSE, respectively.

9. Add the header files STRING.H and DOS.H to the top of the EXPRTAPP.CPP source file.

10. Add the functionality for each of these new member functions by double-clicking on the appropriate Command members for each of the new events. You then can use the editor window on the bottom of the ClassExpert window to modify the empty member-function stubs.

If you take a look at EXPRTAPP.RH, you'll see the new CM_*XXX* identifiers, and EXPRTAPP.RC contains an updated menu. EXPRTAPP.H has the new Cm*XXX* member functions added to the TExpertApp class, and EXPRTAPP.CPP now has the new code for those member functions. Listing 20.8 shows the new version of EXPRTAPP.CPP with the new member functions that implement the text manipulation.

Type

Listing 20.8. The new source code for the EXPRTAPP.CPP implementation file.

```
1:  //---------------------------------------------------------------
2:  //   Project Expert
3:  //
4:  //   Copyright © 1996. All Rights Reserved.
5:  //
```

```
6:    //   SUBSYSTEM:     Expert Application
7:    //   FILE:          ExprtApp.cpp
8:    //   AUTHOR:
9:    //
10:   //   OVERVIEW
11:   //   ~~~~~~~~
12:   //   Source file for implementation of TExpertApp (TApplication).
13:   //
14:   //-------------------------------------------------------------
15:
16:   #include <owl/pch.h>
17:
18:   #include <dos.h>
19:   #include <stdio.h>
20:   #include <string.h>
21:
22:   #include "ExprtApp.h"
23:   #include "ExprtEdF.h"                    // Definition of client class.
24:   #include "ExprtAbD.h"                    // Definition of about dialog.
25:
26:
27:   //{{TExpertApp Implementation}}
28:
29:
30:   //
31:   // Build a response table for all messages/commands handled
32:   // by the application.
33:   //
34:   DEFINE_RESPONSE_TABLE1(TExpertApp, TApplication)
35:   //{{TExpertAppRSP_TBL_BEGIN}}
36:     EV_COMMAND(CM_FILENEW, CmFileNew),
37:     EV_COMMAND(CM_FILEOPEN, CmFileOpen),
38:     EV_COMMAND(CM_HELPABOUT, CmHelpAbout),
39:     EV_COMMAND(CM_LOWERCASE, CmLowercase),
40:     EV_COMMAND(CM_INSDATE, CmInsertDate),
41:     EV_COMMAND(CM_INSDATETIME, CmInsertDateTime),
42:     EV_COMMAND(CM_INSTIME, CmInsertTime),
43:     EV_COMMAND(CM_REVERSE, CmReverse),
44:     EV_COMMAND(CM_UPPERCASE, CmUppercase),
45:   //{{TExpertAppRSP_TBL_END}}
46:   END_RESPONSE_TABLE;
47:
48:
49:   //-------------------------------------------------------------
50:   // TExpertApp
51:   //
52:   TExpertApp::TExpertApp() : TApplication("Expert")
53:   {
54:
55:     // Common file file flags and filters for Open/Save As dialogs.
56:     // Filename and directory are computed in the member functions
57:     // CmFileOpen, and CmFileSaveAs.
58:     //
59:     FileData.Flags =   OFN_FILEMUSTEXIST ¦ OFN_HIDEREADONLY
60:                      ¦ OFN_OVERWRITEPROMPT;
61:     FileData.SetFilter("All Files (*.*)¦*.*¦");
```

20

continues

Listing 20.8. continued

```
62:     FileData.DefExt = "txt";
63:
64:     // INSERT>> Your constructor code here.
65:   }
66:
67:
68:   TExpertApp::~TExpertApp()
69:   {
70:     // INSERT>> Your destructor code here.
71:   }
72:
73:
74:   //------------------------------------------------------------
75:   // TExpertApp
76:   // ~~~~~
77:   // Application intialization.
78:   //
79:   void TExpertApp::InitMainWindow()
80:   {
81:     if (nCmdShow != SW_HIDE)
82:       nCmdShow = (nCmdShow != SW_SHOWMINNOACTIVE) ? SW_SHOWNORMAL : nCmdShow;
83:
84:     TSDIDecFrame* frame = new TSDIDecFrame(0, GetName(), 0, false);
85:
86:     // Assign ICON w/ this application.
87:     //
88:     frame->SetIcon(this, IDI_SDIAPPLICATION);
89:     frame->SetIconSm(this, IDI_SDIAPPLICATION);
90:
91:     // Menu associated with window and accelerator table associated
92:     // with table.
93:     //
94:     frame->AssignMenu(IDM_SDI);
95:
96:     // Associate with the accelerator table.
97:     //
98:     frame->Attr.AccelTable = IDM_SDI;
99:
100:    SetMainWindow(frame);
101:
102:    frame->SetMenuDescr(TMenuDescr(IDM_SDI));
103:  }
104:
105:
106:
107:  //------------------------------------------------------------
108:  // TExpertApp
109:  // ~~~~~~~~~~
110:  // Menu File New command
111:  //
112:  void TExpertApp::CmFileNew()
113:  {
114:    TExpertEditFile* client = TYPESAFE_DOWNCAST(
115:            GetMainWindow()->GetClientWindow(),
116:            TExpertEditFile);    // Client window for frame
```

```
117:    client->NewFile();
118: }
119:
120:
121: //----------------------------------------------------------
122: // TExpertApp
123: // ~~~~~~~~~~~
124: // Menu File Open command
125: //
126: void TExpertApp::CmFileOpen()
127: {
128:    // Display standard Open dialog box to select a file name.
129:    //
130:    *FileData.FileName = 0;
131:
132:    TExpertEditFile* client = TYPESAFE_DOWNCAST(
133:            GetMainWindow()->GetClientWindow(),
134:            TExpertEditFile);      // Client window for frame
135:    if (client->CanClose())
136:      if (TFileOpenDialog(GetMainWindow(), FileData).Execute() == IDOK)
137:        OpenFile();
138: }
139:
140:
141: void TExpertApp::OpenFile(const char* fileName)
142: {
143:    if (fileName)
144:      strcpy(FileData.FileName, fileName);
145:
146:    TExpertEditFile* client = TYPESAFE_DOWNCAST(
147:            GetMainWindow()->GetClientWindow(),
148:            TExpertEditFile);      // Client window for frame
149:    client->ReplaceWith(FileData.FileName);
150: }
151:
152:
153: //{{TSDIDecFrame Implementation}}
154:
155:
156: TSDIDecFrame::TSDIDecFrame(TWindow* parent,
157:                            const char far* title,
158:                            TWindow* clientWnd,
159:                            bool trackMenuSelection,
160:                            TModule* module)
161: :
162:    TDecoratedFrame(parent,
163:                    title,
164:                      !clientWnd
165:                    ? new TExpertEditFile(0, 0, 0)
166:                    : clientWnd,
167:                    trackMenuSelection,
168:                    module)
169: {
170:    // INSERT>> Your constructor code here.
171:
172: }
```

continues

Listing 20.8. continued

```
173:
174:
175: TSDIDecFrame::~TSDIDecFrame()
176: {
177:   // INSERT>> Your destructor code here.
178:
179: }
180:
181:
182: //----------------------------------------------------------
183: // TExpertApp
184: // ~~~~~~~~~~~
185: // Menu Help About Expert command
186: //
187: void TExpertApp::CmHelpAbout()
188: {
189:   // Show the modal dialog.
190:   //
191:   TExpertAboutDlg(MainWindow).Execute();
192: }
193:
194:
195:
196: int OwlMain(int , char* [])
197: {
198:   TExpertApp   app;
199:   return app.Run();
200: }
201:
202: void TExpertApp::CmLowercase()
203: {
204:     uint startPos, endPos;
205:     int numChars;
206:     char* str;
207:     TExpertEditFile* client = TYPESAFE_DOWNCAST(
208:             GetMainWindow()->GetClientWindow(),
209:             TExpertEditFile);    // Client window of frame
210:
211:     client->GetSelection(startPos, endPos);
212:     if (startPos < endPos)
213:         {
214:         numChars = endPos - startPos + 1;
215:         str = new char[numChars + 1];
216:         client->GetSubText(str, startPos, endPos);
217:         strlwr(str);
218:         client->Insert(str);
219:         client->SetSelection(startPos, endPos);
220:         delete[] str;
221:         }
222:     else
223:         {
224:         numChars = client->GetWindowTextLength();
225:         str = new char[numChars + 1];
226:         client->GetSubText(str, 0, (uint)numChars);
227:         strlwr(str);
```

```
228:        client->DeleteSubText(0, (uint)numChars);
229:        client->SetSelection(0, 0);
230:        client->Insert(str);
231:        delete[] str;
232:        }
233: }
234:
235:
236: void TExpertApp::CmInsertDate()
237: {
238:    struct date dt;
239:    char str[41];
240:    TExpertEditFile* client = TYPESAFE_DOWNCAST(
241:            GetMainWindow()->GetClientWindow(),
242:            TExpertEditFile);    // Client window of frame
243:
244:    getdate(&dt);
245:    sprintf(str, "%02d/%02d/%02d",
246:                dt.da_mon, dt.da_day, dt.da_year % 100);
247:    client->Insert(str);
248: }
249:
250:
251: void TExpertApp::CmInsertDateTime()
252: {
253:    TExpertEditFile* client = TYPESAFE_DOWNCAST(
254:            GetMainWindow()->GetClientWindow(),
255:            TExpertEditFile);    // Client window of frame
256:
257:    CmInsertDate();
258:    client->Insert(" ");
259:    CmInsertTime();
260: }
261:
262:
263: void TExpertApp::CmInsertTime()
264: {
265:    struct time tm;
266:    char str[41];
267:    TExpertEditFile* client = TYPESAFE_DOWNCAST(
268:            GetMainWindow()->GetClientWindow(),
269:            TExpertEditFile);    // Client window of frame
270:
271:    gettime(&tm);
272:    sprintf(str, "%02d:%02d:%02d",
273:                tm.ti_hour, tm.ti_min, tm.ti_sec);
274:    client->Insert(str);
275: }
276:
277:
278: void TExpertApp::CmReverse()
279: {
280:    uint startPos, endPos;
281:    int numChars;
282:    char* str;
283:    TExpertEditFile* client = TYPESAFE_DOWNCAST(
```

20

continues

Listing 20.8. continued

```
284:                GetMainWindow()->GetClientWindow(),
285:                TExpertEditFile);    // Client window of frame
286:
287:     client->GetSelection(startPos, endPos);
288:     if (startPos < endPos)
289:         {
290:         numChars = endPos - startPos + 1;
291:         str = new char[numChars + 1];
292:         client->GetSubText(str, startPos, endPos);
293:         strrev(str);
294:         client->Insert(str);
295:         client->SetSelection(startPos, endPos);
296:         delete[] str;
297:         }
298:     else
299:         {
300:         numChars = client->GetWindowTextLength();
301:         str = new char[numChars + 1];
302:         client->GetSubText(str, 0, (uint)numChars);
303:         strrev(str);
304:         client->DeleteSubText(0, (uint)numChars);
305:         client->SetSelection(0, 0);
306:         client->Insert(str);
307:         delete[] str;
308:         }
309: }
310:
311:
312: void TExpertApp::CmUppercase()
313: {
314:     uint startPos, endPos;
315:     int numChars;
316:     char* str;
317:     TExpertEditFile* client = TYPESAFE_DOWNCAST(
318:                GetMainWindow()->GetClientWindow(),
319:                TExpertEditFile);    // Client window for frame
320:
321:     client->GetSelection(startPos, endPos);
322:     if (startPos < endPos)
323:         {
324:         numChars = endPos - startPos + 1;
325:         str = new char[numChars + 1];
326:         client->GetSubText(str, startPos, endPos);
327:         strupr(str);
328:         client->Insert(str);
329:         client->SetSelection(startPos, endPos);
330:         delete[] str;
331:         }
332:     else
333:         {
334:         numChars = client->GetWindowTextLength();
335:         str = new char[numChars + 1];
336:         client->GetSubText(str, 0, (uint)numChars);
337:         strupr(str);
338:         client->DeleteSubText(0, (uint)numChars);
```

```
339:        client->SetSelection(0, 0);
340:        client->Insert(str);
341:        delete[] str;
342:        }
343: }
```

Note: The line numbers in Listing 20.8 will likely not match the numbers in your generated application because I "prettied them up" a bit so they would fit on the book's page. This involved splitting up long lines, thus changing the line count.

The implementation file in Listing 20.8 shows the definitions of the CmXXX member functions that handle the new menu options. The file contains the #include statements that were added to include the header files STRING.H and DOS.H. Also, notice the response-table macros that were inserted by the ClassExpert utility. I added the code for the following member functions:

1. The member function CmLowercase (defined on lines 202 through 233) responds to the Lowercase menu option by performing the following tasks:

   ☐ Obtains the currently selected text (if any). This task involves calling the client window's member function GetSelection (on line 211). The arguments for this message are the local variables startPos and endPos.

   ☐ Performs the following sequence of subtasks (found on lines 214 through 220) if the value in variable startPos is less than that in endPos (which indicates that there is selected text):

      ☐ Calculates the number of characters in the selected text, and assigns this number to the local variable numChars.

      ☐ Creates a dynamic string with numChars+1 characters, and assigns the address of that string to the local pointer str.

      ☐ Copies the selected text into the dynamic string. This task involves the GetSubText member function. The arguments for this function are str, startPos, and endPos.

      ☐ Converts the characters of the dynamic string to lowercase by using the string function strlwr.

      ☐ Replaces the selected text with the contents of the dynamic string by calling the client window's Insert member function with the argument of str.

      ☐ Selects the newly inserted text with SetSelection. The arguments of startPos and endPos are the same as the original selection, thus having the effect of not deselecting the newly modified text.

20

☐ Deletes the dynamic string accessed by pointer str.

☐ If there is no selection, the function converts all of the characters in the file to lowercase by performing the following subtasks (using the statements in lines 224 through 231):

   ☐ Obtains the size of the edited text with the client window's GetWindowTextLength member function. This task assigns the result to the local variable numChars.

   ☐ Creates a dynamic string with numChars+1 characters and assigns the address of that string to the local pointer str.

   ☐ Obtains the entire edited text with the GetSubText member function. The arguments are str (the text copy buffer), 0, and (uint)numChars.

   ☐ Converts the characters of the dynamic string to lowercase by using the string function strlwr.

   ☐ Deletes the entire edited text with DeleteSubText. The arguments for this member function are 0 and (uint)numChars.

   ☐ Selects the start of the file as the new insertion point by setting both the beginning and ending of the selection to 0 in the SetSelection member function.

   ☐ Inserts the characters of the dynamic string into the client window with the Insert member function.

   ☐ Deletes the dynamic string accessed by pointer str.

> **Note:** The program implements the various text-edit operations using the data member client, which is a pointer to the class TExpertEditFile. This class includes TEdit as one of its base classes. This lineage enables the pointer client to receive C++ editing messages implemented by the member functions of class TEdit.

2. The member functions CmUppercase (starting on line 312) and CmReverse (starting on line 278) are exactly like the CmLowercase member function, except that the strlwr function is replaced with strupr and strrev, respectively.

3. The member function CmInsertDate (defined on lines 236 through 248) responds to the Insert Date menu option by performing the following options:

   ☐ Obtains the current system date by calling the function getdate (prototyped in the DOS.H header file). The argument for this function call is the address of the variable dt. This variable contains the date structure.

☐ Creates a formatted string image of the month number, day number, and year number. This task uses the function `sprintf` and assigns the formatted string to the local string variable `str`.

☐ Inserts `str` into the client window with the `Insert` member function.

4. The member function `CmInsertTime` (defined on lines 263 through 275) responds to the Insert Time menu option by performing the following options:

☐ Obtains the current system time by calling the function `gettime` (prototyped in the DOS.H header file). The argument for this function call is the address of the variable `tm`. This variable contains the `time` structure.

☐ Creates a formatted string image of the hour, minute, and second. This task uses the function `sprintf` and assigns the formatted string to the local string variable `str`.

☐ Inserts `str` into the client window with the `Insert` member function.

5. The member function `CmInsertDateTime` (starting on line 251) responds to the Insert Date/Time menu option. This function simply calls the `CmInsertDate` and `CmInsertTime` functions, inserting a space in between them.

Compile and run the program EXPERT.EXE. Load a small text file and experiment with converting and reversing the characters of selected text and of the entire file. In addition, experiment with inserting the date, the time, or both. When you are done experimenting, exit the file without saving it. Figure 20.15 shows a sample session with the EXPERT.EXE program.

Figure 20.15.

A sample session with the EXPERT.EXE program.

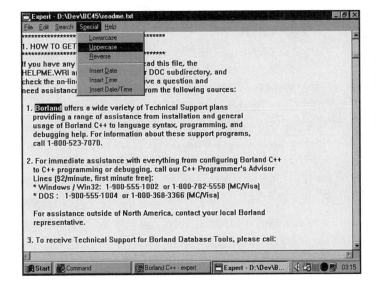

Summary

This chapter introduced you to using the AppExpert and ClassExpert utilities, and it offered a sample SDI-compliant, text-editor application generated by the first utility that was then modified to have additional functionality by the second utility. You learned about the following topics:

☐ Working with the AppExpert utility, which you invoke from inside the IDE.

☐ The Application topics in AppExpert, which enable you to make main selections about the type of application you want AppExpert to generate.

☐ The Main Window topics in AppExpert, which enable you to fine-tune the window styles and the SDI or MDI client windows.

☐ The MDI Child/View options in AppExpert, which enable you to control the creation of the MDI child windows.

☐ The EXPERT project, which implements an SDI-compliant, minimally functioning text editor generated by the AppExpert utility. The project implements the simplest type of text editor that you can create with the AppExpert utility.

☐ Working with the ClassExpert utility, which is invoked from the IDE View menu.

☐ Creating new menu options and response functions using the ClassExpert.

Q&A

Q How does the ClassExpert utility complement the source code generated by AppExpert?

A The ClassExpert enables you to fine-tune the source code of AppExpert by adding new classes and/or member functions that support custom operations of your program.

Q Can I customize the code generated by AppExpert without using ClassExpert?

A Yes. However, depending on how you manually customize the code, it may be difficult to use ClassExpert later for further customization.

Q How can I change the menus and other resources?

A Use the Resource Editor.

Exercises

1. Use the AppExpert utility to create a text editor that supports the drag/drop and printing features. Compare the output code with the listings in this chapter.

2. Use the AppExpert utility to create a text editor that supports the speed bar, status line, drag/drop, and printing features. Compare the output code with the listings in this chapter.

3. Use the AppExpert utility to create a text editor that uses the document/view feature. Compare the output code with the listings in this chapter.

20

21

OLE 2

Object linking and embedding (OLE) is the Windows system for enabling several programs to work together, and OLE 2 represents a further degree of refinement and increase in function over the original OLE system. Borland C++ 5 provides a number of classes to support OLE 2. Today, you explore the following topics:

☐ The Borland solution to implementing OLE 2

☐ Embedding objects the OWL way

What Is OLE 2?

NEW☞ TERM With *object linking and embedding*, objects can be linked together. Thus, a document or other object can be composed of many objects from different applications, and the data that represents the objects can be embedded into the document.

A *linked* object holds sufficient information in the client to invoke another application with the reference for the data to be operated on.

An *embedded* object has the data of the object held in the client itself.

Before going into detail, let's examine why a user would want linking and embedding. From the early days of PC programs, users wanted the capability of joining information from different applications. For example, every word-processed sales report needs that sales-up-in-the-third-quarter pie chart. The original solutions of integration, such as Lotus Symphony, tried to do everything in one large application. Similarly, most of the industry-standard word processors, spreadsheets, and presentation-graphics programs have a tremendous overlap of function—in Excel, you can draw on your spreadsheet; in Word, you can make a simple spreadsheet in a word-processing table. Of course, the user does not want decreased functionality in these add-on features. The solution in Windows is to provide the capability of inserting the output from other applications into documents.

OLE 2 is not just about providing the user with desktop publishing, however. The question could better be phrased, "What *are* OLE 2?" OLE 2 comes in two forms:

☐ A system of data exchange called *Automation* that enables programs to pass data between themselves

☐ A system of joining programs and data together to create a compound document

NEW☞ TERM Throughout the rest of the day, the term *OLE* means OLE 2 unless explicit reference is made to OLE 1. As a matter of fact, Microsoft has decided to start referring to OLE 2 as simply OLE, ignoring the release of the first OLE version.

There is a significant difference between the two activities. With Automation, the two programs must have a defined interface and know about the data that is being passed between them. The client transaction processes the data provided by the Automation server. With object linking and

embedding, the principle is that the container knows nothing about the object being contained; rather, it interacts with the OLE system only. However, an OLE container must provide certain features to enable an object to be inserted.

NEW☛
TERM
The correct terminology for the user of an OLE object is a *container*. The provider of an OLE object is a *server*.

To the user, OLE means being able to edit a document or graphic and place other objects on the screen. An object is inserted into a container either by an Insert Object command, the Clipboard using the special OLE options, or drag-and-drop. The container is responsible for providing the space for the object; the object's server is responsible for drawing it. Similarly, when saving an embedded object, the server is responsible for writing the object to the file provided by the container.

> **Note:** After an OLE object has been linked or embedded, the server is no longer required. The OLE container keeps an image of the object (drawn using a Windows metafile) so it can reproduce the object. This includes scaling to fit the page and printing it—true WYSIWYG (What You See Is What You Get) fashion.

Linking and embedding are two different processes. In linking, the container stores a reference to another application with instructions as to how to access the server. One linked document can be shared among several containers. A change to a linked document can be updated across several containers—and, if the document is moved to another machine, the linked document needs to go with it and the links may need to be reestablished. In embedding, all the data is held in the container document. This means that the object is safely owned by the document, and it can be copied from one place to another without losing the embedded data. Only one document owns the data, however—other documents are not kept up to date. The appropriate method for linking is a user decision, depending on why the object is being inserted.

OLE gets in everywhere. OLE defines a standard for the format for storing objects. The storage is divided into compartments, which can contain other compartments themselves. The main document contains subcompartments, one for each embedded object. The advantages of the standardization of the storage are that containers can identify the server data mixed in with its own data and that the container can use the OLE file structure so that it reads only objects that are needed. For example, if the object is a 24-bit image that is displayed on the second page of a document, it may not be necessary to read the picture when opening a document to view the first page. More importantly, the storage structure is hierarchical and can be used by an object to contain other objects. Finally, the storage concept is independent of the medium in which the objects are saved; a storage can be on disk or in memory or held in a blob on a Paradox database, for example.

21

NEW ☞ The OLE name for a compartment is a *storage*.
TERM

An OLE object is made of two separate components: the data and the view. As you have seen, the data can be stored separately from the application that displays the object. An object can also be viewed in a number of different ways, as with Clipboard formats. So, for an extreme (but actual) example, an embedded wave file may provide a visual "view" for its representation in a document and a sound "view" to play it.

The level of integration in OLE is very high. A true OLE container embedding or linking an OLE object enables its menu, toolbar, and status bar to be taken over by the server for in-place editing, effectively appearing to be the server application. The object, when activated (when it has focus, rather than being edited), can add options to menus, provide for pop-up menus over the object, and can be moved and sized within a document.

OLE applications can work as containers, servers, or both. Even more confusing is that an OLE embedded object with in-place editing can itself open an in-place edited object, as in Figure 21.1. The newer OLE 2 provides backwards compatibility with the original OLE 1 so that you can embed OLE 2 objects in an OLE 1 application (without in-place editing). Similarly, OLE 2 can insert OLE 1 objects—but they can't provide in-place editing.

There are two ways you can provide an OLE server: as an executable and as a DLL. Even as an executable, you may not want to provide your object as a standalone application (to save implementing the standalone requirements of printing and file management, for example). Providing a server as a DLL has large performance improvements. This enables OLE to call server functions directly. With an OLE executable, OLE has a problem. Because OLE is designed for true multitasking systems, it has to organize calls between tasks properly; it cannot simply send messages. Therefore, OLE has to convert its commands into task-independent messages to ensure that it can edit the object without having the container aware of the object implementation. Furthermore, the intention is that the OLE implementation can be extended to enable objects to be implemented across networks so that the OLE tasks might run on different computers—all transparent to the user and the programmer.

Figure 21.1.
The OLE 2 way of embedding.

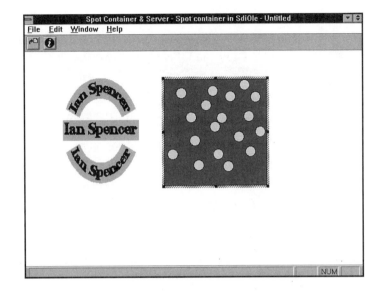

How Does Borland Implement OLE 2?

OLE contains many features. However, "there ain't no such thing as a free lunch." To provide all these features, a container application must provide the correct interaction with OLE. This, as you might imagine, is hard work, considering the tremendous number of different situations with which the application has to cope. OCF simplifies the work required by providing a number of classes that support the basic function in the same way that OWL supports the Windows API. Aside from the classes, OCF provides a number of macros to simplify the definition of the OLE registration data and class definitions. It does so in a way similar to the way that OWL uses macros for the window response tables, and it also defines its own special messages to enable a simplified OCF event to be handled.

NEW☞ *OCF* stands for *Object Components Framework*. This is Borland's high-level C++ wrapper
TERM around OLE, which converts between a simplified C++ object-oriented interface and the OLE API. It is similar to the ObjectWindows Library that acts as a wrapper around the standard Windows API.

21

Note: OCF is a separate set of classes from OWL. OWL provides classes that make use of OCF to build OLE applications, but OCF does not require the use of OWL.

OCF provides class support for OLE servers, OLE containers, and OLE Automation. OCF helps implement the following:

☐ *Linking and embedding.* OCF provides support for both server and container.

☐ *The Clipboard.* OCF provides all the cut-and-paste options.

☐ *Drag-and-drop.* This is the capability of dragging an object and, when placed in a drag-and-drop enabled window, placing the object in that window.

☐ *OLE interface.* OCF provides standard components to build OLE dialog boxes, and it also provides the capability of modifying the container window if it is written to conform to OCF's requirements.

☐ OLE compound files.

OCF places a layer of abstraction over the standard Microsoft OLE interface. If you were to program in straight C++ without OWL, OCF would provide a simplified way of programming OLE. For OLE Automation, OCF provides all the functionality required to pass data between a client and server object. OCF also provides additional help to the application to enable it to handle the command line correctly, which is used to instruct an OLE application as to the mode in which it should run. However, there is still a lot of work to do in managing a linking and embedding application.

Building on the OCF classes, OWL then provides a number of classes to ease the programming of OLE via OCF. There are OLE-enabled frames, `TOleFrame` and `TOleMDIFrame`, and OLE container windows—for example, `TOleWindow`. `TOleDocument` and `TOleView` represent the container and views of the container. There also have been some modifications to the `TApplication` class to enable it to run in the different ways required by OLE.

OWL provides support for these OCF functions, but wraps them further still to the point that you need very little code in your program to support OLE. The best way to use this is with the AppExpert (discussed on Day 20). AppExpert can quickly generate the framework of an OLE application for both an OLE container and server.

OLE *Doc/View*

For the rest of this look at OLE linking and embedding, you'll study the `TOleDocument` and `TOleView` implementation of OLE. The `Doc/View` model has been present in OWL since its original version. The principle of the `Doc/View` model is that the storing of data and the

presentation of data are two different tasks. For example, as was mentioned earlier, you might have a sound document. The document is considered to be just the raw data that makes up the sound. There can be two views of this particular document: a visual representation that can be used for insertion into something like a word processor or an icon in a folder on the system, and a "view" that plays the sound.

NEW☞ TERM For simplicity, *Doc/View* refers to TOleDocument and TOleView throughout the rest of today's lesson.

Defining a *TOleDocument* Class

There are several steps to follow in defining a TOleDocument class.

Step 1: Define the Document Storage

TOleDocument understands how to store OLE documents and provides the container with access to the storage medium so that the programmer can easily add specific data to the document.

OWL Note: Transparently, you write to the special OLE storage format. This means that you do not need to do anything special to store data in either embedded or standalone file format.

Normally, you derive a class and provide Open and Commit functions to enable the document to read and write its data. You also provide a Close function to clear the document, and you may want to provide a Revert function to reset your document to a cleared or as-originally-read state. In each of these, you need to call the base TOleDocument function. You access the file by using the Instream function to return a TInStream for reading and the OutStream function for getting a TOutStream. When writing the file, you should place markers or read a fixed number of objects, which you note before writing so that you can safely reread the data.

Warning: At the end of writing out data in the Commit function, make sure you call TOleDocument::CommitTransactedStorage, which updates the storage to disk. If you do not do this, the file you write will be incomplete and can't be opened.

21

Step 2: Define Notifications to Tell Views to Update Themselves

You are likely to need some notifications to tell the document views of any changes to the document that might affect them. At any time, a document may have several views open, although only one will be active. When a document changes, it uses the `NotifyViews` function, which sends the notification to all the views that are open; it does this via the standard message-response table. There are a number of standard notifications. You can also define your own document-specific notifications for which you need to define a notification value, a response-function signature (via a macro that OWL provides), and a response-table entry. The following code snippet, for example, defines document notifications for when the document has been added to or been cleared:

```
//
// Custom Doc/View notifications
//
const int vnDrawAppend = vnCustomBase+0;
const int vnDrawClear = vnCustomBase+1;
//
// Custom Doc/View signatures
//
NOTIFY_SIG(vnDrawAppend, uint)
NOTIFY_SIG(vnDrawClear, void)
//
// Response table macros
//
#define EV_VN_DRAWAPPEND VN_DEFINE(vnDrawAppend, VnAppend, int)
#define EV_VN_DRAWCLEAR VN_DEFINE(vnDrawClear, VnClear, void)
```

Step 3: Provide Data-Access Functions for Views

In order to provide data-access functions for views, you must define a `TOleView` class. This is described in the next section.

Defining a *TOleView* Class

Next, you need to provide access functions so that the various views can get at the data. Their exact form is up to you, but you will normally require at least something to add data and to get the data from the document. More sophisticated applications provide more functions.

Creating a `TOleView` class requires a bit more work. How much work depends on whether or not the view is intended to contain OLE objects (remember that an OLE server can itself contain objects if you want). `TOleView` contains all the work to contain objects.

> **OWL Note:** When building your `TOleView` class, you should store a pointer or reference to your document class. There is already such a pointer, but it is of the generic `TOleDocument` type and needs down-casting to use.

Step 1: Define the Presentation

Defining the presentation is based on accessing data from the document. Generally, this consists of having the Paint member function retrieve data from the document. You may have more than one method of presenting the data. If so, you can either create separate TOleView classes or, more likely, derive further classes from a common class of your own design. The special trick to an OLE server is that the view may not be presented in device units. OWL looks after the scaling, but it means that any interaction you have with the screen needs to be managed in logical window units—not pixels as you would expect.

Step 2: Add Data-Editing Methods

How the view accepts data is up to the view. However, because there may be several views open on the document at once, take care how you handle this. The general approach is to handle the editing in the view and, when the object is complete, store it in the document using the document access functions you provide. The document accepts the data and sends a notification message. In a Paintbrush example, you might type text on the picture only in the active view and when the text is accepted by the user, add the text to the document. Then, in the notification response, invalidate the window to ensure that the screen is redisplayed. By using custom notifications, you can refine the process so that when adding data, all the views can, if possible, modify their window rather than entirely redraw it.

Step 3: Add Notification Responses

The view should handle all document notifications to ensure that the display matches the document data. The normal response is often to invalidate the window (by calling Invalidate), but, if the object is a server, the view should also call InvalidatePart to ensure that the container is kept in step with the editing.

Note: It's important to remember that if you edit an OLE object (rather than opening for in-place editing), you can observe your embedded object being updated as you edit the object in a separate application.

Step 4: Support Embedded Objects, if Required

OWL supports embedded objects for you in TOleView; however, you need to avoid interfering with how it works. Essentially, OWL provides a default place to dump new objects, then uses EvLButtonDown, EvMouseMove, and EvLButtonUp to manage moving and sizing of the embedded objects. There are a few traps to mouse handling:

☐ You need to enable the mouse messages to be responded to by the base class to enable contained objects to be handled.

☐ The `EvLButtonDown` and `EvMouseMove` messages convert the `TPoint` mouse position parameter into logical units, dependent on the view. The DC view is provided by the `DragDC` member of the view. The mouse down always creates a `DragDC` for you. If you are drawing on the view, you need to use the `DragDC` to get the correct scaling for an embedded edit. If you are storing the position of the object based on the `EvLButtonUp`, you need to convert the mouse coordinates to logical units yourself.

☐ You should use the mouse only if the mouse hasn't selected an embedded object. You can test for this by testing whether a `DragDC` exists (it will unless your mouse has been moved over the window, having first been pressed outside). Then you should check whether the mouse is holding the object. You do this by calling `SelectEmbedded`, which returns `true` if the `TOleView` is currently handling an embedded object.

By default, you have no control over the placement of the objects (which is normal for many embedding applications). You can provide a current position for insertion by providing a `GetInsertPosition` function (for example, this might return the current cursor position in a word processor).

You provide the rest of the OLE container functionality by giving the appropriate menu options—all the OLE function is built in, whether you are building a server or a container.

As you can see, the steps using the Doc/View model are nearly identical for a container or server.

The OLE Registry

The first thing an OLE application does when it starts is to register itself with Windows, letting the operating system know just what parts of OLE the program can handle. The standard method has been to fill in all sorts of long complicated parameters to all manner of OLE API functions. With OCF, the information is easier to supply, though it can still can be rather complicated; the information is created in a structure with the aid of special registration macros. The structure then is passed into the OCF object constructors, which make sure that your application's program is registered properly with the operating system.

Note: The actual registry information is stored in the REG.DAT file in Windows 3.1. In Windows NT and Windows 95, the information is stored in the system registry.

Although there are several registry functions, the most common ones—the ones in which you're interested—are listed in Table 21.1. These are used to build the registration structures that describe both the application and the various document formats.

Table 21.1. OCF registry macros.

Macro	Meaning
BEGIN_REGISTRATION	Used to start defining a structure. This is similar to the DEFINE_RESPONSE_TABLEX macro used in OWL. The single parameter to this macro is the name of the structure to be defined.
END_REGISTRATION	Used to end the definition of a structure. It's similar to OWL's END_RESPONSE_TABLE macro.
REGDATA	The main workhorse macro that adds a keyed entry to the structure. The first parameter to this macro is the key. The second parameter is a value to associate with the key.
REGDOCFLAGS	Adds an entry containing flags for a document template. These flags are used in the Doc/View model of OLE programming. The parameter is an ORed-together bunch of dtXXX flags.
REGFORMAT	Each document needs to let the OLE registry know which formats, such as metafiles, bit maps, and so on, it can handle. This adds information regarding a document's capabilities to the structure.
REGISTRATION_FORMAT_BUFFER	Some of the macros used to create the registration structure require some temporary space in order to properly expand. This macro provides that temporary space, the size of which is based on its single parameter.

In the description of the REGDATA macro, I mentioned that it registers keyed entries. There are quite a number of keys available to be registered, some of which are required for various structures. Table 21.2 describes some of the keys.

21

Table 21.2. OCF registry keys.

Key Name	Entry Value
clsid	Defines the Globally Unique Identifier (GUID) needed to differentiate OLE applications from one another. The GUIDs are generated automatically by the IDE's AppExpert. If you create an OLE application on your own, you can use the GUIDGEN.EXE program supplied with the compiler to generate a GUID for this field.
progid	A string that identifies the structure. This is used for both documents and for applications, and it typically consists of three parts: a program name, an object name, and a version number.
description	When OLE puts up a string for the user to see, it shows the contents of this entry, which can be up to 40 characters long.
cmdline	Describes the arguments that OLE should place on the program's command line when OLE starts the application. It's often just an empty string.
appname	Usually the title that shows up in the application's main window.
docfilter	Represented as a file mask, such as `*.SPT`, and generally uses the same letters as in the document's extension. That file mask is used in the common dialogs, along with a file type (see `menuname` and `description`) when OLE asks the user to open or save files.
usage	A flag that lets OLE know whether it should start up a new instance of the application server for each client that requests it. If `ocrSingleUse` is used here, the application will be started once for each OLE client that needs it. `ocrMultipleUse` means that the server application will be opened only once, no matter how many clients ask for it.
insertable	The key for this entry is always an empty string; its presence is used in a structure to identify a document as one that can be inserted into other container documents. It will appear in the list of available documents when the user selects the Insert Object menu item.
menuname	A short name that shows up as a menu item in container programs. In order to keep menu sizes short and readable, the suggested maximum length for this entry is 15 characters.
verbN	Describes the verbs used for documents, ones that will appear in pop-up menus. N represents a number that should begin with 0 and go no further than 7. Typical entries are `"&Edit"` and `"&Open"`.
extension	Used to identify filename extensions for OLE documents. When OLE is asked to open a file, it matches the extension of the file with the various servers associated with extensions and then uses the matching one.

It's important to note that this list is by no means complete. There are a number of other keys that can be used, but the ones listed so far are enough to get a program up and running with full OLE functionality.

Creating an OLE Application

The previous discussion has created only the Doc/View components and described the registry in general terms, but this has not explained how documents and views are managed. OWL provides a document manager, called TDocManager. It is this class (which you normally don't need to amend in any way) that looks after documents and views. There are a few simple steps that you take to enable the document manager to understand your class.

Step 1: Declare a *Doc/View* Template and Register its Details

You do not need to worry about the internals of declaring a Doc/View template. There are three components you need to define. (You don't use these yourself; they are used by the TDocManager.) The DEFINE_DOC_TEMPLATE_CLASS macro associates the documents and the views. You declare one of these for each combination:

```
DEFINE_DOC_TEMPLATE_CLASS(SpotDoc, SpotView, SpotTemplate);
```

Then you need to declare some important OLE registration details for each document.

```
BEGIN_REGISTRATION(__SpotRegistration)
   REGDATA(progid, "Spot.Container.1")
   REGDATA(description, "Spot Container Version 1")
   REGDATA(extension, "SPT")
   REGDATA(docfilter, "*.SPT")
   REGDOCFLAGS(dtAutoDelete | dtUpdateDir
               | dtAutoOpen | dtRegisterExt)
   REGDATA(menuname, "Spot container")
   REGDATA(insertable, "")
   REGDATA(verb0, "&Edit")
   REGDATA(verb1, "&Open")
   REGFORMAT(0, ocrEmbedSource, ocrContent,
                ocrIStorage, ocrGet)
   REGFORMAT(1, ocrMetafilePict, ocrContent,
                ocrMfPict | ocrStaticMed, ocrGet)
   REGFORMAT(2, ocrBitmap, ocrContent,
                ocrGDI | ocrStaticMed, ocrGet)
   REGFORMAT(3, ocrDib, ocrContent,
                ocrHGlobal | ocrStaticMed, ocrGet)
   REGFORMAT(4, ocrLinkSource, ocrContent,
                ocrIStream, ocrGet)
END_REGISTRATION
```

This table is passed to Windows so that your application is entered into the system. This enables other applications to know of your existence. Important entries (well, they are all important!)

are progid and description, which appear when the user accesses the object (for example, via Insert Object). insertable is a placeholder to indicate that this object can be inserted—that is, the document is an OLE server. extension, docfilter, and the REGDOCFLAGS lines all tell the document manager (and OLE) which files can be handled by the Doc/View combination. The REGFORMATs tell OLE which formats the server can produce for linking and embedding. OWL Doc/View can provide all these formats for you.

Having created this information, you then declare a global static instance of the Doc/View template. The instance takes care of associating itself with the manager, so you can call it whatever you like. It takes the registration information as a parameter (you pass the registration details even if you decide not to provide OLE support).

```
SpotTemplate __spotTemplate(__SpotRegistration);
```

You now have created your Doc/View classes.

Step 2: Add the Application Registration Details

Next, you need to sort out the application. There are a number of features for this. First, you need a static TAppDictionary. This manages OWL internal information. This must be called AppDictionary to ensure that certain OWL features work.

Second, you need to register the application (by the way, place this before your Doc/View registration).

```
//
// Ole 2 linking and embedding apps need a TOcRegistrar
//
static TPointer<TOcRegistrar> Registrar;

REGISTRATION_FORMAT_BUFFER(100)

BEGIN_REGISTRATION(ApplicationReg)
    //
    // The following must be unique per Ole 2 application
    //
    REGDATA(clsid, "{FE91A8E0-DBDA-101B-A585-040224007802}")
    REGDATA(appname, "Spot Container & Server")
    REGDATA(description, "Spot Container & Server Application")
    REGDATA(cmdline, "")
    REGDATA(usage, ocrMultipleUse)
END_REGISTRATION
```

Create a TOcRegistrar pointer, which must be called Registrar. OCF uses templates that rely on this. You will set up the Registrar in OwlMain.

Note: The `TPointer` class is a cunning ruse to ensure that dynamically allocated objects get cleaned up. It accepts a pointer of the type of the object specified and deletes the object if the instance goes out of scope, a new object is assigned to it, or zero is assigned to it. This improves the capability of cleaning up objects if something goes wrong. You can use this class yourself. Typically, you use it where you would declare a variable, but, because of size, you want to declare it using `new`. One place it works well is where an exception may be thrown—objects declared on the stack are cleaned up, but dynamically allocated objects are not. By wrapping the pointer in an object, dynamically allocatable objects can now be cleaned up.

Next, create the application registration. `appname` and `description` are self-explanatory. `usage` enables multiple clients to use the same application, and `cmdline` indicates that there are no arguments needed on the command line. The important one is `clsid`.

Warning: The class `id` must be absolutely unique to ensure that OLE starts the correct program. The Globally Unique IDentifier is unique around the world, and you should never copy someone else's—especially if you are going to distribute your application.

This horribly long number can easily be generated. Merely run GUIDGEN (which lives in your Borland C++ BIN directory). This places a new GUID in your Clipboard, and you can then paste it into your code.

Step 3: Implement the Application Class

You now can move and look at the class. A `Doc/View` application handles a couple of responses for the document manager:

```
DEFINE_RESPONSE_TABLE1(SpotApp, TApplication)
    EV_OWLVIEW(dnCreate, EvNewView),
    EV_OWLVIEW(dnClose, EvCloseView),
    EV_COMMAND(CM_HELPABOUT, CmHelpAbout),
END_RESPONSE_TABLE;
```

The application itself is multiply-derived from `TApplication` and `TOcModule`. The `TOcModule` is transparent, but you do need to use a special `TApplication` constructor:

```
SpotApp::SpotApp ()
    : TApplication(::ApplicationReg["description"],
                   ::Module,
                   &::AppDictionary )
{
    SetDocManager(new TDocManager(dmSDI ¦ dmMenu, this));
}
```

The constructor is identical for any OLE application you write, using the global objects you created earlier. In the constructor, set up the document manager. This needs to be set for whether you are using SDI or MDI (it controls whether multiple documents can be open).

InitMainWindow is fairly standard, except that you cannot create a client at this point; OLE is not yet ready. You use a TOleFrame, which is a special TDecoratedFrame that can handle the OLE toolbar interface. You would create your toolbar for a standalone application here, setting the toolbar's Attr.Id to IDW_TOOLBAR. This enables OWL to swap it if another application takes over your application.

In TApplication::InitInstance, the application can now have its client window set up if required. If the application is not embedding, you can open the file based on the command line, or you can open a blank document. To open files, you ask the document manager. In the following snippet, if not embedding, the application finds out whether the document manager recognizes the filename that has been sent via MatchTemplate. If so, it attempts to open the file by creating a document. It uses the document template to construct an empty document, then uses the document manager to initialize it, which, in turn, opens a view. Similarly, if there is no document, the application merely opens a new view.

```
if (!::Registrar->IsOptionSet(amEmbedding))
{
    TDocTemplate* tpl = GetDocManager()
            ->MatchTemplate(GetCmdLine().c_str());
    if (tpl)
        {
        TDocument* doc = tpl->ConstructDoc();
        if (doc)
            {
            doc->SetTemplate(tpl);
            GetDocManager()->InitDoc(doc,
            GetCmdLine().c_str(), 0);
            return;
            }
        }
    GetDocManager()->CreateAnyDoc(0, dtNewDoc);
}
```

The document manager opens the view. Recall that the application response table defined two document notifications. After a view has been created, it has to be associated with a window. Because the application may operate in an embedded mode, this view may be a window in the container document. So, to handle the notification, the application needs to test whether the document is embedded. If the document is embedded, it creates a view parented to a special window; otherwise, the view is created as a standard client (in this case, an SDI client).

```
TOleView* ov = dynamic_cast<TOleView*>(&view);
if (ov && view.GetDocument().IsEmbedded() &&
    !ov->GetOcRemView()->IsOpenEditing())
  {
  //
  // Embedded view window
  //
  TWindow* vw = view.GetWindow();
  vw->SetParent(dynamic_cast<TOleFrame*>(GetMainWindow())
                                    ->GetRemViewBucket());
  vw->Create();
  }
else
  {
  //
  // Normal window - associate with MainWindow
  //
  GetMainWindow()->SetClientWindow(view.GetWindow());
  if (!view.IsOK())
    GetMainWindow()->SetClientWindow(0);
  else if (view.GetViewMenu())
    GetMainWindow()->MergeMenu(*view.GetViewMenu());
  }
```

Note: In Doc/View, menu merging is used even in an SDI application, because different views can be placed as a client.

Step 4: Implement an OLE *OwlMain*

The OwlMain is changed around. This is to enable the OLE system to call your application correctly. When you run an OLE application, it receives a variety of command-line options. It is responsible for registering and unregistering itself, and also for interpreting the command-line options that OLE might have passed. OWL strips these out for you, leaving a simplified command line with only non-OLE information. This saves you from having to decode the flags yourself. You can interrogate the flags by calling TRegistrar::IsOptionSet. This tests for any flags you send, which are enumerated. The main test you need is to decide whether your application is operating in embedded mode. Normally, the command line can contain the filename to enable the operating system to start your application via its associations. It also normally passes the filename and a flag to request printing a document.

```
int OwlMain (int, char* [])
{
   try
      {
      ::Registrar = new TOcRegistrar(::ApplicationReg,
                                  TOleDocViewFactory<SpotApp>(),
                                  TApplication::GetCmdLine(),
                                  ::DocTemplateStaticHead);
```

21

```
        if (!::Registrar->IsOptionSet(amAnyRegOption))
          ::Registrar->Run();
        ::Registrar = 0;
        return 0;
        }
    catch (xmsg& x)
        {
        ::MessageBox(0, x.why().c_str(), "Exception", MB_OK);
        }
    return -1;
}
```

The main trick here is the use of the `::Registrar` object. For an OLE application that does linking and embedding, you need a `TOcRegistrar` object. The `::ApplicationReg` and `TApplication::GetCommandLine()` are all standard objects that you use. `::DocTemplateStaticHead` represents a special link for the registration to find the document template registration details. The special part is the `TOleDocViewFactory`. This is a template class that generates a hidden callback function. This callback function is what actually is called by the `::Registrar->Run()` call. OWL provides a number of different callbacks depending on the sort of application you are building. The name `Factory` implies that this is the OLE object generator. When building an OLE application, your target needs to include the OCF libraries. (When distributing an OLE application, you also need to distribute the OLE libraries.)

Put all that together, and then run your application. However, before you run an OLE-enabled server, you should run it in register mode. The proper way to do this is to run it with a `-RegServer` command line. The IDE makes this easy for you; there are two special commands on the SpeedMenu for a target node. Choose SpeedMenu | Special | Register or Unregister, and the IDE will run your application in registration mode. In this mode, it does not create windows; it merely performs the registration and then immediately exits.

Creating OLE Applications with AppExpert

The following application was initially generated using AppExpert, although it has been substantially tidied up. With Borland C++ 5, AppExpert is OLE-enabled. You can create `Doc/View` servers or containers with all the usual features that you would expect to be able to generate. ClassExpert understands the OLE `Doc/View` model. You are familiar with AppExpert, so you will find it simple to amend OLE applications. At the time of writing, AppExpert gives a derived `TOleView` object to work with, but it does not provide a derived `TOleDocument` class. This always is required for all but trivial examples and can easily be derived by using ClassExpert. (Remember to use the SpeedMenu from the class pane; this enables you to derive from any class that the ClassExpert knows about.)

Another suggestion is to amend the derived `TOleView` class manually so that it accepts a derived `TOleDocument` as a parameter rather than the `TOleDocument` set as the parameter. This saves down-casting the document each time you access it.

If you want to create an OLE container to play with, press the generate button and compile the result. You will find that you can make an application that provides a nearly complete OLE implementation. AppExpert is useful, because an OLE application normally needs to support toolbars and status bars, and it will generate all the different menus and registration tables.

Note: Do not select Automation support in the OLE 2 options yet. This option is covered in the second part of today's lesson.

The listings for SPOT.EXE, included as Appendix B, provide a practical and stimulating example.

First, ensure that you have registered the server. You may want to build some of the OLE samples in the EXAMPLES directory to give yourself a test bed, unless you have a modern application. Running it as a standalone application might give you a result like the one in Figure 21.2. Running in another OLE application, STEP14.EXE (provided as an example in the OWL tutorial directory), gives the appearance shown in Figure 21.3.

Figure 21.2.

The SPOT application running as a standalone application.

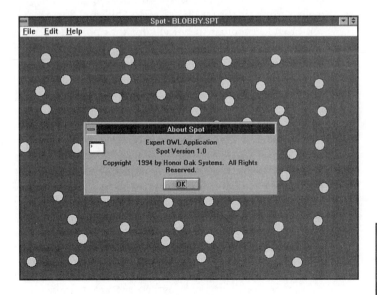

Figure 21.3.
The SPOT application running with in-place editing.

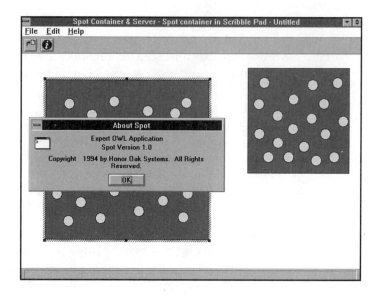

Looking first to the application class in Listing B.2 (SPOTAPP.CPP), you see that there was no toolbar created in the InitMainWindow. This emphasizes that, when running as an in-place editor, you provide a toolbar specifically for the application. In fact, if you can guarantee that the instance will be only single-use (set by the registration option usage for the application), you can borrow the control bar for your main application. OWL TOleView does this by default in response to EvOcShowTools. You should always provide a toolbar; if you don't, the screen jumps about while switching in the container application as the client window is repositioned.

Note also that OWL expects to use menu merging even for an SDI application. For OWL to manage the menus for you, you merely need to create menus of the correct identity. OWL creates the TMenuDescr objects for you, except for the main menu, as long as you use the predefined menu identifiers.

Take a look at the InitInstance. If the application starts as an embedding application, OWL looks after creating the view. In this SDI application, there should always be a client view by first attempting to open a command-line document (this could be optimized to avoid opening for obviously invalid command lines).

The trivialities of the About box bring out an important point about embedded objects. You may want to bring up dialog boxes. GetCommandTarget can be used to provide a suitable parent in place of GetMainWindow, which may, in fact, be hidden during embedding. This should ensure that the dialog stays modal over the container application.

In Listing B.4 (SPOTDOC.CPP), the first catch is in writing the Open function. Although the path appears to be passed in as a parameter, it is not used. You should use GetDocPath, which is filled in before Open is called in TOleDocument::InitDoc.

You can detect a failure to open a file by using the result of the `InStream` function. In `SpotDoc`, the spots are held in a `TArray` container. They can easily be read in from and out to this container.

> **Warning:** Failure to read a document can occur because the document was improperly written. Check that the `Commit` function is properly structured and ends with a call to `TOleDocument::CommitTransactedStorage`.

`AddSpot` uses a custom notification to get the views updated. This is a good optimization, because, for this application, the views need to add the item to their current display rather than redraw the entire screen. Note the interaction of the view and the document. The view captures the data and passes it to the document, which then tells the view to draw it.

Moving on to `Paint` in Listing B.6 (SPOTVIEW.CPP), the drawing here requires care. Your `Paint` functions up to now have almost always been able to rely on having the mapping mode be `MM_TEXT` when drawing to a window. Because the OLE container may have scaled the image, when you edit in place your window may not be pixel-based. OWL sorts out the scaling for you. However, this means that you must be careful that you draw in logical units, not pixels. The `Paint` function also is called by OWL to create the metafile that OLE stores in the embedded document for viewing and printing. This does not provide the usual functions you might expect to determine the drawing area—it is up to you to define the drawing area. The view always obtains its data from the document; it does not store its own data. The other unusual thing to note is the call to `TOleView::Paint`. This is how the embedded objects that are not active get redisplayed. (Therefore, it is not required for a server-only application.)

The mouse handling needs consideration. `TOleView` handles matching the mouse with the current display-mapping mode. To handle its embedded objects, it provides a DC to enable it to draw and to scale its mouse movements. The tricky part is in the use of the `EvLButtonUp` response. Unlike the other two mouse events, `TOleView` does not scale the mouse coordinates. Also, unlike the other two responses, your code needs to happen before the base-class processing so that you can test for the presence of the DC. (Again, if the application is not a container, it does not need to worry about the base-class processing.)

There are two OCF events you might like to handle, which are specific for an OLE server.

The first is declaring the size of your view to OLE with `EvOcViewPartSize`. The implementation here is quick and dirty. Normally, good programming practice dictates avoiding recalculating the view size each time the message is called. In this case, the view expands if data is placed outside the declared bounds. To avoid problems, the minimum view is declared to be a two-inch square.

21

NEW☞ In OCF, the embedded objects are known as *parts*.
TERM

Second, there is the placing of the toolbar. This is requested when OLE opens the object for in-place editing. You create a standard toolbar. (By default, TOleView assumes that it can borrow the application MainWindow toolbar on the assumption that the application instance is single-use.) This toolbar is likely to be slightly different from a normal standalone application toolbar, leaving out File Save and other items. Hidden away is the OWL processing, which updates the menu and manages the status bar. Much of the processing is enabled merely by placing the correct options on the menu and toolbar.

There is a whole raft of functions that OWL provides. You should spend some time experimenting with the effects of the different embedding options. Try dragging objects around, resizing their borders when selected, resizing when open for editing, pasting links, and so on. It is worth remembering that, in OWL, most of the Doc/View control is provided by the document manager (TDocManager). The controlling of the window is mainly provided by TOleView through TOleWindow. With luck, investigating these classes should provide you with the information you need to go beyond this quick look at OLE linking and embedding.

Consider what the changes would be to take away the container functionality—a very few statements, removing a few menu items and a few base class calls. Consider what it would take to take away server function—some registration options and some spare notifications. Finally, compare that with a standalone application—using the Doc/View model. OLE Doc/View provides a surprisingly high degree of implementation independence. It is possible to write OWL OLE applications without the Doc/View model; however, your application needs to be quite specialized to make it worthwhile.

A wealth of issues are not covered here. OLE 2 provides language independence for the interface. Doc/View is a very high-level abstraction—OWL does enable closer control of the OLE process. You can go on to explore enabling your application to control object positioning or laying out objects around the embedded parts. Finally, don't get so involved with providing OLE support that you forget to develop a useful application. There already are a lot of container applications out there; what is needed are useful servers.

Summary

Today, you got a taste of OLE. Specifically, you explored the following topics:

- ☐ OLE as a method for communicating between programs and for linking and embedding views and data

- ☐ How ObjectWindows and Object Components Framework work together to provide a high-level programming solution to OLE

- ☐ How OWL provides tremendous support for OLE embedding via its OLE Doc/View model (you can concentrate on your application rather than OLE)

Q&A

Q How do I find out more about OLE?

A If possible, work through the examples in the Borland manuals on OCF that do not use the OWL classes. These highlight some of the mechanics of OLE. I recommend that you avoid books on pure OLE; these will not explain the OCF interface. There is a full tutorial included with the Borland package, and it is well worth working through it. The OWL manuals and online help are full of information about OLE and OCF.

Workshop

The Workshop provides quiz questions to help you consolidate your understanding of the material covered, and exercises to provide you with experience in using what you've learned. Try to understand the quiz and exercise answers before continuing on to the next day's lesson. Answers are provided in Appendix A.

Quiz

1. Which method of joining documents should a user use to place a document in several other documents?
2. Which OWL class is responsible for managing the display of embedded objects?
3. What must you do before you can access an OLE server from a container?

Exercise

Using AppExpert, generate a copy of the SPOT application with all the decorations.

For this review, you look at the Turbo Cribbage game supplied with the Borland C++ 5 package in the BC5\EXAMPLES\OWL\GAMES\CRIBBAGE directory. As the name suggests, this implements the card game of cribbage. It includes routines for displaying cards and a pegboard, and routines for totaling scores.

How to Play

Before beginning a discussion of the program that implements the game, it probably would be useful (if not downright required) to first have a discussion about how to play the game.

The roots of cribbage extend back to the 1600s and Briton John Suckling. Cribbage is a two-person card game (actually, up to six people could play, but this version is for two players, known as the *Dealer* and the *Pone*). The rules are rather simple, but the variety and strategy still continue to make the game exciting. The numbers and point-counting make it an ideal game for children as well as adults.

Here are the stages of the game:

- ☐ The deal
- ☐ The discard
- ☐ The turn
- ☐ The play
- ☐ Counting player hands
- ☐ Counting the crib

The stages of the game are repeated until one player has acquired 121 points. As soon as 121 points are achieved, the game is over; there is no need to wait until the end of a hand.

Scoring

Different stages of the game involve different scoring possibilities, but most are used throughout the game.

15	Any combination of two or more cards whose sum is 15 (face cards count as 10). Two points are awarded.
Two, three, or four of a kind	If two, three, or four cards have the same face value, 2 points are awarded for each pair combination—the points awarded for 2, 3, and 4 of a kind are 2, 6, and 12 points, respectively.
Run	A sequential series of three or more cards. One point is awarded for each card in the run.
His Nobs	If a player holds a Jack in his or her hand (or in the crib while the dealer) that has the same suit as the turned extra card, one point is awarded.
His Heels	If the Starter (extra card) revealed by the Pone is a Jack, the Dealer receives two points.
31	Any combination of cards whose sum is 31 (again, face cards count as 10) scores 2 points.
Flush	Four or more cards of the same suit. One point is awarded for each card in the flush. The crib allows only a five-card flush.
Go	During the play, a player who cannot play declares "Go" and his or her opponent can receive one point if they cannot play.
Last Card	The last player to lay down a card during the play receives one point for the last card.

The Deal

The deal alternates between players every hand. In the two-player version, each player receives six cards face down.

The Discard

Each player selects two cards to discard (face down) into the *crib*. The crib is a bonus hand that awards the points to the Dealer. Because the deal alternates between players, so do the points in the crib. Throwing to the crib involves a bit of strategy because neither player can control the other's crib contribution, and the Starter, which is used as a fifth card for scoring, will not be revealed until after the throw has been made. The Pone will not want to throw obvious points to the crib, but the Dealer has the capability to throw away points to be received when they count the crib. The scoring combinations are explained in a later section ("Counting Player Hands"), but a couple of obvious bad throws would be a 5, cards which add up to 15, or a pair (all of which give points or guarantee points for the Dealer).

The Turn

After both players have thrown to the crib, the Pone cuts the remaining (undealt) cards and the top card is turned over and then is known as the *Starter*. This card is used as a fifth card for counting points in each player's hand and the crib. If a Jack (of any suit) is revealed, then the Dealer receives two points for *His Heels*.

The Play

The Play is an opportunity for both players to play the four cards they kept in their hands in a head-to-head duel. Play begins with the Pone, who plays a card face up from his or her hand and continues with each player alternating cards. Scoring occurs during The Play by looking at the cards played by each player as a single sequence of cards—one big hand. Scoring opportunities are available for each player in the form of sums of 15; two, three, or four of a kind; runs; Go, Last Card, and 31. Play continues until neither player has any cards left in his or her hand.

Each cycle of play ends when neither player can legally make a play because to do so would cause the total value of upturned cards to exceed the limit of 31 (face cards are counted as 10) or a total of 31 occurs. At the end of each playing cycle, the upturned cards are turned over and a new cycle begins with the remaining cards.

As the total approaches 31, a player who cannot play declares, "Go!" and the opponent can continue playing cards (and collecting points, if possible) or collect 1 point for the Go. If a player plays a card that causes the total to become 31, then that player receives 2 points and all overturned cards are turned over for the next playing cycle.

Counting Player Hands

After the play, each player counts the points in his or her hand, using the Starter as a fifth, extra card. Players can earn points for 15s (commonly counted aloud as "Fifteen-two, fifteen-four", and so on); 2, 3, or 4 of a kind; a flush; runs (of 3 or more cards); or Nobs. Because the Dealer has the advantage of counting the crib's points, the Pone counts his or her hand first.

Counting the Crib

After both players have counted their hands, the Dealer picks up the crib and counts the points (again, including the Starter). The scoring opportunities available when counting the crib are the same as a regular player hand except for the Flush, which is awarded only if all five cards are the same suit.

The Cribbage Example

The base of the program starts in the CARDS.H and CARDS.CPP files where the TCard, TCardGroup, and TDeck classes are declared and defined. The first class models a single card and has data members to describe the card's face value (ace through king), its suit (hearts, spades, diamonds, and clubs), its back style (the card can have one of 13 styles on its back), and whether the card is face up. All these data members are public, and the two constructors are there simply to make the object's creation simpler.

The TCardGroup class is used to model several cards together as a unit (such as a player's hand or a specific pile of cards). The maximum number of cards allowable in the group must be specified when instances of the class are created, and then you can insert and remove cards from the group via the Insert and Remove member functions, respectively. The Insert member function is overloaded to enable you to add either a single card or another group. This class also defines the array operator (operator[]) in order to provide easy access to the cards contained in the group.

Finally, `TDeck` is a descendant of `TCardGroup` that is used to model an entire deck of cards. Because it's derived from `TCardGroup`, it can make use of all the insertion and removal methods of its base, and `TDeck` also adds a little extra functionality. The new class has methods for shuffling, cutting, and initializing the deck. This last method, `Initialize`, is called by the class constructor and simply inserts a card for each member of a standard 52-card deck. The `DealCard` member function acts to simply remove the top card from the deck.

`TDeck` also has the two methods `EncodeDeck` and `DecodeDeck`. The first function creates a 52-byte string with the contents of the current deck encoded into it. This encoding is done by placing the suit of each card into the upper four bits of a byte while filling the lower four bits with the card's face value. The encoding is done so that the contents of the deck can be saved into an INI file for future retrieval.

So far, these classes model cards and card groups only in general terms. In a Windows program, you're going to want to display it. Here's where your friendly neighborhood VBX comes in. Borland C++ 5 automatically installs the MHCD200.VBX file that provides routines for displaying playing cards. For each of these cards you can specify which face value and suit it's to have, and you can select from a variety of back styles. In order to use the VBX, Borland C++ 5 also supplies the VBXGEN program. This reads in a VBX file and automatically creates a header file with the appropriate classes and definitions for using the VBX file. This has been done to create the MHCD2001.H header file, which declares the class `TVbxMhCardDeck` as a descendant of `TVbxControl`.

The files that make use of this to actually display cards are CARDDISP.H and CARDDISP.CPP. These declare and define the `TCardDisplay` class as a descendant of both `TWindow` and `TCardGroup`. This particular window has its style set to that of a child in the constructor, thus making it easy to include within other windows in much the same way as child controls (pushbuttons, list boxes, and so on) can be included within windows; just create a `TCardDisplay` object in the desired location, and then use it the same way you use other controls, calling member functions to change aspects of its appearance.

The data members of the `TCardDisplay` class include a list of pointers to VBX card display objects (`cardvbx`); whether to draw a rectangle around the outside of the control (`rectangle`); the size of the border between the edge of the control and any rectangle that gets drawn (`borderSize`); a label for the control and a position for that label (`label` and `labelPos`); an array of positions for the cards in the group (`cardPos`); and an ID that can be used to distinguish this control from others (`id`).

Table R3.1 lists the member functions of the `TCardDisplay` class.

Table R3.1. TCardDisplay member functions.

Member Function	Usage
TCardDisplay	Initializes the members of the class and sets the size of the window to that specified by the parameters to the function. Also creates arrays to hold the VBX card objects and their positions.
~TCardDisplay	Cleans up the arrays allocated in the constructor.
Paint	Displays the main parts of the card display, including its border (if specified) and the label.
SetupWindow	Sets the background color for the window, and then hides all the VBX cards while setting their backs' colors to the background.
FaceUp	Resets the specified card to its face-up value.
SetCardPosition	Sets the position of the specified card.
Show	This is the function that actually shows a card by setting the VBX properties for the rank, suit, and back style. The function then calls the VBX's ShowWindow member function.
SetLabel	Resets the label of the card display window.
Insert	Calls the base class TCardGroup's Insert member function, and then calls the Show member function to display the newly inserted card.
Remove	Like Insert, this calls the base class's version of this function, and then proceeds to update the display with the new status of the cards.
operator[]	Accesses a card without removing it.
VBXEventHandler	This is the main entry from the VBX controls. In this case, the function checks to see if it was triggered by a mouse click. If so, it then passes that message along to its parent in the form of a WM_CARD_SELECTED message.

The overall effect of all these member functions, especially with the inclusion of the base classes' functionality and member functions, is that of presenting an encapsulated object that provides for all the needs of an apparent card-display control. As you will see shortly, you create this near-control only in a window, and the cards will show themselves with very little prompting.

The cribbage game also includes a pegboard that keeps track of the scoring. Like the card display, this is achieved in the program via a special child window encapsulated in a single

object `TCribbageBoard` as defined in the BOARD.H and BOARD.CPP files. The data members of the `TCribbageBoard` class consist of an array to hold the players' names (`playerName`), an array to hold the players' current points (`points`), an array to hold the players' previous points (`oldpoints`), and an array that holds the locations of all the holes in the pegboard (`holes`). There also is an enum (`PegType`) that defines the various peg types that can be used (`ptPlayer0`, `ptPlayer1`, and `ptEmpty`). Table R3.2 describes the member functions in this `TWindow` descendant.

Table R3.2. Member functions of `TCribbageBoard`.

Member Function	Usage
TCribbageBoard	This constructor initializes several members and sets its window to a specific size. Most of all, though, it fills in the `holes` array with the locations of all the holes in the pegboard.
SetupWindow	Simply calls the base class' `SetupWindow` and then initializes the background color for the window.
Reset	Resets the point values to their initial values of `0` for the current points and `-1` for the previous points.
PegHole	This is what actually draws an individual peg hole. It does this by referring to the `holes` array and then either drawing red boxes for Player 0, drawing blue boxes for Player 1, or copying the `EMPTY_HOLE` bit map into the specified location. Note the addition of an extra `PegHole` function that takes an `int` type for the `pegType` parameter, and then simply calls the real version of the function, casting `pegType` to the appropriate `PegType` enumeration.
AddToScore	Calling this member function adds a specific amount to a specific player's score. At the same time, the pegboard's peg display is updated along with the textual representation of the score. Note how the window's DC is obtained simply by declaring an instance of `TClientDC`, which then is passed to the `PegHole` and `TextOut` functions for drawing.
SetPlayerName	A simple function that sets a specific player's name and then makes sure it's reflected properly in the window.
GetPlayerName	An even simpler function that returns a specific player's name.
Paint	This begins by copying the `PEGBOARD` bit map into the window, followed immediately by writing the two players' names and their scores. Finally, the member function calls `PegHole` to display the two players' scores on the pegboard.

Throughout the course of the game, a number of dialog boxes need to be displayed, the source code for which can be found in the DIALOGS.H and DIALOGS.CPP files. The dialog boxes include one that prompts the user to cut the cards (TCutDeckDialog); it displays the backs of 52 cards and responds to a user's click by returning to the position in the deck where the user clicked. After the user has selected a card from the deck, the TCutResultDialog is displayed, which shows both the card the user selected and the one selected by the computer.

The TGoDialog class opens a simple dialog with a single button that reads either OK or Take 1 Point, depending upon whether the player can play more cards. This is used when the computer has signified that it cannot play any more cards.

The TQuickPointsDialog displays a number of buttons that enable the player to select the number of points he or she is entitled to. It's rather a simple dialog box, but the interesting part is where the constructor creates an array of 15 TButton objects to represent buttons 15 through 29. These objects will be used to hide those buttons in certain versions of the dialog, when it wouldn't be possible to select more than 14 points.

When it's time to display the total points for either the computer's hand or a hand in which the player miscounted, the TShowPointsDialog appears. This consists of a simple text box filled with the number of points counted and a button that enables the player to request details. If that button is pressed, the height of the dialog box is increased, and the extra space at the bottom is filled with a new list box. That list box is filled with the details of the points as passed to the class constructor in the aDetail parameter.

Up to now I've discussed only the lower-level tools that help get the game running. The real meat is contained in the TGameWindow class, as defined and declared in the CRIBBAGE.H and CRIBBAGE.CPP files. Just as a simple deck of cards doesn't define the game of cribbage, neither does the TDeck class define the cribbage game in this program; the TGameWindow class has all the actual functionality that defines the cribbage game itself. You should take careful note here of how the lower-level classes have been designed to model real-world objects that are then used in the main game itself. This is the kind of thing for which C++ and other object-oriented programming languages were designed.

Table R3.4 contains a brief list of the member functions contained in the TGameWindow class and their usage. They all act on the data members described in Table R3.3.

Table R3.3. TGameWindow data members.

Member Data	Meaning
handCardPos	An array holding the positions of all the cards that can be displayed in a player's hand
cribCardPos	An array holding the positions of all the cards that can be displayed in the crib

Member Data	Meaning
pegCardPos	An array holding the positions of all the cards that can be displayed in the playing field
topCardPos	An array (of one element) that holds the position of the extra card
player	An array holding the two TCardDisplay objects used as the two players' hands
crib	The crib display
pegCards	The playing field cards
topCards	The extra card
board	The pegboard display
deal	One of the buttons used during game play
go	One of the buttons used during game play
done	One of the buttons used during game play
take1	One of the buttons used during game play
take2	One of the buttons used during game play
instructions	A static control that is updated throughout the game with instructions concerning the next move for the player
state	The current state of the game, as defined by the TGameState enumeration
dealer	A number that indicates the current dealer
deck	The main deck of cards being played
currentCribPos	Indicates the current owner of the crib
cardBackStyle	Holds the current style of the card backs
pegCardOwner	Keeps track of the owner of each card played. This is used after the game play is over to move the played cards back to their original players for point scoring.
greenBrush	Because green is such a heavily used color in this game (ever played at a real gambling table *without* green felt?), it's saved here to keep it from being recreated all the time.
detail	As points are tallied by the computer, their details are recorded here for the player to examine upon request.
detailCount	Holds the current number of lines in the detail list

Table R3.4. `TGameWindow` member functions.

Member Function	Usage
`TGameWindow`	The constructor initializes the window to its set size and inserts all the player controls, buttons, static text areas, and so on
`~TGameWindow`	Deallocates the objects created in the constructor
`SetupWindow`	Sets the background color of the window to green and initializes the game state to that of waiting for a new game
`FaceValue`	Returns the face value of a card (1 through 10 for Ace through 10 and 10 for all the face cards)
`RunSize`	Checks to see if a sequence of cards forms a run (a sequential list of cards)
`ComputeHandPoints`	Adds up the points in a given hand and lists the breakdown of those points in a details buffer. This looks for all combinations that total 15, series that form runs, pairs of cards, flushes, and Nobs (a Jack that matches the extra card's suit).
`ComputePegPoints`	Computes any points that might have been generated by the last card played on the playing field
`ResetPegCardDisplay`	Clears out the arrays used to keep track of the playing field and the cards' original owners
`ReclaimPegCards`	Redistributes the cards from the playing field back into their original decks
`PegCard`	Adds a card from a player to the playing field
`ScoreComputerPegPoints`	Adds points to the computer's peg score, displaying a message box to let the user know the amount of points
`ComputerPlayPegCard`	Plays a card onto the playing field for the computer
`TurnOverPegCards`	Turns over the cards on the playing field to hide their faces
`PlayableCards`	Searches a group of cards for all that can be played on the playing field without going over the maximum total of 31. It returns an index to the first one playable, and optionally fills in an array with the indices of all those that are playable.
`SetState`	Changes the game state, showing the appropriate buttons and filling the instruction box with appropriate text

Member Function	Usage
Deal	Shuffles the deck and deals the top card out as the extra card. Then, if it's the computer's turn to deal, Deal actually deals the cards to the two players. If it's the player's turn to deal, this just sets the game state to gsDeal and waits for the player to click the Deal button.
ShowPoints	Moves the playing-field cards back into their respective decks and then counts the total points for each hand. If the player miscounts, the computer takes the missing points.
NewGame	Responds to the New | Game menu item by reinitializing the playing field and deck, asking the player for his or her name, asking the player to cut the deck, and then dealing the first hand
DealButton	Responds to the Deal button (which is visible during the gsDeal game state) by dealing the hands, discarding the computer's two cards, and then waiting for the user to discard
FixDeck	Moves all the cards from the playing field, as well as the players' hands, the crib, and the extra card back into the deck
SaveGame	Saves the current game state
Exit	Exits the program
SaveGameEnabler	Enables/disables the Save | Game menu item depending upon whether or not a game is currently in progress
AboutBox	Displays the About dialog box
LoadGame	Loads a saved game
Paint	Draws the DECK bit map. Note that all the other painting is done automatically by the other classes created.
EvCtlColor	Ensures that the background looks green, especially with regard to a slight idiosyncrasy with button controls (described in the source code)
CardSelected	This is a handler for the WM_CARD_SELECTED message generated by the TCardDisplay class in response to a VBX message. If the player currently is discarding cards to the crib, this moves the selected cards. If the player is playing a card to the playing field, this moves the selected card appropriately.

continues   **633**

Table R3.4. continued

Member Function	Usage
PegCardsSum	Computes the total value of all the cards in the playing field
CanClose	This function, which is called whenever the program is asked to quit, checks to make sure the user doesn't want to abandon any game that might currently be in progress
GoButton	Responds to the Go button and checks to see if the player is capable of playing a card. If this verifies that the player is capable at this point, then it issues a warning. Otherwise, it just sends the game play over to the computer.
DoneButton	Responds to the Done button, which is available while the player is moving cards into the crib. This checks to make sure the player moved exactly two cards into the crib. It then turns the crib cards face down, the extra card face up, and has the computer play a card.
Take1Button	When the computer can't play any more cards and the player can, the player is allowed to take either one or two points (if they're below or at 31 points, respectively). The Take 1 and Take 2 buttons are visible at these points and simply add the corresponding number of points to the player's score.
Take2Button	*See Take1Button*
ComputerDiscard	Discards two cards from the computer's hand to the crib
ComputerPlayCard	Has the computer play a card. This includes logic to account for the times when the player has specified that he or she can't play any more cards to the playing field.
CountPoints	Counts the points in the playing field after the player has just played a card. This then displays a dialog box that enables the player to select the number of points gained in the last turn, and it checks to make sure the player counted properly.

There are many interrelationships within the TGameWindow class. Many of the functions are there simply for the use of other functions, which is evidenced by the fact that there are so few listed in the response table. The most important lesson to learn here is how all the other classes are brought together in the main window and used to represent the various parts of the game to the user. It also is an interesting game to learn to play.

Variations and Expanding the Game

A number of variations in the game exist, including the number of players and how many points to play for in a game (achieving 121 points before your opponent scores 61 or scoring 61 before they get 31 is known as a *lurch*). Tournaments are available, and special awards exist for those who receive a perfect hand (containing 29 points), those who have zero-point hands, receiving a hand whose digits are those of their ZIP code, and so on. Other variations include awarding points overlooked by one player and discovered by the other in an act known as *Muggins*.

A good project for you now would be to figure out how to implement some of these variations or, better yet, to give the computer a little more strategy when it plays its game against you. I mean, you don't want to be able to win *all* the time, do you?

Extra Credit

1+

Debugging

No matter how well you may try to write a program, and no matter how good at writing programs you ever become, you will always make mistakes and cause bugs to appear in your program. The easiest bugs to locate and fix are those caught by the compiler as it shows you your syntax and other related errors. However, it is quite possible to have a program compile flawlessly, even without any warnings, and still fail in some miserable ways. When a program fails, a debugger can be the best tool for figuring out what went wrong. In today's lesson, you learn about the following:

- ☐ The integrated debugger commands
- ☐ How to debug a simple program
- ☐ Other debugging tools

The Integrated Debugger

Built into the Integrated Development Environment (IDE) are several debugging functions. You can use these to stop a running program in the middle of its execution, to view the values of variables and member data, and to watch how programming constructs are executed on a line-by-line basis.

In the IDE's top-level menu are two submenus that can be used in debugging. The first is the Debug menu. This menu provides a number of commands that control the execution of programs and enable you to view individual variables and structures. The second menu is the View menu. Inside this menu are, among other items, commands to open various debugging windows.

The Debug Menu

The principal commands for debugging are located in the Debug menu. These are the commands that enable you to execute your program on a line-by-line basis, to set breakpoints, and evaluate individual expressions.

NEW☞ TERM A *breakpoint* is a point in a program at which execution will stop or break. After a breakpoint is set, you can go ahead and let the program run. When the line of code where the breakpoint is set is reached, the program will pause, and the debugger will come up with the specified line highlighted. At this point, you can evaluate expressions and execute the code one line at a time.

- ☐ The Run command starts a program's execution. If the source code has changed and the program isn't already in a suspended state of execution, the IDE goes through the rebuild process, compiling and linking as necessary.

- ☐ The Load... command loads a process or program from disk for debugging. When the program is loaded, its startup code isn't executed (as is normal for programs you

write). The startup code is that portion of code that sets up the program for running before calling the parts that you might have written. You can use this command to debug the startup code of a program.

☐ The Attach... command enables you to attach to a program that's already running on the system and begin debugging it.

☐ The Run to... command enables you to have the debugger start running the program at its current execution point (or start the program at the beginning if there is no execution point yet) and continue until a specific source line in a specific source file is reached (the current cursor location in the current file is the default). At that point, the program will stop as if there was a breakpoint on that line.

☐ Sometimes, you might have started a program running, and then later decided that you need to pause the program, but you didn't set any breakpoints. You can use the Pause process command to pause the program at its current execution point. At this point, you will be able to evaluate expressions and look at various global variables. Unfortunately, you will not always be able to locate the current execution point in the code.

☐ The Reset this process command essentially performs a Terminate Process (discussed next) and then a Load on the current program being debugged.

☐ The Terminate process command stops the program's execution and then removes it from memory, essentially closing it out.

☐ If your program is paused and you move the cursor around, or perhaps you look at some other files, you might lose track of the line of code at which the program was paused. In this case, you can use the Source at execution point command to place the cursor on the current line of executing code. Note that if there is no particular source-code line where the execution point is, this command won't move you anywhere. At that point you can use the View menu's CPU command to bring up the CPU window and show exactly where in memory the execution point lies.

☐ Figure EC1.1 shows the dialog box that is brought up when you select the Add breakpoint... command. This enables you to set a breakpoint in your code. If you have an editor window up when you select this command, the dialog box will be initialized with the location of your current editing position. You also have the option of selecting the Advanced button in order to get the dialog that is brought up by the Breakpoint Options... menu command and apply the options from that dialog to the specific breakpoint being edited.

When a breakpoint is set, you'll notice that the specified line is highlighted, and a red dot appears in the gray area to the left of the edit window. Instead of using the menus to set breakpoints, you can simply click in that gray area on the left. This will toggle the breakpoints on and off for the line at which you click.

Note that there are other types of breakpoints that aren't covered in this short tutorial. As always, in order to get more information, you should consult the online help files.

☐ The Breakpoint Options... command brings up the Breakpoint Condition/Action Options dialog box (see Figure EC1.2). You can create and edit all sorts of general breakpoint options and save them in specific profiles.

Figure EC1.1.
The Add Breakpoint dialog box.

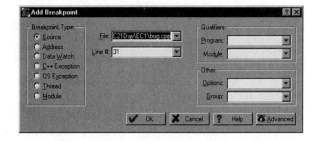

Figure EC1.2.
The Breakpoint Condition/ Action Options dialog box.

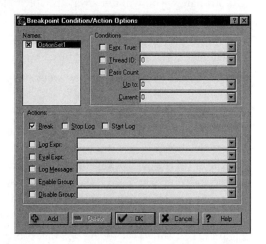

☐ There is a window in the debugger called the Watch window. When you use the Add watch... command, you are given a dialog box, shown in Figure EC1.3, that enables you to add an expression. This expression is placed in the Watch window and updated as the program continues execution. The Watch expressions are excellent ways to see how certain variables change over the course of the program. You can also set special display options for the Watch expression by clicking the Advanced button; the Watch Properties appears, as shown in Figure EC1.4.

☐ The Evaluate... command opens a window that enables you to enter expressions and see what they evaluate to. It also enables you to change the value of certain variables by first evaluating them and then changing their contents.

Figure EC1.3.
The Add Watch dialog box.

Figure EC1.4.
*The Watch Properties
dialog box.*

☐ The `Inspect...` command yields a window for each item you inspect. This window is customized to the type of variable being inspected. If you're looking at a variable, for example, you get simple information showing the name of the variable, its location in memory, and its value. Classes, on the other hand, display all the same data in addition to their member data, their values, and the locations and names of their member functions. Figure EC1.5 shows a sample inspection window.

Figure EC1.5.
*A sample session in the
IDE's debugger with an
inspection window.*

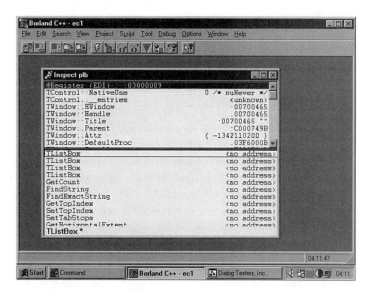

The View Menu

The View menu contains commands that display different windows. One section of that menu enables you to display windows associated with debugging. These are the CPU, Process, Watch, Breakpoint, and Call Stack windows.

☐ Although you are using C++ here, the machine itself actually operates at a much lower level, with machine code and assembly language. The CPU window enables you to go debug through this lower level, stepping through the basic assembly statements rather than the higher-level C++ statements. Note, however, that this really is a completely different language. In many ways, the lower-level assembly code is simpler in that it has many fewer commands, but then that makes it a more complex task to get useful things done. This is the reason why such higher-level languages were created: to simplify the task of writing complex programs.

☐ The Process window lists the different processes currently being run by the IDE. Because the IDE is written in a 32-bit environment, it is capable of running and keeping track of multiple processes in the system. This is extremely useful when you need to debug how different processes interact with each other.

☐ The Watch window shows a list of expressions you've entered and their evaluation. As the program runs and the variables mentioned in the expressions change, so will the evaluations.

☐ The Breakpoint window shows a list of all the breakpoints set in the program. Also, when you double-click a breakpoint entry in this window, you are allowed to bring up the breakpoint properties window, enabling you to modify the breakpoint's settings.

☐ When you've stopped in the middle of a program, it's often helpful to see where you've come from. For example, if you find yourself in a function that could be called by any of a number of other locations, it is useful to know which particular function called the current function and, in turn, who called that. This progression of calls is in the Call Stack window, along with the parameters of the functions for which debugging information is available.

In addition to all these menu commands, there are also the **B**rowse symbol... and **L**ocate symbol... commands found under the Search menu. These bring up dialog boxes that prompt you to enter a symbol's name. The IDE's browser then attempts to find the requested symbol and, in the case of the first menu command, open a window that shows all sorts of information about the symbol (see Figure EC1.6). The second menu command places the cursor at the point in the source code where that symbol is defined. In order for the browser to find the symbol, it must be listed in the loaded debugging information, which means that the source code must be compiled.

Figure EC1.6.
The Browsing window.

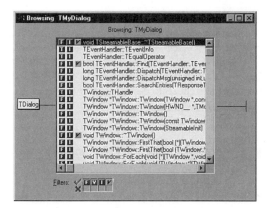

The Speedbar Buttons

Some of the most important debugging functions aren't available from the menus. These are the Run to Here, Statement Step Over, and Statement Step Into, and they're all available on the speedbar just under the menu. Their image and location (and even whether or not they're visible at all) change on the speedbar, depending upon which section of the IDE you're currently in and on whether or not a program is currently running. In order to find the button, you can move the cursor over the buttons, looking at the status bar for descriptions of the buttons. The following are descriptions of the buttons:

☐ The Run to Here button shows a little rectangle with several horizontal lines, one of which is highlighted and has a large arrow pointing to it. To use this command, go to an edit window and place the current edit position on a particular line. When you click the Run to Here button, the program will start or continue execution and keep going until it reaches the current edit position.

☐ The Statement Step Over button has a picture of a pair of open and close braces. The command is used to *single-step* through the program code on a line-by-line basis. Each time you select Statement Step Over, the current code line is executed. If that line contains a function call, the function is called, and when it returns, the debugger will stop again on the next line.

☐ If you want to actually go into the function instead of skipping over it, you can use the Statement Step Into command. The button for this one looks exactly like the previous button, except the arrow points *into* the object rather than passing completely over it. This command is the same as stepping over lines of code, except that this will follow into function calls, enabling you to step through them. If there is no function call, the trace acts exactly like a step. Note, however, that some function calls

aren't as visible as others. For example, when an object is created, its constructor function will be called, even if there doesn't appear to be any direct call to that function.

You can also get to these commands from the pop-up menu that appears when you click the right mouse button in the source-code window. The menu also shows the currently mapped keystroke that will execute the command.

Debugging a Program

When debugging a program, you must first make sure that debugging information is included when the program is compiled and built. With that done, you'll be able to step through the program a line at a time, view the contents of variables as you go, set breakpoints, and so on.

Unfortunately, the standard libraries (the runtime library, the class library, and the Object Windows Library) don't come with debugging information included in them by default. Because of this, you won't be able to step or trace into its source code, just as you won't be able to step or trace into the internal Windows source code (though you can go through its assembly code with the CPU window if you're truly brave). You can, however, rebuild the Borland libraries to include debugging information if you have the source code. The class library and OWL source code is included with the Borland C++ for Windows package, but the runtime library source code is available only on the CD version or at an extra cost.

The best way to learn how to debug a program is to sit down and do it. To start, type in and compile the program in Listings EC1.1 and EC1.2. You'll notice that it compiles with no warnings or errors, but if you try to run it and select the Dialog menu item, you'll get either a GPF or, barring that, an hourglass that doesn't go away. In any case, the program certainly isn't doing what you would want it to do.

Listing EC1.1. Script for the BUG.RC resource file.

```
 1:  #include <windows.h>
 2:  #include <owl\window.rh>
 3:
 4:  TheDialog DIALOG 6, 15, 207, 111
 5:  STYLE DS_MODALFRAME ¦ DS_3DLOOK ¦ WS_POPUP ¦ WS_VISIBLE \
 6:          ¦ WS_CAPTION ¦ WS_SYSMENU
 7:  CAPTION "Dialog of the Century"
 8:  FONT 8, "MS Sans Serif"
 9:  BEGIN
10:     LISTBOX 101, 27, 8, 49, 88, LBS_STANDARD ¦ WS_TABSTOP
11:     DEFPUSHBUTTON "OK", IDOK, 148, 6, 50, 14
12:     PUSHBUTTON "Cancel", IDCANCEL, 148, 24, 50, 14
13: END
14:
15: MainMenu MENU LOADONCALL MOVEABLE PURE DISCARDABLE
```

```
16: BEGIN
17:     MENUITEM "E&xit", CM_EXIT
18:     MENUITEM "&Dialog", 100
19: END
```

Listing EC1.2. Source code for the BUG.CPP program file.

```
1:  #include <stdio.h>
2:  #include <owl\applicat.h>
3:  #include <owl\dialog.h>
4:  #include <owl\framewin.h>
5:  #include <owl\listbox.h>
6:  #include <owl\window.h>
7:  #include <owl\window.rh>
8:
9:  class TMyDialog : public TDialog
10: {
11: public:
12:     TMyDialog(TWindow* parent, TModule* module = 0);
13:
14:     void SetupWindow();
15:
16: private:
17:     TListBox* numbers;
18: };
19:
20: TMyDialog::TMyDialog(TWindow* parent, TModule* module)
21:     : TDialog(parent, "TheDialog", module)
22: {
23: }
24:
25: void fill_lb(TListBox* plb, int count)
26: {
27:     for (int ix = 0; ix < count; ++count)
28:         {
29:         char str[25];
30:         sprintf(str, "%d", ix + 1);
31:         plb->AddString(str);
32:         }
33: }
34:
35: void TMyDialog::SetupWindow()
36: {
37:     fill_lb(numbers, 20);
38: }
39:
40: class TMyWindow : public TWindow
41: {
42: public:
43:     TMyWindow(TWindow* parent = 0);
44:
```

continues

Listing EC1.2. continued

```
45: protected:
46:     void CmExit();
47:     void CmDialog();
48:
49: private:
50:     DECLARE_RESPONSE_TABLE(TMyWindow);
51: };
52: DEFINE_RESPONSE_TABLE1(TMyWindow, TWindow)
53:     EV_COMMAND(CM_EXIT, CmExit),
54:     EV_COMMAND(100, CmDialog),
55: END_RESPONSE_TABLE;
56:
57: TMyWindow::TMyWindow(TWindow *parent)
58:     : TWindow(parent)
59: {
60: }
61:
62: void TMyWindow::CmExit()
63: {
64:     SendMessage(WM_CLOSE);
65: }
66:
67: void TMyWindow::CmDialog()
68: {
69:     TMyDialog(this).Execute();
70: }
71:
72: class TDialogApp : public TApplication
73: {
74: public:
75:     TDialogApp() : TApplication()
76:         { nCmdShow = SW_SHOWMAXIMIZED; }
77:
78:     void InitMainWindow()
79:         {
80:         SetMainWindow(new TFrameWindow( 0,
81:                             "Dialog Testers, Inc.",
82:                             new TMyWindow ));
83:         GetMainWindow()->AssignMenu("MainMenu");
84:         }
85: };
86:
87: int OwlMain(int, char *[])
88: {
89:     return TDialogApp().Run();
90: }
```

If you run the program from the IDE and then select the Dialog menu item, you are likely to get a dialog box that comes up with the message that the current thread (the program) has stopped due to a fault caused by an access violation. By clicking OK, the IDE will come back up and place you on line 31 of the BUG.CPP file.

NEW **TERM** An *access violation* occurs when some code attempts to read or write to a part of memory that it isn't allowed. In C++, this usually means that a pointer is used that hasn't been initialized or is still pointing at memory that has been deleted and no longer exists.

Line 31 of BUG.CPP contains the following code:

```
plb->AddString(str);
```

So, remembering that an access violation exception usually has something to do with accessing memory that is off limits, you might think that the str variable is probably at fault because it's a pointer. The only problem with that theory is that str is really a pointer to a local area of memory that's just been set up. You know that it still exists because it's still in scope.

The only other pointer here is the plb parameter. Considering, however, that you're just calling one of its member functions, how could it possibly be the problem? Take a look at the function it is calling: AddString. This function is declared in the TListBox class in the following manner:

```
virtual int AddString(const char far* str);
```

Note that the function is declared as virtual. This means that when the code to call it is compiled, a direct call to the member function isn't generated; rather, code to look up the location of the function is generated. The reason is that because a derived class could have written its own version of the function, the base class will need to be able to access that new function without necessarily knowing where this function resides. So, when the pointer is used to call AddString, it really does use plb as a pointer, by looking up the function's address in the virtual table.

NEW **TERM** The *virtual table* is a list of pointers to virtual functions. Each class has a virtual table associated with it, in which all the virtual functions have their addresses listed. Along with each object is a *virtual table pointer*, which points to the virtual table for the appropriate class. When some code attempts to call a virtual function, the generated assembly code first looks up the virtual table, then the virtual function's address, and then actually calls the function.

The only possibility at this point is the plb parameter. This pointer appears to be invalid for some reason. The next step is to see who gave us this pointer. Go into the View menu and select Call Stack. A window appears that shows the current function fill_lb at the top. The next function down is TMyDialog::SetupWindow. Double-click that next line to position the cursor at the place where the fill_lb function was called.

You now are placed directly into the middle of the SetupWindow function on the following line:

```
fill_lb(numbers, 20);
```

It appears that the numbers member data is invalid, because that is the parameter that becomes plb in the fill_lb function. If you take a look around, you'll notice that you forgot to set numbers to anything. It's declared in the class, but nothing ever assigns it any value. Oops! This must be fixed before you can continue trying to run the program. Obviously, you need to initialize

numbers in the constructor to connect with the list-box interface element in the dialog box you load from the resource. Go up to the constructor and add the following line:

```
numbers = new TListBox(this, 101, module);
```

At this point, you'll want to test the program again to see if you've found and removed all the bugs. You'll have to recompile the program first, though, so use the Terminate Process option to stop the program and then rebuild and run the application.

This time when you select the Dialog menu item, an hourglass that seems to hang around forever appears. After a while, you may get the idea that something is wrong. The only way to stop the program is to use the Terminate Process menu option, so use it now.

In finding this problem, you're going to have to look at a bit of code to help narrow down where the problem might be. You know the bug occurs after you select the Dialog menu option but before the dialog box actually appears on-screen. At times like this, it's a good idea to set breakpoints on some likely areas and run through the code, one line at a time, to see what happens.

Position the cursor on the `TMyWindow::CmDialog` function and select Add Breakpoint from the Debug menu. Notice how the line changes color to reflect the state of the breakpoint, and a red circle appears next to it in the gray area to the left of the edit space. Now set breakpoints on the `TMyDialog` constructor and its `SetupWindow` function, and then run the program.

When you select the Dialog menu item now, you are returned to the IDE with the cursor on the line where you set the breakpoint, the line where `TMyWindow::CmDialog` is declared. Select the `Step Over` command. The cursor moves on to the next line, where the dialog is actually created and executed. This line looks okay, so you can step over it as well.

Now look at the `TMyDialog` constructor; the code doesn't seem to show anything out of the ordinary. Here you run into the nonlinearity of Windows. If you simply keep stepping, you'll end up running through all sorts of code in which you're not particularly interested at this time, so it's a good idea to just continue running from here by selecting the Run command in the Debug menu.

When next you break into the source code, you're on the `TMyDialog::SetupWindow` function. There's only one function call in here, and it's something you wrote, so there probably is good reason to suspect that that might have inadvertently caused a problem. Use the Step Into function now. Your first step takes you onto the call to `fill_lb`, and your next step takes you right inside it.

Here you will see a `for` loop. It might be a good idea to walk through that one step at a time, watching the relevant variables `plb`, `count`, `ix`, and `str`. Place the cursor on each of these variables and select the Add Watch item from the Debug menu. You are not particularly interested in any fancy displays at this point, so just click OK on the resulting Watch Properties dialog box. You

may notice that some of the values are weird or possibly even undefined, but that's okay for right now. You are not really in the function yet, so the debugger hasn't had a chance to figure out what those values are. Also, because the str variable has not been declared yet, it is listed as undefined until you get to where it is declared, at which point the Watch window becomes synchronized properly.

Step over the beginning of the function. The cursor is placed on the first line of the for loop, and the count variable shows up as the number 20 in the Watch window. This is good. You specified 20 when you called this function. Step again and see that the ix variable is now set to 0 and the str variable is now recognized.

Notice how str is uninitialized at this point, showing random data. Stepping once more fills str with what should be more reasonable data.

Stepping again calls the AddString member function and brings you back to the for loop. Once again takes you to the line with the sprintf. Take another look at the Watch window and see how things are doing.

Wait a minute! Why is count now 21, and why is ix still 0? Take a look at that for loop again.

```
for (int ix = 0; ix < count; ++count)
```

Oops, again! Incrementing the limit rather than the counter is a common mistake. No wonder the program seemed to have stopped. It was never leaving the loop and was trying to keep filling the list box with ever-increasing numbers. To fix that, change the line to the following:

```
for (int ix = 0; ix < count; ++ix)
```

Now terminate the application, remove the breakpoints, rebuild, and start over again. When you select the Dialog menu item now, the dialog box at least appears on-screen. Unfortunately, the list box appears to be completely empty.

The question here comes down to figuring out from where the failure is coming. You know that the pointer to the list box is valid; otherwise, you would have had another general protection exception. So the problem must be somewhere with the portion that is adding the string. Set a breakpoint on the line that reads

```
plb->AddString(str);
```

Now go back to the program, dismiss the dialog, and select the Dialog menu item again. When you reach the breakpoint, take a closer look at the plb parameter. Place the cursor over the plb variable and select the Inspect item from the Debug menu.

Looking at the inspection window, you can clearly see that, although you were obviously capable of creating the class object, it doesn't appear to be hooked up to the actual Windows interface item. The TWindow::HWindow data member is NULL, and the TWindow::Attr data member is mostly empty, except for the 101 that you passed to it earlier.

If you remember, the `SetupWindow` function is the location in which class objects become associated with their Windows counterparts. Taking a look at the `TMyDialog`'s version of the function, you can see that you forgot to call the parent's version of the `SetupWindow` function. Without that call, the actual work that connects the class with the interface element never gets done. To fix this, simply change the function to look like the following:

```
void TMyDialog::SetupWindow()
{
   TDialog::SetupWindow();
   fill_lb(numbers, 20);
}
```

Now, when you next compile and run the program, you will see a fully functional, if boring, application that enables you to display a dialog box that contains a list box of numbers 1 to 20. Of course, before running again, you might want to remove the breakpoints so you don't keep stopping in the middle of the program.

Other Debugging Tools

Along with the integrated debugger included in the IDE, other tools are useful in finding and fixing problems with your applications. The first is *WinSight.* This program can display a listing of all the windows currently registered with Windows, whether those windows are visible or not. You can even see the hierarchy of the windows—which windows are children of which others. From there, you can select one or more windows and watch the messages received by them.

Of course, WinSight requires some knowledge of the lower-level Windows API that hasn't been covered in this book. OWL really does do an admirable job of hiding some of the truly messy details of the Windows API, enabling you to use an easy interface. The drawback is that, when there are problems with your code that involve the lower-level Windows API, it sometimes is difficult to track them down due to OWL's interface hiding.

Another useful program if you're testing your program on a 16-bit version of Windows is WinSpector. Normally, whenever you run your application from outside the IDE, general-protection (GP) faults simply will display a nasty error window and terminate your program. If you have WinSpector running when that GP fault occurs, WinSpector records the location in your application that caused the GP fault. WinSpector also attempts to figure out which other sections of your application had been executed immediately prior to the fault occurring, by performing a stack trace. The results of this then can be run through the DFA program to match up the memory locations with the debugging information of your program. The final results often can tell you exactly which line in your application's source code died and which functions had been called before.

But the most important utility is sold separately by Borland. It's called CodeGuard, and it integrates seamlessly with the Borland C++ IDE, adding its options to the existing options

dialogs, including the TargetExpert. When you run a program, CodeGuard sits in the background and watches for such things as writing to an array past its limits and validating parameters in function calls (for example, making sure certain parameters aren't 0 when they need to be valid). If you're planning on doing any real heavy programming work, I strongly urge you to acquire CodeGuard and start making use of it.

Summary

Today's lesson presented a short tutorial on some of the debugging techniques provided by the IDE. You learned about the following subjects:

☐ The debugging commands available in the Integrated Development Environment

☐ Examples of some of the more common programming mistakes

☐ Some of the techniques used to track down and exterminate bugs

Q&A

Q Do my watches need to be limited to variables?

A No. You may supply whole expressions, such as `(count + 1) * 2`.

Q If I set a breakpoint on a line of code, do I have to stop there every single time the program comes to that line?

A No. You can set up conditions on the breakpoint so that, for example, if you are in the middle of a loop, the debugger will break in only when the iterator is equal to a certain value.

Extra Credit

2+

Common Dialog Boxes

This extra-credit chapter presents three of the five common dialog boxes supported by both Windows and the ObjectWindows library. In addition, it presents the input dialog box supported by the ObjectWindows library. In this extra-credit chapter, you will learn about the following topics:

- [ ] Software requirements for using the common dialog boxes.
- [ ] The ObjectWindows `TInputDialog` class.
- [ ] The file-selection dialog box class `TFileOpenDialog`. This class creates dialog boxes that support opening a file.
- [ ] The file-selection dialog-box class `TFileSaveDialog`. This class creates dialog boxes that support saving a file.
- [ ] The color-selection dialog-box class `TChooseColorDialog`.
- [ ] The text-search dialog-box class `TFindDialog`. This class creates dialog boxes that support finding text.
- [ ] The text-replacement dialog-box class `TReplaceDialog`. This class creates dialog boxes that support replacing text.

I would like to emphasize that the common dialog boxes merely offer to the user interfaces for the respective tasks of the common dialog boxes. You are responsible for providing the associated operations based on the information supplied or selected by the user of these common dialog boxes. Many of the examples in this chapter are kept short to focus on creating, invoking, and accessing the data of the common dialog boxes.

The *TInputDialog* Class

Some of the programs presented in earlier chapters required input from the user. This was usually done with a simple edit box in a window. OWL provides a simple mechanism for doing this automatically via the `TInputDialog` class. The constructor for this class is as follows:

```
TInputDialog(TWindow*          parent,
             const char far* title,
             const char far* prompt,
             char far*         buffer,
             int               bufferSize,
             TModule*          module = 0,
             TValidator*       valid = 0);
```

The constructor requires the parameters for the parent window `parent`, the pointer to the dialog box title `title`, and a pointer to the DLL module `module` (as you've come to expect from a constructor descended from `TDialog`). The new parameters are `prompt` (which supplies the text to use in prompting the user), `buffer` (which supplies the buffer into which the user's response should be saved), and `bufferSize` (which lets OWL know how big `buffer` is). There's also the `valid` parameter, which will be discussed later.

You should note that this constructor automatically calls the TDialog constructor in order to load the SD_INPUTDIALOG dialog from the program's resources. This means that you need to make sure to include the INPUTDIA.RC file inside your own resource file with the #include directive. If you don't do this, the dialog box will mysteriously fail to appear.

In addition to this constructor are four public member functions of use:

```
void TransferData(TTransferDirection direction);

const char far* GetPrompt() const;
const char far* GetBuffer() const;
int             GetBufferSize() const;
```

EC2

The last three are there simply to let you have access to the parameters you passed to the constructor. They're really of little use, because while the dialog is active the buffer you supplied won't reflect the contents of the window. This buffer is set when the dialog terminates due to the automatic call to the TransferData member function.

TrasferData is perhaps the most noteworthy member function. It transfers the data between the edit control of the input dialog box and the text buffer. If the caller passes the argument tdSetData to the direction parameter, the function transfers data from the text buffer to the edit control. The function moves data in the reverse direction when a caller passes the tdGetData argument. You will probably never have any use for calling this function directly, but it's a useful one to know about. It's called by TDialog after the CanClose function has okayed the dialog's closure. By overriding it, you can create your own transfers in and out of the dialog.

Let's look at a simple number-guessing game that uses the input dialog box to prompt you for a new guess. The program generates a secret number between 0 and 1,000 and enables you make up to 10 guesses. To assist you in refining your guess, the program displays hints in the dialog box that tell you whether your last guess was higher or lower than the secret number. You can stop the game at any time by clicking the Cancel button.

 Listing EC2.1. The source code for the INPUTDLG.H header file.

```
1:  #define CM_GAME     101
2:  #define IDM_MAINMENU 400
```

 Listing EC2.2. The script for the INPUTDLG.RC resource file.

```
1:  #include <windows.h>
2:  #include <owl\window.rh>
3:  #include <owl\inputdia.rh>
4:  #include <owl\inputdia.rc>
5:  #include "inputdlg.h"
```

continues

655

Listing EC2.2. continued

```
 6:
 7:    IDM_MAINMENU MENU LOADONCALL MOVEABLE PURE DISCARDABLE
 8:    BEGIN
 9:        MENUITEM "E&xit", CM_EXIT
10:        MENUITEM "&Game", CM_GAME
11:    END
```

Listing EC2.3. The source code for the INPUTDLG.CPP program file.

```
 1: // Program illustrates using the input dialog box in a
 2: // number-guessing game
 3:
 4: #include <owl\applicat.h>
 5: #include <owl\framewin.h>
 6: #include <owl\inputdia.h>
 7: #include <stdlib.h>
 8: #include <stdio.h>
 9: #include "inputdlg.h"
10:
11: const int MaxBuffer = 81;
12: const int MaxIter = 10;
13:
14: // expand the functionality of TWindow by deriving class TGameWindow
15: class TGameWindow : public TWindow
16: {
17: public:
18:     TGameWindow() : TWindow(0, 0, 0) {}
19:
20: protected:
21:     void CmGame();                     // handle the Game menu item
22:
23:     DECLARE_RESPONSE_TABLE(TGameWindow);
24: };
25: DEFINE_RESPONSE_TABLE1(TGameWindow, TWindow)
26:     EV_COMMAND(CM_GAME, CmGame),
27: END_RESPONSE_TABLE;
28:
29: void TGameWindow::CmGame()
30: {
31:     char s[MaxBuffer] = "500";
32:     const char* prompt = "Enter a number between 1 and 1000";
33:     bool ok = true;
34:     int ix;
35:     int number, guess = -1;
36:
37:     randomize();
38:     number = random(1000) + 1;
39:
40:     for (ix = 0; ok && guess != number && ix < MaxIter; ++ix)
41:         {
42:         ok = IDOK == TInputDialog(this, "Hi-Lo Guessing Game",
```

```
43:                                    prompt, s, sizeof(s)).Execute();
44:         guess = atoi(s);
45:         prompt =   (guess > number)
46:                     ? "Enter a lower guess"
47:                     : "Enter a higher guess";
48:         }
49:
50:     sprintf(s, "The secret number was %d.", number);
51:     if (!ok)
52:         MessageBox(s, "Quitter!", MB_OK);
53:     else if (ix < MaxIter)
54:         {
55:         MessageBeep(MB_ICONEXCLAMATION);
56:         MessageBeep(MB_ICONEXCLAMATION);
57:         MessageBox(s, "Congratulations!", MB_OK);
58:         }
59:     else
60:         {
61:         MessageBeep(-1);
62:         MessageBox(s, "Sorry!", MB_OK);
63:         }
64: }
65:
66: class TMyApp : public TApplication
67: {
68: public:
69:     TMyApp() : TApplication()
70:         { nCmdShow = SW_SHOWMAXIMIZED; }
71:
72:     void InitMainWindow()
73:         {
74:         SetMainWindow(new TFrameWindow( 0,
75:                               "Hi-Lo Number-Guessing Game",
76:                               new TGameWindow ));
77:         GetMainWindow()->AssignMenu(IDM_MAINMENU);
78:         }
79: };
80:
81: int OwlMain(int, char*[])
82: {
83:    return TMyApp().Run();
84: }
```

Figure EC2.1 shows a sample session with the INPUTDLG.EXE application.

The program in Listing EC2.3 declares two classes: the main window class TGameWindow and the application class TMyApp.

657

Figure EC2.1.
A sample session with the INPUTDLG.EXE application.

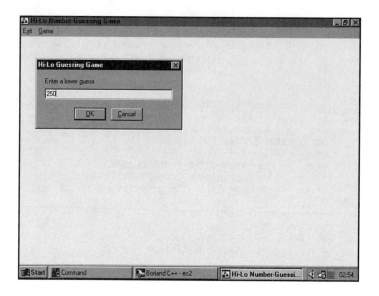

The most relevant part of the program is the member function CmGame, which executes the number-guess game. The function, whose definition starts on line 29, performs the following tasks:

☐ Assigns the string "500" to the text buffer (implemented using the local variable s).

☐ Randomizes the seed for the random-number generating function, using the statement on line 37.

☐ Obtains a random number in the range of 1 to 1,000 and stores that number in the local variable number.

☐ Begins the loop that continues until either the user guesses correctly, presses the Cancel button, or runs out of tries.

☐ Executes the opening dialog box by calling its Execute member function, on lines 42 and 43, to create an instance of the TInputDialog class. The result is checked to make sure the user pressed the OK button, assigning the comparison with IDOK to ok.

☐ Converts the contents of the text buffer into an int and stores that value in the local variable guess. This task calls the function atoi on line 44.

☐ Compares the guess to the secret number on line 45 and then assigns the appropriate message into the prompt variable for use in the next iteration.

☐ Displays a congratulatory message on line 57 if you guessed the secret number within the allowed number of iterations. Otherwise, the program displays the secret number using the statement on line 62.

 **Note:** Although the `TInputDialog` has just been presented in this chapter about Common Dialogs, it isn't really one of the Windows common dialogs. Rather, it's a special window that OWL provides (that's the reason for including INPUTDIA.RC in the resource file). The rest of the dialogs presented in this chapter are all derived from the common class `TCommonDialog`—which is, itself, a descendant of the `TDialog` class. `TCommonDialog` acts as the root of the common dialog-class hierarchy that models color selection, font selection, input-file selection, output-file selection, printing, text search, and text-replacement dialog boxes.

The File Dialog Classes

The ObjectWindows library offers the classes `TFileOpenDialog` and `TFileSaveDialog` to implement the common modal dialog boxes that support opening a file and saving data in a file. Both of these classes are descendants of the abstract class `TOpenSaveDialog`—which is, in turn, a descendant of class `TCommonDialog`. You should take note that the `TOpenSaveDialog` class cannot be instantiated by itself, but rather you need to instantiate one of the other two. The Open and Save As dialog boxes have the following controls:

☐ A Look in combo box

☐ A number of toolbar buttons

☐ A file list window

☐ A File name edit box

☐ A Files of type combo box

☐ An Open/Save button (on Windows NT, the Open is labeled OK)

☐ A Cancel button

The Supporting Classes and Structures

All three of the `TOpenSaveDialog`, `TFileOpenDialog`, and `TFileSaveDialog` classes take the same parameters in their constructors, mainly because the latter two are both directly descended from the first. There are no other member functions that you will have any real use for—especially since these common dialogs are typically used modally, which means that you won't even have a chance to access it while it's executing.

```
TOpenSaveDialog(TWindow*        parent,
                TData&          data,
                TResId          templateId = 0,
                const char far* title = 0,
                TModule*        module = 0);
```

The first parameter parent, of course, is a pointer to the parent window that's opening the dialog. The data parameter contains a number of elements that describe how the dialog should be constructed. templateId is used when you want to override the default dialog box that comes up with your own. This substitute dialog needs to follow certain guidelines, and you should look at the GetOpenFileName Windows API function in the reference manual for more information regarding the creation of your own substitute templates. The next two parameters, title and module, are fairly obvious and are used just as you've come to expect.

The interesting parameter here is the data parameter of type TData. The TData class is a nested class of TOpenSaveDialog, and it has the following definition:

```
class TData {
  public:
    uint32          Flags;
    uint32          Error;
    char*           FileName;
    char far*       Filter;
    char far*       CustomFilter;
    int             FilterIndex;
    const char far* InitialDir;
    const char far* DefExt;
    int             MaxPath;

    TData(uint32 flags=0, char far* filter=0, char far* customFilter=0,
          const char far* initialDir=0, const char far* defExt=0,
          int maxPath=0, int filterIndex = 0);
    TData(const TData& src);
    ~TData();

    TData& operator =(const TData& src);

    void    SetFilter(const char far* filter = 0);

    void    Write(opstream& os);
    void    Read(ipstream& is);
};
```

You should note that all of the members of this class are public, making it more akin to a structure than a class (remember, a structure is really just a class in which the default protection level is public, whereas a class's default protection level is private).

First take note that almost all of the data members are initialized by parameters to the constructor. The two data members that aren't, Error and FileName, are meant to be read in by you after sending an object of type TData to a function. Table EC2.1 describes the data members of the TData class.

Table EC2.1. `TData` member items.

Member	Meaning
Flags	Holds a combination of the OFN_*xxx* flags that identify dialog options to be used.
Error	Gets set by the dialog to an error code if one occurs during the dialog's execution.
FileName	Gets set by the dialog to the filename selected by the user.
Filter	Holds a list of items to be used as available filters when listing files. These are stored as a single string made up of a number of substrings, each separated by the vertical bar character (¦). The first substring contains the name of a filter, the second the filter itself, then the substrings repeat until two vertical bars are placed next to each other. An example is "All files (*.*)¦*.*¦C++ files¦*.cpp¦Header files (*.h)¦*.h¦¦".
CustomFilter	Holds a user-specified file filter. This is changed by the dialog if the user specifies a filter not listed in `Filter`.
FilterIndex	Holds the index of the filter (in `Filter`) to use initially.
InitialDir	Holds the directory to use initially when the dialog first starts up.
DefExt	Holds the default extension.
MaxPath	Holds the maximum number of characters to use in a path.

The `Flags` member of the `TData` class uses the OFN_*XXXX* constants, as shown in table EC2.2.

Table EC2.2. `OFN_XXX` constants.

Constant	Meaning
OFN_ALLOWMULTISELECT	Allows for multiple selections of filenames.
OFN_CREATEPROMPT	Asks if the user wants to create a file if it doesn't already exist.
OFN_ENABLEHOOK	Enables a special hook function. This is an advanced function that goes slightly beyond the scope of this book; look to the online help for more information.
OFN_ENABLETEMPLATE	This enables a special template, allowing you to create your own version of the dialog class. This is an advanced function; look to the online help for more information.

continues

Table EC2.2. continued

Constant	Meaning
OFN_ENABLETEMPLATEHANDLE	Affects how a template is named. This is an advanced function; look to the online help for more information.
OFN_EXPLORER	(Win32 only) Uses a Windows 95 Explorer-like dialog box instead of the older Win16 version. The Explorer version is what's used in this book.
OFN_EXTENSIONDIFFERENT	Set by the dialog to indicate the user entered a filename different from the one specified in DefExt.
OFN_FILEMUSTEXIST	Restricts the user to selecting names of existing files, disallowing them from entering nonexistent names.
OFN_HIDEREADONLY	Hides the Read Only checkbox from the Save dialog.
OFN_LONGNAMES	(Win32 only) Allows long filenames to be displayed if the older dialog is used. This flag is ignored if OFN_EXPLORER is set.
OFN_OVERWRITEPROMPT	Has the Save dialog ask the user about overwriting a file if it already exists.
OFN_NOCHANGEDIR	Resets the current directory back to what it was when the dialog was first executed.
OFN_NODEREFERENCELINKS	(Win32 only) Gives the actual filename of the shortcut file if selected by the user. If this flag isn't set, the dialog returns the actual file referenced by the shortcut.
OFN_NOLONGNAMES	Specifies that no long names should be used. This flag is ignored if OFN_EXPLORER is set.
OFN_NONETWORKBUTTON	Keeps the Network button from appearing.
OFN_NOREADONLYRETURN	Set by the dialog to indicate that the selected file isn't read-only and isn't in a write-protected directory.
OFN_NOTESTFILECREATE	The Save dialog normally creates a file when it exits, but it can fail in such cases as a drive door open, and so on. This flag stops the creation from being tested.
OFN_NOVALIDATE	Doesn't perform any check on the filename.

Constant	Meaning
OFN_PATHMUSTEXIST	Forces the user to enter only valid path names, warning the user when an invalid one is entered.
OFN_READONLY	Causes the read-only checkbox to be checked initially. Upon return, reflects the state of the read-only checkbox.
OFN_SHAREAWARE	Allows the Open dialog to select files even if they're already open.
OFN_SHOWHELP	Shows the Help button in the dialog.

EC2

The File Statistics Program

The next program enables you to obtain file statistics (file size and date/time stamp) using the standard File dialog box. Listing EC2.4 shows the contents of the OPENFILE.H header file. Listing EC2.5 shows the script for the OPENFILE.RC resource file. Listing EC2.6 shows the source code for the OPENFILE.CPP program file.

Compile and run the OPENFILE.EXE program. Click the File Stats menu item to invoke the Open dialog box. The file-filter combo box has two items: all the files and the .CPP files. You can select a file from the current directory or move to another directory. When you have selected a file, click the OK button. The Open dialog box disappears and a message box appears with the selected filename, size, and date/time stamp.

Listing EC2.4. The source code for the OPENFILE.H header file.

```
1:  #define CM_FILESTAT  100
```

Listing EC2.5. The script for the OPENFILE.RC resource file.

```
1:  #include <windows.h>
2:  #include <owl\window.rh>
3:  #include "openfile.h"
4:
5:  MainMenu MENU LOADONCALL MOVEABLE PURE DISCARDABLE
6:  BEGIN
7:     MENUITEM "E&xit", CM_EXIT
8:     MENUITEM "&File Stats", CM_FILESTAT
9:  END
```

Listing EC2.6. The source code for the OPENFILE.CPP program file.

```
1:    // Program to test the Open File common dialog box.  The program
2:    // displays the basic statistics for the file you select
3:
4:    #include <owl\applicat.h>
5:    #include <owl\framewin.h>
6:    #include <owl\opensave.h>
7:    #include <stdlib.h>
8:    #include <stdio.h>
9:    #include <string.h>
10:   #include <dos.h>
11:   #include <dir.h>
12:   #include "openfile.h"
13:
14:   class TMyWindow : public TWindow
15:   {
16:   public:
17:     TMyWindow();
18:
19:     void CmFileStat();
20:     void CmExit();
21:
22:   private:
23:     TOpenSaveDialog::TData FileData;
24:
25:     DECLARE_RESPONSE_TABLE(TMyWindow);
26:   };
27:   DEFINE_RESPONSE_TABLE1(TMyWindow, TWindow)
28:     EV_COMMAND(CM_FILESTAT, CmFileStat),
29:     EV_COMMAND(CM_EXIT, CmExit),
30:   END_RESPONSE_TABLE;
31:
32:   TMyWindow::TMyWindow()
33:     : TWindow(0, 0, 0),
34:       FileData( uint32(  OFN_HIDEREADONLY
35:   #if(WINVER>=0x0400)
36:                       | OFN_EXPLORER          // Win32 only
37:   #endif
38:                       | OFN_OVERWRITEPROMPT),
39:                 "All Files (*.*)|*.*|"
40:                 "C++ Programs (*.cpp)|*.cpp|"
41:                 "Batch files (*.bat)|*.bat||",
42:                 "*.cpp", "", "*.cpp")
43:   {
44:   }
45:
46:   void decode_filetime(unsigned short stamp,
47:                        int& hour, int& minute, int& second)
48:   {
49:     second = 2 * (stamp & 0x001F);
50:     minute = (stamp >> 5) & 0x003F;
51:     hour = (stamp >> 11) & 0x001F;
52:   }
53:
54:   void decode_filedate(unsigned short stamp,
```

```
55:                          int& day, int& month, int& year)
56: {
57:    day =  stamp & 0x001F;
58:    month = (stamp >> 5) & 0x000F;
59:    year = (stamp >> 9) & 0x007F;
60: }
61:
62: void TMyWindow::CmFileStat()
63: {
64:    char str[256];        // 256 should be big enough
65:    ffblk fileInfo;
66:    int Hour, Minute, Second, Day, Month, Year;
67:
68:    // Ask the user to open a file
69:    if (TFileOpenDialog(this, FileData).Execute() != IDOK)
70:       return;
71:
72:    // Get and display file's directory information
73:    findfirst(FileData.FileName, &fileInfo, 0xFF);
74:    decode_filetime(fileInfo.ff_ftime, Hour, Minute, Second);
75:    decode_filedate(fileInfo.ff_fdate, Day, Month, Year);
76:    sprintf(str,
77:            "Filename: %s\n"
78:            "Time Stamp: %02u:%02u:%02u\n"
79:            "Date Stamp: %02u/%02u/%u\n"
80:            "Size: %ld bytes\n",
81:            fileInfo.ff_name,
82:            Hour, Minute, Second,
83:            Month, Day, Year + 1980,
84:            fileInfo.ff_fsize );
85:    MessageBox(str, "File Statistics", MB_OK | MB_ICONINFORMATION);
86: }
87:
88: void TMyWindow::CmExit()
89: {
90:    Parent->SendMessage(WM_CLOSE);
91: }
92:
93: class TMyApp : public TApplication
94: {
95: public:
96:    TMyApp() : TApplication() {}
97:
98:    virtual void InitMainWindow()
99:       {
100:       SetMainWindow(new TFrameWindow(0, "File Statistics", new TMyWindow));
101:       GetMainWindow()->AssignMenu("MainMenu");
102:       }
103: };
104:
105: int OwlMain(int, char*[])
106: {
107:    return TMyApp().Run();
108: }
```

EC2

Figure EC2.2 shows a Windows 95 File dialog box in the open-file mode.

Figure EC2.2.

A sample session with the OPENFILE.EXE program.

Let's examine the code for the program in Listing EC2.6. The window class TMyWindow declares a constructor, two member functions, and a data member. The data member FileData is the supporting structure of type TOpenSaveDialog::TData (note that, in order to use the nested class, a scoping operator is required to access the type). The TMyWindow constructor initializes member FileData starting on line 34. This instance is initialized using the ORed constants OFN_HIDEREADONLY, OFN_OVERWRITEPROMPT, and OFN_EXPLORER. You should take special note that the OFN_EXPLORER flag is set only if the Windows version is v4.00 or greater. This is one way of telling if the Explorer form of the common open-file dialog is valid, as this is available only in Windows 95 and Windows NT 3.51 or greater. In each of these, the WINVER macro is greater than or equal to 0x0400.

In addition to the flags, the creation of FileData specifies the arguments for the parameters filter (the long string that spans over three lines), customFilter (the string "*.cpp"), initialDir (the empty string), and defExt (the string "*.cpp"). The rest of the parameters to TOpenSaveDialog::TData's constructor are default.

The most relevant component of the class is the CmFileStat member function, whose definition starts on line 62. The function declares a number of local variables. The function also declares the ffblk-typed fileInfo variable on line 65. This variable contains the structure for the DOS file data obtained when searching a directory. The function executes the TFileOpenDialog on line 69, checking its return to make sure the user pressed the OK button. If not, the function exits.

The results of the function are stored in the `FileData` data member. What the `CmFileStat` function is most concerned with is the filename selected by the user, and this is stored in `FileData.FileName`. This value is used in the call to `findfirst` on line 73. The `findfirst` function is used to search a directory, and its results contain the file information stored in that directory (essentially, the information you see when you type `dir` on the MS-DOS command line). Lines 74 and 75 call the functions `decode_filetime` and `decode_filedate`, respectively. These functions convert the special MS-DOS file time and dates into something a little more useful. This information is stored into the character array `str`, which is then used in the `MessageBox` call on line 85.

The rest of the program is pretty much what you've seen before.

The *TChooseColorDialog* Class

The `TChooseColorDialog` class supports the color-selection common dialog box. The dialog box contains various controls to select colors, define custom colors, and add to custom colors. As with every other dialog box, the Color dialog box has OK and Cancel buttons.

The `TChooseColorDialog`'s constructor is defined as follows:

```
TChooseColorDialog(TWindow*      parent,
                   TData&        data,
                   TResId        templateId = 0,
                   const char far* title = 0,
                   TModule*      module = 0);
```

The `parent` parameter represents the parent window that's creating the dialog. The `templateId` parameter is used to load a programmer-defined version of the dialog, and the `title` and `module` parameters act as you'd expect. The `data` parameter is where the meat comes from. As with the File Open and Save dialogs, the data is passed to and from the dialog via a `TData` that's defined as a nested class or structure of the dialog class. In this case, the `TChooseColorDialog::TData` class has the following definition:

```
class TData {
  public:
    uint32    Flags;
    uint32    Error;
    TColor    Color;
    TColor*   CustColors;
};
```

Note that this doesn't have any constructor, so you need to assign each member of the class separately. The `Error` data member is set to an error code if the dialog, after being executed, returns `IDCANCEL`. The `Color` data member holds the initial color to be selected in the dialog when it first executes, and then it holds the color that was selected afterwards. `CustColors` holds a list of 16 custom colors to be displayed in addition to the usual list. The `Flags` member holds a list of flags that are used in generating the dialog box. These are listed in Table EC2.3.

Table EC2.3. CC_XXX **constants.**

Constant	Meaning
CC_ENABLEHOOK	Enables a special hook function. This is used internally by OWL.
CC_ENABLETEMPLATE	Enables the programmer to specify a special template to replace the standard dialog.
CC_ENABLETEMPLATEHANDLE	Specifies how the template should be loaded.
CC_FULLOPEN	Opens up the full dialog box. If this isn't set, then the section where the user creates custom colors isn't initially displayed, but rather a Define Custom Color button is displayed. When pressed, this button opens up the extra section.
CC_PREVENTFULLOPEN	Disables the Define Custom Color button, preventing the user from defining any extra colors.
CC_RGBINIT	Tells the dialog to use the Color member of TData as the initial color value.
CC_SHOWHELP	Shows the Help button in the dialog.

Invoking a Color dialog box is similar to invoking an Open or Save As dialog box. The OK button, the Cancel button, and the Close system menu item play the same role in influencing the result returned by the Execute member function.

A Sample Program

The following is a simple program that invokes the Color dialog box and then displays the numeric value for the selected color. Listing EC2.7 contains the script for the GETCOLOR.RC resource file. Listing EC2.8 shows the GETCOLOR.H header file. Listing EC2.9 contains the source code for the GETCOLOR.CPP program file.

Compile and run the GETCOLOR.EXE program. Click the Colors menu item to invoke the Color dialog box. Experiment with selecting different colors. Click the OK button to close the dialog box. The program then displays a message box that contains the integer code for the currently selected color.

Listing EC2.7. The script for the GETCOLOR.RC resource file.

```
1: #include <windows.h>
2: #include <owl\window.rh>
3: #include "getcolor.h"
4:
```

```
5: MainMenu MENU LOADONCALL MOVEABLE PURE DISCARDABLE
6: BEGIN
7:    MENUITEM "E&xit", CM_EXIT
8:    MENUITEM "&Colors", CM_COLORCHANGE
9: END
```

 Listing EC2.8. The source code for the GETCOLOR.H header file.

```
1: #define CM_COLORCHANGE 100
```

 Listing EC2.9. The source code for the GETCOLOR.CPP program file.

```
1: // Program to test the Choose Color common dialog box.
2:
3: #include <owl\applicat.h>
4: #include <owl\framewin.h>
5: #include <owl\chooseco.h>
6: #include <stdio.h>
7: #include <string.h>
8: #include "getcolor.h"
9:
10: class TMyWindow : public TWindow
11: {
12: public:
13:    TMyWindow();
14:
15:    void CmColors();        // handle Colors menu item
16:    void CmExit();          // handle Exit menu item
17:
18: private:
19:    TChooseColorDialog::TData colorData;
20:    static TColor custColors[16];
21:
22:    DECLARE_RESPONSE_TABLE(TMyWindow);
23: };
24: DEFINE_RESPONSE_TABLE1(TMyWindow, TWindow)
25:    EV_COMMAND(CM_COLORCHANGE, CmColors),
26:    EV_COMMAND(CM_EXIT, CmExit),
27: END_RESPONSE_TABLE;
28:
29: TColor TMyWindow::custColors[16] =
30:    {
31:    TColor(0,0,0), TColor(255, 255, 255), TColor(128, 128, 128),
32:    TColor(255, 0, 0), TColor(0, 255, 0), TColor(0, 0, 255),
33:    TColor(255, 128, 0), TColor(128, 255, 0), TColor(128, 0, 255),
34:    TColor(255, 0, 128), TColor(0, 255, 128), TColor(0, 128, 255),
35:    TColor(255, 128, 128), TColor(128, 255, 128),
36:    TColor(128, 128, 255), TColor(64, 64, 64)
37:    };
```

continues

669

Listing EC2.9. continued

```
38:
39: TMyWindow::TMyWindow()
40:     : TWindow(0, 0, 0)
41: {
42:     colorData.Flags = CC_FULLOPEN | CC_RGBINIT;
43:     colorData.Color = TColor(255, 0, 0);
44:     colorData.CustColors = custColors;
45: }
46:
47: void TMyWindow::CmColors()
48: {
49:     if (IDOK != TChooseColorDialog(this, colorData).Execute())
50:         return;
51:
52:     char str[100];        // Ought to be big enough
53:     sprintf(str,
54:             "Hexadecimal color code: 0x%081X\n"
55:             "Decimal color code: %lu",
56:             colorData.Color.GetValue(),
57:             colorData.Color.GetValue());
58:     MessageBox(str, "Color Metrics", MB_OK | MB_ICONINFORMATION);
59: }
60:
61: void TMyWindow::CmExit()
62: {
63:     Parent->SendMessage(WM_CLOSE);
64: }
65:
66: class TMyApp : public TApplication
67: {
68: public:
69:     TMyApp() : TApplication() {}
70:
71:     virtual void InitMainWindow()
72:         {
73:         SetMainWindow(new TFrameWindow(0, "Colors Dialog Box Tester",
74:                                     new TMyWindow));
75:         GetMainWindow()->AssignMenu("MainMenu");
76:         }
77: };
78:
79: int OwlMain(int, char*[])
80: {
81:     return TMyApp().Run();
82: }
```

Figure EC2.3 shows the Color dialog box.

Figure EC2.3.
A sample session with the GETCOLOR.EXE program.

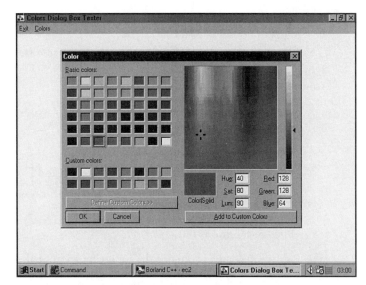

Let's examine the source code shown in Listing EC2.9. The window class TMyWindow declares a constructor, some data members, and a number of member functions. The data member colorData is a TChooseColorDialog::TData class and is involved in passing information to and from the color-selection dialog box.

The first relevant member function is the constructor whose definition starts on line 39. The constructor simply initializes colorData by filling in the Flags, Color, and CustColors data members. The Color data member is initialized to the color blue, and CustColors is set to the static array of custom colors.

The CmColors function starts on line 47. Its first task is to execute the Choose Color dialog, passing the colorData member. If the user doesn't press the OK button in the dialog, the result won't be IDOK and CmColors will exit. If the user does press the OK button, a message box shows the value of the color selected in both hexadecimal and decimal. When you play with this program, you'll notice that the hexadecimal version is actually a lot more useful. The first two digits are used to store special color flags, but the remaining six each represent the blue, green, and red elements of the color, separated into two digits each.

The Find and Replace Dialog Classes

The ObjectWindows library offers the classes `TFindDialog` and `TReplaceDialog` to support modeless dialog boxes for finding and replacing text. The Find dialog box contains the following controls:

- ☐ Find What edit control, which contains the search text
- ☐ Match Whole Word Only check box
- ☐ Match Case check box
- ☐ Direction group box, which contains the Up and Down radio buttons
- ☐ Find Next pushbutton, which acts like the OK button of a typical modal dialog box
- ☐ Cancel pushbutton
- ☐ Help pushbutton

The Replace dialog box contains the following additional controls:

- ☐ Replace With edit control, which contains the replacing text
- ☐ Replace pushbutton
- ☐ Replace All pushbutton

Both the `TFindDialog` and the `TReplaceDialog` are directly derived from `TFindReplaceDialog`, which is, in turn, derived from `TCommonDialog`. You might recognize this hierarchical structure from the Open and Save dialogs earlier in this chapter. The `TFindReplaceDialog` class contains most of the actual functionality of the two dialogs, whereas `TFindDialog` and `TReplaceDialog` contain overrides to work with the specialized portions of the two dialogs.

The constructors for all three are similar to the earlier `TCommonDialog` derivatives you've seen already:

```
TFindReplaceDialog(TWindow*       parent,
                   TData&         data,
                   TResId         templateId = 0,
                   const char far* title = 0,
                   TModule*       module = 0);
```

This time, of course, the `TData` member is a nested class of `TFindReplaceDialog` and has the following definition:

```
class TData {
  public:
    uint32   Flags;
    uint32   Error;
    char*    FindWhat;
    char*    ReplaceWith;
    int      BuffSize;

    TData(uint32 flags = 0, int buffSize = 81);
```

```
    TData(const TData& src);
    ~TData();

    TData& operator =(const TData& src);

    void    Write(opstream& os);
    void    Read(ipstream& is);
};
```

Again, you should notice that all the members are public, and there aren't any member functions to get or set the data, so you have to do it manually. The `Flags` member holds flags for passing Boolean data to and from the dialog as well as to give the dialog special setup instructions; these flags are shown in Table EC2.4. `Error`, as usual, stores an error code if the dialog had any problems. The `FindWhat` and `ReplaceWith` entries are pointers to dynamic memory that contains the contents of the Find and Replace edit boxes in the dialog, and `BuffSize` contains the maximum number of characters allowable in the edit controls. Note that the constructor takes parameters only to set `Flags` and `BuffSize`; that's all you really need to set before starting the dialog.

Table EC2.4. `FR_XXX` flag values.

Flag	Meaning
FR_DIALOGTERM	This flag is set by the dialog when it terminates. You can use this to determine whether or not the window handle you received when creating the dialog is still valid.
FR_DOWN	If this flag is set, then the search should be done down, otherwise up. This reflects the state of the Up and Down radio buttons.
FR_ENABLEHOOK	Enables a special hook function. This is used internally by OWL.
FR_ENABLETEMPLATE	Enables the programmer to specify a special template to replace the standard dialog.
FR_ENABLETEMPLATEHANDLE	Specifies how the template should be loaded.
FR_FINDNEXT	Indicates that the application should search for the next occurrence of what's in `FindWhat`.
FR_HIDEUPDOWN	Hides the Direction group box and the Up and Down radio buttons.
FR_HIDEMATCHCASE	Hides the Match Case check box.
FR_HIDEWHOLEWORD	Hides the Whole Word check box.
FR_MATCHCASE	Indicates that the Match Case check box is checked.

continues

Table EC2.4. continued

Flag	Meaning
FR_NOMATCHCASE	Disables the Match Case check box.
FR_NOUPDOWN	Disables the Up and Down radio buttons.
FR_NOWHOLEWORD	Disables the Whole Word check box.
FR_REPLACE	Indicates that the application should replace the current occurrence of what's in FindWhat with what's in ReplaceWith.
FR_REPLACEALL	Indicates that the application should replace all occurrences of what's in FindWhat with what's in ReplaceWith.
FR_SHOWHELP	Displays the Help button.
FR_WHOLEWORD	Indicates that the Whole Word check box is checked.

Using the Find and Replace Dialogs

Because the TFindDialog and TReplaceDialog are modeless dialog boxes, it takes a little different method to use them than you've seen for the other dialogs. For one thing, a modeless dialog sticks around while the application might be doing something else. Clicking on any button other than Cancel keeps the dialog displayed. It stays visible on top of whatever window starts it up, even when the focus is on that other window.

This also means that the communication with the dialog is a little different as well. Instead of just executing the dialog and then waiting for it to return, you have to create the dialog and have some method of responding to notification messages. There are two ways of responding to the notifications. The simplest is to derive your own version of TFindDialog or TReplaceDialog and override the CmFindNext, CmReplace, and CmReplaceAll member functions. This, however, keeps the processing in the derived dialog classes, when you would probably want to process the messages in the parent window. You could have the derived dialog class notify the parent window class, but there's already a mechanism for this.

The TFindDialog and TReplaceDialog send the FINDMSGSTRING message whenever one of the action buttons are pressed. In order to define an entry in the response table for this message, you should have a line that looks like the following:

```
EV_REGISTERED(FINDMSGSTRING, EvFindMsg);
```

where EvFindMsg is the name of a response function that has the following signature:

```
TResult EvFindMsg(TParam1, TParam2 p2);
```

The second parameter is a pointer to a FINDREPLACE structure, a Windows structure that's supplanted by the OWL classes you're using. This FINDREPLACE structure can be used in the TFindReplaceDialog member function UpdateData. This function makes sure the TData instance that was passed to the dialog is kept up to date with the contents of the dialog itself. Inside that response function, you can test the Flags data member of the TData class for the FR_DIALOGTERM flag, zeroing your pointer to the dialog.

A Sample Program

Let's put all of the preceding information to work in a test program. Here I present a simple menu-driven program that enables you to invoke a Find or Replace dialog box. Listing EC2.10 shows the FINDREP.RC resource script file. Listing EC2.11 contains the FINDREP.H header file. Listing EC2.12 contains the source code for the FINDREP.CPP program file.

Compile and run the FINDREP.EXE test program. The program has two main menu items: Exit and Search. When you select the Search menu item, a pull-down menu appears with the Find and Replace options. The first option invokes the Find dialog box; the second one invokes the Replace dialog box. Select either option and experiment with making new selections and typing new text in the corresponding dialog box. Click the Find Next button (available in both the Find and Replace dialog boxes) and watch the program display a message box that contains the data for the Find or Replace dialog box. When you finish experimenting with one dialog box, select the other. When you are done testing the program, click the Cancel button of the current dialog box to exit.

Listing EC2.10. The script for the FINDREP.RC resource file.

```
 1:  #include <windows.h>
 2:  #include <owl\window.rh>
 3:  #include "findrep.h"
 4:
 5:  MainMenu MENU LOADONCALL MOVEABLE PURE DISCARDABLE
 6:  BEGIN
 7:      MENUITEM "E&xit", CM_EXIT
 8:      POPUP "&Search"
 9:      BEGIN
10:        MENUITEM "&Find...", CM_FIND
11:        MENUITEM "&Replace...", CM_REPLACE
12:      END
13:  END
```

Listing EC2.11. The source code for the FINDREP.H header file.

```
 1:  #define CM_FIND       100
 2:  #define CM_REPLACE    101
```

Listing EC2.12. The source code for the FINDREP.CPP program file.

```
1:   // Program to test the Find and Replace common dialog boxes.
2:
3:   #include <owl\applicat.h>
4:   #include <owl\framewin.h>
5:   #include <owl\findrepl.h>
6:   #include <stdio.h>
7:   #include <string.h>
8:   #include "findrep.h"
9:
10:  const char* btoa(bool b)
11:  {
12:      return b ? "true" : "false";
13:  }
14:
15:  class TMyWindow : public TWindow
16:  {
17:  public:
18:      TMyWindow();
19:
20:  protected:
21:      TFindReplaceDialog::TData FRdata;
22:      TFindDialog* pFindDlg;
23:      TReplaceDialog* pReplaceDlg;
24:
25:      void CmFind();
26:      void CmReplace();
27:      void CmExit();
28:
29:      // handle clicking the Find Next button
30:      TResult EvFindMsg(WPARAM, LPARAM);
31:
32:      DECLARE_RESPONSE_TABLE(TMyWindow);
33:  };
34:  DEFINE_RESPONSE_TABLE1(TMyWindow, TWindow)
35:      EV_COMMAND(CM_FIND, CmFind),
36:      EV_COMMAND(CM_REPLACE, CmReplace),
37:      EV_COMMAND(CM_EXIT, CmExit),
38:      EV_REGISTERED(FINDMSGSTRING, EvFindMsg),
39:  END_RESPONSE_TABLE;
40:
41:  TMyWindow::TMyWindow()
42:      : TWindow(0, 0, 0)
43:  {
44:      pFindDlg = 0;
45:      pReplaceDlg = 0;
46:  }
47:
48:  void TMyWindow::CmFind()
49:  {
50:      if (!pFindDlg && !pReplaceDlg)
51:          {
52:          FRdata.Flags |= FR_DOWN;
53:          pFindDlg = new TFindDialog(this, FRdata);
54:          pFindDlg->Create();
```

```
55:            }
56:    }
57:
58:    void TMyWindow::CmReplace()
59:    {
60:        if (!pFindDlg && !pReplaceDlg)
61:            {
62:            FRdata.Flags = FR_DOWN ¦ FR_MATCHCASE ¦ FR_WHOLEWORD;
63:            pReplaceDlg = new TReplaceDialog(this, FRdata);
64:            pReplaceDlg->Create();
65:            }
66:    }
67:
68:    void TMyWindow::CmExit()
69:    {
70:        Parent->SendMessage(WM_CLOSE);
71:    }
72:
73:    TResult TMyWindow::EvFindMsg(TParam1, TParam2 p2)
74:    {
75:        char s[256];
76:
77:        if (pFindDlg)
78:            {
79:            pFindDlg->UpdateData(p2);
80:            if (!(FRdata.Flags & FR_DIALOGTERM))
81:                {
82:                sprintf(s, "Find String: %s\n"
83:                           "Search Down: %s\n"
84:                           "Match Case: %s\n"
85:                           "Whole Word: %s",
86:                           FRdata.FindWhat,
87:                           btoa(FRdata.Flags & FR_DOWN),
88:                           btoa(FRdata.Flags & FR_MATCHCASE),
89:                           btoa(FRdata.Flags & FR_WHOLEWORD) );
90:                MessageBox(s, "Find Dialog Box Data",
91:                           MB_OK ¦ MB_ICONINFORMATION);
92:                pFindDlg->SetFocus();
93:                }
94:            else
95:                pFindDlg = 0;
96:            }
97:        if (pReplaceDlg)
98:            {
99:            pReplaceDlg->UpdateData(p2);
100:           if (!(FRdata.Flags & FR_DIALOGTERM))
101:               {
102:               sprintf(s, "Find String: %s\n"
103:                          "Replace String: %s\n"
104:                          "Search Down: %s\n"
105:                          "Match Case: %s\n"
106:                          "Whole Word: %s\n"
107:                          "Replace Button Clicked: %s\n"
108:                          "Replace All Button Clicked: %s",
109:                          FRdata.FindWhat,
```

continues

Listing EC2.12. continued

```
110:                        FRdata.ReplaceWith,
111:                        btoa(FRdata.Flags & FR_DOWN),
112:                        btoa(FRdata.Flags & FR_MATCHCASE),
113:                        btoa(FRdata.Flags & FR_WHOLEWORD),
114:                        btoa(FRdata.Flags & FR_REPLACE),
115:                        btoa(FRdata.Flags & FR_REPLACEALL) );
116:         MessageBox(s, "Replace Dialog Box Data",
117:                     MB_OK | MB_ICONINFORMATION);
118:         pReplaceDlg->SetFocus();
119:             }
120:         else
121:             pReplaceDlg = 0;
122:         }
123:     return 0;
124: }
125:
126: class TMyApp : public TApplication
127: {
128: public:
129:     TMyApp() : TApplication() {}
130:
131:     virtual void InitMainWindow()
132:         {
133:         SetMainWindow(new TFrameWindow(0,
134:                                     "Find/Replace Dialog Box Tester",
135:                                     new TMyWindow));
136:         GetMainWindow()->AssignMenu("MainMenu");
137:         }
138: };
139:
140: int OwlMain(int, char*[])
141: {
142:     return TMyApp().Run();
143: }
```

Figure EC2.4 shows the FINDREP application with the Find dialog box, and Figure EC2.5 shows the Replace dialog box.

The FINDREP.CPP source code in Listing EC2.12 is very much like all the other code listings in this chapter, with a few exceptions. In this case, there are dialog pointers for the separate TFindDialog and TReplaceDialog classes so that the parent window can keep track of them. Then there's the extra event function EvFindMsg, which responds to the registered FINDMSGSTRING message.

Figure EC2.4.
A sample Find dialog box.

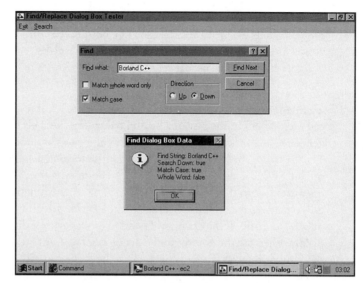

Figure EC2.5.
A sample Replace dialog box.

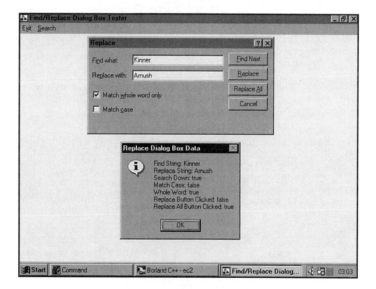

The two functions CmFind and CmReplace, defined starting on lines 48 and 58, respond to the Find and Replace menu selections. They both do basically the same thing, except the former creates a TFindDialog and the latter creates a TReplaceDialog. These are stored in the two dialog pointers pFindDlg and pReplaceDlg, respectively. After the dialogs have been created with new, they're created and displayed with the call to Create.

The EvFindMsg function starts its definition on line 73. It responds to the two dialogs when they call their parent in the case of a button being pressed. This function here can tell which dialog generated the message because this particular program doesn't allow both the Find and the Replace dialogs to be up at the same time; this means that a simple check of the pFindDlg pointer on line 77 and a check of the pReplaceDlg pointer on line 97 lets the function know on which one to act. With that information safely in hand, the function updates the FRdata class with a call to UpdateData on lines 79 and 99, then checks to see if the dialog has been terminated on lines 80 and 100. If the dialog still exists, a message box is displayed with information from the dialog; otherwise the pointer to the dialog is set to 0. After the message box has been displayed, the Find or Replace dialog is set back as the focus window on lines 92 and 118.

Summary

This chapter presented you with powerful dialog boxes that serve as input tools. You learned about the following:

- [ ] The ObjectWindows TInputDialog class, which enables you to prompt the user for an input.
- [ ] The file-selection dialog box classes TFileOpenDialog and TFileSaveDialog. These classes create dialog boxes that support either opening or saving a file.
- [ ] The color-selection dialog box class TChooseColorDialog.
- [ ] The text find/replace dialog box classes TFindDialog and TReplaceDialog. These classes create dialog boxes that support either finding or replacing text.

Note: There are two other common dialog boxes that haven't been covered in this chapter: TChooseFontDialog and TPrintDialog. These bring up dialogs for choosing a font and for printing, respectively. For more information about using these dialogs, read the online help that comes with Borland C++.

Q&A

Q **Is it easy to access the folder bit maps that appear in the File Open/Save dialog box?**

A No. Accessing these bit maps requires advanced programming skills.

Q **Can I use the Find and Replace dialog boxes to search for text patterns?**

A Yes. However, using such patterns may not be obvious to the dialog-box user. Using a check box that indicates whether to use pattern search is highly recommended. This additional control requires that you create your own version of the Find and Replace dialog boxes.

Exercises

1. Extend the class `TInputDialog` to create the class `TIntegerInput`. The new class supports integer input with validation.

2. Use the class `TIntegerInput` to replace the class `TInputDialog` in the number-guessing game, program INPUTDLG.EXE.

3. Write a program that uses the File dialog boxes to copy a file, possibly using a different name for the copy.

Extra Credit

3+

Windows 95 and Windows NT Common Controls

When Microsoft introduced Windows 95, it also introduced a whole new collection of Windows controls. This collection of controls has become known as the *Common Controls* because, like the Common Dialogs before them, they provide a common interface to all programs that make use of them. This Extra Credit Day takes a look at some of them and at how you can use them in your OWL programs.

The controls to be discussed include:

- ☐ Tool tips
- ☐ Progress indicators
- ☐ Updown controls
- ☐ Tab controls

Due to the constraints of space, only the most useful features of each of these controls will be presented. In most instances, you will not need any further information beyond that which is presented here. If you wish to implement something more exotic, please refer to the appropriate sections of the Object Windows and Win32 SDK help files that come with Borland C++ 5.

Tool Tips

Tool tips are used to provide instant information on the item underneath the cursor. These are the little text rectangles that pop up when the cursor is allowed to stop over a control. (See Figure EC3.1.) The item in question can be either a window, a control (this is most typical), or a rectangular area. Typically, tool tips will be provided for buttons, but they can also be provided for any control or window, including edit boxes and list boxes.

Figure EC3.1.

A tool tip on the Windows 95 tool bar.

With OWL, putting tool tips into your program is so easy that there is very little reason not to. All of the work is performed by two classes: `TToolTip` and `TToolInfo`. `TToolTip`, handles all of the dirty work of making the tool tip pop up properly. `TToolInfo` is used to provide the program with the tool tip data. We will take a quick look at each.

In short, here are the minimum number of steps that you must take to add tool tips to your program.

1. Instantiate a `TToolTip` object for your application.
2. For each window or dialog that will have tool tips, create `TToolInfo` objects for each individual tool tip and add them to the `TToolTip` object using the `AddTool` member

function. You need to do this in the dialog's or window's `SetupWindow` member function.

3. If the window or dialog will be destroyed prior to the end of the program, you will also need to delete any tool tips using the `DeleteTool` function. You can do this during the dialog's or window's `CloseWindow` member function.

> **Warning:** Failure to delete tool tips when a dialog is closed will cause your program to use more and more memory every time the dialog is created.

4. For each window or dialog that will have tool tips, install a message filter to relay mouse messages to the `TToolTip` object. (Refer to the `RelayEvent` member function of `TToolTip` for further information.)

The *TToolTip* Class

The `TToolTip` class is used to provide the tool-tip functionality and to control how tool tips are displayed. Among the things that you can do are add new tool tips, turn tool tips on and off, and change the delay time before the tool tip information is shown.

Syntax

The *TToolTip* Constructor

There are two constructor declarations:

```
TTooltip(TWindow* parent,
         bool alwaysTip = true,
         TModule* module = 0);
TTooltip(HWND hWnd,
         TModule* module = 0);
```

The first form of the constructor is the one that you will usually use in OWL. The second form of the constructor can be used to alias a control that provides its own tool tips, for instance, a Tab Control with the `TCS_TOOLTIPS` style.

Here are the parameters that are passed to the constructors. `parent` is the `TWindow` object that will be the parent window for all tool tips. `alwaysTip` is set to `true` if the tool tip should be displayed regardless of whether the window is active or inactive. `module` is the `TModule` for the application.

Examples:

```
TToolTip* pToolTip = new TTooltip(this);
TToolTip* pToolTip = new TToolTip( GetDlgItem(IDC_TABS) );
```

There are a large number of member functions declared for the TToolTips class. Here are some of the more important ones:

The *Activate* Function

The declaration of the Activate member function is

```
void Activate(bool activate = true);
```

This function activates and deactivates the tool-tip control. The activate parameter is set to true to activate the tool-tip control and false to deactivate it.

Example:

```
pToolTip->Activate(false);
```

The *AddTool* Function

The declaration of the AddTool member function is

```
bool AddTool(const TToolInfo& toolInfo);
```

This function is used to add new tool tips to the tool-tip control. toolInfo contains the information about the tool tip to be added. Refer to the following section on the TToolInfo class for further information. The function returns true if the function succeeded in adding the tool tip.

Example:

```
TToolInfo saveBtnTip(*this,
                     GetDlgItem(IDC_SAVE),
                     "Save File");
pToolTip->AddTool(saveBtnTip);
```

Warning: The AddTool function does not check for duplicate tool IDs!

The *DeleteTool* Function

The declaration of the DeleteTool member function is

```
void DeleteTool(const TToolInfo& toolInfo);
```

toolInfo identifies the tool tip that is to be deleted. Use the SetToolHandle or SetToolId member functions of TToolInfo (see the following) to set the tool ID.

Example:

```
TToolInfo saveBtnTip;
saveBtnTip.SetToolInfo(*this, IDC_SAVE);
pToolTip->DeleteTool(saveBtnTip);
```

The *RelayEvent* Function

The declaration of the RelayEvent member function is

```
void RelayEvent(MSG& msg);
```

This function is rather special. You will use it to pass mouse messages to the tool-tip control. This is the mechanism through which the tool-tip control finds where the mouse cursor is and whether the mouse is clicked. The best time to relay these massages is the PreProcessMsg function.

EC3

Example:

```
bool ToolTipDlg::PreProcessMsg(MSG& msg)
{
    ToolTipApp* appPtr
        = TYPESAFE_DOWNCAST(GetApplication(), ToolTipApp);
    if (appPtr != NULL)
    {
        TTooltip* pToolTip = appPtr->pToolTip;
        if (pToolTip && pToolTip->IsWindow())
        {
            // Relay the mouse messages...
            switch(msg.message)
            {
                case WM_MOUSEMOVE:
                case WM_LBUTTONDOWN:
                case WM_LBUTTONUP:
                case WM_MBUTTONDOWN:
                case WM_MBUTTONUP:
                case WM_RBUTTONDOWN:
                case WM_RBUTTONUP:
                    pToolTip->RelayEvent(msg);
                    break;
            }
        }
    }
    return false;
}
```

The *TToolInfo* Class

This class provides an encapsulation of everything needed by the tool-tip control for each individual tool tip. There are a few member functions declared for this class, but only rarely will you actually need to call one of them. This being the case, we will not look at these member functions. Instead, we will concentrate on the multitude of constructors that this class offers.

The constructors fall into two categories: window tool tips and rectangular areas. In each category, there are three constructors. One constructor is used when the tool-tip text is passed directly to the constructor. Another constructor is used when the tool-tip text will be supplied by a message-event handler. The last constructor is used when the tool-tip text is contained within a string table resource. There is also a default constructor that is mainly used when tool-tip information is retrieved from a tool-tip control or when a tool tip is deleted.

The *TToolInfo* Constructors

Syntax

The declaration of these constructors is

```
TToolInfo();
TToolInfo(HWND parent,
          const TRect& rect,
          uint toolId,
          char far* txt = LPSTR_TEXTCALLBACK);
TToolInfo(HWND parent,
          const TRect& rect,
          uint toolId,
          int resId,
          HINSTANCE txtResModule);
TToolInfo(HWND parent,
          HWND toolHwnd,
          char far* txt = LPSTR_TEXTCALLBACK);
TToolInfo(HWND parent,
          HWND toolHwnd,
          int resId,
          HINSTANCE strResModule);
```

The first form of constructor is the default constructor. It creates an empty TToolInfo object. Normally, you will want to call either SetToolInfo immediately after using this constructor.

Example of First Form:

```
TToolInfo toolInfo;
```

The second form creates a tool tip for a rectangular area. The tool-tip text can be supplied directly to the constructor as the txt parameter. Alternatively, if txt is set to LPSTR_TEXTCALLBACK, then the parent window will receive a TTN_NEEDTEXT notification in order to retrieve the text. parent specifies the parent window. rect is used to define the boundaries of the rectangular area. toolId is an arbitrary value, but it must be unique and, in the case where the parent window gets notified, it must match the ID used in the EV_TTN_NEEDTEXT event handler.

Examples of Second Form:

```
TToolInfo toolInfo(*this, rect,
                   IDC_BLUERECT, "Blue Rectangle");
TToolInfo toolInfo(*this, rect,
                   IDC_REDRECT);
```

The third form of constructor also creates a tool tip for a rectangular area. This tool tip, however, gets its text out of a string table resource. The parent, rect, and toolId parameters are the same as above. resId is the string identifier and txtResModule is the instance handle of the .EXE or .DLL file that contains the string table.

Example of Third Form:

```
TToolInfo toolInfo(*this, rect,
                   IDC_GREENRECT, IDS_GREENRECT,
                   GetModule()->GetInstance());
```

The fourth form creates a tool tip for a control or window. The tool-tip text can be supplied directly to the constructor as the txt parameter. Alternatively, if txt is set to LPSTR_TEXTCALLBACK, then the parent window will receive a TTN_NEEDTEXT notification in order to retrieve the text. parent specifies the parent window. toolHwnd is the window handle of the control that will receive the TTN_NEEDTEXT notification.

Examples of Fourth Form:

```
TToolInfo toolInfo(*this, IDC_SAVE, "Save File");
TToolInfo toolInfo(*this, IDC_SAVE);
```

The fifth form of constructor also creates a tool tip for a control or window. This tool tip, however, gets its text out of a string table resource. The window and toolWnd parameters are the same as before. resId is the string identifier and txtResModule is the instance handle of the .EXE or .DLL file that contains the string table.

Example of Fifth Form:

```
TToolInfo toolInfo(*this, IDC_SAVEAS, IDS_SAVEAS,
                   GetModule()->GetInstance());
```

TToolTip Demonstration Program

TOOLTIP.EXE is a demonstration program that shows the creation and use of several kinds of tool tips. The main program window has a number of different kinds of controls. Each of the controls has a tool tip associated with it. In addition, the upper-right and lower-right corners of the main window are rectangular areas that have their own tool tips. The source code for the demonstration is shown in listings EC3.1, EC3.2, and EC3.3.

Listing EC3.1. Source code for the TOOLTIP.H header file.

```
1:  #define IDS_HELP          201
2:  #define IDS_CHECKBOX      202
3:  #define IDS_TOPRT         203
4:
```

continues

Listing EC3.1. continued

```
 5: #define IDE_EDIT          101
 6: #define IDC_CHECKBOX       102
 7: #define IDR_RADIOBUTTON1   103
 8: #define IDR_RADIOBUTTON2   104
 9:
10: #define ID_TOPRT           199
11: #define ID_BOTRT           200
```

Type

Listing EC3.2. Source code for the TOOLTIP.RC resource file.

```
 1: #include "tooltip.h"
 2:
 3: MainDlg DIALOG 6, 15, 136, 119
 4: STYLE WS_CHILD ¦ WS_VISIBLE ¦ WS_BORDER ¦ DS_3DLOOK
 5: FONT 8, "MS Sans Serif"
 6: {
 7:    CONTROL "Edit", IDE_EDIT, "EDIT",
 8:       WS_BORDER ¦ WS_TABSTOP, 12, 9, 50, 80
 9:    CONTROL "&Select This", IDR_RADIOBUTTON1, "BUTTON",
10:       BS_AUTORADIOBUTTON ¦ WS_GROUP ¦ WS_TABSTOP, 69, 10, 60, 12
11:    CONTROL "&Or This", IDR_RADIOBUTTON2, "BUTTON",
12:       BS_AUTORADIOBUTTON ¦ WS_TABSTOP, 69, 22, 60, 12
13:    CONTROL "&Check Here", IDC_CHECKBOX, "BUTTON",
14:       BS_AUTOCHECKBOX ¦ BS_CENTER ¦ BS_VCENTER ¦
15:       WS_CHILD ¦ WS_VISIBLE ¦ WS_TABSTOP, 69, 36, 64, 13
16:    DEFPUSHBUTTON "&Quit", IDOK, 12, 96, 50, 14
17:    CONTROL "&Help", IDHELP, "BUTTON",
18:       BS_PUSHBUTTON ¦ BS_CENTER ¦ BS_VCENTER ¦
19:       WS_CHILD ¦ WS_VISIBLE ¦ WS_TABSTOP, 68, 96, 50, 14
20: }
21:
22: STRINGTABLE
23: {
24:    IDS_HELP, "Help Button"
25:    IDS_CHECKBOX, "Check Box"
26:    IDS_TOPRT, "Top Right Rectangle"
27: }
```

Type

Listing EC3.3. Source code for the TOOLTIP.CPP program file.

```
 1: // Tooltip Class Example
 2: //
 3: #include <owl/pch.h>
 4: #include <owl/tooltip.h>
 5: #include "tooltip.h"
 6:
 7: class ToolTipMainDlg : public TDialog
 8: {
 9: public:
10:    ToolTipMainDlg (TWindow *parent)
```

```
11:          : TDialog(parent, "MainDlg", 0)       {}
12:     virtual ~ToolTipMainDlg()                   {}
13:
14:  protected:
15:     bool            PreProcessMsg(MSG& msg);
16:     void            SetupWindow();
17:     void            CloseWindow(int retval = 0);
18:     void            GetBottomRightTipText(TTooltipText& tiptext);
19:
20:  DECLARE_RESPONSE_TABLE(ToolTipMainDlg);
21:  };
22:  DEFINE_RESPONSE_TABLE1(ToolTipMainDlg, TDialog)
23:     EV_TTN_NEEDTEXT(ID_BOTRT, GetBottomRightTipText),
24:  END_RESPONSE_TABLE;
25:
26:  class ToolTipApp : public TApplication
27:  {
28:  public:
29:     ToolTipApp () : TApplication()       {}
30:     virtual        ~ToolTipApp()         {}
31:     virtual void   InitMainWindow();
32:
33:     TTooltip*      toolTip;
34:  };
35:
36:  void ToolTipMainDlg::SetupWindow()
37:  {
38:     TDialog::SetupWindow();
39:
40:     // Get a pointer to the application's tool tip handler
41:     ToolTipApp* appPtr = TYPESAFE_DOWNCAST(GetApplication(),
42:                                            ToolTipApp);
43:     if (appPtr)
44:         {
45:         TTooltip* tooltip = appPtr->toolTip;
46:
47:         // Make sure that it is legit...
48:         if (tooltip && tooltip->IsWindow())
49:             {
50:             // Tool tips using explicit strings
51:             //
52:             TToolInfo quitButton(*this, GetDlgItem(IDOK), "Quit Button");
53:             tooltip->AddTool(quitButton);
54:
55:             TToolInfo RadButton1(*this, GetDlgItem(IDR_RADIOBUTTON1),
56:                               "Radio Button");
57:             tooltip->AddTool(RadButton1);
58:
59:             TToolInfo radButton2(*this, GetDlgItem(IDR_RADIOBUTTON2),
60:                               "Another Radio Button");
61:             tooltip->AddTool(radButton2);
62:
63:             TToolInfo editBox(*this, GetDlgItem(IDE_EDIT), "Edit Box");
64:             tooltip->AddTool(editBox);
65:
66:             // Tool tip using String Resources
```

continues

691

Listing EC3.3. continued

```
67:            //
68:            TToolInfo helpButton(*this,
69:                            GetDlgItem(IDHELP),
70:                            IDS_HELP,
71:                            GetModule()->GetInstance());
72:            tooltip->AddTool(helpButton);
73:
74:            TToolInfo checkBox(*this,
75:                            GetDlgItem(IDC_CHECKBOX),
76:                            IDS_CHECKBOX,
77:                            GetModule()->GetInstance());
78:            tooltip->AddTool(checkBox);
79:
80:            // Tool tips for rectangles
81:            //
82:            TRect windRect = GetWindowRect();
83:            TRect bottomRtRect((windRect.Width() / 2),
84:                            (windRect.Height() / 2),
85:                            windRect.Width(),
86:                            windRect.Height());
87:            TToolInfo bottomRt(*this, bottomRtRect, ID_BOTRT);
88:            tooltip->AddTool(bottomRt);
89:
90:            TRect topRtRect(windRect.Width() / 2,
91:                            0,
92:                            windRect.Width(),
93:                            windRect.Height() / 2);
94:            TToolInfo topRt(*this,
95:                            topRtRect,
96:                            ID_TOPRT,
97:                            IDS_TOPRT,
98:                            GetModule()->GetInstance());
99:            tooltip->AddTool(topRt);
100:           }
101:       }
102: }
103:
104: // Remove tool tips on dialog close.
105: //
106: void ToolTipMainDlg::CloseWindow(int retval)
107: {
108:     // Get a pointer to the application's tool tip handler
109:     ToolTipApp* appPtr = TYPESAFE_DOWNCAST(GetApplication(),
110:                                        ToolTipApp);
111:     if (appPtr)
112:         {
113:         TTooltip* toolTip = appPtr->toolTip;
114:
115:         // Make sure that it is legit...
116:         if (toolTip && toolTip->IsWindow())
117:             {
118:             TToolInfo toolInfo;
119:
120:             toolInfo.SetToolInfo(*this, IDOK);
121:             toolTip->DeleteTool(toolInfo);
```

```
122:
123:            toolInfo.SetToolInfo(*this, IDR_RADIOBUTTON1);
124:            toolTip->DeleteTool(toolInfo);
125:
126:            toolInfo.SetToolInfo(*this, IDR_RADIOBUTTON2);
127:            toolTip->DeleteTool(toolInfo);
128:
129:            toolInfo.SetToolInfo(*this, IDE_EDIT);
130:            toolTip->DeleteTool(toolInfo);
131:
132:            toolInfo.SetToolInfo(*this, IDHELP);
133:            toolTip->DeleteTool(toolInfo);
134:
135:            toolInfo.SetToolInfo(*this, IDC_CHECKBOX);
136:            toolTip->DeleteTool(toolInfo);
137:
138:            toolInfo.SetToolInfo(*this, ID_BOTRT);
139:            toolTip->DeleteTool(toolInfo);
140:
141:            toolInfo.SetToolInfo(*this, ID_TOPRT);
142:            toolTip->DeleteTool(toolInfo);
143:            }
144:        }
145:    TDialog::CloseWindow(retval);
146: }
147:
148: // ----------------------------------------------------------
149: // Supplies the tip text when the mouse is in the bottom right
150: // corner of the main window.
151: //
152: void
153: ToolTipMainDlg::GetBottomRightTipText(TTooltipText& tiptext)
154: {
155:    tiptext.CopyText("Bottom Right Corner");
156: }
157:
158: // --------------------------------------------------
159: // Relay the mouse movements to the tip handler so that
160: // it knows what is going on.
161: //
162: bool ToolTipMainDlg::PreProcessMsg(MSG& msg)
163: {
164:    ToolTipApp* appPtr = TYPESAFE_DOWNCAST(GetApplication(),
165:                                            ToolTipApp);
166:    if (appPtr)
167:        {
168:        TTooltip* tooltip = appPtr->toolTip;
169:        if (tooltip && tooltip->IsWindow())
170:            {
171:            // Relay the mouse messages...
172:            switch(msg.message)
173:                {
174:                case WM_MOUSEMOVE:
175:                case WM_LBUTTONDOWN:
176:                case WM_LBUTTONUP:
```

continues

Listing EC3.3. continued

```
177:                case WM_MBUTTONDOWN:
178:                case WM_MBUTTONUP:
179:                case WM_RBUTTONDOWN:
180:                case WM_RBUTTONUP:
181:                    tooltip->RelayEvent(msg);
182:                    break;
183:            }
184:        }
185:    }
186:    // Pretend that we didn't do anything...
187:    return false;
188: }
189:
190: void ToolTipApp::InitMainWindow ()
191: {
192:    // Dialog as main window.
193:    SetMainWindow(new TFrameWindow(0,
194:                                   "ToolTip Demo",
195:                                   new ToolTipMainDlg(0),
196:                                   true));
197:    GetMainWindow()->Attr.Style |= (WS_DLGFRAME);
198:    GetMainWindow()->Attr.Style &= ~(WS_MAXIMIZEBOX |
199:                        WS_THICKFRAME);
200:
201:    // Create the tool tip handler for this application.
202:    toolTip = new TTooltip(GetMainWindow()->GetClientWindow());
203: }
204:
205: int OwlMain(int, char* [])
206: {
207:    return ToolTipApp().Run();
208: }
```

A sample session with the ToolTip program is shown in Figure EC3.2.

Figure EC3.2.
The ToolTip demonstration program.

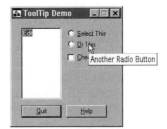

Analysis
The program shown in Listing EC3.3 consists of one dialog box used as a main window. Each of the controls in the program is defined in a dialog template. This template is shown on lines 7–19 of Listing EC3.2. Each of these controls has a tool tip assigned to it. In addition, the upper- and lower-right corners of the main dialog each have their own tool tip.

The tool-tip control itself is created, on line 202, when the main window of the program is initialized.

The tool tips for the dialog are created in the dialog's SetupWindow member function. Lines 52-64 show several tool tips being created using explicit strings. Lines 68-78 show the creation of a couple of tool tips that use string resources. Lines 82-99 show the creation of tool tips for the upper-right and lower-right corners of the dialog box. The first tool tip uses a TTN_NEEDTEXT notification to get its tool-tip text. The response table for this is shown on lines 22-24, and the event-handler function is shown on lines 152-156. The second tool tip gets its text from the string table resource.

The destruction of the tool tips for this dialog is shown in the function CloseWindow starting on line 106. For this program, this step is not really necessary; closing the dialog will cause the program to end. Nevertheless, it is shown here to illustrate how one can go about destroying tool tips that are no longer needed.

The PreprocessMsg filter function on lines 162-188 demonstrates the use of RelayEvent to pass mouse messages to the tool-tip control.

Progress Indicator Controls

Progress indicators are also known as *gauge* or *meter* controls. Visually, they consist of a rectangular bar that grows (or shrinks) according to an amount that corresponds with some process. They are usually used to show how much of a task has been completed, but they can also be used to show analog data. For example, a gauge control can be used to show the amount of free space left on a hard disk. Figure EC3.3 shows a Windows 95 progress indicator control.

Figure EC3.3.
A Windows 95 Progress Indicator.

The progress indicator is new to Windows 95, but it is not new to OWL. OWL has had a TGauge class ever since OWL version 2.0 was released. This class implemented its own gauge control and still does if you compile and run the application that uses it on a 16-bit version of Windows. If, however, you create the control itself in the dialog and then associate the TGauge class in a dialog's constructor code, OWL will make use of the common control.

There is some question as to which version of the control is better: the OWL or the Windows 95 version. The two versions are different visually in that the Windows 95 control can only be horizontal, it doesn't display a textual version of the current value, and its progress indicator is displayed with vertical stripes along its length. On the other hand, the OWL control can be either horizontal or vertical, displays a textual version of the progress embedded in the meter, and uses a smooth meter.

In order to decide which control you wish to use, you have to weigh the pros and cons as they pertain to your particular situation. Obviously, if you use a vertical control anywhere in your application, you should probably use the OWL controls for the horizontal ones as well to help keep a consistent visual appearance throughout the program. Also, if you care about a textual indicator for the gauge, then you should go with OWL. If, on the other hand, you wish your control to adhere to Microsoft's vision of a meter control or you wish to insert the control in the dialog box from the resource editor rather than manually from the source code, then you should go with the common control.

The *TGauge* Class

The TGauge class provides a very flexible interface for gauges and progress indicators. Here I will show how to create gauges and how to manipulate them using the member functions of the TGauge class.

The *TGauge* Constructor

Syntax

The declarations of the TGuage constructors are as follows:

```
TGauge(TWindow* parent,
       const char far* title,
       int id,
       int x, int y, int w, int h = 0,
       bool isHorizontal = true,
       int margin = 1,
       TModule* module = 0);
TGauge(TWindow* parent,
       int id,
       int x, int y, int w, int h = 0,
       TModule* module = 0);
TGauge(TWindow* parent,
       int resId,
       TModule* module = 0);
```

Both of the first two constructors will create an OWL gauge with a minimum value of 0 and a maximum value of 100. The first form of the constructor is the full-featured version. It allows for the inclusion of text within the control, and it allows for vertical as well as horizontal gauges. The second form of the constructor is a simplified version that gives you only the capabilities of the Windows 95 control. In fact, it will actually create the gauge using the Windows 95 progress indicator if it can. The parent parameter is a TWindow pointer to the parent dialog or window. title is the text that will be placed in the gauge. If this text string contains %d, this will be replaced with the current gauge value. x, y, w, and h are the *x* and *y* origins and the width and height of the control. margin is the space between the bevel and the graphic.

The third version of the constructor is for use in connecting to an existing control embedded in the dialog resource. This is the constructor that should be used for the common control.

Example:

```
secondsGauge = new TGauge( this, "%d Seconds",
                           IDC_SECONDS,
                           20,20,30,116,
                           false);      // Vertical Gauge
```

Syntax

The *DeltaValue* Function

The declaration of the DeltaValue member function is as follows:

```
void DeltaValue(int delta);
```

This function changes the current position of the gauge by the relative amount, delta.

Example:

```
pGauge->DeltaValue(-5); // Subtracts 5 from current value.
```

EC3

Syntax

The *GetRange* and *SetRange* Functions

The declaration of the GetRange and SetRange functions is as follows:

```
void GetRange(int& min, int& max) const;
void SetRange(int min, int max);
```

The GetRange function retrieves the minimum and maximum values that the gauge can display. SetRange is used to set the minimum and maximum values that the gauge can display. If max is less than min, SetRange will set the maximum value to min+1.

Examples:

```
pGauge->GetRange(minVal, maxVal);
pGauge->SetRange(50, 100);
```

Syntax

The *GetValue* and *SetValue* Functions

The declaration of the GetValue and SetValue functions is as follows:

```
int GetValue() const;
void SetValue(int value);
```

The GetValue function retrieves the current value of the gauge. SetValue is used to set the new value for the gauge. The value parameter will be constricted to the minimum and maximum values of the gauge.

Examples:

```
curVal = pGauge->GetValue();
pGauge->SetValue(73);          // Current value set to 73.
```

The *SetColor* and *SetLed* Functions

The declaration of the SetColor and SetLed member functions is as follows:

```
void SetColor(const TColor& color);
void SetLed(int spacing, int thickPercent = 90);
```

These two functions are used to control the appearance of the OWL gauge. SetColor sets the color of the gauge to the value specified in the color parameter. SetLed is used to give the gauge an *LED* or dashed look (this is the look that the Windows 95 progress indicator has.) The spacing parameter determines the distance between the LED elements, in gauge units, and the thickPercent parameter determines the width of each LED. When the gauge is set to the LED look, no text will be displayed. Note that neither of these functions have any effect on the common control.

Examples:

```
pGauge->SetColor( TColor::LtRed );    // Sets bar to red.
pGuage->SetLed( 1 );                  // Sets LED spacing to 1
```

The Gauge Clock Program

This program uses gauges to implement a simple Windows clock applet. It uses two TGauge objects and one Windows 95 progress-indicator control. The Windows 95 progress indicator displays the hours. A horizontal TGauge shows the minutes, and the seconds are displayed by a vertical TGauge. The source code for the demonstration is shown in Listings EC3.4, EC3.5, and EC3.6.

Listing EC3.4. Source code for the GAUGE.H header file.

```
1: #define IDC_SECONDS         1000
2: #define IDC_MINUTES         1001
3: #define IDC_HOURS           1002
4: #define IDC_HOURTEXT        1003
5:
6: #define IDT_TIMER           12
```

Listing EC3.5. Source code for the GAUGE.RC resource file.

```
1:  #include "gauge.h"
2:
3:  MainDlg DIALOG 0, 0, 214, 118
4:  STYLE DS_MODALFRAME ¦ WS_CHILD ¦ WS_CAPTION ¦ WS_SYSMENU
5:  FONT 8, "MS Sans Serif"
6:  {
7:     CONTROL "Progress3", IDC_HOURS, "MSCTLS_PROGRESS32",
8:         WS_CHILD ¦ WS_VISIBLE ¦ WS_BORDER, 52,70,138,14
```

```
 9:    DEFPUSHBUTTON "&Quit", IDOK, 96,97,50,14
10:    CTEXT "10 Hours", IDC_HOURTEXT, 100, 56, 48, 12
11: }
```

Type **Listing EC3.6. Source code for the GAUGE.CPP program file.**

```
 1:  // Gauge Class Example
 2:
 3:  #include <owl/pch.h>
 4:  #include <owl/Gauge.h>
 5:  #include <winsys/color.h>
 6:  #include <classlib/time.h>
 7:  #include "Gauge.h"
 8:
 9:  class GaugeMainDlg : public TDialog
10:  {
11:  public:
12:      GaugeMainDlg(TWindow *parent);
13:      virtual ~GaugeMainDlg()          {}
14:
15:  protected:
16:      virtual void SetupWindow();
17:      virtual void CloseWindow(int retval = 0);
18:      virtual void EvTimer(uint timerId);
19:
20:  private:
21:      TGauge* secondsGauge;
22:      TGauge* minutesGauge;
23:      TGauge* hoursGauge;
24:
25:  DECLARE_RESPONSE_TABLE(GaugeMainDlg);
26:  };
27:  DEFINE_RESPONSE_TABLE1(GaugeMainDlg, TDialog)
28:      EV_WM_TIMER,
29:  END_RESPONSE_TABLE;
30:
31:  class GaugeApp : public TApplication
32:  {
33:  public:
34:      GaugeApp() : TApplication()       {}
35:      virtual       ~GaugeApp()         {}
36:      virtual void   InitMainWindow();
37:  };
38:
39:  GaugeMainDlg::GaugeMainDlg (TWindow *parent)
40:        : TDialog(parent, "MainDlg", 0)
41:  {
42:      // Create a vertical gauge for the seconds...
43:      secondsGauge = new TGauge( this, "%d",
44:                                 IDC_SECONDS,
45:                                 20, 20, 30, 116,
46:                                 false);     // Vertical Gauge
47:      secondsGauge->SetRange(0, 59);
```

continues

EC3

Listing EC3.6. continued

```
48:
49:        // Create a horizontal gauge for the minutes.
50:        // Ignore the size and position here. We'll fix that
51:        // in SetupWindow()...
52:        minutesGauge = new TGauge( this, "%d Minutes",
53:                                   IDC_MINUTES,
54:                                   104, 20, 80, 28 );
55:        minutesGauge->SetRange(0, 59);
56:        minutesGauge->SetColor(TColor::LtRed);
57:
58:        // Create an interface for the Win32 common control
59:        hoursGauge = new TGauge(this, IDC_HOURS);
60:        hoursGauge->SetRange(0, 23);
61:        hoursGauge->SetLed(1, 1);    // Fixes a bug in OWL
62:    }
63:
64:    void GaugeMainDlg::SetupWindow()
65:    {
66:        TDialog::SetupWindow();
67:
68:        TRect hourRect(hoursGauge->GetWindowRect());
69:        ScreenToClient(hourRect.TopLeft());
70:        ScreenToClient(hourRect.BottomRight());
71:        minutesGauge->SetWindowPos(0, hourRect.Left(), 20,
72:                                   hourRect.Width(),
73:                                   hourRect.Height(),
74:                                   SWP_NOZORDER);
75:
76:        // Set a one second timer
77:        SetTimer(IDT_TIMER, 1000);
78:    }
79:
80:    void GaugeMainDlg::CloseWindow(int retval)
81:    {
82:        KillTimer(IDT_TIMER);
83:        TDialog::CloseWindow(retval);
84:    }
85:
86:    void GaugeMainDlg::EvTimer(uint /*timerId*/)
87:    {
88:        // When this goes off, fetch the time and transfer it
89:        // to the gauges.
90:        //
91:        TTime timenow;
92:        secondsGauge->SetValue(timenow.Second());
93:        minutesGauge->SetValue(timenow.Minute());
94:        hoursGauge->SetValue(timenow.Hour());
95:
96:        // The common control doesn't supply any text, so
97:        // let's add it ourselves.
98:        //
99:        char buffer[15];
100:       ::wsprintf(buffer, "%d Hours", timenow.Hour() );
101:       SetDlgItemText(IDC_HOURTEXT, buffer);
102:   }
```

```
103:
104: void GaugeApp::InitMainWindow ()
105: {
106:     SetMainWindow(new TFrameWindow(0,
107:                                    "Gauge Demo",
108:                                    new GaugeMainDlg(0),
109:                                    true));
110:     GetMainWindow()->Attr.Style |= WS_DLGFRAME | WS_CLIPCHILDREN;
111:     GetMainWindow()->Attr.Style &= ~(WS_MAXIMIZEBOX | WS_THICKFRAME);
112: }
113:
114: int OwlMain(int, char* [])
115: {
116:     return GaugeApp().Run();
117: }
```

A sample session of the Gauge Clock demonstration program is shown in Figure EC3.4.

Figure EC3.4.

The Gauge Clock demonstration program.

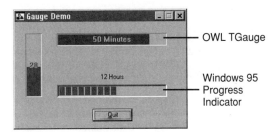

The Windows 95 gauge is created according to the specification in lines 7-8 of the dialog template in GAUGE.RC (see Listing EC3.5). The two OWL gauges are created in the main dialog constructor on lines 43-56 of Listing EC3.6. The ranges of the two gauges are set at this time, and the color of the minutes gauge is also set to red. Immediately following these, the OWL object is created to reference the Windows 95 progress indicator on lines 59-61. As of this writing, there is a bug in the OWL code that prevents TGauge from interfacing with the common-control properly unless the statement on line 61 is executed.

When the SetupWindow function of the main dialog is called (lines 64-78), the minutes gauge is resized and moved to align it with the Windows 95 progress indicator. (This is a handy technique. Often it is easier to resize things on the fly rather than try to tweak them until they are exactly right.) Also in SetupWindow, a one-second timer is started.

The timer's message handler (lines 86-102) handles all of the details of ensuring that the gauges display the correct time. A TTime object is instantiated with the current time. The values of the hours, minutes, and seconds are then used to set the three gauges. Then, on lines 99-100, a static-text box is updated with a textual version of the current hour.

Updown Controls

An *updown control* is a small window containing up and down arrows. These arrows are used to increment and decrement a value associated with the updown control, sometimes referred to as a *spinner* control. The updown control can be used by itself, but more often it will be paired with some other control like an edit box. This combination is sometimes referred to as a *spinbox*. The paired control is referred to as a *buddy control*. See Figure EC3.5 for an example of an updown control.

Figure EC3.5.

An updown control.

When creating updown controls in the resource editor, you can set several different options that affect its look and operation. These options are described in Table EC3.1.

Table EC3.1. Updown control options.

Section	Style	Description
Orientation	Horizontal, Vertical	These cause the updown control to have its arrows either pointing left and right or pointing up and down.
Alignment	Unattached, Left, Right	Selecting Left causes the updown control to align itself with the left edge of its buddy window. The width of the buddy window is reduced by the width of the updown control. Selecting Right causes the control to align itself with the right edge of its buddy window. Again, the width of the buddy window is modified. Selecting Unattached allows the updown control to be free-standing.
UpDown Flags	Auto Buddy	This flag causes the control, when it is created, to select the previous control in the dialog as its buddy. An alternative to this flag is to set the buddy control explicitly (see the SetBuddy function).
	Wrap	This flag causes the value of the updown control to wrap around when it reaches its upper or lower limit.
	Arrow Keys	This flag causes the updown control to respond to the arrow keys on the keyboard. If the updown control has a buddy, then the arrow keys will operate on the updown control when the buddy control has the focus.

Section	Style	Description
	Set Buddy Int	When the updown control's value changes, this flag causes the updown control to set the caption of its buddy control. If the buddy control is a list box or a combo box, this flag will cause a change of selection.
	No Thousands	This flag has no effect unless the Set Buddy Int flag is also used. Normally, when the caption of a buddy control is set, commas will be inserted every three digits. This flag suppresses this behavior.

The *TUpDown* Class

EC3

Unlike the TGauge class already described, there is no difference between the 16-bit version of the TUpDown class that OWL emulates and the common-control version that is directly supported by Windows 95. All of the operations desirable for controlling an updown control are available through this class.

The *TUpDown* Constructor

The declarations of the TUpDown constructors are as follows:

```
TUpDown(TWindow* parent,
        int id,
        int x, int y, int w, int h,
        TWindow* buddy = 0,
        TModule* module = 0);
TUpDown(TWindow* parent,
        int resourceId,
        TWindow* buddy = 0,
        TModule* module = 0);
```

The first form of the constructor is used to create an updown control where one does not already exist. The second form is used when the control already exists in a dialog resource and a TUpDown alias is desired. Most of the parameters should be familiar by now (if not, it is time to review the chapters on the basic Windows controls). The buddy parameter is used to select the buddy control.

Examples:

```
TEdit* pEdit = new TEdit(this, IDC_EDIT);      // Alias a buddy
TUpDown* pUpDown = new TUpDown(this, IDC_UPDOWN1,
                              20,20,6,12,
                              pEdit);

TUpDown* pUpDown = new TUpDown(this, IDC_UPDOWN);
```

The UpDown Demonstration Program

This program demonstrates a couple of updown controls. One updown control is paired with an edit box as a buddy. The other updown control is coupled with a progress indicator by responding to the updown-control notifications. The source code for the demonstration is shown in Listings EC3.7, EC3.8, and EC3.9.

Listing EC3.7. Source code for the UPDOWN.H header file.

```
1: #define IDC_UDBUDDY     1000
2: #define IDC_EDIT        1001
3: #define IDC_PROGRESS1   1002
4: #define IDC_UDGAUGE     1003
5: #define IDC_GAUGE1      1004
```

Listing EC3.8. Source code for the UPDOWN.RC resource file.

```
1:  #include "updown.h"
2:
3:  MainDlg DIALOG DISCARDABLE  0, 0, 186, 94
4:  STYLE DS_MODALFRAME | WS_CHILD | WS_CAPTION | WS_SYSMENU | DS_3DLOOK
5:  FONT 8, "MS Sans Serif"
6:  BEGIN
7:      DEFPUSHBUTTON "&Quit",IDOK,129,7,50,14
8:      CONTROL       "Spin1",IDC_UDBUDDY,"msctls_updown32",
9:                    UDS_ARROWKEYS | WS_CHILD | UDS_SETBUDDYINT,
10:                   57,15,10,14
11:     EDITTEXT   IDC_EDIT,17,15,40,14,ES_AUTOHSCROLL
12:     CONTROL       "Spin2",IDC_UDGAUGE,"msctls_updown32",
13:                   UDS_ARROWKEYS | UDS_WRAP | UDS_HORZ | WS_CHILD,
14:                   153,50,16,14
15: END
```

Listing EC3.9. Source code for the UPDOWN.CPP program file.

```
1:  // UpDown Class Example
2:
3:  #include <owl/pch.h>
4:  #include <owl/updown.h>
5:  #include <owl/gauge.h>
6:  #include "updown.h"
7:
8:  class UpDownMainDlg : public TDialog
9:  {
10: public:
11:     UpDownMainDlg(TWindow *parent);
12:     virtual ~UpDownMainDlg()        {}
13:
14: protected:
```

```
15:     virtual void SetupWindow();
16:     bool EvBump(TNmUpDown& not);
17:
18: private:
19:     TUpDown* gaugeUpDown;
20:     TUpDown* buddyUpDown;
21:     TGauge*  gauge;
22:
23: DECLARE_RESPONSE_TABLE(UpDownMainDlg);
24: };
25: DEFINE_RESPONSE_TABLE1(UpDownMainDlg, TDialog)
26:     EV_UDN_DELTAPOS(IDC_UDGAUGE, EvBump),
27: END_RESPONSE_TABLE;
28:
29: class UpDownApp : public TApplication
30: {
31: public:
32:     UpDownApp() : TApplication()      {}
33:     virtual         ~UpDownApp()      {}
34:     virtual void    InitMainWindow();
35: };
36:
37: UpDownMainDlg::UpDownMainDlg (TWindow *parent)
38:     : TDialog(parent, "MainDlg", 0)
39: {
40:     // Bind to the up/down controls in the dialog template.
41:     gaugeUpDown = new TUpDown(this, IDC_UDGAUGE);
42:     buddyUpDown = new TUpDown(this, IDC_UDBUDDY);
43:
44:     // Create the guage control.
45:     gauge = new TGauge(this, "%d", IDC_GAUGE1, 70, 70, 240, 24);
46: }
47:
48: void UpDownMainDlg::SetupWindow()
49: {
50:     TDialog::SetupWindow();
51:
52:     // Attach the buddy control...
53:     buddyUpDown->SetBuddy(GetDlgItem(IDC_EDIT));
54:     buddyUpDown->SetRange(0, 10);
55:     buddyUpDown->SetPos(0);
56:
57:     // Resize and move the horizontal gauge so that it
58:     // lines up with the updown control.
59:     TRect udRect = gaugeUpDown->GetWindowRect();
60:     ScreenToClient(udRect.TopLeft());
61:     ScreenToClient(udRect.BottomRight());
62:     gauge->SetWindowPos( 0,
63:                          udRect.left-200, udRect.top,
64:                          200, udRect.Height(),
65:                          SWP_NOZORDER );
66:
67:     gauge->SetRange(0, 20);
68:     gauge->SetValue(10);
69:     gaugeUpDown->SetRange(0, 20);
70:     gaugeUpDown->SetPos(10);
```

continues

Listing EC3.9. continued

```
71: }
72:
73: bool UpDownMainDlg::EvBump(TNmUpDown& not)
74: {
75:    gauge->SetValue(not.iPos + not.iDelta);
76:    return false;
77: }
78:
79: void UpDownApp::InitMainWindow ()
80: {
81:    SetMainWindow(new TFrameWindow(0, "Up/Down Demo",
82:                                 new UpDownMainDlg(0), true));
83:    GetMainWindow()->Attr.Style |= WS_DLGFRAME | WS_CLIPCHILDREN;
84:    MainWindow->Attr.Style &= ~(WS_MAXIMIZEBOX | WS_THICKFRAME);
85:
86: }
87:
88: int OwlMain(int, char* [])
89: {
90:    return UpDownApp().Run();
91: }
```

A sample session of the UpDown Control demo is shown in Figure EC3.6.

Figure EC3.6.

The UpDown Control demonstration program.

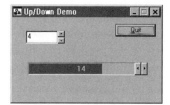

The most important thing to note here is just how little code there is for the updown control associated with the edit box. There are just four lines of code (42, 53-55) in UPDOWN.CPP, and all of them are there for initialization purposes. The lines encapsulate these steps:

1. Alias an OWL TUpDown object to the updown control.

2. Set the buddy control.

3. Set the range and set the initial value.

That's it. Everything else is handled internally to the updown control itself.

The updown control that is associated with the gauge is a little more involved. First, there is code (line 41) that binds the control to the OWL TUpDown object. Then there is some code (lines

59-65) that creates a TGauge object and aligns it to the updown control. Finally, on lines 67-70, you set the range for the gauge, set the range for the updown control, set the initial value for the updown control, and initialize the gauge to the updown control value.

After the initialization things get a little easier, but there is still one more thing to do. Every time the updown control changes value, you must set the gauge to match. This is handled in the EvBump notification handler (lines 73-77.) Here, you read the value of the updown control and set the gauge to match.

The Tab Control

The last control that we will look at in depth is the *tab control*. This control is based on the file folder tab metaphor. Looking at a tab control is a lot like looking at an open filing-cabinet drawer. An alternate way to think about the tab control is that of a collection of buttons. Each button, or tab, causes a particular event to occur. This control shows up a lot in Windows 95, particularly in conjunction with another Windows 95 Common Control, the property sheet. Figure EC3.7 shows the tab control.

Figure EC3.7.

The tab control.

| Name & Location | Date Modified | Advanced |

Tab controls are a bit more involved than the previous controls in this chapter. Table EC3.2 demonstrates the wide variety of flags that the tab control has.

Table EC3.2. Tab-control styles.

Section	Option	Description
Type	Tabs, Buttons	You have the option of making the tab control look like a collection of folder tabs or a collection of buttons.
Alignment	Right, Fixed, Ragged	Sets the tab styles to either right-justified, fixed width (as opposed to variable width), or ragged right.

continues

Table EC3.2. continued

Section	Option	Description
Focus Control	Normal, Never, Button	The normal setting for this resets the focus to the last control when any other control is pressed, including a tab. The Never setting means that the tab will never gain the focus. If the On Button Down option is selected, then a tab will receive the focus only when it's selected.
TabControl Flags	Tool Tips	This style causes the tab to create a tool-tip control to handle tool tips for each of the tabs.
	Multi-Line	Normally, the tab control keeps all of its tabs in one row. If there are too many tabs to be shown all at once, a horizontal updown control is used to scroll the line of tabs back and forth. This style causes the tab control to display the tabs in multiple rows.
	Border	Setting this flag causes the tab control to have a border.
	Force Icon Left	If icons are used in the tabs, then this will force their display into the left of the tab.
	Force Label Left	This forces the label text of the tabs to the left.
	Owner Draw	When set, the application will be responsible for drawing the individual tabs.

The tab control has three even notifications that you may want to handle. These are shown in Table EC3.3.

Table EC3.3. Tab control event notifications.

Event Notification	OWL Event Handler	Description
TCN_SELCHANGE	EV_TCN_SELCHANGE	This event indicates that the tab selection has just changed.
TCN_SELCHANGING	EV_TCN_SELCHANGING	This event is sent when the tab selection is about to change. To allow the change to occur, the handler should respond with `false`. To prevent the change, the handler responds with `true`.
TCN_KEYDOWN	EV_TCN_KEYDOWN	This event notifies the parent of a tab control that a key has been pressed.

OWL provides a couple of classes that encapsulate the tab-control functionality. These classes are TTabControl and TTabItem.

The *TTabControl* Class

The TTabControl class provides member functions that let you manipulate a tab control. Among the things that you can do are add new tabs, remove existing tabs, change the text on tabs, and so forth. Here are the TTabControl member functions.

The *TTabControl* Constructor

The declarations of the TTabControl constructors are as follows:

```
TTabControl(TWindow* parent, int id,
            int x, int y, int w, int h,
            TModule* module = 0);
TTabControl(TWindow* parent,
            int resourceId,
            TModule* module = 0);
```

The first form of the constructor is used to create a tab control from scratch. This tab control will have only a single line of tabs. If needed, though, the style can be changed to multiline by modifying the control window's attributes to include the TCS_MULTILINE style before the control is created.

The second form of the constructor is used to alias a tab control in a dialog resource to a TTabControl object.

Examples:

```
tabControl1 = new TTabControl(this, IDC_TAB1, 10, 10, 360, 40);
tabControl2 = new TTabControl(this, IDC_TAB2);
```

The *Add* Function

Syntax

The declarations of the Add member functions are as follows:

```
int Add(const char far* tabText);
int Add(const TTabItem& tabItem);
```

The Add function adds a new tab to the tab control. The first version creates a tab using the specified text string. The second version creates a tab using a TTabItem object (to be described momentarily). The index of the new tab is returned if successful. If unsuccessful, a -1 is returned.

Examples:

```
index = tabControl->Add("New Tab");
tabControl->Add( tabItem );
```

The *Delete* Function

Syntax

The declaration of the Delete member function is as follows:

```
bool Delete(int index);
```

This function deletes the tab specified by the index value. The function returns true if successful. The first tab is index zero.

Example:

```
tabControl->Delete(5);
```

The *DeleteAll* Function

Syntax

The declaration of the DeleteAll member function is as follows:

```
bool DeleteAll();
```

This function deletes all of the tabs. The function returns true if successful.

Example:

```
tabControl->DeleteAll();
```

The *GetCount* Function

Syntax

The declaration of the GetCount member function is as follows:

```
int GetCount() const;
```

This function returns the number of tabs in the tab control.

Example:

```
int count = tabControl->GetCount();
```

The *GetItem* Function

Syntax

The declaration of the GetItem member function is as follows:

```
bool GetItem(int index, TTabItem& item) const;
```

This function returns all of the information about the tab specified by the index. The first tab index is zero.

EC3

Example:

```
TTabItem tabItem;
tabControl->GetItem(0,tabItem);
```

The *GetRowCount* Function

Syntax

The declaration of the GetRowCount member function is as follows:

```
int GetRowCount() const;
```

This function returns the number of rows in the tab control. Only tab controls with the TCS_MULTILINE style can have more than one row.

Example:

```
int rows = tabControl->GetRowCount();
```

The *GetSel* Function

Syntax

The declaration of the GetSel member function is

```
int GetSel() const;
```

This function returns the index of the currently selected tab. If no tab is selected, the function returns -1.

Example:

```
int index = tabControl->GetSel();
```

Syntax

The *GetToolTips* Function

The declaration of the GetToolTips member function is

```
HWND GetToolTips() const;
```

If the tab control has the TCS_TOOLTIPS style, this function will return the window handle of the tool-tip control. This window handle can be used to construct a TToolTip object. The function returns 0 if there is no tool-tip control associated with the tab control.

Example:

```
toolTip = new TToolTip( tabControl->GetToolTips() );
```

Syntax

The *Insert* Function

The declarations of the Insert member functions are as follows:

```
int Insert(const char far* tabText, int index);
int Insert(const TTabItem&, int index);
```

The Insert function inserts a new tab into the tab control. The index specifies the location of the new tab. The first version creates a tab using the specified text string. The second function creates a tab using a TTabItem object. The index of the new tab is returned if successful. If unsuccessful, -1 is returned.

Examples:

```
index = tabControl->Insert("Newer Tab", 5);
tabControl->Add( tabItem, 5 );
```

Syntax

The *SetItem* Function

The declaration of the SetItem member function is as follows:

```
bool SetItem(int index, const TTabItem& item);
```

This function sets some or all of the information for a particular tab. The *mask* member of TTabItem object determines which information is set. (Refer to the following TTabItem section for further information.) The function returns true if the function was successful.

Example:

```
TTabItem tabItem(TCIF_TEXT);
tabItem.SetLabel("Changed Text");
tabControl->SetItem(4, tabItem);
```

The *SetSel* Function

The declaration of the SetSel member function is as follows:

```
int SetSel(int index);
```

This function sets a new current index. The function returns the previously selected index or -1 if the function was unsuccessful.

Example:

```
tabControl->SetSel(5);
```

> **Note:** The TCN_SELCHANGE or TCN_SELCHANGING notifications are *not* sent when the selected tab is changed by using the SetSel function.

The *TTabItem* Class

The TTabItem class is a handy way to carry around the bits of information associated with each tab in a tab control.

The *TTabItem* Constructor

The declarations of the TTabItem constructors are as follows:

```
TTabItem(uint mask);
TTabItem(const TC_ITEM& tbItem);
TTabItem(const TTabControl& ctl, int index,
        uint mask, int buffLen = 0,
        char far* buffer = 0);
```

The first form of the constructor is used to create a TTabItem with a particular mask. See Table EC3.4 for a list of mask values. Mask values can be ORed together.

The second form of the constructor is used to create a TTabItem object from a TC_ITEM structure. This structure is what TTabItem is based on, what the actual Win32 SDK uses; it's useful to have the ability to create a TTabItem object from its basic building block.

The third form of the constructor is used to create a TTabItem object from the contents of a particular tab in a tab control. ctl is a reference to the TTabControl in question. index is the index of the tab item. mask specifies which information to get. buffer and buffLen specify a buffer, in case the desired information is the tab text.

713

Examples:

```
TTabItem tabItem(TCIF_TEXT);
TTabItem item(*tabControl,
              tabControl->GetSel(),
              TCIF_TEXT,
              sizeof(tabText), tabText);
```

Table EC3.4. Tab-item mask values.

Mask Value	Meaning
TCIF_TEXT	Get or set tab text information.
TCIF_PARAM	Get or set lParam. lParam is an LPARAM-sized piece of user-defined data associated with each tab.
TCIF_IMAGE	Get or set the tab's image data.

The *SetIcon* Function

Syntax

The declaration of the SetIcon function is as follows:

```
void SetIcon(int imageIndex);
```

This function sets the TTabItem's image information. imageIndex is an index to the tab image.

Example:

```
tabItem.SetIcon(IDX_LION);
```

The *SetLabel* Function

Syntax

The declaration of the SetLabel function is as follows:

```
void SetLabel(const char far* str, int len = 0);
```

This function sets the TTabItem's tab text.

Example:

```
tabItem.SetLabel("The Lion");
```

The *SetParam* Function

Syntax

The declaration of the SetParam function is as follows:

```
void SetParam(TParam2 lParam);
```

This function sets the TTabItem's user defined lParam value.

Example:

```
tabItem.SetParam(lionCount);
```

The Tab-Control Demonstration Program

This is a program that exercises many of the different features of the tab control. New tabs can be added with the New Tab button and removed with the Remove Tab button. To change the text that is on a tab, select that tab, enter the desired text into the edit box, and then click on the *Set Text* button. The source for the tab-control demonstration is shown in Listings EC3.10, EC3.11, and EC3.12.

 Listing EC3.10. Source code for the TABS.H header file.

```
1: #define IDC_TAB        1001
2: #define IDC_ADD        1002
3: #define IDC_REMOVE     1003
4: #define IDC_EDIT       1004
5: #define IDC_SETTEXT    1005
6: #define IDC_TABSEL     1006
```

Listing EC3.11. Source code for the TABS.RC resource file.

```
1:  #include "tabs.h"
2:
3:  #ifndef SS_ETCHEDFRAME
4:  #   define SS_ETCHEDFRAME (0x12)
5:  #endif
6:
7:  MainDlg DIALOG 0, 0, 262, 138
8:  STYLE DS_MODALFRAME ¦ DS_3DLOOK ¦ WS_CHILD ¦ WS_CAPTION ¦ WS_SYSMENU
9:  FONT 8, "MS Sans Serif"
10: {
11:     PUSHBUTTON "&New Tab", IDC_ADD, 35, 71, 50, 15
12:     PUSHBUTTON "&Remove Tab", IDC_REMOVE, 35, 89, 50, 13
13:     LTEXT "&Tab Text", -1, 144, 74, 20, 8
14:     EDITTEXT IDC_EDIT, 168, 71, 72, 14, ES_AUTOHSCROLL
15:     PUSHBUTTON "&Set Text", IDC_SETTEXT, 144, 86, 96, 14
16:     DEFPUSHBUTTON "&Quit", IDOK, 106, 117, 50, 14
17:     CTEXT "Selected Tab is ""%s""", IDC_TABSEL, 44, 48, 170, 10
18:     CONTROL "", -1, "static", SS_ETCHEDFRAME ¦ WS_CHILD ¦ WS_VISIBLE,
19:         42, 46, 174, 12
20:     CONTROL "Tab1", IDC_TAB, "SYSTABCONTROL32", WS_CHILD ¦ WS_VISIBLE,
21:         0,0,262,138
22: }
```

Listing EC3.12. Source code for the TABS.CPP program file.

```
1:   // Tabs Class Example
2:
3:   #include <owl/pch.h>
4:   #include <owl/tabctrl.h>
5:   #include <owl/edit.h>
6:   #include <owl/checkbox.h>
7:   #include "tabs.h"
8:
9:   class TabsMainDlg : public TDialog
10:  {
11:  public:
12:     TabsMainDlg(TWindow *parent);
13:     virtual ~TabsMainDlg() {}
14:
15:  protected:
16:     virtual void SetupWindow();
17:
18:     void TabSelChange(TNotify& selChange);
19:
20:     void AddTab(WPARAM wParam=0);
21:     void RemoveTab(WPARAM wParam=0);
22:     void SetTabText(WPARAM wParam=0);
23:
24:  private:
25:     TTabControl*    tabControl;
26:     int             tabCount;
27:
28:  DECLARE_RESPONSE_TABLE(TabsMainDlg);
29:  };
30:  DEFINE_RESPONSE_TABLE1(TabsMainDlg, TDialog)
31:     EV_TCN_SELCHANGE(IDC_TAB, TabSelChange),
32:     EV_CHILD_NOTIFY_ALL_CODES(IDC_ADD, AddTab),
33:     EV_CHILD_NOTIFY_ALL_CODES(IDC_REMOVE, RemoveTab),
34:     EV_CHILD_NOTIFY_ALL_CODES(IDC_SETTEXT, SetTabText),
35:  END_RESPONSE_TABLE;
36:
37:  class TabsApp : public TApplication
38:  {
39:  public:
40:     TabsApp() : TApplication()          {}
41:     virtual      ~TabsApp()             {}
42:     virtual void   InitMainWindow();
43:  };
44:
45:  TabsMainDlg::TabsMainDlg (TWindow *parent)
46:     :  TDialog(parent, "MainDlg", 0),
47:        tabCount(6)
48:  {
49:     tabControl = new TTabControl(this, IDC_TAB);
50:  }
51:
52:  void TabsMainDlg::SetupWindow()
53:  {
54:     TDialog::SetupWindow();
55:
```

```
56:     //Initialize the tabs to 5 buttons, single line.
57:     tabControl->Add("Quince");
58:     tabControl->Add("Snug");
59:     tabControl->Add("Bottom");
60:     tabControl->Add("Flute");
61:     tabControl->Add("Snout");
62:
63:     // Update the static display.
64:     TabSelChange(TNotify());
65: }
66:
67: // ----------------------------------------
68: // Selection just changed
69: //
70: void TabsMainDlg::TabSelChange(TNotify& /*selChange*/)
71: {
72:     // Retrieve the text of the selected item
73:     // and display it.
74:     //
75:     char textBuf[128] = "No tabs are selected";
76:     if (tabControl->GetCount() > 0)
77:         {
78:         char tabText[50];
79:         TTabItem item(*tabControl,
80:                     tabControl->GetSel(),
81:                     TCIF_TEXT,
82:                     sizeof(tabText), tabText);
83:         ::wsprintf( textBuf,
84:                     "The Selected Tab is \"%s\"",
85:                     tabText);
86:         }
87:     SetDlgItemText(IDC_TABSEL, textBuf);
88: }
89:
90: void TabsMainDlg::AddTab(WPARAM /*wParam*/)
91: {
92:     // Add a new tab...
93:     char tabText[50];
94:     ::wsprintf(tabText, "Tab #%d", tabCount++);
95:     int newTab = tabControl->Add(tabText);
96:     tabControl->SetSel(newTab);
97:     TabSelChange(TNotify());
98: }
99:
100: void TabsMainDlg::RemoveTab(WPARAM /*wParam*/)
101: {
102:     int selectedTab = tabControl->GetSel();
103:     tabControl->Delete(selectedTab);
104:     tabControl->SetSel(0);
105:     TabSelChange(TNotify());
106: }
107:
108: void TabsMainDlg::SetTabText(WPARAM /*wParam=0*/)
109: {
110:     // Get the edit box's content...
```

continues

717

Listing EC3.12. continued

```
111:    char buffer[50];
112:    GetDlgItemText(IDC_EDIT, buffer, sizeof(buffer));
113:
114:    TTabItem tabItem(TCIF_TEXT);
115:    tabItem.SetLabel(buffer);
116:
117:    // Change the text on the selected tab.
118:    int    selectedTab = tabControl->GetSel();
119:    tabControl->SetItem(selectedTab, tabItem);
120:
121:    TabSelChange(TNotify());
122: }
123:
124: void TabsApp::InitMainWindow ()
125: {
126:    SetMainWindow(new TFrameWindow(0,
127:                                   "Tabs Demo",
128:                                   new TabsMainDlg(0),
129:                                   true));
130:    MainWindow->Attr.Style |= WS_DLGFRAME;
131:    MainWindow->Attr.Style &= ~(WS_MAXIMIZEBOX | WS_THICKFRAME);
132: }
133:
134: int OwlMain(int, char* [])
135: {
136:    return TabsApp().Run();
137: }
```

A sample session of the Tab Control demonstration is shown in Figure EC3.8.

Figure EC3.8.
*The Tab Control demon-
stration program.*

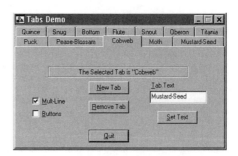

Analysis　The actual tab control in this program is specified in the TABS.RC file on lines 20-21. A couple of things to note about it are that it is sized to take up the entire dialog and that it is listed last. Sizing it to the dialog gives the dialog a nice, raised edge that makes it look as if all of the other controls are on the tab page. Listing the tab control last insures that all of the other controls will be drawn on top of the tab. If the tab control were first, you could still operate the other controls, but they would be difficult to see.

The tab control is aliased to an OWL TTabControl object on line 49 of TABS.CPP. Five initial tabs are created in the SetupWindow function on lines 57-61.

The program contains an event handler for TCN_SELCHANGE. Upon receipt of this event, the program will retrieve the text of the newly selected tab and copy it into a static text control. This is shown on lines 70-88.

The AddTab and RemoveTab functions are called when the Add Tab and Remove Tab buttons are clicked, respectively. Those functions add and remove tabs, just as one would expect. The code for these functions is on lines 90-98 and 100-106.

The SetTabText function on lines 108-122 is used to change the tab's text. It is called when the Set Text button is pressed. The function reads the contents of the edit box and sets the currently selected tab to this string.

Other Windows 95 Common Controls

There are several other controls included with the Windows 95 Common Controls collection. Most of these controls have a corresponding OWL class. Exceptions are noted here. For further information on how to program using these classes, refer to the ObjectWindows Reference.

Animation Control—Use the TAnimateCtrl class. This control displays an .AVI file. Often you will want to use this to indicate to the user that a slow operation, such as a file copy, is still proceeding. Figure EC3.9 shows an example of an animation control.

Figure EC3.9.
An animation control.

Header Control—Use the TColumnHeader class. This control is a convenient way to head up columns of data in a ListView control (see the following). Features of this control allow for varying the column widths and selecting a particular column for sorting. Figure EC3.10 shows an example of a column header control.

Figure EC3.10.
A column header control.

Name		Size	Type	Modified	

Hotkey Control—Use the THotKey class. This control enables the user to enter a key combination that the application will assign to a specific action. As you can see from Figure EC3.11, the hotkey control is essentially just a special-purpose edit box.

Figure EC3.11.
A hotkey control.

ListView Control—Use the TListWindow, TListColumn, and TListItem classes. These controls can be used to display a list of items. An example of the use of a ListView control is the file window in the Windows Explorer. Figure EC3.12 shows a ListView control.

Figure EC3.12.
A ListView control.

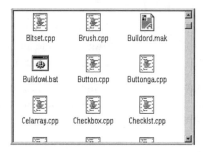

Warning: Do not confuse the OWL TListView class with the Windows 95 List View control. The TListView class was part of OWL before the Windows 95 controls were released. It is unfortunate that they share this name.

Property Sheets—Use the TPropertyPage and TPropertySheet classes. Property sheets are the tab-controlled, multilayered dialogs that can be seen all over Windows 95. The property-sheet control is used in conjunction with the tab control to implement these. The property-sheet control is also used extensively (without the tab control) to implement *Wizards*—those helpful, multipaged dialogs that guide you through tricky processes. Figure EC3.13 shows a property-sheet control used to implement a property sheet.

Status Bar Control—OWL provides its own status-bar class, TStatusBar. It does not use the Windows 95 status-bar control. The application user won't care which you use. Most of the time, it will be easier to use TStatusBar in place of the Windows 95 common control. See Figure EC3.14 for an example of a Status Bar.

ToolBar Control—OWL provides its own tool-bar class, TControlBar, as well. Again, the Windows 95 ToolBar control is not used. Most of the time it will be easier to use TControlBar in place of the Windows 95 common control. See Figure EC3.15 for an example of a tool bar.

Figure EC3.13.

A property-sheet control.

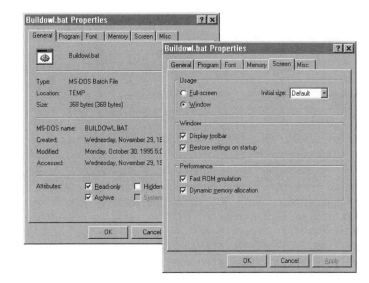

EC3

Figure EC3.14.

The OWL status bar.

Figure EC3.15.

An example of a tool bar.

TrackBar Control—Track bars are also referred to as *sliders*. Including track bars in your program, as it turns out, is a lot like including the progress indicators/gauges discussed earlier in this chapter. You can use either the Windows 95 track-bar control or the OWL THSlider and TVSlider classes. The benefit of the Windows 95 track bar is that you can manipulate it using the resource editor. On the other hand, the OWL sliders have a larger feature set. Neither situation is optimal. Figure EC3.16 shows a horizontal and a vertical track bar.

Figure EC3.16.

Track bars.

> **Tip:** If you do use the OWL sliders, make sure that your resource script contains the line #include <owl/slider.rc>. This file contains bit maps that are used for the OWL slider knobs. (Or you can provide your own customized slider-knob bit maps!)

TreeView Control—Use the TTreeView class. This control can be used to display information in a hierarchical format. The Windows Explorer uses this for its directory window. See Figure EC3.17 for an example of a TreeView control.

Figure EC3.17.
A TreeView control.

Summary

This extra-credit chapter took a look at several of the new Windows 95 Common Controls. It covered the most useful features of the tool-tip, progress-indicator, updown-control, and tab controls. It then took a cursory look at the rest of the new Windows 95 Common Controls. Along the way, you saw that OWL does not always provide a one-to-one mapping of functionality with the native Windows API.

Q&A

Q Why is the RelayEvent member function of the TToolTips class special?

A Because it is used to relay mouse messages to the tool-tip control.

Q What are the advantages to using the OWL emulation version of the TGauge class over the Windows 95 Progress Indicator version?

A The emulated TGauge class can be vertical as well as horizontal. The color of the bar can be changed by the program. The TGauge can have text inside it.

Q What is the advantage of using the Windows 95 Progress Indicator instead of the OWL TGauge?

A The Windows 95 Progress Indicator can be edited using the resource editor.

Q Why should a tab control be listed last in a resource script?

A Because, if it is not, it will hide any of the controls that are placed "on top of" the tab control.

Q Where can I get further information about the Windows 95 Common Controls?

A Look in the *Win32 Online Help* file and the *Object Windows Reference* file, which are included with Borland C++ 5.

Exercise

1. Write a program that uses the TSlider class to change the contents of a TGauge object.

Extra Credit

4+

The Resource Editor

Many PC users who worked with DOS applications have come to appreciate Windows applications. Windows (along with the Apple Macintosh) has popularized the graphical user interface (GUI). This interface is simpler to use and is more compatible across diverse applications than the character-based user interface of MS-DOS and PC-DOS. In addition, software vendors such as Microsoft and Borland have shaped the development of programming for the masses by incorporating visual programming tools in their software-development packages. Although visual programming did exist in the 1980s, it was restricted to special university projects. This chapter looks at the visual programming aspects of Borland C++ 5 that are significantly supported by the Integrated Resource Editor. The Resource Editor employs visual tools to help you create resources that can be used by all Windows-compliant programming languages, not just Borland C++. In this extra-credit chapter, you will learn about the following topics:

- General functions of the Resource Editor
- Types of resources supported by the Resource Editor
- Resource files
- Visual editing
- Image-based picture editing
- Menu editing
- String tables and version-information editing
- Dialog-box editing

Resource Overview

Resources are special ingredients of Windows applications. Using resources, you can modify messages, menus, and icons, and even use different human languages without having to change the source code or recompile it. Thus, for example, you can employ resources in different human languages with the same source code.

In order to achieve this, Windows provides a scripting language to describe resources. These are what you've been typing in for the .RC files for the chapters in this book so far. You can develop resources by typing their script in .RC and .DLG files, in a manner that is typical of any programming language. In order to get a full listing of the script commands, consult the help files.

The Resource Editor is a powerful tool that enables you to develop resources using visual programming techniques. In other words, you can "draw" the resources you need using a mouse, visual tools, and a set of menus and dialog boxes. The Resource Editor then translates your drawings into the proper resource files, such as the script resource .RC files or the precompiled .RES files.

This chapter does not discuss the Resource Editor from A to Z. Instead, it serves to illustrate how to use this graphical tool in creating significant (and generally visual) ingredients of Windows programs. As usual, for the full story, go to the reference manuals.

Types of Resources

The Resource Editor supports the following kinds of resources:

- ☐ Accelerators
- ☐ Bit maps
- ☐ Cursors
- ☐ Dialog boxes and extended dialog boxes
- ☐ Icons
- ☐ Menus and extended menus
- ☐ String tables
- ☐ User-defined and RCDATA resources
- ☐ VERSIONINFO

These resources are briefly defined in the following subsections.

EC4

Accelerators

Accelerators are basically "hot keys" that enable you to invoke a command without first choosing its parent menus and options. Accelerators offer a quick and direct way to perform a task and are very useful for invoking nested commands.

Bit maps

Bit maps are binary representations of a graphical image. The popular Windows controls—pushbuttons, radio buttons, and scroll bars—use bit maps. The Resource Editor enables you to create bit maps using the Paint editor. This editor supports the drawing, coloring, and editing of bit maps.

Cursors

Cursors are special bit maps of a specific size (32×32 pixels). A cursor displays the location of the mouse on the screen. Windows supports using different cursor shapes to signal various tasks. For example, the hourglass cursor indicates that a Windows application is busy processing data. The Resource Editor enables you to create cursors with the Paint editor.

Dialog Boxes and Extended Dialog Boxes

Dialog boxes are special windows that interact with the application user. Typically, dialog boxes prompt you to enter or confirm current data. The Resource Editor supports creating dialog-box resources and visually drawing their controls. This feature is the highlight of this chapter. Extended dialog boxes are special dialog boxes supported by the 32-bit versions of Windows.

Icons

Icons are special bit maps, each being 16×16, 32×32, or 64×64 (for high-resolution devices) pixels in size. Windows uses icons to represent minimized windows and programs on the Start menu. Windows also supports inserting icons in windows and dialog boxes to incorporate small visual images.

Menus and Extended Menus

Menus are resources that offer selections and options for the diverse operations of a Windows application. Because menus are resources, you can create different menu resources in different human languages. This enables you to distribute your applications to various countries. Extended menus are special menus supported by the 32-bit versions of Windows.

String Tables

String tables are resources that contain text for various messages, prompts, and descriptions. Like menu resources, you can create different string tables in different human languages to support multinational versions of your software. This requires that you avoid embedding string literals in your source code and instead rely on the string table resources.

User-Defined and RCDATA Resources

The user-defined and RCDATA resources support special information that is incorporated into the executable files. This kind of information provides read-only data used by the host program to initialize itself.

VERSIONINFO

The VERSIONINFO resource is a special version-stamp resource for applications.

Resource Files

The Resource Editor works with the following kinds of resource files:

□ *The resource script files with .RC extensions.* These text files contain resource statements, which define various kinds of resources, such as menus, accelerators, string tables, and dialog boxes.

□ *The binary .RES files,* which contain compiled resources. The Resource Editor can read and produce either .RC or .RES files. In other words, you can ask the Resource Editor to read a .RES file, decompile it, and then create a corresponding .RC file that you can edit.

□ *The bit-mapped resource files .BMP, .ICO, and .CUR files,* which contain bit map, icon, and cursor resources. Note that these could also be stored directly in the .RC or .RES file.

□ *The dialog-box script resource files, with the extension .DLG.* Typically, these files contain resource scripts for reusable dialog boxes. You can include the .DLG files (and also other .RC files) in an .RC file using the special preprocessing directive #include.

□ *The executable .EXE and dynamic-link library .DLL files,* which contain executable code bound together with compiled resources. The Resource Editor enables you to read resources in .EXE and .DLL files, decompile them, edit them, and then save the new resources back to the .EXE and .DLL binary files. Note that this also applies to the various other file extensions that are really just forms of dynamic-link libraries (.DRV, .SCR, and so on).

Visual Editing

The editor itself is integrated into the IDE in the same way as the source-code editor, the compiler, and the debugger. As I'm sure you've noted, when you create a new project, one of the nodes that is automatically added is the .RC node. If you now double-click on this node, the resource editor loads and you are presented with a window that contains a list of the resource items.

By default, this window starts out as having two sections separated by a vertical bar. The section on the left contains a hierarchical list of the objects in the resource file, and the section on the right contains a preview area. This preview area shows an image or source listing of the item highlighted in the left section. This division of sections can be changed to a horizontal division, or the preview section can be removed altogether.

The window starts out initially empty, save for a single, empty entry for holding identifiers as shown in Figure EC4.1. You might also notice that the menu at the top of the IDE has changed to accommodate a new menu item: Resource. The contents of the Resource menu are listed in Table EC4.1.

Figure EC4.1.
The empty Resource window.

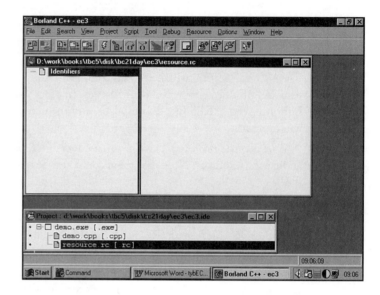

Table EC4.1. The Resource menu options.

Menu Item	Meaning
New	Creates a new resource item.
Edit...	Opens up a resource item for editing visually.
Edit as text...	Opens up a resource item for editing textually. This lets you edit the script itself.
View...	Views the resource item.
Save resource as...	Saves the resource item as a separate file. You can then include this item in the .RC file with an external reference.
Resource attributes...	Modifies such things as the name of the resource item, its memory options, and its language options.
Identifiers	Edits the list of identifiers used for resources.

Obviously, the key menu command here is New, which enables you to create new items. When you select this, you are presented with the New Resource dialog box containing a list box with the various resource types you are allowed to create—in addition to an all-important Options... button, which enables you to set specifics of the new resource item.

Note that after you start editing a resource, the IDE's menu acquires a new pop-up menu with the type of resource being edited. This menu contains various commands specific to the resource.

Pictures

There are a number of resources that can be classed as pictures or image-based resources. These include bit maps, cursors, and icons. Each of these are visual picture elements that are edited in essentially the same manner, with only a few differences in features applicable to them.

The first difference in features is evident in the options available when creating them. Figures EC4.2, EC4.3, and EC4.4 show the different dialogs for the bit map, cursor, and icon option screens, respectively.

Figure EC4.2.
The Bitmap Options dialog.

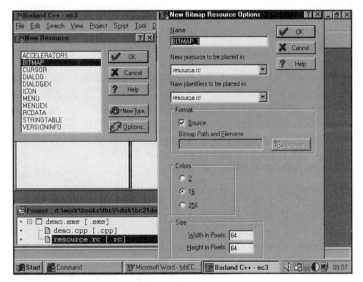

Figure EC4.3.
The Cursor Options dialog.

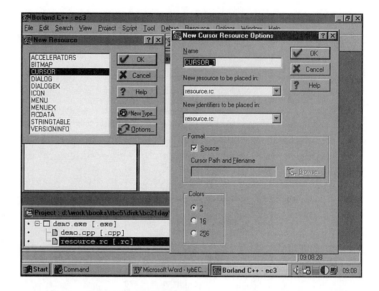

Figure EC4.4.
The Icon Options dialog.

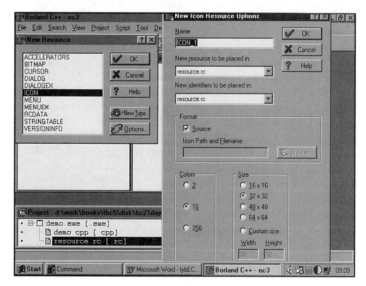

You should note a general pattern of providing options to set the name of the bit map as well as where new resources and identifiers will be placed. These options are the same for virtually all of the resources, image-based or not. The ones that vary with the image-based resources are the Format, Colors, and Size options.

The Format option enables you to specify whether the image will be stored in an ASCII script format or as a binary file. If you accept the default of the Source box being checked, then a block of incomprehensible ASCII representations (in hexadecimal) of the image is stored in the .RC file. If the Source box is unchecked, then the Path and Filename edit box are available, and you are able to specify the file in which to store the appropriate binary resource (.BMP for bit maps, .CUR for cursors, and .ICO for icons). In the .RC file, this binary resource is referred to by an appropriate inclusion statement.

The Colors option gives you the option of specifying either two colors (black and white), 16 colors (for standard Windows 3.x and earlier applications) or 256 colors (for more modern applications). When selecting the color depth to use, you need to keep in mind a few things. Number one is that the 16-bit versions of Windows are incapable of handling cursors of more than two colors. Also, they are incapable of handling icons of greater than 16 colors.

The Size option varies slightly between the three image-based resources. For bit maps, you can specify any size you desire. Cursors are always the same size, and so this option doesn't even show up for cursors. When it comes to the size of an icon, however, you are presented with some very specific size options, including the ability to specify a custom size. The 16-bit versions of Windows made use of only the 32×32 size icons. With the advent of the newer 32-bit versions, other sizes of icons are possible. The old standard 32×32 is still available, but now there is also a 16×16 size; this is the icon that is displayed in the upper-left corner of windows in Windows 95. The larger-sized icons are used for higher resolution screens.

Editing the images themselves is fairly similar to any paint application you might have used, including the Paint program that comes with Windows. There are, however, a few key differences. For one thing, instead of presenting a single, unified window with all the various toolbars, the default has the color and tools bars as floating windows. These can, however, be docked with the main IDE window by dragging the smaller windows to the various edges. Figure EC4.5 shows an example of a cursor being edited.

There are two special features—one of which applies to both icons and cursors, the other of which applies only to cursors. The first special feature is the ability to specify both a background and an inverse section of the image. That's what those two large X symbols on the right side of the color bar are. The top symbol, when selected as the drawing color, paints portions of the image that are to be transparent; that is, whenever the cursor or icon is drawn, the portions that contain the transparent color show whatever was beneath that location on the screen. Similarly, the inverse color inverts whatever was on the background when the image is drawn on the screen.

The cursor's special feature is its hot spot. This is the set of coordinates on the cursor that specify where it's supposed to be pointing. For example, on a standard arrow cursor, the hot spot is at the tip of the arrow. You can set the cursor's hot spot from the Cursor menu's Set Hot Spot... command.

Figure EC4.5.
The Cursor editor.

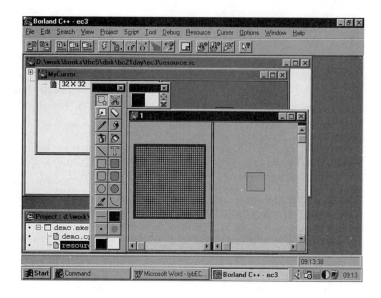

Menus

The interface for creating menus is quite different from that of painting images. The first differences you come to are the options available for the new menu, as shown in Table EC4.2. As you can see, these options are contained in four radio buttons separated into two groups: Menubar Styles, for the types of menus that are attached to windows; and Pop-up Menu Styles, for menus that are meant to pop up at the press of the right mouse button.

Table EC4.2. New Menu resource options.

Style	Meaning
Simple Menubar	Creates a very simple menu bar containing a simple pop-up item that, itself, contains a single menu item. These can then be modified, and you can add to them.
Full Application Menubar	Creates a menu filled with a good set of initial entries useful for an application's menu bar. These entries include the File, Edit, Window, and Help drop-down menus as well as various appropriate entries for each.
Simple Pop-up Menu	Creates a pop-up menu that's initially empty, save for a single, initial menu item that's meant to be changed.
Full Pop-up Menu	Creates a pop-up menu that initializes with Cut, Copy, Paste, and Properties menu items.

The menu editor consists of a window containing the menu to be edited and a property inspector, as shown in Figure EC4.6. As you select the various menu items and pop-ups in the menu window, you'll note that the property inspector changes its values to display the appropriate information for the selected item, as detailed in Table EC4.3. You can type directly into the menu editor to modify menu entry names, and you can right-click on items to obtain a pop-up menu with, among other things, commands for inserting new items and pop-ups into the menu.

Figure EC4.6.

The menu resource editor.

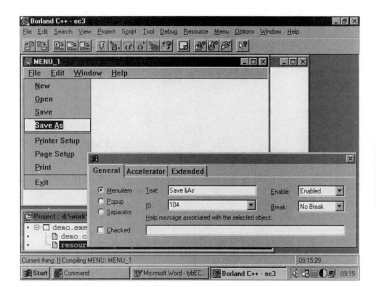

Table EC4.3. Menu property inspector.

Tab	Control	Meaning
General	Menuitem, Popup, Separator	These radio buttons select the type of the selected menu item. A menu item is a standard command, a pop-up opens up to reveal a new submenu, and separators are used to visually separate menu commands.
	Checked	When this check box is checked, so will be the menu item.

continues

Table EC4.3. continued

Tab	Control	Meaning
	Text	This is the text of the item as it appears in the menu. If there is an ampersand character (&) in the text item, the character immediately following it will be underlined. Note that if there are mul-tiple ampersands, only the last item will appear under-lined.
	ID	This applies only to menu items and is the ID that will be returned from the menu when the item is selected.
	Enable	This combo box enables you to select whether or not the menu is initially Enabled, Disabled, or Grayed.
	Break	The break options are No Break, Menu Bar Break, Menu Break, and Help Break.
	Help message	The help message typed here can be used by the application for display on its status bar.
Accelerator	Key	This holds the key value to be used as an accelera-tor (these are the accelerator items you typically see on the right side of a menu next to a command).
	ASCII, Virtual Key Control, Alt, Shift, Invert	These are the key modifiers used when pressing the accelerator key. For example, if Control is checked and the key is "N", then the accelerator is Ctrl+N.
	Record	By clicking this button, you are presented with a dialog asking you to press the keystroke combina-tion you wish for the accelerator; the properties are updated automatically.
Extended	Default	Sets a menu item as the default.
	Highlight	Highlights the menu item.

Tab	Control	Meaning
	Radio checkmark	Displays a radio button next to a checked menu item.
	Help ID	Specifies the help text ID associated with the selected menu item.

You'll quickly note that you are able to insert new menu items only before current ones. This can be somewhat inconvenient (at least it is for me) when you want to create the menu in a top-down fashion. Rest assured, however, that you can easily create any menu item you wish, then you can drag it to its final destination.

String Tables and Version Information

The string tables should be pretty much self-explanatory. For each string table you create, you are presented with the text script source code for the string table. The first item is created for you to help you with the format of the entries, which simply consists of a string ID followed (after a comma) by the string to be associated with that ID.

The version information is similar in that you edit the script source code directly. Again, given what the fields are initialized to, you should be able to figure out what they're for. The slightly cryptic header can usually be safely ignored; just concentrate on the lines in the first block of statements that begin with the term `"VALUE"`. For information on other fields that can be added here, consult the reference material.

Dialogs

Now we get to the meat of the resource editor. Although the other items will get used for various applications, it's the dialog section that gets the most use. Figure EC4.7 shows a sample session with the dialog resource editor. There's a property Inspector, as you've seen in previous editors. For the main dialogs (sometimes referred to as forms), this property inspector provides five property tabs, each with several settings, as shown in Table EC4.4. There are also two other tool bars: the Tools palette and the Controls palette. The former provides a number of buttons enabling you to align controls, and the latter provides numerous controls that can be applied to the dialog box. These controls are separated into sections to help make them easier to locate.

Figure EC4.7.

The dialog resource editor.

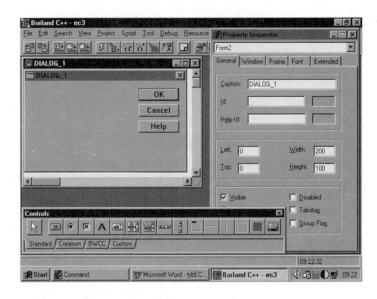

Table EC4.4. The Dialog property inspector.

Tab	Control	Meaning
General	Caption	This is the text that will appear in the dialog's title bar.
	Id	This is the ID that is used to identify the dialog in the resources, the value that is used to load it.
	Help Id	The help ID is used in calling up the appropriate help topic in the help file.
	Left, Top, Width, Height	These specify the position and size of the dialog. You can enter the values here, but you will usually set the dialog's size by stretching the dialog itself in the editor.
	Visible	If this isn't checked, then the dialog won't be initially visible and will have to be shown by the loading application.
	Horizontal Scrollbar	This, when checked, provides a horizontal scroll bar at the bottom of the dialog.
	Vertical Scrollbar	This, when checked, provides a vertical scroll bar at the right of the dialog.

Tab	Control	Meaning
	Disabled	If applied to a dialog, disables the dialog, thus preventing user input. This flag is more commonly applied to a control in a dialog that grays it out and prevents user input to that one control.
	Tabstop	Specifies that a particular control can be selected in the dialog when the user presses the Tab key.
	Group Flag	Indicates the first control in a group. This mostly affects such things as groups of radio buttons.
Window	Class	This is the window class used for the dialog. Normally, you won't ever want to touch this; it's mainly used for such things as subclassing the dialog window, a topic much too advanced for this book.
	Menu	If you want to place a menu in the dialog, you can do so by specifying its ID in this edit box.
	Window Type	The window lets you specify the kind of window the dialog should be. If you want to use the dialog as a part of another window, then you should set this to Child.
	Initial State	This specifies how the dialog should be shown when initially displayed. This, though, is often superseded when it's brought up by the application.
	Positioning	The names of these four options are pretty self-explanatory; they affect how the dialog will be positioned on the screen.
	Clipping	The clipping attributes determine how the dialog will affect and be affected by other windows.
Frame	Frame Type	The standard dialog frame is simply a border. Thick frames are what allow users to resize a window.
	Frame Attributes	These affect what will appear at the top of the dialog. Note that most of these won't show up at all unless the Caption box is checked.

EC4

continues

Table EC4.4. continued

Tab	Control	Meaning
	Misc Flags	These flags deserve the designation of miscellaneous. The 3-D Look option, it should be noted, makes a difference only in Windows 3.*x*; Windows 95 and Windows NT automatically give dialogs the 3-D look.
Font	Name	Sets the name of the font to use for the dialog. Note that this font applies to everything appearing in the dialog; you cannot select different fonts for different controls in the same dialog from the resource editor.
	Size	Sets the size of the font used in the dialog.
	Styles	Sets the various styles for the dialog's font.
Extended	General Alignment	Determines where text will be placed with respect to the controls (either on its right or left).
	Reading Order	Use this to set the reading order. For example, English is read left-to-right, and Hebrew is read right-to-left.
	Scrollbar Alignment	This places the scroll-bar (if any) on either the right or left side of the dialog; it's used for the same reason as the previous two settings.
	Window Flags	These describe a variety of extended dialog flags, including those available only in 32-bit versions of Windows.

You should take careful note of the fact that the tabs and options in the property inspector change, depending upon what object is selected. The items listed in Table EC4.4 are associated with the main dialogs themselves. If you select a different object, like a button control or an edit box, you will be presented with a different set of properties. Space requirements make a comprehensive list prohibitive here. The reference documentation provides a complete list.

Summary

Today's lesson presented the Integrated Resource Editor. It made a light pass at describing some of the more common features you use in creating your resources. You learned about the following topics:

- [ ] The different types of resources
- [ ] The different types of resource files
- [ ] The Integrated Resource Editor basics
- [ ] The different types of images
- [ ] The transparent and inverse sections of icons and cursor
- [ ] The hot spots of cursors
- [ ] Menu-resource editing
- [ ] How the resource editor enables you to add string tables and version information
- [ ] The tools available when editing dialogs

Q&A

Q How can I fine-tune the location and dimensions of multiple controls in a dialog?

A The resource editor provides the alignment tools for this task. Select the controls you wish to modify and then press the appropriate alignment button. You could also manually edit the .RC file, modifying the numbers for the coordinates and dimensions for each control.

Q Does the resource editor support custom VBX controls?

A Yes. You can install new VBX libraries by going to the Options | Environment... dialog, then selecting the Resource Editors | Control Libraries page.

Answers

Answers

> **Note:** Because of space limitations, not every Exercise has an answer presented here.

Answers to Day 1, "Getting Started"

Quiz

1. The program generates the string C++ in 21 Days?.

2. The program generates no output because the cout statement appears inside a comment! The function main simply returns 0.

3. The cout statement is missing the semicolon.

Exercise

```
#include <iostream.h>

int main()
{
    cout << "I am a C++ Programmer";
    return 0;
}
```

Answers to Day 2, "The C++ Preprocessor, Variables, and Operators"

Quiz

1. The following table indicates which identifiers are valid and which are not (and why).

Identifiers	Valid?	Reason (If Invalid)
numFiles	Yes	
n0Distance_02_Line	Yes	
0Weight	No	Starts with a digit
Bin Number	No	Contains a space
static	No	Reserved keyword
Static	Yes	

2. The output is

```
12
8
2
3.64851
150.5
```

3. The output is

```
12
-19
2
```

4. The output is

```
12
27
```

5. The output is

```
TRUE
TRUE
TRUE
FALSE
```

Exercise

1. `int maxVal = (i > j) ? i : j;`

2. `int minVal = (i < j) ? i : j;`

3. `int absVal = (i > 0) ? i : -i;`

. `bool isOdd = (i % 2 != 0) ? true : false;`

   or

   `bool isOdd = (i % 2 != 0);`

Answers to Day 3, "The Decision-Making Constructs and Loops"

Quiz

1. The simpler version is

```
if (i > 0 && i < 10)
    cout << "i = " << i << endl;
```

2. The simpler version is

```
if (i > 0)
    {
    j = i * i;
    cout << "j = " << j << endl;
    }
else if (i < 0)
    {
    j = 4 * i;
    cout << "j = " << j << endl;
    }
else
    {
    j = 10 + i;
    cout << "j = " << j << endl;
    }
```

3. False. When the variable i stores values between -10 and -1, the statements in the clauses of the two if statements execute. In this case, all the assignment statements are executed. By contrast, it is impossible to execute the statements in both the if and else clauses of the supposedly equivalent if-else statement.

4. The simplified version is

```
if (i > 0 && i < 100)
    j = i * i;
else if (i >= 100)
    j = i;
else
    j = 1;
```

Notice that I eliminated the original first else if clause because the tested condition is a subset of the first tested condition. Consequently, the condition in the first else if never gets examined and the associated assign statement never gets executed. This is an example of what is called *dead code*.

5. The tested condition is always false. Consequently, the statements in the clause never are executed. This is another example of dead code.

6. The statements inside the loop fail to alter the value of i. Consequently, the tested condition is always true and the loop iterates endlessly.

7. The output of the program is an endless sequence of lines that display the value of 3. The reason for the indefinite looping is that, although the loop-control variable has 2 added to it, the result of that operation isn't stored back into the variable. Consequently, the variable never gets modified and the loop continues forever.

8. The output of the program is the same as the last question. This time it's a little more obvious that the loop-control variable isn't modified.

9. The nested for loops use the same loop-control variable. This outer loop will execute only long enough for the inner loop to run.

10. The condition of the while loop is always true. Therefore, the loop iterates endlessly.

11. The program lacks a statement that explicitly initializes the variable `factorial` to 1. Without this statement, the program automatically initializes the variable `factorial` to 0—the wrong value. Consequently, the `for` loop ends up assigning 0 to the variable `factorial` in every iteration. Here is the correct version of the code:

```
int n;
double factorial = 1;
cout << "Enter positive integer: ";
cin >> n;
for (int i = 1; i <= n; i++)
    factorial *= i;
cout << n << "! = " << factorial;
```

Exercises

1. Here is my version of the program SWITCH2.CPP.

```cpp
// C++ program which uses the switch statement to implement
// a simple four-function calculator program

#include <iostream.h>

int main()
{
    double x, y, z;
    char op;
    bool error = false;

    cout << "Enter the first operand: ";
    cin >> x;
    cout << "Enter the operator: ";
    cin >> op;
    cout << "Enter the second operand: ";
    cin >> y;

    switch (op)
        {
        case '+':
            z = x + y;
            break;
        case '-':
            z = x - y;
            break;
        case '*':
            z = x * y;
            break;
        case '/':
            if (y != 0)
                z = x / y;
            else
                error = true;
            break;
        default:
            error = true;
        }
```

```
        if (!error)
            cout << x << " " << op << " " << y << " = " << z << endl;
        else
            cout << "Bad operator or division-by-zero error" << endl;

        return 0;
    }
```

2. Here is my version of program FOR5.CPP.

```cpp
// Program to gather numbers and calculate an average
//
#include <iostream.h>

int main()
{
    int ix, count;
    float sum = 0.0;

    cout << "Enter the total number to be averaged: ";
    cin >> count;
    for (ix = 0; ix < count; ++ix)
        {
        float f;
        cout << "  Enter number " << ix + 1 << ": ";
        cin >> f;
        sum += f;
        }
    cout << "The average is " << sum / count << endl;
    return 0;
}
```

3. Here is my version of program WHILE2.CPP.

```cpp
// Program  to gather numbers and calculate an average
//
#include <iostream.h>

int main()
{
    int ix, count;
    float sum = 0.0;

    cout << "Enter the total number to be averaged: ";
    cin >> count;
    ix = 0;
    while (ix < count)
        {
        float f;
        cout << "  Enter number " << ix + 1 << ": ";
        cin >> f;
        sum += f;
        ++ix;
        }
    cout << "The average is " << sum / count << endl;
    return 0;
}
```

4. Here is my version of program DOWHILE2.CPP.

```cpp
// Program to gather numbers and calculate an average
//
#include <iostream.h>

int main()
{
    int ix, count;
    float sum = 0.0;

    cout << "Enter the total number to be averaged: ";
    cin >> count;
    ix = 0;
    if (count > 0)
        do
            {
            float f;
            cout << "  Enter number " << ix + 1 << ": ";
            cin >> f;
            sum += f;
            } while (++ix < count);
    cout << "The average is " << sum / count << endl;
    return 0;
}
```

Note the check before the do-while loop to make sure that count is greater than 0. This is done because the check of ix against count is done at the end of the loop. If the user were to enter something less than or equal to 0, then the loop should never be run in the first place; the for and while loops will pick up on that immediately, but the do-while loop won't.

Answers to Day 4, "User-Defined Types and Pointers"

Quiz

1. The enumerated values on and off appear in two different enumerated types. Here is a correct version of these statements:

```cpp
enum State { state_on, state_off };
enum YesNo { yes, no };
enum DiskDriveStatus { drive_on , drive_off };
```

2. False. The enumerated type YesNo is correctly declared.

3. The program lacks a delete statement before the return statement. Here is the correct version:

```cpp
#include <iostream.h>
int main()
{
    int *p = new int;
```

```
     cout << "Enter a number: ";
     cin >> *p;
     cout << "The square of " << *p << " = " << (*p * *p);
     delete p;
     return 0;
}
```

Exercises

1. Here is a union for storing words:

```
union word
{
    unsigned short w;
    struct b
    {
        unsigned char lo;
        unsigned char hi;
    };
};
```

2. Here is my version of structure `intArrStruct`:

```
struct intArrStruct
{
    unsigned size;
    int* dataPtr;
};
```

3. Given the following:

```
intArrStruct ias;
ias.size = 100;
ias.dataPtr = new int[ias.size];
```

Here are a few different versions:

```
int myInt = ias.dataPtr[ix];
int myInt = *(ias.dataPtr + ix);
```

Answers to Day 5, "Functions"

Quiz

1. The output of the program is

```
a = 10 and b = 3
```

The function swap fails to swap the arguments a and b because it swaps only a copy of their values.

2. The output of the program is

```
a = 3 and b = 10
```

The function swap succeeds in swapping the arguments a and b because it uses reference parameters. Consequently, the changes in the values of parameters i and j go beyond the scope of the function itself.

3. The second version of function `inc` has a default argument, which, when used, hinders the compiler from determining which version of `inc` to call. The compiler flags a compile-time error for such functions.

4. Because the second parameter has a default argument, the third one must also have a default argument. Here is one version of the correct definition of function `volume`. Also, the `return` statement is missing a semicolon.

```
double volume(double length,
              double width = 1,
              double height = 1)
{
    return length * width * height;
}
```

5. The parameter `i` is a lowercase letter. However, the function uses the uppercase `I` in the assignment statement. The compiler complains that the identifier `I` is not defined.

6. The function main requires a prototype of function `sqr`. The correct version of the program is

```
#include <iostream.h>

// declare prototype of function sqr
double sqr(double);

int main()
{
    double x = 5.2;
    cout << x << "^2 = " << sqr(x);
    return 0;
}

double sqr(double x)
{ return x * x; }
```

7. The function is

```
double factorial(int i)
{
    return (i > 1) ? double(i) * factorial(i - 1) : 1;
}
```

Exercises

Here is my version of program OVERLOD2.CPP.

```
// C++ program illustrates function overloading
// and default arguments

#include <iostream.h>

// inc version for int types
void inc(int& i, int diff = 1)
{
    i = i + diff;
}
```

751

```
// inc version for double types
void inc(double& x, double diff = 1)
{
    x = x + diff;
}

// inc version for char types
void inc(char& c, int diff = 1)
{
    c = c + diff;
}

int main()
{
    char c = 'A';
    int i = 10;
    double x = 10.2;

    // discplay initial valus
    cout << "c = " << c << endl
         << "i = " << i << endl
         << "x = " << x << endl;

    // invoke the inc functions using default arguments
    inc(c);
    inc(i);
    inc(x);

    // display updatecd values
    cout << "After using the overloaded inc function" << endl
         << "c = " << c << endl
         << "i = " << i << endl
         << "x = " << x << endl;
    return 0;
}
```

Answers to Day 6, "Arrays"

Quiz

1. The program displays the factorials for the numbers 0 to 4.

```
x[0] = 1
x[1] = 1
x[2] = 2
x[3] = 6
x[4] = 24
```

2. The program displays the squares for the numbers 0 to 4.

```
x[0] = 0
x[1] = 1
x[2] = 4
x[3] = 9
x[4] = 16
```

3. Just checking to see if you're awake; the cout statement is missing a semicolon.

Exercise

The source code to SEARCH2.CPP can be found in the electronic source code.

Answers to Day 7, "Strings and Managing I/O"

Quiz

1. The output statement cannot contain the inserter operator >>. The statement can be corrected as follows:

   ```
   cout << "Enter a number ";
   cin >> x;
   ```

2. Because the variable x appears in the first and last items, the last number overwrites the first number.

3. The string s1 is smaller than string s2. Consequently, the call to function strcpy causes a memory overwrite.

4. Using the function strncpy to include the constant MAX as the third argument ensures that string s1 receives MAX characters (excluding the null terminator) from string s2:

   ```
   #include <iostream.h>
   #include <string.h>
   const in MAX = 10;
   int main()
   {
     char s1[MAX+1];
     char s2[] = "12345678901234567890123456789";
     strncpy(s1, s2, MAX);
     cout << "String 1 is " << s1
          << "\nString 2 is " << s2;
     return 0;
   }
   ```

5. Because the string in variable s1 is less than that in variable s2, the statement assigns a negative number (-13, to be exact) in variable i.

6. The call to function strcmp compares the substrings " C++" with " Pascal" because the arguments include an offset value. Because " C++" is less than " Pascal", the statement assigns a negative number (-13 again) in variable i.

7. True.

Exercises

1. Here is my version of program OUT3.CPP.

   ```
   // C++ program uses the printf function for formatted output

   #include <stdio.h>
   #include <math.h>
   ```

```
int main()
{
    double x;

    // display table heading
    printf("       X          Sqrt(X)\n");
    printf("-----------\n");
x = 2;
    printf("     %3.0lf          %3.4lf\n", x, sqrt(x));
    x++;
    printf("     %3.0lf          %3.4lf\n", x, sqrt(x));
    x++;
    printf("     %3.0lf          %3.4lf\n", x, sqrt(x));
    x++;
    printf("     %3.0lf          %3.4lf\n", x, sqrt(x));
    x++;
    printf("     %3.0lf          %3.4lf\n", x, sqrt(x));
    x++;
    printf("     %3.0lf          %3.4lf\n", x, sqrt(x));
    x++;
    printf("     %3.0lf          %3.4lf\n", x, sqrt(x));
    x++;
    printf("     %3.0lf          %3.4lf\n", x, sqrt(x));
    x++;
    printf("     %3.0lf          %3.4lf\n", x, sqrt(x));
    return 0;
}
```

2. Here is my version of program OUT4.CPP.

```
// C++ program which displays octal and hexadecimal integers

#include <iostream.h>
#include <stdio.h>

int main()
{
    long i;
    cout << "Enter an integer : ";
    cin >> i;

    printf("%ld = %lX (hex) = %lo (octal)\n", i, i, i);
    return 0;
}
```

3. Here is my version of function strlen.

```
int strlen(const char* s)
{
  int i = 0;
  while (s[i] != '\0')
    i++;
  return i;
}
```

4. Here is the other version of function strlen.

```
int strlen(const char* s)
{
```

```
    char *p = s;
    while (p++ != '\0')
        /* do nothing */;
    return p - s;
}
```

5. Here is my version of program STRING5.CPP.

```cpp
#include <stdio.h>
#include <string.h>

int main()
{
    char str[] = "2*(X+Y)/(X+Z) - (X+10)/(Y—5)";
    char strCopy[41];
    char* tkn[3] = { "+-*/ ()", "( )", "+-*/ " };
    char* ptr;

    strcpy(strCopy, str); // copy str into strCopy
    printf("%s\n", str);
    printf("Using token string %s\n", tkn[0]);
    // the first call
    ptr = strtok(str, tkn[0]);
    printf("String is broken into: ");
    while (ptr)
        {
        printf(", %s", ptr);
        // must make first argument a NULL character
        ptr = strtok(NULL, tkn[0]);
        }

    strcpy(str, strCopy); // restore str
    printf("\nUsing token string %s\n", tkn[1]);
    // the first call
    ptr = strtok(str, tkn[1]);
    printf("String is broken into: ");
    while (ptr)
        {
        printf(", %s", ptr);
        // must make first argument a NULL character
        ptr = strtok(NULL, tkn[1]);
        }

    strcpy(str, strCopy); // restore str
    printf("\nUsing token string %s\n", tkn[2]);
    // the first call
    ptr = strtok(str, tkn[2]);
    printf("String is broken into: ");
    while (ptr)
        {
        printf(", %s", ptr);
        // must make first argument a NULL character
        ptr = strtok(NULL, tkn[2]);
        }
    printf("\n\n");
    return 0;
}
```

Answers to Day 8, "Object-Oriented Programming and C++ Classes"

Quiz

1. By default, the members of a class are private. Therefore, the class declaration has no public member and cannot be used to create instances. Also, the two constructors that take an `unsigned` for their first parameter are ambiguous due to the default argument of the second of the two.

2. The fourth constructor has a default argument, which makes it redundant with respect to the fifth constructor. The C++ compiler detects such an error.

3. True. `String("Hello Borland C++")` creates a temporary instance of class `String` and then assigns it to the instance `s`.

4. Yes. The new statements are valid.

Exercise

Here is the implementation of function `main` in my version of program OARRAY.CPP:

```
int main()
{
   String s[3];

   s[0] = String("Kevin");
   s[1] = String(" Hay");

   s[2] = s[0] + s[1];
   cout << "\"" << s[0] << "\" + \"" << s[1]
        << "\" = \"" << s[2] << "\"" << endl;
   return 0;
}
```

Answers to Day 9, "Namespaces"

Quiz

1. True. With the use of RTTI, you can prevent such things as inadvertent casts from one type to another incompatible one.

2. That all depends upon the template you wish to use. Each template has its own requirements for the objects it uses. Typically, though, the templates require such rudimentary things as proper copy constructors and equivalency operators.

Exercise

Consult the downloadable source code for QUEUE.CPP. (See the introduction of this book for information on acquiring the source code.)

Answers to Day 10, "Basic Stream File I/O"

Quiz

1. False. The read and write functions cannot store and recall the dynamic data, which is accessed by a pointer member of a structure or a class.

2. True.

3. True.

4. False.

Exercise

Please see the online source code for VSEARCH.CPP.

Answers to Day 11, "The Standard Template Library's *string* Class"

Quiz

1. STRING must be included to use the STL string class.

2. A string class variable can be declared either with or without an initial value, such as the following:

```
string s1;
string s2("Initial Value");
```

3. The string class includes functions for comparing it to a C-style string.

   Operators ==, >, <, >=, <= and != have versions that compare string class variables to C-style strings.

   Another way is to compare the C-style element of the string class variable to the C string, as in the following:

```
result = strcmp(CStyleStr, stringClassVar.c_str());
```

4. The task performed by the replace member function substitutes one set of text for another in one call.

5. The second character in a string class variable is at index 1. Addressing is the same as with any array, with index 0 being the first item.

6. This can be done with the following declaration:

```
string myString("12");
```

7. Given string s1 = "11"; string s2 = "2112";

    a. The result of s1 + s2 is "112112"

    b. s2.find(s1); returns 1 because "11" is found in "2112"

    c. s1 > s2 is false

    d. s2.find(s1, 0); returns 1 because "11" is located beginning at index 1 in "2112"

Exercises

1. A C-style string of value "12" can be:

```
char myCStyleString[] = "12";
```

A C++ string class item of value "12" can be either one of the following:

```
string myString("12");
string myString = "12";
```

2. The following is a function that accepts a C++ string as a calling argument and writes its value to the computer screen:

```
void ShowString(string& myString)
{
    cout << myString;
}
```

3. The following function writes out each character of the passed string individually and then returns the size of the string:

```
size_t ShowString(string& myString)
{
    size_t index;
    size_t len = myString.length();

    // write each char from the string to the screen
    // one for each pass through the loop

    for (index = 0; index < len; ++index)
        cout << myString[index];

    return len; // return the length of the string
}
```

4. There's a simple way to do this using the strrev function:

```
strrev(myString.c_str());
```

The only real problem with this method is that it produces a compiler error to the effect that a const char* can't be converted to a char*. This is because the string

class's `c_str` method returns a const `char*`, whereas the `strrev` function takes a `char*` parameter. Well, this is easy to fix with a cast:

```
strrev((char*)myString.c_str());
```

This works. It compiles, and it even runs properly. The problem now is that this is bad programming, and something that can potentially lead to some very dangerous and hard-to-find bugs.

To understand the problem, you should first realize why the `c_str` member function returns a constant pointer instead of a standard one. As per object-oriented reasoning, the interior of a class should be hidden; nobody but the class itself and other special friends should know what's in there. This is so that the class can implement things in one way, have something else make use of it, then completely change its implementation so long as it leaves the interface the same.

Okay, that's all very generic, you say, but how does it apply in this instance? I'm glad you asked. Because you're not supposed to know how the internals of the "string" class work, you can't be sure of how the text is stored inside it. You know that `strrev` takes a character array and reverses its contents. Well, that's what `c_str` returns, a character array, but how do you know that's not just some temporary area set up for the specific request? How do you know that changing the contents of that array will actually modify the contents of the string class?

The answer is that you don't. In this particular case, it turns out that the previous code works, but if you try that with some other compiler and its implementation of the string class, you could very well be writing code that causes severe problems. The `c_str` member function returns a constant pointer for a reason: you're not supposed to modify what you get back.

A proper solution to this problem would be as follows:

```
string& strrev(string& str)
{
    // First we allocate a temporary string and copy
    // the contents of the original into it.
    //
    char* tmpstr = new char[str.length() + 1];
    strcpy(tmpstr, str.c_str());

    strrev(tmpstr);        // reverse the temporary string
    str = tmpstr;          // copy the reversal back
    delete[] tmpstr;       // We're done with the temp string
    return str;
}
```

What you're essentially doing here is creating a temporary area that you know is compatible with the `strrev` function, a character array. Then you just make use of the tools available to you. The only thing that might be unclear is why you bother to

return the string at the end of the function. This is so that you can use the result in expressions such as the following:

```
cout << strrev(myString) << endl;
```

You might also be confused concerning the name of the function. It's allowed to be the same as the one that acts on character arrays because of the C++ function over-loading feature. So long as the function arguments are different in type and/or there's a different number of arguments, then the compiler knows how to differentiate between them and lets you make multiple functions with the same name. Of course, the ideal solution would be to create a descendent MyString class and add the strrev function as a member.

Answers to Day 12, "Programming Windows with OWL5"

Quiz

1. False. The type's already changed between the 16-bit versions of Windows and the 32-bit versions. (WORD, for example, changed from an unsigned int to an unsigned short.) The idea, however, is that if you use the Windows types, you won't have to make any changes to your own code.

2. True. Even though OWL uses C++ classes, OWL itself is still written using the same functions that a C program would. Using OWL, you get to let the Borland programmers do the work for you.

Exercises

You can create REAL2.CPP by simply inserting the following lines at line 166 in REAL.CPP, just after the else clause for the carriage return:

```
else
    {
    char str[50];
    sprintf(str, "You pressed an invalid key: ASCII %d", key);
    MessageBox(str);
    }
```

Answers to Day 13, "Basic Windows"

Quiz

1. True.
2. True.
3. False.

Answers to Day 14, "OWL Controls"

Quiz

1. False. Only the text for controls with SS_SIMPLE style is unchangeable.
2. True.
3. True.
4. True.
5. True, because every control is a window.
6. True, but the OWL-prescribed method is to use the EV_BN_CLICKED macro.

Answers to Day 15, "Dialog Boxes"

Quiz

1. False. You don't need the .RES file until after linking the object modules and libraries.
2. True. There does, however, need to be a method by which the user can signal the dialog box to close itself. This is often done with buttons that, though labeled differently, return IDOK and IDCANCEL.
3. True.
4. False. The best examples of nested dialogs are those related to setting up the printer.
5. False. Dialog boxes can be standalone windows.

Answers to Day 16, "Grouped Controls"

Quiz

1. False. The check box can replace the two radio buttons only if these buttons offer opposite alternatives.

2. True.

3. True. Each check box can be independently toggled.

4. False.

Answers to Day 17, "List-Box Controls"

Quiz

1. True.

2. True.

3. False. `LBN_SELCHANGE` indicates that a new item is selected.

4. False. `LBN_DBLCLICK` indicates that a list item is selected with a double mouse click.

5. False. `LBS_STANDARD` includes the `LBS_SORT` style and therefore creates sorted list boxes.

Answers to Day 18, "Scroll Bars, Combo Boxes, and VBX Controls"

Quiz

1. True.

2. False. You need to respond to the `CBN_EDITUPDATE` message.

3. False. The items are sorted, but not unique. You can insert multiple copies of the same string.

4. True. In order to maintain a chronological order, you must prevent automatic sorting.

5. False.

6. True.

7. False.

Answers to Day 19, "MDI Windows"

Quiz

1. False. MDI child windows cannot have their own menus.

2. False. MDI child windows are confined to the frame area of their parent window.

3. False. You cannot nest MDI child windows.

Answers to Day 21, "OLE 2"

Quiz

1. Linking. This ensures that there is one source document only.

2. `TOleWindow`. `TOleView` is derived from `TOleWindow`.

3. The server must be registered.

Answers to Extra Credit Day 3, "Windows 95 and Windows NT Common Controls"

Exercises

1. Here are the key elements for one way to solve this exercise.

   First, here is the class declaration. Take note of the `TGauge` and `THSlider` pointer members and the `UpdateGauge` function.

   ```
   class GaugeSliderMainDlg : public TDialog
   {
   private:
      TGauge*   gauge;
      THSlider* horizSlider;

   protected:
      DECLARE_RESPONSE_TABLE(GaugeSliderMainDlg);
      void UpdateGauge(WPARAM wParam=0);
      void SetupWindow();

   public:
      GaugeSliderMainDlg (TWindow *parent);
      virtual ~GaugeSliderMainDlg () {};
   };
   ```

   The response table contains an entry for the `UpdateGauge` function.

   ```
   DEFINE_RESPONSE_TABLE1(GaugeSliderMainDlg, TDialog)
     EV_CHILD_NOTIFY_ALL_CODES(IDC_H_OWLSLIDER, UpdateGauge),
   END_RESPONSE_TABLE;
   ```

Here is the code that creates the TGauge and THSlider objects. In this particular answer, the slider and gauge have ranges from zero to twenty five.

```
horizSlider = new THSlider( this, IDC_H_OWLSLIDER,
                            20,20,150,26 );
gauge = new TGauge( this, "Position=%d", IDC_H_OWLGAUGE,
                    20,50,150,26 );
horizSlider->SetRange(0, 25);
horizSlider->SetRuler(1, false);
gauge->SetRange(0,25);
```

The last element that is needed is the actual response function that updates the gauge every time that slider changes its position. Here is the UpdateGauge function:

```
void GaugeSliderMainDlg::UpdateGauge(WPARAM /*wParam*/)
{
    gauge->SetValue(horizSlider->GetPosition());
}
```

Source Code for SPOT Project

Source Code for SPOT Project

The following is the source code for the SPOT project as described on Day 21, "OLE 2."

Listing B.1. Source code for the SPOTAPP.H header file.

```
#if !defined(__spotapp_h)
#define __spotapp_h
//      Class definition for SpotApp (TApplication).


#include <owl\pch.h>
#pragma hdrstop


#include "spotapp.rh"
//
// For OLE2 linking & embedding, need TOcModule
// which coordinates with OCF
//
class SpotApp : public TApplication, public TOcModule
  {
    public:
      SpotApp ();
      virtual void InitMainWindow ();
      virtual void InitInstance ();
    protected:
      void EvNewView (TView& view);
      void EvCloseView (TView& view);
      void CmHelpAbout ();
    DECLARE_RESPONSE_TABLE(SpotApp);
};

#endif
```

Listing B.2. Source code for the SPOTAPP.CPP program file.

```
#include <owl\pch.h>
#pragma hdrstop
#include "spotdoc.h"
#include "spotapp.h"
#include "spotview.h"
#include "sptabtdl.h"
//
// Ole 2 linking & embedding apps (may need to) use a special
// dictionary.
//
DEFINE_APP_DICTIONARY(AppDictionary);
//
// Ole 2 linking and embedding apps need a TOcRegistrar
//
static TPointer<TOcRegistrar> Registrar;
```

```
REGISTRATION_FORMAT_BUFFER(100)

BEGIN_REGISTRATION(ApplicationReg)
//
// The following must be unique per Ole 2 application
//
    REGDATA(clsid, "{FE91A8E0-DBDA-101B-A585-040224007802}")
    REGDATA(appname, "Spot Container & Server")
    REGDATA(description, "Spot Container & Server Application")
    REGDATA(cmdline, "")
    REGDATA(usage, ocrMultipleUse)
END_REGISTRATION

//
// This builds the relationship between the document
// and the view.
//
DEFINE_DOC_TEMPLATE_CLASS(SpotDoc, SpotView, SpotTemplate);

BEGIN_REGISTRATION(__SpotRegistration)
    REGDATA(progid, "Spot.Container.1")
    REGDATA(description, "Spot Container Version 1")
    REGDATA(extension, "SPT")
    REGDATA(docfilter, "*.SPT")
    REGDOCFLAGS(dtAutoDelete ¦ dtUpdateDir ¦ dtAutoOpen ¦ dtRegisterExt)
    REGDATA(menuname, "Spot container")
    REGDATA(insertable, "")
    REGDATA(verb0, "&Edit")
    REGDATA(verb1, "&Open")
    REGFORMAT(0, ocrEmbedSource,  ocrContent,  ocrIStorage, ocrGet)
    REGFORMAT(1, ocrMetafilePict, ocrContent,  ocrMfPict ¦ ocrStaticMed, ocrGet)
    REGFORMAT(2, ocrBitmap, ocrContent,  ocrGDI ¦ ocrStaticMed, ocrGet)
    REGFORMAT(3, ocrDib, ocrContent,  ocrHGlobal ¦ ocrStaticMed, ocrGet)
    REGFORMAT(4, ocrLinkSource, ocrContent,  ocrIStream, ocrGet)
END_REGISTRATION
SpotTemplate __spotTemplate(__SpotRegistration);


//
// Build a response table for all messages/commands handled
// by the application.
//
DEFINE_RESPONSE_TABLE1(SpotApp, TApplication)
    EV_OWLVIEW(dnCreate, EvNewView),
    EV_OWLVIEW(dnClose,  EvCloseView),
    EV_COMMAND(CM_HELPABOUT, CmHelpAbout),
END_RESPONSE_TABLE;

//
// Note the special constructor
//
SpotApp::SpotApp () : TApplication
   (::ApplicationReg["description"], ::Module, &::AppDictionary)
{
    //
```

continues

Listing B.2. continued

```
          // Tell the doc manager what sort of application it is
          // dealing with - SDI in this case
          //
          SetDocManager(new TDocManager(dmSDI | dmMenu, this));
    }


    //
    // Application intialization.
    //
    void SpotApp::InitMainWindow ()
    {
    //
    // AppExpert likes to set this in a complicated way...
    //
        if (nCmdShow != SW_HIDE)
          nCmdShow = (nCmdShow != SW_SHOWMINNOACTIVE) ? SW_SHOWNORMAL : nCmdShow;

        TOleFrame *frame = new TOleFrame(GetName(), 0, false, this);
        //
        // Assign ICON w/ this application.
        //
        frame->SetIcon(this, IDI_SDIAPPLICATION);
        //
        //  Menu and accelerator
        //
        frame->AssignMenu(SDI_MENU);
        frame->Attr.AccelTable = SDI_MENU;

        SetMainWindow(frame);
        //
        // OLE 2 needs to use menu descriptors for
        // easy merging of menus
        //
        frame->SetMenuDescr(TMenuDescr(SDI_MENU));
        EnableCtl3d(true);
        }
    void SpotApp::InitInstance ()
    {
        TApplication::InitInstance();

        if (!::Registrar->IsOptionSet(amEmbedding))
          {
            TDocTemplate* tpl = GetDocManager()->MatchTemplate(GetCmdLine().c_str());
            if (tpl)
              {
                TDocument* doc = tpl->ConstructDoc();
                if (doc)
                  {
                    doc->SetTemplate(tpl);
                    GetDocManager()->InitDoc(doc, GetCmdLine().c_str(), 0);
                    return;
                  }
              }
```

```
            GetDocManager()->CreateAnyDoc(0, dtNewDoc);
        }

}
// Response Table handlers:
//
void SpotApp::EvNewView (TView& view)
{
    //
    // When a new view is opened - need to associate with
    // correct window. If the object is embedded and is
    // using in place editing - get the in-place window.
    // (Can be embedded and do full screen editing)
    //
    // Only OLE servers need this test
    //
    TOleView* ov = dynamic_cast<TOleView*>(&view);
    if (ov && view.GetDocument().IsEmbedded() &&
        !ov->GetOcRemView()->GetState() == TOcRemView::OpenEditing)
      {
        //
        // Embedded view window
        //
        TWindow* vw = view.GetWindow();
        vw->SetParent(dynamic_cast<TOleFrame*>(GetMainWindow())
                     ->GetRemViewBucket());
        vw->Create();
      }
    else
      {
        //
        // Normal window - associate with application
        // main window frame.
        //
        GetMainWindow()->SetClientWindow(view.GetWindow());
        if (!view.IsOK())
          GetMainWindow()->SetClientWindow(0);
        else
          if (view.GetViewMenu())
            GetMainWindow()->MergeMenu(*view.GetViewMenu());
      }
}


void SpotApp::EvCloseView (TView&)
{
    GetMainWindow()->SetClientWindow(0);
    //
    // Set caption back to just title
    //
    GetMainWindow()->SetCaption("Spot");
}

/////////////////////////////////////////////////////////
// SpotApp
// ===========
```

continues

Listing B.2. continued

```
// Menu Help About spot.exe command
void SpotApp::CmHelpAbout ()
{
    //
    // Show the modal dialog.
    //
    SpotAboutDlg(&TWindow(GetMainWindow()->GetCommandTarget())).Execute();
}


int OwlMain (int , char* [])
{
    try
      {
        ::Registrar = new TOcRegistrar(::ApplicationReg,
➥TOleDocViewFactory<SpotApp>(), TApplication::GetCmdLine(),
::DocTemplateStaticHead);
        if (!::Registrar->IsOptionSet(amAnyRegOption))
        // If this is an exe server normal run, run the app now.
         ::Registrar->Run();
        ::Registrar = 0; // Explicitly free registrar
        return 0;
      }
    catch (xmsg& x)
      {
        ::MessageBox(0, x.why().c_str(), "Exception", MB_OK);
      }

    return -1;
}


/*** new code ***
void OpenDoc(const char * fileName)
  {
    char* newFile =
    PostMessage
  }
        if (!spotDoc.CanClose())         // normally calls back to FlushDoc()
          return;
        spotDoc.Close();
        TDocument* doc = &spotDoc;
        delete doc;
        doc = tpl->ConstructDoc();
        if (doc)
          {
            doc->SetTemplate(tpl);
            GetApplication()->GetDocManager()->InitDoc(doc, fileName, 0);
            return;
          }
      }
  }
*/
```

```
#if !defined(__spotdoc_h)
#define __spotdoc_h

//    Class definition for SpotDoc (TOleDocument).

#include <owl\pch.h>
#pragma hdrstop
#include "spotapp.rh"
//
// Custom doc/view notifications
//
const int vnDrawAppend = vnCustomBase+0;
const int vnDrawClear = vnCustomBase+1;
//
// Custom doc/view signitures
//
NOTIFY_SIG(vnDrawAppend, uint)
NOTIFY_SIG(vnDrawClear, void)
//
// Response table macros
//
#define EV_VN_DRAWAPPEND  VN_DEFINE(vnDrawAppend,  VnAppend,  int)
#define EV_VN_DRAWCLEAR   VN_DEFINE(vnDrawClear,   VnClear,   void)

typedef TArray<TPoint> Points;
//
// Underlying OLE capable document - uses OLE2 storage
// format
//
class SpotDoc : public TOleDocument
  {
    public:
      SpotDoc (TDocument* parent = 0);
      virtual ~SpotDoc ();
//
// SpotView helper functions
//
      TPoint* GetSpot(uint index);
      void    AddSpot(TPoint& point);
      void    Clear();
//
// Document manager functions
//
      virtual bool Open (int mode, const char far* path = 0);
      virtual bool Commit (bool force);
      virtual bool Close ();
    protected:
      Points* points;
  };
#endif
```

Listing B.4. Source code for the SPOTDOC.CPP program file.

```cpp
#include <owl\pch.h>
#pragma hdrstop
#include "spotdoc.h"
SpotDoc::SpotDoc (TDocument* parent):
    TOleDocument(parent)
{
    points = new Points(10,0,10);
}


SpotDoc::~SpotDoc ()
{
    delete points;
}
//
// Warning! Open is called and path is never
// populated!
//
bool SpotDoc::Open (int mode, const char far* path)
{
    points->Flush();
    //
    // If new - GetDocPath() will return 0
    //
    if (GetDocPath())
      {
        //
        // Read base storage for any contained
        // objects
        //
        TOleDocument::Open(mode,path);
        //
        // Get the file stream
        //
        TInStream* is = (TInStream*)InStream(ofRead);
        //
        // If cannot open file is will be zero
        //
        if (!is)
          return false;
        // reference for convenience
        TInStream& in = *is;
        //
        // Check how many points to read - NB assume
        // not a corrupt file
        //
        uint pointCount;
        in >> pointCount;
        //
        // Read specified number of points
        //
        TPoint p;
        for (int i = 0; i < pointCount; i++)
```

```
            {
               in >> p;
               points->Add(p); // Add to container
            }
            delete is;

        }
       SetDirty(false);        // Mark as unchanged
       return true;
    }
bool SpotDoc::Commit (bool force)
{
    //
    // Write out contained objects
    //
    TOleDocument::Commit(force);
    //
    // Get output stream to write own data
    //
    TOutStream* os = OutStream(ofWrite);
    if (!os)
      return false;
    TOutStream& out = *os; // reference for convenience
    //
    // Write out number of points
    //
    out << points->GetItemsInContainer();
    //
    // For each point, write out to stream
    //
    for (int i = 0; i < points->GetItemsInContainer();i++)
      out << (*points)[i];
    delete os;
    //
    // Mark document as matching
    //
    SetDirty(false);
    //
    // Very important line! This forces write to disk
    // without this, the file IS created but is corrupt
    //
    TOleDocument::CommitTransactedStorage();
    return true;
}

//
// Close document
//
bool SpotDoc::Close()
  {
    points->Flush();
    return TOleDocument::Close();
  }
//
// View service functions
```

continues

Listing B.4. continued

```cpp
//
//  GetSpot returns a point at index
//
TPoint* SpotDoc::GetSpot(uint index)
  {
    if (points && index < points->GetItemsInContainer())
      return &(*points)[index];
    else
      return 0;
  }
//
// Add spot to collection
//
void SpotDoc::AddSpot(TPoint& point)
  {
    points->Add(point);
    // Picture has changed - set dirty flag
    SetDirty(true);
    //
    // Notify all views that the view has changed
    // Pass the index of the new point so that the
    // views can draw the new spot without redrawing
    // the entire screen.
    //
    // vnDrawAppend is defined in the header
    //
    NotifyViews(vnDrawAppend, points->GetItemsInContainer() - 1);
  }
//
// Entirely clear document
//
void SpotDoc::Clear()
  {
    //
    // Clear the document data
    //
    points->Flush();
    SetDirty(true);
    //
    // Tell view to empty container
    //
    // (At time of writing I couldn't determine a safe
    // way of emptying the document - ask the view to
    // do it)
    //
    // TOleDocument::Revert(true);

    NotifyViews(vnDrawClear,0);
  }
```

Type

```
#if !defined(__spotview_h)
#define __spotview_h
#include <owl\pch.h>
#pragma hdrstop


#include "spotapp.rh"              // Definition of all resources.
#include "spotdoc.h"
//
// View class (may be several instances of this per
// document)
//
class SpotView : public TOleView
  {
    public:
      SpotView (SpotDoc& doc, TWindow* parent = 0);
      virtual ~SpotView ();
      virtual void Paint (TDC& dc, bool erase, TRect& rect);
      virtual const char far* GetViewName ();
      static const char far* StaticName ();
    protected:
      SpotDoc& spotDoc;  // Parent document
      TBrush* backBrush;
      TBrush* spotBrush;
      TPoint storePoint;
      TControlBar * toolBar;
      //
      // Draw a spot from a view
      //
      void SpotView::DrawSpot(TDC& dc, const TPoint& point);
      void EvLButtonDown (uint modKeys, TPoint& point);
      void EvMouseMove (uint modKeys, TPoint& point);
      void EvLButtonUp (uint modKeys, TPoint& point);
      void CmClear ();
      void CmEditCopy ();
      void CmEditCut ();
      bool EvOcViewPartSize(TOcPartSize far& ps);
      bool EvOcViewShowTools(TOcToolBarInfo far& tbi);

    // Document notifications
      bool VnCommit(bool force); // Document saved
      bool VnRevert(bool clear); // Document restored
      bool VnAppend(uint index); // Document amended
      bool VnClear();            // document blanked
      DECLARE_RESPONSE_TABLE(SpotView);
  };


#endif
```

Listing B.6. Source code for the SPOTVIEW.CPP program file.

```cpp
#include <owl\pch.h>
#pragma hdrstop

#include "sptabtdl.h"
#include "spotapp.h"
#include "spotview.h"
#include "spotapp.rh"
#include <stdio.h>

const int spotRadius = 10; // Spot size
//
// Build a response table for all messages/commands handled
// by the application.
//
DEFINE_RESPONSE_TABLE1(SpotView, TOleView)
    EV_WM_LBUTTONDOWN,
    EV_WM_MOUSEMOVE,
    EV_WM_LBUTTONUP,
    EV_COMMAND(CM_EDITCLEAR, CmClear),
    EV_COMMAND(CM_EDITCOPY, CmEditCopy),
    EV_COMMAND(CM_EDITCUT, CmEditCut),
  EV_VN_COMMIT,
  EV_VN_REVERT,
  EV_VN_DRAWAPPEND,
  EV_VN_DRAWCLEAR,
  EV_OC_VIEWPARTSIZE,
  EV_OC_VIEWSHOWTOOLS,
END_RESPONSE_TABLE;

// SpotView
// ==========
// Construction/Destruction handling.
SpotView::SpotView (SpotDoc& doc, TWindow* parent)
    : TOleView(doc, parent),
      spotDoc(doc)
{
    backBrush = new TBrush(TColor::LtMagenta);
    spotBrush = new TBrush(TColor::LtYellow);
    toolBar = 0;
}


SpotView::~SpotView ()
{
    delete backBrush;
    delete spotBrush;
}
//
// Class and View names
//
const char far* SpotView::GetViewName ()
{
    return "SpotViewClass";
```

```
}
const char far* SpotView::StaticName ()
{
    return "Spot View";
}
//
// Paint is not only called for window, but also to update
// OLE2 metafile
//
void SpotView::Paint (TDC& dc, bool /*erase*/, TRect& rect)
{
    TPoint* spot;
    //
    // At time of writing could not determine a good way
    // of determining the size of window display - especially
    // when painting to a DC.
    //
    //      bool metafile = dc.GetDeviceCaps(TECHNOLOGY) == DT_METAFILE;
    //      if (metafile)
    //          {
    TRect clientRect(0,0,GetSystemMetrics(SM_CXSCREEN),
                         GetSystemMetrics(SM_CYSCREEN));
    dc.FillRect(clientRect,*backBrush);
    //          }
    //      else
    //          dc.FillRect(rect,*backBrush);

    //
    // This line paints the OLE embedded objects
    // (note: OLE objects are painted from a metafile and
    // do not require the server to be present)
    //
    TOleView::Paint(dc, false, rect);
    //
    // Spots before your eyes...
    //
    dc.SelectObject(*spotBrush);
    int i = 0;
    do
      {
        spot = spotDoc.GetSpot(i++);
        if (spot)
          DrawSpot(dc,*spot);
      }
    while (spot);

    dc.RestoreBrush();
}
void SpotView::DrawSpot(TDC& dc, const TPoint& point)
  {
    int radius = spotRadius;
    TRect spotRect(point.x - radius,
                   point.y - radius,
                   point.x + radius,
                   point.y + radius);
```

continues

Listing B.6. continued

```
        dc.Ellipse(spotRect);

    }


    void SpotView::EvLButtonDown (uint modKeys, TPoint& point)
    {
        //
        // Base call sets up DragDC - it also modifies point
        // to be in logical units. This allows in-place editing
        // to work when the window has been stretched
        //
        TOleView::EvLButtonDown(modKeys, point);
        if (DragDC && !SelectEmbedded())
          {
            //
            // If haven't hit an OLE object -
            // capture mouse and draw temporary spot
            //
            SetCapture();
            DragDC->SetROP2(R2_XORPEN);     // Invert drawing
            storePoint = point;            // store point
            DragDC->SelectObject(*spotBrush);
            DrawSpot(*DragDC,storePoint);  // Draw spot inverted
          }
    }


    void SpotView::EvMouseMove (uint modKeys, TPoint& point)
    {
        TOleView::EvMouseMove(modKeys, point); // point modified
        if (DragDC&& !SelectEmbedded())  // If not dragging OLE object
          {
            DrawSpot(*DragDC,storePoint); // Clear up spot
            storePoint = point;
            DrawSpot(*DragDC,storePoint); // Spot breaks out again
          }

    }


    void SpotView::EvLButtonUp (uint modKeys, TPoint& point)
    {
        if (DragDC && !SelectEmbedded()) // Not OLE2 object
          {
            DrawSpot(*DragDC,storePoint); // Clear up spot
            storePoint = point;           // Store point
            DragDC->DPtoLP(&storePoint);  // Convert to LPs
            ReleaseCapture();
            spotDoc.AddSpot(storePoint);
          }
                                          // Inconsistant:
        TOleView::EvLButtonUp(modKeys, point); // Does not convert point
                                          // except if using itself
```

```
}
//
// Let container know about the server view size in pixels
//
bool
SpotView::EvOcViewPartSize(TOcPartSize far& ps)
{
  TClientDC dc(*this);
  // Set minimum size...
  TRect rect(0, 0, 0, 0);
  // a 2" x 2" extent for server
  //
  rect.right  = dc.GetDeviceCaps(LOGPIXELSX) * 2;
  rect.bottom = dc.GetDeviceCaps(LOGPIXELSY) * 2;
  //
  // Note: this would be better calculated on open of
  // view and when data added - but for simplicity I have
  // just done it a nasty way.
  //
  // Declare picture size to be a minimum of 2" x 2"
  // but allow user to add more points for scaling
  //
  // Iterate through all the points and calculate the
  // most extreme
  //
  uint i = 0;
  // *** remember Logical Units ***
  TPoint* tempPoint = spotDoc.GetSpot(i++);
  while (tempPoint)
    {
      TPoint point = *tempPoint;
      dc.DPtoLP(&point);
      if (point.x > rect.bottom)
        rect.bottom = point.x;
      if (point.y > rect.right)
        rect.right = point.y;
      tempPoint = spotDoc.GetSpot(i++);
// ***

    }
  ps.PartRect = rect;
  return true;
}
//
// Give toolbar to container application.
// Note: to emphasise the point, the when executing, the
// server does not have a toolbar - only when embedding.
// For the application, create a toolbar in the standard
// fashion. (Give it an Attr.Id of IDW_TOOLBAR)
//
bool
SpotView::EvOcViewShowTools(TOcToolBarInfo far& tbi)
{
  //
  // Construct & create a control bar for show, destroy our bar for hide
```

continues

Listing B.6. continued

```
    //
    if (tbi.Show)
      {
        if (!toolBar)
          {
            toolBar = new TControlBar(this);
            toolBar->Insert(*new TButtonGadget(CM_EDITCLEAR, CM_EDITCLEAR,
➥TButtonGadget::Command));
            toolBar->Insert(*new TSeparatorGadget);
            toolBar->Insert(*new TButtonGadget(CM_HELPABOUT, CM_HELPABOUT,
➥TButtonGadget::Command));
          }
        toolBar->Create();
        tbi.HTopTB = (HWND)*toolBar;
      }
    else {
      if (toolBar) {
        toolBar->Destroy();
        delete toolBar;
        toolBar = 0;
      }
    }
    return true;
}

bool
SpotView::VnCommit(bool /*force*/)
{
  // nothing to do here, no data held in view
  return true;
}

bool
SpotView::VnRevert(bool /*clear*/)
{
  Invalidate();  // force full repaint
  return true;
}
//
// View notification that the document has been
// emptied
//
bool
SpotView::VnClear()
  {
  Invalidate();  // force full repaint
  //
  // Component parts are held in a collection
  // iterate the collection to remove the data
  //
  for (TOcPartCollectionIter i(GetOcDoc()->GetParts()); i; i++)
    {
      TOcPart* p = i.Current();
      TOcPartChangeInfo changeInfo(p, invData¦invView);
```

```
      EvOcViewPartInvalid(changeInfo);
      GetOcDoc()->GetParts().Detach(p,true);
    }
  InvalidatePart(invData¦invView);
  return true;
}
//
// View notiification that the document has been added to
//
bool
SpotView::VnAppend(uint index)
{
  //
  // Append a spot onto current views - could be a metafile
  //
  // Get a dc for the view window
  TClientDC dc(*this);
  //
  // Get the spot notified at index
  //
  const TPoint* spot = spotDoc.GetSpot(index);
  bool metafile = dc.GetDeviceCaps(TECHNOLOGY) == DT_METAFILE;
  //
  // If drawing to metafile, need to scale
  //
  SetupDC(dc, !metafile);
  dc.SelectObject(*spotBrush);
  DrawSpot(dc,*spot);
  //
  // Tell container to redraw
  //
  InvalidatePart(invView);
  return true;
}


void SpotView::CmClear ()
{
    //
    // Tell document to clear down
    //
    spotDoc.Clear();

}


void SpotView::CmEditCopy ()
{
  //
  // Supposed to be able to copy view to clipboard
  //
  // Not implemented at time of writing
  //
  //   TOcRemView* orv = GetOcRemView();
  //   if (orv)
```

continues

Listing B.6. continued

```
//    orv->Copy();

}


void SpotView::CmEditCut ()
{
    // Do nothing... nothing sensible to do
}
```

Type **Listing B.7. Source code for the SPOTAB.H header file.**

```cpp
#if !defined(__sptab_h)
#define __sptab_h

#include <owl\pch.h>
#pragma hdrstop

#include "spotapp.rh"
class SpotAboutDlg : public TDialog
 {
  public:
    SpotAboutDlg (TWindow *parent, TResId resId = IDD_ABOUT, TModule *module = 0);
    virtual ~SpotAboutDlg ();
  public:
    void SetupWindow ();
};
// Reading the VERSIONINFO resource.
class ProjectRCVersion
  {
    public:
      ProjectRCVersion (TModule *module);
      virtual ~ProjectRCVersion ();

      bool GetProductName (LPSTR &prodName);
      bool GetProductVersion (LPSTR &prodVersion);
      bool GetCopyright (LPSTR &copyright);
      bool GetDebug (LPSTR &debug);

    protected:
      LPBYTE      TransBlock;
      void FAR    *FVData;

    private:
    // Don't allow this object to be copied.
    ProjectRCVersion (const ProjectRCVersion &);
    ProjectRCVersion & operator =(const ProjectRCVersion &);
  };


#endif
```

Type **Listing B.8. Source code for the SPOTAB.CPP program file.**

```cpp
#include <owl\pch.h>
#pragma hdrstop

#if !defined(__FLAT__)
#include <ver.h>
#endif

#include "spotapp.h"
#include "spotab.h"
//
// AppExpert generated About box
//
ProjectRCVersion::ProjectRCVersion (TModule *module)
{
    char    appFName[255];
    char    subBlockName[255];
    DWORD   fvHandle;
    UINT    vSize;

    FVData = 0;

    module->GetModuleFileName(appFName, sizeof(appFName));
    DWORD dwSize = ::GetFileVersionInfoSize(appFName,&fvHandle);
    if (dwSize)
      {
        FVData  = (void FAR *)new char[(UINT)dwSize];
        if (::GetFileVersionInfo(appFName, fvHandle, dwSize,
                                 FVData))
          {
            strcpy(subBlockName, "\\VarFileInfo\\Translation");
            if (!::VerQueryValue(FVData, subBlockName,
                        (void FAR* FAR*)&TransBlock, &vSize))
              {
                delete FVData;
                FVData = 0;
              }
            else
                *(DWORD *)TransBlock =
                            MAKELONG(HIWORD(*(DWORD *)TransBlock),
                            LOWORD(*(DWORD *)TransBlock));
          }
      }
  }


ProjectRCVersion::~ProjectRCVersion ()
  {
    if (FVData)
        delete FVData;
  }
```

continues

```
bool ProjectRCVersion::GetProductName (LPSTR &prodName)
  {
    UINT    vSize;
    char    subBlockName[255];

    wsprintf(subBlockName, "\\StringFileInfo\\%08lx\\%s",
       *(DWORD *)TransBlock, (LPSTR)"ProductName");
    return FVData ? ::VerQueryValue(FVData, subBlockName,
                       (void FAR* FAR*)&prodName, &vSize) : false;
  }


bool ProjectRCVersion::GetProductVersion (LPSTR &prodVersion)
  {
    UINT    vSize;
    char    subBlockName[255];

    wsprintf(subBlockName, "\\StringFileInfo\\%08lx\\%s",
          *(DWORD *)TransBlock, (LPSTR)"ProductVersion");
    return FVData ? ::VerQueryValue(FVData, subBlockName,
          (void FAR* FAR*)&prodVersion, &vSize) : false;
  }


bool ProjectRCVersion::GetCopyright (LPSTR &copyright)
  {
    UINT    vSize;
    char    subBlockName[255];

    wsprintf(subBlockName, "\\StringFileInfo\\%08lx\\%s",
          *(DWORD *)TransBlock, (LPSTR)"LegalCopyright");
    return FVData ? ::VerQueryValue(FVData, subBlockName,
          (void FAR* FAR*)&copyright, &vSize) : false;
  }


bool ProjectRCVersion::GetDebug (LPSTR &debug)
{
    UINT    vSize;
    char    subBlockName[255];

    wsprintf(subBlockName, "\\StringFileInfo\\%08lx\\%s",
          *(DWORD *)TransBlock, (LPSTR)"SpecialBuild");
    return FVData ? ::VerQueryValue(FVData, subBlockName,
          (void FAR* FAR*)&debug, &vSize) : false;
}


SpotAboutDlg::SpotAboutDlg (TWindow *parent, TResId resId, TModule *module)
    : TDialog(parent, resId, module)
 {
 }

SpotAboutDlg::~SpotAboutDlg ()
```

```
  {
    Destroy();
  }

void SpotAboutDlg::SetupWindow ()
{
    LPSTR prodName = 0, prodVersion = 0, copyright = 0, debug = 0;

    // Get the static text for the value based on VERSIONINFO.
    TStatic *versionCtrl = new TStatic(this, IDC_VERSION, 255);
    TStatic *copyrightCtrl = new TStatic(this, IDC_COPYRIGHT, 255);
    TStatic *debugCtrl = new TStatic(this, IDC_DEBUG, 255);

    TDialog::SetupWindow();

    // Process the VERSIONINFO.
    ProjectRCVersion applVersion(GetModule());

    // Get the product name and product version strings.
    if (applVersion.GetProductName(prodName) &&
        applVersion.GetProductVersion(prodVersion)) {
        char    buffer[255];
        char    versionName[128];

        buffer[0] = '\0';
        versionName[0] = '\0';

        versionCtrl->GetText(versionName, sizeof(versionName));
        wsprintf(buffer, "%s %s %s", prodName,
                 versionName, prodVersion);

        versionCtrl->SetText(buffer);
    }

    //Get the legal copyright string.
    if (applVersion.GetCopyright(copyright))
        copyrightCtrl->SetText(copyright);

    if (applVersion.GetDebug(debug))
        debugCtrl->SetText(debug);
}
```

Listing B.9. Source code for the SPOTAPP.RH resource header file.

```
//#if !defined(__spotapp_rh)         // Sentry use file only if it's not
                                     //already included.

//#define __spotapp_rh

//
// Application specific definitions:
//
#define IDI_SDIAPPLICATION    1001              // Application icon
```

continues

Listing B.9. continued

```
#define SDI_MENU                    100           // Menu resource ID and Accelerator
                                                  //IDs

#define IDM_DOCMANAGERFILE          32401         // Menu for DocManager merging.
#define IDM_EDITVIEW                32581         // Menu for TEditView merging.
#define IDM_LISTVIEW                32582         // Menu for TListView merging.


//
// OleView merged menus (include\owl\oleview.rh)
//
#define IDM_OLEPOPUP                32405
#define IDM_OLEVIEW                 32406


//
// CM_FILEnnnn commands (include\owl\editfile.rh except for CM_FILEPRINTPREVIEW)
//
#define CM_FILENEW                  24331         // SDI New
#define CM_FILEOPEN                 24332         // SDI Open
#define CM_FILECLOSE                24339
#define CM_FILESAVE                 24333
#define CM_FILESAVEAS               24334
#define CM_FILEREVERT               24335
#define CM_VIEWCREATE               24341


//
// Window commands (include\owl\window.rh)
//
#define CM_EXIT                     24310


//
// CM_EDITnnnn commands (include\owl\window.rh)
//
#define CM_EDITUNDO                 24321
#define CM_EDITCUT                  24322
#define CM_EDITCOPY                 24323
#define CM_EDITPASTE                24324
#define CM_EDITDELETE               24325
#define CM_EDITCLEAR                24326
#define CM_EDITADD                  24327
#define CM_EDITEDIT                 24328
#define CM_EDITPASTESPECIAL         24311
#define CM_EDITPASTELINK            24312
#define CM_EDITINSERTOBJECT         24313
#define CM_EDITLINKS                24314

#define CM_EDITOBJECT               24370
#define CM_EDITFIRSTVERB            24371         // 20 verbs at most
#define CM_EDITLASTVERB             24390

#define CM_EDITCONVERT              24391
#define CM_EDITSHOWOBJECTS          24392
```

```
//
// Search menu commands (include\owl\editsear.rh)
//
#define CM_EDITFIND              24351
#define CM_EDITREPLACE           24352
#define CM_EDITFINDNEXT          24353


//
// Help menu commands.
//
#define CM_HELPABOUT             2009


//
// About Dialogs
//
#define IDD_ABOUT                22000
#define IDC_VERSION              22001
#define IDC_COPYRIGHT            22002
#define IDC_DEBUG                22003


//
// OWL defined strings
//

// Statusbar
#define IDS_MODES                32530
#define IDS_MODESOFF             32531


// EditFile
#define IDS_UNABLEREAD           32551
#define IDS_UNABLEWRITE          32552
#define IDS_FILECHANGED          32553
#define IDS_FILEFILTER           32554

// EditSearch
#define IDS_CANNOTFIND           32540


//
// General & application exception messages (include\owl\except.rh)
//
#define IDS_UNKNOWNEXCEPTION     32767
#define IDS_OWLEXCEPTION         32766
#define IDS_OKTORESUME           32765
#define IDS_UNHANDLEDXMSG        32764
#define IDS_UNKNOWNERROR         32763
#define IDS_NOAPP                32762
#define IDS_OUTOFMEMORY          32761
#define IDS_INVALIDMODULE        32760
#define IDS_INVALIDMAINWINDOW    32759
#define IDS_VBXLIBRARYFAIL       32758
```

continues

Listing B.9. continued

```
//
// Owl 1 compatibility messages
//
//#define IDS_INVALIDWINDOW       32756
//#define IDS_INVALIDCHILDWINDOW  32755
//#define IDS_INVALIDCLIENTWINDOW 32754


//
// TXWindow messages
//
#define IDS_CLASSREGISTERFAIL   32749
#define IDS_CHILDREGISTERFAIL   32748
#define IDS_WINDOWCREATEFAIL    32747
#define IDS_WINDOWEXECUTEFAIL   32746
#define IDS_CHILDCREATEFAIL     32745

#define IDS_MENUFAILURE         32744
#define IDS_VALIDATORSYNTAX     32743
#define IDS_PRINTERERROR        32742

#define IDS_LAYOUTINCOMPLETE    32741
#define IDS_LAYOUTBADRELWIN     32740


//
// TXGdi messages
//
#define IDS_GDIFAILURE          32739
#define IDS_GDIALLOCFAIL        32738
#define IDS_GDICREATEFAIL       32737
#define IDS_GDIRESLOADFAIL      32736
#define IDS_GDIFILEREADFAIL     32735
#define IDS_GDIDELETEFAIL       32734
#define IDS_GDIDESTROYFAIL      32733
#define IDS_INVALIDDIBHANDLE    32732


// ListView (include\owl\listview.rh)
#define IDS_LISTNUM             32584


// DocView (include\owl\docview.rh)
#define IDS_DOCMANAGERFILE      32500
#define IDS_DOCLIST             32501
#define IDS_VIEWLIST            32502
#define IDS_UNTITLED            32503
#define IDS_UNABLEOPEN          32504
#define IDS_UNABLECLOSE         32505
#define IDS_READERROR           32506
#define IDS_WRITEERROR          32507
#define IDS_DOCCHANGED          32508
#define IDS_NOTCHANGED          32509
#define IDS_NODOCMANAGER        32510
#define IDS_NOMEMORYFORVIEW     32511
#define IDS_DUPLICATEDOC        32512
```

```
#define IDS_EDITOBJECT          32600
#define IDS_EDITCONVERT         32601
#define IDS_CLOSESERVER         32602
#define IDS_EXITSERVER          32603

// Text for clipboard format names
#define IDS_CFTEXT              32610
#define IDS_CFBITMAP            32611
#define IDS_CFMETAFILE          32612
#define IDS_CFSYLK              32613
#define IDS_CFDIF               32614
#define IDS_CFTIFF              32615
#define IDS_CFOEMTEXT           32616
#define IDS_CFDIB               32617
#define IDS_CFPALETTE           32618
#define IDS_CFPENDATA           32619
#define IDS_CFRIFF              32620
#define IDS_CFWAVE              32621
#define IDS_CFUNICODETEXT       32622
#define IDS_CFENHMETAFILE       32623

#define IDS_IN                  32700


// TInputDialog DIALOG resource (include\owl\inputdia.rh)
#define ID_PROMPT               4091
#define ID_INPUT                4090


// TSlider bitmaps (horizontal and vertical) (include\owl\slider.rh)


// Validation messages (include\owl\validate.rh)
#define IDS_VALINVALIDCHAR      32521
#define IDS_VALNOTINRANGE       32522
#define IDS_VALNOTINLIST        32523


//#endif          // __spotapp_rh sentry.
```

Type Listing B.10. Script for the SPOTAPP.RC resource file.

```
#if !defined(WORKSHOP_INVOKED)
#include <windows.h>
#endif
#include "owl/except.rh"
#include "spotapp.rh"

SDI_MENU MENU
{
 POPUP "&File"
 {
  MENUITEM "&New", CM_FILENEW
```

continues

789

Listing B.10. continued

```
         MENUITEM "&Open...", CM_FILEOPEN
         MENUITEM SEPARATOR
         MENUITEM "&Save", CM_FILESAVE, GRAYED
         MENUITEM "Save &As...", CM_FILESAVEAS, GRAYED
         MENUITEM SEPARATOR
         MENUITEM "E&xit\tAlt+F4", CM_EXIT
         }

      MENUITEM SEPARATOR
      POPUP "&Edit"
      {
      MENUITEM "&Undo\tAlt+BkSp", CM_EDITUNDO, GRAYED
      MENUITEM SEPARATOR
      MENUITEM "Cu&t\tShift+Del", CM_EDITCUT, GRAYED
      MENUITEM "&Copy\tCtrl+Ins", CM_EDITCOPY, GRAYED
      MENUITEM "&Paste\tShift+Ins", CM_EDITPASTE, GRAYED
      MENUITEM "Paste &Special...",    CM_EDITPASTESPECIAL
      MENUITEM "Paste &Link",          CM_EDITPASTELINK
      MENUITEM SEPARATOR
      MENUITEM "Clear &All\tCtrl+Del", CM_EDITCLEAR, GRAYED
      MENUITEM Separator
      MENUITEM "&Insert Object...",    CM_EDITINSERTOBJECT
      MENUITEM "&Links...",            CM_EDITLINKS
      MENUITEM "&Object",              CM_EDITOBJECT
      MENUITEM Separator
      MENUITEM "&Show Objects",        CM_EDITSHOWOBJECTS
      }

      MENUITEM SEPARATOR
      MENUITEM SEPARATOR
      MENUITEM SEPARATOR
      MENUITEM SEPARATOR
      POPUP "&Help"
      {
      MENUITEM "&About...", CM_HELPABOUT
      }

      }


      // Accelerator table for short-cut to menu commands. (include\owl\editfile.rc)
      SDI_MENU ACCELERATORS
      BEGIN
        VK_DELETE, CM_EDITDELETE, VIRTKEY
        VK_DELETE, CM_EDITCUT, VIRTKEY, SHIFT
        VK_INSERT, CM_EDITCOPY, VIRTKEY, CONTROL
        VK_INSERT, CM_EDITPASTE, VIRTKEY, SHIFT
        VK_DELETE, CM_EDITCLEAR, VIRTKEY, CONTROL
        VK_BACK,   CM_EDITUNDO, VIRTKEY, ALT
        VK_F3,     CM_EDITFINDNEXT, VIRTKEY
      END
```

B

```
IDM_DOCMANAGERFILE MENU LOADONCALL MOVEABLE PURE DISCARDABLE
BEGIN
    MENUITEM "&New", CM_FILENEW
    MENUITEM "&Open...", CM_FILEOPEN
    MENUITEM "&Close", CM_FILECLOSE
    MENUITEM SEPARATOR
    MENUITEM "&Save", CM_FILESAVE, GRAYED
    MENUITEM "Save &As...", CM_FILESAVEAS, GRAYED
    MENUITEM SEPARATOR
    MENUITEM "E&xit\tAlt+F4", CM_EXIT
END


// Menu merged in when TOleView is active, notice the extra MENUITEM SEPARATORs
//which are
// for menu negotiation.  These separators are used as group markers by OWL.
IDM_OLEVIEW MENU
{
 MENUITEM SEPARATOR
 POPUP "&Edit"
 {
  MENUITEM "&Undo\aCtrl+Z", CM_EDITUNDO
  MENUITEM SEPARATOR
  MENUITEM "&Cut\aCtrl+X", CM_EDITCUT
  MENUITEM "C&opy\aCtrl+C", CM_EDITCOPY
  MENUITEM "&Paste\aCtrl+V", CM_EDITPASTE
  MENUITEM "Paste &Special...", CM_EDITPASTESPECIAL
  MENUITEM "Paste &Link", CM_EDITPASTELINK
  MENUITEM "Clear &All\aCtrl+Del", CM_EDITCLEAR
  MENUITEM Separator
  MENUITEM "&Insert Object...",    CM_EDITINSERTOBJECT
  MENUITEM "&Links...",            CM_EDITLINKS
  MENUITEM "&Object",              CM_EDITOBJECT
  MENUITEM Separator
  MENUITEM "&Show Objects",        CM_EDITSHOWOBJECTS

 }

 MENUITEM SEPARATOR
 MENUITEM SEPARATOR
 MENUITEM SEPARATOR
 MENUITEM SEPARATOR
 POPUP "&Help"
 {
  MENUITEM "&About...", CM_HELPABOUT
 }

}

IDM_OLEPOPUP MENU LOADONCALL MOVEABLE PURE DISCARDABLE
BEGIN
    POPUP "OLE"
    BEGIN
```

continues

791

Listing B.10. continued

```
            MENUITEM "&Cut\aCtrl+X", CM_EDITCUT
            MENUITEM "C&opy\aCtrl+C", CM_EDITCOPY
            MENUITEM "&Delete\aDel", CM_EDITDELETE
            MENUITEM SEPARATOR
            MENUITEM "&Object", CM_EDITOBJECT
        END
    END


//
// Table of help hints displayed in the status bar.
//
STRINGTABLE
BEGIN
    -1,                        "File/document operations"
    CM_FILENEW,                "Creates a new document"
    CM_FILEOPEN,               "Opens an existing document"
    CM_VIEWCREATE,             "Create a new view for this document"
    CM_FILEREVERT,             "Reverts changes to last document save"
    CM_FILECLOSE,              "Close this document"
    CM_FILESAVE,               "Saves this document"
    CM_FILESAVEAS,             "Saves this document with a new name"
    CM_EXIT,                   "Quits Spot and prompts to save the documents"
    CM_EDITUNDO-1,             "Edit operations"
    CM_EDITUNDO,               "Reverses the last operation"
    CM_EDITCUT,                "Cuts the selection and puts it on the Clipboard"
    CM_EDITCOPY,               "Copies the selection and puts it on the Clipboard"
    CM_EDITPASTE,              "Inserts the clipboard contents at the insertion
 point"
    CM_EDITPASTESPECIAL,       "Select paste option and format"
    CM_EDITPASTELINK,          "Link with object on the clipboard"
    CM_EDITDELETE,             "Deletes the selection"
    CM_EDITCLEAR,              "Clear the document"
    CM_EDITLINKS,              "Edit links to the document"
    CM_EDITINSERTOBJECT,       "Insert an object into the document"
    CM_EDITOBJECT,             "Ask the selected object to perform an action"
    CM_EDITSHOWOBJECTS,        "Hilight selected object"
    CM_EDITADD,                "Insert a new line"
    CM_EDITEDIT,               "Edit the current line"
    CM_EDITFIND-1,             "Search/replace operations"
    CM_EDITFIND,               "Finds the specified text"
    CM_EDITREPLACE,            "Finds the specified text and changes it"
    CM_EDITFINDNEXT,           "Finds the next match"
    CM_HELPABOUT-1,            "Access About"
    CM_HELPABOUT,              "About the Spot application"
END


//
// OWL string table
//

// EditFile (include\owl\editfile.rc and include\owl\editsear.rc)
```

```
STRINGTABLE LOADONCALL MOVEABLE DISCARDABLE
BEGIN
    IDS_CANNOTFIND,               "Cannot find ""%s""."
    IDS_UNABLEREAD,               "Unable to read file %s from disk."
    IDS_UNABLEWRITE,              "Unable to write file %s to disk."
    IDS_FILECHANGED,              "The text in the %s file has changed.\n\nDo you
➥want to save the changes?"
    IDS_FILEFILTER,               "Text files (*.TXT)¦*.TXT¦AllFiles (*.*)¦*.*¦"
END


// ListView (include\owl\listview.rc)
STRINGTABLE LOADONCALL MOVEABLE DISCARDABLE
BEGIN
  IDS_LISTNUM,   "Line number %d"
END


// Doc/View (include\owl\docview.rc)
STRINGTABLE LOADONCALL MOVEABLE DISCARDABLE
BEGIN
    IDS_DOCMANAGERFILE,           "&File"
    IDS_DOCLIST,                  "--Document Type--"
    IDS_VIEWLIST,                 "--View Type--"
    IDS_UNTITLED,                 "Document"
    IDS_UNABLEOPEN,               "Unable to open document."
    IDS_UNABLECLOSE,              "Unable to close document."
    IDS_READERROR,                "Document read error."
    IDS_WRITEERROR,               "Document write error."
    IDS_DOCCHANGED,               "The document has been changed.\n\nDo you want to
➥save the changes?"
    IDS_NOTCHANGED,               "The document has not been changed."
    IDS_NODOCMANAGER,             "Document Manager not present."
    IDS_NOMEMORYFORVIEW,          "Insufficient memory for view."
    IDS_DUPLICATEDOC,             "Document already loaded."
END


// OLEView (include\owl\oleview.rc)
STRINGTABLE LOADONCALL MOVEABLE DISCARDABLE
BEGIN
    IDS_EDITOBJECT,               "&Object"
    IDS_EDITCONVERT,              "Convert..."
    IDS_CLOSESERVER,              "Close and Return to "
    IDS_EXITSERVER,               "Exit and Return to "
END

STRINGTABLE LOADONCALL MOVEABLE DISCARDABLE
BEGIN
    IDS_CFTEXT,                   "Text\nplain text"
    IDS_CFBITMAP,                 "Bitmap\na bitmap image"
    IDS_CFMETAFILE,               "Metafile Picture\na static picture"
    IDS_CFSYLK,                   "Sylk\na spreadsheet"
    IDS_CFDIF,                    "DIF\na document"
    IDS_CFTIFF,                   "Tagged Image File Format\na TIFF image file"
```

continues

Listing B.10. continued

```
        IDS_CFOEMTEXT,              "OEM Text\nan OEM text"
        IDS_CFDIB,                 "DIB\na device independent bitmap image"
        IDS_CFPALETTE,             "Palette\na color palette"
        IDS_CFPENDATA,             "Pen Data\npen data"
        IDS_CFRIFF,                "RIFF\na RIFF media file"
        IDS_CFWAVE,                "Wave\na sound wave file"
        IDS_CFUNICODETEXT,         "UniCode Text\nUnicode text"
        IDS_CFENHMETAFILE,         "Enhanced Metafile\nan enhanced metafile picture"
        IDS_IN,                    " in "
END


// Exception string resources (include\owl\except.rc)
STRINGTABLE LOADONCALL MOVEABLE DISCARDABLE
BEGIN
        IDS_OWLEXCEPTION,          "ObjectWindows Exception"
        IDS_UNHANDLEDXMSG,         "Unhandled Exception"
        IDS_OKTORESUME,            "OK to resume?"
        IDS_UNKNOWNEXCEPTION,      "Unknown exception"

        IDS_UNKNOWNERROR,          "Unknown error"
        IDS_NOAPP,                 "No application object"
        IDS_OUTOFMEMORY,           "Out of memory"
        IDS_INVALIDMODULE,         "Invalid module specified for window"
        IDS_INVALIDMAINWINDOW,     "Invalid MainWindow"
        IDS_VBXLIBRARYFAIL,        "VBX Library init failure"

        IDS_INVALIDWINDOW,         "Invalid window %s"
        IDS_INVALIDCHILDWINDOW,    "Invalid child window %s"
        IDS_INVALIDCLIENTWINDOW,   "Invalid client window %s"

        IDS_CLASSREGISTERFAIL,     "Class registration fail for window %s"
        IDS_CHILDREGISTERFAIL,     "Child class registration fail for window %s"
        IDS_WINDOWCREATEFAIL,      "Create fail for window %s"
        IDS_WINDOWEXECUTEFAIL,     "Execute fail for window %s"
        IDS_CHILDCREATEFAIL,       "Child create fail for window %s"

        IDS_MENUFAILURE,           "Menu creation failure"
        IDS_VALIDATORSYNTAX,       "Validator syntax error"
        IDS_PRINTERERROR,          "Printer error"

        IDS_LAYOUTINCOMPLETE,      "Incomplete layout constraints specified in window
➥%s"
        IDS_LAYOUTBADRELWIN,       "Invalid relative window specified in layout
➥constraint in window %s"

        IDS_GDIFAILURE,            "GDI failure"
        IDS_GDIALLOCFAIL,          "GDI allocate failure"
        IDS_GDICREATEFAIL,         "GDI creation failure"
        IDS_GDIRESLOADFAIL,        "GDI resource load failure"
        IDS_GDIFILEREADFAIL,       "GDI file read failure"
        IDS_GDIDELETEFAIL,         "GDI object %X delete failure"
        IDS_GDIDESTROYFAIL,        "GDI object %X destroy failure"
```

```
        IDS_INVALIDDIBHANDLE,        "Invalid DIB handle %X"
END


// General Window's status bar messages. (include\owl\statusba.rc)
STRINGTABLE
BEGIN
    IDS_MODES                    "EXT¦CAPS¦NUM¦SCRL¦OVR¦REC"
    IDS_MODESOFF                 "    ¦    ¦   ¦    ¦   ¦   "
    SC_SIZE,                     "Changes the size of the window"
    SC_MOVE,                     "Moves the window to another position"
    SC_MINIMIZE,                 "Reduces the window to an icon"
    SC_MAXIMIZE,                 "Enlarges the window to it maximum size"
    SC_RESTORE,                  "Restores the window to its previous size"
    SC_CLOSE,                    "Closes the window"
    SC_TASKLIST,                 "Opens task list"
    SC_NEXTWINDOW,               "Switches to next window"
END


// Validator messages (include\owl\validate.rc)


//
// Misc application definitions
//

// Application ICON
IDI_SDIAPPLICATION ICON "applsdi.ico"


// About box.
IDD_ABOUT DIALOG 12, 17, 204, 65
STYLE DS_MODALFRAME ¦ WS_POPUP ¦ WS_CAPTION ¦ WS_SYSMENU
CAPTION "About Spot"
FONT 8, "MS Sans Serif"
BEGIN
    CTEXT "Version", IDC_VERSION, 2, 14, 200, 8, SS_NOPREFIX
    CTEXT "Expert OWL Application", -1, 2, 4, 200, 8, SS_NOPREFIX
    CTEXT "", IDC_COPYRIGHT, 2, 27, 200, 17, SS_NOPREFIX
    RTEXT "", IDC_DEBUG, 136, 55, 66, 8, SS_NOPREFIX
    ICON IDI_SDIAPPLICATION, -1, 2, 2, 34, 34
    DEFPUSHBUTTON "OK", IDOK, 82, 48, 40, 14
END

CM_EDITCLEAR BITMAP LOADONCALL MOVEABLE
{
 '42 4D 66 01 00 00 00 00 00 00 76 00 00 00 28 00'
 '00 00 14 00 00 00 14 00 00 00 01 00 04 00 00 00'
 '00 00 F0 00 00 00 00 00 00 00 00 00 00 00 00 00'
 '00 00 00 00 00 00 00 00 00 00 00 00 00 80 00 00 80'
 '00 00 00 80 80 00 80 00 00 00 80 00 80 00 80 80'
 '00 00 80 80 80 00 C0 C0 C0 00 00 00 FF 00 00 FF'
 '00 00 00 FF FF 00 FF 00 00 00 FF 00 FF 00 FF FF'
 '00 00 FF FF FF 00 88 88 88 88 88 88 88 88 88 88'
```

continues

Listing B.10. continued

```
'40 00 88 88 88 88 88 88 88 88 88 88 90 00 88 88'
'88 88 88 88 88 88 88 88 20 00 88 88 88 88 88 88'
'88 88 88 88 40 18 88 88 88 88 88 88 88 88 88 88'
'00 00 88 88 88 88 88 88 88 88 88 88 00 00 88 88'
'88 88 88 88 88 88 88 88 00 00 88 88 88 88 88 88'
'88 88 88 88 0B 00 88 80 08 88 88 88 88 88 88 88'
'00 00 88 80 08 88 88 88 88 88 88 88 00 00 88 80'
'08 88 88 84 44 44 44 48 00 00 88 80 08 80 88 84'
'EF EF EF 48 0B 00 88 80 07 80 08 84 FE FE FE 48'
'00 00 88 87 00 00 00 84 EF EF EF 48 00 00 88 88'
'70 00 00 84 FE FE FE 48 00 00 88 88 88 80 08 84'
'EF EF EF 48 0B 00 88 88 88 80 88 84 FE FE 44 48'
'FF FF 88 88 88 88 88 84 EF EF 44 88 FF FF 88 88'
'88 88 88 84 44 44 48 88 00 00 88 88 88 88 88 88'
'88 88 88 88 0B 00'
}
CM_HELPABOUT BITMAP
{
'42 4D 66 01 00 00 00 00 00 00 76 00 00 00 28 00'
'00 00 14 00 00 00 14 00 00 00 01 00 04 00 00 00'
'00 00 F0 00 00 00 00 00 00 00 00 00 00 00 00 00'
'00 00 00 00 00 00 00 00 00 00 00 00 80 00 00 80'
'00 00 80 80 00 80 00 00 00 00 80 00 00 80 80 80'
'00 00 80 80 80 00 C0 C0 C0 00 00 00 FF 00 00 FF'
'00 00 00 FF FF 00 FF 00 00 00 FF 00 FF 00 FF FF'
'00 00 FF FF FF 00 88 88 88 88 88 88 88 88 88 88'
'00 00 88 88 88 84 44 44 48 88 88 88 00 00 88 88'
'84 44 44 44 44 48 88 88 00 00 88 88 44 46 FF 64'
'44 44 88 88 00 00 88 84 44 4F FF F6 44 44 48 88'
'00 00 88 44 44 4F F6 48 44 44 44 88 00 00 88 44'
'44 46 FF 44 44 44 44 88 01 01 84 44 44 44 FF 64'
'44 44 44 48 08 33 84 44 44 44 6F F4 44 44 44 48'
'00 00 84 44 44 44 4F F6 44 44 44 48 00 00 84 44'
'44 48 46 FF 44 44 44 48 00 00 84 44 44 46 FF FF'
'44 44 44 48 00 00 84 44 44 44 6F F6 44 44 44 48'
'00 00 88 44 44 44 44 44 44 44 44 88 00 00 88 44'
'44 44 44 66 44 44 44 44 88 00 00 88 84 44 44 46 FF'
'64 44 48 88 00 00 88 88 44 44 46 FF 64 44 88 88'
'00 00 88 88 84 44 44 66 44 48 88 88 00 00 88 88'
'88 84 44 44 48 88 88 88 00 00 88 88 88 88 88 88'
'88 88 88 88 00 00'

}
// Version info.
//
#if !defined(__DEBUG_)
// Non-Debug VERSIONINFO
1 VERSIONINFO LOADONCALL MOVEABLE
FILEVERSION 1, 0, 0, 0
PRODUCTVERSION 1, 0, 0, 0
FILEFLAGSMASK 0
FILEFLAGS VS_FFI_FILEFLAGSMASK
FILEOS VOS__WINDOWS16
FILETYPE VFT_APP
```

B

```
BEGIN
    BLOCK "StringFileInfo"
    BEGIN
        // Language type = U.S. English (0x0409) and Character Set = Windows,
        //Multilingual(0x04e4)
        BLOCK "040904E4"                                    // Matches VarFileInfo Transla-
                                                            //tion hex value.

        BEGIN
            VALUE "CompanyName", "Honor Oak Systems\000"
            VALUE "FileDescription", "Spot for Windows\000"
            VALUE "FileVersion", "1.0\000"
            VALUE "InternalName", "Spot\000"
            VALUE "LegalCopyright", "Copyright   1994 by Honor Oak Systems.  All
➡Rights Reserved.\000"
            VALUE "LegalTrademarks", "Windows (TM) is a trademark of Microsoft
➡Corporation\000"
            VALUE "OriginalFilename", "Spot.EXE\000"
            VALUE "ProductName", "Spot\000"
            VALUE "ProductVersion", "1.0\000"
        END
    END

    BLOCK "VarFileInfo"
    BEGIN
        VALUE "Translation", 0x0409, 0x04e4         // U.S. English(0x0409) &
                                                    // Windows Multilingual(0x04e4)
                                                    // 1252

    END

END
#else

// Debug VERSIONINFO
1 VERSIONINFO LOADONCALL MOVEABLE
FILEVERSION 1, 0, 0, 0
PRODUCTVERSION 1, 0, 0, 0
FILEFLAGSMASK VS_FF_DEBUG ¦ VS_FF_PRERELEASE ¦ VS_FF_PATCHED ¦ VS_FF_PRIVATEBUILD ¦
➡VS_FF_SPECIALBUILD
FILEFLAGS VS_FFI_FILEFLAGSMASK
FILEOS VOS__WINDOWS16
FILETYPE VFT_APP
BEGIN
    BLOCK "StringFileInfo"
    BEGIN
        // Language type = U.S. English (0x0409) and Character Set = Windows,
        //Multilingual(0x04e4)
        BLOCK "040904E4"                                    // Matches VarFileInfo Transla-
                                                            //tion hex value.

        BEGIN
            VALUE "CompanyName", "Honor Oak Systems\000"
            VALUE "FileDescription", "Spot for Windows\000"
            VALUE "FileVersion", "1.0\000"
            VALUE "InternalName", "Spot\000"
            VALUE "LegalCopyright", "Copyright   1994 by Honor Oak Systems.  All
➡Rights Reserved.\000"
            VALUE "LegalTrademarks", "Windows (TM) is a trademark of Microsoft
```

continues

797

Listing B.10. continued

```
➡Corporation\000"
                VALUE "OriginalFilename", "Spot.EXE\000"
                VALUE "ProductName", "Spot\000"
                VALUE "ProductVersion", "1.0\000"
                VALUE "SpecialBuild", "Debug Version\000"
                VALUE "PrivateBuild", "Built by Ian Spencer\000"
            END
        END

        BLOCK "VarFileInfo"
        BEGIN
            VALUE "Translation", 0x0409, 0x04e4      // U.S. English(0x0409) &
                                                     //Windows Multilingual(0x04e4)
                                                     // 1252
        END

    END
    #endif

    IDM_OLEVIEW ACCELERATORS
    {
     VK_DELETE, CM_EDITDELETE, VIRTKEY, CONTROL
    }
```

Listing B.11. Source code for the SPOTAPP.DEF definition file.

```
NAME spot

DESCRIPTION 'Spot Application - Copyright © 1996 by Honor Oak Systems.  All Rights
➡Reserved.'
EXETYPE     WINDOWS
CODE        PRELOAD MOVEABLE DISCARDABLE
DATA        PRELOAD MOVEABLE
HEAPSIZE    65536
STACKSIZE   65536
```

Listing B.12. Contents of the SPOT.IDE project file.

The following files need to exist in the project window. Note, however, that they need to be added to the project as usual, with SPOT.EXE as the target and all the other files as nodes.

```
SPOT[.EXE] OWL + OCF LIBRARIES
    SPOTAPP[.CPP]
    SPOTDOC[.CPP]
    SPOTVIEW[.CPP]
    SPOTAB[.CPP]
    SPOTAPP[.RC]
    SPOTAPP[.DEF]
```

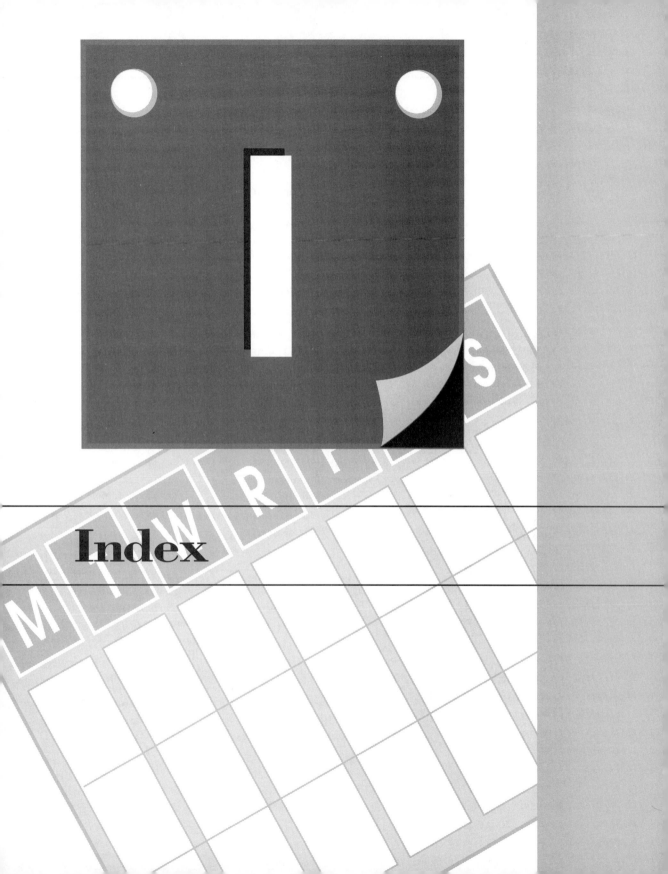

Index

Symbols

A

functions

listings

SAMS
PUBLISHING

Sams
Learning
Center

listings

Add to Your Sams Library Today with the Best Books for Programming, Operating Systems, and New Technologies

The easiest way to order is to pick up the phone and call

1-800-428-5331

between 9:00 a.m. and 5:00 p.m. EST.

For faster service please have your credit card available.

ISBN	Quantity	Description of Item	Unit Cost	Total Cost
0-672-30791-X		Peter Norton's Complete Windows 95 Guide	$29.99	
0-672-30762-6		32-Bit Windows Programming (Book/CD)	$39.99	
0-672-30602-6		Programming Windows 95 Unleashed (Book/CD)	$49.99	
0-672-30474-0		Windows 95 Unleashed (Book/CD)	$39.99	
0-672-30685-9		Windows NT 3.5 Unleashed, 2E	$39.99	
0-672-30611-5		Your Windows 95 Consultant	$19.99	
0-672-30655-7		Developing Your Own 32-Bit Operating System (Book/CD)	$49.99	
0-672-30704-9		Delphi Developer's Guide (Book/CD)	$49.99	
0-672-30617-4		The World Wide Web Unleashed	$35.00	
❑ 3 ½" Disk		Shipping and Handling: See information below.		
❑ 5 ¼" Disk		TOTAL		

Shipping and Handling: $4.00 for the first book, and $1.75 for each additional book. Floppy disk: add $1.75 for shipping and handling. If you need to have it NOW, we can ship product to you in 24 hours for an additional charge of approximately $18.00, and you will receive your item overnight or in two days. Overseas shipping and handling adds $2.00 per book and $8.00 for up to three disks. Prices subject to change. Call for availability and pricing information on latest editions.

201 W. 103rd Street, Indianapolis, Indiana 46290

1-800-428-5331 — Orders   1-800-835-3202 — FAX   1-800-858-7674 — Customer Service

Book ISBN 0-672-30756-1